Lecture Notes in Computer Science   15378

Founding Editors

Gerhard Goos
Juris Hartmanis

The series Lecture Notes in Computer Science (LNCS), including its subseries Lecture Notes in Artificial Intelligence (LNAI) and Lecture Notes in Bioinformatics (LNBI), has established itself as a medium for the publication of new developments in computer science and information technology research, teaching, and education.

LNCS enjoys close cooperation with the computer science R & D community, the series counts many renowned academics among its volume editors and paper authors, and collaborates with prestigious societies. Its mission is to serve this international community by providing an invaluable service, mainly focused on the publication of conference and workshop proceedings and postproceedings. LNCS commenced publication in 1973.

Panayiotis Zaphiris · Andri Ioannou ·
Robert A. Sottilare · Jessica Schwarz ·
Matthias Rauterberg
Editors

HCI International 2024 – Late Breaking Papers

26th International Conference on
Human-Computer Interaction, HCII 2024
Washington, DC, USA, June 29 – July 4, 2024
Proceedings, Part V

 Springer

Editors
Panayiotis Zaphiris (iD)
Cyprus University of Technology
Limassol, Cyprus

Robert A. Sottilare
Soar Technology, Inc.
Orlando, FL, USA

Matthias Rauterberg
Eindhoven University of Technology
Eindhoven, The Netherlands

Andri Ioannou (iD)
Cyprus University of Technology
Limassol, Cyprus

CYENS
Nicosia, Cyprus

Jessica Schwarz
Fraunhofer FKIE
Wachtberg, Germany

ISSN 0302-9743   ISSN 1611-3349 (electronic)
Lecture Notes in Computer Science
ISBN 978-3-031-76814-9   ISBN 978-3-031-76815-6 (eBook)
https://doi.org/10.1007/978-3-031-76815-6

Foreword

This year we celebrate 40 years since the establishment of the HCI International (HCII) Conference, which has been a hub for presenting groundbreaking research and novel ideas and collaboration for people from all over the world.

The HCII conference was founded in 1984 by Prof. Gavriel Salvendy (Purdue University, USA, Tsinghua University, P.R. China, and University of Central Florida, USA) and the first event of the series, "1st USA-Japan Conference on Human-Computer Interaction", was held in Honolulu, Hawaii, USA, 18–20 August. Since then, HCI International is held jointly with several Thematic Areas and Affiliated Conferences, with each one under the auspices of a distinguished international Program Board and under one management and one registration. Twenty-six HCI International Conferences have been organized so far (every two years until 2013, and annually thereafter).

Over the years, this conference has served as a platform for scholars, researchers, industry experts and students to exchange ideas, connect, and address challenges in the ever-evolving HCI field. Throughout these 40 years, the conference has evolved itself, adapting to new technologies and emerging trends, while staying committed to its core mission of advancing knowledge and driving change.

As we celebrate this milestone anniversary, we reflect on the contributions of its founding members and appreciate the commitment of its current and past Affiliated Conference Program Board Chairs and members. We are also thankful to all past conference attendees who have shaped this community into what it is today.

The 26th International Conference on Human-Computer Interaction, HCI International 2024 (HCII 2024), was held as a 'hybrid' event at the Washington Hilton Hotel, Washington, DC, USA, during 29 June – 4 July 2024. It incorporated the 21 thematic areas and affiliated conferences listed below.

A total of 5108 individuals from academia, research institutes, industry, and government agencies from 85 countries submitted contributions, and 1271 papers and 309 posters were included in the volumes of the proceedings that were published just before the start of the conference. Additionally, 222 papers and 104 posters were included in the volumes of the proceedings published after the conference, as "Late Breaking Work". The contributions thoroughly cover the entire field of human-computer interaction, addressing major advances in knowledge and effective use of computers in a variety of application areas. These papers provide academics, researchers, engineers, scientists, practitioners and students with state-of-the-art information on the most recent advances in HCI. The volumes constituting the full set of the HCII 2024 conference proceedings are listed on the following pages.

I would like to thank the Program Board Chairs and the members of the Program Boards of all thematic areas and affiliated conferences for their contribution towards the high scientific quality and overall success of the HCI International 2024 conference. Their manifold support in terms of paper reviewing (single-blind review process, with a minimum of two reviews per submission), session organization and their willingness to act as goodwill ambassadors for the conference is most highly appreciated.

This conference would not have been possible without the continuous and unwavering support and advice of Gavriel Salvendy, founder, General Chair Emeritus, and Scientific Advisor. For his outstanding efforts, I would like to express my sincere appreciation to Abbas Moallem, Communications Chair and Editor of HCI International News.

September 2024   Constantine Stephanidis

HCI International 2024 Thematic Areas
and Affiliated Conferences

- HCI: Human-Computer Interaction Thematic Area
- HIMI: Human Interface and the Management of Information Thematic Area
- EPCE: 21st International Conference on Engineering Psychology and Cognitive Ergonomics
- AC: 18th International Conference on Augmented Cognition
- UAHCI: 18th International Conference on Universal Access in Human-Computer Interaction
- CCD: 16th International Conference on Cross-Cultural Design
- SCSM: 16th International Conference on Social Computing and Social Media
- VAMR: 16th International Conference on Virtual, Augmented and Mixed Reality
- DHM: 15th International Conference on Digital Human Modeling & Applications in Health, Safety, Ergonomics & Risk Management
- DUXU: 13th International Conference on Design, User Experience and Usability
- C&C: 12th International Conference on Culture and Computing
- DAPI: 12th International Conference on Distributed, Ambient and Pervasive Interactions
- HCIBGO: 11th International Conference on HCI in Business, Government and Organizations
- LCT: 11th International Conference on Learning and Collaboration Technologies
- ITAP: 10th International Conference on Human Aspects of IT for the Aged Population
- AIS: 6th International Conference on Adaptive Instructional Systems
- HCI-CPT: 6th International Conference on HCI for Cybersecurity, Privacy and Trust
- HCI-Games: 6th International Conference on HCI in Games
- MobiTAS: 6th International Conference on HCI in Mobility, Transport and Automotive Systems
- AI-HCI: 5th International Conference on Artificial Intelligence in HCI
- MOBILE: 5th International Conference on Human-Centered Design, Operation and Evaluation of Mobile Communications

Conference Proceedings – Full List of Volumes

https://2024.hci.international/proceedings

26th International Conference on Human-Computer Interaction (HCII 2024)

The full list with the Program Board Chairs and the members of the Program Boards of all thematic areas and affiliated conferences of HCII2024 is available online at:

http://www.hci.international/board-members-2024.php

HCI International 2025 Conference

The 27th International Conference on Human-Computer Interaction, HCI International 2025, will be held jointly with the affiliated conferences at the Swedish Exhibition & Congress Centre and Gothia Towers Hotel, Gothenburg, Sweden, June 22–27, 2025. It will cover a broad spectrum of themes related to Human-Computer Interaction, including theoretical issues, methods, tools, processes, and case studies in HCI design, as well as novel interaction techniques, interfaces, and applications. The proceedings will be published by Springer. More information is available on the conference website: https://2025.hci.international/.

General Chair
Prof. Constantine Stephanidis
University of Crete and ICS-FORTH
Heraklion, Crete, Greece
Email: general_chair@2025.hci.international

https://2025.hci.international/

Contents – Part V

New Cultural and Tourism Experiences

Design for Learning

On Students' Perception of Compiler Syntax Error Messages: A Human Factors Approach

Sana Algaraibeh[1] , Clinton Jeffery[1] , and Terence Soule[2]([⊠])

[1] New Mexico Institute of Mining and Technology, 801 Leroy Place, Socorro, NM 87801, USA
{sanaa.algaraibeh,clinton.jeffery}@nmt.edu
[2] University of Idaho, 875 Perimeter Drive, Moscow 83844, USA
tsoule@uidaho.edu
https://www.cs.nmt.edu/~jeffery/ , https://webpages.uidaho.edu/tsoule

Abstract. Error messages play a crucial role in helping developers, especially novices. The main job of error messages is to help users find and fix errors. This paper explores students' perceptions of using compiler syntax error messages to find and repair erroneous programs. We conducted an experiment in which participants had to find and fix errors, followed by reflection on their experiences with three tasks. In task one, participants evaluated the error messages using a proposed rubric for user experiences with compiler error messages. In task two, they described the error messages through open-ended questions, while in task three, they suggested alternative messages. Eighteen error messages from three compilers were ranked based on the rubric. The results indicate that users prefer error messages that are informative, human-centric, and provide accurate and precise information about the error and its resolution. Reported difficulties with error messages include lack of clarity and misdirection.

Keywords: Syntax errors · Error messages · Human factors · HCI · User experience

1 Introduction

Novice programmers heavily rely on compiler error messages, which are crucial for their learning process. Many studies describe error messages as often cryptic and unhelpful. This study investigates the user/learner perspective and input about error messages. User-driven design is used to produce messages based on the expressed needs of computer science students. The research objective is *to understand undergraduate students' needs and difficulties using compiler error messages to find and fix errors in C/C++ programs.*

© The Author(s), under exclusive license to Springer Nature Switzerland AG 2025
P. Zaphiris et al. (Eds.): HCII 2024, LNCS 15378, pp. 3–16, 2025.
https://doi.org/10.1007/978-3-031-76815-6_1

2   Methodology

We conducted an experiment where students found and fixed erroneous C++ programs using error messages from three compilers, one of which was customized to generate enhanced error messages. After that, the participants completed three reflection tasks. First, they rated the friendliness of the error messages. Next, they described the error messages in response to an open-ended question. Finally, they produced alternative error messages for the ones they had encountered. The participants in the experiment were 55 undergraduate students from the Computer Science and Engineering department at the New Mexico Institute of Mining and Technology. We used eighteen error messages and nine programs for the experiment, and each student worked on two error messages with two programs.

The compilers used to generate error messages in this study are GNU GCC version 10.3.1 (GCC), Microsoft Visual C++ Compiler version 2019 (MSVC), and a compiler prototype called EduCC. In previous work, we proposed a global, local, and expression-level (GLE) parsing technique that aims to enhance compiler error messages for novice programmers. GLE is a 3-phase parsing technique that prioritizes the parsing of the large code components over diving into all the details. The EduCC prototype for the C++ language implements key parts of the GLE for evaluation purposes [1].

The experiment utilized nine programs from Soule's textbook [9]. These programs were deliberately seeded with common novice syntax errors and were all of equivalent complexity. The order of the programs and compilers was randomized, and participants were randomly assigned to work with different sets of programs. The experiment took the form of an online self-administered questionnaire using Qualtrics.

In the experiment, there were two parts. In the first part, participants gained some experience in using error messages to identify and fix erroneous programs in C++. The success of the task was recorded in another study [1]. The goal of the second part was to examine the user experience of utilizing compiler syntax error messages. In the second part, participants reflected on their experience with error messages in the first part through three tasks. Task one involved rating the friendliness of error messages using a rubric. Task two required participants to describe the error messages through an open-ended question. Task three involved writing alternative messages for the ones that were used.

2.1   Task One: Rating the Friendliness of Error Messages

We assessed eighteen error messages to determine their friendliness using a rubric that we designed. The main question we asked was: "How friendly are the compiler error messages?" Participants were required to choose one option from the rubric. The rubric items can be found in Table 1. Each participant rated two messages, and we then calculated the median and mode for each message.

Table 1. Rubric for user experiences with syntax error messages

6	These error messages feel familiar, which makes me comfortable and encouraged to continue working on my program.
5	These error messages sound familiar to me favorably.
4	I understand most of the content of these error messages.
3	These messages are unclear or disorganized; the messages use unfamiliar vocabulary or obscure terms.
2	These error messages make me uncomfortable while I am programming; I feel like I did something wrong I must not do.
1	These error messages are intimidating and have a long scary list of errors.

2.2 Task Two: Self-reported Metrics for Error Messages

In task two, participants were asked to describe the error messages they encountered using their own words. Researchers used the qualitative content analysis method to analyze the responses. Themes and codes emerged from the analysis. Two researchers independently categorized the students' responses according to the codes, and the level of agreement in assigning categories was measured using inter-coder reliability.

2.3 Task Three: Participants Suggested Alternative Error Messages

For task three, participants provided alternative error messages to the ones originally used. The participants' messages were compared with the original ones and used to validate the results from tasks one and two. This task's purpose is to gain an understanding of how compiler error messages should be written from the perspective of undergraduate computer science students. It serves as a catalyst for an innovative initiative, inviting users/students to co-design educational compiler error messages. The objective is to investigate users' preferences regarding error messages. The fundamental concept of co-design involves the joint creation between users and design experts in order to harness the collective creativity of potential users [11].

3 Results and Discussion

3.1 Task One: Rating Friendliness of Error Messages

In Table 3, you can find the ranked error messages from task one, and Table 2 shows the related programs. The highest scores were given to error messages that had a friendly tone and provided accurate information. Messages 1, 2, and 3, which were generated by the EduCC compiler, received the highest median and mode scores of 6 in the friendliness rubric. According to the rubric, a score of 6 means that "These error messages feel familiar, which makes me comfortable and encouraged to continue working on my program." Most of the error messages received a median score of 4, indicating that "I understand most of the content of

Table 2. Abbreviated erroneous C++ programs that were used in the experiment

prog1.cpp

```
 7  int main() {
...
18  lucky = ((abs(favorite-disliked))*13) % 10;}
19  cout << endl << "Your secret, lucky number is: " << lucky << endl;}
20  if (lucky < 0){
21  cout << "Try to be less negative." << endl;}
...
36 }
```

prog2.cpp

```
37 void area(double r, double *area){
38 cout << "pointer\n";
39 *area = 3.1417 * r * r;
40 }
```

prog3.cpp

```
52 int room2(){
  ...
58 if(choice == 1)
59 return 2;
60 }
61 if(choice == 2){
62 return 1;
63 }
64 if(choice == 3){
65 return 3;
66 }
```

prog4.cpp

```
  ...
4 int main(){
  ...
27 if(choice == 3){
28 result=value1*value2;
29 cout << value1 << " * " << value2 << " = " << result << endl;
30 }
31 if(choice == 4)&&(value2 != 0){
32 result=value1/value2;
33 cout << value1 << " / " << value2 << " = " << result << endl;
34 }
35 }
```

prog5.cpp

```
33 int roll(int n){
34 int die = 0;
35 for(i < n){
36 die = die + (rand() % 6)+1;
37 cout << i << ":" <<die << " ";
38 }
39 cout << endl;
40 return die;
41 }
```

(*continued*)

Table 2. (*continued*)

prog6.cpp

```
33 int roll(int n){
34 int die = 0;
35 for(  i = 0, i < n,  i++)
36 die = die + (rand() % 6)+1;
37 cout << i << ":" <<die << " ";
38
39 cout << endl;
40 return die;
41 }
```

prog7.cpp

```
...
5 int main(){
   ...
14 while(HorL !=3)
15 }
16 cout << "I guessed: " << computerguess << endl;
17 cout <<"(1)higher or (2)lower or (3)correct?\n";
...
```

prog8.cpp

```
...
6 int main()
7 {
...
14 if (current_player == 1) {
            ...
20 }
21 } else {
22 do {
23 move =  1+ rand() % 3;
24 } while((move < 1) || (move > 3)) || (move > num_objects));
25 cout << "Computer removed " << move << endl;
26 }
...
```

prog9.cpp

```
...
34 int roll(int n){
35 int die = 0;
36 int i;
37 for(  i = 0; i < n; i+
38 cout << i << ":" <<die << " ";
39 die = die + (rand() % 6)+1;
40 cout << endl;
41 return die;
42 }
```

this error message." The lowest scores were given to Message 17 that is generated by MSVC, with a score of 3, indicating that "These messages are unclear or disorganized; the messages use unfamiliar vocabulary or obscure terms," and to Message 18 that is generated by GCC, with a score of 2.5, indicating that "These error messages make me uncomfortable while I am programming; I feel like I did something wrong I must not do." Messages 17 and 18 were observed to contain a long list of incorrect information and used compiler writer jargon. It was also noted that the last item of the rubric was rarely used by participants. Two out of 55 participants gave a score of 1 to Messages 15 and 18, which indicates that "These error messages are intimidating and have a long scary list of errors."

3.2   Task Two: Self-Reported Metrics for Error Messages

For task two, two main themes emerged from the content analysis: Theme 1: difficulties/ complaints; Theme 2: needs. The categories of *"difficulties"* theme were ordered according to their frequencies in the students' answers as shown in Table 4. "Unclear" was the dominant category and had the highest frequency, at 43%, where the message fails to explain the problem. The next category was "misdirected," with a 13% frequency, where the message points to the wrong error location.

The categories of the *"needs"* theme were ordered according to their frequencies as shown in Table 5. "Informative" was the dominant category among the "needs" categories, with 86% frequency. In this category, a message tells the problem, points to the correct direction correctly and precisely, and helps fix errors. Additionally, some responses are not categorized as "difficulties" or "needs" categories. In these responses, students said their experiences helped them find and fix errors when using bad error messages, and express a list of feelings, especially in the responses that are categorized as overwhelming, where compilers give long cascading lists of error messages, some of which are incorrect and misleading. They express their feelings using words such as: "irritating message," "intimidating message," "very frightening," "very confusing," and "That sounds terrifying." However, in the responses that are categorized as "informative," they used words such as "feel comfortable" and "encouraging". These results can help compiler writers in designing human-centric and better error messages. Finally, these categories can be used for future studies to create a rubric to evaluate error messages.

3.3   Task Three: Participants Suggested Alternative Error Messages

Most of the suggested error messages are short, informative, concise, and written in a language that is easily understandable by humans. For example, the following two messages were alternatives for Message 6 in Table 3

"A program terminates unexpectedly."
"(underline "cout «") prog1.cpp:19:5: error: standalone expressions should be placed inside functions."

The following alternative message for Message 9:

"Main function ends prematurely. Did you add an extra }?"

Table 3. Prompt Templates

$ **prog7.cpp**

Compilation of: (prog7.cpp)

Error message: look at line 15, in the program "prog7.cpp".
Do you mean open bracket '{' instead of close bracket '}'? because usually
while statement start with '{' , or any other correct statement before: "}".

Message#: Message 1, Compiler: EduCC, Median: 6, and Mode: 6.

$ **prog9.cpp**

Compilation of: (prog9.cpp)

Error message: look at line 38, in the program "prog9.cpp".
Missing close parenthesis ')' of for header.

Message#: Message 2, Compiler: EduCC, Median: 6, and Mode: 6.

$ **prog6.cpp**

Compilation of: (prog6.cpp)

Error message: look at line 35, in the program "prog6.cpp".
Semicolons is required in the for header, expected two semicolons inside the for's
parentheses (i.e for(int x=1;x<10;x++). You may fix that by adding two ';' in the
propoer places: for (statement; condition ; statment) before   "i".

Message#: Message 3, Compiler: EduCC, Median: 6, and Mode: 6.

(continued)

Table 3. (*continued*)

$ **prog4.cpp**
Compilation of: (prog4.cpp)
Error message: look at line 31, in the program "prog4.cpp". Is the following operator continuing the condition of an if, for, while, do-while, or switch statment? In that case, you need additional parentheses around the whole condition. The operator is "&&".
Message#: Message 4, Compiler: EduCC, Median: 5, and Mode: 6.

$ **prog3.cpp**
Compilation of (prog3.cpp):
Error message: A statement is written outside function boundaries that start with the word: "if". Look at line: 61, in the program: "prog3.cpp". Function room2() ends at line 60 is that what you intend?
Message#: Message 5, Compiler: EduCC, Median: 5, and Mode: 5.

$ **prog1.cpp**

```
prog1.cpp:19:5: error: 'cout' does not name a type
  19 |    cout << endl << "Your secret, lucky number is: " << lucky << endl;
     |    ^~~~
prog1.cpp:20:5: error: expected unqualified-id before 'if'
  20 |    if(lucky < 0){  // conditional, clause less than 0
     |    ^~
prog1.cpp:23:5: error: expected unqualified-id before 'if'
  23 |    if(lucky >= 0 && lucky < 5){// 0 to 4 inclusive
     |    ^~
prog1.cpp:26:5: error: expected unqualified-id before 'if'
  26 |    if(lucky >= 5 && lucky < 9){ // 5 to 8 inclusive
     |    ^~
prog1.cpp:29:5: error: expected unqualified-id before 'if'
  29 |    if(lucky == 9){ // exactly 9
     |    ^~
```

Message#: Message 6, Compiler: GCC, Median: 4.5, and Mode: 5.

$ **prog7.cpp**

```
prog7.cpp: In function 'int main()':
prog7.cpp:15:6: error: expected primary-expression before '}' token
  15 |    }
     |    ^
```

Message#: Message 7, Compiler: GCC, Median: 4, and Mode: 4.

(*continued*)

Table 3. (*continued*)

Description	Project	File	Line
no operator "+" matches these operands	ErrExample	prog9.cpp	37
expected a ')'	ErrExample	prog9.cpp	38
expected a statement	ErrExample	prog9.cpp	43
binary '+': no operator found which takes a right-hand operand of type 'std::ostream' (or there is no acceptable conversion)	ErrExample	prog9.cpp	37
syntax error: missing ')' before identifier 'die'	ErrExample	prog9.cpp	39
syntax error: ';'	ErrExample	prog9.cpp	39

Message#: Message 8, Compiler: MSVC, Median: 4, and Mode: 4.

$ **prog1.cpp**

Compilation of (prog1.cpp):

Error message: A print statement is written outside function boundaries that start with the word: "cout".
Look at line: 19, in the program: "prog1.cpp".
Function main() ends at line 18 is that what you intend?

Message#: Message 9, Compiler: EduCC, Median: 4, and Mode: 4.

$ **prog8.cpp**
prog8.cpp: In function 'int main()':
prog8.cpp:24:46: error: expected ';' before '||' token
   24 | } while((move < 1) || (move > 3)) || (move > num_objects));
      | ^ ~ ~
      | ;
prog8.cpp:24:47: error: expected primary-expression before '||' token
   24 | } while((move < 1) || (move > 3)) || (move > num_objects));
    _ | ^ ~

Message#: Message 10, Compiler: GCC, Median: 4, and Mode: 4.

Description	Project	File	Line
identifier "i" is undefined	ErrExample	prog6.cpp	35
expected a ';'	ErrExample	prog6.cpp	35
'i': undeclared identifier	ErrExample	prog6.cpp	35
'i': undeclared identifier	ErrExample	prog6.cpp	35
'i': undeclared identifier	ErrExample	prog6.cpp	35
syntax error: missing ';' before ')'	ErrExample	prog6.cpp	35
'i': undeclared identifier	ErrExample	prog6.cpp	36
syntax error: missing ')' before identifier 'cout'	ErrExample	prog6.cpp	39
syntax error: ';'	ErrExample	prog6.cpp	39

Message#: Message 11, Compiler: MSVC, Median: 4, and Mode: 4.

(*continued*)

Table 3. (*continued*)

Description	Project	File	Line
expected a declaration	ErrExample	prog3.cpp	61
syntax error: 'if'	ErrExample	prog3.cpp	61
syntax error: missing ';' before '('	ErrExample	prog3.cpp	61
'(': missing function header (old-style formal list?)	ErrExample	prog3.cpp	61
syntax error: 'if'	ErrExample	prog3.cpp	64
syntax error: missing ';' before '('	ErrExample	prog3.cpp	64
'(': missing function header (old-style formal list?)	ErrExample	prog3.cpp	64

Message#: Message 12, Compiler: MSVC, Median: 4, and Mode: 3.

Description	Project	File	Line
i is not a template	ErrExample	prog5.cpp	35
expression must have a constant value	ErrExample	prog5.cpp	35
expected a '>'	ErrExample	prog5.cpp	35
'i': undeclared identifier	ErrExample	prog5.cpp	35
syntax error: missing ';' before ')'	ErrExample	prog5.cpp	35
syntax error: missing ';' before '('	ErrExample	prog5.cpp	35
syntax error: missing ')' before '('	ErrExample	prog5.cpp	35
'i': undeclared identifier	ErrExample	prog5.cpp	37

Message#: Message 13, Compiler: MSVC, Median: 4, and Mode: none.

Description	Project	File	Line
expected a ';'	ErrExample	prog8.cpp	25
syntax error: missing ';' before '||'	ErrExample	prog8.cpp	25
syntax error: '||'	ErrExample	prog8.cpp	25
syntax error: ')'	ErrExample	prog8.cpp	25

Message#: Message 14, Compiler: MSVC, Median: 3.5, and Mode: none.

```
$      prog4.cpp
prog4.cpp: In function 'int main()':
prog4.cpp:31:20: error: expected identifier before '(' token
   31 |   if(choice == 4)&&(value2 != 0){
      |                    ^
```

Message#: Message 15, Compiler: GCC, Median: 3.5, and Mode: 3.

(*continued*)

Table 3. (*continued*)

```
$       prog2.cpp
prog2.cpp:37:34: error: initializer provided for function
  37 | void area(double r, double *area)(
     |                                  ^
prog2.cpp:39:9: error: expected constructor, destructor, or type conversion
before '=' token
  39 |   *area = 3.1417 * r * r;
     |         ^
prog2.cpp:40:1: error: expected declaration before '}' token
  40 | }
     | ^
```

Message#: Message 16, Compiler: GCC, Median: 3, and Mode: 3.

Description	Project	File	Line
declaration is incompatible with "int *area" (declared at line 39)	ErrExample	prog2.cpp	16
"cout" is ambiguous	ErrExample	prog2.cpp	23
"cout" is ambiguous	ErrExample	prog2.cpp	26
"cout" is ambiguous	ErrExample	prog2.cpp	27
"cout" is ambiguous	ErrExample	prog2.cpp	28
"cout" is ambiguous	ErrExample	prog2.cpp	34
unexpected parenthesis after declaration of function "area(double, double *)" (malformed parameter list or invalid initializer?)	ErrExample	prog2.cpp	37
expected a ';'	ErrExample	prog2.cpp	42
syntax error: '('	ErrExample	prog2.cpp	37
syntax error: missing ')' before '<<'	ErrExample	prog2.cpp	38
syntax error: missing ';' before '<<'	ErrExample	prog2.cpp	38
missing type specifier - int assumed. Note: C++ does not support default-int	ErrExample	prog2.cpp	38
missing type specifier - int assumed. Note: C++ does not support default-int	ErrExample	prog2.cpp	39
'area': redefinition; previous definition was 'function'	ErrExample	prog2.cpp	39
'r': undeclared identifier	ErrExample	prog2.cpp	39
'r': undeclared identifier	ErrExample	prog2.cpp	39
syntax error: '}'	ErrExample	prog2.cpp	40
syntax error: missing ';' before '}'	ErrExample	prog2.cpp	40
syntax error: missing ';' before '['	ErrExample	prog2.cpp	42
'[': missing function header (old-style formal list?)	ErrExample	prog2.cpp	42
'cout': ambiguous symbol	ErrExample	prog2.cpp	48
'<<': illegal, right operand has type 'const char [29]'	ErrExample	prog2.cpp	48

Message#: Message 17, Compiler: MSVC, Median: 3, and Mode: 3.

(*continued*)

Table 3. (*continued*)

```
$          prog5.cpp
prog5.cpp: In function 'int roll(int)':
prog5.cpp:35:7: error: 'i' was not declared in this scope
  35 |  for(i < n){
     |      ^
prog5.cpp:40:3: error: expected primary-expression before 'return'
  40 |  return die;
     |  ^~~~~~
prog5.cpp:39:16: error: expected ')' before 'return'
  39 |  cout << endl;
     |               ^
     |               )
  40 |  return die;
     |  ~~~~~~
prog5.cpp:35:6: note: to match this '('
  35 |  for(i < n){
     |      ^
```

Message#: Message 18, Compiler: GCC, Median: 2.5, and Mode: 3.

Table 4. The categories of *"difficulties"* theme were ordered according to their frequencies.

Order	Categories	Frequencies
1	Unclear	43%
2	Misdirected	13%
3	Overwhelming	9%
4	Computer-centric	7%
5	Non-directed	7%
6	Overcomplicated	7%
7	Misleading	4%
8	Too verbose	4%
9	Imprecise	2%
10	Incomplete	2%
11	Incorrect	2%
12	Misinterpreted	2%
13	Unhelpful	2%

The following are alternative messages for Message 17, which got the lowest score in task one:

"I was expecting ")" on line 42. Instead, I see you put "void." Maybe you're missing a parenthesis somewhere between lines 37 and 42."
"Bracket mismatch line 37."
"Syntax error: unexpected parenthesis after the declaration of the function. should be '{'."

Table 5. The categories of the *"needs"* theme were ordered according to their frequencies.

Order	Categories	Frequencies
1	Informative	86%
2	Human-centric	8%
3	Not-overwhelming	2%
4	Suitable to the user level	2%
5	Understandable	2%

The following are alternative messages for Message 16:

"Unmatched (did you mean {?"

The following are alternative messages for Message 16:

"Syntax Error at line 35 of "prog5.cpp". "For" loops require 3 statements separated by a semicolon: initialization, comparison, incrementation."

4   Related Work

A rich literature on designing compiler error messages from a Human-Computer Interface perspective has failed to result in consistently adequate messages from mainstream compilers. Molich and Nielsen emphasize that any system designed for people should be easy to learn and remember, effective, and pleasant to use [7]. Based on HCI guidelines for designing user interfaces, Traver proposed a set of principles that should guide compiler error message design: clarity and brevity, specificity, context insensitivity, locality, proper phrasing, consistency, suitable visual design, and extensible help [10]. Shneiderman explored the impact of error messages on users [8]. The study enhanced the error messages of a COBOL compiler and compared the user repair score of erroneous programs. Based on the author's experience, they suggested guidelines for effective error messages. Brown analyzed the compiler error messages of fifteen Pascal programs and proposed guidelines [3]. Lewis and Mulley studied the usefulness of error and warning messages for different types of users and took into account user feedback to improve the compiler error messages [5]. They developed a set of merits for useful compiler warning and error messages, although they did not measure their effectiveness. Marceau et al. investigated the effectiveness of error messages in the DrScheme environment [6], and suggested a rubric that measures the effectiveness of good error messages. Barik and his colleagues hypothesized that the quality of compiler error messages would improve if they contained explanations that applied explanation theories, such as Toulmin's model of argument [2]. They tested the helpfulness of explanatory error messages by conducting a survey among professional developers from software companies, who were asked to rate error messages from OpenJDK and Jikes, some of which followed the reasoning model and others did not. Denny et al. studied the readability of error messages and conducted experiments to investigate the factors influencing error message readability. They incorporated user input with close- and open-ended questions and asked the users to rate groups of error messages [4]. What this study does differently is that we asked the users to rate the friendliness of the error messages using a proposed rubric for specific error messages after they had an experience using these error messages. We also incorporated user input on how the compiler error message should be, asking open-ended questions on not only the readability but all aspects of the error messages. Also, we asked users to suggest alternative error messages. This study will help future researchers develop metrics for how the compiler should report errors.

5   Conclusion

In this study, we analyzed error messages from the perspective of users/learners. An experiment was conducted in which students were given erroneous C++ programs and were asked to identify and correct them using error messages from three different compilers. After completing the tasks, participants were asked to reflect on their experience using the error messages. We evaluated 18 error messages using a rubric designed for user experiences with syntax error messages. The study provides insights into the difficulties and requirements of users, which can be helpful for future studies on improving compiler error messages.

References

1. Algaraibeh, S.M.: Techniques for Enhancing Compiler Error Messages. Phd dissertation, University of Idaho (2023)
2. Barik, T., Ford, D., Murphy-Hill, E., Parnin, C.: How should compilers explain problems to developers? In: Proceedings of the 2018 26th ACM Joint Meeting on European Software Engineering Conference and Symposium on the Foundations of Software Engineering, pp. 633–643 (2018)
3. Brown, P.J.: Error messages: the neglected area of the man/machine interface. Commun. ACM **26**(4), 246–249 (1983)
4. Denny, P., et al.: On designing programming error messages for novices: readability and its constituent factors. In: Proceedings of the 2021 CHI Conference on Human Factors in Computing Systems, pp. 1–15 (2021)
5. Lewis, S., Mulley, G.: A comparison between novice and experienced compiler users in a learning environment. ACM SIGCSE Bull. **30**(3), 157–161 (1998)
6. Marceau, G., Fisler, K., Krishnamurthi, S.: Measuring the effectiveness of error messages designed for novice programmers. In: Proceedings of the 42nd ACM Technical Symposium on Computer Science Education, pp. 499–504 (2011)
7. Molich, R., Nielsen, J.: Improving a human-computer dialogue. Commun. ACM **33**(3), 338–348 (1990)
8. Shneiderman, B.: Designing computer system messages. Commun. ACM **25**(9), 610–611 (1982)
9. Soule, T.: A Project-Based Introduction to C++. Kendall Hunt (2014)
10. Traver, V.J.: On compiler error messages: what they say and what they mean. Adv. Hum. Comput. Interact. **2010**, 1–26 (2010)
11. Zamenopoulos, T., Alexiou, K.: Co-design as collaborative research. Bristol University/AHRC Connected Communities Programme (2018)

Enhancing Engagement Prediction in Online Environment Using Temporal Features

Eman Almotairi[✉], Amani Alzahrani, and Danda B. Rawat

Department of Electrical Engineering and Computer Science, Howard University, Washington, DC, USA
{aeman.almotairi,amani.alzahrani}@bison.howard.edu,
Danda.Rawat@howard.edu

Abstract. The COVID-19 crisis has hastened the uptake of educational classes on online platforms such as Zoom. To ensure the success of the educational process, instructors should monitor their students' engagement levels during sessions. By assessing learners' emotional and behavioral states, educators can refine their teaching strategies to improve the learning experience. However, accurately observing emotions and behaviors in a virtual environment is challenging. Therefore, there is a demand to automate engagement detection and prediction. Developing automatic detection systems to predict student engagement is crucial. This paper proposes a robust video-based engagement detection model that utilizes temporal feature extraction through the optical flow technique, combined with a pre-trained model. We experimented with various pre-trained Convolutional Neural Network (CNN) models, including MobileNetV2, ResNet101, EfficientNet, DenseNet161, VGG19, and InceptionV3. These models were fine-tuned using two public video datasets, DAiSEE and EmotiW23-EN, which are designed to evaluate student engagement in real-life online learning scenarios. Our research findings indicate that integrating optical flow with DenseNet161 significantly enhances engagement detection accuracy.

Keywords: emotion · engagement detection · Facial expression · human computer interaction · spatial features · temporal features · machine learning · deep learning · artificial intelligence (AI) tool · 'online learning' · 'CNN'

1 Introduction

The COVID-19 pandemic has accelerated the use of online platforms such as Zoom and Google Meet for educational purposes. Engagement in online learning encompasses the combined emotional and behavioral states of students [4]. Student engagement can be classified into two categories: Engaged and "Not Engaged". The engaged category includes positive emotions and behaviors such as happiness, focusing, and actively looking at the screen. The Not Engaged class comprises negative emotions and actions, such as boredom, distraction, looking away, and yawning. Tracking engagement in virtual settings is crucial for ensuring effective learning outcomes. By measuring students' emotions and behaviors, instructors can monitor engagement levels and implement strategies to enhance the learning experience outcomes [15].

Detecting learners' engagement precisely and efficiently is essential. As a result, there is a demand to automate engagement detection and prediction. Developing automatic detection systems to predict student engagement is crucial. Researchers have turned to artificial intelligence (AI) tools for automatic attendance monitoring to address this need. Early studies initially focused on extracting emotions from chat texts and self-reports. However, the field has evolved. Now, researchers are exploring more sophisticated methods, including analyzing images of attendees to discern their feelings through facial image processing.

Computer vision techniques, machine learning (ML), and deep learning (DL) algorithms provide practical means to analyze user engagement. These methods can be classified into image-based and video-based approaches. The image-based method extracts engagement features from individual images or frames taken from the video [15]. Processing is carried out independently for each frame, resulting in spatial features. In contrast, Video-based methods identify engagement features or motion patterns within a series of frames over time. The features extracted in this case are known as temporal features [6]. However, attendance engagement is not limited to static facial expressions. There is a need to explore video data and dynamic information from video content.

Engagement prediction involves two tasks: feature extraction and classification. We utilize the Optical Flow technique [2] to extract temporal features from frames in the video. The feature vectors obtained from Optical Flow represent the motion and movement of various facial features, such as eyebrows, eyes blink, mouth, and overall facial expression. We use the machine and deep learning algorithms to monitor emotions during sessions for classification purposes. Among these, the Convolutional Neural Network (CNN) model stands out as a prevalent deep learning algorithm, exhibiting significant success in this domain. In comparison, CNN models have traditionally been widely used in emotion classification. In our experiment, we adopt the Vision Transformer model based on CNN architecture and fine-tune the models for the engagement classification task. We leverage popular pre-trained CNN models known for their success in image and video classification, including ResNet101 [10], Inception [24], EfficientNet [25], DenseNet161 [11], VGG19 [22]and MobileNetV2 [19].

The primary contributions offered in this study are as follows:

- Investigate video-level engagement information such as motions and behavior presentation.
- Enhance engagement prediction by adopting temporal features.
- Conducting our experiment on real-life datasets shows that our proposed method outperforms the state-of-the-art Engagement Prediction approaches.

The subsequent sections are structured as follows: Literature Review on Student Engagement Recognition in Sect. 2. Section 3 outlines the methodology, and section 4 presents the study's outcomes and discusses those results. The paper's final section summarizes key findings and provides a conclusive perspective.

2 Related Work

Recent progressions in machine learning (ML) and deep learning (DL) algorithms have made it possible to utilize valuable data, including education, healthcare, and intelligent transportation. Within the education domain, the research efforts have focused on improving engagement prediction by employing ML and DL methods. There are two distinct approaches for engagement detection: frame-level and video-level prediction. The former entails capturing static snapshots from the video and analyzing features within individual frames, such as facial expressions, commonly denoted as spatial information [15]. Conversely, the latter methodology focuses on movement and actions observed over time, depicted across multiple frames extracted from video content, termed temporal information [6].

2.1 Frame-Based Engagement Prediction

Various researchers have explored the prediction of engagement levels by leveraging frames extracted from video content. Bhardwaj et al. [3] introduced a CNN-based model for estimating engagement by analyzing facial expressions extracted from single images. Their model was tested on the FER-2013 dataset, comprising images labeled with emotions such as happiness, anger, sadness, and neutrality. Their results showed a 50% accuracy in engagement estimation. Nezami et al. [15] employed a CNN-based model for face detection, followed by utilizing the engagement histogram of oriented gradients (HOG) and support vector machines (SVM) to classify faces into engaged and disengaged categories. Their model was tested on their ER dataset, achieving an accuracy of 59.88% on the test set. The authors [18] suggest a transfer learning method named ATL-BP that predicts student engagement by analyzing faces in videos of students working in an E-Learning environment. They utilize the pre-trained VGG-Face for extracting facial features and the ResNet50 network for addressing the engagement prediction issue in the target domain. Their final model, ATL-BP for Affect Transfer Learning for Behavior Prediction, achieves an improvement in the mean F-score of 50% over the state-of-the-art method on this new dataset. Zheng et al. [31] introduced a transfer learning approach to estimate learners' engagement in online learning. They utilized time-series facial and bodily expressions, extracted upper-body key points using OpenPose, and addressed noise issues through the moving average method. They applied a long short-term memory (LSTM) based CNN model on the DAiSEE dataset. Their proposed method achieved 63.7% accuracy in their experiments. Sharma et al. [20] utilized a convolutions neural network (CNN) trained on the FER 2013 data set and applied a transfer method inspired by the VGG16 architecture. Kamath et al. [13] employed the Viola-Jones face detection algorithm to examine the input images, followed by the utilization of a Histogram of Oriented Gradients (HOG) to represent the facial features within the image patches, resulting in the creation of a final feature vector. The system used a Multiple Kernel Learning Support-Vector Machine (MKL-SVM) to construct a trained model with extracted features. After that, the system's performance was evaluated, and the results showed an average accuracy of 43.98% with a maximum accuracy of 51%.

2.2   Video-Based Engagement Prediction

This methodology focuses on movement and actions observed over time, depicted across multiple frames extracted from video content, termed temporal information. Sharma et al. [21] evaluated students' engagement level in an educational context by analyzing their real-time facial expressions, head and eye movements. They employed the Viola and Jones algorithm to extract facial expressions and eye regions from images. Subsequently, they trained (CNN)based model on eye images to determine if the student was attentive "Focused" or "Distracted". When attention was confirmed, they used a mini-Xception CNN to classify emotions into seven categories: Neutral, Happy, surprised, Sad, disgusted, Anger, and scared. However, their system faced challenges with "face occlusion," when a student's face is partially obscured, such as by their hand or glasses. Huang et al. [12] introduced a Deep Engagement Recognition Network, a model that integrates LSTM and an attention mechanism to extract features from facial expressions and gauge the degree of engagement. OpenFace is utilized to extract facial expression, head posture, facial action, and eye gaze. It operates in real-time video analysis, tracking changes in facial position from a spatial standpoint and analyzing eye gaze angles. Their model achieved 60 % accuracy in detecting engagement levels using the DAiSEE dataset. Wu et al. [28] extracted motion and emotion features from video clips within the EmotiW dataset, followed by the application of Gated Recurrent Unit (GRU) methods and Long short-term memory (LSTM) to predict learners' emotional responses within the context of online educational environments. A multi-feature engineering approach was employed to forecast emotions in extended videos under diverse conditions, including low light and dark backgrounds. Their result showed the MSE:0.061 on the test set). Abedi and Khan [1] propose an innovative hybrid neural network architecture that combines a Residual Network (ResNet) and a Temporal Convolutional Network (TCN) for detecting students' engagement levels in videos. They employ the ResNet to extract spatial features and the TCN to capture motion information from video frames using the DAiSEE dataset. Their findings indicate an accuracy of 64%.

Based on the literature review, several distinct techniques of computer vision, machine learning (ML), and deep learning (DL) have emerged as popular methods for engagement recognition. Previous researchers have experimented with various models, and a summary of these techniques and approaches has been presented in Table 1.

Table 1. Engagement prediction methodologies in previous research.

Author	Approach	Dataset	Proposed Model
Bhardwaj,et al. [3]	Frame-level	FER-2013	Haar-cascade + CNN
Nezami,et al. [15]	Frame-level	ER dataset	HOG+ SVM
Ruiz,et al. [18]	Frame-leve	Private dataset	VGG-Fac + ResNet50
Zheng ,et al. [31]	Frame-level	DAiSEE	OpenPose+ LSTM
Sharma,et al. [20]	Frame-level	FER-2013 + CK+	Voila-Jones+ VGG16
Kamath,et al. [13]	Frame-level	private dataset	HOG+ (MKL-SVM)
Sharma,et al. [21]	Video-level	Private dataset	Voila-Jones + mini-Xception CNN
Huang,et al. [12]	Video-level	DAiSEE	Attention mechanism + LSTM
Wu,et al. [28]	Video-level	EmotiW	GRU+ LSTM
Abedi,et al. [1]	Video-level	DAiSEE	ResNet+ TCN

3   Proposed Approach

To confirm the validity of our findings, we employed various pre-trained models renowned for their efficacy in image classification on two widely available engagement datasets: DAiSEE [8] and Emotiw23-EN [23]. We utilized the Optical Flow technique to capture temporal information from the video. The pre-trained models we used are convolutional neural network (CNN) architectures trained on extensive datasets for tasks like image classification and engagement recognition. We then fine-tuned these models specifically for the task of engagement classification. Our proposed architecture is shown in Fig. 1. The subsequent section will provide an overview of the datasets utilized in training our model.

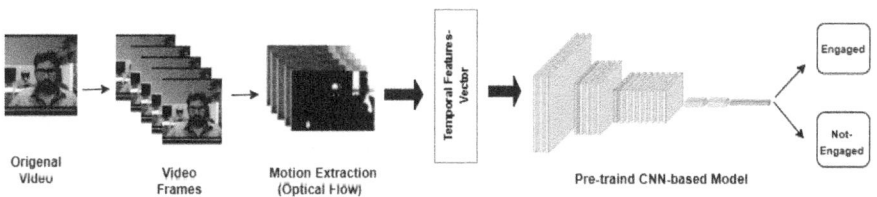

Fig. 1. The Proposed Architecture

3.1   Datasets Overview

We executed our experiment utilizing two public datasets: **DAiSEE** [8]: This publicly available dataset consists of 9086 (10-second) video clips captured from 112 students aged between 18 and 30, observed during online classes. The dataset includes 32 females and 80 males and is classified into four categories: engagement, frustration, confusion, and boredom. However, the dataset is imbalanced regarding class distribution, as shown in Fig. 3.

Fig. 2. DAiSEE dataset [8]

EmotiW23-EN [23]: This public dataset audio-video group emotion recognition challenge. It comprises 11,206 videos, divided into training, validation, and test videos. Each video has an approximate length of 10 sec. It has 127 participants representing different illumination conditions as shown in Fig. 4. It is fitting to examine a range of features, such as action units, eye gaze, and head pose.

3.2   Data Pre-processing

We utilize two publicly available datasets to assess the models: DAiSEE and EmotiW2023-EN.It is important to highlight that there is a notable imbalance in the datasets, as depicted in Figs. 3 and 4. To address this challenge, we implemented an oversampling technique. However, it does not impact the overall accuracy of the models. In addressing the DAiSEE distribution class discrepancy, we merged boredom, confusion, and frustration into a single category termed "disengaged," illustrated in Fig. 6. This decision aligns with real-world scenarios where these states are typically classified as non-engagement. By grouping them, we create a more balanced representation of engagement levels, allowing models to better capture the nuances of user interactions [30]. Despite implementing augmentation techniques as a solution to address the imbalance problem, as

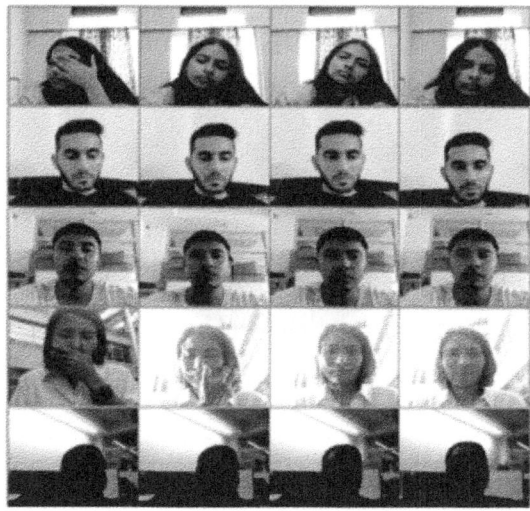

Fig. 3. EmotiW23-EN dataset [23]

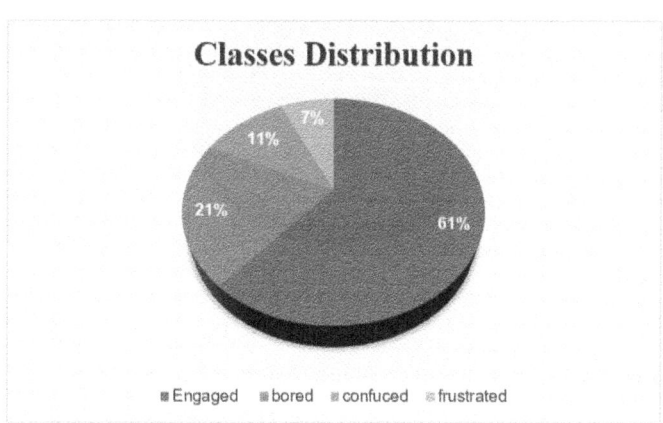

Fig. 4. DAiSEE Distribution Classes

suggested by Mohan et al. [16], the impact on the model's accuracy was not significant, indicating their inadequacy in our specific case.

On the other hand, the EmotiW23-EN is also an imbalanced dataset as shown in Fig. 5. To address this challenge, we implemented an oversampling technique. However, it does not impact the overall accuracy of the models. In our efforts to handle the imbalance in engagement classes, we select a fixed number of videos from each category to tackle this. For this experiment, we select two classes: Highly engaged and Disengaged. In this work, we select specific subsets of the datasets. The reason behind this selection is constraints on computational resources. These subsets were randomly chosen from the two datasets to ensure

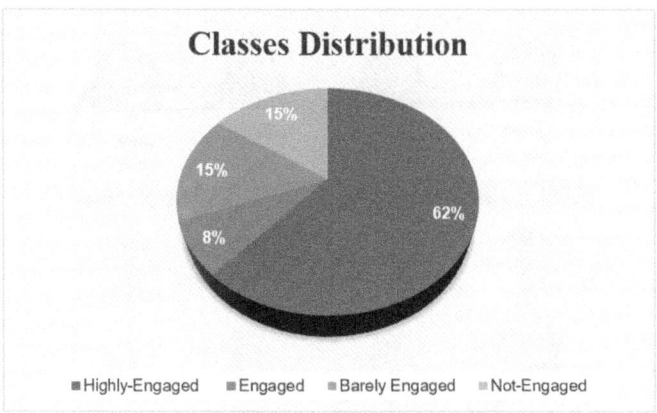

Fig. 5. EmotiW23 Distribution Classes

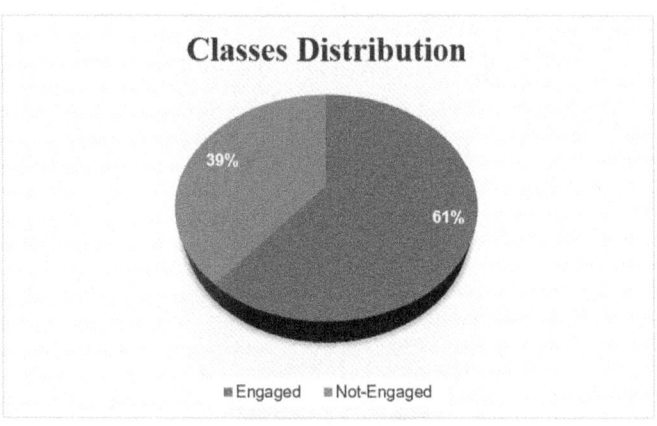

Fig. 6. DAiSEE Class Distribution after the merging process.

they represent a diverse range of engagement scenarios while keeping the computational demands manageable. To prepare the datasets for model training, we extract fixed numbers of frames from each video. Our experiment comprised 4,000 frames for the Train set and 800 for the validation set for both datasets.

3.3 Features Extraction

Two methods exist for extracting video content: spatial and temporal information.**Spatial Features**: We opted to extract crucial features from each frame. In our experiment, we specifically extracted static facial features and disregarded others, as emotions can be effectively detected through facial expressions in real scenarios. We utilize the OpenCV library to employ a Haar Cascades-based classifier [17] to extract facial features. Paul Viola and Michael Jones proposed the

Viola and Jones object detection algorithm in 2001, employing the Haar Cascade algorithm to speedily and effectively extract features from images [26]. This approach has gained significant popularity and is widely utilized for various object detection tasks [15]. The dataset's training and validation sets are initially in color, and for compatibility with pre-trained models, we resize them to become suitable for each model configuration. **Temporal features:** We focus on facial actions, head, eye, and lip movements. Our approach involves utilizing the Optical Flow technique [2] to extract motion between frames. This method captures motion information between consecutive frames by computing motion vectors, which represent changes in movement over time. The motion vectors obtained from Optical Flow represent the movement of various facial features, such as eyebrows, eyes, mouth, and overall facial expression.

3.4   Pre-traind Models and Fine-Tuning Vision Transformer

To overcome limited data, we're utilizing a strategy of retraining pre-trained models known for their excellence in computer vision, especially in classifying videos and images. Specifically, we employed pre-trained version of Vision Transformer (ViT) models, available in the Hugging Face library [27]. This library facilitates the download and loading of a model known as google/vit-basepatch16-224-in21k [27], which has undergone pre-training on the ImageNet-21k dataset [5]. The models encompass MobileNetV2, ResNet 101, Inception V3, EfficientNet, DenseNet 161 and VGG19. Subsequently, these models underwent fine-tuning on the datasets to enhance their performance in predicting user engagement. Below is an overview of each model employed in our study:

1. MobileNetV2 [19] is a lightweight CNN comprising 53 layers, designed for classifying images such as mouse, cat, and pen and for object detection tasks. It has developed intricate feature representations for diverse image types. Operating with image inputs of 224 by 224 pixels, it boasts a modest memory requirement, making it well-suited for real-time applications like the one at hand.
2. ResNet101 [10] is a deep residual network that has 101 layers. It is a famous architecture for image classification tasks and operating with image inputs of 224 by 224 pixels.
3. InceptionV3 [24] is CNN architecture that GoogleNet developed. It is known for efficiently processing images with varying sizes and aspect ratios.
4. EfficientNet [25] is a family of CNNs designed to achieve state-of-the-art accuracy while minimizing the number of parameters and computational resources required.
5. DenseNet161 [11] is a densely connected CNN that has 161 layers. It is known for extracting features from images at multiple scales.
6. VGG19 [22] is a CNN with 16 convolutional layers, three fully connected layers, five max-pooling layers, and one softmax layer.

When fine-tuning pre-trained models for classification tasks, we froze the weights of the convolutional layers in the base model. These layers will not be updated during training. Freezing the convolutional layers helps preserve the learned features while allowing us to train new layers on top [29]. We adjusted the output layer to align with the necessary number of outputs for our specific task. Since we are working with two engagement classes from the datasets (Engaged and Disengaged), we fine-tuned the model with different settings. We analyzed the performance of pre-trained models with different hyperparameters by fine-tuning them with varying numbers of epochs, batch size, and learning rates. Each model was evaluated on dataset validation using the following metrics: Accuracy, precision, Recall, and F1 score. The computational resources required for engagement prediction were acquired through the Google Colab Pro platform. This platform has a Tensor Processing Unit (TPU) processor with high RAM. These robust resources enable efficient and powerful model training and inference, ensuring accurate predictions.

Initially, Each model was trained to utilize the Adam optimizer [14]. During the training stage, diverse loss functions were employed, including cross-entropy loss, and a learning rate of 0.0001 was utilized. The training process was configured for 20 epochs with early stopping, ceasing when there was no discernible improvement in model accuracy. In addition, we incorporated a dropout rate of 0.5 during our training process. This regularization technique [9] is crucial for preventing over-fitting by randomly deactivating neurons during training. Upon concluding the training phase, a comprehensive assessment of the model's performance was conducted, utilizing various metrics, including Precision, Recall, F1, and accuracy.

3.5   Model Training

Our methodology is structured into two distinct stages. In the initial stage depicted in Fig. 1, we focus on extracting spatial features from individual frames. We utilize the OpenCV library to detect faces within every single frame of the video sequences. A Haar Cascades-based classifier is employed for accurate face detection. The detected faces are then utilized to feed pre-trained models designed explicitly for spatial feature extraction and emotion classification. These models are fine-tuned using the datasets to enhance their performance. Each trained model is evaluated using performance metrics: accuracy, precision, recall, and F1 score to assess its efficacy in engagement detection.

In the subsequent stage, as illustrated in Fig. 2, attention shifts to extracting temporal features by utilizing motion tracking across multiple frames within each video clip. We extract temporal features by tracking various motions across several frames within each video clip, including hand movement, head movement, eye movement, and lip motion. The optical flow technique is employed for precise motion extraction. The extracted motion vectors feed pre-trained models designed for engagement classification. Similar to the first stage, the pre-trained models are fine-tuned using the extracted temporal features on the datasets. The experiment was conducted twice, each time utilizing two distinct datasets. The objective was to compare the efficacy of spatial and temporal features and determine which yields superior performance. Notably, the experiment maintains consistency by employing an equal number of samples from each dataset.

4   Results and Discussion

We trained and fine-tuned models on a subset of the datasets, consisting of 4000 frames in the training set and 800 in the validation set. Table 2 summarizes an overview of the performance of different models based on spatial features 'for DAiSEE'. Regarding spatial feature extraction, InceptionV3 demonstrates superior performance compared to other models, achieving the highest accuracy, precision, recall, and F1 score. MobileNetV2 and EfficientNet exhibit similar performance closely behind, while ResNet101, DenseNet161, and VGG19 display comparatively lower scores across all metrics, as depicted in Fig. 7.

Table 2. The performance results on DAiSEE for spatial features.

Model	Accuracy	Precision	Recall	F1-score
MobileNetV2	0.52	0.52	0.52	0.48
ResNet101	0.50	0.50	0.25	0.33
InceptionV3	**0.57**	**0.59**	**0.54**	**0.55**
EfficientNet	0.51	0.51	0.51	0.51
DenseNet161	0.51	0.52	0.51	0.46
VGG19	0.50	0.25	0.50	0.33

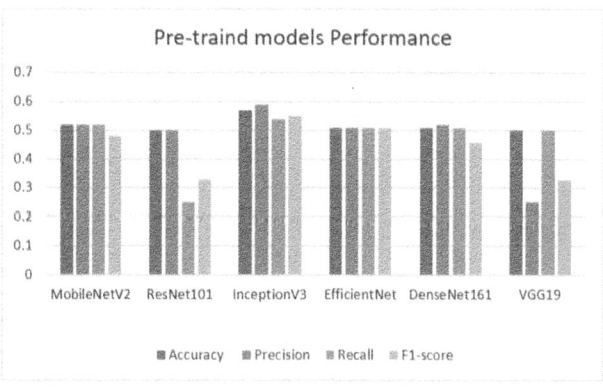

Fig. 7. The performance comparison on DAiSEE for spatial features

The performance comparison of models based on spatial features extracted from facial expressions for the EmotiW23-EN dataset is elaborated in Table 3.

To maintain consistency, we fine-tuned these models on a subset of the dataset, comprising 4000 frames in the training set and 800 in the validation set, aligning with the approach used in the previous DAiSEE dataset. Subsequently, we assessed the models' performance. InceptionV3 achieved the highest accuracy of 0.53. Meanwhile, MobileNetV2 and EfficientNet exhibited relatively lower scores across all metrics, as illustrated in Table 3 (Fig. 8).

Table 3. The performance results on Emotiw23 for spacial-Features

Model	Accuracy	Precision	Recall	F1-score
MobileNetV2	0.48	0.49	0.49	0.48
ResNet101	0.50	0.51	0.50	0.46
InceptionV3	**0.55**	**0.54**	**0.54**	**0.54**
EfficientNet	0.48	0.48	0.48	0.48
DenseNet161	0.51	0.50	0.51	0.49
VGG19	0.51	0.51	0.51	0.49

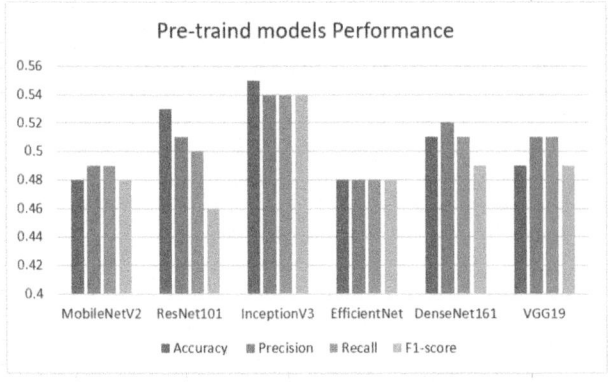

Fig. 8. The Performance caparison on EmotiW23 for spacial-Features

In contrast, fine-tuning was conducted on a subset of the DAiSEE dataset, specifically targeting frames capturing motion data to extract temporal features. As depicted in Table 4, MobileNetV2, ResNet101, DenseNet161, and VGG19 consistently display powerful performance across all evaluation metrics, achieving an accuracy, precision, recall, and F1-score of 0.60 or higher. However, EfficientNet lags behind other models' accuracy and F1-score, indicating relatively lower performance in leveraging temporal features for classification tasks within the DAiSEE dataset as shown in Fig. 9.

Table 4. The performance results on DAiSEE for Temporal-Features

Model	Accuracy	Precision	Recall	F1-score
MobileNetV2	**0.61**	**0.61**	**0.61**	**0.61**
ResNet101	0.60	0.60	0.60	0.60
InceptionV3	0.60	0.60	0.60	0.60
EfficientNet	0.50	0.25	0.50	0.33
DenseNet161	0.60	0.60	0.60	0.60
VGG19	0.60	0.60	0.60	0.60

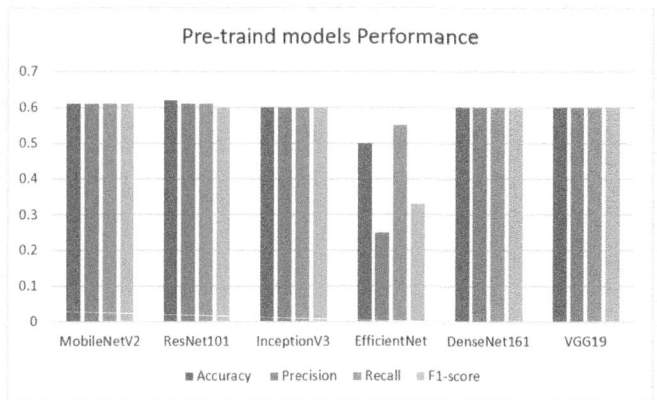

Fig. 9. The Performance Comparison on DAiSEE for Temporal-Features

The comparison of results based on temporal features extracted from motion data in the Emotiw23 dataset reveals notable variations among the models, as shown in Table 5. DenseNet161 exhibits the highest accuracy of 0.66, alongside precision, recall, and F1-score values at 0.66, indicative of robust overall performance across all metrics. MobileNetV2 and InceptionV3 achieve an accuracy of 0.65, accompanied by consistent precision, recall, and F1-score values, indicating competitive performance. Moreover, VGG19 presents balanced results across all metrics, with an accuracy of 0.61 and precision, recall, and F1 score values at 0.61. ResNet101 also delivers reasonable performance, with an accuracy of 0.60 and precision, recall, and F1-score metrics at 0.60. In contrast, EfficientNet demonstrates the lowest performance among the models, with an accuracy of 0.50 and relatively lower precision, recall, and F1-score metrics. Overall, these findings highlight the varying effectiveness of different models in leveraging temporal features for classification tasks in the Emotiw23-EN dataset, shown in Fig. 10.

Generally, models trained on both datasets typically exhibit stronger performance when leveraging temporal features rather than spatial features for engagement detection, as depicted in Figs. 11 and 12. DenseNet161 consistently outper-

Table 5. The performance results on EmotiW2023 for Temporal-Features

Model	Accuracy	Precision	Recall	F1-score
MobileNetV2	0.64	0.64	0.64	0.64
ResNet101	0.60	0.60	0.60	0.60
InceptionV3	0.65	0.65	0.65	0.65
EfficientNet	0.50	0.25	0.50	0.33
DenseNet161	**0.66**	**0.66**	**0.66**	**0.66**
VGG19	0.60	0.60	0.60	0.60

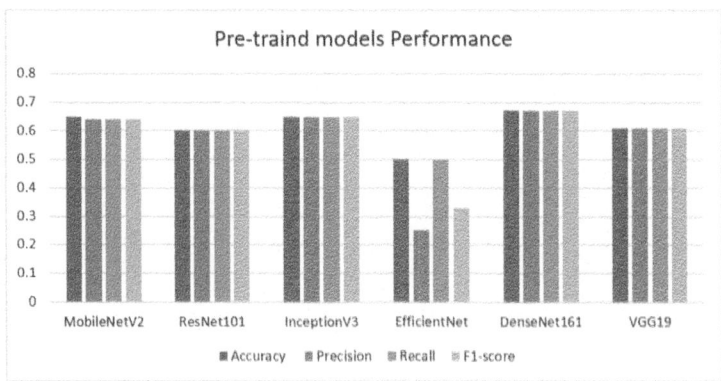

Fig. 10. The Performance Comparison on EmotiW2023 for Temporal-Features

forms other models across both spatial and temporal features in both datasets, showcasing its ability to effectively capture and utilize feature representations for engagement detection. Conversely, EfficientNet consistently lags behind other models in terms of performance, especially when utilizing both spatial and temporal features. Moreover, the Emotiw23-EN dataset generally displays higher performance scores across all models compared to the DAiSEE dataset, indicating potential disparities in data characteristics and quality between the two datasets (Fig. 11).

We compared our approach with various studies in the field of engagement recognition. Gupta et al. [8] utilized InceptionNet on the DAiSEE dataset, achieving an accuracy of 46.4%. Geng et al. [7] employed a C3D convolution network on the same dataset, achieving a higher accuracy of 56.2%. Huang et al. [12] enhanced performance further on DAiSEE by implementing an LSTM with an attention mechanism, achieving an accuracy of 60%. On the EmotiWEP23 dataset, Singh et al. [23] utilized OpenFace 2.0 with TCN, achieving an accuracy of 65.60%. Our team introduced Optical-Flow with MobileNet2, achieving an accuracy of 61% on the DAiSEE dataset. Additionally, on the EmotiWEP23 dataset, our approach integrated Optical-Flow with DenseNet161, reaching the highest accuracy of 66%. These comparisons demonstrate the efficacy and com-

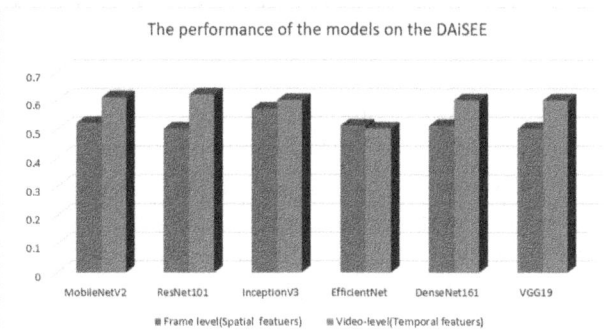

Fig. 11. Models' performance on the DAiSEE dataset in terms of spatial and temporal features

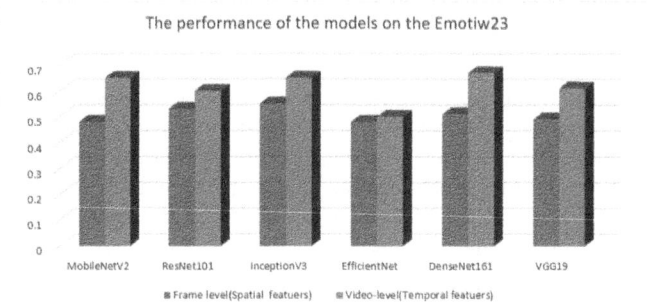

Fig. 12. Models' performance on the EmotiW23-EN dataset in terms of spatial and temporal features

petitiveness of our proposed methodology in the realm of engagement recognition (Table 6).

5   Conclusions

In conclusion, the shift towards online platforms for educational delivery, accelerated by the COVID-19 pandemic, underscores the importance of monitoring and assessing student engagement during virtual sessions. Educators can adapt their teaching approaches to optimize learning outcomes by gauging attendees' emotional states. Therefore, automating the prediction of engagement poses a significant challenge, prompting the development of robust models leveraging spatial and temporal features from video data. However, the video-based approaches outperform the frame-based approaches in student engagement detection because they capture temporal dynamics information that frames alone may miss. Additionally, the video-based approach can leverage motion cues and movements, which are important indicators of engagement, further enhancing its

Table 6. Comparison with other studies

Paper	Dataset	Proposed Model	Accuracy
[8]	DAiSEE	InceptionNet	46.4%
[7]	DAiSEE	C3D convolution network	56.2%
[12]	DAiSEE	LSTM +Attention mechanism	60%
[23]	EmotiW23-EN	OpenFace 2.0+ TCN	65.60%
	DAiSEE	Optical-Flow + MobileNet2	61%
Our approach	EmotiW23-EN	Optical-Flow + DenseNet161	66%

effectiveness in detecting student engagement. In the future, investigating the integration of multi-modal data, including audio and textual information, alongside video data could provide a more comprehensive understanding of students' engagement levels.

Acknowledgments. This research was funded partly by the Center of Excellence in AI and Machine Learning (CoE-AIML) at Howard University under Contract Number W911NF-20-2-0277 with the U.S. Army Research Laboratory, and Meta Research Gift Funds at Howard University. However, any opinion, findings, conclusions, or recommendations expressed in this document are those of the authors and should not be interpreted as representing the official policies, either expressed or implied, of the funding agencies.

References

1. Abedi, A., Khan, S.S.: Improving state-of-the-art in detecting student engagement with Resnet and TCN hybrid network. In: 2021 18th Conference on Robots and Vision (CRV), pp. 151–157. IEEE (2021)
2. Beauchemin, S.S., Barron, J.L.: The computation of optical flow. ACM Comput. Surv. (CSUR) **27**(3), 433–466 (1995)
3. Bhardwaj, P., Gupta, P., Panwar, H., Siddiqui, M.K., Morales-Menendez, R., Bhaik, A.: Application of deep learning on student engagement in e-learning environments. Comput. Electr. Eng. **93**, 107277 (2021)
4. Brown, A., Lawrence, J., Basson, M., Redmond, P.: A conceptual framework to enhance student online learning and engagement in higher education. High. Educ. Res. Dev. **41**(2), 284–299 (2022)
5. Deng, J., Dong, W., Socher, R., Li, L.J., Li, K., Fei-Fei, L.: ImageNet: a large-scale hierarchical image database. In: 2009 IEEE Conference on Computer Vision and Pattern Recognition, pp. 248–255. IEEE (2009)
6. D'Mello, S., Dieterle, E., Duckworth, A.: Advanced, analytic, automated (AAA) measurement of engagement during learning. Educational psychologist **52**(2), 104–123 (2017)
7. Geng, L., Xu, M., Wei, Z., Zhou, X.: Learning deep spatiotemporal feature for engagement recognition of online courses. In: 2019 IEEE Symposium Series on Computational Intelligence (SSCI), pp. 442–447. IEEE (2019)

8. Gupta, A., D'Cunha, A., Awasthi, K., Balasubramanian, V.: DAiSEE: towards user engagement recognition in the wild. arXiv preprint arXiv:1609.01885 (2016)
9. Hahn, S., Choi, H.: Understanding dropout as an optimization trick. Neurocomputing **398**, 64–70 (2020)
10. He, K., Zhang, X., Ren, S., Sun, J.: Deep residual learning for image recognition. In: Proceedings of the IEEE Conference on Computer Vision and Pattern Recognition, pp. 770–778 (2016)
11. Huang, G., Liu, Z., Van Der Maaten, L., Weinberger, K.Q.: Densely connected convolutional networks. In: Proceedings of the IEEE Conference on Computer Vision and Pattern Recognition, pp. 4700–4708 (2017)
12. Huang, T., Mei, Y., Zhang, H., Liu, S., Yang, H.: Fine-grained engagement recognition in online learning environment. In: 2019 IEEE 9th International Conference on Electronics Information and Emergency Communication (ICEIEC), pp. 338–341. IEEE (2019)
13. Kamath, A., Biswas, A., Balasubramanian, V.: A crowdsourced approach to student engagement recognition in e-learning environments. In: 2016 IEEE Winter Conference on Applications of Computer Vision (WACV), pp. 1–9. IEEE (2016)
14. Kingma, D.P., Ba, J.: Adam: a method for stochastic optimization. arXiv preprint arXiv:1412.6980 (2014)
15. Mohamad Nezami, O., Dras, M., Hamey, L., Richards, D., Wan, S., Paris, C.: Automatic recognition of student engagement using deep learning and facial expression. In: Joint European Conference on Machine Learning and Knowledge Discovery in Databases, pp. 273–289. Springer (2020)
16. Mohan, K., Seal, A., Krejcar, O., Yazidi, A.: Facial expression recognition using local gravitational force descriptor-based deep convolution neural networks. IEEE Trans. Instrum. Meas. **70**, 1–12 (2020)
17. Pandey, A.K., Mishra, R.: Deep learning based facial recognition using H aar cascade technique. In: 2023 3rd International Conference on Advance Computing and Innovative Technologies in Engineering (ICACITE), pp. 2109–2113. IEEE (2023)
18. Ruiz, N., et al.: Atl-bp: a student engagement dataset and model for affect transfer learning for behavior prediction. IEEE Trans. Biometrics Behav. Identity Sci. **5**, 411–424 (2022)
19. Sandler, M., Howard, A., Zhu, M., Zhmoginov, A., Chen, L.C.: MobilenetV2: inverted residuals and linear bottlenecks. In: Proceedings of the IEEE Conference on Computer Vision and Pattern Recognition, pp. 4510–4520 (2018)
20. Sharma, A., Mansotra, V.: Deep learning based student emotion recognition from facial expressions in classrooms. Int. J. Eng. Adv. Technol. **8**(6), 4691–4699 (2019)
21. Sharma, P., et al.: Student engagement detection using emotion analysis, eye tracking and head movement with machine learning. In: International Conference on Technology and Innovation in Learning, Teaching and Education, pp. 52–68. Springer (2022)
22. Simonyan, K., Zisserman, A.: Very deep convolutional networks for large-scale image recognition. arXiv preprint arXiv:1409.1556 (2014)
23. Singh, M., Hoque, X., Zeng, D., Wang, Y., Ikeda, K., Dhall, A.: Do i have your attention: a large scale engagement prediction dataset and baselines. In: Proceedings of the 25th International Conference on Multimodal Interaction, pp. 174–182 (2023)
24. Szegedy, C., Vanhoucke, V., Ioffe, S., Shlens, J., Wojna, Z.: Rethinking the inception architecture for computer vision. In: Proceedings of the IEEE Conference on Computer Vision and Pattern Recognition, pp. 2818–2826 (2016)

25. Tan, M., Le, Q.: Efficientnetv2: smaller models and faster training. In: International conference on machine learning, pp. 10096–10106. PMLR (2021)
26. Viola, P., Jones, M.J.: Robust real-time face detection. Int. J. Comput. Vision **57**, 137–154 (2004)
27. Wu, B., et al.: Visual transformers: token-based image representation and processing for computer vision. arXiv preprint arXiv:2006.03677 (2020)
28. Wu, J., Yang, B., Wang, Y., Hattori, G.: Advanced multi-instance learning method with multi-features engineering and conservative optimization for engagement intensity prediction. In: Proceedings of the 2020 International Conference on Multimodal Interaction, pp. 777–783 (2020)
29. Xiao, X., Mudiyanselage, T.B., Ji, C., Hu, J., Pan, Y.: Fast deep learning training through intelligently freezing layers. In: 2019 International Conference on Internet of Things (iThings) and IEEE Green Computing and Communications (GreenCom) and IEEE Cyber, Physical and Social Computing (CPSCom) and IEEE Smart Data (SmartData), pp. 1225–1232. IEEE (2019)
30. Zhang, H., Xiao, X., Huang, T., Liu, S., Xia, Y., Li, J.: An novel end-to-end network for automatic student engagement recognition. In: 2019 IEEE 9th International Conference on Electronics Information and Emergency Communication (ICEIEC), pp. 342–345. IEEE (2019)
31. Zheng, X., Hasegawa, S., Tran, M.T., Ota, K., Unoki, T.: Estimation of learners' engagement using face and body features by transfer learning. In: International Conference on Human-Computer Interaction, pp. 541–552. Springer (2021)

Metaverse Mastery: Enhancing Public Speaking Skills in Linguistic High School Students Through Advanced Technologies

Alessandro Aloisio$^{(\boxtimes)}$ [iD], Antonella Cavallaro [iD], and Marco Romano [iD]

Dipartimento di Scienze Umanistiche e Sociali Internazionali, Università degli Studi Internazionali di Roma, 00147 Rome, Italy
{alessandro.aloisio,antonella.cavallaro,marco.romano}@unint.eu

Abstract. Developing cross-cutting skills for graduating students is a key objective outlined in the Italian National Recovery and Resilience Plan (PNRR), aimed at addressing school dropout rates and encouraging further academic pursuits. This research explores solutions grounded in interactive systems to engage students more effectively and facilitate the development of these skills. Specifically, our focus is on public speaking, and we investigate how metaverse and virtual reality platforms can impact anxiety levels, enhance the sense of empowerment in public speaking, and influence the level of engagement and acceptance of this technology as training tools. To achieve this, we organized and conducted a pilot study involving one workshops in a linguistic high school, engaging a cohort of 19 students. During this workshop, students prepared a 5-minute speech to be delivered in a virtual forum using 3D avatars. We employed a metaverse solution developed by Università degli Studi Internazionali di Roma - UNINT, named UNINTVERSE, featuring diverse environments. Students were instructed to enter a waiting room and then proceed to the speaking venue, mimicking real-world actions to provide them with a heightened sense of realism and immersion. Preliminary results indicate that the metaverse and virtual reality can be complementary tools to enhance cross-cutting skills, such as public speaking, rather than substitutes for traditional methods. They can be used to alleviate the anxiety and fear typically experienced by young and untrained individuals. This study highlights two main properties of these technologies: creating a layer between the speaker and the public and experiencing different scenarios that may be difficult or impossible to reproduce in the real world.

Keywords: Metaverse · Virtual reality · Public speaking

1 Introduction

The *metaverse* is a term that refers to a concept of a shared three-dimensional virtual environment where people can interact with each other and with digital

P. Zaphiris et al. (Eds.): HCII 2024, LNCS 15378, pp. 35–45, 2025.
https://doi.org/10.1007/978-3-031-76815-6_3

objects in an immersive way. The main features of the metaverse include: *multiple scenarios*: the metaverse offers a wide range of scenarios and virtual environments, which can be created by users themselves or by developers; *social interaction*: people can communicate and interact with each other through avatars or digital representations of themselves; *virtual economy*: in the metaverse, users can buy and sell digital goods, such as objects, virtual property, clothing for avatars, and services; *customization*: users can customize their avatars, appearance, clothing, and the virtual environment around them; *continuity*: the metaverse is a persistent and continuous environment that continues to exist even when users disconnect.

As a thriving field, the metaverse promises to revolutionise various aspects of life, including entertainment, education, and commerce. It offers a platform for unprecedented levels of creativity and interaction, enabling users to overstep physical boundaries and experience new forms of social engagement and collaboration.

In recent years, the metaverse and virtual reality (VR) have transcended traditional boundaries, serving not only as tools for entertainment and education but also as powerful avenues for honing cross-cutting skills [7,17,35]. Among all cross-cutting skills, public speaking stands out as a vital competency that significantly influences personal and professional success. The ability to articulate thoughts, convey ideas with confidence, and connect with an audience is a hallmark of effective communication [12,28]. The metaverse and VR are emerging as innovative means to refine these skills [6,13,20].

Public speaking anxiety is a common challenge faced by individuals across various walks of life, which hit among the 20% of the population [20,34]. The fear of speaking in front of an audience can hinder career advancement, limit personal growth, and impede effective communication. Recognizing the potential of the metaverse and VR to provide immersive and realistic environments, tailored experiences are being developed to specifically address the nuances of public speaking [6,20,37].

Furthermore, the significant reduction in the price of VR visors and applications, as reported in [19], has ushered in a transformative era for public speaking research. As these cutting-edge technologies become more accessible, researchers now have unprecedented opportunities to explore the dynamics of communication in immersive virtual environments. The affordability of VR visors and applications has democratized access to tools that were once confined to specialized labs or high-budget projects. This shift opens doors for extensive research into public speaking, allowing scholars to conduct experiments and gather data in diverse settings without the constraints of expensive equipment.

As technology continues to advance, the integration of the metaverse and VR in public speaking training programs offers a unique opportunity to create realistic scenarios where individuals can practice and refine their abilities in a safe and controlled virtual space. From simulated boardroom presentations to large auditorium settings, they not only offer risk-free environments for individuals to conquer their fear of public speaking but also provide platforms for targeted skill development.

The intersection of technology and cross-cutting skills development, particularly in the context of public speaking, represents a promising frontier with the potential to reshape how individuals approach and master this critical aspect of effective communication.

As shown later in this paper, the students validated our hypothesis that the metaverse and virtual reality can be used as tools for honing public speaking skills. On one hand, these technologies enable individuals to practice without exhibiting part of the signs of anxiety, thanks to the use of an avatar mask. On the other hand, they also provide opportunities to challenge individuals with varying levels of difficulty. Indeed, one can practice before audiences of different sizes, from a single person to thousands, and in diverse public settings.

1.1 Related Work

In this section, we will add more references about the metaverse and VR. As mentioned in the previous section, over the last ten years, the reduction in prices and technological improvements have led to an ever-growing community studying how the metaverse and VR can enhance cross-cutting skills and education. We will not include many older papers, as their results are often outdated [24,29].

More in detail, the metaverse and VR have been studied across various educational fields, including heritage education [41], language learning [14,21,40], history [39], engineering [16], and surgical education [15,23].

Unlike augmented reality and mixed reality [31], VR uniquely transports users from the physical world into a fully simulated environment [22,24,25,29, 32], providing a strong sense of presence [30]. This property of VR, which also applies to the metaverse, is clearly useful for many educational goals [22,24], including public speaking [6,13]. This enhanced presence allows interaction with simulated settings that are often difficult or impossible to recreate in reality [25,27].

Another property of both the metaverse and VR is their immersive nature, which is quite useful for cross-cutting skills and educational training. For example, being part of an artificial environment can increase the effectiveness of distance learning [18] and public speaking [20,37].

Recent meta-analyses and reviews by scholars such as [38,41], and [36] are particularly noteworthy. For instance, [38] investigates the application of the metaverse in education, while [36] focuses on K-12 and higher education.

A recent novel study, [33], involved 120 Italian high school teachers participating in a practical workshop to evaluate their knowledge, skills, and intention to use VR in teaching following a brief training. The findings suggest that teachers are interested in incorporating VR into their lessons, believing it can improve teaching practices by fostering active student engagement and experiential learning.

2   Workshop

The workshop was developed in collaboration among the Virtual and Augmented Reality for Learning working group at UNINT, the Disability Research Center (DRC) at UNINT, and the high school Istituto San Giuseppe del Caburlotto in Rome, Italy.

The structure of a single workshop session comprised several phases. In the initial phase, there was a 30 min introduction to metaverse and VR in education. The second phase (around 20 min) provided an overview of metaverse and VR in connection to other extended digital realities and detailed the technical functioning of the Meta Oculus Quest 2 VR headset[1], which was utilized for the practical segment of the workshop. The final phase, spanning around 90 min, involved an explanation and hands-on experience with the UNINTVERSE application[2]. This metaverse was developed by the Virtual and Augmented Reality for Learning working group at UNINT using the immersive social platform Spatial.io[3]. The idea was to build an environment where UNINT students can meet to collaborate in studying and socializing while also familiarizing themselves with emerging technologies. Moreover, UNINT also decided to offer services such as curriculum counseling, a student service office, and more on the UNINTVERSE application. It was conceived as an auxiliary opportunity that will never substitute the university's goal of in-person socializing. The UNINTVERSE platform was developed not only to familiarize students with VR and the metaverse but also for research purposes in various areas, specifically in social sciences. Figure 1 shows four different areas in this metaverse.

The workshop took place in one of the school's rooms. The first two phases were common for the whole audience since they were basically theoretical, while the third phase was divided into three practical sessions. The first two sessions accommodated six students each, while the last one accommodated seven students. The practical sessions were held in a main hall inside UNINTVERSE.

Additionally, two technical personnel from UNINT were in attendance. For the final phase, students were divided into groups of at most seven participants to streamline workshop management and prevent overloading the network connection, since managing multiple VR headsets requires significant resources. We utilized a portable Wi-Fi router.

In the workshop, most participants, accounting for 52.6%, were female, while the remainder 47.4% were male. In terms of age, about 68.4% were 17 years old, 26.3% were 18 years old, while 5.3% were 20 years old. In terms of educational levels, all the students were in the fourth year of high school.

Students who did not wear the VR headsets, along with the teacher, had the opportunity to observe the activities inside the metaverse through projection on a screen.

---

[1] https://www.meta.com/it/quest/products/quest-2/, accessed on 18 May 2024.

[2] https://www.spatial.io/s/UNINTVERSE-Base-Camp-6561e893efb5938bda0458cb.

[3] https://spatial.io.

Fig. 1. Sample pictures of UNINTVERSE.

Tools. A questionnaire based on the Personal Report of Public Speaking Anxiety Scale (PRPSA) is used. The PRPSA is a self-report questionnaire comprising 34 items on a 5-point Likert scale, designed to assess perceived anxiety in public speaking. It is particularly utilized in educational settings [26]. Each item is rated on a scale from 1 (strongly disagree) to 5 (strongly agree). The PRPSA measures two dimensions of fear of public speaking: (a) anxiety prior to and during a public speech and (b) feelings of helplessness and lack of control during a speech [26]. The questionnaire was adapted for use before and after a public speaking experience in the metaverse. Therefore, the questionnaire comprises 17 items derived from the PRPSA scale, an item on a five-point Likert scale used to assess the level of anxiety experienced during the speaking engagement in the metaverse.

We delved into the realm of the metaverse with 19 students to explore the impact of immersive experiences on public speaking anxiety. As mentioned in the previous paragraph (Tools), the workshop commenced with a pre-assessment, shown in Table 1, gauging the students' anxiety levels regarding public speaking. This pre-assessment was conducted by the students the day before, which is why there are 20 students in Table 1 instead of 19. We chose this approach due to the limited time available at school. Armed with VR visors, the students were introduced to the metaverse named UNINTVERSE.

As the participants moved through this digital environment, they were directed to gather in the main hall of our metaverse application. The immersive nature of UNINTVERSE aimed to effectively replicate the pressures of real-world public speaking, allowing us to observe firsthand the students' reactions and responses. Throughout the experience, students received constructive feedback from virtual audiences, enhancing their communication skills. Following the virtual presentations, a post-assessment, shown in Table 2, was conducted to measure any changes in anxiety levels. The results demonstrated a somewhat noticeable reduction in public speaking anxiety among the participants, highlighting the potential of the metaverse and VR technologies in alleviating performance-related stress. This workshop not only showcased the transformative power of the metaverse and virtual reality in education but also laid the groundwork for future research on the psychological and educational benefits of leveraging immersive technologies in the high school setting. The UNINT-VERSE workshop underscored the importance of incorporating cutting-edge tools to enhance learning experiences and build essential life skills.

Table 1. First questionnaire (pre-assessment).

ID	Item	N.	Mean	S.D.
1	When I prepare to speak in public, I feel tense and nervous.	20	3.2	1.06
2	I feel tense when I see the words 'Conference' or 'Public Speaking' as examination methods for a course.	20	2.75	1.02
3	I become anxious when I think that my public speech is approaching.	20	3.75	1.02
4	I am not afraid of speaking in public.	20	2.6	1.05
5	When a teacher assigns me a task ending with a public presentation, I begin to feel tense.	20	2.5	0.95
6	I enjoy preparing for a public speech.	20	2.4	0.68
7	I get anxious when someone asks me a question I don't know the answer to.	20	2.9	1.12
8	I feel fully in control of myself when I give a speech.	20	3.15	0.99
9	I am not afraid of giving a public speech.	20	2.7	0.86
10	Just before speaking in public, my heart started beating faster.	20	3.9	1.12
11	Realizing that there is only a little time left in a speech makes me very tense and anxious.	20	3.1	1.21
12	While giving my presentation, I felt I could control my anxiety and tension.	20	3.05	1.28
13	I feel relaxed and comfortable in the hours immediately before a speech	20	2	0.79
14	I give a few public talks because I'm anxious.	20	3.3	1.22
15	If I make a mistake during the speech, I find it difficult to concentrate on the next part.	20	3	1.12
16	During an important speech, I feel a sense of helplessness inside me.	20	2.25	0.91
17	While giving a speech, I get so nervous that I forget things I know.	20	2.75	1.21

Table 2. Second questionnaire (post-assessment).

ID	Item	N.	Mean	S.D.
0	During the simulation with the VR headset, did you have the opportunity to present your talk to an audience?	19	0.95	0.23
1	I felt tense and nervous when I learned that I had to present in the metaverse.	19	1.89	1.05
2	I would experience tension if I required to speak in public in the metaverse as an exam modality.	19	2.21	1.18
3	When my turn to speak in public in the metaverse was approaching, I felt anxious.	19	2.37	1.34
4	I have been fearless of public speaking in the metaverse.	19	3.89	1.15
5	I felt tense when the teacher assigned me to present in public in the metaverse.	19	2.11	1.05
6	I enjoyed preparing the public speech for the metaverse exercise.	19	3.63	0.83
7	I got anxious when someone asked me a question that I couldn't answer (if it didn't happen, answer if you would have gotten anxious if someone had asked you the question).	19	2.32	1.42
8	I felt I was entirely in control of myself when I gave the public speech with the avatar.	19	3.95	1.08
9	I wasn't afraid to give a public talk in the Metaverse.	19	4.05	1.03
10	Just before I started speaking in public, my heart started beating faster.	19	2.26	1.19
11	While giving a talk in the metaverse, realizing there was	19	2.16	1.07
12	While giving my presentation in the metaverse, I felt like I could control my anxiety and tension.	19	3.74	1.10
13	I felt relaxed and comfortable before the speech.	19	3.47	1.26
14	I would give a few public speeches in the metaverse because I am anxious.	19	2.58	1.12
15	If I made a mistake during my speech, I found concentrating on the next part difficult. (If that didn't happen, try to imagine what it would have been like.)	19	2.42	1.35
16	During an important speech (in the metaverse), I would feel a sense of helplessness within me.	19	2.16	1.26
17	While speaking in the metaverse, I became so nervous that I forgot what I wanted to say.	19	1.74	1.15

3   Conclusion and Future Works

In conclusion, our pilot workshop in a high school utilizing the metaverse and VR for public speaking demonstrated promising potential. The innovative use of immersive virtual environments engaged students and facilitated a more inter-active and supportive atmosphere for developing public speaking skills. While these initial results are encouraging, they are preliminary and based on a small sample size.

To build on this foundation, we plan to conduct more advanced experimenta-tion with students from our university. This next phase will involve a larger, more diverse cohort and employ comprehensive methodologies to assess the effective-ness of metaverse-based public speaking training. By refining our approach and expanding our research, we aim to generate robust data that will provide deeper insights into the educational benefits and limitations of using the metaverse in this context. Ultimately, our goal is to establish a well-substantiated framework for integrating the metaverse and VR into public speaking curricula, potentially improving how these skills are taught and learned.

Another line of research that we think is worth exploring is the use of multi-agent game theory models [1–5] and artificial intelligence [8, 10] to create models that describe the strategies adopted by the involved actors (agents) while increas-ing personal utility in the field of cross-cutting skills, such as public speaking. An example of using game theory in education can be found in [9], while two applications of artificial intelligence in public speaking can be found here [10, 11]

Disclosure of Interests. The statements, opinions and data contained in this paper are solely those of the individual author(s) and contributor(s) and not of HCII and/or the editor(s). HCII and/or the editor(s) disclaim responsibility for any injury to people or property resulting from any ideas, methods, instructions or products referred to in the content.

References

1. Aloisio, A.: Distance hypergraph polymatrix coordination games. In: Proceedings of the 22nd Conference Autonomous Agents and Multi-Agent Systems (AAMAS), pp. 2679–2681 (2023)
2. Aloisio, A., Flammini, M., Kodric, B., Vinci, C.: Distance polymatrix coordina-tion games. In: Proceedings of the 30th International Joint Conference Artificial Intelligence (IJCAI), pp. 3–9 (2021)
3. Aloisio, A., Flammini, M., Kodric, B., Vinci, C.: Distance polymatrix coordination games (short paper). In: SPIRIT co-located with 22nd International Conf. AIxIA 2023, 7-9 November 2023, Rome, Italy, vol. 3585 (2023)
4. Aloisio, A., Flammini, M., Vinci, C.: The impact of selfishness in hypergraph hedo-nic games. In: Proceedings of the 34th Conference Artificial Intelligence (AAAI), pp. 1766–1773 (2020)
5. Aloisio, A., Flammini, M., Vinci, C.: Generalized distance polymatrix games. In: Proceedings of the 49th International Conference Current Trends in Theory & Practice of Computer and Science (SOFSEM). Springer (2024)

6. Bachmann, M., Subramaniam, A., Born, J., Weibel, D.: Virtual reality public speaking training: effectiveness and user technology acceptance. Front. Virtual Reality **4** (2023). https://doi.org/10.3389/frvir.2023.1242544, https://www.frontiersin.org/articles/10.3389/frvir.2023.1242544
7. Bartolotta, S., Gaggioli, A., Riva, G.: The meta-learning project: design and evaluation of an experiential-learning intervention in the metaverse for soft skills improvement. Cyberpsychology Behav. Soc. Netw. **26**(3), 221–224 (2023). https://doi.org/10.1089/CYBER.2023.29268.CEU, https://doi.org/10.1089/cyber.2023.29268.ceu
8. Battistoni, P., et al.: Using artificial intelligence and companion robots to improve home healthcare for the elderly. In: HCI International 2023 - Late Breaking Papers - 25th International Conference on Human-Computer Interaction, HCII 2023, Copenhagen, Denmark, 23-28 July 2023, Proceedings, Part II. LNCS, vol. 14055, pp. 3–17. Springer (2023). https://doi.org/10.1007/978-3-031-48041-6_1
9. Beltadze, G.N.: Game theory - basis of higher education and teaching organization. Int. J. Mod. Educ. Comput. Sci. **8**(6), 41–49 (2016)
10. Chen, Y.: Effects of technology-enhanced language learning on reducing EFL learners' public speaking anxiety. Comput. Assisted Lang. Learn. **37**, 1–25 (2022)
11. Cherner, T., Fegely, A., Hou, C., Halpin, P.: AI-powered presentation platforms for improving public speaking skills: takeaways and suggestions for improvement **34**(2), 1–25 (2023)
12. Dunbar, N., Brooks, C., Tara, K.M.: Oral communication skills in higher education: using a performance-based evaluation rubric to assess communication skills. Innov. High. Educ. **31**(2), 115–128 (2006). https://doi.org/10.1007/s10755-006-9012-x, funding Information: This research was funded by a California State University Long Beach Assessment Grant received by the first two authors
13. Frisby, B.N., Kaufmann, R., Vallade, J.I., Frey, T.K., Martin, J.C.: Using virtual reality for speech rehearsals: an innovative instructor approach to enhance student public speaking efficacy. Basic Commun. Course Ann. **32**(1), 6 (2020)
14. García-Del-Toro, E., Más-López, M., Quijano, M., García Salgado, S.: Virtual laboratories as an educational tool to promote the SDGS of the 2030 agenda. In: INTED2023 Proceedings, pp. 657–666. 17th International Technology, Education and Development Conference, IATED (6-8 March 2023) (2023). https://doi.org/10.21125/inted.2023.0225
15. Gonzalez-Romo, N.I., et al: Virtual neurosurgery anatomy laboratory: a collaborative and remote education experience in the metaverse. Surg. Neurol. Int. **14**(90), (2023). https://doi.org/10.25259/SNI_162_2023. PMID: 37025523; PMCID: PMC10070459
16. Huang, Y., Richter, E., Kleickmann, T., Richter, D.: Virtual reality in teacher education from 2010 to 2020, pp. 399–441. Springer Fachmedien Wiesbaden, Wiesbaden (2023). https://doi.org/10.1007/978-3-658-37895-0_16
17. Hwang, Y., Lee, J.H.: "Yes, i am more confident with my avatars": Integrating EFL students' speaking practice into metaverse. RELC J. (2024). https://doi.org/10.1177/00336882241251952
18. Hák, T., Janoušková, S., Moldan, B.: Sustainable development goals: a need for relevant indicators. Ecol. Ind. **60**, 565–573 (2016). https://doi.org/10.1016/j.ecolind.2015.08.003
19. Knuth, D.E.: AR VR headsets market share (2023)
20. Kroczek, L.O., Mühlberger, A.: Public speaking training in front of a supportive audience in virtual reality improves performance in real-life. Sci. Rep. **13** (2023). https://doi.org/10.1371/journal.pone.0216288

21. Lafuente-Lechuga, M., Cifuentes-Faura, J., Úrsula Faura-Martínez: Mathematics applied to the economy and sustainable development goals: a necessary relationship of dependence. Educ. Sci. **10**(11) (2020). https://doi.org/10.3390/educsci10110339, https://www.mdpi.com/2227-7102/10/11/339

22. Leder, J., Horlitz, T., Puschmann, P., Wittstock, V., Schütz, A.: Comparing immersive virtual reality and Powerpoint as methods for delivering safety training: impacts on risk perception, learning, and decision making. Saf. Sci. **111**, 271–286 (2019). https://doi.org/10.1016/j.ssci.2018.07.021, https://www.sciencedirect.com/science/article/pii/S0925753518302832

23. Liu, Y., Fan, X., Zhou, X., Liu, M., Wang, J., Liu, T.: Application of virtual reality technology in distance higher education. In: Proceedings of the 2019 4th International Conference on Distance Education and Learning, pp. 35–39. ICDEL 2019, Association for Computing Machinery, New York, NY, USA (2019). https://doi.org/10.1145/3338147.3338174

24. Makransky, G., Borre-Gude, S., Mayer, R.E.: Motivational and cognitive benefits of training in immersive virtual reality based on multiple assessments. J. Comput. Assist. Learn. **35**(6), 691–707 (2019). https://doi.org/10.1111/JCAL.12375

25. Mikropoulos, T.A., Natsis, A.: Educational virtual environments: a ten-year review of empirical research (1999–2009). Comput. Educ. **56**(3), 769–780 (2011). https://doi.org/10.1016/j.compedu.2010.10.020

26. Mörtberg, E., Jansson-Fröjmark, M., Pettersson, A., Hennlid-Oredsson, T.: Psychometric properties of the personal report of public speaking anxiety (PRPSA) in a sample of university students in Sweden. Int. J. Cogn. Ther. **11**(4), 421–433 (2018)

27. Nations, U.: Transforming our world: the 2030 agenda for sustainable development (2023). https://sdgs.un.org/2030agenda

28. Pathak, A., Vasan, M.L.: Oral communication skills in higher education: using a performance-based evaluation rubric to assess communication skills. Int. J. Eval. Res. Educ. (IJERE) **4**(4), 179–184 (2015). https://doi.org/10.11591/ijere.v4i4.4509

29. Pellas, N., Mystakidis, S., Kazanidis, I.: Immersive virtual reality in k-12 and higher education: a systematic review of the last decade scientific literature. Virtual Reality **25**(3), 835–861 (2021). https://doi.org/10.1007/s10055-020-00489-9

30. Polcar, J., Horejsi, P.: Knowledge acquisition and cyber sickness: a comparison of VR devices in virtual tours, pp. 613–616. (2015). https://api.semanticscholar.org/CorpusID:17423238

31. Romano, M., Díaz, P., Aedo, I.: Empowering teachers to create augmented reality experiences: the effects on the educational experience. Interact. Learn. Environ. **31**(3), 1546–1563 (2023). https://doi.org/10.1080/10494820.2020.1851727

32. Romano, M., Díaz, P., Ignacio, A., D'Agostino, P.: Augmenting smart objects for cultural heritage: a usability experiment. In: Augmented Reality. Virtual Reality, and Computer Graphics, pp. 186–204. Springer International Publishing, Cham (2016)

33. Romano, M., et al.: Exploring the potential of immersive virtual reality in Italian schools: a practical workshop with high school teachers. Multimodal Technol. Interact. **7**(12), 111 (2023). https://doi.org/10.3390/MTI7120111

34. Ruscio, A.M., Brown, T.A., Chiu, W.T., Sareen, J., Stein, M.B., Kessler, R.C.: Social fears and social phobia in the USA: results from the national comorbidity survey replication. Psychol. Med. **38**(1), 15–28 (2007)

35. Stewart, C., Wall, A., Marciniec, S.: Mixed signals: do college graduates have the soft skills that employers want? Competition Forum **14**(2), 276 (2016)

36. Sá, M.J., Serpa, S.: Metaverse as a learning environment: some considerations. Sustainability **15**(3) (2023). https://doi.org/10.3390/su15032186, https://www.mdpi.com/2071-1050/15/3/2186

37. Takac, M., Collett, J., Blom, K.J., Conduit, R., Rehm, I., Foe, A.D.: Public speaking anxiety decreases within repeated virtual reality training sessions. PLOS ONE **14**(5), 1–17 (2019). https://doi.org/10.1371/journal.pone.0216288

38. Tlili, A., et al.: Is metaverse in education a blessing or a curse: a combined content and bibliometric analysis. Smart Learn. Environ. **9**(1), 24 (2022). https://doi.org/10.1186/s40561-022-00205-x

39. University, K., Virtual Rights Policy Institute, J.y.: The potential of virtual reality for the SDGS: infrastructure development through content and cultural policies Yuto Kunitake (2023). https://sdgs.un.org/

40. Wu, J.G., Zhang, D., Lee, S.M.: Into the brave new metaverse: envisaging future language teaching and learning. IEEE Trans. Learn. Technol. **17**, 44–53 (2024). https://doi.org/10.1109/TLT.2023.3259470

41. Yue, K.: Breaking down the barrier between teachers and students by using metaverse technology in education: based on a survey and analysis of Shenzhen city, China, p. 40–44. IC4E 2022, Association for Computing Machinery, New York, NY, USA (2022). https://doi.org/10.1145/3514262.3514345

Research on the Transformation of Digital Teaching and Learning Methods in Higher Education and Its Influencing Factors

Huiqian He[1,2], Salwa Hanim Abdul-Rashid[2], Raja Ariffin Raja Ghazilla[2(✉)], and Huijie He[3]

[1] Guangdong Technology College, Guangdong 526100, Zhaoqing, China
[2] University of Malaya, 50603 Kuala Lumpur, Malaysia
r_ariffin@um.edu.my
[3] Shishan Senior High School, Guangdong 528200, Foshan, China

Abstract. With the development of digital intelligence technology, digital teaching and talent training have become important issues in global education and have received widespread attention from society. To deepen the comprehensive reform of higher education and accelerate the digitalization process of higher education, it is necessary to clarify the factors that promote and hinder the transformation of digital teaching and learning methods in higher education. This study aims to seek effective digital education strategies, and through a series of in-depth user research and influencing factor analysis, it obtains the main influencing factors of the transformation of digital teaching and learning methods in higher education. Based on the literature research on the digitalization of higher education and combined with the current status of digitalization of higher education, an initial model of influencing factors was constructed. Conduct reliability and validity analysis and structural equation model analysis on the questionnaire survey results. The research results show that teacher factors, student literacy, technology diffusion, policy support, and data security have a positive impact on the transformation of digital teaching and learning methods in higher education. However, infrastructure and university support have no significant impact on it. The research results have reference value for institutions and governments to formulate relevant digital education strategies.

Keywords: Digitalization of Higher Education · Learning Behavior · Influencing Factors · Structural Equation Model

1 Introduction

Digitalization of education is an inevitable choice to achieve fair and high-quality development of education. General Secretary Xi Jinping clearly stated in the report of the 20th National Congress of the Communist Party of China to "promote the digitalization of education and build a learning society and a learning country with lifelong learning for all." The digitalization of higher education is through thorough and comprehensive digital transformation and ecological reconstruction to form a data-driven, human-technical integration, cross-border and open educational ecosystem, and to build a more agile, appropriate, fair and sustainable higher education system [1]. The core of education digital transformation is knowledge and data-driven, and the key is collaborative sharing [2].

Digital gaps and challenges to quality education exist in higher education. Environmental factors play a decisive role in ensuring the quality of education [3]. Motivation, feedback from teachers and students, evaluation of results, reasonable supervision, etc. are very important in closing the digital gap [4].

Although digital teaching can make the classroom lively and easy to download, it may also cause teachers to suffer from the workload and anxiety of "technology overload", which will have a negative impact on teachers' teaching, thinking and working methods. At the same time, students also need to pay additional fees for digital hardware such as computers, tablets, Internet, etc. [5]. Personal information also faces risks of being misappropriated, stolen, and leaked [6]. Current digital education has deficiencies in resource allocation, teacher-student cognition, training mechanisms, evaluation systems, and policy systems. Teachers are lacking in comprehensive information literacy, and the digital ecosystem has not been fully formed [7].

This study mainly answers the following questions: What are the differences and changes between digital teaching and traditional teaching in higher education? What are the main influencing factors of the transformation of digital teaching and learning methods in higher education? What are the strategies to promote high-quality digital development of higher education?

2   Literature Review

The world is undergoing digital transformation, and some universities are following the trend while others are lagging behind in digital development. The digital transformation of higher education is a complex systematic project, which is affected by many factors [8]. This article mainly identifies the main influencing factors affecting the digital development and transformation of universities. In a study on the digital transformation of business schools, it was concluded that student capabilities have the greatest impact on the adoption of digitalization in business schools, followed by faculty capabilities and technology dissemination, while industry expectations have no significant impact [9]. The extent and effectiveness of digital teaching will be affected by digital capabilities in teaching, university support, ICT self-efficacy, and ICT perceptions. These factors will promote the digitalization of higher education institutions in a variety of practical ways [10]. Similarly, another study also showed that digital policies and commitments, university management, institutional equipment, technology and educational support, self-assessment of basic digital skills, self-assessment of technology-related teaching skills, all explain the huge level of digital learning activities difference [11]. He Sheng-sheng pointed out that the degree of coupling between higher education and digitalization in China is low and development is slow, showing the geographical characteristics of gradation and agglomeration. The degree of development of the technology market, the intensity of government support, and the intensity of school-enterprise connections will promote the digital development of higher education. However, the impact of social human capital and regional economic development level is not significant [12]. Research by Wang Ping and others concluded that the digital transformation of universities is affected by multiple factors concurrently, including digital perception, digital innovation, digital learning, resource construction, resource integration and resource utilization, and proposed to strengthen dynamic capabilities, integrate resource orchestration, and build a multi-element collaboration mechanism, etc. [13].

At present, research on the digitalization of higher education mainly focuses on its connotation, dilemmas, strategies, transformation paths, and enlightenment of the digitalization of international higher education. There is less research on the transformation of digital teaching and learning methods in higher education and its influencing factors, and there is a lack of systematic research. In the process of educational transformation, teachers and students play an important role.

3 Research Framework and Hypotheses

The essence of digital transformation is the transformation of people. Teachers and students, as the main bodies of education and teaching, need to be focused on in the process of digital transformation of higher education [14]. The cognitive level of teachers and students will affect the effectiveness of the digitalization of higher education. Students need to adapt to learning in the digital era, and teachers need to have the ability to teach digitally and be competent in work in the digital era in order to effectively promote the digital transformation of higher education. Institutions also need to provide supporting conditions for digital transformation, and the government also needs to introduce a series of policies to support the digital development of higher education, combining advanced technologies such as artificial intelligence, big data technology, cloud computing, and the Internet of Things to ensure the construction of digital infrastructure and ensure the safety of users. Privacy and data security. Higher education is a complex systemic project that requires extensive participation from social organizations and active cooperation from enterprises to jointly promote the digital transformation of higher education. Therefore, this article initially proposes that the factors influencing the digital transformation of higher education include: teacher factors, student literacy, technology dissemination, institutional support, infrastructure, policy support and data security.

3.1 Teacher Factors (TF)

As the leader of teaching, teachers play a key role in curriculum teaching. Teachers' digital teaching capabilities are mainly reflected in their awareness, ability, literacy and research on integrating digital technology into teaching [14], making the series of processes such as teaching objectives, teaching content and activities, teaching situation construction, teaching evaluation, and student feedback more dynamic, intuitive, and visual, which helps to reconstruct the curriculum and accurately meet the needs of social talent training. The continuous improvement of teachers' digital teaching capabilities is the core content and prerequisite for digital transformation. It requires the coordinated efforts of social organizations, institutions of higher learning, government departments, and teachers themselves to promote the development of teachers' digital teaching capabilities [14]. In addition, Teacher beliefs are also a key factor in the successful use of technology in education. Self-efficacy is defined as a person's belief in his or her success in performing certain behaviors or tasks. Digital education self-efficacy mainly refers to teachers' confidence in their ability to effectively use technology to achieve educational goals [10]. Therefore, this article proposes the following hypotheses:

H1: Teacher factors play a key role in the digital transformation of higher education.

3.2 Student Literacy (SL)

The ultimate goal of the digital transformation of higher education is to realize the learning and development of students in the digital age and enable students to keep pace with the times. Reconstruct traditional learning methods and cognitive methods, provide students with digital learning situations, build intelligent, open, and shared learning resources, create a diverse and social learning community, and provide personalized and precise learning support services [14], to meet the learning needs of students in the digital era and create conditions for cultivating compound talents. Therefore, students need to master basic digital technology knowledge and skills, information and data literacy, be able to use digital technology to communicate and collaborate, solve problems, create content and self-improvement, and have basic digital security and ethical awareness [15]. The autonomy of students' digital learning includes communication between the digital learning environment and the learning community. Students need to have a certain degree of subjective initiative and be able to actively acquire knowledge, which mainly depends on the student's experience and ability [16], can also be summarized as factors related to students. Therefore, this article proposes the following hypotheses:

H2: Student literacy has a positive impact on the digital transformation of higher education.

3.3 Technology Diffusion (TD)

Diffusion refers to how a specific technology spreads among a wide range of people. This article refers to the extent to which digital education technology is used by users [9]. For some colleges and universities, data technology has not been fully integrated. Teachers and students do not know how to obtain data and are "unclear, do not understand, and do not know how to use" the obtained data. There are also "reluctance to use" when using data. "Not good" and other quality issues, some teaching or learning data are missing and standards are inconsistent, etc. [17]. In addition, various units and functional departments have differences in data update time, frequency and standards, which to a certain extent hinders the integration and effective use of data and limits users' willingness to use digital education systems. To a certain extent, digital technology also requires matching smart devices with subject guides and teaching content, analyzing user information, evaluating data, and providing adaptive personalized teaching methods. Therefore, this article proposes the following hypotheses:

H3: Technology diffusion has a positive impact on the digital transformation of higher education.

3.4   University Support (US)

Major universities and higher education institutions are the initiators and guarantors of educational digitalization. School leaders, faculty and staff, and service personnel all play a proactive role in reform, proactively empowering learning and cultivation, and taking the initiative from policy planning, technology Systematic deployment and implementation of conditions, teaching implementation, learning atmosphere, digital literacy and other aspects. Institutional support not only includes the support and internal coordination of teachers' units, but also involves efficient collaboration between universities and sister institutions, enterprises, governments and other institutions [18], relying on the efforts of all parties to jointly promote the digital transformation of higher education, and orderly link subject knowledge, education and teaching resources, and social resources [19]. In addition, colleges and universities should adopt a systematic model, with teachers and students as the main body, formulate strategic plans, gather forces from multiple parties, lead the digital transformation of higher education, break information barriers, and build a digital higher education ecosystem that is co-constructed, co-governed, collaborative and shared [20].

H4: University support has a positive impact on the digital transformation of higher education.

3.5   Infrastructure (iN)

There are still serious gaps in digital education infrastructure, and the digital divide has increased significantly [20]. Infrastructure is a necessary condition for the integration of information and communication technology into teaching classrooms, but it is not a sufficient condition and has a direct impact on digital learning technology [21]. Good infrastructure, equipment and support are more conducive to promoting a wider range of learning activities and more frequently transferring knowledge and skills to related digital learning activities [11]. Infrastructure includes talents, systems, goals and assessments. Currently, there is a serious shortage of information technology professionals in the market, and an even greater shortage of artificial intelligence talents [20]. Therefore, colleges and universities should strengthen the construction of information infrastructure, actively develop digital education resources, and build a safe, stable, and efficient digital governance environment [22], it is also necessary to provide faculty with more extensive and practical information and communication technology training to adapt to the development of the digital era. In terms of digital education evaluation, compared with the staged, one-sided and fixed evaluation of traditional education, digital education can integrate teaching content and establish a systematic knowledge map, making teaching objectives and learning objectives clearer and clearer, using the whole process, all-round, normalized, and open evaluation, which helps teach students in accordance with their aptitude and allows underachievers to follow up on teaching progress in a timely manner.

H5: Infrastructure has a positive impact on the digital transformation of higher education.

3.6 Policy Support (PS)

The national "14th Five-Year Plan" outline and the report of the 20th National Congress of the Communist Party of China have both proposed policies to accelerate the digital transformation of education and promote high-quality development of education [7]. Driven by the national strategy, local governments and universities have also followed the policy and initially built hardware and software facilities for the digitalization of higher education. However, there are still some problems such as coordination, matching, and recognition. Universities also need to strengthen policy support for digitalization in the field of higher education and guide the coordinated development of digitalization and higher education [12].

H8: Policy support has a positive impact on the digital transformation of higher education.

3.7 Data Security (DS)

In the process of digital transformation, universities also need to be vigilant to prevent privacy leaks and personal surveillance [22]. In the era of big data and artificial intelligence, users' private lives are exposed in smart devices and smart platforms. Colleges and universities should do a good job in data confidentiality, protect devices, content, personal data and privacy in the digital environment, and protect users' mental health, and understand the social well-being brought by digital technology and its impact on the environment, and popularize data security knowledge.

H7: Data security has a positive impact on the digital transformation of higher education.

3.8 Digital Transformation of Higher Education (DTHE)

Assuming that the digital transformation of higher education will be affected by the above dimensional variables, the questionnaire questions are set around the user's behavioral intention and actual usage behavior. The model of factors influencing the digitalization of higher education proposed in this study is shown in Fig. 1.

4 Research Design

A total of 203 valid questionnaires were obtained in this survey, of which 73 were male and 130 were female. The age group was basically concentrated in 18–25 years old, accounting for 83.74%. Since the model of influencing factors of higher education digitalization proposed in this article is mainly based on various dimensional variables summarized from literature research, the model is relatively complex. CB-SEM is mainly used to verify relatively simple models that have little changes based on the original model, while PLS-SEM is suitable for complex models or to verify the impact of key factors and can represent key indicators of prediction. Therefore, PLS-SEM is more suitable for this study than CB-SEM. This article uses Smart PLS 4 for structural equation model analysis.

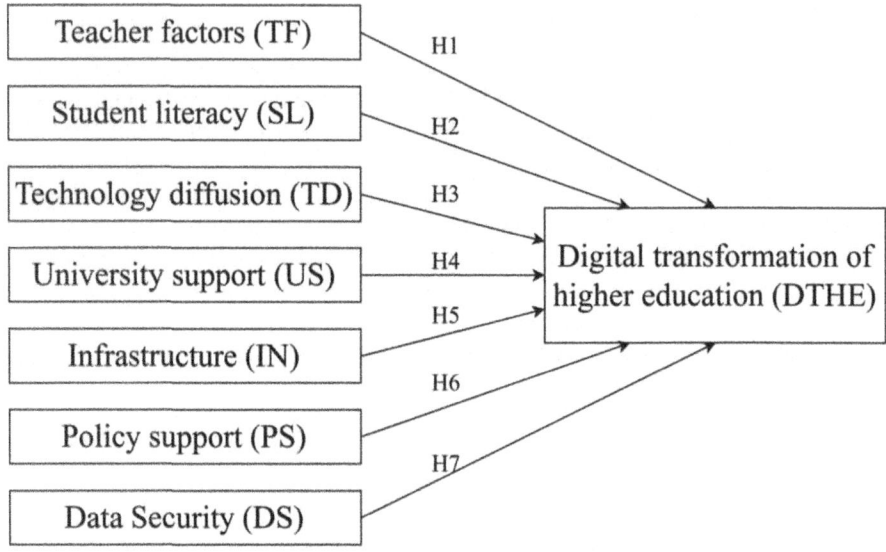

Fig. 1. Factors influencing the digitalization of higher education

We used a reflective measurement model for all seven latent variables, and analyzed and evaluated the reliability and convergent validity of the measurement model through confirmatory factor analysis, excluding those with loading values not exceeding 0.7 [23]. The internal consistency of the construct was tested by a Cronbach's alpha coefficient greater than 0.7, which is an acceptable critical value. All AVE values are higher than 0.5 and verify the convergent validity of the measurement items. Table 1 shows the results of the measurement model.

Table 1. The measurement model

Item		Loadings	Composite reliability (rho_a)	Average variance extracted (AVE)	Cronbach alpha
Teacher factors (TF)	TF1	0.865	0.903	0.826	0.895
	TF2	0.940			
	TF3	0.920			
Student literacy(SL)	SL1	0.900	0.934	0.735	0.832
	SL2	0.830			
	SL3	0.842			

(*continued*)

Table 1. (*continued*)

Item		Loadings	Composite reliability (rho_a)	Average variance extracted (AVE)	Cronbach alpha
Technology diffusion (TD)	TD1	0.859	0.908	0.765	0.898
	TD2	0.876			
	TD3	0.892			
	TD4	0.870			
University support (US)	US1	0.718	0.833	0.704	0.789
	US2	0.885			
	US3	0.901			
infrastructure (IN)	IN1	0.787	0.878	0.771	0.850
	IN2	0.928			
	IN3	0.911			
policy support (PS)	PS1	0.920	0.861	0.759	0.838
	PS2	0.923			
	PS3	0.760			
Data Security (DS)	DS1	0.754	0.884	0.768	0.847
	DS2	0.934			
	DS3	0.928			
Digital transformation of higher education (DTHE)	DTHE1	0.889	0.895	0.760	0.894
	DTHE2	0.891			
	DTHE3	0.856			
	DTHE4	0.849			

Then, using Fornell–Larcker to conduct discriminant validity analysis, the square root of a construct's AVE must be higher than the correlation value of the cross construct [23]. Table 2 shows the correlation matrix and square root of AVE, and it can be seen that all variables are satisfied.

Table 2. Correlation matrix and square root of the AVE (Fornell–Larcker)

	DS	DTHE	IN	PS	SL	TD	TF	US
DS	0.876							
DTHE	0.609	0.872						
IN	0.607	0.502	0.878					

(*continued*)

Table 2. (*continued*)

	DS	DTHE	IN	PS	SL	TD	TF	US
PS	0.580	0.578	0.687	0.871				
SL	0.283	0.230	0.452	0.380	0.858			
TD	0.496	0.557	0.578	0.546	0.517	0.874		
TF	0.288	0.475	0.433	0.457	0.342	0.535	0.909	
US	0.224	0.292	0.366	0.262	0.222	0.422	0.360	0.839

5   Results and Discussion

Structural equation model analysis is mainly used to identify the relationships between structures. The significance of the hypothesis is judged based on a significance level less than 0.05. Table 3 shows the test of hypotheses. The research results show that teacher factors (p = 0.011, t = 2.540), student literacy (p = 0.047, t = 1.985), technology diffusion (p = 0.003, t = 2.934), policy support (p = 0.016, t = 2.418), data security (p = 0.000, t = 4.445) have a positive impact on the reform of digital teaching and learning methods in higher education. But infrastructure (p = 0.630, t = 0.482) and univeristy support (p = 0.621, t = 0.494) is not significant impact. The digital transformation of higher education is an extremely complex process, and changes in teachers' teaching methods and students' learning behaviors may be affected by many factors. Because universities have not fully implemented the digitalization of higher education, teachers and students have not truly enjoyed the benefits of higher education digitalization and lack a certain understanding of it. The infrastructure is imperfect, the digital talent pool is insufficient, and some colleges and universities have not fully supported digitalization. In education, most colleges and universities in China are still in the traditional face-to-face teaching mode, and use online teaching platforms as teaching aids. In the future, when promoting the digital development of higher education, we need to focus on cultivating the digital skills of teachers and students, disseminating digital technology, and ensuring user data security. The government needs to promulgate relevant policies to promote the

Table 3. Hypotheses test

Hypothesis	Path	t value	p value	Comments
H1	TF → DTHE	2.540	0.011	Support
H2	SL → DTHE	1.985	0.047	Support
H3	TD → DTHE	2.934	0.003	Support
H4	US → DTHE	0.494	0.621	Not support
H5	IN → DTHE	0.482	0.630	Not support
H6	PS → DTHE	2.418	0.016	Support
H7	DS → DTHE	4.445	0.000	Support

adoption of digital education in various institutions and introduce digital technology talents.

6 Conclusion

Through literature review, the influencing factors of higher education digitalization were summarized, an influencing factor model was constructed, and the research hypothesis was proved using questionnaire survey and data analysis. The results show that teacher factors, student literacy, technology diffusion, policy support, and data security have a positive impact on the transformation of digital teaching and learning methods in higher education. However, infrastructure and university support have no significant impact on it. This paper clarifies the reasons for the changes in digital teaching and learning methods in higher education, and comprehensively analyzes the influencing factors that hinder or promote the development of digital education from multiple dimensions such as awareness, ability, ecology, governance system, and mechanism, which will help to provide guidance for the digitalization of higher education quality development. In short, digitally empowering the transformation of higher education requires the linkage of multiple resources. Major universities, teachers and students need to actively respond to the challenges and opportunities brought about by the digital era with an attitude of recognizing, and with the spirit of co-construction. Determined to effectively promote the process of digital transformation. In addition, colleges and universities also need to avoid falling into the trap of digitalization and neglecting emotional communication in real life.

Acknowledgments. This study was funded by Guangdong Provincial Association of Higher Education's "14th Five-Year Plan" 2023 Higher Education Research Topic "Research on the Transformation of Digital Teaching and Learning Methods in Higher Education and Its Influencing Factors (23GQN44)", "Research on application strategies of online learning evaluation system for design majors under the digital background (23GQN46)"; 2023 Guangdong Technology College's "Quality Engineering" project "VI Image Design Based on OBE Concept" Curriculum Reform and Practice (JXGG202351)"; 2023 Guangdong Technology College Science and Technology Project and 2023 "Innovation Strengthening School Project" scientific research project "Research on the Innovation Mechanism of Industry-Education Integration of Design Courses under the Perspective of Rural Revitalization (2023YBSK085)"; Guangdong Technology College's 2024 College Student Innovation and Entrepreneurship Training Plan Project "Influencing factors and service system design for the transformation of higher education digital student learning behavior patterns (CXCY202401070)".

Disclosure of Interests. The authors have no competing interests.

References

1. Yang, Z.: Digital development of higher education: connotation, stages and implementation paths. China High. Educ. **02**, 16–20 (2023)
2. Cheng, J., Cui, Y., Li, M., Han, X.: Analysis on the core elements of digital transformation in higher education teaching and learning——from the perspectives of institution, academic program and curriculum. China Educ. Technol. **07**, 31–36 (2022)
3. Rodriguez-Abitia, G., Martinez-Perez, S., Ramirez-Montoya, M.S., Lopez-Caudana, E.: Digital gap in universities and challenges for quality education: a diagnostic study in Mexico and Spain [Article]. Sustainability **12**(21), 14, 9069 (2020)
4. Drugova, E., Zhuravleva, I., Aiusheeva, M., Grits, D.: Toward a model of learning innovation integration: TPACK-SAMR based analysis of the introduction of a digital learning environment in three Russian universities. Educ. Inf. Technol. **26**(4), 4925–4942 (2021)
5. Wang, X.: Digital transformation and high-quality development of higher education: coupling logic and realization path. Soc. Sci. Front **2023**(01), 236–244 (2023)
6. Qu, D., Tao, Z., Deng, Y.: On the security protection of information data in the digitalization of higher education——highlights and reflections on 2021 EDUCAUSE horizon action plan: privacy. Educ. Res. Monthly **03**, 29–36 (2023)
7. Sun, Z., Gan, Y.: Realistic foundation and optimization path of digital empowerment for high-quality development of online teaching in higher education. Modern Educ. Manag. **12**, 122–128 (2023)
8. Zhu, Z.T., Zheng, H., Xu, Q.X., Wu, Y.H.: Policy Orientation and ecological development strategies for digital transformation of education. Mod. Educ. Technol. **32**(09), 5–18 (2022)
9. Gupta, R., Seetharaman, A., Maddulety, K.: Critical success factors influencing the adoption of digitalisation for teaching and learning by business schools. Educ. Inf. Technol. **25**(5), 3481–3502 (2020)
10. Nagy, J.T., Dringó-Horváth, I.: Factors influencing university teachers' technological integration. Educ. Sci. **14**(1), 55 (2024)
11. Lohr, A., et al.: On powerpointers, clickerers, and digital pros: investigating the initiation of digital learning activities by teachers in higher education. Comput. Hum. Behav. **119**, 106715 (2021)
12. He, S.: Evaluation and influencing factors of the coupling coordination degree of digitalization and higher education in China. J. Northeastern Univ. (Soc. Sci.) **25**(02), 128–135 (2023).
13. Wang, P., Peng, L., Jin, H., Zhang, S., Liu, T.: Influence factors and pathway analysis of digital transformation of universities: based on the dynamic capabilities and resource orchestration theory. J. Dist. Educ. **42**(01), 41–49 (2024)
14. Han, X., Chen, X., Diao, J., Zhou, Q.: Analysis on the core elements of digital transformation in higher education teaching and learning——from the perspectives of students and teachers. China Educ. Technol. **07**, 37–42 (2022)
15. Law, N., Woo, D., de la Torre, J., Wong, K.: A global framework of reference on digital literacy skills for indicator 4.4. 2 (2018)
16. Engel, O., Zimmer, L.M., Lörz, M., Mayweg-Paus, E.: Digital studying in times of COVID-19: teacher-and student-related aspects of learning success in German higher education. Int. J. Educ. Technol. High. Educ. **20**(1), 12 (2023)
17. Qian, H., Wang, M., Xiong, Y.: Digital transformation in higher education: a systematic review. Big Data Res. **9**(03), 56–70 (2023)
18. Chen, W., Zhang, Z., Yun, X., Zhao, Y., Zhang, Y.: First-class university's practice and exploration of digital transformation: experience and model of Zhejiang university. Chin. J. ICT Educ. **28**(05), 3–12 (2022)

19. Li, X., Zhang, T., Wang, Z.: Qualitative comparative analysis of digital transformation construction paths of higher education in China. J. Dist. Educ. **42**(01), 32–40 (2024)
20. Lili, D., Hui, J., Huineng, L.: New prospect of digital education in the post-epidemic era: challenges, actions and reflections: analysis of European union's digital education action plan (2021–2027). J. Dist. Educ. **39**(01), 16–27 (2021)
21. Gil-Flores, J., Rodríguez-Santero, J., Torres-Gordillo, J.-J.: Factors that explain the use of ICT in secondary-education classrooms: the role of teacher characteristics and school infrastructure. Comput. Hum. Behav. **68**, 441–449 (2017)
22. Shen, G., Zhou, X.: The motivation, connotation and path of digitalization empowering modernization of internal governance in universities. Modern Educ. Manag. **10**, 62–71 (2023)
23. Sarstedt, M., Ringle, C.M., Hair, J.F.: Partial least squares structural equation modeling. In: Handbook of Market Research, pp. 587–632. Springer (2021)
24. Fornell, C., Larcker, D.F.: Structural equation models with unobservable variables and measurement error: algebra and statistics. In: Sage Publications Sage CA: Los Angeles, CA (1981)

Review of the Factors That Influence Learners Motivation in Using AI-Enabled Gamification for Collaborative Learning

Ajrina Hysaj[1](✉) , Sara Azeem Khan[2] , Doaa Hamam[3] ,
and Georgina Farouqa[4]

[1] UOWD College, University of Wollongong in Dubai, Dubai, UAE
ajrinahysaj@uowdubai.ac.ae
[2] University of Wollongong in Dubai, Dubai, UAE
[3] Higher Colleges of Technology, Dubai, UAE
dhamam@hct.ac.ae
[4] CEHE, Dubai, UAE
dr.georginafarouqa@cehe.ae

Abstract. This study aimed to explore the effective and ethical use of GenAI gamification tools in higher education. GenAI gamification tools are commonly and constantly used by multicultural undergraduate students in higher education to search information and easily accessible data. This research aims to identify the GenAI gamification tools that are currently in use by teachers in higher education and examining the impact of these tools on educational, discipline and subject related outcomes. A thorough literature review was conducted to explore faculty perceptions on the effectiveness of GenAI gamification tools in higher education. This study aimed to contribute to the ongoing discussion about the role of GenAI gamification tools in higher education and its potential to transform the traditional educational system while upholding academic integrity. The selection of the papers was conducted through Springer or SCOPUS indexed databases. Journal articles and conference proceedings were chosen based on their suitability and the purpose chosen by the researchers. The main purpose of choosing the articles was to provide an updated insight into the current uses of GenAI gamification tools in HE. There were a number of keywords and combinations of terms used to allocate the appropriate research sources. These keywords included GenAI, games, ESL games, higher education and a variety of combinations of these terms.

Keywords: GenAI Gamification Tools · Games in Higher Education · Faculty Perceptions · Academic Integrity

1 Introduction

The use of gamification in teaching and learning has come a long way starting with the work of Prensky [38] and continuing with the works of Majuri, Koivisto and Hamari [30] and Oliveira et al. [33] just to name a few. Digital game-based learning is no longer a new

P. Zaphiris et al. (Eds.): HCII 2024, LNCS 15378, pp. 58–69, 2025.
https://doi.org/10.1007/978-3-031-76815-6_5

learning platform and the concepts of learning and gaining knowledge through fun are used in a variety of institutions [51]. Educational games are designed to teach learners of different age-groups specific subjects and help them develop individual skills [31]. Furthermore, GenAI gamification tools are designed to be very interactive and with the main purpose of teaching learners to set goals, adapt to evolving circumstances, follow guidelines and rules and/or solve varied problems [3]. The narrative of GenAI games resembles that of an actual story and the concepts behind these games are of educational and personal perspectives [44]. Therefore, learners benefit from the use of educational games in more than one aspect and in a number of levels [26, 27, 34]. GenAI games offer crucial components of learning while providing learners with an acceptable level of joy. These games allow learners to collaborate purposefully in completing tasks and learning through fun. GenAI games offer fundamental requirements of learning while providing - enjoyment, passionate involvement, structure, motivation, ego gratification, adrenaline, creativity and emotion [3, 44]. As technology evolves rapidly so does the gaming industry that offers quite a rich and diverse range of possibilities to choose from [34].

Digital natives or Gen Z are becoming increasingly active learners when it comes to using new technologies in applying what they learn in different contexts [11, 12, 45]. Understandably, Gen Z become actively and innovatively more engaged in a positive way that leaves no space for boredom caused by redundancy [11, 12, 35]. Learning through games encompasses infinite tools and options that make learners fascinated by the number of opportunities they have to prove their creativity in the process of learning [10, 55]. In digital games, learning occurs through fun and enjoyment which makes it more memorable. Moreover, learning through games is a good opportunity for students to think and process information from different angles, which leads to development of a sense of individualism and improvement of individual learning skills [10, 35, 45]. Game-based learning develops learners' collaborative work, enhances strategic thinking and communicative skills and provides them with the tools needed to apply the gained knowledge in real world contexts. Finally, online games use very close to reality 3D images that make it possible for users to readily engage with their worlds [10]. If empowered with learners' creativity online gaming can prove to be a very useful authentic learning tool.

Richards, Min and Games [41] developed a continuum of authentic characteristics to gauge effective dimensions of interactive learning on the Web. This continuum advanced and included a large number of online educational games that can be classified as authentic tasks on a number of counts and for a number of reasons [35, 45]. Learners see GenAI online games more like entertainment products rather than useful educational tools [10]. One of the drawbacks of GenAI gamification tools is that it makes it difficult to design multiple assessment measures being those formative or summative ones [52]. Another drawback of GenAI games is that the more complex ones are paid and usually they are the ones that provide a better learning platform for the undergraduate students [32]. Although paid online games provide to a certain extend a degree of expert skill and performance; even they leave the path for disputable levels of expertise and professional practice [28]. As a result, ideas are not articulated enough, leaving a narrow understanding and as a result student are unable to compare their thoughts and ideas to those of experts [10, 52]. Quite often students lack time and possibility to reflect on the learned matter and to create their own version of online gaming, therefore, learning process does not consolidated and the possibility of knowledge transference is limited [28, 52]. Another drawback of GenAI games is that even though there are growing numbers of multi-player games, most games are designed for one or two players, which make the real- life reflection process difficult to be achieved [46, 47].

Another noticeable disadvantage of GenAI games is that knowledgeable students may not given the chance of empowering themselves while playing or while assisting weaker students by coaching them during the gaming process [32]. Furthermore, the reflection process is another characteristic that online gaming is commonly scarce. This aspect is required to be taken into consideration by us educators when choosing online games for our students [52]. One way of addressing this deficiency could be by supplementing these games with reflective exercises [28, 32]. The process of reflection is known to be crucial in development of critical and analytical thinking, hence it could benefit students in a variety of ways. For instance, GenAI games could integrate the process of reflection which coupled with creativity tasks have the potential to complete the requirement set for classification of any given tool as an authentic one [27, 28]. However, this task requires careful consideration as online games are a representation of a very high degree of reality' resembles which is their main strength, hence, very often the inclusion of other follow-up tasks may prove to be more disadvantageous than advantageous [46].

Online games can be used as educational tools in a countless of perspectives [29, 30, 33]. Learners of all levels get participate effectively in the learning process due to the use of GenAI games. In many instances, students are unaware of their learning taking place due to the high degree of excitement that they experience while learning through games [32]. Not only do the students thoroughly enjoy the play but they are also being encouraged to go through different levels and learn progressively. This gives them a sense of accomplishment and encourages purposeful and active participation in the learning process. It goes without saying that a screen of an iPad is more appealing to students than a traditional notebook. Understandably students are more willing to type than to write just like they are to solve problems in the virtual world than they are in the real world [52–54]. Increased levels of motivation can support students to open up with their peers and discuss issues that they may have faced while playing these educational GenAI games, which can ultimately support to develop their social and emotional skills [29].

This study aimed at exploring the effective and ethical use of GenAI games in higher education. The rationale is that GenAI gamification tools constant used by multicultural undergraduate students in higher education to search information and easily accessible data. Furthermore, this study aimed at exploring the use GenAI games in supporting teaching and learning in higher education as well as exploring the impact that these Gen AI tools have on students personal and academic development. The research questions for this study are as follows:

a) What are the potential benefits and drawbacks of implementing GenAI gamification in HE?

b) What are the potential benefits and drawbacks of GenAI gamification on students personal and academic aspects?

2   Literature Review

2.1   Theoretical and Practical Perspectives on the Use of GenAI Gamification in HE

The concept of learning through play has been gaining more popularity for the last decade or so mainly thanks to the positive feedback received over time. For example, if GenAI games have some scientific background, this may have a positive effect on students' development of critical and analytical thinking [31, 33]. Higher education level of teaching and learning is another successful example of the use of online games in the education field. In many instances, students might not necessarily like to study subjects e.g., literature or science but learning through games gives them the possibility of exploring their own potential while empowering themselves with knowledge needed for their essays, assignments and projects [31, 43]. Moreover, some games provide platforms which can be utilized by learners to create their own games and demonstrate their own talent. Although this may not suit all the students, it is yet, another form of engaged and purposeful learning.

The continues spread of GenAI gamification tools and their diversification has created the need to teaching staff in higher education to explore their use and functionality in facilitating teaching and learning process [35, 45–47]. This exploration needs to consider aspects of positive and negative nature such as usefulness, purposefulness, uncertainty, ethical implications and ways of regulating the use of these tools in higher education (HE) [56]. The degree of designing GenAI tools is constantly increasing and the purpose and use of these tools is constantly evolving [57]. While faculty in HE may vary in the degree of skepticism about the ethical implications of these tools, it is valuable to emphasise that majority of educators acknowledge the constant use of these gamification tools by students in HE, therefore, agree on the necessity of opening a path to discussion about the benefits and drawbacks of these tools [35].

Exploration of GenAI gamification tools needs to include aspects of personal and academic nature. For instance, when students in HE use GenAI tools to learn concepts of educational nature they should be able to connect these with notions that they are subsequently exploring in their discipline related subjects. This relationship needs to be explored by educators and incorporated in the teaching and process [13, 51, 55, 56]. As the curriculum design is an evolving process, it is important that educators explore GenAI games through experiential and theoretical frameworks aiming to create an inclusive classroom environment online and on campus [13, 47–50]. GenAI tools games can be utilized for a variety of reasons e.g., to explore new concepts, break down complex notions as we all to develop critical and analytical thinking. While utilizing the GenAI games in higher education, it is important to focus on the personal and academic implications that the use of these tools can have for students [35, 46]. Although the general understanding and common expectation are that Gen Z students are well-aware of notions related to games and their functionalities, this does not seem to be always the case with all the students [56]. Moreover, many students may find the use of games as too challenging and do not enjoy learning through them.

Another issue with the use of GenAI games in higher education is related to the usefulness of these games in preparing undergraduate students to find employment and in general to compete in the business world [4, 7]. Just like everything else taught and learned in higher education, GenAI games are used to empower students with a variety of notions and concepts and should serve their purpose to support undergraduate students academic and personal learning experiences [4, 46] Exploration of the diversity of uses of GenAI games in higher education needs to take into consideration the use of such tools in serving as a bridge between the academic perspectives and work environment [13, 42–45]. This requires a careful consideration of effectiveness of these tools in relation to aspects of teaching and learning such as alignments of the curriculum design and learning outcomes with the purpose of these tools and subsequently the transfer of the acquired knowledge on the completion of the assessment tasks [4, 7, 41].

The exploration of Gen AI needs to not only inclusive but also well-researched and purposefully utilized for the benefit of teaching and learning in a short-term and in a long-term [46, 53, 57]. A crucial aspect connected with the use of GenAI gamification tools is related to the ethical utilization of these tools [40, 47]. As notions of plagiarism and academic integrity evolve based on the widespread use of technological advances, it is the responsibility of the educators and policy makers to develop and apply guidelines that ensure the use of these tools in an ethically and morally appropriate formats [4, 22, 39]. The exploration of the use the tools can facilitate an improved understanding of their functionalities and support the design of guidelines for their appropriate utilization. It is crucial to explore the diversity of uses of GenAI Gamification tools in higher education as well as their and their outcomes related to functionalities that these tools possess, categories by which undergraduate students can benefit from using them and finally examples of how the usefulness of these tools can match with the purposefulness of their utilization for the personal and academic benefits of undergraduate students [7, 13]. While exploring the tools, educators move away from notions of patrolling undergraduate students when using the GenAI gamification tools and step forward towards creating an environment of learning and knowledge sharing through challenges and achievements [26, 27, 38, 46, 47].

2.2 Implications of GenAI Gamification in English as Second Language Classes

GenAI games are frequently been incorporated in language teaching as they can stimulate motivation and authenticity making communicative practices more efficient and enjoyable [42]. GenAI games can provide a convenient environment that develops cognitive, language and literacy skills. They can serve as authentic tasks if learners themselves get involved in designing them by developing computational thinking skills [37, 53, 54]. Feature of repetition seems inseparable by a correct approach towards second language acquisition [29]. Digital games make it possible for extrovert and introvert student to play in their own terms, go as fast or slow as they prefer [29, 30, 32]. Gaming can be customized more than any other conventional teaching method and makes learning process easier for all adult students [17, 18, 36]. Dziorny [9] makes a thoughtful statement based on research carried out in US higher education. According to the same half million students with learning disabilities were enrolled in higher education system in year 2006 and this number is expected to go up in the coming years. This finding coincides with that of Abu Rabia and Maroun [1] who pointed out that 17.6% of Emirati female students suffer from dyslexia. Dyslexia is a learning disability involving difficulty with reading, writing and spelling [9, 33, 35]. This figure is aggravated further more when considering the fact that the UAE population (citizens and expatriates alike) study English as a second or third language. Dyslexic adults have a very hard time learning English language as they lack short term memory skills and confuse the order of the words in sentences. Digital games repeat the words and introduce simple and complex sentence structures by making learning possible without the need of rote learning and memorization [32, 43].

GenAI games help students to increase their attention span, to facilitate learning of slow learners, to keep learners motivated, and finally, to provide fun filled and goal-oriented activities and learning experience [26, 27, 30, 53, 54]. Bunts-Anderson [6] noticed the need for public and government awareness in institutionalizing the use of GenAI games. It is commonly accepted that GenAI are mainly created respecting cultural diversity as a prerequisite [53]. Furthermore, these educational games designed with a neutral thought based on the variety of religions, cultures and traditions are more likely to be successful [4]. Nevertheless, in the paper by Ruphina and Liu [42] Chinese learners complained of lack of cultural element on games design. Males and females differ in their motivation on using digital games. Lee, Cheon and Key [29] asserted the difference between genders in degrees and factors of motivation and persistency in second language learning. Males to be more motivated to find the meaning of new words and continue playing irrespective of the difficulties or barriers blocking their way. On the other hand, females tended to look at the usefulness of online games and pay attention to skills development. Digital game designers should keep into consideration the gender factor when designing educational games to support L2 learning process [20, 28, 35, 43].

It is a well-known fact that English as a second language teaching provides a very diverse and useful array of online games [13]. These games help in making students of English feel citizens of a global classroom, practicing communication on a global level [13, 26, 27, 43]. For instance, GenAI games can be skills based e.g., reading and writing, listening and speaking or more specialized ones that provide support with pronunciation and spelling. Moreover, these games can introduce vocabulary quizzes and puzzles and can offer an introduction and review of complex linguistic, comprehension and composition tasks [55, 56]. Multicultural students hail from different parts of the world and their educational needs are interconnected with a myriad of educational systems worldwide [10, 12, 21, 22, 55, 56]. Online games have the power of serving as an authentic learning tool to cater to their unique needs and connect them virtually with many more people around the globe [10, 26, 43].

3   Methodology

For this study, the authors conducted a comprehensive literature review that covered the areas of GenAi gamification tools from its initial stages until the current year of this study. The approach was to formulate an understanding of the background information related to gamification and its use in HE. The authors focused on giving background information on the use of GenAI gamification tools in HE in a variety of contexts and purposes. The selection of the papers was conducted through Springer or SCOPUS indexed databases. Journal articles and conference proceedings were chosen based on their suitability and the purpose chosen by the researchers. The main purpose of choosing the articles was to provide an updated insight into the current uses of GenAI gamification tools in HE. There were a number of keywords and combinations of terms used to allocate the appropriate research sources. These keywords included GenAI, games, ESL games, higher education and a variety of combinations of these terms. The first stage of sources collection was achieved through assembling a collection of articles that seemed relevant to the research questions. The second stage of sources analysis involved a careful analysis of the articles and a subsequent exclusion of the articles that lacked substantial discussion related to the content of this study. The focus was on analysing more recent papers; and the papers were categorised based on recurring themes that emerged while reading the articles thoroughly. Finally, as a result of this careful selection process, a total of 57 papers were included in this review and analysed in details for this study.

4   Discussion

This study analysed the GenAI gamification tools from pedagogical and cognitive perspectives aiming to facilitate the process of teaching and learning in higher education [24, 25]. Studies analysed for this research paper examined the efficacy of GenAI gamification tools from a curriculum and instructional design perspective [23, 43]. Furthermore, GenAI games were explored to understand the effects that they may have in improving students' motivation and retention [14, 15, 22]. These GenAI gamification tools were also explored based on constructivist principles aiming to increase the amount of shared knowledge and knowledge acquisition through students' active participation the learning process [23]. This study found that it is important to explore the possibilities of training faculty to utilize these gamification tools for the benefit of the teaching and learning process. Moreover, it becomes valuable to necessitate professional development strategies in not only empowering faculty with the use of these tools but most importantly empowering them with the required skills to recognize students learning difficulties which can help in choosing appropriate GenAI games [14, 15, 50]. GenAI games are not to be seen as the ultimate threat or the opposite, they are generally meant to support teaching staff in delivering the material efficiently and in supporting students' learning process [21, 23, 50]. It goes without saying that emphasis has to be put to recognize learners' individual strengths and needs, as well as to facilitate instructional efficacy through digital educational games [20, 43, 50].

GenAI games can help with a variety of aspects of second language acquisition process [19, 36–40]. In 2012 Wu and Richards enumerated that digital games help ESL learners develop an array of skills related to literacy e.g., spelling, pronunciation, reading and/ writing skills, sentence formation and grammar. Based on the papers by Bunts-Anderson [6], Dziorny [9], Hoge, Hughes and Myers [17], Howard, Morgan and Ellis [18] digital games help students with constructive and communicative skills. As GenAI gamification tools change continuously it is difficult if not impossible to keep up with the diversity of functions that they may present [16, 17, 43]. Nevertheless, it is important that these tools are used to enhance the communication between students as well as the communication between students and teachers [15, 23]. These tools should be utilized not only to create an immersive learning experience but most importantly to equip students with transferable skills required outside academia [14, 50]. These transferable skills should be related to a variety of disciplines that students may be studying in their universities and could equip them with skills required in medicine, engineering, computer science, humanities or other fields [13, 20].

Since GenAI games evolve rapidly it is important to look into the long-term outcomes of these tools [12, 43]. A variety of studies focus on short-term effect of these tools while not many studies have aimed at exploring the long-term effect of the tools [8, 23]. Also, studies need to explore the effect of immersive learning experiences and the possible life-long learning that may occur due to the active involvement of undergraduate students in the learning process through the utilization of GenAI gamification tools [7, 19, 46]. Exploration of short and long-term outcomes from the use of tools can facilitate the appropriate use of the tools and influence positively students' academic performance and knowledge retention [6, 23, 46]. While the use of these tools should be encouraged across all educational levels, it is important to investigate the effectiveness of the tools and explore the research that provides nuanced insights into which tools could be used in generic subjects and in discipline related subjects [5, 8]. Understanding which games can better support teaching and learning in a given context; can support the optimization of the benefits that may occur as the result of their use. Furthermore, strategizing the exploration of the functions of the Gen AI games in consideration to students' learning needs works towards the long-term of students' benefits from the use of games [4, 8]. Furthermore, it is important to explore the potential of GenAI gamification tools to encourage effective collaboration in group work [3, 43, 46]. In a nutshell, GenAI gamification tools are a possible alternative in addressing learners' different levels of motivation, sense of independence and linguistic needs [2, 56, 57].

5 Conclusion and Recommendations

Although the use of GenAI gamification tools has been explored, more needs to be done in this regard considering the pace of designing these tools and the widespread of their utilisation in the education system. The ways that these tools should be analysed should include pedagogical and instructional domains of all the aspects of teaching and learning in higher education. The research indicates that there is a shift from an awareness about the GenAI gamification tools stage to a stage where these tools are explored based on their functionalities and the purpose of their uses. Understandably, more new tools will be designed and more thorough research about the most recent games will be done in the years to come. Further discussion should consider how to design GenAI online games more effectively and how to integrate them into teaching and learning. The range of GenAI games has to be in accordance with the needs of the learners' abilities and skills.

There is a clear need for more rigorous research in understanding the efficacy of GenAI games and how to use them appropriately in the ESL field and in higher education in general. More studies need to contribute in building the bridge between the diverse use of GenAI games in higher education and their potential challenges and drawbacks. Furthermore, with the spread of hybrid learning, it is important to address the implementation of GenAI gamification in the online platform. These categories of studies can contribute to the ongoing discussion about the role of GenAI tools in shaping the present and future educational landscapes, ensuring that these tools support the foundations of academic work and academic integrity and do not hinder them. Moreover, aspects of faculty perceptions with regard to gamification and the general use of AI tools in higher education should be researched and required framework for the ethical use of these tools should be formalised. There is a need to initiate exploration of approaches that can help to capitalise on the usefulness of GenAI gamification tools in all disciplines in higher education.

References

1. Abu Rabia, S., Maroun, L.: Consanguinity linked to reading disability in Arab community. Dyslexia **11**, 1–21 (2009). https://doi.org/10.1002/dys.271, https://doi.org/10.1002/dys.271
2. Al Shammari, M.H, Albalawi, I.: Technology in learning english as a foreign language in Saudi Arabia. In: Barton, S., et al. (eds.), Proceedings of Global Learn 2011, pp. 1669–1678. AACE (2011)
3. Alam, A.: A digital game based learning approach for effective curriculum transaction for teaching-learning of artificial intelligence and machine learning. In: 2022 International Conference on Sustainable Computing and Data Communication Systems (ICSCDS), pp. 69–74. IEEE (2022)
4. All, A., Castellar, E.N.P., Van Looy, J.: Digital Game-based learning effectiveness assessment: reflections on study design. Comput. Educ. **167**, 104160 (2021)
5. Bataineh, R., Baniabdelrahman, A.: Jordanian EFL students' perceptions of their computer literacy. Int. J. Educ. Dev. Using ICT **2**(2), 35–50. UWI (2006)
6. Bunts-Anderson, K.: The emergence of game based learning (GBL) from informal to formal contexts in Gulf higher education. In: Proceedings of World Conference on E-Learning in Corporate, Government, Healthcare, and Higher Education 2011, pp. 1079–1084. Chesapeake, VA: AACE (2011)
7. Breien, F.S., Wasson, B.: Narrative categorization in digital game-based learning: engagement, motivation & learning. Br. J. Edu. Technol. **52**(1), 91–111 (2021)
8. Coleman, T.E., Money, A.G.: Student-centred digital game–based learning: a conceptual framework and survey of the state of the art. High. Educ. **79**(3), 415–457 (2020)
9. Dziorny, M.: Digital game-based learning and dyslexia in higher education. In: Carlsen, R., et al. (eds.), Proceedings of Society for Information Technology & Teacher Education International Conference 2007, pp. 1189–1197. Chesapeake, VA: AACE (2007)
10. Erolin, C.: Interactive 3D digital models for anatomy and medical education. Biomed. Visual. **2**, 1–16 (2019)
11. Farouqa, G., Hysaj, A.: Exploring faculty members perception of utilizing technology to enhance student engagement in the united Arab Emirates: technology and the ICAP modes of engagement. In: Meiselwitz, G. (eds.) Social Computing and Social Media: Applications in Education and Commerce. HCII 2022. Lecture Notes in Computer Science, vol. 13316, pp. 67–76. Springer, Cham (2022). https://doi.org/10.1007/978-3-031-05064-0_5
12. Farouqa, G., Hysaj, A.: Active learning in the lenses of faculty: a qualitative study in universities in the United Arab Emirates. In: Meiselwitz, G. (eds.) Social Computing and Social Media: Applications in Education and Commerce. HCII 2022. Lecture Notes in Computer

Science, vol 13316, pp. 77–90. Springer, Cham (2022). https://doi.org/10.1007/978-3-031-05064-0_6

13. Fu, Q.K., Lin, C.J., Hwang, G.J., Zhang, L.: Impacts of a mind mapping-based contextual gaming approach on EFL students' writing performance, learning perceptions and generative uses in an English course. Comput. Educ. **137**, 59–77 (2019)

14. Hamam, D., Hysaj, A.: The aftermath of COVID 19: future insights for teachers' professional development in higher education. J. Asia TEFL **19**(1), 303 (2022)

15. Hamam, D., Hysaj, A.: Technological pedagogical and content knowledge (TPACK): higher education teachers' perspectives on the use of TPACK in online academic writing classes. In: Stephanidis, C., Antona, M., Ntoa, S. (eds.) HCI International 2021 - Posters. HCII 2021. Communications in Computer and Information Science, vol 1421, pp. 51–58. Springer, Cham (2021). https://doi.org/10.1007/978-3-030-78645-8_7

16. Herrington, J., Reeves, T.C., Oliver, R.: A Guide to Authentic E-Learning. Routledge, New York (2010)

17. Hoge, B., Hughes, F., Myers, J.: The future of game-based learning as project-based learning in the classroom. In: Resta, P., (Ed.), Proceedings of Society for Information Technology & Teacher Education International Conference 2012, pp. 2548–2553. Chesapeake, VA: AACE (2012)

18. Howard, C., Morgan, M., Ellis, K.: Games and learning ... does this compute?. In: Pearson, E., Bohman, P., (eds.), Proceedings of World Conference on Educational Multimedia, Hypermedia and Telecommunications 2006, pp. 1217–1224. Chesapeake, VA: AACE (2006)

19. Hysaj, A.: Group reports in the online platform: a puzzle, a ride in the park or a steep slope: a case study of multicultural undergraduate students in the United Arab Emirates. In: 2021 IEEE International Conference on Engineering, Technology & Education (TALE), pp. 745–750. IEEE (2021)

20. Hysaj, A.: COVID-19 pandemic and online teaching from the lenses of K-12 STEM teachers in Albania. In: 2021 IEEE International Conference on Engineering, Technology & Education (TALE), pp. 01–07. IEEE (2021)

21. Hysaj, A., Freeman, M., Khan, Z.R.: Theory of planned behaviour in higher education: exploring the perceptions of multicultural ESL students about cheating. In: Coman, A., Vasilache, S. (eds.) Social Computing and Social Media. HCII 2023. Lecture Notes in Computer Science, vol 14026, pp. 58–71. Springer, Cham (2023). https://doi.org/10.1007/978-3-031-35927-9_5

22. Hysaj, A., Hamam, D.: What does it take to develop critical thinking? the case of multicultural students in a digital learning platform. In: Coman, A., Vasilache, S. (eds.) Social Computing and Social Media. HCII 2023. Lecture Notes in Computer Science, vol. 14026, pp. 49–57. Springer, Cham (2023). https://doi.org/10.1007/978-3-031-35927-9_4

23. Greenhalgh, S.P.: Influences of game design and context on learners' trying on moral identities. In: Virtual Learning Environments, pp 9–26. Routledge (2024)

24. Jonassen, D.H.: Technology as cognitive tools: Learners as designers. IT Forum paper (1994). http://itech1.coe.uga.edu/itforum/paper1/paper1.html

25. Johnson, L., Adams Becker, S., Cummins, M., Estrada V., Freeman, A., Ludgate, H.: NMC Horizon Report: 2014 K-12 edition. The New Media Consortium, Austin, Texas (2013)

26. Khan, Z.R., et al.: Initiating count down-gamification of academic integrity. Int. J. Educ. Integr. **17**, 1–15 (2021)

27. Khan, Z.R., Sivasubramaniam, S., Anand, P., Hysaj, A.: 'e'-thinking teaching and assessment to uphold academic integrity: lessons learned from emergency distance learning. Int. J. Educ. Integr. **17**, 1–27 (2021)

28. King, D.L., Delfabbro, P.H., Gainsbury, S.M., Dreier, M., Greer, N., Billieux, J.: Unfair play? video games as exploitative monetized services: an examination of game patents from a consumer protection perspective. Comput. Hum. Behav. **101**, 131–143 (2019)

29. Lee, Y.Y., Cheon, J., Key, S.: Learners' perceptions of video games for second/foreign language learning. In: McFerrin, K., et al. (eds.), Proceedings of Society for Information Technology & Teacher Education International Conference 2008, pp. 1733–1738. Chesapeake, VA: AACE (2008)

30. Majuri, J., Koivisto, J., Hamari, J.: Gamification of education and learning: a review of empirical literature. In: Proceedings of the 2nd international GamiFIN conference, GamiFIN 2018. CEUR-WS (2018)

31. Manzano-León, A., et al.: Between level up and game over: a systematic literature review of gamification in education. Sustainability 13(4), 2247 (2021)

32. Mayer, R.E.: Computer games in education. Annu. Rev. Psychol. 70(1), 531–549 (2019)

33. Oliveira, W., et al.: Tailored gamification in education: a literature review and future agenda. Educ. Inf. Technol. 28(1), 373–406 (2023)

34. Ofosu-Ampong, K.: The shift to gamification in education: a review on dominant issues. J. Educ. Technol. Syst. 49(1), 113–137 (2020)

35. Onjewu, A.K.E., Godwin, E.S., Azizsafaei, F., Appiah, D.: The influence of technology use on learning skills among generation Z: a gender and cross-country analysis. Ind. High. Educ. 09504222241263227 (2024)

36. O'Rourke, J., Main, S., Ellis, M: So the kids are busy, what now? teacher perceptions of the use of hand-held game consoles in West Australian primary classrooms. Australas. J. Educ. Technol. 29(5) (2013)

37. Peridore, S., Lines, C.: An online educational framework for second language teaching. In: Proceedings of World Conference on E-Learning in Corporate, Government, Healthcare, and Higher Education 2011, pp. 365–368. Chesapeake, VA: AACE (2011)

38. Prensky, M.: Digital natives, digital immigrants part I. On Horizon 9(5), 1–6 (2001)

39. Prensky, M.: Don't bother me mom – I'm learning! Minnesota, Paragon House (2006)

40. Prensky, M.: Teaching digital natives – Partnering for real learning. Corwin, USA. Prensky, M. (2001a) Digital game based learning. St Paul, MN: Paragon (2010)

41. Richards, K., Min, W., Games, A.: Examining digital game-based learning through the lens of 21st century gamers. In: Koehler, M., Mishra, P., (eds.), Proceedings of Society for Information Technology & Teacher Education International Conference 2011, pp. 45–52. Chesapeake, VA: AACE (2011)

42. Ruphina, A., Liu, M.: Digital games: potential integration of mingoville games in learning english as a foreign language. In: Koehler, M., Mishra, P., (eds.), Proceedings of Society for Information Technology & Teacher Education International Conference, pp. 2216–2222. Chesapeake, VA: AACE (2011)

43. Rustamov, I., Mirza ogli, A.I.: Advantages and methods of using games in foreign language teaching. Журналиностранныхязыковилингвистики, 5(5) (2023)

44. Sailer, M., Homner, L.: The gamification of learning: a meta-analysis. Educ. Psychol. Rev. 32(1), 77–112 (2020)

45. Saxena, M., Mishra, D.K.: Gamification and Gen Z in higher education: a systematic review of literature. Int. J. Inf. Commun. Technol. Educ. (IJICTE) 17(4), 1–22 (2021)

46. Schöbel, S., Saqr, M., Janson, A.: Two decades of game concepts in digital learning environments–a bibliometric study and research agenda. Comput. Educ. 173, 104296 (2021)

47. Sicart, M.: Game, player, ethics: a virtue ethics approach to computer games. In: The Ethics of Information Technologies, pp. 427–432. Routledge (2020)

48. Sinitskaya Ronda, N., Owston, R., Sanaoui, R.: Voulez-Vous Jouer? [Do you want to play?]: game development environments for literacy skill enhancement. In: Siemens, G., Fulford, C., (eds.), Proceedings of World Conference on Educational Multimedia, Hypermedia and Telecommunications 2009, pp. 3795–3802. Chesapeake, VA: AACE (2009)

49. Sørensen, B.H., Meyer, B.: Design for game based learning platforms - in a global perspective. In: Gibson, D., Dodge, B., (eds.), Proceedings of Society for Information Technology & Teacher Education International Conference 2010, pp. 2071–2078. Chesapeake, VA: AACE (2010)

50. Sousa, M.J., Rocha, Á.: Leadership styles and skills developed through game-based learning. J. Bus. Res. **94**, 360–366 (2019)

51. Tay, J., Goh, Y.M., Safiena, S., Bound, H.: Designing digital game-based learning for professional upskilling: a systematic literature review. Comput. Educ. **184**, 104518 (2022)

52. Westera, W.: Why and how serious games can become far more effective: accommodating productive learning experiences, learner motivation and the monitoring of learning gains. J. Educ. Technol. Soc. **22**(1), 59–69 (2019)

53. Wu, M.L., Richards, K.: Massively multiplayer online role-playing games as digital game-based English learning platforms: a study of the effects of digital game play on ESL students' English use. In: Bastiaens, T., Marks, G., (eds.), Proceedings of World Conference on E-Learning in Corporate, Government, Healthcare, and Higher Education 2012, pp. 1370–1373 (2012)

54. Wu, M.L., Richards, K.: Learning with educational games for the intrepid 21st century learners. In: Resta, P., (ed.), Proceedings of Society for Information Technology & Teacher Education International Conference 2012, pp. 55–74. Chesapeake, VA: AACE (2012)

55. Yeo, X.W.: The game plan: using gamification strategies to engage learners as active players. J. Appl. Learn. Teach. **2**(2), 71–75 (2019)

56. Yu, Z., Gao, M., Wang, L.: The effect of educational games on learning outcomes, student motivation, engagement and satisfaction. J. Educ. Comput. Res. **59**(3), 522–546 (2021)

57. Zakariah, N.M, Huda, N., Mohd Yusoff, N.: Design factors of learning disabilities in emotional design model for dyslexic learners. In: Amiel, T., Wilson, B., (eds.), Proceedings of World Conference on Educational Multimedia, Hypermedia and Telecommunications (2012)

Can Facial Expressions Predict Performance?: A Machine Learning Approach

Sameeran G. Kanade[1]([✉]), Jun He[1], Sogand Hasanzadeh[2], Brandon Pitts[1], Behzad Esmaeili[1,2], and Vincent G. Duffy[1,3]

[1] School of Industrial Engineering, Purdue University, 315 N. Grant Street, West Lafayette 47907, IN, USA
{kanade,he184,bjpitts,besmaei,duffy}@purdue.edu
[2] Lyles School of Civil Engineering, Purdue University, 550 Stadium Mall Drive, West Lafayette 47907, IN, USA
sogandm@purdue.edu
[3] Agricultural and Biological Engineering, Purdue University, 225 S. University Street, West Lafayette 47907, IN, USA

Abstract. Emotional responses play a crucial role in decision-making processes and human interactions. This study used the FaceReader technology to investigate the correlation between emotional expressions (fear, anger, happiness, sadness, disgust, surprise and arousal) and hazard recognition performance. The facial expressions of the participants during the hazard identification test were recorded and then analyzed using machine learning methodologies. The results highlighted the significant relationship between emotional response and hazard identification performance, with heightened anger and happiness indicating higher hazard identification scores, while increased arousal and fear was associated with decreased performance. These findings demonstrate the relationship between emotional states and hazard identification performance. This study highlights the potential of integrating FaceReader technology with machine learning tools to predict the safety behavior of employees in the workplace and prevent hazards before they occur and offers a data-driven approach using objective measures in improving workplace safety.

Keywords: FaceReader · Machine learning · Emotional response · Construction safety · Accident prevention

1 Introduction

Emotional responses play a significant role in various fields, including marketing, consumer behavior, and human-computer interaction. Understanding and analyzing emotional expressions can provide valuable insights into individuals'

J. He—This author contributed equally to this work.

P. Zaphiris et al. (Eds.): HCII 2024, LNCS 15378, pp. 70–84, 2025.
https://doi.org/10.1007/978-3-031-76815-6_6

reactions and preferences. Research has shown that eliciting positive emotions in consumers is crucial for impacting product/service evaluation, purchase intentions, impulsive purchases, and word-of-mouth [1]. Figure 1 demonstrates the increased interest in research related to emotional response.

FaceReader technology, which involves the automatic coding of facial expressions to detect emotional responses, has emerged as a powerful tool in this regard. FaceReader technology has been effective in detecting emotional responses in various contexts, such as user's responses to different orange juices [2], different salt levels in food [3], urban sound perception [4], and YouTube videos [5]. This technology has been instrumental in measuring emotional valence and arousal, which are essential dimensions in understanding human emotional states and behavioral tendencies [6]. Moreover, the integration of FaceReader technology in studies related to health claims, food preferences, and advertising has provided valuable insights into how emotional responses influence decision-making processes [7,8]. By analyzing facial expressions, researchers have been able to detect pleasant and unpleasant emotions with high probabilities, highlighting the sensitivity and specificity of automatic facial coding [6]. FaceReader technology has also been utilized in human-computer interaction research, where advancements in electroencephalogram (EEG) technology have enabled a better understanding of brain-computer interaction. This interdisciplinary field focuses on designing interfaces that enhance the effectiveness, efficiency, and satisfaction of interactions between humans and computers [9]. The utilization of FaceReader technology in analyzing emotional responses offers a deeper understanding of human behavior, decision-making processes, and interaction patterns. By leveraging this technology, researchers can gain valuable insights into the impact of emotions on various aspects of human life, from consumer preferences to user experience in human-computer interaction.

Game-based learning has the potential to enhance learner engagement and improve training outcomes [10]. This approach is particularly beneficial in the construction industry, where human error due to inadequate training often leads to hazards [11]. Additionally, interruptions are known to disrupt cognitive function [12]. In our previous study, we examined the impact of game-based learning on construction safety knowledge and how interruptions affect participants' hazard identification abilities. Participants' baseline knowledge was assessed with a pre-training test, followed by game-based training. Post-training knowledge was then evaluated using the same hazard identification test. Results showed significant improvement in safety knowledge due to game-based training. In the current study, we assessed participants' safety knowledge one year after the game-based training to evaluate long-term knowledge retention. During this retention test, we recorded participants' facial expressions and analyzed their emotional responses with the Noldus FaceReader tool. This article explores whether the FaceReader tool's results can predict participants' performance on the hazard identification test.

Documents by year

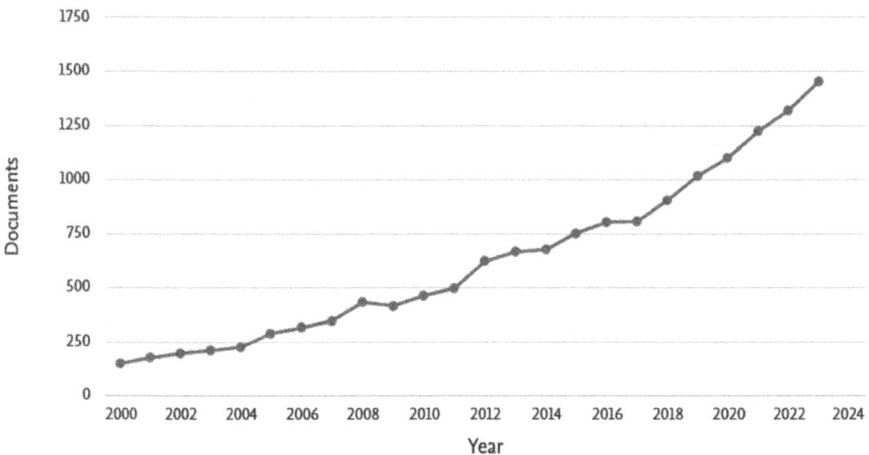

Fig. 1. Trend diagram demonstrating increased interest in research related to emotional response. This diagram was generated by analyzing results generated by Scopus when the keyword "emotional response" was used. [13]

2   Methods

2.1   Data Collection

The data used for analysis in this article was collected as a part of a larger study designed to evaluate the effectiveness of game-based learning for improved retention of safety knowledge in the construction industry. The results of the larger study are outside the scope of this article. 10 graduate students (23–30 years old, mean age 26.2 years, 7 males, 3 females) who had previously undergone game-based training for construction safety volunteered to participate in this research. A hazard identification test was designed to test the safety knowledge of these participants in the context of construction safety. This test consisted of 10 images of various construction sites. Each image was displayed for one minute and had multiple hazards. These images were displayed using a Tobii TX300 eye-tracker device which captured the eye movements of the participants during the hazard identification test. The analysis of the eye-tracker data is beyond the purview of this article. The participants were instructed to identify as many hazards as possible on each image and talk out. The participants' responses were recorded using a voice recorder. These responses were then analyzed to calculate the number of hazards identified by each participant. The comparison of the number of hazards identified by the participants in the retention test compared to the post-training test is outside the scope of this article. The facial expressions of the participants during the hazard recognition test were recorded. These videos were then analyzed using the FaceReader tool licensed from Noldus.

2.2 FaceReader

FaceReader (version 9.1), an advanced automated system developed by Noldus, was used to analyse facial expressions. This software has the ability to identify six fundamental or universal expressions: happiness, sadness, anger, surprise, fear, and disgust [14]. The classification process within FaceReader involves a series of sequential steps. Firstly, a deep learning-based face-finding algorithm is used to locate the position of the face in an image by detecting facial features at various scales. Subsequently, FaceReader employs a facial modeling technique based on deep neural networks to generate an artificial face model, detailing the location of nearly 500 key points on the face, learned from a database of annotated images. Finally, facial expression classification is conducted using a trained deep artificial neural network that identifies patterns in the face, directly analyzing image pixels. The neural network was trained on a dataset comprising over 20,000 manually annotated images to classify emotions according to Ekman's six basic emotions, including a neutral state, and to recognize the set of Facial Action Units available in FaceReader [14]. This comprehensive approach ensures the accurate and reliable analysis of facial expressions, providing insights into individuals' emotional states. Apart from the six fundamental expressions, the participant's arousal during the hazard identification test was measured using the FaceReader tool.

2.3 Machine Learning

The subsequent approach after data collection was to use machine learning techniques for further data analysis. The application of machine learning techniques in our study serves as a pivotal methodological approach to comprehensively analyze the complex dataset derived from the hazard identification test and facial expression recordings. The adoption of machine learning methodologies arises from the intrinsic capability to identify intricate patterns and relationships within multidimensional datasets, thereby facilitating a nuanced understanding of human behavior and cognition. In our research, machine learning, and more specifically supervised learning, offers a robust framework to unravel the underlying mechanisms governing hazard recognition and emotional responses. Moreover, machine learning techniques are inherently flexible and adaptable, capable of accommodating diverse types of data and accommodating complex interactions between predictors. This flexibility aligns seamlessly with the multifaceted nature of our research problem, where traditional statistical methods may fall short in capturing the intricate interplay between variables.

Within the realm of supervised learning, linear regression emerges as the most appropriate choice for its simplicity, and efficiency in modeling linear relationships between predictors and outcomes. By employing linear regression models, we aimed to identify the level of influences of different factors, such as demographic attributes, training and emotional expressions among participants. More complicated approaches can also be adapted to our analysis, including ensemble methods such as Random Forest and Gradient Boosting, as well as deep learning architectures like Convolutional Neural Networks (CNNs) and Long Short-Term Memory networks (LSTMs). These advanced techniques enable us to capture nonlinearities and interactions inherent in the data, thereby enhancing the predictive accuracy and robustness of our models. However, due to the limitation of our sample data size ($N = 10$), these complex approaches may be subject to overfitting, which is a common issue in many machine-learning problems. Although such issues can be addressed by regularization or feature selection, we find that using these advanced techniques defeats the purpose of learning the relationship between participants' hazard identification performance and the expression data, making the results impossible to interpret.

One additional concern for using machine learning is privacy, as discussed in [15] in which federated learning can be used to better protect users' private information. Inspired by this, we first replace all participants' names with randomly assigned participant ID numbers, and use that as the reference to match all data. We further pre-process the data using a similar approach to the average pooling method on each expression category to further decrease the exposure of too many details that may cause privacy concerns, and in the meantime reduce the dimension of features as a simple remedy to potential overfitting issues. The details of this have been explained in the next section.

3   Data Analysis

In this section, we use the machine learning technique of linear regression to analyze the data. We randomly select 10 samples and feed the data into the regression model to demonstrate the learning results. The structure of this section is as follows. First, we introduce the descriptive statistics of the data set, and we take necessary steps to pre-process the data through methods such as averaging and pre-conditioning to address or mitigate any issues related with feature dimension and large condition numbers. Then, we present the regression model that is used to fit the data. Finally, we present the results.

3.1   Sample Data

3.1.1 Data Structure
As the purpose of the analysis is to demonstrate the effectiveness of machine learning in our research, here we randomly select 10 samples ($N = 10$) from our overall data set. Each sample corresponds to one participant, labeled with participant ID to avoid researchers' subjective bias, as well as to protect participants' privacy. For each sample, the data to collect is listed in Table (1). The first attribute "Participant ID" is used as the reference key to ensure each data is connected with the correct participant. The second attribute "HII score" is the outcome (dependent variable) that we aim to predict from our model. The rest of the data attributes are the predictors (independent variables) and can be further separated into 2 groups: demographic and time series. The demographic information refers to each participant's personal information such as gender and age, which is fixed at the time of data collection. The time series data refers to data that depends on time, which is in the format of a list. All types of time series data are collected by the FaceeReader. Due to the fact that each participant spent different amount of time in

Table 1. Sample data features (with data types and data structures).

Attribute	Type	Data structure	Note
Participant ID	Reference key	`string`	–
HII score	Outcome	`float`	–
Gender	Demographic	`binary`	Base category is female
Age	Demographic	`integer`	–
Previous education	Demographic	`binary`	Base category is no education
Previous work experience	Demographic	`binary`	Base category is no experience
Neutral	Time series	`list[float]`	Size varies across samples
Happy	Time series	`list[float]`	Size varies across samples
Sad	Time series	`list[float]`	Size varies across samples
Angry	Time series	`list[float]`	Size varies across samples
Surprised	Time series	`list[float]`	Size varies across samples
Scared	Time series	`list[float]`	Size varies across samples
Disgusted	Time series	`list[float]`	Size varies across samples
Valence	Time series	`list[float]`	Size varies across samples
Arousal	Time series	`list[float]`	Size varies across samples

their experiment, the data length sampled from the FaceReader varies. This will be addressed during the pre-processing step. Last but not least, we assign binary values to handle non-quantitative data based on the categories. For example, we assign 0 to female gender which is the base case, and 1 to male gender. This approach is called one-hot encoding or dummy variables and is commonly used in regression analysis.

3.1.2 Pre-processing

One major problem of the data is the varying sizes of all time series attributes collected by the FaceReader that reflects the levels of different emotions it detects. The length of the data depends on how long that participant spent on the experiment. Although the experiment was designed to be in identical length, manually turning on and off the sensors may perturb the total time length. As the FaceReader samples the recording on a discrete time interval, longer time results in more data entries for that sample. To address this issue, we take the approach to instead average each emotion category for each participant. As a result, we focus on estimating the relationship between the average level of each emotion and the final performance score.

Another problem identified from the data is an ill-conditioned matrix. Let X be the matrix (augmented with an all-one vector for the bias term) that contains all the data except the outcomes, in which each row represents a participant, and each column refers to a predictor. Let y be the vector of outcomes, in which each entry represents the HII score of each participant. The regression analysis aims to use this to find out the weights and bias of the model, denoted as w. Mathematically, we solve $Xw = y$, which implies $X^T X w = X^T y$. Assuming the matrix $X^T X$ is full rank, we can get $W = (X^T X)^{-1} X^T y$. We observe that most of our data falls in between -1 and 1, except the age which ranges from 23 to 30. As a result, the matrix $X^T X$ may contain numbers that are either too large or too small. Such matrix is often ill-conditioned, and taking an inverse of it may cause numerical issues from computer hardware and further lead to a wrong answer. To remedy this, we perform a pre-conditioning by offsetting the age by -23 (age is therefore ranging from 0 to 7), which greatly reduce the size of the numerical value. Also this does not impact the weights since the offset part is now part of the bias term.

3.1.3 Descriptive Statistics

The detailed descriptive statistics are shown in Table (2). The minimum HII score over the 10 samples is 0.4038 and maximum 0.6538, with the mean and variance being 0.5519 and 0.0088, respectively. We also include a column "Base Count" for the 3 binary variables and counts the number of the base categories (which has value 0, as defined in Table (1).) For example, the base count for previous education is 4, meaning 4 participants did not receive any training of hazard identification at the moment of the experiment, while the other 6 participants did. The age attribute, after offsetting, should be interpreted as how much older the participant is from age 23 for its mean, minimum and maximum values. All emotion-related attributes are replaced by their average values over the experiment time. As a result, the statistics should be interpreted as the mean, variance, minimum and maximum values of the average emotion.

3.2   Machine Learning Model

The regression model is a linear combination of the pre-processed data. Let the variable of each predictor be denoted as in Table (2), where we use y as the outcome, and z for static demographic information and x for emotion-related data. Let b be the bias (or constant term/intercept) of the model, and ε be the unknown error term which is assumed to be normally distributed ($\varepsilon \sim \mathcal{N}(0, 1)$.) Each variable is indexed with subscript i that represents the sample index. The true model is presented as follows in Eq. (1):

$$
\begin{aligned}
y_i =\, & b + w_1 z_{g,i} + w_2 z_{a,i} + w_3 z_{e,i} + w_4 z_{w,i} \\
& + w_5 x_{n,i} + w_6 x_{h,i} + w_7 x_{s,i} + w_8 x_{a,i} + w_9 x_{p,i} \\
& + w_{10} x_{c,i} + w_{11} x_{d,i} + w_{12} x_{v,i} + w_{13} x_{r,i} + \varepsilon_i
\end{aligned}
\tag{1}
$$

Linear regression aims to learn the relationship between the predictors and the outcome by estimating the weights w's and bias b through minimizing the least squares loss of the model given a data set. Let $\hat{w}, \hat{b}, \hat{y}$ be the estimated weights, bias and predicted outcome of the regression model. Equation (2) below shows the regression model we would learn through machine learning.

$$
\begin{aligned}
\hat{y}_i =\, & \hat{b} + \hat{w}_1 z_{g,i} + \hat{w}_2 z_{a,i} + \hat{w}_3 z_{e,i} + \hat{w}_4 z_{w,i} \\
& + \hat{w}_5 x_{n,i} + \hat{w}_6 x_{h,i} + \hat{w}_7 x_{s,i} + \hat{w}_8 x_{a,i} + \hat{w}_9 x_{p,i} \\
& + \hat{w}_{10} x_{c,i} + \hat{w}_{11} x_{d,i} + \hat{w}_{12} x_{v,i} + \hat{w}_{13} x_{r,i}
\end{aligned}
\tag{2}
$$

Table 2. Sample data descriptive statistics. The "Variable" column indicates how each attribute is denoted in the regression analysis. The last column "Base Count" for binary variables indicates number of samples in the base categories as defined in Table (1). All emotion-related attributes are replaced by their average values over the experiment time. The Age attribute is offset by -23 as a result of matrix pre-conditioning.

Attribute	Variable	Mean	Variance	Min	Max	Base Count
HII score	y	0.5519	0.0088	0.4038	0.6538	–
Gender	z_g	0.7	0.2333	0	1	3
Age	z_a	3.2	4.6222	0	7	–
Previous education	z_e	0.6	0.2667	0	1	4
Previous work experience	z_w	0.3	0.2333	0	1	7
Average Neutral	x_n	0.6871	0.0421	0.2651	0.9210	–
Average Happy	x_h	0.0274	0.0015	0.0002	0.1067	–
Average Sad	x_s	0.0469	0.0044	0.0012	0.2304	–
Average Angry	x_a	0.1557	0.0320	0.0224	0.4864	–
Average Surprised	x_p	0.1021	0.0183	0.0005	0.3675	–
Average Scared	x_c	0.0222	0.0005	0.0037	0.0618	–
Average Disgusted	x_d	0.0101	0.0002	0.0001	0.0357	–
Average Valence	x_v	−0.1581	0.0261	−0.4840	0.0147	–
Average Arousal	x_r	0.2842	0.0003	0.2646	0.3093	–

The regression problem is defined in (3), where we minimize the total sum of squared residuals (difference between the predicted outcome and true outcome.)

$$\text{minimize} \sum_{i=1}^{N} (\hat{y}_i - y_i)^2 \text{subject to} (2) \tag{3}$$

In addition, the complete machine learning model is shown in Fig. 2. The first layer of the model consists of all raw data. Different machine learning techniques are applied to each data attribute to generate the second layer of data, as described in previous section. Finally, the linear regression is performed to predict the outcome.

3.3   Results

The result of the learned regression model is presented in Table (3). We observe that most (average) emotion can significantly impact the final score. The one with the highest impact is the average scared level, with -3.3509, indicating an increase in the scared level of 0.1 detected by the FaceReader can lower participant's final score by 0.33509. Similarly, an increase of 0.1 in the level of average angry, neutral, arousal and happy can affect the final score by 0.20714, 0.14236, -0.13359 and 0.12954, respectively. We also pay attention to the demographic information, especially the previous education attribute. We can see that the

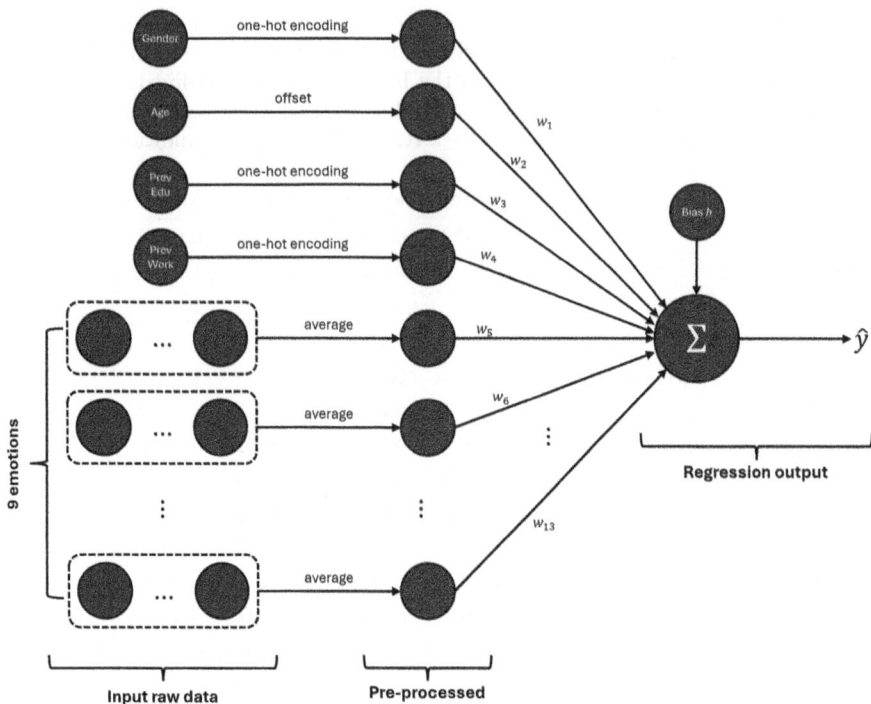

Fig. 2. The complete machine learning model. The first layer is the raw input data; the second layer is data after pre-processing; and the last layer is the linear regression with predicted output.

Table 3. Regression result learned from the 10 samples.

Attribute	Variable	Value
Bias	$\hat{b}$	−0.3485
Gender	$\hat{w}_1$	−0.0071
Age	$\hat{w}_2$	0.0611
Previous education	$\hat{w}_3$	−0.2160
Previous work experience	$\hat{w}_4$	−0.1312
Average Neutral	$\hat{w}_5$	1.4236
Average Happy	$\hat{w}_6$	1.2954
Average Sad	$\hat{w}_7$	0.6409
Average Angry	$\hat{w}_8$	2.0714
Average Surprised	$\hat{w}_9$	0.5453
Average Scared	$\hat{w}_{10}$	−3.3509
Average Disgusted	$\hat{w}_{11}$	0.1795
Average Valence	$\hat{w}_{12}$	0.5736
Average Arousal	$\hat{w}_{13}$	−1.3359

impact is not as significant in comparison to the emotions. It is also interesting to see that, in these 10 samples, the score is lower for the participant who received training prior to the experiment. The counter-intuitive observation is highly likely a result of small sample size. More data is needed if we want to achieve a more accurate result.

To better illustrate the results, we next present the graphs. However, it is impossible to graph the learned model as it has 13 predictors and thus 13 dimensions. We utilize an important property of regression that the average value of the predictors and the outcome must be on the fitted line. In other words, if we set all predictors to be their sample mean as listed in Table (2), through the regression model of Equation (3), the predicted value $\hat{y}$ must be the average HII score of the 10 samples. Therefore, for each variable, we fix all other variables to their mean, and draw a 2D graph that focus only on the HII score and that single variable. The slope of each line is the estimated weight of each variable, which is $\frac{\partial \hat{y}}{\partial x}$, where x is any of the 13 predictors. Intuitively, each line tells us that "if all other values are average, how much I would gain or lose in my HII score according to that single variable". Figure 3 shows how different emotion levels each affects the final score. We can see that the steeper the line is, the more sensitive the final score is to any perturbation in that emotion. The top 5 most influential emotions are scared, angry, neutral, arousal and happy. Figure 4 shows how changes in age are associated with the final score. And we can see a positive trend in the graph. This indicates in the 10 samples, the older the participant is, the more he/she scores in the end. Finally, for the 3 categorical variables (gender, previous education, and previous work experience), we compare each of them by setting the binary variable to 1 and 0. The result is shown in Fig. 5, in which each category has different colors. Keeping everything else at their sample mean values, we can see that female participants score slightly better than male participants, and to our surprise that participants without prior education about hazard identification and/or without professional work experience score higher than those who has education and/or work experience.

4 Discussion

Our study explored the relationship between emotional responses, demographic factors, and hazard recognition performance in the hazard identification test. By collecting facial expression data and employing machine learning techniques to analyze it, we aimed to investigate the relationship between emotional response and participants' performance in the hazard identification test to check if emotional response can predict performance. Our findings underscore the significant impact of emotional expressions on participants' hazard identification scores. We observed that emotions such as fear, anger, neutrality, arousal, and happiness exerted varying degrees of influence on participants' ability to recognize hazards in construction sites. Higher levels of fear and arousal were associated with decreased hazard identification scores, suggesting a detrimental effect on hazard identification performance. Conversely, increased levels of happiness and anger

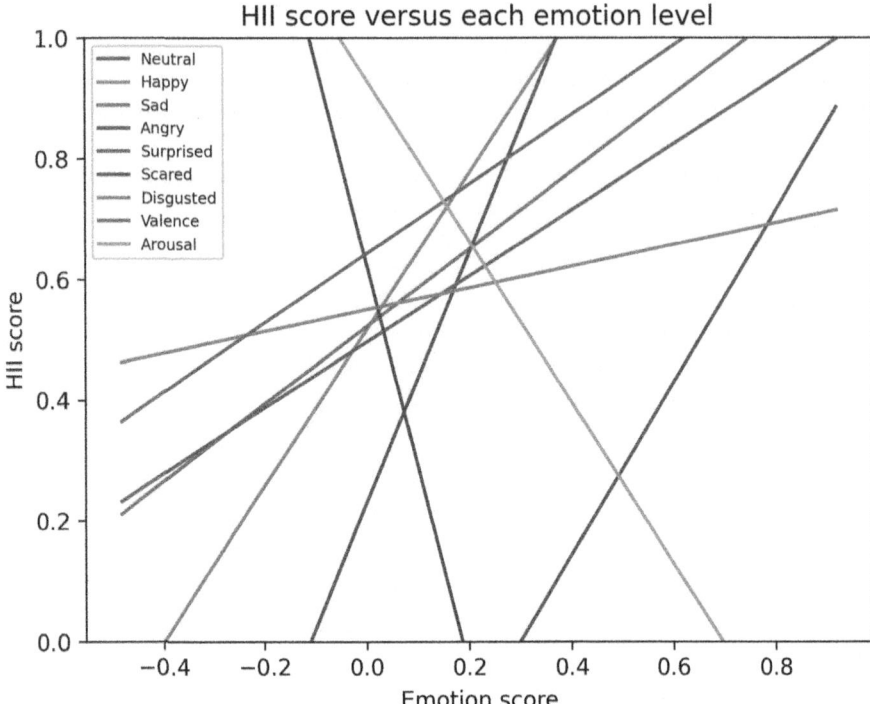

Fig. 3. HII score versus each emotion level. Each line is drawn by setting every other variable to their fixed sample mean value and changing only the corresponding emotion variable.

were positively correlated with higher hazard identification scores, indicating a potential predictive role of certain emotional expressions in enhancing cognitive processes relevant to hazard recognition.

Moreover, our analysis explored the influence of demographic factors on hazard recognition. Contrary to our initial hypotheses, participants with prior education and work experience in hazard identification did not demonstrate superior performance compared to those without such backgrounds. It needs to be noted that these factors were not controlled for during participant recruitment i.e., participants were not selected based on their previous work/educational experience. The participants might also have different levels of experience - someone might have a 10-minute workplace safety training which might not educate them as much. Hence, these findings might not be accurate. This unexpected finding could also be the result of a small sample size. Further investigation is required to establish concrete conclusions regarding the relationship between previous educational/work experience and hazard identification performance.

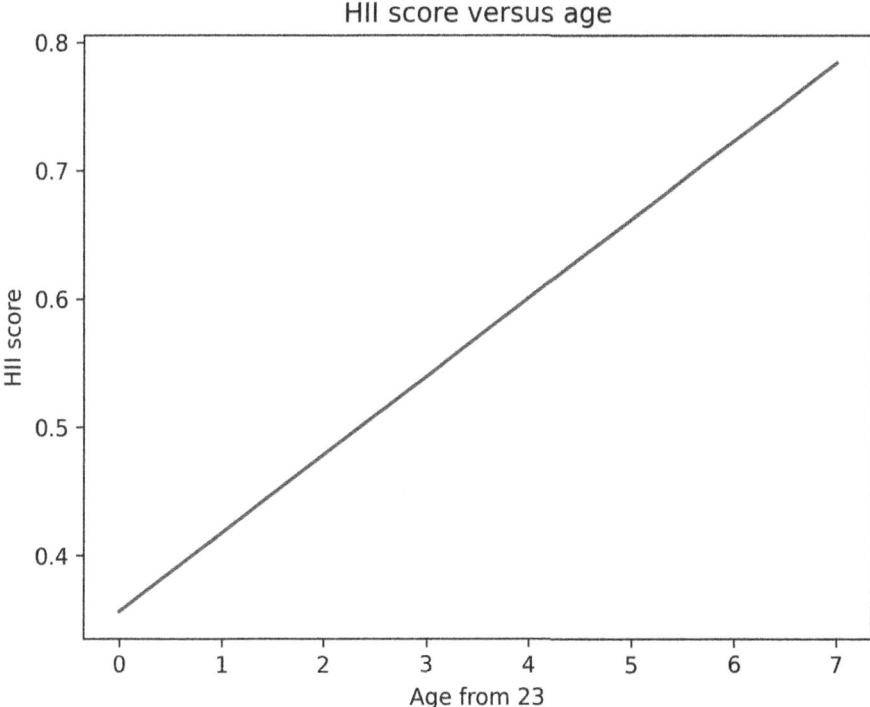

Fig. 4. HII score versus each age. The line is drawn by setting every other variable to their fixed sample mean value and changing only the age variable.

Limitations. The study's small sample size might limit the broader implications of its results. The result lacks a further analysis on its statistics including t-statistics, F-statistics, p-values, R^2, *etc.*. These statistics values are crucial because they could help us understand which variables are significant and how well our model is. Because the number of sample size is smaller than the number of features, these values cannot be computed. Furthermore, the study exclusively involved graduate students as participants. Future research endeavors should explore the potential of combining FaceReader with machine learning on a larger and more diverse sample, thereby enhancing the predictive accuracy of safety performance measures.

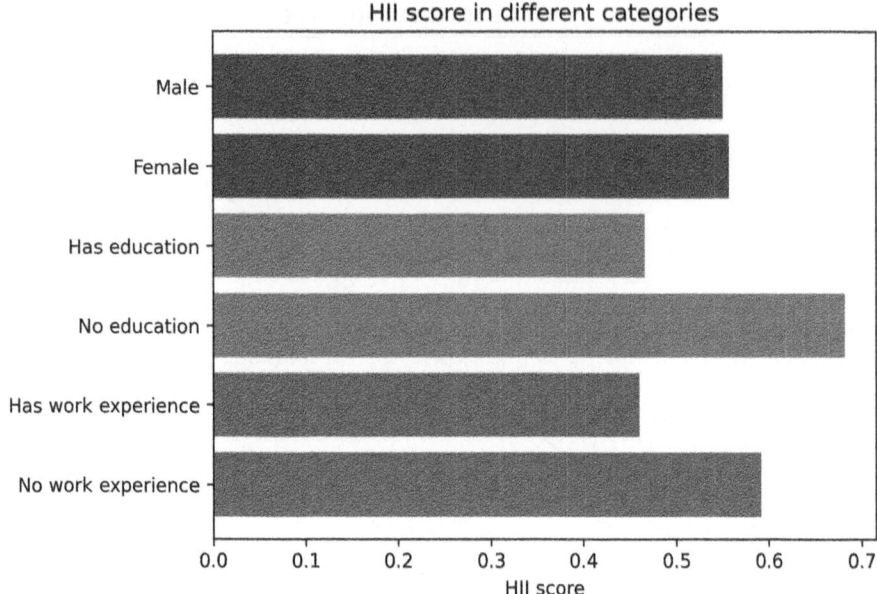

Fig. 5. HII score versus each categorical variable (gender, previous education, and previous work experience. Every two bars of the same color are plotted by setting every other variable to their fixed sample mean value and changing only the corresponding binary variable.

5   Conclusion

In conclusion, this study investigated the efficacy of integrating emotional response analysis, facilitated by FaceReader technology, with machine learning algorithms for predicting safety performance in the context of construction safety. Our findings demonstrate the utility of this approach, highlighting the potential to forecast operator safety based on facial expressions indicative of emotional states that may compromise hazard identification. This predictive framework offers real-time intervention capabilities, alerting workers to potential declines in their hazard detection abilities. Consequently, this approach can contribute to the mitigation of potentially dangerous situations. The successful integration of emotional response analysis and machine learning underscores the promise of this framework for enhancing safety protocols. Furthermore, the study paves the way for the exploration of innovative applications of FaceReader technology for proactive workplace safety interventions and hazard prevention. Future research should focus on further refining the predictive model to maximize its effectiveness and generalizability across various industrial contexts.

6   Future Work

This study's findings unveil several promising directions for future research. Firstly, an investigation into the impact of incorporating real-time feedback mechanisms predicated on emotional cues on safety performance outcomes is warranted. Such an inquiry could yield valuable insights into the effectiveness of these interventions in augmenting hazard identification and prevention capabilities. Additionally, research could explore the feasibility of implementing personalized safety alerts tailored to individual emotional responses. This approach has the potential to offer a more nuanced and potentially productive strategy for improving safety practices across various occupational settings. Future endeavors could also focus on developing adaptive algorithms that can dynamically adjust safety cues based on real-time fluctuations in emotional states to optimize hazard recognition and mitigation strategies. Furthermore, a longitudinal study examining the long-term effects of utilizing emotional analysis with machine learning on overall safety culture and organizational safety climate could provide a comprehensive understanding of the sustained benefits associated with these technological interventions. By addressing these research directions, future studies can contribute significantly to the advancement of innovative approaches to workplace safety, fostering a proactive safety mindset among employees, and ultimately, enhancing overall safety outcomes.

References

1. Lacroix, C., Rajaobelina, L., St-Onge, A.: Impact of perceived experiential advertising on customers' responses: a multi-method approach. Int. J. Bank Mark. **38**(6), 1237–1258 (2020)
2. Danner, L., Sidorkina, L., Joechl, M., Duerrschmid, K.: Make a face! implicit and explicit measurement of facial expressions elicited by orange juices using face reading technology. Food Qual. Prefer. **32**, 167–172 (2014)
3. Kerrihard, A.L., Khair, M.B., Blumberg, R., Feldman, C.H., Wunderlich, S.M.: The effects of acclimation to the united states and other demographic factors on responses to salt levels in foods: an examination utilizing face reader technology. Appetite **116**, 315–322 (2017)
4. Meng, Q., Hu, X., Kang, J., Wu, Y.: On the effectiveness of facial expression recognition for evaluation of urban sound perception. Sci. Total Environ. **710**, 135484 (2020)
5. Lewinski, P.: Don't look blank, happy, or sad: patterns of facial expressions of speakers in banks' Youtube videos predict video's popularity over time. J. Neurosci. Psychol. Econ. **8**(4), 241 (2015)
6. Höfling, T.T.A., Gerdes, A.B., Föhl, U., Alpers, G.W.: Read my face: automatic facial coding versus psychophysiological indicators of emotional valence and arousal. Front. Psychol. **11**, 1388 (2020)
7. Pichierri, M., Peluso, A.M., Pino, G., Guido, G.: Health claims' text clarity, perceived healthiness of extra-virgin olive oil, and arousal: an experiment using facereader. Trends Food Sci. Technol. **116**, 1186–1194 (2021)

8. Bartkiene, E., et al.: Factors affecting consumer food preferences: food taste and depression-based evoked emotional expressions with the use of face reading technology. BioMed Res. Int. **2019**, 2097415 (2019)
9. Gurcan, F., Cagiltay, N.E., Cagiltay, K.: Mapping human-computer interaction research themes and trends from its existence to today: a topic modeling-based review of past 60 years. Int. J. Hum. Comput. Interact. **37**(3), 267–280 (2021)
10. Kanade, S.G., Duffy, V.G.: A systematic literature review of game-based learning and safety management. In: Digital Human Modeling and Applications in Health, Safety, Ergonomics and Risk Management. Human Communication, Organization and Work: 11th International Conference, DHM 2020, Held as Part of the 22nd HCI International Conference, HCII 2020, Copenhagen, Denmark, 19–24 July 2020, Proceedings, Part II 22, pp. 365–377 (2020). Springer
11. Kanade, S.G., Duffy, V.G.: Use of virtual reality for safety training: a systematic review. In: International Conference on Human-Computer Interaction, pp. 364–375 (2022). Springer
12. Kanade, S.G., Duffy, V.G.: Exploring the effectiveness of virtual reality as a learning tool in the context of task interruption: a systematic review. Int. J. Ind. Ergon. **99**, 103548 (2024)
13. Scopus. https://www.scopus.com/standard/marketing.uri, https://www.scopus.com/term/analyzer.uri?sort=plffsrc=ssid=87d87e891ab65f258db53e8805818fc9sot=asdt=asl=33s=TITLE-ABSKEY
14. Lewinski, P., Den Uyl, T.M., Butler, C.: Automated facial coding: validation of basic emotions and FACS AUs in FaceReader. J. Neurosci. Psychol. Econ. **7**(4), 227 (2014)
15. He, J., Cao, T., Duffy, V.G.: Machine learning techniques and privacy concerns in human-computer interactions: a systematic review. In: International Conference on Human-Computer Interaction, pp. 373–389 (2023). Springer. https://doi.org/10.1007/978-3-031-48057-7_23

Developing a Pedagogical Approach to Enhance Learning Experiences for Fostering Soft Skills

Eunyoung Kim[(⊠)] [ID]

Japan Advanced Institute of Science and Technology, Nomi, Ishikawa 9231292, Japan
kim@jaist.ac.jp

Abstract. There are increasing needs of innovating pedagogical approaches to foster soft skills such as creative skill, cognitive skill, innovation skills, etc. Many educational pro-grams have been implemented and assessed in various fields for the last couple of decades, however, there are still lack of pedagogical development research to design learning content to enhance learning experiences. Thus, this study proposes a learning and pedagogical model to enhance learning experience focusing on soft skills.

This research integrates related theories to establish a new model of learning objectives as an expanding cycle of inspiring – illuminating – interacting – incubating – reflecting. Based on the proposed model, we designed an educational program to be implemented for fostering soft skills and evaluated it from students' perspectives to enhance their learning experiences in further steps. To develop educational content for enhancing soft skills, we conducted systematic literature review to extract appropriate topics to learn. Five students voluntarily participated in our pilot educational program, which was conducted in a commonly accepted educational setting as a course with 14 sessions in a semester. The results of evaluation from learners will be utilized to redesign the educational content to enhance the learning experiences.

This study suggests a novel approach to integrate pedagogical methods with the learning objectives of inspiring, illuminating, interacting, incubating, and reflecting to facilitate significant learning experiences. In future research, we will redesign the learning content and collect larger sample data to conduct empirical research.

Keywords: Pedagogical Development · Learning Model · Innovations in Education · Soft Skills · Learning Experiences

1 Introduction

Numbers of educators in higher education institutes (HEIs) are facing challenges from the changes in learning behaviors of Generation Z, drastic changes of socio-technical environment such as post-Covid [1], and the imbalances of learning styles between the educator generation and the learner generation [2]. In line with this, there are increasing needs of innovating pedagogical approaches to foster soft skills such as creative skill,

© The Author(s), under exclusive license to Springer Nature Switzerland AG 2025
P. Zaphiris et al. (Eds.): HCII 2024, LNCS 15378, pp. 85–93, 2025.
https://doi.org/10.1007/978-3-031-76815-6_7

cognitive skill, innovation skills, etc. Many educational programs have been implemented and assessed in various fields for last couple of decades, however, there are still lack of pedagogical development research to design learning content to enhance learning experiences. Thus, this study is to propose a learning model to enhance learning experience focusing on soft skills.

2   Literature Review

2.1   Objectives and Benefits of Learning

Bloom's taxonomy of educational objectives [3] is the one of most widely recognized framework for categorizing educational goals, as a pyramid of remembering – understanding – applying – analyzing – evaluating – creating. This taxonomy has been modified in several versions considering the levels of processing and the domains of knowledge [4, 5]. Souitaris et al. [6] classified the benefits of entrepreneurship education program into three dimensions: inspiration; learning; and incubating resource.

This research integrates related theories to establish a new model of learning objectives as shown in Fig. 1: Inspiring – An instructor introduces key conceptual words to motivate learners to learn; Illuminating - An instructor explains the key concepts with various case studies, theoretical findings, related research design to let learners acquire knowledge and have insight; Interacting – An instructor encourages learners to facilitate and participate in various learning activities and discussion; Incubating – Learners take time to process, combine, and integrate the acquired knowledge; Reflecting – Learners engage in self-reflection on their learning process.

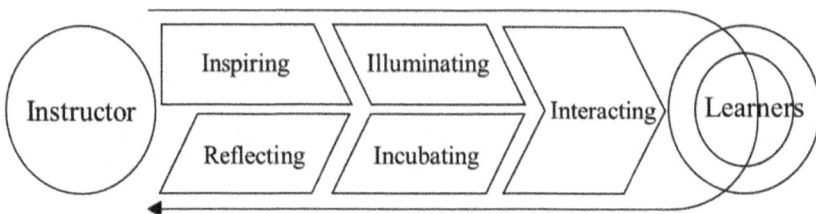

Fig. 1. IIIIR (Inspiring, Illuminating, Interacting, Incubating, and Reflecting) model of learning objectives.

2.2   Creating Significant Learning Experiences

Fink [7] defined the significant learning experiences as results of meaningful changes in lives of learners. He highlighted the importance of human interaction and motivation and categorized six major types of significant learning as foundational knowledge, application, integration, human dimensions, caring, learning how to learn.

This study focuses on fostering soft skills such as creative thinking skills which allow us to have aha experience of insight moment [8, 9], optimal experience of flow moment

[10], peak experience [11, 12], wow experience [13], hmm experience of incubation [14] and reflection [15]. Those learning experiences can be resulted through mental activities in learning process. Thus, this study will suggest pedagogical methods to engage students in the mental activities to bring them significant learning experiences.

3   Methods

Synthesizing the objectives of learning and the cognitive process for creating significant learning experiences, this study proposes an integrated model of cognitive process for enhancing learning experiences as show in Fig. 2. Furthermore, this paper develops a pedagogical approach to engage learners in the mental activities of inspiration, incubation, illumination, reflection, and interaction that lead them to create wow, hmm, aha moment in their learning experiences.

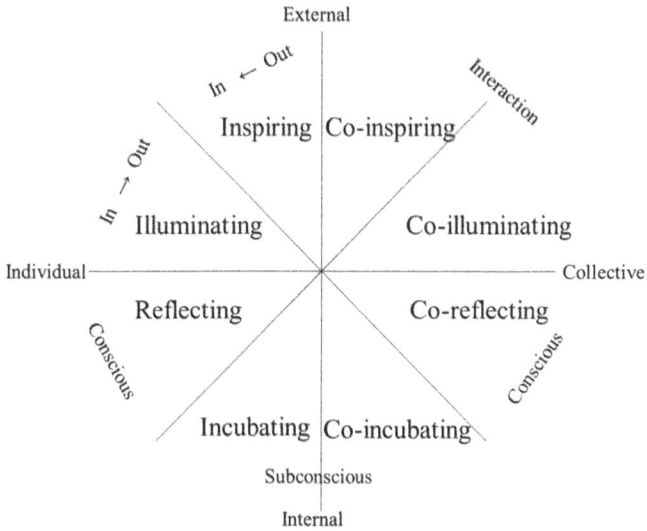

Fig. 2. An integrated model of cognitive process for learning experiences.

3.1   Learning Design for Inner Process

Inspiration. Instructors need to utilize inspiration stimuli that influence 'hearts and minds' of learners to motivate them to actively engage in learning, apart from learning the curriculum itself [6]. The inspirational methods can be designed with high level of emotional intelligence of educational designers who can utilize relevant resources in diverse fields for their educational content development. It can be forms of raising a fundamental question, introducing emotional stories, motivating cases, and novel research design methods and their results; posing a challenge; envisioning future; etc. In addition, we suggest to assesses the level of inspiration by self-report from the learners.

Incubation. Incubation can be defined as a "period of preconscious, fringe-conscious, off-conscious, or perhaps even unconscious mental activity" [16]. Incubation usually occurs while thinker is engaged in other activities of their daily routine. Instructors can intentionally distract learners with changing topics in various fields different from the domain the thinker are working on, letting learners to take a break, refreshing the atmosphere, inducing learners to take certain actions such as playing a simple game or puzzle, chatting, take a walk outside, meditating, etc. Due to its natural characteristics, this stage is difficult to evaluate.

Illumination. Educators can devise a pedagogical method that creates situations during which their students experience illumination, or referred to as insight that brings "aha!" moment [17]. These experiences are mostly engaged in problem solving process [18]. Illuminating the learners can be promoted by designing appropriate classroom activities such as quizzes, simple and complex tasks, group activities, assignments.

Reflection. Reflection helps learner to develop abstract concepts from concrete experiences [19]. It allows students to engage in debriefings, reframing, seeking feedback, drawing lessons, discussing, etc. [20]. Instructor needs to facilitate learners' reflection and their meta-cognitive skills by designing a series of assignments that structurally interconnected with each other.

3.2   Learning Design for Interactive Process

Learning can occur at individual level, group level, institutional level, and social level. In many cases, the classroom settings of higher education institute are for group learning. Many educators are focused on learner-centered course design, which facilitates interactions among learners or between students and instructors in nearly all courses.

Four stages of learning explained in previous sub-section can be co-developed through proper interactions. To facilitate co-learning by interactions among learners, educators need consider the diversity of classroom members, and utilize various pedagogical methods to design classroom activities for engaging and co-learning including setting appropriate discussion agenda, providing opportunities to give constructive peer feedback with each other.

3.3   Implementation and Assessment

Five students voluntarily participated in our pilot educational program, which was conducted in a commonly accepted educational setting as a course with 14 sessions in a semester. We implemented 159 educational practices based on the combination of five types of pedagogical methods and the keywords of ten topics to learn. In the last session of the program, all participants evaluated their learning experiences of each learning practice based on the criteria relevant to its designated learning objectives.

4 Results and Conclusion

4.1 Designing the Learning Content and Learning Experiences

Based on an extensive literature review, we identified ten topics to learn to enhance soft skills, 37 inspiring key conceptual words, 80 related theories, case studies, educational practices, and related research design methods, 21 tasks and quizzes, 12 themes for group activities and discussion, and eight assignments were designed for learners, as shown in Fig. 3, for example.

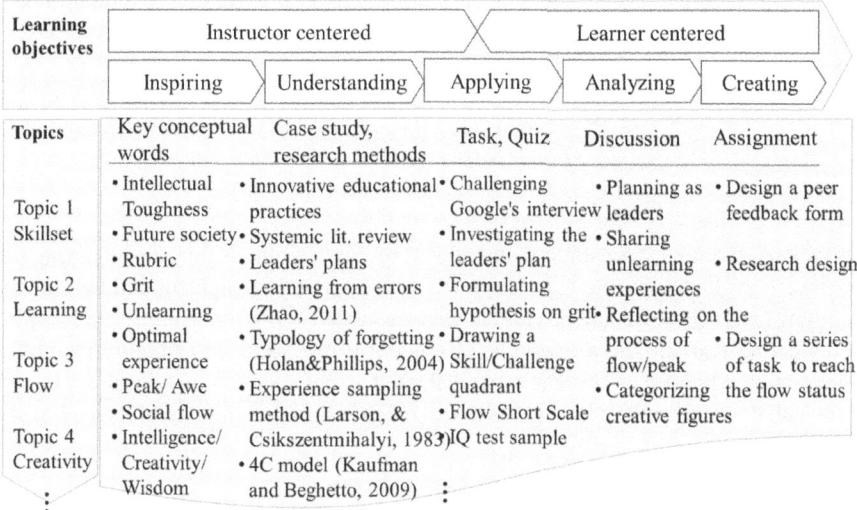

Fig. 3. An example list of the designed learning content and learning experience.

4.2 Assessment on the Learning Experiences

A pilot course was implemented with five students. Each session was a class of two hours, including introducing inspiring keywords, related theories, conducting individual tasks, group activities and discussions, and individual assignments. In the final session, participants were asked to review all the list of learning content they had encountered since the start of the course, engaging them in the feedback and assessment process. The reflection survey questionnaire on the learning content was created using Google Forms. Learners were prompted to indicate the extent to which the learning objectives were achieved by the learning content presented and explained by the instructor.

37 inspiring keywords introduced during the course were evaluated by the learners in three level: highly inspiring, inspiring, not so much inspiring. As result, 19 keywords were evaluated as highly inspiring, 8 keywords were evaluated as inspiring, and 10 keywords were evaluated as less inspiring (See Table 1).

Table 1. An example list of the inspiring keywords.

	Examples
Highly inspiring keywords (19)	Creativity in daily life; Difficulty in new product development; Creative thinking; "Wow!" experience; Awe experience; Social flow; Future society; Generative AI and Creativity; Importance of diffusion over invention; Objective of learning; Rubric evaluation; Hacks and pranks of students; Presentation formats: Pechakucha, Ignite, Ted talk, Elevator pitch; Workshop process, etc
Inspiring keywords (8)	Flow; Optimal experience; Peak experience; Idea evaluation; Originality; Tech-driven philanthropy; Analogical thinking; Design thinking as a cultural process
Less inspiring keywords (10)	intellectual toughness; Unlearning; GRIT; Hype cycle for emerging tech; IDEO cases; ME310 course; Eureka myth; Insight; Concept of mental activities; Impasse

80 related theories, case studies, and related research methods introduced during the course were evaluated by the learners in two dimensions of insightful and helpful for conducting research. As result, 53 content were evaluated as highly insightful and helpful for conducting learner's own research, 11 content were evaluated as highly insightful but not so much helpful, 7 content were evaluated as not so much insightful but highly helpful, and 9 content were evaluated as not so much insightful either helpful (see Fig. 4).

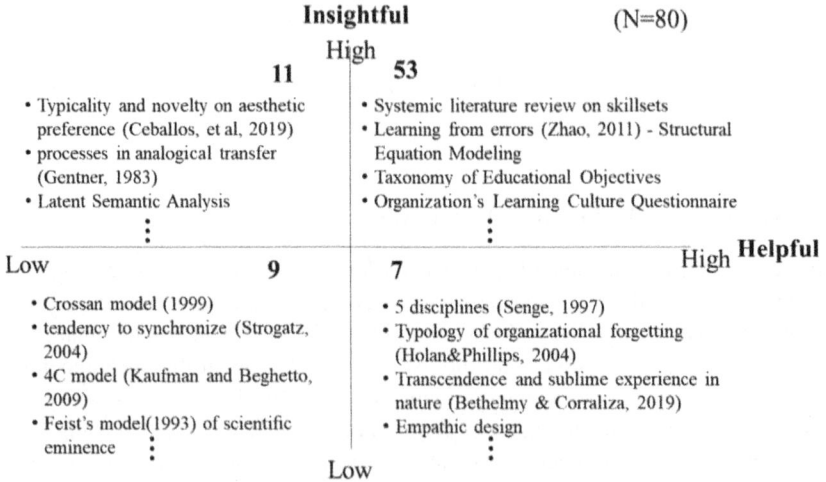

Fig. 4. Assessment result and an example list of learning content.

Learning experiences on each task and group activity will be assessed by learners as shown in Fig. 5, in two dimensions of enjoyability and meaningfulness learned from the key conceptual word "optimal experience" [10].

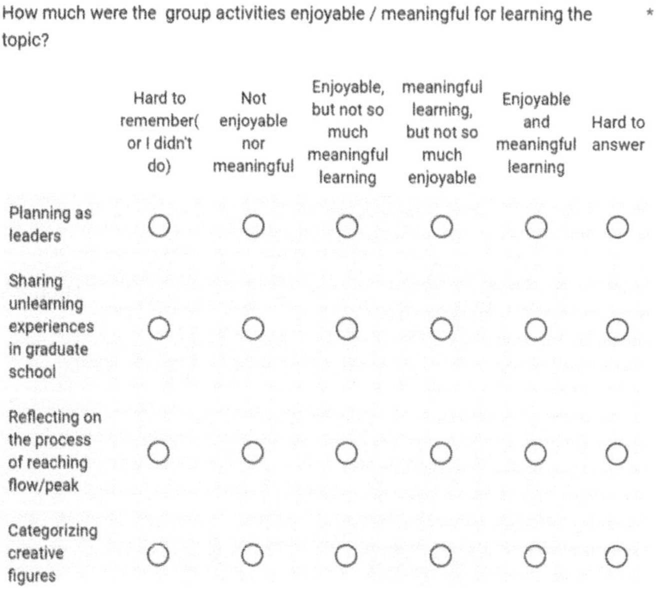

How much were the group activities enjoyable / meaningful for learning the   *
topic?

	Hard to remember(or I didn't do)	Not enjoyable nor meaningful	Enjoyable, but not so much meaningful learning	meaningful learning, but not so much enjoyable	Enjoyable and meaningful learning	Hard to answer
Planning as leaders	O	O	O	O	O	O
Sharing unlearning experiences in graduate school	O	O	O	O	O	O
Reflecting on the process of reaching flow/peak	O	O	O	O	O	O
Categorizing creative figures	O	O	O	O	O	O

Fig. 5. Survey questionnaire on the learning experiences.

As a result, learners evaluated their learning experiences as highly meaningful and enjoyable while they were conducting 11 out of 21 individidual takses (52%) in the qudrant I in Fig. 6.

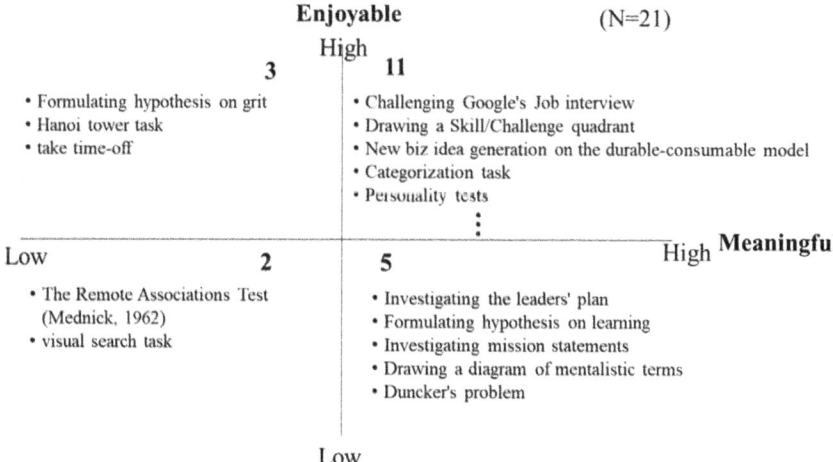

Fig. 6. Assessment result and an example list of learning experience of individual tasks.

Regarding the group activities, learners evaluated their learning experiences as highly meaningful and enjoyable while they were conducting 8 out of 12 group activities (67%) in the qudrant I in Fig. 7.

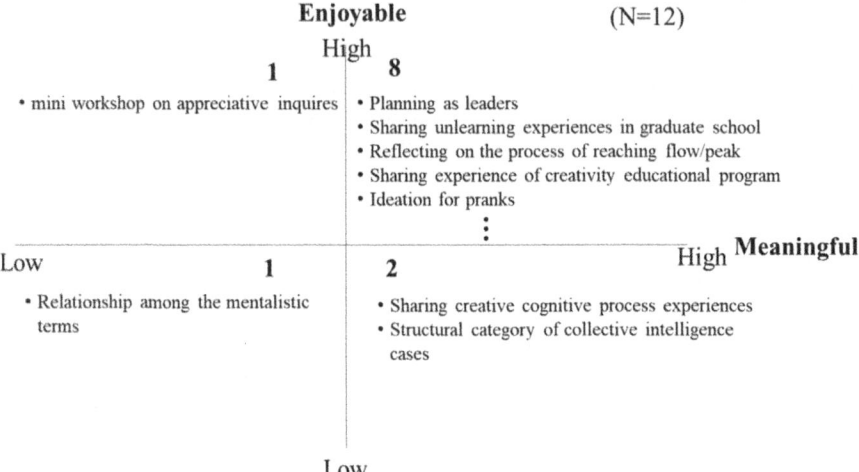

Fig. 7. Assessment result and an example list of learning experience of group activities.

4.3 Conclusion

This study suggests a novel approach to integrate pedagogical methods with the learning objectives of inspiring, illuminating, interacting, incubating, and reflecting for facilitate significant learning experiences. It elaborated theory-based practical methods in each stage as a level of conceptual research. The significance of this research lies in all learners evaluated each educational content learned from the instructor and their learning experience on conducting each individual task and group activity adopting reflective session.

However, it lacks enough empirical data to validate our proposals. The target learners of this pilot study were five international graduate students with three different nationalities majoring three different fields. In our future research, we will recruit larger sample of groups to implement our educational practices and evaluate the learning experiences of learners to further develop the pedagogical methods to fulfill the objectives of learning. In addition, we will conduct further analysis on learning which types of educational content in prior influences on creating significant learning experiences.

Acknowledgments. This study was funded by KAKEN22K13754, Japan Society for the Promotion of Science.

Disclosure of Interests. The author has no competing interests to declare that are relevant to the content of this article.

References

1. Neuwirth, L.S., Jović, S., Mukherji, B.R.: Reimagining higher education during and post-COVID-19: challenges and opportunities. J. Adult Continuing Educ. **27**, 141–156 (2021)
2. Cilliers, E.J.: The challenge of teaching generation Z. People Int. J. Soc. Sci. **3**, 188–198 (2017)
3. Bloom, B.S., Krathwohl, D.R.: Taxonomy of Educational Objectives: Volume 2 Affective Domain. David McKay Company Incorporated (1971)
4. Dubas, J.M., Toledo, S.A.: Taking higher order thinking seriously: using Marzano's taxonomy in the economics classroom. Int. Rev. Econ. Educ. **21**, 12–20 (2016)
5. Anderson, L.W., et al.: A Taxonomy for Learning, Teaching, and Assessing: A Revision of Bloom's Taxonomy of Educational Objectives, abridged Longman, White Plains, NY (2001)
6. Souitaris, V., Zerbinati, S., Al-Laham, A.: Do entrepreneurship programmes raise entrepreneurial intention of science and engineering students? the effect of learning, inspiration and resources. J. Bus. Ventur. **22**, 566–591 (2007)
7. Fink, L.D.: Creating Significant Learning Experiences: An Integrated Approach to Designing College Courses. John Wiley & Sons (2013)
8. Weisberg, R.W.: Toward an Integrated Theory of Insight in Problem Solving. Insight and Creativity in Problem Solving, pp. 5–39. Routledge (2019)
9. Shen, W., Yuan, Y., Liu, C., Luo, J.: In search of the 'Aha!' experience: elucidating the emotionality of insight problem-solving. Br. J. Psychol. **107**, 281–298 (2016)
10. Csikszentmihalyi, M.: Flow: The psychology of optimal experience (1990)
11. Maslow, A.H.: Peak experiences in education and art. Theory Into Pract. **10**, 149–153 (1971)
12. Raettig, T., Weger, U.: Learning as a shared peak experience: interactive flow in higher education. Int. J. Appl. Positive Psychol. **2**, 39–60 (2018)
13. Gordon, J.: The Wow Factors: The Assessment of Practical Media and Creative Arts Subjects. Perspectives on Learning Assessment in the Arts in Higher Education, pp. 169–183. Routledge (2021)
14. Ellwood, S., Pallier, G., Snyder, A., Gallate, J.: The incubation effect: hatching a solution? Creat. Res. J. **21**, 6–14 (2009)
15. Sogunro, O.A.: Efficacy of role-playing pedagogy in training leaders: some reflections. J. Manage Dev. **23**, (2004)
16. Davis, G.A.: Creativity is forever. Kendall/Hunt Pub. (2004)
17. Kizilirmak, J.M., Galvao Gomes da Silva, J., Imamoglu, F., Richardson-Klavehn, A.: Generation and the subjective feeling of "aha!" are independently related to learning from insight. Psychol. Res. **80**, 1059–1074 (2016)
18. Harris, K.R., Graham, S.E., Urdan, T.E., Bus, A.G., Major, S.E., Swanson, H.: APA Educational Psychology Handbook, Vol 3: Application to Learning and Teaching. American Psychological Association (2012)
19. Kolb, D.A.: Experiential Learning: Experience as the Source of Learning and Development. Pearson Education (2014)
20. Roskos, K., Vukelich, C., Risko, V.: Reflection and learning to teach reading: a critical review of literacy and general teacher education studies. J. Lit. Res. **33**, 595–635 (2001)

DCLA: Towards Distributed Cooperative Learning Analytics for Developing Communities

Shin'ichi Konomi[1]([✉]), Lulu Gao[2], Doreen Mushi[3], and Baofeng Ren[1]

[1] Kyushu University, 744 Motooka, Fukuoka 819-0395, Japan
konomi@artsci.kyushu-u.ac.jp
[2] School of Blockchain Industry (Xin Gu Industrial College),
Chengdu University of Information Technology, Chengdu 610225, China
[3] The Open University of Tanzania, Dar es Salaam, Tanzania

Abstract. The rapid advancement of smart technologies is arguably widening the digital divide, making the lives of people without easy access to the Internet increasingly challenging. This digital divide can exacerbate the educational gap between communities with and without reliable digital infrastructures, as learning increasingly relies on smart digital technologies such as learning management systems, learning analytics and artificial intelligence tools. In this paper, we discuss a distributed cooperative learning analytics approach for developing communities without reliable Internet access based on our look into the cases of Tanzania. To enable management of digital learning contents, learning analytics, and interaction with AI agents based on slowly transmitted and shared learning data, we propose Distributed Cooperative Learning Environments for Development (DCL4D), which provides mechanisms for supporting teachers and learners in distributed environments by extending and integrating Delay-Tolerant Networking, Semi-supervised Federated Learning, and Progressive Visual Analytics techniques. This is a first step towards the provision of distributed cooperative learning analytics for developing communities and helps to identify key challenges to pave the way for smart learning support systems accessible to all.

Keywords: Distributed cooperative learning · learning analytics · intermittent networking · federated learning · progressive analytics

1 Introduction

The rapid advancement of smart technologies is arguably widening the digital divide, making the lives of people without easy access to the Internet increasingly challenging. This is relevant to many facets of people's lives including not only healthcare, work, and leisure activities but also education and learning. Indeed, such digital divide can exacerbate the educational gap between communities with and without reliable digital infrastructures, as learning increasingly relies on smart digital technologies such as learning management systems, learning analytics and artificial intelligence tools.

As we will discuss in the subsequent section in the context of technology-enhanced learning in Tanzania, the disparities in access to technology and digital literacy skills,

P. Zaphiris et al. (Eds.): HCII 2024, LNCS 15378, pp. 94–106, 2025.
https://doi.org/10.1007/978-3-031-76815-6_8

which persist, particularly in rural areas, necessitates efforts to tackle relevant technological and social challenges. Based on our look into the cases of Tanzania, we discuss a distributed cooperative learning analytics approach for developing communities without reliable Internet access. To enable management of digital learning contents, learning analytics, and interaction with AI agents based on slowly transmitted and shared learning data, we propose Distributed Cooperative Learning Environments for Development (DCL4D). DCL4D provides mechanisms for supporting teachers and learners in distributed environments by providing meaningful preliminary analytics for timely actions. These mechanisms are enabled by extending and integrating three technological components. Firstly, Delay-Tolerant Networking techniques allow for transmission and sharing of learning activity data in intermittent communication environments. Secondly, Semi-supervised Federated Learning enables personalized learning analytics in distributed environments. Finally, Progressive Visual Analytics supports usability and usefulness for teachers and learners even in slow data communication and computation environments. The architecture and mechanisms we propose is a first step towards the provision of distributed cooperative learning analytics for developing communities. As such, it allows for the discussions of the benefits as well as the limitations of the current architecture and mechanisms, thereby helping identify key future challenges to pave the way for smart learning support systems accessible to all.

2 Technology-Enhanced Learning in Tanzania

Tanzania has been undergoing remarkable transformation in the adoption of information and communication technologies across various sectors including education. Ever since the early 2000s, the country has taken initiatives to develop its ICT infrastructure, promote digital literacy, and formulate strategies and policies that can holistically support social development and economic growth [1]. The National ICT policy was first introduced in 2003 and it has been providing directions on the integration of ICTs to bridge the digital divide and foster the growth of the ICT in various sectors [2, 3]. The latest draft of the National ICT policy, has a dedicated section outlining the responsibilities of educational and research institutions in the country regarding the policy [3]. Specifically, Sect. 5.12 outlines three core responsibilities: the development of digital and emerging technologies, the promotion of digital content, and scientific research to support the country's digital advancement [3].

Tanzania is a low-income country with a population of over 69.04 million, predominantly distributed, with 68% residing in the rural regions and 362% in urban areas [4]. The national communications statistics report by the Tanzania Communication and Regulatory Authority highlights that digital device usage is a key driver in promoting and scaling the use of technology services in the country [4]. In their 2023 -2024 report, phones had the largest penetration rate at 83%, followed by smartphones at 30.71% [5]. At the same time, TCRA reports on 55% of geographical coverage by mobile network signal which indicates there is still a gap in terms of infrastructure and penetration. The statistics regarding internet network coverage and smartphone usage highlight the role that technology can play in improving access to educational opportunities and resources.

Technology enhanced learning in Tanzanian higher learning institutions can be traced back to the early 2000's with the Open University of Tanzania (OUT) and the University of Dar es Salaam (UDSM) being the first adopters of the initiatives [6]. In the latest years this implementation has been going through significant strides, with universities striving to adopt educational technology solutions that meet the needs and demands of their respective student populations. For instance, in the study reported by [7], over 80% of the universities have learning management systems for supporting instruction and learning activities. It is also important to note that this acceleration of e-learning has been influenced by the COVID-19 pandemic [8], with many institutions transitioning to online learning modalities to support continuity of education during lockdowns and social distancing measures [9].

Efforts have been made to address the challenges facing technology enhanced learning in Tanzanian higher learning institutions [10]. These include government initiatives to improve internet infrastructure and access, partnerships with telecommunications companies to provide discounted data packages for students, and provision of capacity building programs for academic staff and administrators to enhance their digital literacy and educational technology competencies [10, 11].

Despite these efforts, disparities in access to technology and digital literacy skills persist, particularly in rural areas [12].

3   Related Works

Our earlier efforts [13, 14] to explore distributed approaches for addressing disparities in access to technology highlighted the importance of three key areas of technological developments. Firstly, intermittent networking methods such as *Delay-Tolerant Networking* to enable data transmission and sharing, even without reliable internet access, although the process may be slower. Secondly, machine learning techniques for distributed environments such as *Semi-supervised Federated Learning* to construct personalized models of learners' activities efficiently. Finally, *Progressive Analytics* to provide useful insights and visualizations to teachers and learners even when relevant data are transmitted and shared slowly.

3.1   Delay-Tolerant Networking and Their Applications

The idea to use intermittent networking methods such as Delay-Tolerant Networking (DTN) for the support of education in developing communities is not entirely new. Brewer et al., for example, discussed DTN-based technologies for education, and proposed an easy-to-use local content repository for students and teachers in developing regions [15]. CAM provides mobile environments for people in rural areas by exploiting barcodes and mobile cameras to enable paper-based navigation and offline interaction [16]. The Digital Study Hall system [17] uses intermittent networking techniques to support lectures, homework and QA sessions in rural India. More recently, a decentralized data infrastructure for off-grid networks has been proposed based on state-of-the-art Web 3.0 technologies [18]. Existing solutions that use intermittent networking techniques for the support of education in developing and/or rural communities mainly focus on traditional learning contents and interactions; they are not designed to fully support learning analytics involving collection, processing, and communication of learning activity data.

3.2 Semi-supervised Federated Learning

Personalization is an extremely powerful approach for the technologies that monitor and support diverse learners. However, devising personalized analytics for distributed learning activity data is a challenging task. Some of the recent machine learning mechanisms consider the requirements of distributed environments. Federated Learning (FL) is a distributed framework that enables multiple parties to collaboratively train a shared generic model based on their own data, benefiting all the participants involved. FL was proposed as an alternative to traditional centralized deep learning, which has been widely adopted in many applications, including activities recognition [19, 20]. Sozinov et al. introduced a FL based human activity recognition (HAR) system that demonstrates robust performance, achieving accuracy levels comparable to those of centralized learning systems [20]. Similarly, an FL-based HAR system designed for activity and health monitoring is developed by Zhao et al. in [21]. Most of the established FL systems for activity recognition, however, assume that the ground-truth of the data on each participant are known to perform training in supervised manners. In practice, it is too labor-intensive and time-consuming to annotate data manually. What can make things even worse is that some annotators may lack the expertise and/or resource to annotate data properly. All in all, existing FL-based activity recognition systems are likely to face the so-called label scarcity problem.

To address the label scarcity problem in FL, Semi-Supervised Learning (SSL) is broadly explored, which combines supervised learning with unsupervised learning to tackle model training with limited labeled data [22]. Generating pseudo labels for unlabeled data to construct labeled data for model training in a supervised fashion has been extensively researched [22–24]. For instance, Diao et al. propose SemiFL to ensure the accuracy of pseudo labels based on "fine-tune global model with labeled data" and "generate pseudo-labels with the global model" to conduct SSL [22]. Liu et al. use labeled data on the FL server to train a model through supervised learning and then send this model to FL clients to generate labels on their local data [24]. Another direction of semi-supervised FL is to perform unsupervised learning on clients to derive robust feature representation learning from the unlabeled data for downstream tasks with limited labeled data. Van Berlo et al. introduce federated unsupervised representation to pretrain the model using unlabeled data to solve the label scarcity problem [25]. Zhao et al. proposed a semi-supervised FL framework for HAR, in which clients conduct unsupervised learning on autoencoders with unlabeled local data for representation learning, and a server conducts supervised learning on an LSTM classifier with labeled data [26]. However, the challenging data heterogeneity of activity recognition in FL setting due to the different physical characteristics and various contextual information are not properly considered in these proposals. Since the meaning of the learning activity in individuals are different, and thus, it is necessary to build a personalized model on a particular client for unique information precisely identified to firmly enable the establishment of evidence-based pedagogical approaches.

Recently, FedHAR was proposed to build the global model by aggregating the computed unsupervised and supervised gradients, in which a small number of clients own labeled data and a large number of clients only have unlabeled data [27]. FedAR, assuming that there are labeled data in each client, combines active learning and label propagation to semi-automatically annotate the local unlabeled sensor data [28]. Different from these works, we do not rely on the assumption of labeled data stored on clients. For the more realistic case of storing only limited labeled data contributed by volunteers on the server, we propose a practical solution to continuously improve model performance by integrating representation learning and pseudo-labeling.

3.3 Progressive Analytics

When we transmit and share learning activity data slowly in intermittent networking environments, it is desirable to provide meaningful preliminary analytics quickly to support timely actions by teachers and learners. Existing techniques for managing, analyzing and visualizing data under slow computation and communication environments can be useful in this context.

Progressive Visualization (PV) and progressive visual analytics (PVA) allow immediate feedback and interaction with large datasets and complex computations by using partial results improving with time [29]. Progressive Insights [30], for example, use a modified implementation of the Sequential Pattern Mining (SPAM) algorithm to meet the progressive and user-driven requirements in the context of healthcare, and provide a user interface with multiple coordinated views that are integrated with this algorithm. PVA starts by producing a fist meaningful partial result, proceeds to show a reliable result within an accceptable margin of errors, then presents a stable result, and finally presents a completed result [31].

Database researchers have discussed closely-related techniques including the early work on online aggregation, including methods for returning the output in random order, controlling relative rate at which different aggregates are computed, and computing running confidence intervals [32]. In the context of online analytical processing (OLAP), special statistical summaries or synopses of the original data can be precomputed to provide fast approximate answers to aggregate queries [33].

Despite these developments in the last decades, there is still scarcity of research that targets machine learning-based intelligent analytics based on *slow* data and/or computation.

4   Distributed Cooperative Learning Environments for Development

To address the challenges of digital technology-based learning in developing communities, we have developed and refined the overall design of distributed cooperative learning environments for development (DCL4D). It is based on the key insights we learned by looking at specific cases in Tanzania and by analyzing datasets from areas in East Africa.

Figure 1 shows the overview of DCL4D. The large rectangle on the right shows a centralized environment involving four schools. As students learn in classes in these schools, their learning activity data are upload to a centralized cloud server and processed by the centralized machine intelligence in the middle. The processing results are delivered to teachers and students using different forms of Dashboard visualizations as well as AI agents' notifications, advice, and recommendations. The large rectangle on the left shows a distributed environment involving a larger school, three smaller schools, and a group of learners without a shared physical space for learning. Learning activity data at each site is accumulated locally, and slowly transferred to other sites based on a Delay-Tolerant Networking (DTN) environment that exploits pedestrians, bikes, cars, buses, and other vehicles as "data mules". Local machine intelligence at each site processes the local data and the data received from other sites to provide progressive visualizations and AI-based feedback to local teachers and students. To boost local machine intelligence, models learned in the centralized environment can be transferred to the sites in the distributed environment.

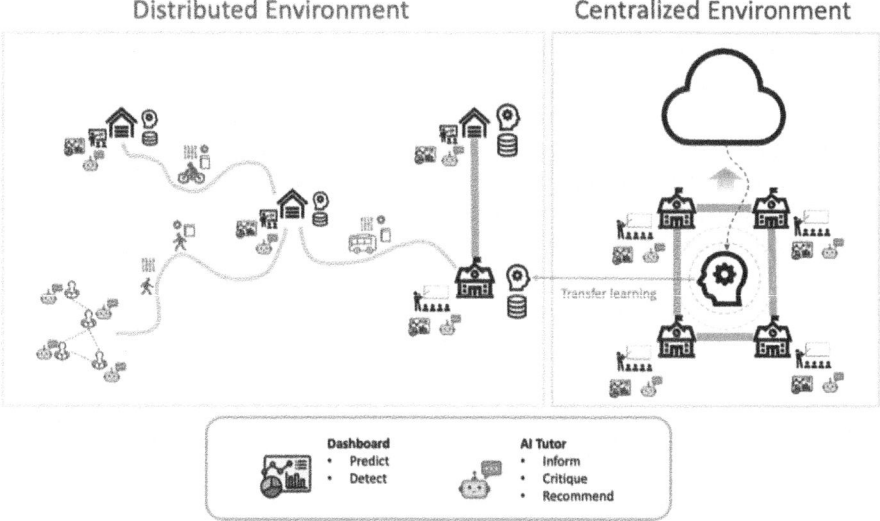

Fig. 1. Overview of the distributed cooperative learning environments for development (DCL4D).

The data collected by mobile tools are shared through intermittent *ad hoc* peer-to-peer exchange of data across mobile devices in proximity. To cope with the sparsity of mobile devices in unpopulated areas, we also introduced embedded micro servers that receive, store, and send data to/from mobile devices in proximity, thereby enabling asynchronous communications across mobile devices. Embedded micro servers are small devices with computing, storage and wireless networking capabilities that can be embedded in public spaces. We used Raspberry Pi to develop a preliminary prototype micro server having the capability of transferring data via wireless communication and USB memory sticks.

5   Delay-Tolerant Learning Analytics

We next propose a Delay-Tolerant Learning Analytics mechanism to integrate and extend a distributed framework for machine learning and progressive analytics for teachers and learners.

5.1 Federated Learning Analytics

Federated learning analytics is based on a scheme that follows the Federated Learning (FL) paradigm, using a distributed framework for machine learning. An overview of the proposed scheme is presented in Fig. 2. The server periodically sends the weights of a global learning analytics model to the available clients for model updating. The same deep neural network structure is established on the server and clients with representation layers, W_a, and classification layers, W_{cls}, for learning analysis. The global server model is initialized with the limited labeled data on the server, while the network on each client side is implemented with an SSL strategy to personalize the server model. In each communication round t, the global model $W_g^t = (W_{a_g}^t, W_{cls_g}^t)$, which has already been fine-tuned with the server-side labeled data, is sent to connected clients for further updating. After receiving the global model, each client would perform unsupervised learning for representation learning and then send the updated representation model to the server. The server averages the uploaded parameters from active clients to update the representation model, which is further trained in conjunction with a classification model to construct a new complete model W_g^{t+1} on the server for following communications. Each client can further learn a personalized model through pseudo-labeling, where both confidence and uncertainty are considered in selecting the right samples with the help of the best global models in history.

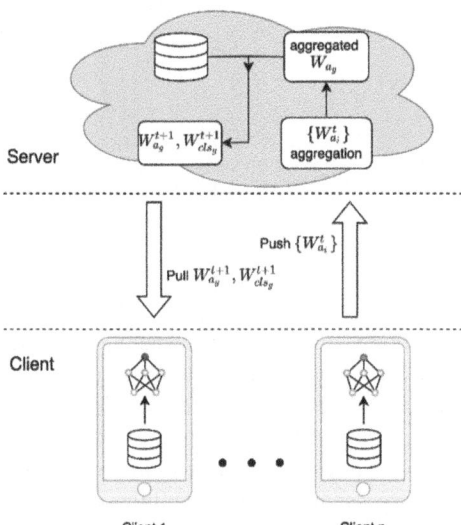

Fig. 2. Overview of the proposed scheme, involving a resourceful server with labeled samples and distributed clients with totally unlabeled data.

Representation Learning. The universal features extracted from input with the representation part of the deep learning model significantly affect the performance of the learning tasks [34]. In practical scenarios, there are many unlabeled data collected by different users, and unsupervised feature extraction has been proposed and studied to comprehensively utilize the target data. The autoencoder relies on reconstructing unlabeled data using unsupervised neural networks. The data is encoded into its latent representation as the extracted features, and then, the decoder part tries to reconstruct the original data from the learned representation. To facilitate the feature design and selection, various autoencoders are proposed, such as the villa autoencoder [35] and the stacked autoencoder [36]. Moreover, van Berlo et al. show promising potential for using autoencoders to implement semi-supervised FL and Zhao et al. apply autoencoders to unlabeled local data to learn general representations [26].

Therefore, in order to address the lack of labels on clients in learning analysis with learning log data and achieve a strong generalization ability while leveraging heterogeneous data, our proposed system applies SSL in an FL architecture. The server and clients use unsupervised learning to jointly train autoencoders with their own data in an unsupervised fashion for further recognition, and the server uses supervised learning to train a classifier that can map encoded representations to learning activities with a labeled dataset. Besides, the data or experience of learning analytics from developed communities with centralized servers can be leveraged to pre-train the learning model, and then, the model will be fine-tuned based on the context of developing community and the locally collected and annotated data to achieve more precise learning analysis.

Personalization with Uncertainty-Aware Pseudo Labeling. Although the shared global model is fine-tuned with a small number of labeled samples, it is not adaptive for all clients due to the possible heterogeneity between local data on the client side and labeled data on the server side. Hence, the server model with general representation extraction and a shared classifier would be personalized for a specific person. To obtain the information of local data as much as possible for model personalization, the pseudo labels for some samples are inferred. Typically, for each unlabeled data sample, it would pick the class with the maximum predicted confidence as a prediction to be used as a pseudo label. For sample x^i, $y_k^i = 1$ denotes that class k is present in the corresponding input as a potential label and $y_k^i = 0$ represent the class's absence. We set the p_k^i represents the probability of class k being present in the samples. With this prediction probability, the pseudo-label can be generated for x^i as:

$$\tilde{y}_k^i = \mathbb{1}\left[p_k^i \geq \gamma\right]$$

where $\gamma \in (0,1)$ is a threshold used to produce hard labels and $\mathbb{1}[\cdot]$ produce one-hot labels with given values.

In that setting, it is essential for determining the criteria used to select how many and which samples are transferred from unlabeled data to labeled data during training at each round. When starting to personalize, the client would pull several of the best models in history from the server to achieve well-performed models for conducting pseudo-labeling. Then, the pseudo-labels would be generated based on the agreements and uncertainty of the model prediction [24, 37]. Let $g^i = \left[g_1^i, g_2^i, \ldots, g_K^i\right] \subseteq \{0,1\}^K$ be a binary vector representing the selected pseudo-labels in sample x^i, where $g_k^i = 1$ when $\tilde{y}_k^i$ is selected and $g_k^i = 0$ when $\tilde{y}_k^i$ is not selected. This vector is obtained as follows:

$$\tilde{g}_k^i = \mathbb{1}\left[p_k^i \geq \gamma\right] + \mathbb{1}\left[u(p_k^i) \leq \sigma\right]$$

where $u(p)$ is the uncertainty of a prediction p, and σ are the uncertainty thresholds. The uncertainty part ensures the network prediction is sufficiently certain to be selected. Therefore, to maintain stability in each model, we retain artificial labels whose largest class probability is above a predefined threshold γ_t for communication round t, and the uncertainty of corresponding class probability should lower than a preset threshold σ_t. Since the imbalance of training would degrade the model performance, we also made adjustments with class balance for samples selection.

5.2 Progressive Learning Analytics

We next discuss progressive analytics for learners and teachers as well as their integration with the federated learning mechanism. As a first step, we explore the uses of progressive visual analytics for a teacher's dashboard for monitoring and predicting students' activities. This includes incrementally-updated bar charts showing students' "dropout rates" and "course pass rates", which can be combined with corresponding error bars easily, as shown in Fig. 3.

To provide meaningful preliminary analytics quickly to support timely actions by teachers and learners, we exploit an user-centered approach to design first *meaningful* partial results in addition to the provision of supplemental statistical information through dedicated UI components such as incrementally updatable error bars. We plan to refine the underlying DTN mechanism of DCL4D to suit the user interface and educational requirements of progressive learning analytics.

In order to support scenarios involving machine learning tasks, we can exploit easy-to-interpret evaluation metrics for machine learning models, including MSE, MAE, and F1-score, and present their slow progression through dedicated UI components for incremental updates.

6 Discussion and Conclusion

Again, our aim is to enable management of digital learning contents, learning analytics, and interaction with AI agents based on slowly accumulated and communicated learning data. We thus introduced Distributed Cooperative Learning Environments for Development (DCL4D) based on the key insights we learned by looking at the cases in Tanzania and relevant data. DCL4D use DTN techniques involving "data mules" to transmit and share learning activity data slowly across distributed learning sites with different technological constraints and use delay-tolerant learning analytics mechanism for providing intelligent feedback in progressive manners based on semi-supervised federated learning and progressive visual analytics.

Building on the approaches proposed in this paper, we are in the process of completing the first generation DCL4D environment by engaging in subsequent activities to refine the progressive analytics UI components and adjusting relevant aspects of the DTN mechanism. Our current work is just a step towards addressing disparities in access to technology in developing communities. Addressing the closely related challenges of disparities in digital literacy skills is an important direction for our future work.

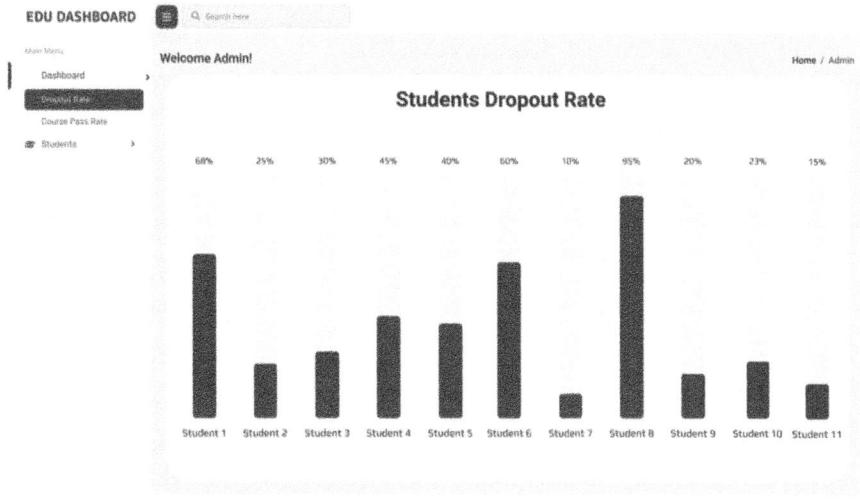

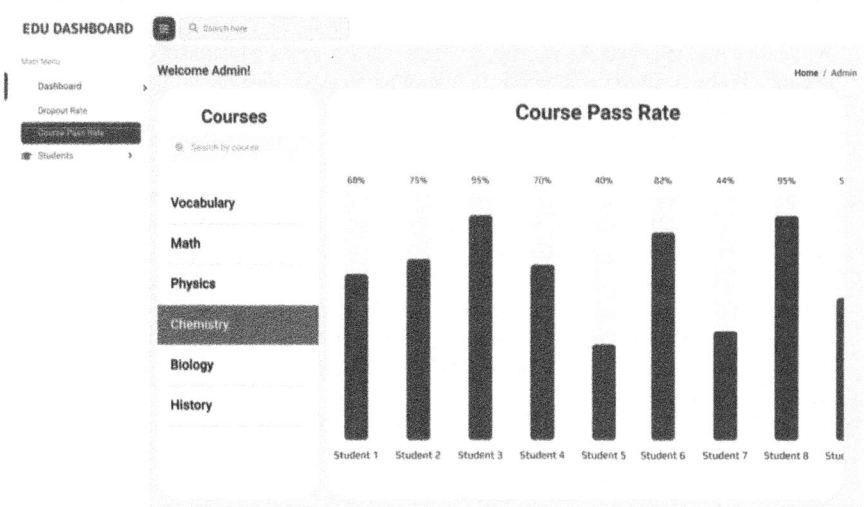

Fig. 3. Visualizing students' dropout rates and course pass rates as components of an educational dashboard.

Acknowledgments. This work was supported by JSPS KAKENHI Grant Number 20H00622.

References

1. Lubua, E.W., Maharaj, M.: ICT policy and e-Transparency in Tanzania. In: IST-Africa 2012 Conference Proceedings, pp. 1–10. IIMC International Information Management Corporation (2012)

2. Tanzania National ICT Policy. https://dict.mzumbe.ac.tz/wp-content/uploads/2019/03/3.Nat ional-ICT-Policy-of-2003.pdf. Accessed 18 May 2024

3. Drafted National ICT Policy 2023. https://www.mawasiliano.go.tz/uploads/documents/sw-1693455522-DOCUMENT%20TO%20UPLOAD%20DRAFT%20AUGUST%20NICTP. pdf. Accessed 18 May 2024

4. United Nations Population Fund. https://www.unfpa.org/data/world-population/TZ. Accessed 18 May 2024

5. Tanzania – TCRA. https://www.tcra.go.tz/uploads/text-editor/files/TCRA Communications Statistics 2023 -2024-Q1_1698210303.pdf. Accessed 18 May 2024

6. Mushi, R.M., Lashayo, D.M.: E-learning readiness assessment on distance learning: a case of tanzanian higher education institutions. Int. J. Inf. Commun. Technol. Hum. Dev. (IJICTHD) **14**(1), 1 (2022). https://doi.org/10.4018/IJICTHD.299409

7. Mtebe, J., Raphael, C.: A decade of technology enhanced learning at the University of Dar es Salaam, Tanzania: Challenges, achievements, and opportunities. Int. J. Educ. Dev. Using ICT **13**(2) (2017)

8. Mtebe, J.S., Fulgence, K., Gallagher, M.: COVID-19 and technology enhanced teaching in higher education in Sub-Saharan Africa: a case of the university of Dar es Salaam, Tanzania. J. Learn. Dev. **8**(2), 383–397 (2021)

9. Kisanjara, S.: Factors influencing e-learning implementation in Tanzanian universities. Online J. Distance Educ. E-Learn. **8**(1), 37–54 (2020)

10. Semlambo, A.A., Sengati, F., Angalia, B.: Factors affecting the adoption of e-learning systems in public higher learning institutions in Tanzania: a case of institute of accountancy arusha (IAA). J. Comput. Commun. **10**(9), 113–126 (2022)

11. Innocent, W.A., Masue, O.S.: Applicability of E-learning in higher learning institutions in Tanzania. Int. J. Educ. Dev. Using Inf. Commun. Technol. **16**(2), 242–249 (2020)

12. Mahai, L.S.: Overcoming the odds: Online learning experiences from Open University of Tanzania's regional centre rural-based students. University of Dar es Salaam Library J. **17**(1), 114–128 (2022). https://orcid.org/0000-0002-7557-221X

13. Konomi, S., Gao, L., Mushi, D.: An intelligent platform for offline learners based on model-driven crowdsensing over intermittent networks. In: Rau, P.L., (eds.) Cross-Cultural Design. Applications in Health, Learning, Communication, and Creativity. HCII 2020. Lecture Notes in Computer Science(), vol. 12193, pp. 300–314. Springer, Cham (2020). https://doi.org/10. 1007/978-3-030-49913-6_26.

14. Konomi, S., Hu, X., Gu, C., Mushi, D.: Designing a distributed cooperative data substrate for learners without internet access. In: Streitz, N.A., Konomi, S. (eds.) Distributed, Ambient and Pervasive Interactions. Smart Living, Learning, Well-being and Health, Art and Creativity. HCII 2022. Lecture Notes in Computer Science, vol. 13326, pp. 137–147. Springer, Cham (2022). https://doi.org/10.1007/978-3-031-05431-0_10

15. Brewer, E., et al.: The case for technology in developing regions. IEEE Comput. **38**(6), 25–38 (2005)

16. Parikh, T.S., Lazowska, E.D.: Designing an architecture for delivering mobile information services to the rural developing world. In: Proceedings of the 15th international conference on World Wide Web, pp. 791–800. ACM Press, New York (2006)

17. Wang, R., et al.: The digital study hall. Computer Science Department, Princeton University, Tech. Rep. TR-723–05 (2005)

18. Niavis, H., Papadis, N., Reddy, V., Rao, H., Tassiulas, L.: A blockchain-based decentralized data sharing infrastructure for off-grid networking. In: 2020 IEEE International Conference on Blockchain and Cryptocurrency (ICBC), pp. 1-5 (2020). https://doi.org/10.1109/ICBC48 266.2020.9169441

19. Li, L., Fan, Y., Tse, M., Lin, K.-Y.: A review of applications in federated learning. Comput. Ind. Eng. **149**, 106854 (2020). https://doi.org/10.1016/j.cie.2020.106854

20. Sozinov, K., Vlassov, V., Girdzijauskas, S.: Human activity recognition using federated learning. In: 2018 IEEE International Conference on Parallel & Distributed Processing with Applications, Ubiquitous Computing & Communications, Big Data & Cloud Computing, Social Computing & Networking, Sustainable Computing & Communications (ISPA/IUCC/BDCloud/SocialCom/SustainCom), pp. 1103–1111 (2018). https://doi.org/10.1109/BDCloud.2018.00164

21. Zhao, Y., Haddadi, H., Skillman, S., Enshaeifar, S., Barnaghi, P.: Privacy-preserving activity and health monitoring on databox. In: Proceedings of the Third ACM International Workshop on Edge Systems, Analytics and Networking, in EdgeSys '20. New York, NY, USA: Association for Computing Machinery, pp. 49–54 (2020)

22. Diao, E., Ding, J., Tarokh, V.: SemiFL: Semi-Supervised Federated Learning for Unlabeled Clients with Alternate Training (2022). arXiv. https://doi.org/10.48550/arXiv.2106.01432

23. Long, Z., et al.: FedSemi: An Adaptive Federated Semi-Supervised Learning Framework (2020). ArXiv, Accessed 24 Apr 2023

24. Lin, H., Lou, J., Xiong, L., Shahabi, C.: SemiFed: Semi-supervised Federated Learning with Consistency and Pseudo-Labeling. arXiv (2021). https://doi.org/10.48550/arXiv.2108.09412

25. van Berlo, B., Saeed, A., Ozcelebi, T.: Towards federated unsupervised representation learning. In: Proceedings of the Third ACM International Workshop on Edge Systems, Analytics and Networking, in EdgeSys 2020. New York, NY, USA: Association for Computing Machinery, pp. 31–36 (2020). https://doi.org/10.1145/3378679.3394530

26. Zhao, Y., Liu, H., Li, H., Barnaghi, P., Haddadi, H.: Semi-supervised Federated Learning for Activity Recognition. arXiv, (2021). https://doi.org/10.48550/arXiv.2011.00851

27. Yu, H., et al.: FedHAR: semi-supervised online learning for personalized federated human activity recognition. IEEE Trans. Mob. Comput. 1 (2021). https://doi.org/10.1109/TMC.2021.3136853

28. Presotto, R., Civitarese, G., Bettini, C.: Semi-supervised and personalized federated activity recognition based on active learning and label propagation. Pers. Ubiquitous Comput. **26**(5), 1281–1298 (2022). https://doi.org/10.1007/s00779-022-01688-8

29. Ulmer, A., Angelini, M., Fekete, J.D., Kohlhammer, J., May, T.: A survey on progressive visualization. IEEE Trans. Visual. Comput. Graph. (2023)

30. Stolper, C.D., Perer, A., Gotz, D.: Progressive visual analytics: user-driven visual exploration of in-progress analytics. IEEE Trans. Visual Comput. Graph. **20**(12), 1653–1662 (2014)

31. Angelini, M., Santucci, G., Schumann, H., Schulz, H.J.: A review and characterization of progressive visual analytics. Informatics **5**(3), 31. MDPI (2018)

32. Hellerstein, J.M., Haas, P.J., Wang, H.J.: Online aggregation. In: Proceedings of the 1997 ACM SIGMOD International Conference on Management of Data, pp. 171–182 (1997)

33. Acharya, S., Gibbons, P.B., Poosala, V., Ramaswamy, S.: The aqua approximate query answering system. In: Proceedings of the 1999 ACM SIGMOD International Conference on Management of data, pp. 574–576 (1999)

34. Oh, J., Kim, S., Yun, S.Y.: FedBABU: Towards Enhanced Representation for Federated Image Classification. arXiv (2022). https://doi.org/10.48550/arXiv.2106.06042

35. Thakur, D., Biswas, S., Ho, E.S.L., Chattopadhyay, S.: ConvAE-LSTM: convolutional autoencoder long short-term memory network for smartphone-based human activity recognition. IEEE Access **10**, 4137–4156 (2022). https://doi.org/10.1109/ACCESS.2022.3140373

36. Moya Rueda, F., Grzeszick, R., Fink, G.A., Feldhorst, S., Ten Hompel, M.: Convolutional neural networks for human activity recognition using body-worn sensors. Informatics **5**(2), 2 (2018). https://doi.org/10.3390/informatics5020026

37. Rizve, M.N., Duarte, K., Rawat, Y.S., Shah, M.: In Defense of Pseudo-Labeling: An Uncertainty-Aware Pseudo-label Selection Framework for Semi-Supervised Learning. acceptable, Apr 19 (2021). https://doi.org/10.48550/arXiv.2101.06329

Meta-Analysis of the Application of Artificial Intelligence and Spiritual Science in Guiding Learner Imagery Transformation: An Action Research on Quantum Resonance Design Course in University General Education Curriculum

Lin-mei Lin[1(✉)], Wen-Ko Chiou[2], Po-Chen Shen[2], Szu-Erh Hsu[2], Hao Chen[1], and Chao Liu[1]

[1] Department of Industrial Design, Chang Gung University, Taoyuan City, Taiwan
march19670324@gmail.com
[2] Department of Management, Chang Gung University, Taoyuan City, Taiwan
wkchiu@mail.cgu.edu.tw

Abstract. This meta-analysis investigates the concurrent application of artificial intelligence (AI) and spiritual science in guiding the transformation of self-cognitive imagery among higher education learners. The study encompasses 35 learners from two institutions, including non-design majors from an unconventional wilderness arts university and undergraduates taking the "Quantum Resonance Design" course in a university general education curriculum. Through the fusion of AI tools, such as ChatGPT and Bing AI Image, with Eastern and Western philosophies, including Jungian psychology and dynamic meditation activities, the research explores their integration into teaching planning and design. Results show the significant positive impact of AI tools on design thinking education for non-design majors and the profound transformation and deep self-awareness brought about by the intervention of spiritual science.

Challenges in integrating spiritual science elements into teaching, particularly among STEM students, highlight the need for open dialogue and inclusion of potential curricula, such as life design workshops. Under the guidance of life philosophy, students engage in profound self-exploration through activities like mandala painting and free writing, empowered by AI techniques to create impressive sketches based on text-based concepts with sustainable design principles. This study underscores the significant changes in learners' future learning imagination through ongoing spiritual inspiration and design technology intervention, ultimately promoting positive changes in learner mental imagery and aligning with the goal of fostering interdisciplinary talents in higher education. ⌋

Keywords: AI · spiritual science · sustainable design · learner imagery · interdisciplinary education

P. Zaphiris et al. (Eds.): HCII 2024, LNCS 15378, pp. 107–119, 2025.
https://doi.org/10.1007/978-3-031-76815-6_9

1 Introduction

1.1 Integration of Sustainable Design, AI Tools, and Spiritual Science in Multifaceted Educational Models

Achieving sustainable development is a pressing global concern. Education plays a pivotal role as the nexus where past knowledge intersects with contemporary perspectives, fostering a creative process that can imbue humanity with enduring spiritual vitality and catalyze collective consciousness transformation.

Design serves as a creative avenue to foster harmonious coexistence among humans, nature, and society. Design thinking is recognized within Taiwan's higher education community as a vital component of interdisciplinary education and essential for sustainable development. In "New Directions in Sustainable Design," diverse authors from various fields discuss humanity's challenges and reflections on our planet's future: "Will humanity mature to respect each other and the species older than us, as the Ojibwe people suggest? Or will we recklessly destroy what sustains us?" (Liu, Zhao, & Duan 2019).

Reflecting on Taiwan's higher education landscape, researchers ponder the dominance of instrumental rational thinking, which may lead young adults towards materialistic pursuits that could be overshadowed by AI advancements. Can sustainable education design offer a new direction amidst this dilemma? Are there synchronous principles of sustainable educational design across spirituality, mind, culture, and nature? "Quantum resonance" denotes a state of unified harmony across all levels of existence in nature. Embracing "quantum resonance" in our lives fosters harmony among body, mind, spirit, and the universe, embodying the goal of holistic education. Design thinking education, AI tools, and spiritual science enlightenment view chaos and unpredictability as essential elements of evolution, recognizing the intertwined complexity of the real world. To navigate this complexity, higher education imagery requires diversified educational model integration, reflection, and practice.

1.2 Observation: Transformation and Feedback of Learner Life Imagery

The cross-cultural poet Édouard Glissant (1928–2011) once discussed: "Imagination is a way for us to experience aesthetics. With this idea, it will lead us to think about this world and the universe, leading us back to the poetry of the infinite universe and world." Carl Gustav Jung (1875–1961), the German depth psychologist, proposed synchronicity, based on the simultaneous occurrence of two different psychic states, or phenomena of resonance between the self and the other. When symmetry breaks and recombines suddenly, new forms appear after mental resonance. From the perspective of spirituality and aesthetic imagination, the subjective moves involuntarily yet freely from the subject to the object.

The subjects of this study are forty university students from various disciplines who enrolled in the "Quantum Resonance Design" course as part of the general education curriculum at Chang Gung University in Taiwan, along with self-study students. Based on the research objectives, the study follows the action research trilogy. Firstly, "pre-action research" is conducted, where Carl Gustav Jung's individual mandala coloring activity is redesigned to cooperative mandala coloring and post-coloring free writing for artistic and spiritual transformation. Subsequently, "action research" is carried out, guiding these university students to utilize AI tools for altruistic social design and creation in the classroom, with teachers participating in participatory observation. Finally, "post-action research" involves teaching reflection and analysis through learning outcomes, end-of-term student feedback, and the goal of promoting learners' self-transformation and social welfare.

Our educational team focuses on the philosophy of the interconnectedness of all things. In addition to understanding and utilizing science, we reflect on how instrumental rationality binds our flow of consciousness and consider how to maintain our unique spiritual beauty and mindfulness dreams. We learn to engage in social improvement and the sustainable projects of the unified world, promoting the evolution of "body, mind, and spirit" while addressing global issues through quantum AI technology and innovative design. By facilitating dialogue between AI artificial intelligence and humans, we aim to break barriers and create a better future.

1.3 Exploration: Reflection on Action Research in Interdisciplinary Design Teaching

The sustainability of educational design advocated in this action research, along with the synchronicity principles of sustainability education design derived from the researcher's years of field practice, serve as the teaching beliefs. These principles aim to create profound learning experiences for learners, helping them to pay attention to the impacts of internal and external events without clinging to observed singular phenomena. Learners are encouraged to establish collective subconscious connections between their current sensory perceptions and their past, present, and future cognitive states. The ultimate goal of this research is to integrate design education, artificial intelligence, and spiritual science into an integrated Quantum Resonance Design course, transforming learners' self-organization into the driving force for social design. It also aims to embody the educational aesthetics of diverse subject-object dialogues through metadialectics, literature dialogues, and reflective practices, presenting research findings to provide feedback to all teachers and learners seeking educational innovation and scientific-spiritual resonance.

2   Literature Review

Sample Heading (Third Level). Only two levels of headings should be numbered. Lower-level headings remain unnumbered; they are formatted as run-in headings.

2.1 Principles of Sustainable Design, Eastern Philosophy, and Jungian Psychology in Teaching Individualization and Collective Subconscious

In the 18th century, German aesthetic educator Schiller posited that "beauty" not only results from achieving a perfect balance between reality and form but also serves the function of fostering harmony in human nature (Feng Zhi, Fan Dachan 1989). Consequently, Schiller laid the groundwork for aesthetic education as a means of enhancing social systems.

Originating from aesthetic endeavors, design science saw rapid development in Europe following the Industrial Revolution of the 18th century. Initially focused on creating tools for material existence, designers in the 19th century shifted their attention to studying the structures and behaviors of organisms, leading to abstraction and biomimetic design. Throughout the 20th century, designers began considering planning methods, governmental roles, efficiency, fairness, and sustainability. This shift led to non-material design innovations such as service design, experience design, and sustainable design. The contemporary aim of design has evolved towards facilitating human coexistence through sustainable practices, involving fields like science, philosophy, and ecology (Xu Chunmei 2017).

The International Union for Conservation of Nature (IUCN) published the first international declaration on human sustainable development in 1987, emphasizing the importance of meeting present needs without compromising future generations' ability to meet their own. Design thinking, rooted in a desire to improve the world, has progressed from being designer-centric to user-centric, ultimately aiming for Earth-centered "design for good."

The integration of design thinking into education has gained international prominence, with institutions like Stanford University and National Taiwan University establishing design schools. This approach breaks traditional frameworks to embrace innovation.

Jung's concept of synchronicity, seen as "timely creative action," aligns with the imagery of design education, suggesting that universities should be viewed as ecosystems conducive to exploration. This exploration requires a philosophical examination of theories related to sustainable development, including complex adaptive systems and spiritual changes. Implementing spiritual science in practice marks the inception of visualizing design education philosophy and learners' mental aesthetics.

2.2 Complexity Adaptation Systems for Sustainability

Sustainability development is both scientific and philosophical, emphasizing the necessity of uncertainty. It resists fixed frameworks and embraces uncertainty as a sign of ecological health (Liu, Zhao, & Duan 2019). Sustainable development and complex thinking share the goal of resisting traditional structures.

The concept of Sustainable Design, proposed in 1980, incorporates uncertainty and presents strategies for sustainable solutions. This study advocates replacing uncertainty with sustainability in educational aesthetics research and embracing uncertainty in sustainable educational design (Lin 2017b). Transitioning from uncertainty to sustainability promotes diversity, synchronicity, and departure from rigid boundaries in complex world design thinking.

Sustainable design encompasses natural, social, economic, and technological attributes. It seeks to optimize ecosystems, improve human quality of life, maximize economic benefits while preserving natural resources, and promote cleaner and more efficient technologies to minimize waste and pollution. Whether it's green design, ecological design, circular design, or educational design, they all contribute to rational design without deviating from the essence of self-organized action in complex science and rational exploration in educational philosophy.

2.3 Synchronistic Meaning Connections of Sustainability

Unprecedented transformations in organisms and educational environments have plunged us into chaos. Sustainability, intricately linked with human cultivation education and well-being, defies quantification but encompasses life, nature, culture, justice, and aesthetics. Emphasizing decentralization, sustainability extends beyond human-centric perspectives to embrace ecology, the universe, and sustainable educational development. It embodies a spiritual movement towards "common progress" and "co-evolution" (Wang, 2004; Ji & Lei 2000; Song 2005; Yeh 2017; Qiu 2003; Liu, Zhao, & Duan 2019).

Carl Jung, the German psychoanalyst, was inspired by Albert Einstein's theories of relativity and space-time, leading him to develop the concept of synchronicity over thirty years later. Synchronicity, introduced by Jung in 1930, represents meaningful coincidences and non-causal correlations, bridging the gap between the mental and material worlds. It symbolizes resonance between self and others, sudden reorganization after symmetry fracture, and emergence of new forms, facilitating the journey toward individuation and collective unconsciousness.

The theories of complexity and sustainable design, emerging after Jung's time, converge with Jung's synchronicity theory. Sustainability, as a cultural symbol and spiritual movement, embodies self-grounding, evolution, and parallel evolution. It represents external self-sustainability of organisms, evolutionary adaptation, and relative independence, integrity, and diversity in shared environments (Liu, Zhao, & Duan 2019). The connection between sustainability and synchronicity signifies collective evolution and creative progress, akin to acts of creation.

2.4 Social Engagement Improvement for Sustainability

Design thinking is inherently integrative. Asking the right questions often determines a more meaningful starting point for new educational goals or designs. Researchers combine interdisciplinary principles of sustainable development, complex thinking, educational aesthetics, design thinking, and practical experience from various fields step by step, attempting to establish the principles of synchronous sustainability in educational design. They do this by developing problem awareness rather than directive language:

- Introducing dialogue with values, beliefs, philosophical systems, reflection, and contemporary perceptions?
- Initiating the examination of self-worth, future imagination, and the ability to design for self and others?
- Practicing wandering and multiple movements in the world we inhabit?
- Reimagining our position in this world through imagination, creativity, design, and spiritual embodiment?
- Do these processes meet the growth needs of stakeholders (teachers, learners, Mother Earth)?

3   Research Methodology

3.1   Teaching Action Research Design

Philosophy of the Quantum Coherence Design:

1. Strengthening undergraduate students' prerequisite knowledge of quantum technology through interdisciplinary general education.
2. Explaining the superposition property of quantum states through wave functions and wave superposition, elucidating conceptual knowledge such as tunneling effects, energy level quantization, and learning quantum resonance science.
3. Introducing classic works of human history on health preservation and life wisdom as alternative manuals for Integrative Body-Mind-Spirit quantum resonance design, learning to return to the harmonization, balance, and integration of inner and outer aspects in the "here, now, present."
4. Reviving Eastern philosophy of life as a source of wisdom for quantum resonance design.
5. Manifesting the educational goal of holistic well-being through interdisciplinary collaboration and mutual nurturing (Fig. 1).

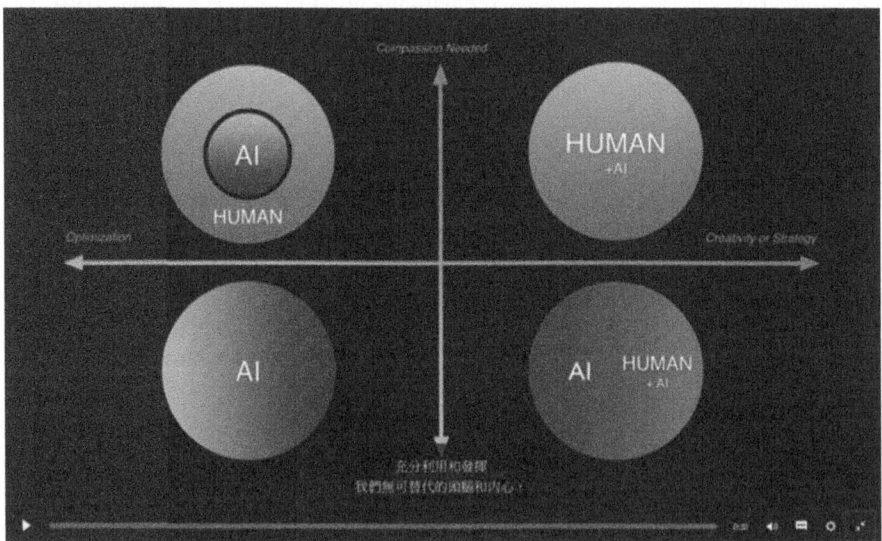

Fig. 1. Philosophy of the Quantum Coherence DesignA (by CGU Ergonomics Design Lab/C-WK, 2023)

The instructional action and research design of the Quantum Coherence Design course in this study are aimed at cultivating a new generation of Earth designers to become "helpers," learning to transform into a positive mindset of body, mind, and spirit. They engage in open-minded imagining of the future society, embrace a passion for narrating life stories, and engage in sincere communication and collaboration with diverse members. In the universe's resonance energy field where belief creates reality, they cultivate humility, grounding, and the development of "Bright" creation views of Oneness, "Moment" experiences of Flow, and the habit of "Event" mindfulness (Fig. 2).

Fig. 2. Philosophy of the Quantum Coherence Design B (by CGU Ergonomics Design Lab/March Lin 2023)

3.2 Participants/Data Collection Procedure/Analysis Method

There was a total of 35 learners from two schools involved in the study, including self-directed learners from the Wilderness Arts University and university students taking the Quantum Coherence Design course as a cross-disciplinary elective at Chang Gung University in Taiwan. Finally, three works from the participants were selected for analysis, providing an interpretation of the learners' psychological image transformation and creative performance using meta-cognitive analysis to ensure both subjective and objective compatibility. Based on the research objectives, a three-step action research approach was adopted. Firstly, "pre-action research" was initiated, where Carl Gustav Jung's individual mandala coloring activity was redesigned to incorporate cooperative mandala coloring and post-coloring free writing for artistic and spiritual transformation. Secondly, "action research" involved guiding these university students to use AI tools for altruistic social design and creation in class, with participatory observation by the teacher. Finally, "post-action research" involved reflective teaching and analysis based on learning outcomes, students' free writing feedback, and whether the intervention could promote self-transformation and the goal of social welfare for the learners.

4   Research Findings

4.1   Analysis of Students' Individual Mandala Coloring Creations

This study adopts the research method proposed by the post-structuralist scholar Rebecca. However, due to constraints on the time of research subjects and the limited energy of the researcher, the narrative length of the subjects was redesigned. Only three of the subject's autobiographical narratives, titled "Me in Reality, Me in Ideal, and Me in synchronicity." along with mandala drawings, were used to invite the participant PH into the research design. The autobiographical narratives produced by PH were deeply sincere and moving, profoundly touching the soul of the researcher. Through expressive artistic creations to illuminate the autobiographical narratives of the learners, this study conducted meta-analysis and interpretation.

Personalization Journey: The Collective Conscious Gift Embedded in PH's. Life. PH is a precocious and thoughtful current college student. He has experienced more growth pains and received more responsibility than his peers. He has also encountered the realities of society and shouldered the burdens of his life earlier than others. With a thinking capacity several times that of his peers, PH's journey of self-awareness and coordination between the inner and outer worlds can be likened to three forests. His personal consciousness stems from traversing the Red River Valley of his primal family, but he seems to have developed an early awareness and can calmly handle crises. In the black forest of his personal unconsciousness, as revealed in his mandala drawings, he longs for truth and awaits the right moment for self-expression. The idealized PH is surrounded by a glow, like a newly built warm nest, ready to spread his wings beyond the forest, awaiting his time to shine. In his simultaneous writing, PH can sense the development of a warm collective unconsciousness with his like-minded group, where everyone loves, listens to, and supports each other like siblings. This is a budding forest of yellow-green, where he no longer needs to hide behind a facade of calmness. PH begins to place life's solidified problems at the periphery, easing the restlessness of losing his true self with confidence. The collective unconsciousness of his companions serves as an external force of co-creative value, quietly opening the door of his heart that once punched into emptiness (Fig. 3).

PH Free Writing: Me in Reality constantly dialectics between sensibility and rationality, amidst self-collision and constant progress. This dynamic reality brings feelings that are sometimes ever-changing and sometimes collapsing at any moment. Doing aerobic exercise in the city, carrying the pulse of the other with every breath, maintaining regularity and self-demand. The apparent imminent collapse seems not at the end, but at the beginning, and in every inhalation and exhalation, where fragmentation and life coexist, although illusory, it also has reality.

PH Free Writing: Me in the Ideal World is static and suffocating, where talent abounds, composed of endless desires. Typically, such restless thoughts are quickly suppressed by the exhaustion from external accusations about the ideal world and the equally passionate tenderness of others, then calm is restored until it falls into emptiness. What remains in the empty ideal world is a dim light, where there is light, there is hope, holding onto one's own phototropism, ideals continue to advance in a silent manner.

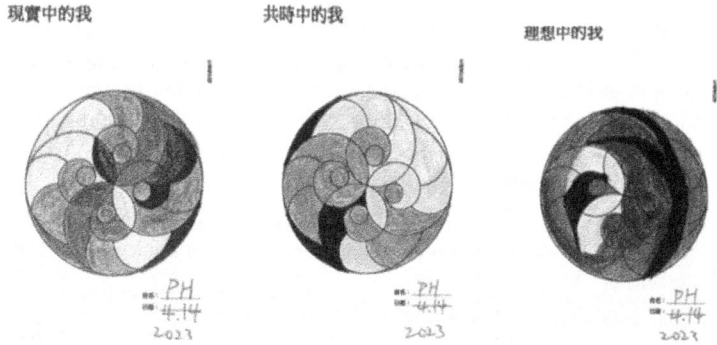

Fig. 3. PH's Individual Mandala Coloring "Me in Reality, Me in Ideal, and Me in synchronicity."

PH Free Writing: Me in synchronicity is like the warm circulation of the heart and lungs, gradually losing attachment to time. In the space of neither fast nor slow, neither moving nor stopping, there is a comforting envelopment, like the misplaced touch of humanity's resonance. Separating the individual from others, separating the person from the individual, led by resonance to return, the happiness of return pours out and generously lingers to eternity. In the state of simultaneity, all shortcomings will be sublimated, and I can strongly feel that all desires converge into pleasantness.

4.2 Advanced Performance Assisted by AI Tools in Conveying Learners' Engagement in Social Welfare

This course focuses on the philosophy of interconnectedness of all things, advocating not only for understanding and utilizing science but also reflecting on how instrumental rationality binds our flow of consciousness. It encourages contemplation on maintaining one's own unique spiritual essence and mindful aspirations, learning to engage in societal improvement and the sustainable development of the interconnected world. Through quantum AI technology and innovative design, it emphasizes evolving the "body, mind, and spirit" while addressing global issues, facilitating dialogue between AI artificial intelligence and humans, and breaking limitations to pave the way for the future.

Learners' Journals and Feedback from the Quantum Resonance Design Workshop

1. **Session One:** Lifelong Learning Motivations
   In the initial session, Teacher March prompted us to reflect on our motivations for learning at different stages of life. Initially, I listed common goals like academic success and career stability. However, this exercise led to introspection, revealing the complexity of identifying our true aspirations and fostering self-awareness.
2. **Session Two:** Mandala Drawing for Mindfulness
   This class introduced mandala drawing as a method to promote mindfulness and mental calmness. Through painting, I experienced a sense of tranquility and focus, clearing my mind of distractions. This practice highlighted the joy of concentration and inner peace.

3. **Session Three:** Chang Gung Wellness Culture Village
   The Chang Gung Wellness Culture Village offers seniors a vibrant environment for holistic well-being, combining medical resources with cultural activities. It promotes lifelong learning and ensures seniors lead enriched lives filled with color and engagement.
4. **Session Four:** Smart Sun Protection Hat
   To address dementia and promote cognitive health in seniors, the Smart Sun Protection Hat provides outdoor exercise opportunities with built-in AI tracking for safety during physical activities.
5. **Session Five:** Four Seasons Spring Observation Deck
   Designed for people of all ages, the observation deck provides a safe and accessible space for recreation and nature appreciation, fostering inclusivity and engagement across generations.
6. **Session Six:** Ocean Heritage Conservation Declaration
   Amid ongoing threats to ocean health, initiatives like marine conservation areas and reducing plastic usage are crucial. Embedding environmental awareness in education promotes a deeper understanding of conservation efforts and individual responsibility.
7. **Session Seven:** Hero's Journey AI Board Game

Fig. 4. Learners' AI Works of Quantum Resonance Design Workshop

In this session, we designed a board game focused on marine conservation, aiming to educate and inspire players about the importance of protecting ocean ecosystems through engaging gameplay and missions promoting environmental stewardship (Fig. 4).

5 Conclusion

5.1 Spiritual Imagery of Mandalas and Positive Self-awareness

As the personal psyche's complexes are based on the archetypes of the collective psyche, a deeper understanding of any complex reveals associations with its archetype. Jungian analysis of art largely relies on expanding the meaning of images, allowing the self to feel its connection to the world of archetypes in a therapeutic manner, without being overwhelmed by a sea of scattered archetypes. Jung stated that when archetypes are invoked, it leads to "insight," surpassing temporal and material awareness. This chapter will present the transformational process of adolescents through self-analysis in free writing after cooperative mandala coloring activities. Through their own reflection and introspection, they no longer rely solely on the traditional role of the teacher, but achieve the following possibilities of self-nurturing. From the mandala artwork of the learners in this study, we can observe the journey of the self from recognizing the collective unconscious within the chaotic complex system to embarking on the path of self-transformation. The repetitive nature of their creations generates a sense of order, allowing individuals to experience a sense of wholeness and soothing of the psyche, leading to profound self-awareness through the symmetrical quantum resonance of harmony.

5.2 The Positive Significance of AI Tools as Interdisciplinary Design Thinking and Innovative Teaching

Ecological system scholars like Fritjof Capra combined quantum mechanics with New Age thought to create quantum mysticism. Ecological cycles require smooth flow of information and feedback, and the spiral journey plays a necessary role in the struggle between individuals and imbalances, shattering our old assumptions and constructing new meanings. Its interpretation of social ecological organization and action can be stated as follows: "The participants in this group, their collective evolution or growth, are driven by the construction of common meanings and knowledge, and involve continuous creation and adaptation."

This study draws upon perspectives from the scientific community on quantum resonance, sustainability design from the design field, as well as views from AI artificial intelligence and educational aesthetics. Starting from the goal of promoting social common good through design education, it traverses the sources of spiritual science and classical wisdom, returning to the ethical framework of sustainable common good in social design. The imagery of holistic education for sustainability relies heavily on the stage of higher education before university students enter the real world. While higher education practitioners are striving to promote interdisciplinary learners and their design thinking outcomes as an "art of possibilities," they should first guide learners in self-awareness and transformation. Through the transformative power of personal growth, learners can engage in social improvement. The use of AI artificial intelligence tools will not be reduced to a tool of science or a means of personal competition, but rather will complement the values of human goodness, resulting in the best outcome for innovative design education.

References

1. Cambray, J.: Synchronicity: Nature and Psyche in an Interconnected Universe, vol. 15. Texas A&M University Press (2009)
2. Davis, B.: Jung, Aquinas, and the Aurora Consurgens: Establishing a Relationship with God (2010)
3. Haaning, A.: Jung's quest for the Aurora consurgens. J. Anal. Psychol. **59**(1), 8–30 (2014)
4. Martusewicz, R.A.: Seeking Passage: Post-Structuralism, Pedagogy, Ethics: Teachers College Press (2001)
5. Wang, H.: Green education: the direction of university education development in the 21st century. J. Petrol. Univ. Soc. Sci. Ed. **20**(3), 98–101 (2004)
6. Ju, K.: Jung's Map of the Soul (Original work by Murray Stein). New Taipei City: Lixi Culture. (Original work published in 1998) (1999)
7. Ji, G., Lei, J.: On the Humanistic Implication of Sustainable Development. Journal of Petroleum University (Social Sciences Edition), 1 (2000)
8. Song, H.: On the integration of science and humanities and the strategy of sustainable development. J. Petrol. Univ. Soc. Sci. Ed. **21**(5), 31–34 (2005)
9. Lin, Z.: The Red Book—Jung Manuscript (Revised) (Original work by Jung). Beijing, China: Central Compilation and Translation Press. (Original work published in 2009) (2012)
10. Lin, M.: Ubiquitous educational wilderness. alternative. Education **4**, 165–170 (2016)
11. Lin, M.: A New Perspective on the Three Natures of Educational Aesthetics: Neurological, Artistic, and Spiritual (Doctoral dissertation, National Chengchi University, Taiwan) (2017a)
12. Lin, M.: Spiritual Transformation—How Francis Bacon Articulates Education into Art. In: Li, G. (ed.) Aesthetic Education: The Art and Teaching from a Spiritual Perspective, pp. 293–310. Wunan Publishing, Taipei City (2017)
13. Jin, H., Yang, Y.: The Faith of Seeds (Original work by Henry D. Thoreau). Taipei City: Da Shu Culture. (Original work published in 1993) (1995)
14. Shi, Z.: Introduction to Complex Thought (Original work by Edgar Morin). Taipei City: Times Culture. (Original work published in 1990) (2000)
15. Hung, C.: Edgar Morin's Theory of Complex Thought and Its Educational Implications. Hong, C (2016)
16. Fan, R.: Wilderness Art University: The Future of Nomadic Learning (Master's thesis, National Central University, Taiwan) (2023)
17. Tang, J.: The Garden of the Gods (Original work by Gerald Durrell). Taipei City: Da Shu Culture. (Original work published in 1978) (1995)
18. Xu, C.: Sustainability and design ethics—essential issues that contemporary designers need to understand and take seriously. Contemp. Artists **3**, 8–11 (2017)
19. Zhang, X.: Life, Education, Learning (Original work by Jiddu Krishnamurti). Taipei City: Fangzhi. (Original work published in 1981) (1995)
20. Zhang, J.: Transforming Sustainable Design: How Designers and Designs Drive the Sustainability Process (Original work by Anne Chick & Paul Micklethwaite). China: Hunan University Press. (Original work published in 2011) (2012)
21. Chen, Y.: Introduction to Complexity Theory and Educational Issues (Original work by Morin, E.). Beijing, China: Peking University. (Original work published in 2000) (2004)

22. Chen, J.: Francis Bacon: The Logic of Sensation (Original work by Deleuze). Taipei City: National Translation Institute. (Original work published in 1981) (2003)
23. Feng, Z., Fan, D.: Aesthetic Education Letters (Original work by Friedrich Schiller). Taipei City: Shuxin Publishing. (Original work published in 1794) (1989)
24. Lin, Z.: Born with Wings—Rumi's Poems of Longing and Ecstasy (Original work by Rumi). New Taipei City: Freedom Hill (2018)
25. Wei, H., et al.: Synchronicity: The Universe of Nature and Psyche (Original work by Joseph Cambray). Taipei City: Mind Workshop. (Original work published in 2009) (2012)
26. Gong, Y.: Jung and the New Era (Original work by David Tacey). Beijing, China: World Book. (Original work published in 2001) (2015)

Optimizing Self-paced Learning in Machine Learning Education for Working Professionals: Strategies, Trends, and Insights

Peiyan Liu[✉][iD]

The George Washington University, Washington, DC 20052, USA
peiyan.liu@gwu.edu

Abstract. As the demand for flexible Machine Learning (ML) education grows among working professionals, optimizing self-paced learning models becomes crucial. This study investigates effective strategies for self-paced ML education by conducting a systematic review of academic literature, analyzing existing course websites, and integrating insights from in-depth interviews with 21 professionals. Key findings reveal that a modular course structure, hands-on projects with real-world datasets, comprehensive learning resources, and ongoing support significantly enhance learning outcomes. By addressing these elements, this research provides actionable recommendations for developing effective self-paced ML courses, ultimately supporting the continuous professional development and career advancement of learners in the field of ML.

Keywords: Machine Learning education · Self-paced learning · Working professionals · Project-based learning · Flexible education · Professional development

1 Introduction

As the field of Machine Learning (ML) continues to advance, the demand for flexible educational opportunities is growing, particularly among working professionals. These individuals often face unique challenges, such as balancing work responsibilities, personal commitments, and the need to stay current with rapidly evolving technologies. Traditional classroom settings and rigid schedules are frequently impractical, leading to an increased interest in self-paced learning models.

Self-paced learning offers several advantages, including flexibility in scheduling, the ability to learn at an individual pace, and the opportunity to revisit complex topics as needed. However, the variability in outcomes due to diverse educational approaches presents a significant challenge. This study aims to explore the nuances of self-paced ML learning, addressing this variability and identifying effective strategies to optimize learning outcomes for professionals.

P. Zaphiris et al. (Eds.): HCII 2024, LNCS 15378, pp. 120–136, 2025.
https://doi.org/10.1007/978-3-031-76815-6_10

By reviewing best practices([6,20,27,31]), analyzing current trends, and presenting a comprehensive case study, this research seeks to enhance the efficacy of self-paced ML education for professionals. I examine various educational tools and methodologies, assessing their impact on learning efficiency and knowledge retention. my study includes insights from interviews with working professionals who have undertaken self-paced ML courses, providing a practical perspective on the challenges and benefits of this learning model.

1.1   Research Questions

This research focuses on three main questions:

- **What effective strategies and tools support self-paced machine learning for professionals?** This question aims to identify the specific techniques and resources that facilitate successful self-paced learning.
- **What trends characterize self-paced learning plans and dataset use in professional machine learning education?** Understanding these trends helps in designing more effective and relevant learning programs.
- **What key lessons emerge from mentoring a professional in self-paced machine learning?** Insights from mentoring experiences can offer valuable guidance for educators and mentors in this field.

My study contributes to the growing body of knowledge on ML education by offering a detailed examination of self-paced learning tailored to the needs of working professionals. The findings aim to provide actionable recommendations for educators, researchers, students, and professionals, ultimately supporting the ongoing development and optimization of ML educational programs.

2   Related Works

2.1   Overview

In the context of the growing demand for Machine Learning (ML) education, this section reviews literature on the integration of ML into professional development, with a particular emphasis on self-paced learning for working professionals [2,7, 9,15,19,28,29]. The increasing need for flexible learning environments that cater to the busy schedules of professionals has been well-documented. Abood et al. (2019) discuss the integration of ML into professional development programs, highlighting the critical role of flexibility and practical application in fostering effective learning [1].

The importance of practical experiences and the use of real-world datasets in improving learning outcomes is emphasized in several [5,34]. Beckman (1997) and Shaw (2005) underline how practical, hands-on experience with real-world data significantly enhances the understanding and application of ML concepts [5,34]. However, there is notable variability in the effectiveness of self-paced learning environments, often influenced by course design, instructional quality, and learner motivation. Winzker et al. (2012) and Daun et al. (2014, 2016) explore these challenges, noting that the design of the learning environment and the intrinsic motivation of learners play crucial roles in determining success [12, 13, 38].

To address these challenges, my study aims to refine self-paced ML education by identifying best practices and insights from a comprehensive professional case study. This includes detailed analyses of interviews conducted with working professionals who have participated in self-paced ML courses. These interviews provide practical insights into the benefits and challenges faced by learners, offering a nuanced understanding of how self-paced learning can be optimized for professional development.

2.2   Project Based

In rapidly evolving fields like deep learning, a subset of Machine Learning, project-based learning has emerged as a particularly effective educational approach. Project-based learning emphasizes the application of theoretical knowledge to real-world problems, fostering deeper understanding and engagement. Huang (2019) and Miller (2019) discuss the integration of hands-on projects into ML courses, highlighting the importance of real-world relevance and practical application in enhancing learning outcomes [8, 17, 30, 39].

Brungel (2020) and Wong (2020) further illustrate the benefits of project-based learning, noting that it helps learners develop critical thinking and problem-solving skills by working on practical projects. This approach not only enhances technical skills but also prepares learners for real-world challenges they are likely to encounter in their professional careers.

This study builds on these findings by incorporating insights from professionals who have benefited from project-based approaches in their self-paced ML learning journeys. These insights are derived from interviews that explore how project-based learning components were integrated into their self-paced courses and how these projects contributed to their overall learning experience and professional development.

2.3   Self Paced

Self-paced learning offers unparalleled flexibility for professionals in machine learning, allowing them to adapt their education to fit their schedules and personal learning paces. This flexibility is crucial for professionals who must balance their education with work and other commitments. Research by Beckman (1997) and Shaw (2005) underscores the importance of flexibility and practical application in self-paced learning environments.

However, the effectiveness of self-paced learning can vary widely. Studies by Winzker et al. (2012) and Daun et al. (2014, 2016) highlight this variability, attributing differences in learning outcomes to variations in course design, the quality of instructional materials, and learner motivation. Effective self-paced learning programs must therefore be carefully designed to maintain engagement and ensure the practical application of ML concepts.

This study aims to bridge these gaps by providing a comprehensive analysis of effective self-paced learning strategies. I draw on qualitative data from interviews with professionals who have successfully navigated self-paced ML courses, offering practical insights into what works and what doesn't in these learning environments. These interviews reveal best practices, common pitfalls, and key strategies for maintaining motivation and ensuring successful learning outcomes.

By detailing these best practices and integrating feedback from working professionals, this research offers actionable insights that can enhance the design and implementation of self-paced ML education programs. This approach ensures that the learning experience is not only flexible but also highly relevant and effective for professionals seeking to advance their ML skills. my findings contribute to the growing body of knowledge on ML education, providing valuable recommendations for educators, researchers, students, and professionals alike.

3   Methods

I conducted a comprehensive review of academic papers on ML-related courses, supplemented by an in-depth survey of relevant course websites. Additionally, I included a reflective analysis of personal self-paced learning experiences over the past three years as a case study. This methodology was structured to provide a robust foundation for understanding the current state of self-paced ML learning and to identify effective strategies tailored for working professionals.

Table 1. Progression of Paper Search Steps: S1 represents initial search results, S2 indicates potentially relevant findings, S3 highlights confirmed relevant results, and S4 enumerates those results after removing duplicates.

Paper Source (Steps)	S1	S2	S3	S4
Google Scholar	300	215	112	112
ACM DIgital Library	100	90	45	40
IEEE Xplore	60	53	37	35
ERIC	30	21	15	12
arXiv	10	6	5	5
subtotal	500	385	214	204

3.1   Keywords

Utilizing the Preferred Reporting Items for Systematic Reviews and Meta-Analyses (PRISMA) approach, I systematically identified pertinent papers over a two-month period, from January to March 2024. The databases explored

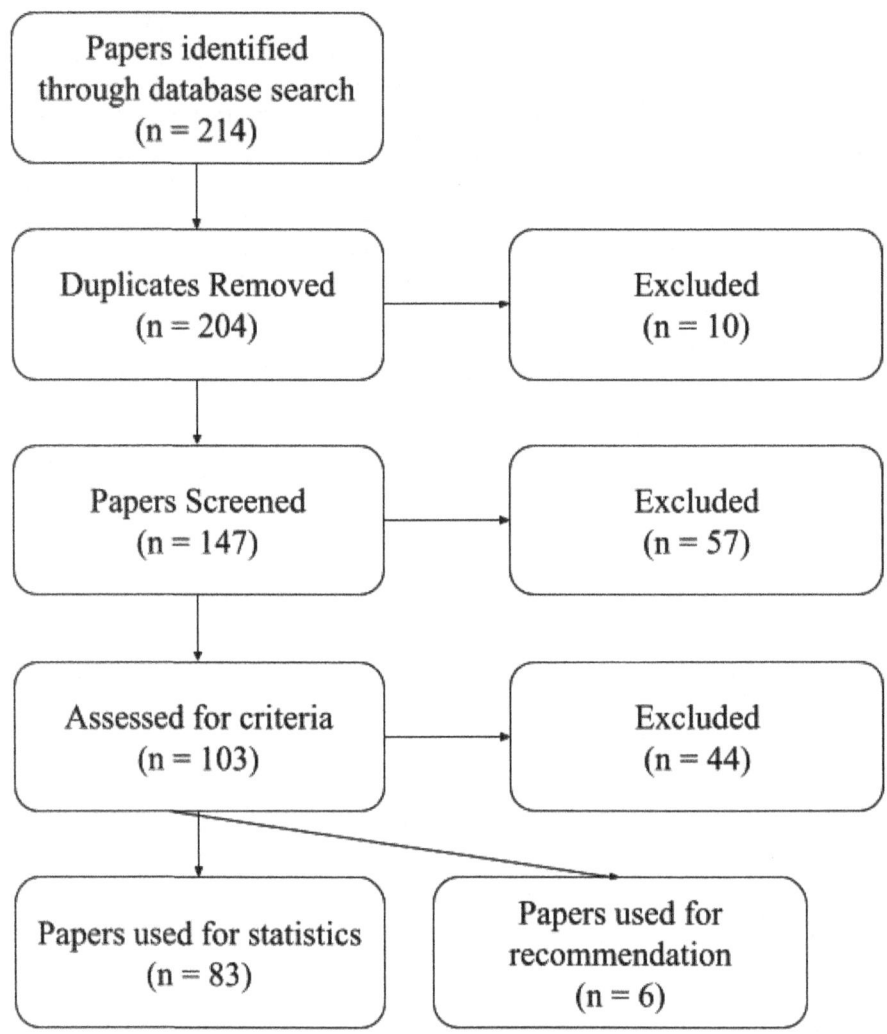

Fig. 1. Selection process for the papers

included Google Scholar, IEEE Xplore, ACM Digital Library, arXiv, and ERIC. My keyword search comprised: (*'Machine Learning' OR 'Deep Learning' OR 'ML' OR 'DL' AND 'project-based' OR 'project-based learning' OR 'PBL' AND 'self-paced' OR 'self-paced learning' AND 'Survey' OR 'Review' OR 'Case Study'*).

My strategy aimed to pinpoint papers aligning with my research questions. Table 1 and Fig. 1 visualize the search trajectory, showcasing the number of papers identified and excluded based on set criteria. To cater to the target audience's time constraints, I curated a concise list of papers encapsulating the prevailing trends in the domain.

3.2   Selection Criteria

To ensure the relevance and quality of my review's content, the following criteria were applied:

- **Project-based:** Papers and courses must emphasize project-based machine learning, detailing their design and execution. This focus ensures that the content is practically relevant and applicable to real-world ML problems.
- **Publication Time frame:** I included papers from 2017 onwards and courses updated after 2020. This time frame ensures that the review encompasses the most recent advancements and trends in ML education.
- **Machine Learning Focus:** Preference was given to content primarily addressing project-based Machine Learning or Deep Learning. This focus aligns with my goal of enhancing practical ML education for professionals.
- **Target Audience:** This work targets non-CS major working professionals seeking to learn machine learning amidst full-time work. It aims to tailor ML education to their unique needs by providing accessible, practical content that accommodates diverse backgrounds and busy schedules, ensuring meaningful learning experiences without requiring a computer science foundation.

3.3   Interview

In addition to the systematic review, I conducted in-depth interviews with 21 professionals from various non-CS backgrounds who have engaged in self-paced machine learning education over the past year. The purpose of these interviews was to uncover insights into their learning strategies, challenges encountered, and the effectiveness of the resources they utilized, providing a nuanced understanding of self-paced ML learning among working professionals.

- **Interview Process:** I conducted semi-structured interviews with 21 professionals from various industries, including technology, finance, healthcare, and education. Each interview lasted approximately 60 min and was conducted via video conferencing. The interviews were recorded and transcribed to ensure accuracy in capturing the participants' experiences and perspectives. Additionally, we applied best practices from Institutional Review Board (IRB) requirements to ensure ethical standards were maintained throughout the interview process.
- **Interview Questions:** The questions focused on several key areas: motivations for choosing self-paced learning, the effectiveness of various learning materials and methods, challenges faced during the course, and the impact of the learning on their professional skills and career progression.
- **Data Analysis:** The interview transcripts were analyzed using thematic analysis to identify common themes and insights. This method allowed us to systematically categorize and interpret the qualitative data, revealing patterns and key findings relevant to self-paced ML learning. These insights were then integrated with the findings from the systematic review and reflective case study to provide a comprehensive understanding of the topic.

3.4   Case Study

I also included a reflective analysis of my personal learning experiences over the past three years, presented as a case study. This case study offers a practical perspective on participating in self-paced ML courses and highlights the lessons learned from balancing these courses with professional responsibilities.

- **Case Study Description:** The case study focuses on a series of self-paced ML courses that I undertook over the past three years. These courses were designed to meet the needs of non-CS major working professionals, emphasizing flexibility, practical relevance, and accessibility. The case study provides detailed descriptions of the course structures, learning strategies employed, and personal feedback, offering a comprehensive view of the learning experience.
- **Lessons Learned:** The case study identifies key lessons and best practices for self-paced ML education from a learner's perspective. These include the importance of flexibility in course scheduling and pacing, the use of real-world datasets to enhance practical learning, and the value of ongoing support and mentorship. The case study also highlights the challenges faced in self-paced learning environments and the strategies used to overcome these challenges, providing valuable insights for other learners and educators.

By combining systematic review, qualitative interviews, and a reflective case study, my methodology provides a comprehensive and multi-faceted understanding of self-paced ML learning for working professionals. This approach ensures that my findings are grounded in both theoretical and practical insights, offering valuable recommendations for educators, researchers, and learners in the field.

4   Results

4.1   Literature Review

Table 2 displays the summarized findings from my literature review. This review focused on identifying best practices in Machine Learning (ML) education, particularly for self-paced learning models aimed at working professionals. I categorized the findings into several key topics, highlighting common best practices across various studies.

1. Machine Learning:

- **Comprehensive Curriculum:** Effective ML courses typically offer a well-rounded curriculum that covers fundamental concepts, advanced techniques, and practical applications. This ensures that learners acquire a broad understanding of ML and can apply their knowledge to real-world problems.
- **Hands-On Projects:** Incorporating hands-on projects is crucial in ML education. Studies indicate that projects involving real-world datasets and practical problems significantly enhance learning outcomes by providing learners with practical experience and reinforcing theoretical knowledge.

Table 2. Paper Results Key: U denotes undergrad-only studies, G for graduate-only, and UG for both levels. R signifies review papers, C indicates case studies, and Best P stands for best practices. Detailed explanations of topics and best practices are provided in the results section.

Paper	Level	Type	Topic(s)	Best P
[1,2,4,7,15,19,20]	U	R	ABC	1,2,3
[5,9,12,14,17,25]	U	C	BC	2,3,4
[3, 6, 11, 18, 21]	UG	R	ABD	3,5
[22, 23,26, 28,31]	UG	C	BC	2,6
[16, 24, 29, 33]	G	R	BCD	1,2,3,5
[8, 10, 13, 16, 34]	G	C	BCDE	1, 3, 4

2. Project-Based Teaching and Learning:

- **Engagement and Motivation:** Project-based learning (PBL) has been shown to increase student engagement and motivation. By working on relevant and challenging projects, learners are more likely to stay motivated and invested in their studies.
- **Collaborative Learning:** Many successful PBL courses encourage collaboration among students. Group projects and peer feedback are effective in promoting deeper understanding and developing teamwork skills.

3. Self-Paced Learning:

- **Flexibility:** One of the primary advantages of self-paced learning is its flexibility. Best practices in this area include offering modular course structures that allow learners to progress at their own pace and revisit challenging topics as needed.
- **Support and Resources:** Providing ample support and resources is critical for self-paced learners. This includes access to online forums, instructional videos, and supplemental materials that help learners overcome obstacles independently.

4. Students' Feedback:

- **Positive Impact of Flexibility:** Students frequently highlight the benefits of the flexible schedule offered by self-paced courses. This flexibility allows them to balance their studies with professional and personal commitments effectively.
- **Need for Interactive Elements:** Feedback often suggests that incorporating interactive elements, such as quizzes and real-time feedback, can enhance the learning experience in self-paced courses.

5. Professors' Feedback:

– **Importance of Course Design:** Professors emphasize the significance of well-structured course design in self-paced learning environments. Clear learning objectives, organized content, and regular assessments are essential for maintaining student engagement and ensuring successful learning outcomes.
– **Challenges in Providing Support:** While self-paced courses offer flexibility, professors note the challenges in providing timely support and feedback to students. Implementing automated systems and leveraging technology can help address these challenges.

4.2   Course Websites Analysis

Table 3 showcases the findings from my analysis of existing course websites. This analysis aimed to identify common elements and best practices in self-paced Machine Learning (ML) courses offered online. I explored several key topics to understand how these courses are structured and what resources they provide to learners.

Table 3. Analysis of Course Websites: U represents undergrad-only courses, G for graduate-only, and UG for both. Key features include E) HCI datasets utilization, F) availability of sample code, G) presentation slides, and H) instructional videos. Best P signifies courses emphasizing best practices.

Course	Level	Institution	Best P
[41, 42]	U	Williams	6, 7,8
[43]	U	Amherst	8
[44,45]	U	Swarthmore	7,9
[46, 47,48]	U	Pomona	7,8,9
[49, 50]	UG	Harvard	6,7,8,9
[50, 51]	UG	Upenn	7,9, 10
[52, 53, 54]	UG	Stanford	6,7,8,9,10
[55, 56]	UG	MIT	8,9,10
[57,58,59]	UG	CMU	6, 8, 9
[60,61,62]	UG	UC B	6, 7,8,9,10

6. Self-paced Learning:

Modular Structure: Many of the analyzed courses feature a modular structure, allowing learners to progress through the material at their own pace. This flexibility is crucial for working professionals who need to balance their studies with other commitments.

Progress Tracking: Effective self-paced courses often include tools for tracking progress, such as dashboards that display completed modules and upcoming tasks. This helps learners stay organized and motivated.

7. Project-Based Teaching and Learning:

Hands-On Projects: A significant number of courses incorporate project-based learning, where students work on real-world projects to apply the concepts they have learned. These projects often involve datasets from industry or research, providing practical experience.

Peer Collaboration: Some courses facilitate peer collaboration through discussion forums or group projects, allowing learners to share insights and provide mutual support.

8. Sample Code:

Code Repositories: Many courses provide access to code repositories, such as GitHub, where learners can find sample code and scripts used in the course. This is particularly useful for understanding practical implementation details.

Code Walkthroughs: Courses that include detailed code walkthroughs, either in written form or through video demonstrations, help learners understand the step-by-step process of developing ML models.

9. Slides:

Comprehensive Lecture Slides: High-quality courses offer comprehensive lecture slides that summarize key concepts and provide visual aids to enhance understanding. These slides are often available for download, allowing learners to review them at their own pace.

Supplemental Materials: In addition to slides, some courses provide supplemental materials such as cheat sheets, reference guides, and additional readings to deepen learners' understanding.

10. Course Videos:

Engaging Video Lectures: Video lectures are a staple of online ML courses. The best courses feature engaging, well-produced videos that clearly explain complex concepts. These videos often include demonstrations, animations, and real-world examples to illustrate key points.

Interactive Elements: Some courses incorporate interactive elements within videos, such as embedded quizzes or coding challenges, to reinforce learning and keep learners engaged.

4.3   Interview

Interviews with Professionals

The interviews conducted with 21 professionals from various non-CS backgrounds provided rich insights into their experiences with self-paced machine learning education. Key themes and findings from these interviews are summarized below:

Motivations for Choosing Self-paced Learning:

Flexibility: The primary motivation for choosing self-paced learning was the flexibility it offers, allowing professionals to balance their studies with work and personal commitments. Self-Directed Learning: Many participants valued the ability to control their learning pace and revisit challenging topics as needed, enhancing their understanding and retention of ML concepts.

Effectiveness of Learning Materials and Methods:

Practical Projects: Hands-on projects were frequently highlighted as one of the most effective learning methods. Participants reported that working on real-world datasets and problems significantly improved their practical skills and confidence in applying ML techniques. Comprehensive Resources: Access to a variety of learning resources, including video lectures, sample code, and comprehensive slides, was deemed essential for effective learning. Participants appreciated courses that provided detailed explanations and supplemental materials.

Challenges Encountered:

Time Management: Balancing study time with professional responsibilities was a common challenge. Participants suggested that clear guidance on time management and setting realistic study goals could help mitigate this issue. Need for Support: While self-paced learning offers independence, many participants noted the need for timely support and feedback. Interactive elements, such as quizzes and forums, were found helpful but not always sufficient.

Impact on Professional Skills and Career Progression:

Skill Enhancement: Participants reported significant improvements in their technical skills and ability to apply ML in their professional roles. This has led to increased confidence and recognition in their respective fields. Career Opportunities: Several participants indicated that their newly acquired ML skills opened up new career opportunities and advancements, underscoring the value of self-paced ML education for professional development.

4.4   Case Study

The reflective case study of my personal learning experiences over the past three years provided practical insights into the implementation and outcomes of self-paced ML courses for working professionals. Key lessons and best practices identified from the case study include:

Course Design and Structure:

Modular Approach: Implementing a modular course structure was effective in providing flexibility and managing my learning progress. Each module focused on specific topics, allowing me to tackle one concept at a time. Clear Learning Objectives: Clearly defined learning objectives and outcomes for each module helped guide me and keep me focused on my goals.

Learning Strategies:

Real-World Relevance: Incorporating real-world datasets and practical projects into the curriculum was crucial for maintaining my engagement and ensuring the practical application of ML concepts. Interactive Elements: Integrating quizzes, coding challenges, and interactive video lectures enhanced my engagement and provided immediate feedback on my understanding.

Support and Mentorship:

Ongoing Support: Receiving ongoing support through online forums, regular check-ins, and mentorship was essential for addressing my questions and challenges. This support system helped maintain my motivation and fostered a sense of community among learners. Feedback Mechanisms: Automated systems for providing timely feedback on assignments and projects were effective in ensuring that I received the guidance I needed to improve.

Challenges and Solutions:

Balancing Flexibility and Structure: While flexibility is a key advantage of self-paced learning, maintaining a balance between flexibility and structured learning paths was challenging. Optional schedules and progress tracking tools helped me stay on track without feeling constrained. Engagement and Motivation: Keeping myself engaged and motivated over the course duration was a persistent challenge. Regular updates, interactive elements, and periodic assessments were employed to maintain my engagement and measure progress.

By reflecting on these experiences, I identified key factors that contributed to the success of self-paced ML courses and the strategies that helped overcome common challenges. These insights provide valuable guidance for other learners and educators aiming to optimize self-paced ML education for working professionals.

4.5   Overall Summary

The combined results from the interviews and case study highlight several critical factors for optimizing self-paced ML learning for working professionals:

Flexibility and Control: Self-paced learning's flexibility allows professionals to manage their learning alongside work and personal commitments. However, this must be balanced with structured guidance and clear objectives to ensure consistent progress. Practical Application: Incorporating real-world projects and practical exercises is essential for effective learning. These hands-on experiences enhance understanding and help learners apply theoretical knowledge in practical scenarios. Comprehensive Resources and Support: Providing a wide range of learning materials, interactive elements, and timely support is crucial for overcoming the challenges of self-paced learning. Continuous mentorship and feedback mechanisms are particularly valuable for maintaining motivation and addressing learner needs. Career Impact: Self-paced ML education can significantly enhance professional skills and open up new career opportunities, making it a valuable investment for working professionals. These insights provide a robust foundation for developing and refining self-paced ML courses, ensuring they meet the unique needs of working professionals and support their continuous learning and career development.

5   Discussion

The findings from my comprehensive literature review, analysis of course web-sites, interviews with professionals, and reflective case study provide a holistic view of the current state and best practices in self-paced Machine Learning (ML) education for working professionals. This discussion synthesizes these insights, highlighting key themes, challenges, and recommendations for optimizing self-paced ML learning.

Key Themes Flexibility and Adaptability: The primary advantage of self-paced learning is its inherent flexibility, which allows professionals to tailor their educational pursuits to fit their busy schedules. This flexibility is particularly valuable for working professionals who must juggle multiple responsibilities. The ability to control the pace of learning and revisit challenging concepts is a sig-nificant benefit, as highlighted by both the literature and interview participants.

Practical Application: A recurring theme across this study is the importance of practical, hands-on learning. Project-based learning, which involves working on real-world datasets and problems, emerged as a highly effective approach. Both the literature and interviews underscored that practical projects not only reinforce theoretical knowledge but also enhance learners' confidence and skills in applying ML techniques in real-world scenarios.

Comprehensive Resources and Support: Effective self-paced ML courses pro-vide a range of learning materials, including video lectures, sample code, com-prehensive slides, and interactive elements. The availability of diverse resources ensures that learners can choose the materials that best suit their learning styles. Additionally, ongoing support through forums, regular check-ins, and mentorship is crucial for addressing learners' questions and maintaining their motivation.

Challenges Balancing Flexibility and Structure: While flexibility is a key advantage of self-paced learning, maintaining a balance between flexibility and structured guidance is challenging. Learners benefit from having clear learning objectives and a modular course structure that allows them to progress system-atically. Tools for tracking progress and setting realistic study goals can help mitigate the risk of learners falling behind.

Time Management: One of the most common challenges faced by working professionals is time management. Balancing study time with professional and personal responsibilities can be difficult. Providing guidance on effective time management strategies and realistic pacing can help learners manage their work-loads better.

Need for Timely Support: Despite the independence offered by self-paced learning, many learners expressed the need for timely support and feedback. Interactive elements, such as quizzes and coding challenges, help maintain engagement, but the availability of mentors and responsive instructors is crucial for addressing more complex questions and providing personalized feedback.

Recommendations Designing Flexible Yet Structured Courses: Educators should design self-paced ML courses that offer flexibility while providing a structured learning path. Modular course designs with clear objectives and progress tracking tools can help learners stay on track. Additionally, incorporating optional schedules and regular assessments can provide the necessary structure without compromising flexibility.

Emphasizing Practical Projects: Incorporating hands-on projects that use real-world datasets should be a priority. These projects should be progressively challenging, starting with basic data analysis and culminating in the development of complex ML models. Providing detailed instructions and sample code can help learners navigate these projects successfully.

Providing Comprehensive Resources and Ongoing Support: Courses should offer a variety of learning materials to cater to different learning styles. This includes video lectures, sample code, comprehensive slides, and supplemental materials like cheat sheets and reference guides. Additionally, establishing a support system that includes online forums, regular check-ins, and mentorship can address learners' questions and challenges promptly.

Enhancing Interactivity and Engagement: Interactive elements, such as quizzes, coding challenges, and real-time feedback, can enhance learner engagement. Embedding these elements within video lectures and course modules can help maintain motivation and ensure learners can apply the concepts they have learned effectively.

Real-World Machine Learning Projects: A significant finding from this study is the crucial role of real-world machine learning projects in self-paced learning environments. These projects provide learners with hands-on experience and practical application of the concepts they have learned. Here is a subset of the projects mentioned in this study that learners practiced ([3, 4, 10, 11, 14, 16, 18, 21–26, 31–33, 35–37, 40, 41, 41–45]).

Implications for Future Research and Practice: The findings from this study provide valuable insights for educators, course designers, and researchers in the field of ML education. Future research should continue to explore the effectiveness of different self-paced learning strategies and the impact of various instructional designs on learner outcomes. Additionally, there is a need for more longitudinal studies that track the long-term career impacts of self-paced ML education on working professionals.

By incorporating these best practices and addressing the identified challenges, educators and course designers can develop more effective and engaging self-paced ML courses that meet the unique needs of working professionals. This will not only enhance the learning experience but also support the continuous professional development and career advancement of learners in the rapidly evolving field of Machine Learning.

6   Conclusion

This study explores the optimization of self-paced Machine Learning (ML) education for working professionals, emphasizing the importance of flexibility, practical application, and comprehensive support. Through a systematic review of literature, analysis of course websites, in-depth interviews, and a reflective case study, I identified best practices and common challenges in self-paced learning environments. Key findings highlight the need for modular course structures, hands-on projects, diverse learning resources, and ongoing support to enhance learning outcomes. By addressing these elements, educators can develop more effective self-paced ML courses, ultimately supporting the professional growth and career advancement of learners in the dynamic field of ML.

References

1. Abood, H.G.: E-learning applications in engineering and the project-based learning vs problem-based learning styles: a critical & comparative study. Eng. Technol. J. **37**(4), 391–396 (2019)
2. Alshahrani, A.: The impact of ChatGPT on blended learning: current trends and future research directions. Int. J. Data Netw. Sci. **7**(4), 2029–2040 (2023)
3. An, S., Bhat, G., Gumussoy, S., Ogras, U.: Transfer learning for human activity recognition using representational analysis of neural networks. ACM Trans. Comput. Healthcare **4**(1), 1–21 (2023)
4. An, S., Tuncel, Y., Basaklar, T., Ogras, U.Y.: A survey of embedded machine learning for smart and sustainable healthcare applications. In: Embedded Machine Learning for Cyber-Physical, IoT, and Edge Computing: Use Cases and Emerging Challenges, pp. 127–150. Springer (2023)
5. Beckman, K., Coulter, N., Khajenoori, S., Mead, N.R.: Collaborations: closing the industry-academia gap. IEEE Softw. **14**(6), 49–57 (1997)
6. Bennett, B.T.: Teaching artificial intelligence in a multidisciplinary computing environment. J. Comput. Sci. Coll. **33**(2), 222–228 (2017)
7. Bhutoria, A.: Personalized education and artificial intelligence in the United States, China, and India: a systematic review using a human-in-the-loop model. Comput. Educ. Artif. Intell. **3**, 100068 (2022)
8. Brüngel, R., Rückert, J., Friedrich, C.M.: Project-based learning in a machine learning course with differentiated industrial projects for various computer science master programs. In: 2020 IEEE 32nd Conference on Software Engineering Education and Training (CSEE&T), pp. 1–5. IEEE (2020)
9. Castro, R.: Blended learning in higher education: trends and capabilities. Educ. Inf. Technol. **24**(4), 2523–2546 (2019)
10. Chen, P., Ding, H., Araki, J., Huang, R.: Explicitly capturing relations between entity mentions via graph neural networks for domain-specific named entity recognition. In: Proceedings of the 59th Annual Meeting of the Association for Computational Linguistics and the 11th International Joint Conference on Natural Language Processing (Volume 2: Short Papers), pp. 735–742 (2021)
11. Chen, P., et al.: HYTREL: hypergraph-enhanced tabular data representation learning. In: Advances in Neural Information Processing Systems, vol. 36 (2024)
12. Daun, M., Salmon, A., Tenbergen, B., Weyer, T., Pohl, K.: Industrial case studies in graduate requirements engineering courses: the impact on student motivation. In: 2014 IEEE 27th Conference on Software Engineering Education and Training (CSEE&T), pp. 3–12. IEEE (2014)

13. Daun, M., Salmon, A., Weyer, T., Pohl, K., Tenbergen, B.: Project-based learning with examples from industry in university courses: an experience report from an undergraduate requirements engineering course. In: 2016 IEEE 29th International Conference on Software Engineering Education and Training (CSEET), pp. 184–193. IEEE (2016)

14. Dou, G., Zhou, Z., Qu, X.: Time majority voting, a PC-based EEG classifier for non-expert users. In: International Conference on Human-Computer Interaction, pp. 415–428. Springer (2022)

15. Fan, Y., Matcha, W., Uzir, N.A., Wang, Q., Gašević, D.: Learning analytics to reveal links between learning design and self-regulated learning. Int. J. Artif. Intell. Educ. **31**(4), 980–1021 (2021)

16. Gui, S., Song, S., Qin, R., Tang, Y.: Remote sensing object detection in the deep learning era-a review. Remote Sens. **16**(2), 327 (2024)

17. Huang, L.: Integrating machine learning to undergraduate engineering curricula through project-based learning. In: 2019 IEEE Frontiers in Education Conference (FIE), pp. 1–4. IEEE (2019)

18. Jiang, C., Hui, B., Liu, B., Yan, D.: Successfully applying lottery ticket hypothesis to diffusion model. arXiv preprint arXiv:2310.18823 (2023)

19. Kazemitabaar, M., Hou, X., Henley, A., Ericson, B.J., Weintrop, D., Grossman, T.: How novices use LLM-based code generators to solve CS1 coding tasks in a self-paced learning environment. In: Proceedings of the 23rd Koli Calling International Conference on Computing Education Research, pp. 1–12 (2023)

20. Kwan, P.: A college freshman's guide to machine learning: short and sweet way to introduce machine learning to college freshman. J. Comput. Sci. Coll. **30**(1), 36–37 (2014)

21. Li, H., et al.: SphereHead: Stable 3D full-head synthesis with spherical tri-plane representation. arXiv preprint arXiv:2404.05680 (2024)

22. Lu, Y., Chen, T., Hao, N., Van Rechem, C., Chen, J., Fu, T.: Uncertainty quantification and interpretability for clinical trial approval prediction. Health Data Sci. **4**, 0126 (2024)

23. Lu, Y., Sato, K., Wang, J.: Deep learning based multi-label image classification of protest activities. arXiv preprint arXiv:2301.04212 (2023)

24. Lu, Y., Shen, M., Wang, H., Wang, X., van Rechem, C., Wei, W.: Machine learning for synthetic data generation: a review. arXiv preprint arXiv:2302.04062 (2023)

25. Ma, X.: Traffic performance evaluation using statistical and machine learning methods. Ph.D. thesis, The University of Arizona (2022)

26. Ma, X., Karimpour, A., Wu, Y.J.: Data-driven transfer learning framework for estimating on-ramp and off-ramp traffic flows. J. Intell. Transp. Syst., 1–14 (2024)

27. Martins, R.M., Gresse Von Wangenheim, C.: Findings on teaching machine learning in high school: a ten-year systematic literature review. Inform. Educ. **22**(3), 421–440 (2023)

28. Martins, R.M., von Wangenheim, C.G., Rauber, M.F., Hauck, J.C.: Machine learning for all-introducing machine learning in middle and high school. Int. J. Artif. Intell. Educ. **34**, 1–39 (2023)

29. Meng, N., Dong, Y., Roehrs, D., Luan, L.: Tackle implementation challenges in project-based learning: a survey study of PBL e-learning platforms. Educ. Tech. Res. Dev. **71**(3), 1179–1207 (2023)

30. Miller, E.C., Krajcik, J.S.: Promoting deep learning through project-based learning: a design problem. Discip. Interdiscip. Sci. Educ. Res. **1**(1), 1–10 (2019)

31. Murungi, N.K., Pham, M.V., Dai, X.C., Qu, X.: Empowering computer science students in electroencephalography (EEG) analysis: a review of machine learning algorithms for EEG datasets. In: The 29th ACM SIGKDD Conference on Knowledge Discovery and Data Mining (KDD) (2023)
32. Qu, X., Liu, P., Li, Z., Hickey, T.: Multi-class time continuity voting for EEG classification. In: Brain Function Assessment in Learning: Second International Conference, BFAL 2020, Heraklion, Crete, Greece, 9–11 October 2020, Proceedings 2, pp. 24–33. Springer (2020)
33. Qu, X., Mei, Q., Liu, P., Hickey, T.: Using EEG to distinguish between writing and typing for the same cognitive task. In: Brain Function Assessment in Learning: Second International Conference, BFAL 2020, Heraklion, Crete, Greece, October 9–11, 2020, Proceedings 2, pp. 66–74. Springer (2020)
34. Shaw, M., Herbsleb, J., Ozkaya, I.: Deciding what to design: closing a gap in software engineering education. In: Proceedings of the 27th International Conference on Software Engineering, pp. 607–608 (2005)
35. Tan, J., Zhang, X., Wu, S., Wang, Y.: State-space model based inverse reinforcement learning for reward function estimation in brain-machine interfaces. In: 2023 45th Annual International Conference of the IEEE Engineering in Medicine & Biology Society (EMBC), pp. 1–4. IEEE (2023)
36. Tang, Y., Song, S., Gui, S., Chao, W., Cheng, C., Qin, R.: Active and low-cost hyperspectral imaging for the spectral analysis of a low-light environment. Sensors **23**(3), 1437 (2023)
37. Wang, J., Chang, R., Zhao, Z., Pahwa, R.S.: Robust detection, segmentation, and metrology of high bandwidth memory 3D scans using an improved semi-supervised deep learning approach. Sensors **23**(12), 5470 (2023)
38. Winzker, M.: Semester structure with time slots for self-learning and project-based learning. In: Proceedings of the 2012 IEEE Global Engineering Education Conference (EDUCON), pp. 1–8. IEEE (2012)
39. Wong, K., Tomov, S., Dongarra, J.: Project-based research and training in high performance data sciences, data analytics, and machine learning. J. Comput. Sci. Educ. **11**(1), 36–44 (2020)
40. Yi, L., Qu, X.: Attention-based CNN capturing EEG recording's average voltage and local change. In: Artificial Intelligence in HCI: 3rd International Conference, AI-HCI 2022, Held as Part of the 24th HCI International Conference, HCII 2022, Virtual Event, June 26–July 1, 2022, Proceedings, pp. 448–459. Springer (2022)
41. Yunoki, I., Berreby, G., D'Andrea, N., Lu, Y., Qu, X.: Exploring AI music generation: a review of deep learning algorithms and datasets for undergraduate researchers. In: International Conference on Human-Computer Interaction, pp. 102–116. Springer (2023)
42. Zhang, Z., Tian, R., Ding, Z.: TREP: transformer-based evidential prediction for pedestrian intention with uncertainty. In: Proceedings of the AAAI Conference on Artificial Intelligence, vol. 37, pp. 3534–3542 (2023)
43. Zhang, Z., Tian, R., Sherony, R., Domeyer, J., Ding, Z.: Attention-based interrelation modeling for explainable automated driving. IEEE Trans. Intell. Veh. **8**(2), 1564–1573 (2022)
44. Zhao, S., et al.: Deep learning based CETSA feature prediction cross multiple cell lines with latent space representation. Sci. Rep. **14**(1), 1878 (2024)
45. Zhao, Z., Zhou, F., Xu, K., Zeng, Z., Guan, C., Zhou, S.K.: LE-UDA: label-efficient unsupervised domain adaptation for medical image segmentation. IEEE Trans. Med. Imaging **42**(3), 633–646 (2022)

Integrating Sustainable Development Goals into Foreign Language Teaching and Learning Contexts with the Use of Technology: A Systematic Literature Review

Semeli Tilemachou(✉), Anna Nicolaou, and Antigoni Parmaxi

Language Centre, Cyprus University of Technology,
3036 Limassol, Cyprus
sh.tilemachou@edu.cut.ac.cy

Abstract. This study reviews recently published scientific literature on the integration of the Sustainable Development Goals (SDGs) adopted by the United Nations (UN) into foreign language (FL) teaching and learning contexts with the use of technology. The aim of this dissertation is to (a) explore the role of technology in the integration of SDGs into FL teaching and learning contexts (b) present a synthesis of the available empirical evidence on the benefits as well as the challenges of using technology as an educational tool with the aim of facilitating the integration of SDGs into FL teaching and learning contexts, and (c) define future research perspectives concerning the integration of SDGs into Computer-Assisted Language Learning (CALL) contexts. The outcomes of this systematic literature review are discussed in terms of their implications for future research, and can provide useful guidance for stakeholders, policymakers, publishers, educators and researchers in the field of CALL.

Keywords: Sustainable Development Goals (SDGs) · Education for Sustainable Development (ESD) · Foreign Language Teaching · Foreign Language Learning · Computer-Assisted Language Learning (CALL) · Technology

1 Introduction

1.1 The UN's Sustainable Development Goals (SDGs)

The Sustainable Development Goals (SDGs) were created in 2015 by the United Nations with the ultimate aim to "eradicate poverty, protect the environment, and guarantee that everyone enjoys freedom and harmony by 2030" [1]. The 2030 Agenda for Sustainable Development consists of the following 17 goals: 1) No poverty 2) Zero hunger 3) Good health and well-being 4) Quality education 5) Gender equality 6) Clean water and sanitation 7) Affordable and clean energy 8) Decent work and economic growth 9) Industry, innovation and infrastructure 10) Reduced inequalities 11) Sustainable cities and communities 12) Responsible consumption and production 13) Climate action 14) Life below water 15) Life on land 16) Peace, justice and strong institutions 17) Partnerships for the Goals [2].

P. Zaphiris et al. (Eds.): HCII 2024, LNCS 15378, pp. 137–155, 2025.
https://doi.org/10.1007/978-3-031-76815-6_11

The planetary emergency that humanity has been facing due to the destruction of ecosystems, the loss of biodiversity, the exhaustion of vital resources, environmental pollution, and extreme poverty for billions of people around the world can be viewed as "primarily an education problem" since, as stated by de la Fuente [3], it has been caused mainly by a "lack of knowledge". As it is widely acknowledged that education can facilitate the process of addressing global issues and achieving the UN's SDGs, it is definitely worth exploring the concept of Education for Sustainable Development (ESD).

1.2   Education for Sustainable Development (ESD)

Education for Sustainable Development (ESD) is defined as a teaching approach or a learning process that is based on principles and ideals that prepare people to plan for, cope with, and find solutions for issues that jeopardise the sustainability of our planet [4]. ESD is therefore "a guide for institutions and educators to redesign curricula and pedagogies around sustainability principles" [3].

Leal Filho [5] suggests that, although ESD is critical at all educational levels, it is most essential at the university level since students will soon pursue careers in different professions, and they will need to know the impact that their professions can have in addressing issues pertaining to sustainability. As a result, ESD will encourage undergraduates "to take action both during their time as students and, later on, as professionals" [5]. However, it is not only HEIs that should be held responsible for the promotion of SDGs since, as stated by Taimur [6], "all education institutions from primary to tertiary education and in nonformal and formal education can and should accept the responsibility to intensively deal with the matters of sustainable development and to nurture sustainability competencies".

Ssossé et al. [7] argue that ESD "aims at interdisciplinarity" while, similarly, Petkutė [8] suggests that sustainable development and its principles should be introduced through various disciplines and already-existing subjects rather than through a newly-introduced subject dedicated exclusively to sustainable development. Thus, incorporating ESD into a variety of fields, including foreign language education, is a fundamental step towards raising awareness about SDGs and fostering their achievement.

1.3   ESD and Foreign Language Education

De la Fuente [3] contends that the most evident connection between ESD and foreign language learning is "the fact that multilingualism and multiculturalism are part of our present reality"; thus, monolingualism and monoculturalism may inhibit sustainability efforts at the global level.

Incorporating ESD into foreign language teaching and learning contexts is also important since, according to Ülker et al. [9], students who are able to express their ideas about social, economic and environmental matters in both their native and non-native languages will feel empowered and motivated to actively participate in decision-making mechanisms which shape the future of the world. The target language can therefore be used for fostering discussions and debates about global challenges, for conducting research about sustainability solutions, and for writing reflective papers which offer suggestions on how to approach sustainability issues, all of which are examples of practices for sustainability education [9].

1.4   ESD, FL Education and the Use of Technology

Literature suggests that there are several benefits to using technology in FL teaching and learning processes where the aim is to incorporate ESD. For instance, Visvizi et al. [10] argue that the use of technology can foster FL learners' critical thinking skills and civic engagement, while Ricard et al. [11] propose that digital tools are "valuable for teacher training through competence acquisition and skill development" as they can provide access to a wide range of training courses for FL teachers. Additionally, digital tools can "make organising training times more flexible" and offer opportunities for "training in and through digital technology" [11]. When it comes to fostering student inclusion in learning processes, digital technologies can be seen as critical in providing educational resources to FL learners who are struggling academically [1]. The aforementioned affordances of using technology in FL education are closely related to ESD and especially to SDG 4 (Quality Education); therefore, exploring the role of technology in the integration of SDGs and ESD into FL teaching and learning contexts can be an illuminating process.

However, "a lack of adaptation to ICT skills, a lack of infrastructure or ICT access, and inadequate training of staff" could impede FL learning and teaching processes and as a result hinder the achievement of SDG 4 [11]. More specifically, literature suggests that FL educators often feel unprepared to include technology in their teaching practice [12] or have a negative attitude towards the use of technology altogether [13]. In addition, FL educators sometimes feel that the administrative and technical support they receive from the higher education institution at which they work is insufficient [14]. Moreover, there are FL educators who feel that working with technology leads to increased workload [15–17], which can also be demotivating for FL instructors. These factors can have a negative impact on the effective use of technology in FL teaching and learning contexts where the aim is to promote SDGs.

1.5   Critical Pedagogy

According to Crookes [18], Critical Pedagogy, founded by Paulo Freire, is "teaching for social justice, in ways that support the development of active, engaged citizens"; thus, it is a movement which takes the side of individuals who are underprivileged and deprived from "social, economic and political opportunities" [19]. Critical Pedagogy is an invaluable approach to learning since, as Giroux [20] points out, educational institutions "must be seen as places where culture, power, and knowledge come together to produce particular identities, narratives, and social practices", and not merely as places where instruction takes place. Sevilla-Pavón and Nicolaou [19] similarly argue that, within the Critical Pedagogy framework, "a social and educational view of justice and equality should be the basis for any kind of didactic initiative, the ultimate goal being the liberation from oppression and human-caused injustices and suffering". According to Freire [21, 22], the application of Critical Pedagogy is crucial as it helps one become aware of the injustices and the oppressions that exist in the world, which is the first step towards one's liberation from them.

1.6 Critical Applied Linguistics

Critical Applied Linguistics is a way of "relating aspects of applied linguistics to broader social, cultural, and political domains" [23]. However, according to Pennycook [23], an essential element of Critical Applied Linguistics is going "beyond mere correlations between language and society" and instead raising "more critical questions to do with access, power, disparity, desire, difference, and resistance". In other words, Critical Applied Linguistics engages with "questions of inequality, injustice, rights, and wrongs" and views social transformation as one of its cores aims [23].

1.7 Critical CALL

Computer-Assisted Language Learning (CALL) has been defined as "the search for and study of applications of the computer in language teaching and learning" [24]. At the same time, Critical Computer-Assisted Language Learning (Critical CALL) is a subfield of Critical Applied Linguistics that is also closely associated with the broader framework of Critical Pedagogy [19], since Critical CALL is concerned with "issues of power and inequality and an understanding of how our classrooms and conversations are related to broader social, cultural and political relations" [25]. Thus, it is evident how Critical CALL relates to the promotion of SDGs, since integrating SDGs into CALL contexts requires the introduction of topics "related to both local and global critical issues" and which refer to "challenges which culturally diverse communities face" [26].

1.8 Rationale

Exploring how technology has been used in FL teaching and learning contexts where the goal was the integration of SDGs is significant, as it could shed light upon the affordances as well as the potential challenges of using digital tools while aiming to foster SDGs in FL education and as a result contribute to the field of CALL. Furthermore, this study could contribute to the field of Critical CALL, since the aims of the SDGs seem to align with the aims of Critical Pedagogy and more specifically with the aims of Critical CALL, which is concerned with "issues of power and inequality and an understanding of how our classrooms and conversations are related to broader social, cultural and political relations" [25].

The significance of this study is also justified by the fact that a systematic literature review that explores the integration of SDGs into CALL contexts does not exist in the current literature to the best of the authors' knowledge. This study aims to fill this gap by carefully reviewing past studies which explore the relationship between the three areas, namely SDGs, FL learning, and technology. Identifying, evaluating, and synthesising research results which examine the relationship between SDGs, FL learning, and technology could be valuable for foreign language educators as it could help them in activity-design processes as well as their overall teaching practice. Moreover, such a review could provide a solid foundation for researchers who wish to conduct follow-up studies in the field of CALL or Critical CALL. Finally, this review could be useful for stakeholders, publishers, and policymakers during decision-making processes.

1.9 Aims

This systematic literature review is led by the following key research question: How has technology been used in foreign language teaching and learning contexts where the goal was the integration of SDGs?

The aim of this study is to carefully review empirical studies conducted in the last five years in order to gain a better understanding of how technology has been used in FL teaching and learning contexts at the primary, secondary, and tertiary level of education where the goal was the integration of SDGs. The following subsidiary research questions are guiding this study:

1. Which SDGs have been promoted the most in CALL contexts in the last five years?
2. What types of technologies have been used while promoting SDGs in foreign language teaching and learning contexts in the last five years?
3. What types of activities have been used while promoting SDGs in CALL contexts in the last five years?
4. At which levels of education have SDGs been introduced the most in the last five years?
5. What are the benefits of using technology while promoting SDGs in FL teaching and learning contexts?
6. What are the challenges of using technology while promoting SDGs in FL teaching and learning contexts?

2 Methods/Methodology

2.1 Keywords and Databases

For the purposes of this study, a systematic literature review was conducted on the 31st of July 2023, in the following international bibliographic databases: (a) IEEE XPLORE, (b) SpringerLink, (c) Web of Science and (d) Scopus. Searches were restricted to peer-reviewed articles, written in English, and published between 2019 and 2023 (research over the last five years), in order for the most recent scientific literature to be included in this study. The same search string (("language learn*" OR "language teach*" OR "language educat*" OR "language classroom") AND ("technolog*" OR "online" OR "ICT" OR "CALL" OR "MALL" OR "TELL" OR "Web 2.0" OR "AR" OR "VR") AND ("SDGs" OR "Sustainable Development Goals" OR "SD" OR "Sustainable Develop-ment" OR "Sustainability" OR "ESD" OR "Education for Sustainable Development")) used was across the four databases. In IEEE XPLORE, the filters applied were: Journals, 2019–2023. In SpringerLink, the filters applied were: Article, Education, English, 2019–2023. In both Web of Science and Scopus, the filters applied were: 2019–2023, English, Article.

2.2 Inclusion and Exclusion Criteria

The following criteria were used to decide which papers would be included in the review (IC):

IC 1: The paper is written in English.

IC 2: The paper was published between the years 2019–2023.

IC 3: The paper has been peer-reviewed.

IC 4: The paper presents an empirical study.

IC 5: The paper explicitly mentions the terms: "sustainable development" (or "SD") or "sustainable development goals (or "SDGs") or "education for sustainable development" (or "ESD") or "sustainability".

IC 6: The paper reports the application of technology in a foreign language teaching/learning context.

Six criteria for excluding articles (EC) were also determined:

EC 1: The paper is not written in English.

EC 2: The paper was published before 2019.

EC 3: The paper has not been peer-reviewed.

EC 4: The paper does not present an empirical study.

EC 5: The paper does not explicitly mention the terms "sustainable development" (or "SD") or "sustainable development goals (or "SDGs") or "education for sustainable development" (or "ESD") or "sustainability" (i.e. the integration of SDGs, ESD or sustainability can only be implied) or the terms "sustainability" and/or "sustainable development" are used but in a different context.

EC 6: The paper does not explicitly mention the application of technology in a foreign language teaching/learning context (i.e. there is no mention of technology or technology is used in a different context/discipline).

2.3 Article Selection Process

The article selection process is depicted in the PRISMA diagram presented in Fig. 1. Initial pre-screening yielded 333 sources. After deduplication, 332 studies were retained and screened based on their title and abstract. Thereafter, 258 articles were excluded based on their title and abstract and 74 studies were sought for retrieval. Since all 74 articles were retrieved, they were all carried over for full-text screening. Full-text assessment resulted in 4 studies being excluded based on EC 4, 22 studies being excluded based on EC 5, 14 studies being excluded based on EC 6, and 8 studies being excluded based on both EC 5 and EC 6 (total number of articles excluded based on the exclusion criteria = 48). During this process, 7 duplicated articles across the four databases were also located and excluded from the final corpus of this study, resulting in 19 articles being included in this study retrieved solely from the four databases used. Following this process, backward and forward search was conducted. Initially, 26 studies were identified from backward search and 12 studies were located from forward search, resulting in 38 studies sought for retrieval. Since all 38 studies were retrieved, they were all subsequently assessed for eligibility. Throughout this process, 8 articles were excluded based on EC 4, 16 articles were excluded based on EC 5, and 10 articles were excluded based on EC 6, resulting in 4 articles being included in the final corpus of this study retrieved solely from backward and forward search. As a result, 23 articles in total were included in this study (databases = 19 articles retrieved, backward/forward search = 4 articles retrieved).

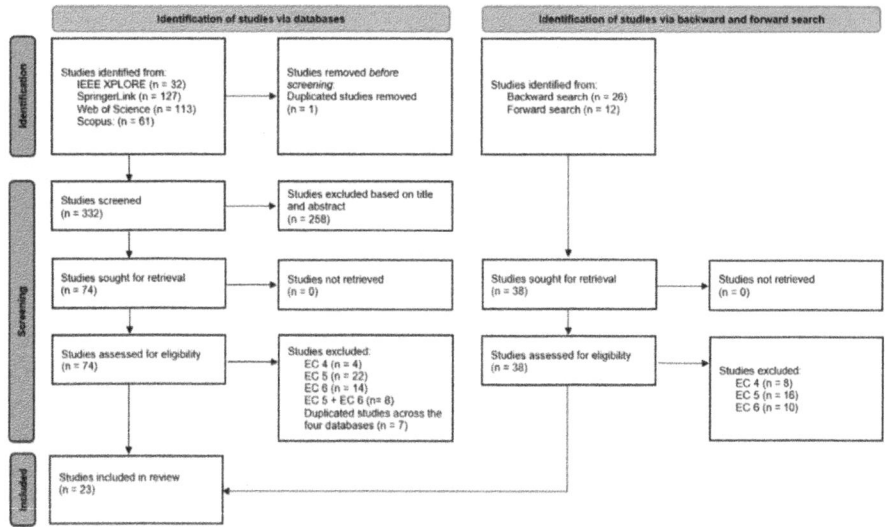

Fig. 1. Process of the article selection

3 Results

3.1 Summary of the Findings Based on the Study's Subsidiary Research Questions

In this section the results of the systematic literature review are summarised and presented, in an attempt to answer the subsidiary research questions found in Sect. 1.9.

RQ1: Which SDGs have been Promoted the Most in CALL Contexts in the Last Five Years? The findings suggest that SDG 4 (Quality Education) has been promoted the most in CALL contexts in the last five years. Specifically, the majority (n = 17) of the articles included in this study focus solely on the achievement of SDG 4 [27–31]. Meanwhile, one study mentions Goal 8 (Decent Work and Economic Growth) as well as Goal 4 [32]. There are also four studies which focus on all the 17 SDGs, including Goal 4 [33–36]. Only one study stands out for focusing on SDGs other than Goal 4; specifically, in the study conducted by Fakhretdinova et al. [37], there is an emphasis on the achievement of Goal 13 (Climate Action) (Fig. 2).

RQ2: What Types of Technologies have been Used While Promoting SDGs in Foreign Language Teaching and Learning Contexts in the Last Five Years? A small number of studies (n = 2) have utilised AR technologies [34, 38], while another two

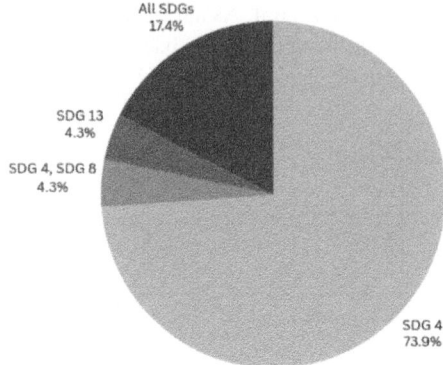

Fig. 2. SDGs promoted in CALL contexts in the last five years

used VR technologies [31, 39]. In addition, eight studies used MALL applications [40–42], while another eight of them included the use of LMS platforms [29, 30, 35, 40, 43, 44]. Gamification tools were employed in three studies [28, 40, 44] while four studies used websites [35, 37, 45, 46]. Six studies included in the final corpus utilised Google tools [28, 33, 40] and a significant proportion of the studies (n = 12) opted for video-conferencing tools [28, 29, 36, 40, 43, 44, 47, 48]. Collaboration tools were used in the majority of the studies (n = 16) [35, 40, 46], while two studies mentioned the use of Information and Communication Technologies (ICT) in general [32, 49] (Fig. 3).

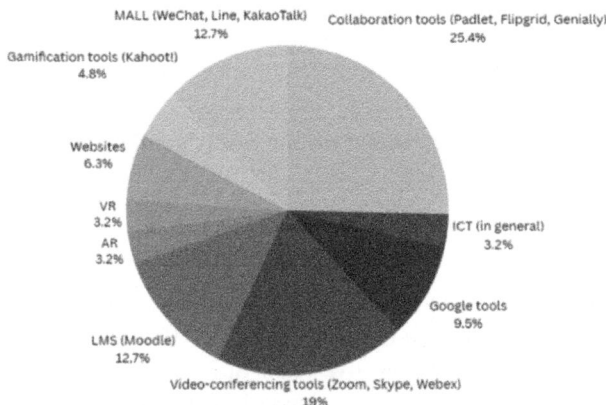

Fig. 3. Technologies used while promoting SDGs in FL teaching and learning contexts in the last five years

RQ3: What Types of Activities have been Used While Promoting SDGs in CALL Contexts in the last Five Years? Online collaborative tasks were predominantly used in the studies (n = 9) [35, 40, 47]. Assessment tasks such as tests and quizzes were included in five of the studies [27, 34, 40]. Task-Based Learning (TBL) activities were used in two of the studies [36, 47] while Project-Based Learning (PBL) activities were used in another two [33, 48], which were all facilitated by virtual exchanges and telecollaboration. There was also one study which included gamification [34].

However, a significant number of studies (n = 7) did not include FL learning activities and focused on corpus analysis [41, 45], observations of the everyday life and activities of the participants [32] and the participants' perceptions instead [28, 39, 44, 49]. Nevertheless, observing the results of such studies could still shed light upon the benefits as well as the challenges of using technology with the aim of promoting SDGs in FL education; therefore, they have not been excluded from this review (Fig. 4).

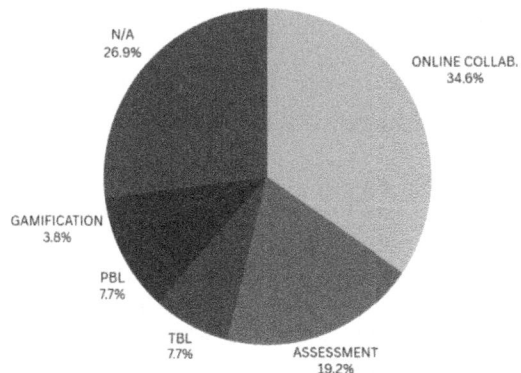

Fig. 4. Activities used while promoting SDGs in CALL contexts in the last five years

RQ4: At Which Levels of Education have SDGs Been Introduced the Most in the Last Five Years? The largest number of studies (n = 16 out of 23) introduce the concept of sustainability and SDGs in tertiary education [28–31, 33] followed by four studies which promote SDGs through FL teacher development [40, 41, 44, 48]. One study included adults that were neither university students nor FL teachers, but stakeholders instead [32]. Only two studies stand out for including participants other than adults; specifically, one study introduces SDGs to high school students [34] and another study's participants are children aged five to twelve [38] (Fig. 5).

RQ5: What are the Benefits of Using Technology While Promoting SDGs in FL Teaching and Learning Contexts? The results of this systematic literature review indicate that using technology while promoting SDGs in foreign language teaching and learning contexts can offer a great number of benefits. For instance, according to Vymetalkova and Milkova [30], the use of ICT tools and, more specifically, the blended learning model used in their study, contributes to sustainable and quality education as it offers access to knowledge 24/7 as well as a more flexible, convenient and inclusive mode of learning, especially regarding "more mature learners with outside commitments" such as family and work. Similarly, Tanabe [29] argues that online learning and, particularly, the flipped learning model used in her study, "can achieve a variety of goals in sustainable education, such as providing access for students, particularly in times of crisis, as well as providing them with opportunities to study interdependently". Likewise, Jeong [27] claims that MALL applications used in her study could facilitate sustainable language

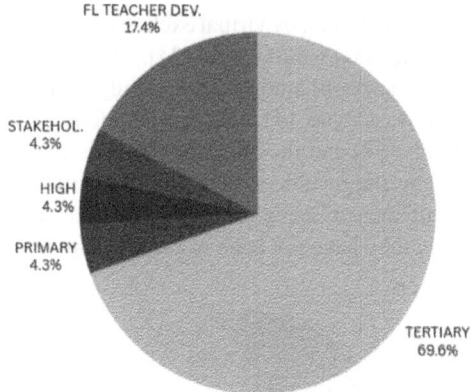

Fig. 5. Levels of education where SDGs have been introduced in the last five years

education due to the "ease of access to learning contents, portability of the learning tools, flexible and self-directed learning environment, better interaction, and improved self-efficacy in English learning performance". Furthermore, according to the findings of the study conducted by Mihai et al. [28], online language learning is perceived to be conducive to student engagement which is "key in reaching sustainable learning outcomes" and sustainable educational development, since it leads to students' "better academic performance and to a decrease in their dropout rate", while also "enhancing belonging and fighting isolation towards students' personal development and well-being", especially during challenging times. Other studies have similarly concluded that the use of technology can increase learners' motivation and engagement in activities as well as their interest in sustainable development [27, 29, 30, 34, 37–39] while also assisting learners in achieving better results pertaining to their language skills [30, 31, 34, 38, 42, 49]. Additionally, Motteram [48] argues that video-conferencing tools such Skype can support effective FL teacher development which is "an important part of providing quality education as a part of Sustainable Development Goal 4". Moreover, Hashim et al. [38] contend that the use of AR for FL learning purposes "offers a lot of potential, in terms of therapy, intervention, and education for children with autism". Furthermore, the use of technology can encourage autonomous learning [30, 42–44]. Also, online FL learning assists in dealing with travel restrictions by freeing teachers and learners from the necessity of travelling to a classroom [29]. In addition, can potentially gain a better understanding of sustainable development principles due to the fact that they are often given the opportunity to collaborate and communicate internationally about global issues such as sustainability [31]. As a result, students expand their civic awareness as well as their intercultural competence and skills [29, 33, 35, 36] and are able to become active participants in sustainable development [37]. Moreover, FL teacher development is also positively affected, since building professional communities online helps FL educators to work together collaboratively in order to navigate their way through unstable or challenging circumstances [40], to discuss and address issues regarding the challenges they face, as well as develop teaching materials [41]. Other benefits include the possibility of instant feedback on students' work [30], the development of learners' critical thinking, communication and collaboration skills [35], and the provision of life-long learning opportunities [32] which are essential to the attainment of SDG 4. Also, the use of technology in FL teaching and learning contexts can aid the development of creative and sustainable language assessment strategies [43]. Finally, the promotion of SDGs through CALL can facilitate the advancement of learners' digital skills [33] and interdisciplinary knowledge [39]; as a result, it can lead to positive experiences in foreign language acquisition [39] as well as foster sustainable language learning, development and use [40].

RQ6: What are the Challenges of Using Technology While Promoting SDGs in FL Teaching and Learning Contexts? Despite the numerous benefits, this study also reveals the several potential challenges of using technology while promoting SDGs in foreign language teaching and learning contexts. First of all, a lack of institutional training and support can lead to FL instructors feeling unprepared and adopting a negative attitude towards online teaching for SDG development [44]. Choi and Chung [40] have also come to a similar conclusion, since the participants of their study found that it was difficult for them to use technology and digital tools effectively "with little experience and training". Moreover, a lack of access to electronic devices or the presence of bugs in mobile applications could disturb the learning experiences of students [34]. Another concern mentioned in one of the studies was the possibility of reduced concentration and continuity of learning caused by eye fatigue and decreased readability due to the small screen size of mobile devices [27]. Similarly, Karataş and Tuncer [46] mention that the use of digital devices could be problematic for the development of reading and writing skills as it may cause eye problems and loss of concentration. As for the development of listening skills, technical issues can be a drawback [46]. In Karataş and Tuncer's study [46], participants also reported that "they had little to no speaking practice compared to face-to-face educational settings". In the same study, participants also referred to "inadequate technological equipment and connection problems" as other major drawbacks [46]. Most importantly, students from low-income social groups who do not have access to the internet or technological tools and devices could potentially be excluded from learning opportunities and as a result be negatively affected from "the digital divide" and "unequal opportunities" [46]; therefore, "this situation creates a threat for realizing SDG 4" [46]. This concern has also been raised by Motteram et al. [41], who argue that issues of internet access could potentially reinforce inequalities. This possibility would contradict some of the most important targets of SDG 4, such as universal access to education and education equality [46]. In addition, although for many students the use of technology in the FL classroom is motivating, for others it can be demotivating; for instance, in the study conducted by Karataş and Tuncer [46] some participants described themselves as being "less motivated, irresponsible, passive, and technologically illiterate" and mentioned they had issues with "time management, study habits, self-discipline, and academic integrity" during distance education [46]. The issue of unequal participation and engagement has also been highlighted in the study undertaken by Motteram et al. [41].

4 Discussion

In this section the results of the systematic literature review are discussed, in an attempt to answer the key research question that is leading this study: How has technology been used in foreign language teaching and learning contexts where the goal was the integration of SDGs? Implications for researchers as well as stakeholders and practitioners in the field of CALL are also introduced in this section.

The results show that in the last five years, technology has extensively been used with the aim of fostering the achievement of SDG 4 (Quality Education) in the context of foreign language education, whereas other SDGs have been promoted to a lesser extent while using technology in the aforementioned context. This is evident since more than 70% of the articles included in this review focus solely on the promotion of SDG 4. These results seem to align with the literature and can be explained by the fact that the significance of SDG 4 is highlighted by the United Nations, who acknowledge Goal 4 as a medium for reaching the remaining SDGs [50]. Nevertheless, it would be interesting to see further studies focusing on the integration of SDGs other than Goal 4 within the same context in the future.

The findings of this study also indicate that a wide range of digital tools have been used in FL teaching and learning contexts where the goal was the integration of SDGs, confirming the popularity of technology-enhanced language learning (TELL) in recent years [51]. Digital collaboration tools as well as video-conferencing tools were predominantly preferred by educators and researchers aiming to integrate SDGs into foreign language education; therefore, it is clear that technology has the potential to facilitate collaboration and communication in FL teaching and learning contexts. These results seem to agree with the literature, which proposes that collaborative learning with the use of ICTs is an effective approach to transforming FL education into Education for Sustainable Development [52, 53]. Educators are therefore encouraged to use technology with the aim of fostering SDGs in foreign language teaching and learning contexts. However, further research could be conducted on how other emerging technologies, such as VR and AR, could potentially facilitate the integration of SDGs into foreign language education, since only a small number of studies included in this review utilised such tools. AR and VR are considered intriguing areas of research since they can have various affordances, including the provision of immersive simulations and opportunities for role play, which allow students to "enter into experiences from authentic situations" [11] and could therefore enhance the integration of SDGs into foreign language teaching and learning contexts.

The results of the study also point to ways in which technology has been used to facilitate the implementation of various activity types employed with the aim of integrating SDGs into foreign language teaching and learning contexts. The fact that online collaborative tasks (i.e. virtual exchanges, video-conferencing) were the predominant choice among the educators and researchers who conducted the studies included in this review indicates that telecollaborative tasks can assist in the integration of SDGs into foreign language education, which aligns with the literature suggesting that collaborative learning with the use of technology can facilitate the implementation of Education for Sustainable Development [52, 53]. Such international collaborative learning initiatives reflect the global efforts to achieve the SDGs and respond to Goal 17 (Partnerships for the Goals). For this reason, it is highly recommended for FL educators to use online collaborative activities in their lessons with the aim of fostering SDGs, especially during times of crisis, such as the COVID-19 pandemic.

The findings of this study also reveal that the level of education in which SDGs have been introduced the most in the last five years is tertiary education. This conclusion seems to agree with the literature since, according to de la Fuente [3], ESD is already used "by hundreds of universities worldwide". These results can be explained by the fact that the UN considers the implementation of the 2030 Agenda for Sustainable Development in Higher Education Institutions (HEIs) critically important, since university teaching and learning is "a crucial enabler of the 2030 agenda's overall success" [54]. In addition, Leal Filho [5] suggests that, although the implementation of ESD is vital at all educational levels, it is most important at the university level, since students will soon pursue careers in different professions, and they will need to know the impact that their professions can have in addressing issues pertaining to sustainability. This way, students will be well-equipped to deal with the challenges they will face in their professional fields and they will be able to take action towards a more sustainable world [3]. This idea is closely related to the notion of Critical Pedagogy, which proposes that learners should be aware of the oppression and injustices that exist in the world, so that they can take action and eventually be liberated from them [21, 22]. In the light of these findings, it is strongly recommended for HEIs to further integrate SDGs and ESD into their curricula. However, despite the great significance of introducing SDGs in FL tertiary education, future studies could also further explore the integration of SDGs in primary and secondary FL education, since less than 10% of the studies included in this review focused on these levels of education. Nevertheless, such studies are deemed necessary, since they could potentially shed light upon the affordances as well as the challenges of introducing SDGs to younger FL learners through the use of technology, which might differ from the ones presented in studies which included adult participants. Furthermore, studies focusing on SDG integration into FL primary and secondary education could benefit younger FL learners since "embedding ESD and SDGs values within primary and secondary education" could yield "positive results on the students both in the short and the long term" as it "enhances their behavior towards their environment and their community, helps them acquire more citizenship values" and equips them with "more sustained mindsets and skillsets" [55].

The findings of this study also indicate that the use of technology in FL teaching and learning contexts can support the promotion of SDGs (especially SDG 4) in several ways. For instance, technology can assist in dealing with travel restrictions as students who live in remote areas can benefit from distance learning [29]. Specifically, online learning "can achieve a variety of goals in sustainable education, such as providing access for students, particularly in times of crisis" [29]. In addition, according to Tanabe [29], intercultural discussions facilitated by video-conferencing technologies and learning management systems "improve the quality of learning". Technology allows FL learners living in different countries to collaborate and communicate with each other about global issues such as sustainability, which can enhance their civic awareness as well as their intercultural competence and skills that could in turn enable them to take action towards a more sustainable world [37]. This potential benefit is aligned with the notion of Critical Pedagogy, which supports "the development of active, engaged citizens [18]. Moreover, FL teacher development, which is crucial in achieving SDG 4, is also positively affected by the use of technology, since building professional communities online fosters collaboration between FL educators worldwide and helps them navigate their way through unstable or challenging circumstances, such as the COVID-19 pandemic [40]. Other major benefits include the accessibility and portability of learning tools as well as the flexible and self-directed learning environment facilitated by the use of technology, which can be convenient especially for learners with family or work commitments [30]. Finally, the use of technology in FL teaching and learning contexts can foster the development of learners' digital skills [33] and interdisciplinary knowledge, which is "necessary to attain the SDG of quality education" [39]. Many of these results seem to align with the literature; for instance, Visvizi et al. [10] suggest that the use of technology can foster learners' civic engagement, as well as motivate and empower them to make the most of their potential. Regarding teacher development, Ricard et al. [11] propose that digital tools are "valuable for teacher training through competence acquisition and skill development" as they can provide access to a wide range of training courses. Finally, digital tools can "make organising training times more flexible" and offer opportunities for "training in and through digital technology" [11]. The affordances that were brought to light through this study imply that it is highly recommended for FL educators to use technology with the aim of integrating SDGs into their lessons and as a result promote "an understanding of how our classrooms and conversations are related to broader social, cultural and political relations" [25], which is one of the cores aims of Critical CALL.

In spite of the numerous benefits, this study also reveals a number of potential challenges of using technology in foreign language teaching and learning contexts where the aim is to foster the achievement of SDGs. First and foremost, a lack of institutional training and support can lead to FL educators feeling unprepared and having a negative attitude towards the use of technology in their lessons [44]. Moreover, a lack of access to electronic devices, as well as the presence of bugs in mobile applications [34] and other technical issues [46] could disturb the learning experiences of students and therefore be "a threat for realizing SDG 4" [46]. Another concern mentioned in the findings was the possibility of reduced concentration and continuity of learning caused by eye fatigue and decreased readability due to the small screen size of mobile devices [27]. Furthermore, students from low-income social groups who do not have access to the internet or digital devices could be excluded from FL learning opportunities [46]. This possibility would jeopardise equitable and inclusive education and as a result compromise the attainment of SDG 4 [46]. In addition, the use of technology in FL learning contexts can be demotivating for some students [46]. Finally, the use of technology could lead to unequal participation and engagement [41]. While these results contradict some of the literature mentioned earlier, there is also literature that seems to have come to similar conclusions. For instance, Ricard et al. [11] suggest that "a lack of adaptation to ICT skills, a lack of infrastructure or ICT access, and inadequate training of staff" could hamper FL learning and teaching processes and as a result inhibit the achievement of SDG 4. Moreover, Oldham et al. [12] argue that FL educators often feel unprepared to include technology in their teaching practice, while Raghunath et al. [13] suggest that FL teachers often adopt a negative attitude towards the use of technology altogether, which could be due to the insufficient administrative and technical support they receive from the institutions at which they work [14]. Overall, the challenges observed in this study imply that FL educators need to be provided with adequate administrative and technical support as well as sufficient training in order to feel prepared to use technology in their lessons with the aim of fostering SDGs. Equal and easy access to digital tools and devices as well as sufficient training should also be provided to FL learners, in order to reduce inequalities and increase students' motivation throughout the learning process.

4.1 Implications for Researchers

Taking the findings of this study into consideration, it is suggested that researchers in the field of CALL conduct further research on the integration of SDGs into CALL contexts, especially with a focus on SDGs other than Goal 4, in an attempt to fill this gap in the literature and explore how other SDGs can be promoted in CALL contexts. In addition, further research could be conducted on how other emerging technologies, such as VR and AR, are utilised in CALL contexts where the aim is the integration of SDGs, in order to further explore the potential of such tools. Future studies could also focus on the integration of SDGs into levels of FL education other than tertiary, such as primary and secondary.

4.2 Implications for Practitioners and Stakeholders

In the light of the results of this study, it is suggested that FL educators use technology with the aim of integrating SDGs into their lessons, especially video-conferencing tools and collaboration tools, as it has the potential to offer a great number of benefits. It is also highly recommended for FL educators to use online collaborative activities in their lessons with the aim of fostering SDGs, especially during times of crisis (such as the COVID-19 pandemic). Moreover, it is strongly recommended for HEIs to further integrate SDGs and ESD into their curricula. However, FL educators need to be provided with adequate administrative and technical support as well as sufficient training in order to feel prepared to use technology in their lessons with the aim of fostering SDGs. Finally, equal and easy access to digital tools and devices as well as sufficient training should also be provided to FL students, so that access to quality FL education is fostered and inequalities in CALL contexts are reduced.

5 Conclusions

This study presents a review of recently published scientific literature on the use of technology in foreign language teaching and learning contexts with the aim of facilitating the integration, promotion, and achievement of the United Nations Sustainable Development Goals (SDGs) by 2030. The study aims to identify the utilisation of technology in such contexts, summarising relevant empirical findings and indicating future research perspectives as well as practical applications.

The review conducted suggests that there are few empirical studies involving the explicit promotion of SDGs in foreign language education with the use of technology, since only 23 articles were located and selected for this study. The results also showed that while technology has the potential to foster the achievement of the UN's SDGs and especially Goal 4, there are also significant potential challenges that need to be considered and addressed, as this study pointed to cases where the use of technology in FL teaching and learning contexts where the aim was to promote the SDGs had a negative impact on FL students' learning experiences as well as FL teachers' professional development and teaching practices.

This study opens a new perspective for future research focused on experience with technology, Education for Sustainable Development (ESD) and foreign language learners under the age of 18, since only two of the articles in this review included studies working with this age group. Another point demonstrated in this study is the lack of empirical research involving the use of technology in FL teaching and learning contexts with the aim of promoting SDGs other than Goal 4. Another suggestion for future research is to further examine how emerging technologies such as VR and AR have been used in FL teaching/learning contexts where the aim was the integration of SDGs, since the studies that have explored these areas in the last five years are currently rather limited.

Overall, this study has demonstrated that technology has enormous potential as a tool which supports the integration of SDGs into foreign language education. It is hoped that the study will provide useful guidance for stakeholders, policymakers, publishers, educators, and researchers in the field of CALL.

Acknowledgements. Portions of this manuscript are drawn from my unpublished master thesis: Semeli Tilemachou. (2023). Integrating Sustainable Development Goals into Foreign Language Teaching and Learning Contexts with the Use of Technology: A Systematic Literature Review. Unpublished Master Thesis. Cyprus University of Technology.

References

1. Saini, M., Sengupta, E., Singh, M., Singh, H., Singh, J.: Sustainable development goal for quality education (SDG 4): a study on SDG 4 to extract the pattern of association among the indicators of SDG 4 employing a genetic algorithm. Educ. Inf. Technol. **28**(2), 2031–2069 (2022). https://doi.org/10.1007/s10639-022-11265-4
2. United Nations. The sustainable development goals report. United Nations (2023). https://unstats.un.org/sdgs/report/2023/The-Sustainable-Development-Goals-Report-2023.pdf
3. De la Fuente, M.J.: Education for sustainable development in foreign language learning: content-based instruction in college-level curricula. Routledge (2022)
4. UNESCO. United Nations Decade of Education for Sustainable Development (2005–2014): International Implementation Scheme. UNESCO, Paris (2005)
5. Leal Filho, W.: Universities and Climate Change: Introducing Climate Change to University Programmes. Berlin: Springer Publishing (2010)
6. Taimur, S.: Pedagogical Training for Sustainability Education. Encyclopedia of the UN Sustainable Development Goals, 1–12 (2020) https://doi.org/10.1007/978-3-319-69902-8_51-1

7. Ssossé, Q., Wagner, J., Hopper, C.: Assessing the impact of ESD: methods, challenges, results. Sustainability **13**(5), 2854 (2021). https://doi.org/10.3390/su13052854

8. Petkutė, R.: Integrating the concept of sustainable development into English language curriculum of environmental engineering sciences. Santalka **20**(1), 65–74 (2012). https://doi.org/10.3846/cpe.2012.07

9. Ülker, N., Gemalmaz, Ö., Yüksek, Y.: Towards 21st century citizenship through sustainable development goals in foreign language education (2022). https://doi.org/10.5821/conference-9788412322262.1315

10. Visvizi, A., Lytras, M.D., Daniela, L.: Education, innovation and the prospect of sustainable growth and development. The Future of Innovation and Technology in Education: Policies and Practices for Teaching and Learning Excellence, pp. 297–305 (2018). https://doi.org/10.1108/978-1-78756-555-520181015

11. Ricard, M., Zachariou, A., Burgos, D.: Digital education, information and communication technology, and education for sustainable development. Radical Solutions ELearning, 27–39 (2020). https://doi.org/10.1007/978-981-15-4952-6_2

12. Oldham, E., et al.: Developing confident computational thinking through teacher twinning online. Int. J. Smart Educ. Urban Soc. **9**(1), 61–75 (2018). https://www.learntechlib.org/p/186431/

13. Raghunath, R., Anker, C., Nortcliffe, A.: Are academics ready for smart learning? Br. J. Edu. Technol. **49**(1), 182–197 (2016). https://doi.org/10.1111/bjet.12532

14. Dobozy, E.: Learning design research: advancing pedagogies in the digital age. Educ. Media Int. **50**(1), 63–76 (2013). https://doi.org/10.1080/09523987.2013.777181

15. Adekola, J., Dale, V.H.M., Gardiner, K.: Development of an institutional framework to guide transitions into enhanced blended learning in higher education. Res. Learn. Technol. **25** (2017). https://doi.org/10.25304/rlt.v25.1973

16. Han, I., Shin, W.S., Ko, Y.: The effect of student teaching experience and teacher beliefs on pre-service teachers' self-efficacy and intention to use technology in teaching. Teach. Teach. **23**(7), 829–842 (2017). https://doi.org/10.1080/13540602.2017.1322057

17. Lochner, B., Conrad, R.-M., Graham, E.: Secondary teachers' concerns in adopting learning management systems: A U.S. perspective. TechTrends, **59**(5), 62–70 (2015). https://doi.org/10.1007/s11528-015-0892-4

18. Crookes, G.: Critical ELT in Action: Foundations, Promises, Praxis. Routledge, New York (2013)

19. Sevilla-Pavón, A., Nicolaou, A.: Artefact co-construction in virtual exchange: youth entrepreneurship for society. Comput. Assist. Lang. Learn. 1–26 (2020). https://doi.org/10.1080/09588221.2020.1825096

20. Giroux, H.A.: Henry Giroux on Critical Pedagogy and the Responsibilities of the Public Intellectual. Palgrave Macmillan US EBooks, pp. 3–20 (2006). https://doi.org/10.1057/978 1403984364_1

21. Freire, P.: Education for Critical Consciousness. Seabury, New York (1973)

22. Freire, P.: Pedagogia do oprimido, 17th edn. Paz e Terra, Rio de Janeiro (1987)

23. Pennycook, A.: Critical Applied Linguistics: A Critical Introduction. Lawrence Erlbaum, Mahwah, NJ (2001)

24. Levy, M.: Computer-Assisted Language Learning: Context and Conceptualization. Clarendon Press, New York (1997)

25. Helm, F.: The practices and challenges of telecollaboration in higher education in Europe. Lang. Learn. Technol. **19**(2), 197–217 (2015). http://llt.msu.edu/issues/june2015/helm.pdf

26. Makarova, E.: Application of sustainable development principles in foreign language education. In: E3S Web of Conferences, vol. 208, p. 09014 (2020). https://doi.org/10.1051/e3s conf/202020809014

27. Jeong, K.-O.: Facilitating sustainable self-directed learning experience with the use of mobile-assisted language learning. Sustainability **14**(5), 2894 (2022). https://doi.org/10.3390/su1405 2894

28. Mihai, M., Albert, C.N., Mihai, V.C., Dumitras, D.E.: Emotional and social engagement in the English language classroom for higher education students in the COVID-19 online context. Sustainability **14**(8), 4527 (2022). https://doi.org/10.3390/su14084527

29. Tanabe, J.: Sustaining language learning through social interaction at a Japanese national university. IAFOR J. Educ. **9**(6), 112–125 (2021). https://doi.org/10.22492/ije.9.6.06

30. Vymetalkova, D., Milkova, E.: Experimental verification of effectiveness of English language teaching using MyEnglishLab. Sustainability **11**(5), 1357 (2019). https://doi.org/10.3390/su1 1051357

31. Wang, C.-C., Hung, J.C., Chen, H.-C.: How prior knowledge affects visual attention of Japanese mimicry and onomatopoeia and learning outcomes: evidence from virtual reality eye tracking. Sustainability **13**(19), 11058 (2021). https://doi.org/10.3390/su131911058

32. Nomnian, S., Trupp, A., Niyomthong, W., Tangcharoensathaporn, P., Charoenkongka, A.: Language and community-based tourism: use, needs, dependency, and limitations. Adv. Southeast Asian Stud. **13**(1), 57–79 (2020). https://doi.org/10.14764/10.ASEAS-0029

33. Casañ-Pitarch, R., Candel-Mora, M.Á., Demydenko, O., Tikan, I.: Telecollaborative projects for teaching english for professional and academic purposes. LFE, **28**(1), 27–41 (2022). https://doi.org/10.20420/rlfe.2022.484

34. Çelik, F., Yangın Ersanlı, C.: The use of augmented reality in a gamified CLIL lesson and students' achievements and attitudes: a quasi-experimental study. Smart Learn. Environ. **9**(1) (2022). https://doi.org/10.1186/s40561-022-00211-z

35. Garcia-Esteban, S.: Telecollaboration for civic competence and SDG development in FL teacher education. Eur. J. Educ. **3**(2), 129 (2020). https://doi.org/10.26417/936ywi19y

36. Lenkaitis, C.A.: Integrating the United Nations' sustainable development goals: developing content for virtual exchanges. Lang. Learn. Technol. **26**(1), 1–20 (2022). https://doi.org/101 25/73470

37. Fakhretdinova, G., Zinnatullina, L.M., Tarasova, E.N.: Integrating sustainability into language teaching in engineering university. In: Auer, M.E., Hortsch, H., Michler, O., Köhler, T. (eds.) Mobility for Smart Cities and Regional Development - Challenges for Higher Education. ICL 2021. Lecture Notes in Networks and Systems, vol. 390, pp. 478–484. Springer, Cham (2022). https://doi.org/10.1007/978-3-030-93907-6_50

38. Hashim, H.U., Yunus, M.M., Norman, H.: "AReal-Vocab": an augmented reality english vocabulary mobile application to cater to mild autism children in response towards sustainable education for children with disabilities. Sustainability **14**(8), 4831 (2022). https://doi.org/10.3390/su14084831

39. Kwee, C.T.T., Dos Santos, L.M.: How can blended learning English-as-a-second-language courses incorporate with cultural heritage, building, and sense of sustainable development goals? a case study. Front. Educ. **7** (2022). https://doi.org/10.3389/feduc.2022.966803

40. Choi, L., Chung, S.: Navigating online language teaching in uncertain times: challenges and strategies of EFL educators in creating a sustainable technology-mediated language learning environment. Sustainability **13**(14), 7664 (2021). https://doi.org/10.3390/su13147664

41. Motteram, G., Dawson, S., Al-Masri, N.: WhatsApp supported language teacher development: a case study in the Zataari refugee camp. Educ. Inf. Technol. **25**(6), 5731–5751 (2020). https://doi.org/10.1007/s10639-020-10233-0

42. Shadiev, R., Wang, X., Halubitskaya, Y., Huang, Y.-M.: Enhancing foreign language learning outcomes and mitigating cultural attributes inherent in asian culture in a mobile-assisted language learning environment. Sustainability **14**(14), 8428 (2022). https://doi.org/10.3390/su14148428

43. Chung, S.-J., Choi, L.-J.: The development of sustainable assessment during the COVID-19 pandemic: the case of the English language program in South Korea. Sustainability 13(8), 4499 (2021). https://doi.org/10.3390/su13084499
44. Sevilla-Pavón, A., Finardi, K.R.: Pandemic language teaching: insights from Brazilian and international teachers on the pivot to emergency remote instruction. J. Lang. Educ. 7(4), 127–138 (2021). https://doi.org/10.17323/jle.2021.11676
45. Kapranov, O.: The discourse of sustainability in English language teaching (ELT) at the University of oxford: analyzing discursive representations. J. Teach. Educ. Sustain. 24(1), 35–48 (2022). https://doi.org/10.2478/jtes-2022-0004
46. Karataş, T.Ö., Tuncer, H.: Sustaining language skills development of pre-service EFL teachers despite the COVID-19 interruption: a case of emergency distance education. Sustainability 12(19), 8188 (2020). https://doi.org/10.3390/su12198188
47. Lenkaitis, C.A., Loranc-Paszylk, B.: Facilitating global citizenship development in lingua franca virtual exchanges. Lang. Teach. Res. 136216881987737 (2019). https://doi.org/10.1177/1362168819877371
48. Motteram, G.: Videoconferencing tools as mediating artefacts in english language teacher development in challenging contexts. J. Educ. Online 16(1) (2019). https://doi.org/10.9743/jeo.2019.16.1.10
49. Maican, M.-A., Cocoradă, E.: Online foreign language learning in higher education and its correlates during the COVID-19 pandemic. Sustainability 13(2), 781 (2021). https://doi.org/10.3390/su13020781
50. Kioupi, V., Voulvoulis, N.: Education for sustainable development: a systemic framework for connecting the SDGs to educational outcomes. Sustainability 11(21), 6104 (2019). https://doi.org/10.3390/su11216104
51. Marijuan, S., Sanz, C.: Technology-assisted L2 research in immersive contexts abroad. System 71, 22–34 (2017). https://doi.org/10.1016/j.system.2017.09.017
52. Roschelle, J., Teasley, S.D.: The construction of shared knowledge in collaborative problem solving. Comput. Support. Collaborative Learn. 128, 69–97 (1995). https://doi.org/10.1007/978-3-642-85098-1_5
53. Vare, P., Scott, W.: Learning for a change. J. Educ. Sustain. Dev. 1(2), 191–198 (2007). https://doi.org/10.1177/097340820700100209
54. Holmes, J., Moraes, O., Rickards, L., Steele, W., Hotker, M., Richardson, A.: Online learning and teaching for the SDGs – exploring emerging university strategies. Int. J. Sustain. High. Educ. 23(3), 503–521 (2021). https://doi.org/10.1108/ijshe-07-2020-0278
55. Fekih Zguir, M., Dubis, S., Koç, M.: Embedding education for sustainable development (ESD) and SDGs values in curriculum: a comparative review on Qatar, Singapore and New Zealand. J. Clean. Prod. 319, 128534 (2021). https://doi.org/10.1016/j.jclepro.2021.128534

LiveLingo: Create Digital Learning Experiences for Kids, Leveraging AI

Ngoc Thuy Dung Vo(✉)

Boston College, Chestnut Hill, MA 02467, USA
thuydungvo3095@gmail.com

Abstract. Learning on mobile devices has demonstrated significant effectiveness in language acquisition for a wide range of learners of English as a second language (ESL) and foreign language (EFL). The integration of advanced technologies, including AI and virtual reality, in language learning apps, has revolutionized engagement and personalized instruction, yet there remains a gap in the application of sound learning theories. Current commercial language learning products are seen as more tech-focused than education-focused. Balancing these two aspects is crucial for developing impactful and engaging learning experiences for learners. Grounded in learning theories and leveraged by AI technologies, Livelingo offers multiple authentic entry points to language learning and supports interactions between the child and their environment, technology, and peers/parents. This working paper calls for greater attention to embedding learning theories into the creation of AI-empowered learning experiences for learners.

Keywords: Edtech · Learning Engineering · Learning Design · Human-centered Design · Digital Learning Product · Language Learning · Learning Technologies · ESL · EFL · AI in Education

1 Introduction

Mobile-assisted learning has proven to be effective in language learning [1], both within and outside traditional classroom settings [2]. It can improve learners' oral fluency, enhance engagement, and reduce anxiety [3]. Zhenzhen Chen et al. [4], after synthesizing 80 experimental and quasi-experimental studies from 2008 to 2018, concluded that mobile devices have a medium-to-high overall effect size on language learning achievement, confirming the positive outcomes of incorporating mobile devices in language learning. Furthermore, mobile-assisted learning holds the promise of providing educational opportunities in rural areas [5] and contributing to a more sustainable and inclusive education [6].

In ESL/EFL learning, quizzes and puzzles were commonly used for vocab and grammar, augmented learning to increase engagement, and virtual reality to help learners create and sustain conversations [7]. With the presence of state-of-art AI in designing language learning systems, natural processing language in converting source language, supporting learning and offering feedback, the use of data-driven approaches to tailor

© The Author(s), under exclusive license to Springer Nature Switzerland AG 2025
P. Zaphiris et al. (Eds.): HCII 2024, LNCS 15378, pp. 156–174, 2025.
https://doi.org/10.1007/978-3-031-76815-6_12

to the current comprehension and skills level of each learner; Automated speech recognition and chatbots to understand produced spoken and written text and interact with learners [8]. However, there is a lack of learning theories embedded in the development and implementation of those AI technologies [9]. Most commercial mobile language learning products present a slow pedagogical shift from behavior towards a communicative approach in language teaching and learning [10] I.e., Apps teach vocabs in isolation with little context; skill levels are not adapted to individuals, and meaningful feedback is not provided to learners. As researchers and education designers, we need to find the best ways to incorporate tech tools into education to ensure an optimal learning experience for learners.

Livelingo significantly contributes to the current research and practice of designing digital language learning products for kids by seriously considering and implementing learning theories throughout its development process. The design directions are driven by cognitive, educational, and motivational theories, as well as guidelines for creating effective educational products for children. Recognizing the gap in contextualized and communicative learning in most commercial apps, Livelingo emphasizes developing systems based on authenticity principles, helping learners make sense of what they learn in real-world contexts, whether it involves learning new vocabulary, sentences, or conversations. In terms of creating a communicative learning environment, Livelingo integrates social interactions with friends and family members to align with the communicative approach in second/foreign language acquisition, supporting both face-to-face and online interactions, whether synchronous or asynchronous. Additionally, the platform tailors' choices and levels to individual learners to enhance motivation, avoiding right/wrong answers in favor of adaptive suggestions for improving language knowledge and skills. Throughout the development process, a conjecture map was created, tracked, and modified to ensure each prototype aligned with pedagogical principles. Finally, learning design goals and engagement were prioritized during observation, testing, and evaluation phases. In summary, Livelingo emphasizes the importance of grounding its tools in educational theory, aiming to bridge the gap between pedagogical approaches and technological development.

2   Research Method and Design Approach

2.1   Research and Data Collection Method

Design-based research method was adopted in this project to explore how relevant variables interact in an authentic learning context [11]. The Livelingo design process (Fig. 1) went through different iterations of investigating, developing, implementing, data collecting, and refining products, eventually, helping us understand more of how learning occurs and what we, as learning designers can do to design and support learning.

The Livelingo design challenge began by identifying and scoping the challenge through a thorough investigation of the context and learners. This initial phase included exploring literature on language learning, technologies in language learning, and designing digital learning experiences for children to determine suitable design approaches. Additionally, an assessment of the affordances and disaffordances of current products and solutions for mobile language learning for children was conducted.

Following the investigation phase, the design process commenced. Ideas were generated, refined, and presented as low-fidelity prototypes. Subsequently, a test plan was devised and executed under controlled in-lab conditions. Data was gathered during these tests, and insights gleaned were utilized to enhance the prototype for the next iteration.

Each iteration involved further research, the collection of data, and the incorporation of insights to refine the design challenge and its solution. Decisions made throughout the process were documented in a design journal, and the conjecture map was updated accordingly. This iterative approach ensured continuous improvement and optimization of the design solution.

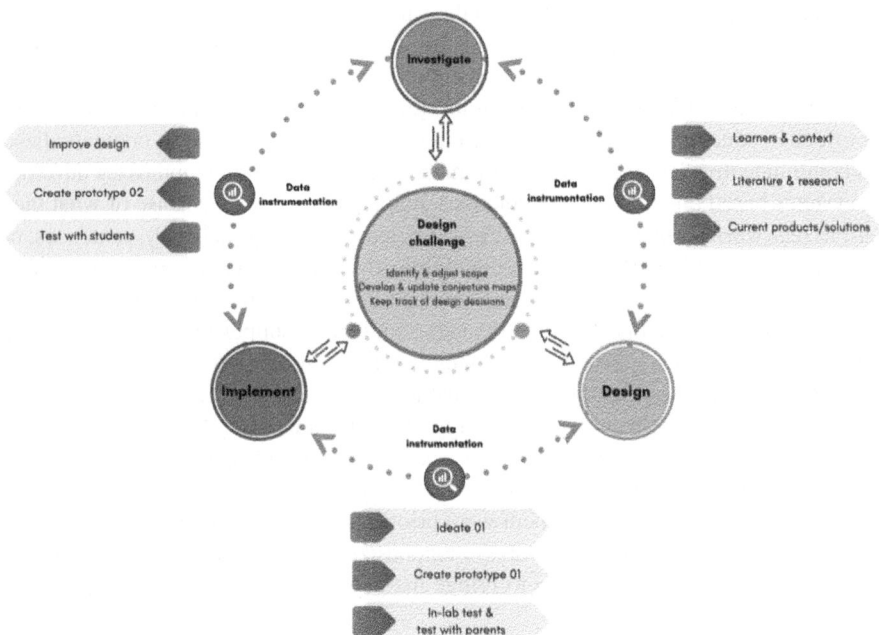

Fig. 1. Livelingo Design Process (Adapted from Learning Engineering Process, CC-BY Aaron Kessler 2022)

As of equal importance, the project employed the learning engineer's approach to draw evidence-based conclusions based on the implementation and analytics of data [12]. In this project, several data collection methods were used:

- Focus groups: A group of 9 Vietnamese students aged 6–12, with their consensus and their parents' permit. A group of 5 parents, 9 learning engineers, teachers, and product managers collectively participated in the project as key stakeholders.
- Experiments: A prototype of a language learning app accompanied by AI platforms was used to help learners and stakeholders understand the design concept. Due to geographical constraints, experiments with learners and their parents were fully conducted online. A total of 3 experiments, each with a participant group: learning engineers, local parents/teachers, and children were conducted during this study.

- Observations: Observations were conducted via recordings in both face-to-face and online experiments. Both the verbal and non-verbal language of participants were analyzed after each experiment.
- Interview: Interviews were conducted throughout the design process in the investigation, design, and implementation phases.

This study was conducted following ethical standards for research involving human subjects. All participants provided informed consent before participating in the study. They were given detailed information about the study's purpose, procedures, potential risks, and benefits, and they were assured that their participation was voluntary and that they could withdraw at any time. Additionally, participants' data were collected and stored securely to ensure privacy and confidentiality. Identifiable objects were anonymized, pseudo-nyms were used, and data access was restricted only to the researcher.

2.2 Literature Research (AKA "Design Lens")

"Design lens" [13] refers to various design concept approaches, primarily rooted in literature and research. Identifying a design lens is a critical research step, guiding the formation of the initial design idea. This process ensures that the design is anchored in scientific principles and evidence. Ultimately, the incorporation of design lenses contributes to a more informed, systematic, and scientifically validated design process.

Learning theories	Descriptions	Design implications
Authenticity *Learning happens in context, with relevance, and personal meaning to learners, as well as the value of real-world connections.* [14]	The authenticity lens emphasizes the importance of creating learning experiences that are real and relatable to learners. The more relevant the content is to learners' communication needs, the easier it becomes to transfer skills into real-life contexts	• Vocab introduction: Learners could create their tailored dictionaries and selectively choose words they truly want to learn to live annotation to capture objects in the surrounding environment and provide descriptive sentences emerged • Language theme: Real-life functional language, such as asking for permission to go out or informing friends about being late for a party • Feedback system: Rather than scoring or ranking, the system provides feedback on strengths and areas for improvement, facilitated by a color system and supportive language

(*continued*)

(*continued*)

Learning theories	Descriptions	Design implications
Social constructivism *Knowledge is constructed by social interactions and expression via language.* [15]	This lens informs designers to create various touchpoints for learners to interact with friends and family members in different ways, providing support for speaking with other learners or in real-life situations	• Language practice: Interactive games where learners can play with their friends and engage in role-playing conversational situations
Self-determination *Human beings are motivated to engage in activities that satisfy three psychological needs: autonomy, competence, and relatedness.* [16]	In the context of an after-school language learning program, self-determination theory emphasizes the need to design for autonomy, offer a wide range of choices, foster relatedness, and sustain learning engagement through the choice of learning content and materials	• Content presentation: Option for students to choose topics • Learning mode: Choice to learn on their own or with a learning partner
Design principles for kids *"Designing for kids means designing for parents and teachers as well. It requires an understanding of their goals and expectations, as well as their concerns around privacy, safety, and appropriate content."* [17]	A successful language learning design must cater to the needs of all stakeholders involved	Based on the insights gathered from discovery interviews with Vietnamese parents, kids, and teachers: • Time: Flexibility in terms of time investment, indicating that the design must allow for different levels of engagement and learning depending on each child's schedule • Type of activities: The need for games and interactive activities, ensuring fun learning experience • Feedback: Instant feedback for learning improvement

2.3   Conjecture Map

A conjecture map, characterized by Sandoval [18] as "an intricate framework for argumentative discourse in design research," functions analogously to an architect's blueprint, offering sophisticated guidance throughout the phases of design, construction, and evaluation (Fig. 2).

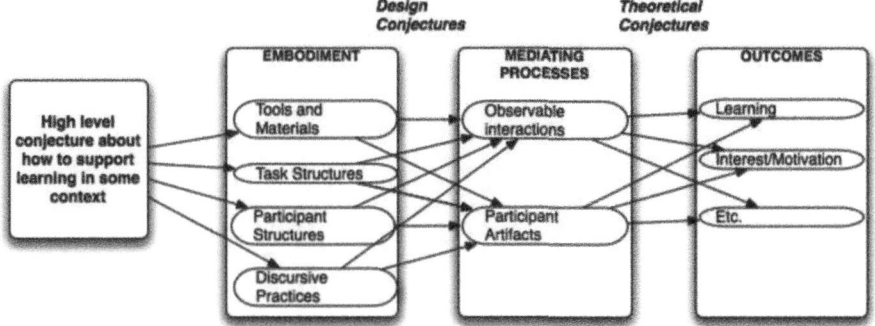

Fig. 2. Generalized conjecture map for educational design research by Sandoval

This map not only facilitates the creation of the design but also provides an advanced mechanism for predicting and addressing deviations from the planned course. Functioning as a logic map, it explains the intentional inclusion of design elements and their intricate connections and predicts how learners progress to the learning goals. It is imperative to iteratively refine the conjecture map during the design process to accommodate nuanced insights. The conjecture map is also a handy tool for fostering transparent communication and making judicious design decisions in collaboration with stakeholders. The adapted form of the conjecture map for LiveLingo can be accessed here.

3 Product Ideas and Final Prototype

LiveLingo's approach to the design challenge prioritizes authentic and effective language acquisition. Recognizing the significance of gradual skill improvement, the platform offers a range of activities designed to enhance learners' abilities. The tasks gradually increase in complexity, allowing learners to master language elements such as syntax and cultural awareness.

- Activities like Word Scavenger (Fig. 3) and Brain Boost (Fig. 4) focus on vocabulary uptake.
- Word Scavenger is an activity inspired by image recognition and annotation by Google Lens [19] that empowers learners to take charge of their vocabulary learning. It encourages learners to explore and observe the objects and things around them and build their dictionary of words that are relevant to their environment.

- Brain Boost is a tool empowered by Wordwalls [20] that helps deep learn vocabulary in Word Scavenger by focusing on a variety of activities that build upon different strengths. By targeting memory, sense-making, pronunciation, spelling, and word order, learners can benefit from a range of exercises that are tailored to their individual learning needs.

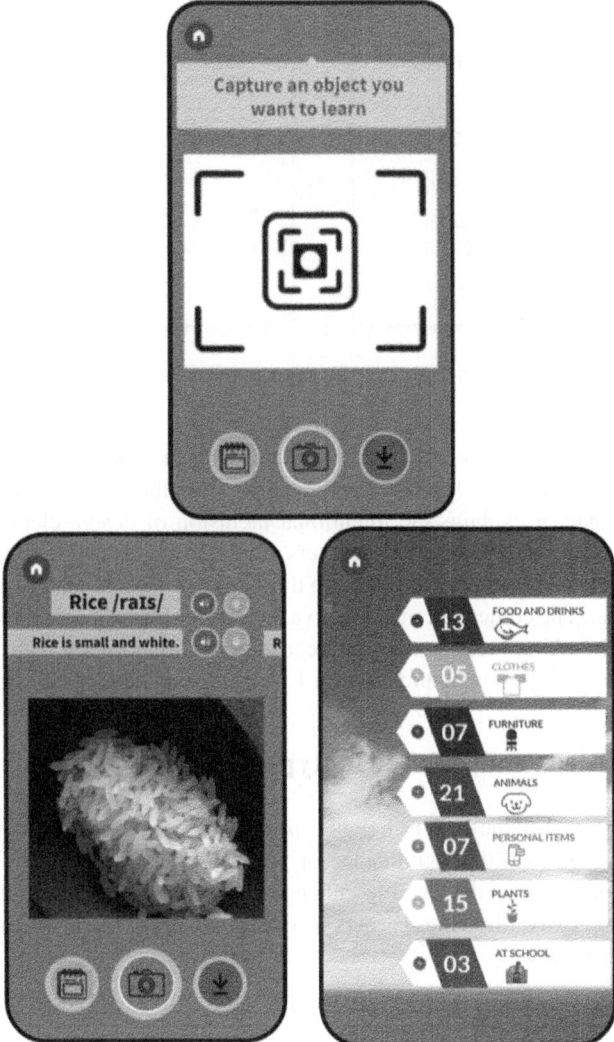

Fig. 3. Word Scavenger interface

- Grammar Guru (Fig. 5) helps strengthen language mental models. The activity allows learners to explore grammar by manipulating control centers and observing changes in sentence structures. Learners discover the rules by figuring out basic changes in sentence structure and how they affect meaning.

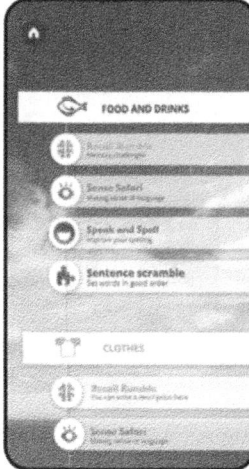
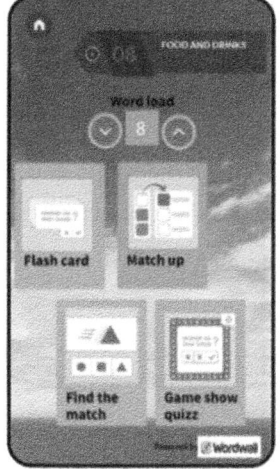
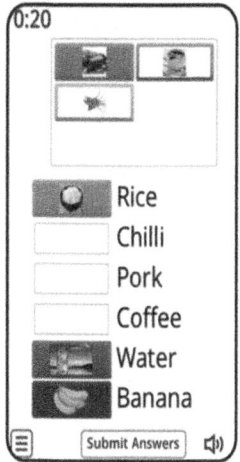

Fig. 4. Brain Boost interface

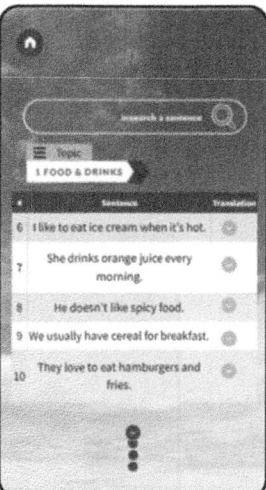

Fig. 5. Grammar Guru interface

- Picture This, AI! (Fig. 6) and Play on! (Fig. 7) engage learning with activities empowered by generative AI

– Picture this, AI! is a tool that allows learners to visualize their language creatively and memorably. Current generative AI technologies like DALL-E2 [21] or MidJourney [22] enable learners to convert their language into imaginative images that can reinforce their short-term memory.

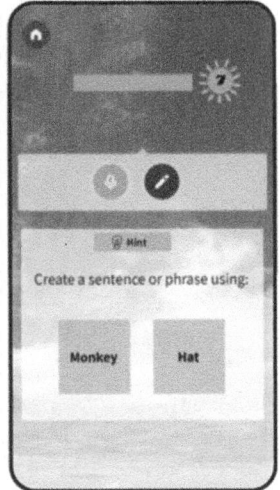

Fig. 6. Picture This, AI! interface

– Play on!, inspired by TikTok [23], is an AR-empowered set of interactive games to
  enhance learners' language skills. The goal is to enhance learners' language reflexes
  by using body gestures and voice to participate in fast-moving interactive games with
  the system and friends/family members.

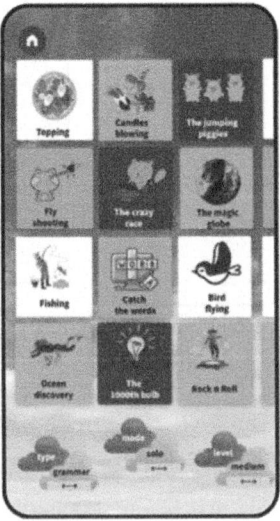

Fig. 7. Play on!! interface

- Lip Sync Legend (Fig. 8) and Meme Master (Fig. 9) offer opportunities for real-life language practice and creativity.

– Lip Sync Legend is an activity that offers learners the flexibility to choose the type of dubbing they want to do empowered by Chat GPT [24] and AI-generative video platform Synthesia [25].

  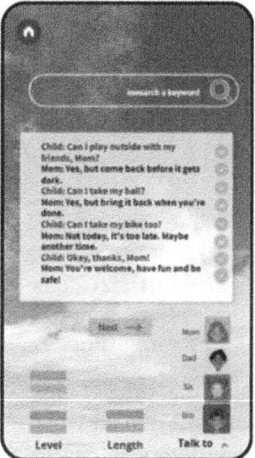

Fig. 8. Lip Sync Legend interface

Whether it's functional English, conversational language, dubbing a song, or reading a story with someone, learners can choose their preferred context, length, level, and speakers/characters.

- Meme Master, inspired by Meme Generator [26] is the last design piece of Livelingo to help learners build up skills, confidence, and interests in language learning, and express themselves to the world.

It is not just a platform for making memes. It is a creative playground that encourages learners to explore their expressive potential through language, imagery, and humor. Meme Master is necessary for students to advance their language learning level.

Fig. 9. Meme Master interface

4   Design Process and Findings

4.1   Investigation

The initial project aimed to create a learning solution for parents and children in rural areas in Vietnam with limited access to English education. To understand their needs, Zoom interviews were conducted with five parents and their 6–12-year-old children. Each interview lasted 45 min. The focus was on exploring the language learning context, parental involvement, and technology accessibility.

Findings from stakeholders led me to an unexpected endeavor. Parents were motivated to support their children's learning but faced challenges in sustaining engagement and developing language competence. Additionally, not all families had computers, but most had at least one or two smartphones. Given a limited three-month timeframe and the challenges of online co-design with parents, I decided to pivot the project towards creating learning experiences primarily for children. One thing I knew certainly was that I needed to create a mobile app that was accessible in rural areas.

This shift in focus was not part of the initial plan but was deemed necessary. I acknowledged the importance of adaptability and openness to changing course when new information or perspectives emerged. The goal remained to address young learners' needs while leaving room for potential future co-design projects involving parents. This experience highlighted *the significance of flexible decision-making in research and design endeavors.*

4.2   Design

First Iteration. Based on my research findings and insights from stakeholders, I did a quick wireframe and then built up the prototype for my app. The first mock-up includes five activities: Live Dictionary, Interactive games, Grammar Master, Dubbing, and Creating Reels, arranged in ways that learners can have freaccess to all contents as they wish (Fig. 10).

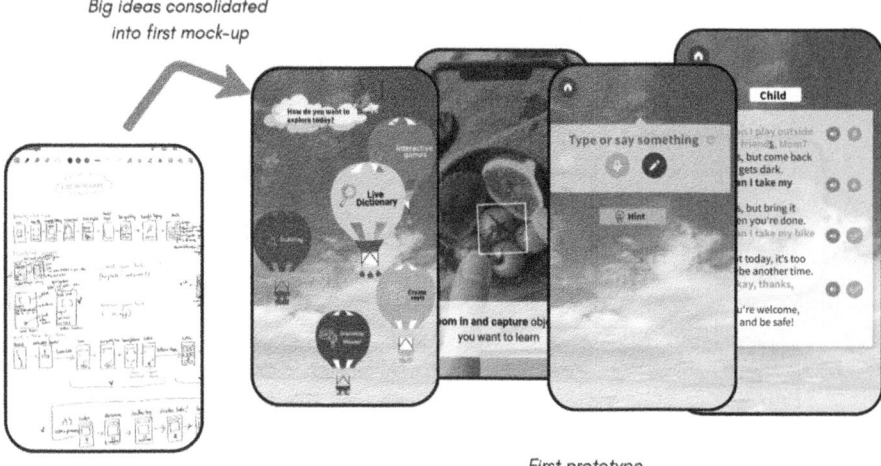

Big ideas consolidated into first mock-up

Initial wireframe

First prototype

Fig. 10. LiveLingo's first prototype

The project underwent three iterations and three tests: an in-lab test, an idea test with parents, and finally, testing with groups of primary school students. In the first test, two groups of professors and students were assigned to interact with the mock-up created by Genially, followed by discussions.

The goal of the first test was first, to see how learners engage with the learning activities and second, to generate insights on how they think learning would be for 6–11-year-old kids. In this first test, it was challenging for learners to see the big picture of how parts are connected and build up knowledge and skills for learners. Reasons were traced down to two factors: Constant perspective change (between users and observers) and partially functioned minimal viable product (MVP) (Fig. 11).

Based on feedback from the first group of testers, I decided to make several adjustments to increase the cohesiveness of the design. Based on feedback from professors and parents, I decided to make several adjustments to increase the cohesiveness of the design. In terms of the testing plan, I decided to shift the goal from testing interactions on MVP to testing design ideas.

Second Iteration. In the second prototype development, I wrote up my scaffolding theory and then moved those ideas into my design. Below are several changes to the mock-up page, taking Live Dictionary as an example. Instructions were added, including suggestions on what to scan in each topic in case learners have little idea where to start. Simple games to reinforce short-term memory were introduced, allowing learners to decide on the number of vocabulary words they wanted to review (Fig. 12).

In this test, testers were able to grasp the product's design logic and offer valuable insights into my research questions. The test plan (combination of presenting, demoing, and organizing activities) helped testers understand my design idea (Fig. 13).

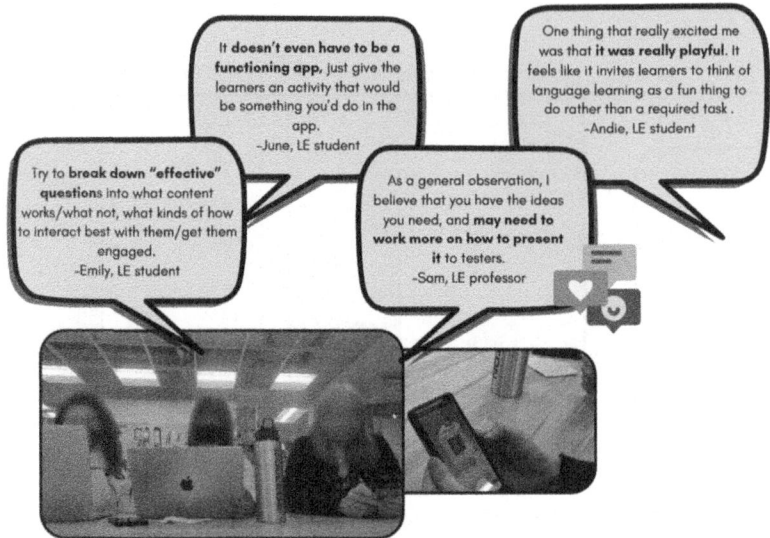

Fig. 11. Testers interact with app mock-up on Genially

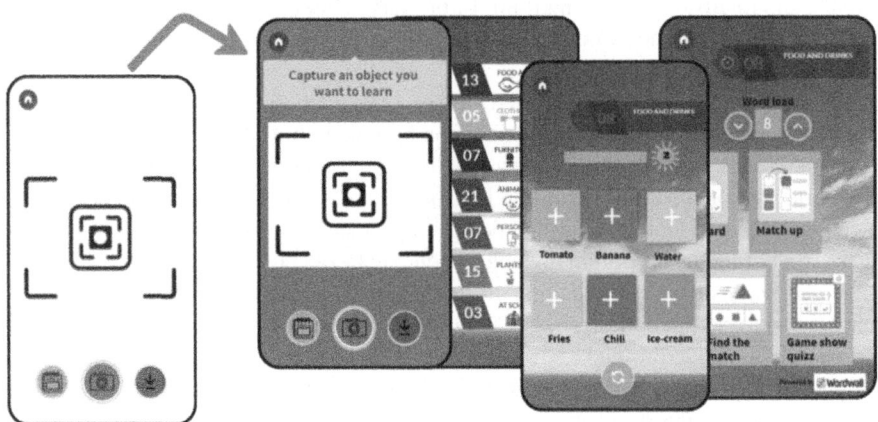

Live dictionary, first mock-up   *Live dictionary, refined mock-up with instructions and scaffolds*

Fig. 12. LiveLingo's second prototype

Findings from recorded videos and interview responses suggested:

1. Elements of engagement are across most sections. My chosen lens of authenticity and social culture helps learners see parts of the engagement conjecture about language learning. I, however, could not show much of the role of self-determination in the design and need to work more on this, especially scaffolding and feedback.

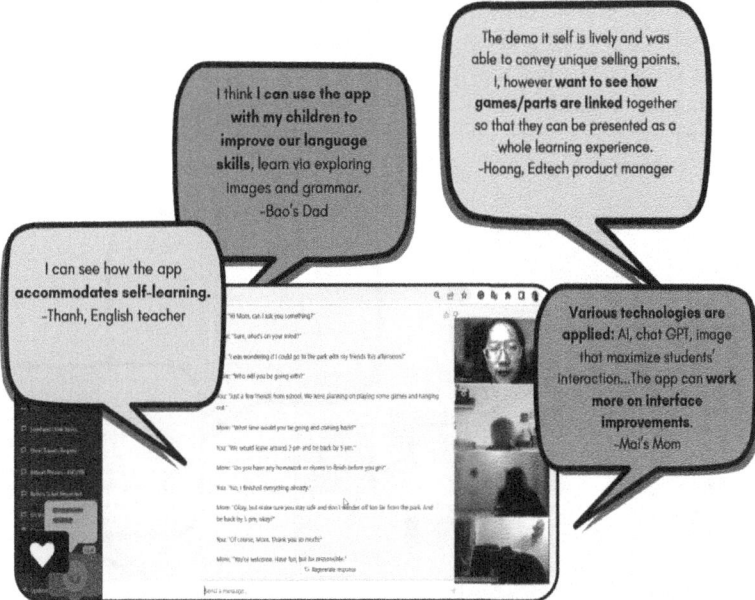

Fig. 13. Testers participated in an app activity by requesting a sample conversation from Chat-GPT

2. My design afforded personalization, which I think, contributed to students' motivation (part of self-determination). Testers' activity engagement and feedback strengthened my conjectures for learning.
3. While there were areas for improvement to further meet learners' needs, my aim for the next prototype is to integrate games/parts to create a seamless learning experience. In the upcoming test, I will prioritize the organization of activities to provide children with a comprehensive experience of the ideas (my role as a "wizard of Oz").

4.3 Implement

Third Iteration. In the third iteration, I conducted five user tests with nine students aged 6–10 whose exposure to English varied (0–5 years of language learning). Testers engaged in activities via Zoom, followed up by semi-structured interviews.

My goals were to explore:

1. How my target audience (elementary school students) think about the test design (what they like, what they do not)
2. Measuring goal 1: How do they see/foresee the learning journey help them improve their knowledge in language? (What can they know?)
3. Measuring goal 2: How do they see/foresee the learning journey to help them improve their language skills? (What can they do/practice doing?)
4. How can my product meet more of their needs?

Verbal and nonverbal feedback from asking questions will help me answer questions about what the testers like or do not like about the design. Verbal cues like questions for clarification and non-verbal cues of interrupting learning can provide ideas for where learning was difficult. Paying attention to verbal cues informs what kind of support is needed. Other verbal responses will inform me of more use cases for the app or questions about what they wish the app could do more and can give me ideas to develop it in the future (Fig. 14).

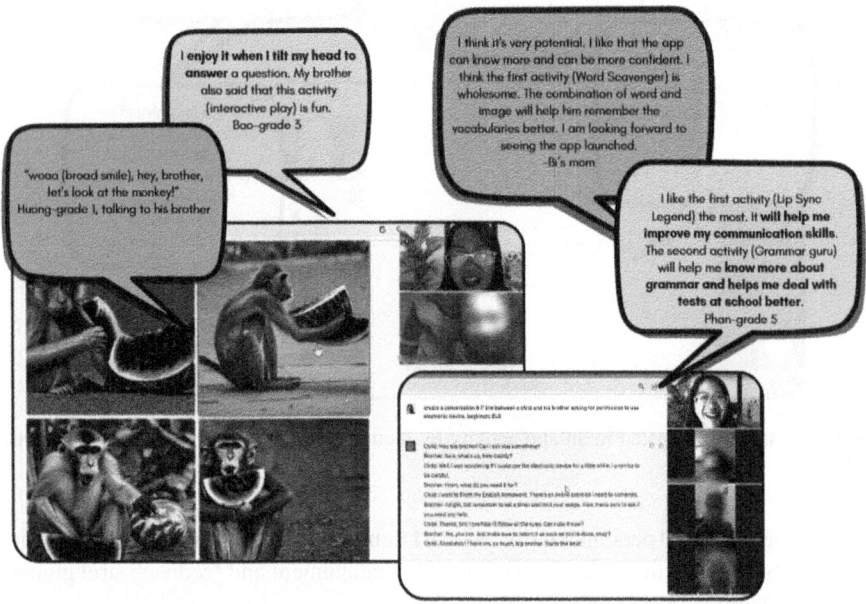

Fig. 14. Testers participated in in-app activities facilitated by researchers and generative AI tools

Main findings:

5. Nine learners were engaged with the design, either via interaction with the surrounding environment, with other learners, having the right challenge and immediate feedback, or having the choice and control over what to learn, and who to learn with.
6. Learners' interactions and feedback inform/strengthen: My conjectures to predict the achievement of my short-term goals [Skills and Confidence], as well as my long-term goal [Attitude]. Since the last iteration, my goal has been to find ways to link games/parts together so that they can be presented as a whole learning experience. I have achieved this goal with the support of the conjecture maps, seeing how parts overlap and supporting different learning experiences for learners.
7. I can further meet their needs by

- Focusing more on the personalization of the learning content for each student (with the support of technology)
- Creating a more dynamic learning experience (with the support of technology)
- The interface needs improvements to suit my target learners

Those will be the focus of future iterations.

5   Discussions and Key Takeaways

5.1   What Worked?

Achieve Design Goals. The LiveLingo project is a constellation of different activities that provide stepping stones for learners to develop their knowledge, skills, and mindsets. Throughout each iteration, feedback showed that learners were engaged and shared that they learned something new through the mock-up interface. The target group expressed their willingness to use it in the future. They recognized the potential of engaging in different activities within the app with their parents, siblings, and friends after school.

Apply Technologies. In Livelingo, technology plays a crucial role in enhancing various aspects of the learning experience. By integrating technology into the language learning program, I aim to enhance sensemaking, foster social-cultural learning, and provide opportunities for creative expression, ultimately creating a dynamic and engaging environment for learners to thrive in their language acquisition journey. Below is a description of how the technology is utilized.

- Sense Making and Mental Model Building:

  - Word Scavenger: Technology creates a space for learners to interact with the learning environment, fostering a social-cultural learning experience. Learners interact with the app to gather vocabulary from their surroundings and apply it in real-life contexts.
  - Interactive Play: Inspired by platforms like TikTok reels, our interactive play feature utilizes technology to encourage collaborative learning among learners. They can engage in language-focused activities together, promoting interaction and social engagement.

- Social-Cultural Learning:

  - Lip Sync Legend: This activity allows learners to interact with other learners, through dubbing and sharing their language practice. Technology facilitates the social aspect of language learning and enables collaboration
  - Picture This, AI: Leveraging technologies like Google Lens and AI-generative arts platforms, learners can unleash their creativity. By converting language into imaginative images, learners can create unique associations and visual representations of vocabulary.

- Creative Expression with Technology and Language:

  - Meme Masters: Through the integration of technology, learners can express theirlanguage skills creatively by creating memes that incorporate linguistic elements. This activity encourages playful language use and sparks creativity.

Design for Social Justice. In designing this language learning program, I have prioritized accessibility, inclusivity, and adaptability. To ensure accessibility, I have developed an app-based platform that allows learners to engage with the program from anywhere, including remote areas where access to traditional language learning resources may be limited.

Throughout the design process, I have actively sought the input and feedback of parents, teachers, and target students, and incorporated their valuable insights into my design. Additionally, options for individual learning or collaborative study were provided, allowing them to choose the learning mode that best suits their preferences and goals. The algorithm embedded in the program is intended to adjust the difficulty level based on learners' progress and performance.

5.2   What Required More Work?

Support Mental Model for Learners. A challenge I encountered in this design process was building a clear mental model for learners, ensuring they understood the purpose of each activity and why they needed to engage in specific tasks. Not until I created the conjecture map, was I able to observe how the different parts overlap and support learners' understanding of the system. As a result, testers started to see how each activity contributed to their comprehension of the content and the trajectory of their language skills. This experience taught me a valuable lesson for future designs: *the importance of building and regularly updating a clear mental model in providing a cohesive learning experience.*

Invite and Sustain Learning. While the concept of learning in my design was intriguing, I recognize that there is room for improvement, particularly in terms of interactions and user experience for young learners. The platform could benefit from further research and exploration to create more intuitive and engaging interactions that cater specifically to the needs and capabilities of young learners. This may involve incorporating elements such as colorful visuals, clear instructions, intuitive icons, and age-appropriate gamification techniques. Additionally, I can explore ways to enhance the interactivity of the platform. This may include incorporating interactive elements like drag-and-drop features, touch interactions, or voice commands to make the learning experience more engaging and interactive for young learners.

5.3   Key Takeaways

Start with Education, Not Technology, in Developing Edtech Products. In developing Edtech products, it is essential to prioritize educational goals over technological capabilities. Designers of digital learning experiences should first establish clear educational objectives and then determine how technology can support and enhance these goals. This approach ensures that the primary focus remains on creating meaningful and effective learning experiences rather than simply incorporating the latest technological advancements.

Thorough research into learning theories and their implications for design should be carefully conducted. A conjecture map can help predict, track, and assess how learning occurs. Additionally, it is crucial to assess both learning and learners' engagement alongside product usability testing. Technology should be viewed as a means to achieve educational aims, not an end itself. This perspective fosters a balanced approach where educational content and technology work together to create impactful and engaging learning experiences for learners.

Testing Digital Learning Designs for Kids. As a designer, it is crucial to test the design to ensure that it meets the desired outcomes. The greatest challenge in initial tests when designing a digital learning experience for kids was that the mockup presentation did not support the expression of ideas, mostly due to the unavailability of technological support. It is important to be creative and flexible in showing the testers my ideas to ensure that testers understand the design and offer feedback in the early stage of the design cycle. *Low-fidelity mock-ups (using papers, or accessible/available technologies tools) should be a potential solution to several first tests. Designers should not rush working with technology.*

From Uncertainty to Confidence: Trusting the Journey of Decision-Making. "It doesn't matter that your decision has changed from your initial plan. What matters is how you arrived at that decision," said Janet Kolodner, my advisor. Initially, my goal was to create a learning app for both children and parents to learn English in an after-school setting. However, after engaging in conversations with parents and witnessing their daily challenges, I decided to shift my focus towards helping children learn the language first. This is how Livelingo came to life.

Janet's wisdom serves as a constant reminder that as learning engineers, we should embrace the fluidity of the design process. *Our decisions may evolve, but it is the thoughtfulness, empathy, and intention behind those decisions that truly matter.* Each decision represents an opportunity for growth, learning, and refining our understanding of how to create meaningful learning experiences.

Acknowledgments. I extend my heartfelt thanks to Elizabeth Rosenzweig for her insightful review of this paper. To my mentors: Janet Kolodner, Cathy Lachapelle, and Brian K Smith, your guidance has been invaluable to my progress. Special appreciation to the Learning Engineering Cohort 2022–2023 at Boston College for your constructed critique and contributions to the project. I am grateful to the participants and my family for their unwavering support.

References

1. Sung, Y.T., Chang, K.E., Yang, J.M.: How effective are mobile devices for language learning? a meta-analysis. Educ. Res. Rev. **16**, 68–84 (2015)
2. Irudayasamy, J., Uba, S.Y., Hankins, C.A.: Exploration and exploitation of mobile apps for english language teaching: a critical review. Engl. Lang. Teach. **14**(4), 43–54 (2021)
3. Sun, Z., Lin, C.H., You, J., Shen, H.J., Qi, S., Luo, L.: Improving the English-speaking skills of young learners through mobile social networking. Comput.-Assist. Lang. Learn. **30**(3–4), 304–324 (2017)

4. Chen, Z., Chen, W., Jia, J., An, H.: The effects of using mobile devices on language learning: a meta-analysis. Educ. Tech. Res. Dev. **68**(4), 1769–1789 (2020)
5. Ulfa, S.: Implementing Mobile Assisted Language Learning in Rural Schools for Enhancing Learning Opportunity ISSN: 2186–5892 – The Asian Conference on Education 2013 – Official Conference Proceedings (2014)
6. Palomino, M.D.C.P.: Implications of mobile learning for sustainable inclusive education: a systematic review. Electr. J. e-Learn. **20**(5), 538–553 (2022)
7. Lim, F.V., Toh, W.: APPS for English language learning: a systematic review. Teach. English Technol. **24**(1) (2024)
8. Son, J.B., Ružić, N.K., Philpott, A.: Artificial intelligence technologies and applications for language learning and teaching. J. China Comput.-Assist. Lang. Learn. (2023)
9. Parmaxi, A., Demetriou, A.A.: Augmented reality in language learning: a state-of-the-art review of 2014–2019. J. Comput. Assist. Learn. **36**(6), 861–875 (2020)
10. Heil, C.R., Wu, J.S., Lee, J.J., Schmidt, T.: A review of mobile language learning applications: trends, challenges, and opportunities. EuroCALL Rev. **24**(2), 32–50 (2016)
11. Brown, A.L.: Design experiments: theoretical and methodological challenges in creating complex interventions in classroom settings. J. Learn. Sci. **2**(2), 141–178 (1992)
12. Goodell, J., Kolodner, J. (eds.). Learning Engineering Toolkit: Evidence-Based Practices from the Learning Sciences, Instructional Design, and Beyond. Taylor & Francis (2022)
13. Norton, P., Hathaway, D.: In search of a teacher education curriculum: appropriating a design lens to solve problems of practice. Educ. Technol. **55**(6), 3–14 (2015). http://www.jstor.org/stable/44430419
14. Shaffer, D.W., Resnick, M.: Thick authenticity: new media and authentic learning. J. Interact. Learn. Res. **10**(2), 195–216 (1999)
15. Glassman, M.: Dewey and Vygotsky: society, experience, and inquiry in educational practice. Educ. Res. **30**(4), 3–14 (2001)
16. Ryan, R.M., Deci, E.L.: Self-determination theory and the facilitation of intrinsic motivation, social development, and well-being. Am. Psychol. **55**(1), 68 (2000)
17. Cantuni, R.: Designing digital products for kids: Deliver user experiences that delight kids, parents, and teachers. Apress (2020)
18. Sandoval, W., sandoval@gseis.ucla.edu.: Conjecture mapping: an approach to systematic educational design research. J. Learn. Sci. **23**(1), 18–36 (2014). https://doi.org/10.1080/10508406.2013.778204
19. Google. Google Lens (2023). https://lens.google/
20. Wordwall. Create better lessons quicker. Wordwall (2023). https://wordwall.net/
21. Open AI. Dall-E2 (2023). https://openai.com/dall-e-2
22. Midjourney Lab. Midjourney (2023). https://www.midjourney.com/home
23. ByteDance, Tiktok (2023)
24. https://play.google.com/store/apps/details?id=com.ss.android.ugc.trill&hl=en&gl=US
25. Open AI. Chat GPT 3.5 (2023). https://chat.openai.com/
26. Synthesia. Synthesia (2023). https://www.synthesia.io/
27. Imgflip LLC. Meme Generator (2023). https://imgflip.com/memegenerator

A Systematic Literature Review on Educational Game Design Research: Based on Bibliometric and Content Analysis (2013–2023)

Xiaoqian Wang and Fan Zou(✉)

College of Computer Science, Sichuan Normal University, Chengdu, China
zoufan@sicnu.edu.cn

Abstract. The design of educational games, as a core part of educational game research, is crucial in promoting practical application and enhancing the educational effectiveness of these games. However, there are still some shortcomings and gaps in current research on educational game design, which urgently need to be systematically sorted and summarized. Therefore, this study adopted a systematic literature review method, based on CNKI and WOS databases, and selected influential journals widely recognized in the field of educational technology as samples. A comprehensive study was conducted on 44 Chinese and 60 English literature on educational game design research published from 2013 to 2023. Firstly, statistical analysis was conducted on the publication and citation status of literature, the distribution characteristics of countries and regions, as well as research hotspots and current trends, using bibliometric methods. Then, the content analysis method was further used to construct a content coding system for educational game design research, including five dimensions: theoretical foundation, specific design, development and implementation, application research, evaluation and reflection, along with secondary coding and specific coding content. Finally, based on this, trends and suggestions for future research on educational game design are proposed, in order to provide useful reference and inspiration for the theoretical and practical development of educational game design.

Keywords: Educational Game Design · Educational Games · Game Design · Game Development · Gamification · Systematic Literature Review

1 Introduction

Educational games serve as an essential teaching method in the field of education. Compared with traditional learning methods, educational games are more conducive to learners' mastery of knowledge and skills [1] reducing learners' cognitive load [2], and enhancing their proactive initiative [3]. However, some studies have also indicated that educational games still pose some challenges, such as the potential for game features to distract students' attention in teaching [4], learners spending more time on game tasks, obscuring the true purpose of learning [5], and inappropriate gamification measures having negative impacts on student engagement and academic performance [6].

P. Zaphiris et al. (Eds.): HCII 2024, LNCS 15378, pp. 175–194, 2025.
https://doi.org/10.1007/978-3-031-76815-6_13

In fact, gamified learning is not simply introducing game elements into the classroom, and educational games are not merely adding a game shell to learning activities [7]. The design of educational games is crucial to achieving a balance between their educational value and gameplay [8]. Under the trend of educational digitization, the development of educational game design research will become a key issue in the field of educational games. Nevertheless, for a long time, research on educational games has focused more on application effects [9] and empirical studies [10], with relatively little attention paid to educational game design research, lacking systematic review and in-depth analysis [11]. Therefore, this study takes this as a starting point, employing bibliometric and content analysis methods to systematically review the current status, hotspots, trends, and content characteristics of educational game design research from 2013 to 2023, aiming to provide theoretical and practical references for the future development of educational game design research. Specific research questions include:

RQ1: What are the current status and trends of educational game design research in the past decade?

RQ2: What are the theoretical foundations of educational game design research?

RQ3: What are the specific design aspects of educational games?

RQ4: Which technologies provide support for the design and development of educational games?

RQ5: What fields and target audiences are educational game design research applied to?

RQ6: What primary methods are used to evaluate and reflect on educational game design research?

2   Research Method

This study employed a systematic literature review methodology, utilizing the *China National Knowledge Infrastructure* (CNKI) and *Web of Science* (WOS) databases. Chinese literature was searched using the key terms " 游戏设计" OR " 游戏开发" in the title field. For English literature, the terms "game design" OR "game development" were used in the title searches. The search spanned from 2013 to 2023. Taking into account factors such as industry recognition and the reference value of the literature, 8 Chinese journals and 11 English journals in the field of educational technology were selected. By applying systematic review and meta-analysis methods [12], a total of 44 eligible Chinese articles and 60 English articles were obtained, summing up to 104 articles.The PRISMA flow diagram is presented in Fig. 1.

3   Research Status

3.1   Publication and Citation of Documents

By sorting the 104 retrieved articles based on their publication dates, we obtained the annual distribution of literature on educational game design research from 2013 to 2023. As shown in Fig. 2, the peaks of Chinese and English literature publications occurred in 2015 and 2018, respectively. After 2019, there was a decline in related research due to

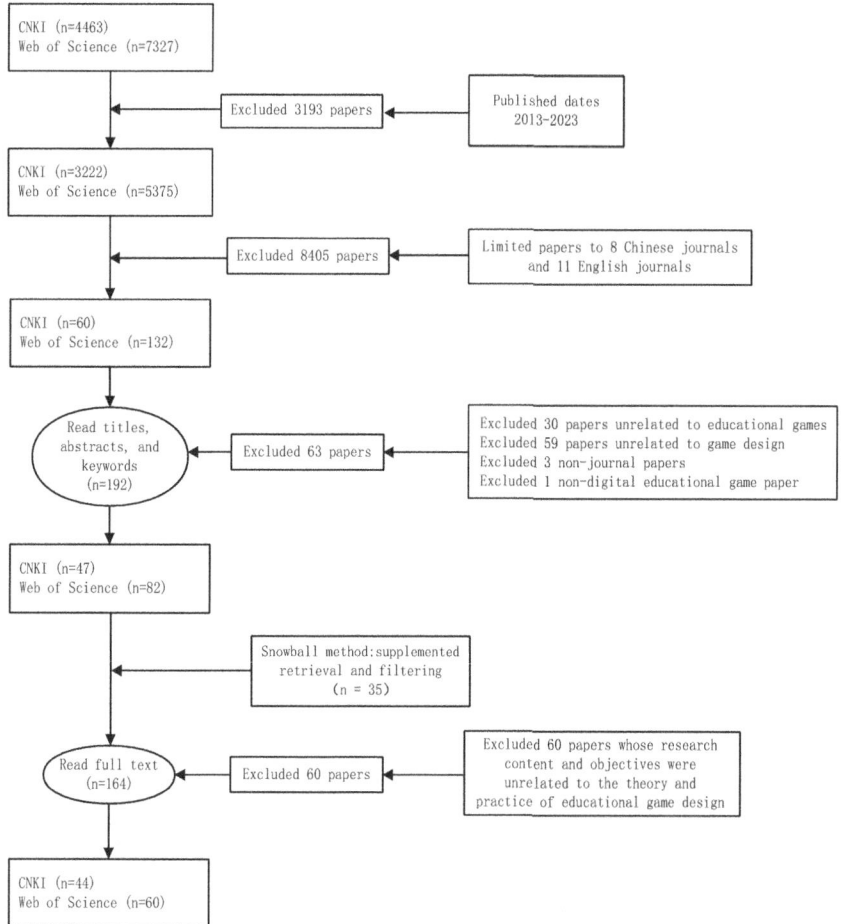

Fig. 1. The PRISMA flow diagram.

the impact of the COVID-19 pandemic. With the advent of the post-pandemic era and the application of technologies such as Big Data, Extended Reality (XR), and Artificial Intelligence (AI) in the education sector, researchers embarked on a new round of discussions and research on educational game design in 2022. By 2023, the number of Chinese publications on educational game design research had declined significantly, while there was still a considerable number of English publications. It is evident that further breakthroughs in educational game design research need to be identified to promote the overall development of the field.

From the perspective of journal distribution, the Chinese journals with the highest number of publications are *"E-education Research"* and *"Modern Educational Technology"*, both with 13 articles; the English journal is *"British Journal of Educational Technology"* with 12 articles in total. In terms of citation rates, 19 articles have a citation rate of over 50, and 7 articles have a citation rate of over 100. Among them, the

English article with the highest number of citations is the one published by Arnab et al. in 2015 (959 citations) [13]. The Chinese article with the highest citation rate is the one published by Wang Yonggu et al. in 2014 (118 citations) [14].

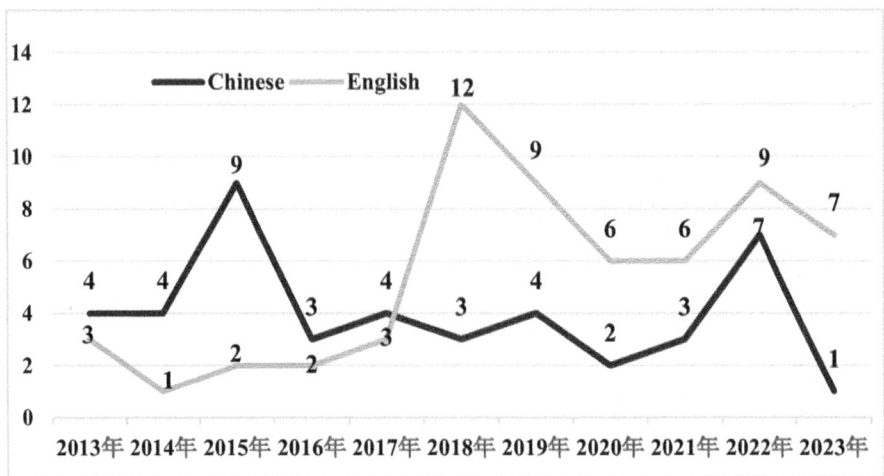

Fig. 2. The number of publications in Chinese and English literature on educational game design research from 2013 to 2023.

3.2 National and Regional Distribution Characteristics

To present the geographical distribution of researchers engaging in the design and research of educational games, a statistical analysis was conducted on 104 articles using CiteSpace software. It was discovered that these researchers originate from a total of 30 countries and regions. Specifically, in terms of the distribution by country and region, apart from Mainland China (46 articles), Taiwan (15 articles), the United Kingdom (7 articles), the United States (6 articles), Finland (5 articles), and Greece (4 articles) are the top five countries or regions with the highest number of publications. And as shown in Fig. 3, Taiwan, as the region with the highest number of English-language publications, does not exhibit a significant trend of collaboration, indicating a lack of international research cooperation and exchange among scholars in Taiwan. In contrast, the regional collaboration networks in the United Kingdom, Finland, and the United States are more prominent, suggesting that authors in these regions have more active international exchanges in the design and research of educational games.

3.3 Research Hotspots and Current Trends

Utilizing the CiteSpace software, a keyword clustering analysis with K-value selection and the "Timeline" visualization option was conducted to reveal the temporal span of each cluster and the interconnectedness between different clusters. A total of five Chinese and six English clusters were obtained. As shown in Figs. 4 and 5, the research

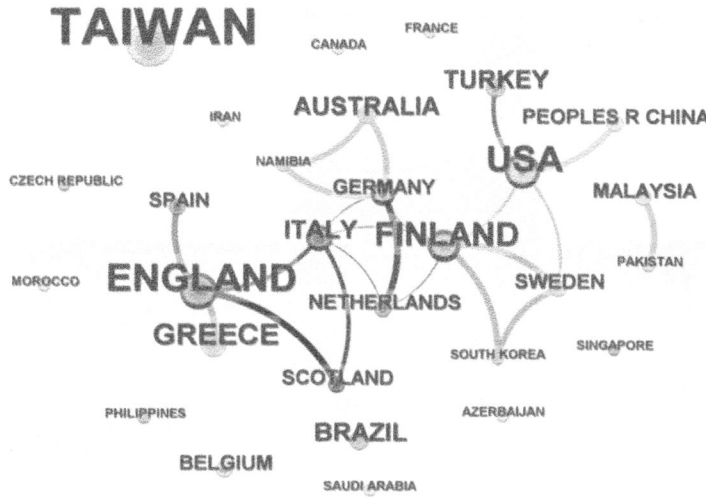

Fig. 3. The national and regional distribution map of English literature on educational game design research from 2013 to 2023.

hotspots in Chinese literature on educational game design include learning sciences, discovery-based learning, puzzle games, and game design strategies, while English literature covers serious games and educational games, flow theory, multimedia learning for young children, design-based research, and neurosciences.

Furthermore, the burst detection algorithm was employed to determine the research frontiers and development trends based on changes in word frequencies. Figures 6 and 7 reveal that: (1) "增强现实" and "framework" are the earliest emerging keywords in Chinese and English literature, respectively; (2) "数学认知" and "performance" have the highest burst strengths in their respective domains; (3) the duration of burst keywords is mostly concentrated in 2–3 years, indicating the rich variety and rapid iteration speed of research topics in educational game design; (4) there are some similar burst keywords in both Chinese and English literature with longer durations, such as "计算思维", "computational thinking", "增强现实", "virtual reality," suggesting that computational thinking learning and extended reality technologies will remain key research areas in educational game design from the present to the future; (5) burst keywords in Chinese and English literature exhibit different characteristics in different periods. Specifically, the earliest burst keywords in Chinese literature appeared in 2017. From 2017 to 2020, researchers discussed "数学学习" and "电子游戏", while since 2021, the focus has shifted to new areas such as "计算思维" and "学习科学".The burst keywords in English literature emerged earlier than in Chinese literature, discussing "framework," "performance," and "interactive learning environments" from 2015 to 2018, and emphasizing "behavior," "challenges," and "knowledge" since 2019. In summary, Chinese literature primarily focuses on the application domains of educational game design, while English literature emphasizes learner performance in the application of educational game design.

Although the focuses differ, it is foreseeable that both directions will advance towards the innovative trend of technology integration, aiming to design and develop quality educational games for learners.

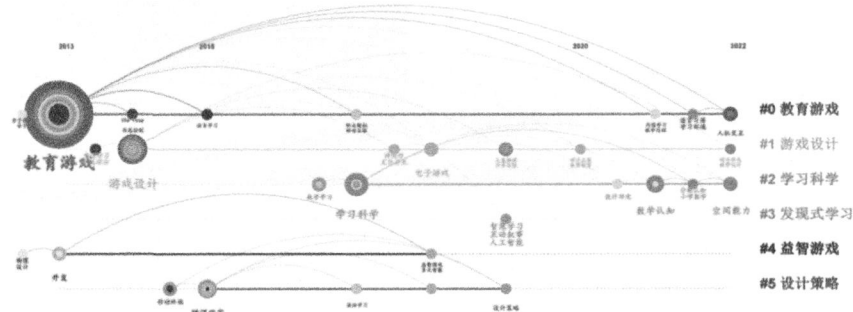

Fig. 4. The timeline clustering map of keywords in Chinese literature on educational game design research from 2013 to 2023.

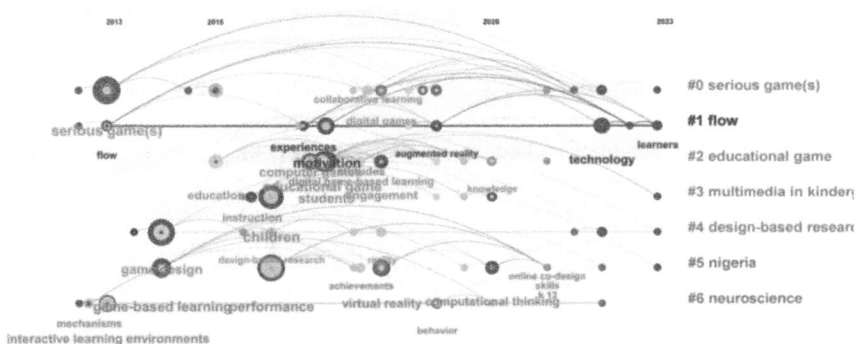

Fig. 5. The timeline clustering map of keywords in English literature on educational game design research from 2013 to 2023.

4   Results

Based on the aforementioned work, to further explore the development process of educational game design research, after referring to relevant analytical frameworks and coding systems [15], this study established a content coding framework encompassing five dimensions: theoretical foundations, specific design, development and implementation, application research, evaluation and reflection. It is worth noting that, considering the multifaceted and multi-angled nature of the literature on the topic of "educational game design," this study permits documents to belong to multiple categories simultaneously, aiming to better capture the interconnections between different aspects. The specific coding results are presented in Table 1.

Top 8 Keywords with the Strongest Citation Bursts

Keywords	Year	Strength	Begin	End	2013 - 2023
增强现实	2015	1.01	2017	2019	
数学学习	2017	0.85	2017	2019	
游戏设计	2014	0.53	2017	2020	
电子游戏	2018	0.91	2018	2020	
儿童编程	2019	0.46	2019	2023	
计算思维	2019	0.46	2019	2023	
数学认知	2021	1.24	2021	2023	
学习科学	2017	1.08	2021	2023	

Fig. 6. The keywords burst map of Chinese literature on educational game design research from 2013 to 2023.

Top 16 Keywords with the Strongest Citation Bursts

Keywords	Year	Strength	Begin	End	2013 - 2023
framework	2015	2.17	2015	2017	
performance	2016	2.71	2016	2018	
design-based research	2016	0.74	2016	2018	
students	2017	2.17	2017	2018	
interactive learning environments	2013	1.07	2017	2018	
education	2015	0.91	2018	2019	
digital game-based learning	2018	0.8	2018	2019	
attitudes	2018	0.61	2018	2020	
educational game	2017	1.42	2019	2020	
game design	2014	1.01	2019	2020	
behavior	2019	0.93	2019	2023	
challenges	2019	0.62	2019	2023	
computational thinking	2020	1.18	2020	2023	
knowledge	2020	1.08	2020	2021	
virtual reality	2018	1.18	2021	2023	
digital games	2018	0.84	2021	2023	

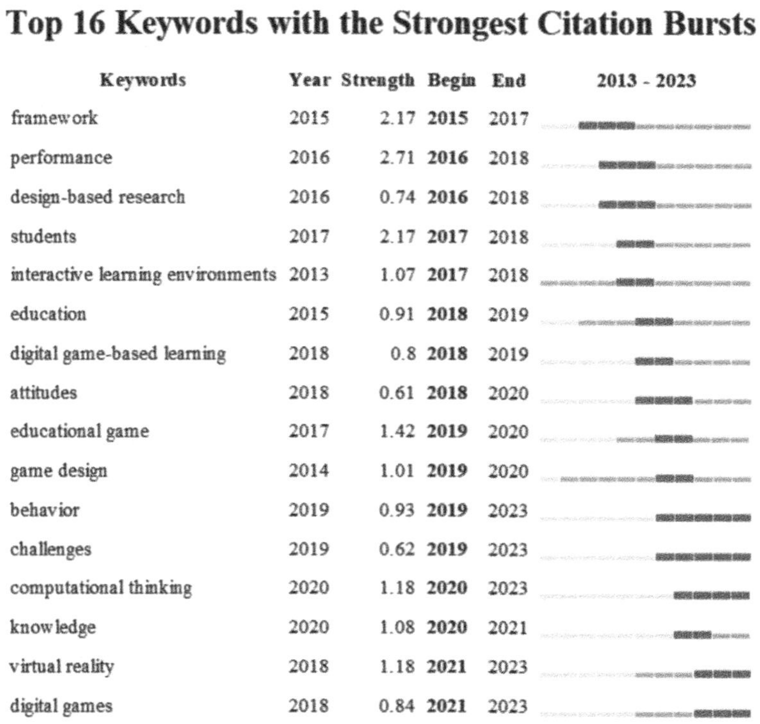

Fig. 7. The keywords burst map of English literature on educational game design research from 2013 to 2023.

Table 1. Content analysis of the coding system.

First-level Category	Second-level Category	Content Code
Theoretical Foundations	Subject Theories	Educational theory, psychological theory, sociological theory, neuroscience theory, computer science theory, interdisciplinary theory
	Design Frameworks/ Models	Classic game design frameworks/models, innovative game design frameworks/models, others
	Design Strategies/Principles	Gameplay strategies and principles, educational strategies and principles, integrative strategies and principles
Specific Design	Game Element Design	Character design, level design, UI design, interaction design, sound and music design, visual arts and animation design, others
	Game Mechanism Design	Game types and characteristics, correlation between game mechanics and learning objectives, optimization and improvement of game mechanics, others
	Game Scenario Design	Story scenario design, social scenario design, reality based design, virtual reality scenario design, cross cultural scenario design, others
	Game Strategy Design	Learning strategy design, adaptive adjustment strategies, personalized learning strategies, team collaboration strategies, individualgrowth strategies, others
Development and Implementation	Developers	Research teams, business, RPP
	Development Tools	Fill in according to actual circumstances

(*continued*)

Table 1. (*continued*)

First-level Category	Second-level Category	Content Code
	Development Technologies	Game engine development technology, graphic rendering technology, augmented reality technology, artificial intelligence and machine learning technology, network communication technology, programming technology, others
	Game Platforms	PC, mobile, web, cross-platform, others
Application Research	Educational Stage	K12, higher education, adult education, lifelong learning, others
	Disciplinary Fields	Natural science field (STEM), humanities and social sciences field, interdisciplinary field, others
	Application Targets	Students, teachers, parents, special education recipients, others
	Application Environments	Formal learning environment, informal learning environment, others
Evaluation and Reflection	Research Design	Experiment and quasi-experiment, case study, survey, design-based research, others
	Research Methods	Qualitative research, quantitative research, mixed methods research
	Number of Participants	Small-scale experiment (<50 people), medium-scale experiment (50–100 people), large-scale experiment (>100 people), extra-large scale experiment (>1000 people)
	Research Duration	Single-time, short-term (<6 months), medium-term (6–12 months), long-term (>12 months)
	Evaluation Indicators	Learning effectiveness, game enjoyment, educational applicability, technological implementation,others

(*continued*)

Table 1. (*continued*)

First-level Category	Second-level Category	Content Code
	Data Collection	Survey, interviews, observation, case studies, log analysis, expert reviews, long term tracking data collection and analysis, others
	Technical Tools	Data collection software, data collection devices,data storage and management tools
	Data Analysis	Content analysis, discourse analysis, descriptive statistics, inferential statistics, data visualization and interactive technology, machine learning anddata mining, emerging technologies, others

4.1 Theoretical Research

Applying Multidisciplinary Theoretical Foundations. The theoretical basis for educational game design incorporates theoretical achievements from multiple disciplines such as education, psychology, and sociology. A total of 37 articles explicitly mentioned the application of relevant theories. Among them, flow theory was the most frequently mentioned, with a total of 8 articles referencing it. These theories not only focus on the learning experience and motivation during gameplay, but also delve into various levels such as cognitive learning and educational design. At the same time, researchers have come to realize that a singular theoretical perspective is insufficient to comprehensively address the complexity of educational game design. Therefore, they have sought new design inspirations from interdisciplinary fields such as educational neuroscience [16] and learning sciences [17]. Additionally, with the development of computer science theory, this perspective can also be explored further to support and optimize the design research of educational games in the future.

Constructing Game Design Framework Models. Utilizing appropriate theoretical guidance in the design and development process of educational games is crucial to ensuring their effectiveness. While existing theories elucidate the learning process within games, they fail to provide specific guidance for the design of different types of educational games. Therefore, researchers have constructed game design models under the framework of these theories to support game development. A total of 40 articles mentioned frameworks and models related to game design, among which the 4DF framework proposed by De Freitas et al. [18] and the LM-GM model introduced by Arnab et al. [13] are widely recognized and utilized. Additionally, numerous studies have constructed more targeted and personalized frameworks and models based on their specific needs, such as the sequence data analysis (SDA)-driven methodological framework implemented by Liu et al. [19]. However, there is still a lack of a perfect framework model suitable for all educational games. Consequently, researchers should focus on integrating teaching elements and game mechanics, balancing educational and gameplay characteristics, to propose a standardized and unified design approach. Future research should strive to construct a robust and comprehensive framework or model to guide the design and development process of educational games.

Integrated Game Design Strategies and Principles. The design strategies and principles of educational games play an essential role in guiding their research, design, and development, and ensure consistency in the research process. This study found that in 21 relevant articles, scholars explored these strategies and principles from various perspectives, including knowledge and skills [18], learning environments [21], and interactive modes [22]. Essentially, these strategies and principles involve discussions on the integration of education and games at different and unified levels. The educational dimension focuses on clarifying teaching objectives and optimizing learning content to ensure that the game experience effectively supports the learning process. Meanwhile, the gaming dimension emphasizes innovative design of game elements and mechanisms, aiming to enhance the attractiveness and fun of the game. Ultimately, these two dimensions are bridged from theory to practice through technological means. In the future, the design research of educational games can incorporate integrated design strategies and principles of education and games, integrate emerging technological tools, fully utilize innovative game elements, and align with educational goals to guide the design and practice of educational games.

4.2 Specific Design Research

Core Elements in Educational Game Design. In the realm of educational game design, game elements and mechanisms constitute the foundation of the gaming experience. Among the 18 pieces of literature that focus on the design of game elements, visual art design has garnered significant attention. Educational game designers are advised to prioritize the creation of engaging visual elements to enhance the attractiveness of educational games. Game mechanisms, as the executors of game elements, ensure the playability and rules of educational games. In 23 articles, researchers not only delve into how game mechanisms can be designed to clarify the type and characteristics of games, but also explore the integration of game mechanisms with game elements [23], educational goals [24] and how they support and influence the game learning process [25]. It is crucial to note that excessive gamification can also lead to suboptimal learning outcomes [26]. Therefore, researchers should base their work on educational objectives, adequately consider learners' information processing capabilities and cognitive load, and streamline and optimize game mechanisms to ensure their substantive educational value.

Context design is a crucial aspect in educational games, involving the interaction between learners and their environment. In 29 articles, researchers emphasize the role of context in stimulating learner engagement and developing capabilities. Through contextual designs such as storylines [27], role interactions [28], and technological tools like virtual reality [29], educational games offer a more immersive learning experience compared to traditional classroom teaching. To enhance the inclusiveness and accessibility of games, future considerations could include the integration of cross-cultural context design and cultural adaptability to cater to learners from diverse cultural backgrounds.

Adaptive and Personalized Learning Strategies in Educational Games. With the evolving educational paradigm, more attention is being paid to individual differences among students. Researchers are actively exploring adaptive and personalized gaming strategies to cater to the behavioral preferences of different learners. Twelve articles highlight the implementation of adaptive and personalized gaming strategies, which not only enhance learning outcomes but also provide new learning opportunities for learners from special groups [30]. Furthermore, with the advancement of intelligent technologies, the design of educational games will become more intelligent through the utilization of advanced data analysis, intelligent assistance, and automated assessment systems. Therefore, in future educational game design, more emphasis will be placed on the application of adaptive and personalized learning strategies, leveraging intelligent technologies to provide learners with a more personalized and equitable learning experience.

4.3   Development Research

Interdisciplinary Teams and Student Involvement in Design. The design teams for educational games are often led by educational technology researchers, but collaboration with multi-expert teams from educational institutions and gaming companies can enhance the diversity and comprehensiveness of designs, benefiting a wider range of game users. The Researcher-Practitioner Partnership (RPP) [31] facilitates knowledge sharing, bidirectional learning, and more effective design of educational games. In this study, 14 pieces of literature emphasize the importance of school-enterprise cooperation and the participation of subject matter experts, with 5 articles involving learners participating in game design themselves.

With the advancement of technology and the increasing complexity of educational game design, the significance of RPP will become even more prominent. Collaboration among interdisciplinary teams will inject new inspiration into the design and development of educational games. Involving learners, as users, throughout the entire game design process will help improve the effectiveness and stickiness of educational games, stimulate learners' creative thinking. Therefore, further research should be conducted to explore how to better promote innovation and development in educational game design research through RPP.

Development Technologies and Game Platforms. The development of information technology has brought significant leaps in the design and development of educational games. In this study, 27 pieces of literature focus on the development technologies of educational games, ranging from Flash [32] to the Unity3D [33]. Additionally, AI [34] and HCI [35] play crucial roles in enhancing game quality and player experience. In the future, with the increasing demands for educational games and technological advancements, more efforts can be made to explore educational game development technologies utilizing advancements in network communication, generative artificial intelligence, and related fields.

On the other hand, the choice of game platforms often depends on the target audience, technical equipment, and the characteristics of game content and design. With the increasing demands of learners and technological advancements, extended reality technologies and wearable devices also provide new development tools and application platforms for educational games. Students can experience educational games through devices such as virtual reality head-mounted displays (HMD) 36. In the future, research on cross-platform educational game design can be further expanded to be compatible with various operating systems and devices, satisfying the seamless transition between formal and informal learning as well as learners' lifelong learning needs.

4.4 Applied Research

Educational Stage and Subject Areas. In the past decade of research on educational game design, applications in different educational stages and subject areas have exhibited certain characteristics. As indicated in the statistical results from Fig. 8 (excluding 22 pieces of literature that did not involve specific educational stages or subjects, and 13 pieces that targeted a broad audience or did not specify the research subjects as "others"), the primary education stage has been the focus of research, with elementary education standing out particularly (30 articles), while research on preschool education (14 articles), secondary education (12 articles), and higher education (11 articles) is relatively balanced. Research in the field of adult education is relatively scarce, with only 2 pieces of literature addressing this area. This distribution may reflect the difficulty of designing and developing educational games for different educational stages, their application effects, and the characteristics of the target audience. It also suggests that further research is needed in the field of adult education and lifelong learning regarding the design of educational games.

In terms of subject areas, research on educational game design covers natural sciences (STEM), humanities and social sciences, as well as interdisciplinary fields. Specifically, the field of "language learning" is the most extensively studied (18 articles), "mathematics education" (10 articles), "science education"(9 articles), "social science education" (9 articles), "computer science education" (9 articles), and "special education" (9 articles). In contrast, research in "art education" (4 articles), "health education" (3 articles), and "vocational education" (2 articles) has increased in recent years, but the number is still relatively small. To better meet the educational needs of different fields, future research can strengthen its focus on these subject areas, and further explore interdisciplinary game design research.

Application Object and Environment. The object and environment of educational game design are closely related to their respective subject areas and educational stages. Educational games targeting basic subjects and the primary education stage are primarily designed for students and teachers to be used in formal learning environments such as classrooms and schoolrooms. Their designs are often closely aligned with curriculum standards and course content. Meanwhile, games focused on literacy cultivation and ability enhancement for a general audience tend to be more inclined towards informal learning environments that are online and connected.

Notably, the design of educational games for special groups has always been a focus of attention. These games aim to meet learning needs in special environments such as families and rehabilitation institutions. For instance, the tabletop game designed by

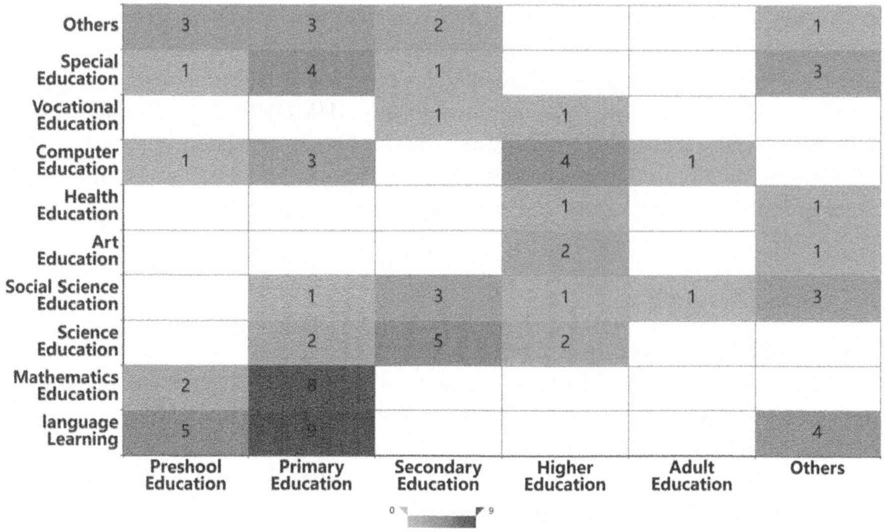

	Preschool Education	Primary Education	Secondary Education	Higher Education	Adult Education	Others
Others	3	3	2			1
Special Education	1	4	1			3
Vocational Education			1	1		
Computer Education	1	3		4	1	
Health Education				1		1
Art Education				2		1
Social Science Education		1	3	1	1	3
Science Education		2	5	2		
Mathematics Education	2	8				
language Learning	5	9				4

0 — 9

Fig. 8. Statistical Classification by Educational Stage and Subject areas for Chinese and English Educational Game Design Research Literature.

Korozi et al. [37] for children with cognitive impairments has been implemented in rehabilitation centers for children with disabilities. The design of educational games for special groups emphasizes customization functions, providing highly inclusive, adaptive, and personalized learning experiences based on an in-depth analysis of the needs of user groups. This feature distinguishes educational games from traditional education, making them powerful tools to help special groups overcome learning barriers and enhance their learning potential.

Overall, in the past decade, the application areas and research objects of educational game design have exhibited a wide range. While research on basic education and basic subjects remains the focus, with the evolution of technological innovation, the goals of talent cultivation in the intelligent era have also changed, with a greater emphasis on fostering learners' thinking activities, innovation, creativity, problem-solving abilities, and comprehensive quality improvement. On this basis, educational game design needs to incorporate deeper and more diverse learning content to meet the diverse needs of learners.

4.5 Evaluation and Reflection

Characteristics of Research Methodology. In the evaluation and reflection studies of educational game design, researchers have adopted a diverse range of research methods, including experimental studies, case studies, and surveys. Among these, experimental and quasi-experimental studies are the most prevalent (39 articles). Additionally, there are 9 case studies focusing on individuals or groups [38] and 5 survey studies that gather, analyze, and interpret data to answer research questions [39]. Design-based research has also gained increasing popularity (7 articles) [40]. Other studies (10 articles) primarily involve testing and evaluating game products from the perspectives of experts and teachers [41]. This evaluation method provides crucial insights into game design and practical application from a professional standpoint, which can be conducted alongside learner testing to ensure a more comprehensive and effective assessment of educational game design.

Overall, most studies have employed quantitative research (37 articles) and mixed-method approaches combining both quantitative and qualitative methods (22 articles). Furthermore, there are 12 purely qualitative analyses, most of which target younger special groups [42]. Due to the special conditions of cognitive abilities and physical development in this group, qualitative methods such as observation and interviews are more suitable. To address this limitation, future researchers need to explore more intelligent and multimodal data collection methods, such as electroencephalography (EEG), eye-tracking, and emotion recognition, to conduct scientific and effective statistical analysis of the research process and results.

Participant Numbers and Research Duration. In the evaluation studies of educational game design over the past decade, small-scale studies with fewer than 50 participants are the most common (31 articles), followed by medium-scale studies with 50–100 participants (13 articles). There are also some studies with sample sizes exceeding 500 participants (3 articles), among which Karoui et al.'s [43] study involving 1,389 students is the largest.

Most studies did not explicitly propose a time period, with 43 studies counting as single-intervention studies measured in class hours. The second largest category is short-term studies (within 6 months) with 19 articles, and there are also 5 long-term studies (over one year). Among them, the longest time period is a four-year multi-round iterative study conducted by Kara et al. [44]. More long-term tracking and diverse testing methods are needed in future research to enhance the reliability and persuasiveness of the findings.

Data Collection and Analysis. In the evaluation of educational game design, researchers have also employed a variety of data collection and analysis methods. For qualitative data, interviews (16 articles) and observations (8 articles) are primarily used to gather students' subjective perceptions and suggestions on the gaming experience, combined with content analysis of game data (6 articles), video materials (5 articles), and other sources. Quantitative data analysis includes descriptive statistics such as testing (33 articles) and questionnaires (27 articles), as well as various statistical analysis methods such as T-tests (21 articles) and ANOVA (19 articles). In the evaluation studies of educational game design, a diverse range of data collection and analysis methods should be selected to increase the reliability and validity of the research.

Moreover, current research on educational game design mostly focuses on evaluating game experience, learning outcomes, and the application value of games, with little attention paid to the assessment of game performance and algorithm optimization from a technical perspective. On the other hand, the advantages of diverse multimodal data collection, acquisition, storage, and management methods are gradually being demonstrated. For instance, Wu et al. [45] employed the State-Space Grid (SSG) measurement method to capture the number of cells when students engage in game experiences. In the future, with the development of emerging technologies such as multimodal data collection and analysis methods, it will become possible to utilize cloud platforms to record, analyze, and manage user behavior data. Combining physiological signal analysis such as eye-tracking [46] can capture learners' dynamic learning processes, enabling a more comprehensive evaluation of educational game design.

5   Conclusion and Outlook

As an essential tool in the digital transformation of education, the design of educational games has garnered significant attention. Through a systematic review of the literature spanning the past decade, this study has thoroughly examined the current research status, hot topics, trends, and content characteristics of educational game design, aiming to provide theoretical and practical references for future research. It is anticipated that with the continuous advancement of technology and the evolution of educational concepts, the design research of educational games will delve deeper into the following aspects in the future.

5.1   Integration of Interdisciplinary Theories

The theoretical foundation of educational game design is no longer confined to education and psychology alone. Disciplines such as neuroscience, cognitive science, biological science, sociology, and even economics will provide a more comprehensive perspective and in-depth theoretical support for educational game design. Furthermore, scholars and practitioners from different fields will strengthen their collaboration and exchanges (RPP), jointly promoting the development and innovation of the field of educational games. This will help break through the limitations of a single discipline, open up new research ideas and methods, and provide broader theoretical support and practical guidance for educational game design.

5.2   Emergence of Boundary-Less Learning

With technological advancements, the design research of educational games will inevitably achieve cross-platform and cloud-based integration, breaking the traditional limitations of classrooms and learning devices. This will enable students to access the cloud at any time and any place through smart devices, seamlessly switching between learning scenarios and content, realizing boundary-less learning.

5.3   Emphasis on Personalized Learning and Adaptive Design

Driven by emerging technologies such as big data, human-computer interaction and artificial intelligence, educational games will be more personalized and adaptive. Related design research will focus on learners and pay more attention to innovative game design frameworks that promote personalized learning, including personalized game element design such as learner preferences, skill levels, and learning styles; inclusive game design for special groups; personalized learning path design; intelligent and adaptive game mechanisms, and collaborative strategy design and optimization to promote learners.

5.4 Deep Integration of Game Mechanics and Educational Goals

The core of educational game design lies in the deep integration of game mechanics and educational goals. Designers need to have a profound understanding of learning theories and skillfully integrate educational goals into game mechanics, enabling learners to achieve learning objectives while enjoying the fun of the game. This integration will help enhance learners' interest and motivation, promoting knowledge construction and transfer.

5.5 Enhancement of Scenario Creation and Emotional Experience

Utilizing technologies such as virtual reality, augmented reality, and mixed reality, educational game design will pay more attention to scenario creation and emotional experience. By designing cross-cultural, collaborative, and social interactive scenarios, real and enriched contexts will be created, enhancing learners' emotional experience, cognitive engagement, and emotional resonance, further strengthening learning outcomes. Additionally, emotional design will also focus more on learners' psychological feelings, making the game process more enjoyable and attractive.

5.6 Normalization of Continuous Evaluation and Reflection

In the future, with the development of data science and machine learning, the evaluation of educational games will be more scientific and objective, and will continue to pay attention to the learning input, emotional experience and learning effect of learners, providing scientific evidence for the improvement and optimization of educational games. By collecting and analyzing learners' multimodal data (e.g., behavioral data, physiological data) in real-time, the learning characteristics and patterns of learners can be deeply explored, providing strong support for the innovation and personalized design of educational games.

Acknowledgments. The work presented in this paper was supported by the Scientific Research Fund of Sichuan Normal University under grant number 22XW071.

Disclosure of Interests. The authors have no competing interests to declare that are relevant to the content of this article.

References

1. Clark, D.B., Tanner-Smith, E.E., Killingsworth, S.S.: Digital games, design, and learning: a systematic review and meta-analysis. Rev. Educ. Res. **86**(1), 79–122 (2016)
2. Chang, C.C., Liang, C., Chou, P.N., Lin, G.Y.: Is game-based learning better in flow experience and various types of cognitive load than non-game-based learning? perspective from multimedia and media richness. Comput. Hum. Behav. **71**, 218–227 (2017)
3. He, W.B., Dong, Y.Q.: Research on the influence of educational games on students' learning effect ——meta-analysis based on 41 experiments and quasi-experiments. Mod. Educ. Technol. **4**, 44–50 (2021)

4. Mayer, R.E., Moreno, R.: Nine ways to reduce cognitive load in multimedia learning. Educ. Psychol. **38**(1), 43–52 (2003)
5. Miranda, A.T., Palmer, E.M.: Intrinsic motivation and attentional capture from gamelike features in a visual search task. Behav. Res. Methods **46**, 159–172 (2014)
6. Hsu, C.C., Wang, T.I.: Applying game mechanics and student-generated questions to an online puzzle-based game learning system to promote algorithmic thinking skills. Comput. Educ. **121**, 73–88 (2018)
7. Shang, J.J., Xiao, H.M., Jia, L.: An empirical research review of international educational games: 2008–2012. E-Educ. Res. **35**(01), 71–78 (2014)
8. Wei, T., Li, Y.: Review of educational game design at home and abroad. J. Dist. Educ. **17**(03), 67–70 (2009)
9. De Freitas, S.: Are games effective learning tools? a review of educational games. J. Educ. Technol. Soc. **21**(2), 74–84 (2018)
10. Gu, Y.W., Zhang, J.Y., Zhang, K.Y., Chiang, F.G.: Literature review of international empirical studies on game-based learning in the past five years. J. Open Learn. **25**(04), 10–18 (2020)
11. Laine, T.H., Lindberg, R.S.: Designing engaging games for education: a systematic literature review on game motivators and design principles. IEEE Trans. Learn. Technol. **13**(4), 804–821 (2020)
12. Page, M.J.,e t al.: The PRISMA 2020 statement: an updated guideline for reporting systematic reviews Bmj, **372** (2021)
13. Arnab, S., et al.: Mapping learning and game mechanics for serious games analysis. Br. J. Educ. Technol. **46**(2), 391–411 (2015)
14. Wang, Y.G., Zhang, T., Li, W., Huang, B.Y.: Elements of educational game designing framework based on flow theory: a case study of the speech learning games for exceptional children. J. Dist. Educ. **32**(03), 97–104 (2014)
15. Zhao, Y.Y., Shun, D.E., Shang, J.J.: A literature review of empirical studies on educational games based on bibliometric and content analysis. J. Open Learn **29**(05), 106–120 (2023)
16. Pei, L.S., Shang, J.J., Zhou, X.L.: The design of educational games based on learning sciences. E-Educ. Res. **10**, 60–69 (2017)
17. Shang, J.J., Zeng, J.L., Zhou, J.Y.: Research on design and application of mathematical spatial games from learning sciences perspective. E-Educ. Res. **43**(07), 63–72 (2022)
18. De Freitas, S., Oliver, M.: How can exploratory learning with games and simulations within the curriculum be most effectively evaluated? Comput. Educ. **46**(3), 249–264 (2006)
19. Liu, Z., Moon, J.: A framework for applying sequential data analytics to design personalized digital game-based learning for computing education. Educ. Technol. Soc. **26**(2), 181–197 (2023)
20. Chen, J.C., Liu, F., Chen, L., Wang, C.R.: Research on the design principle of mobile learning game based on distributed cognition theory. E-Educ. Res. **37**(11), 60–668 (2016)
21. Lan, Y.J., Hsiao, I.Y., Shih, M.F.: Effective learning design of game-based 3D virtual language learning environments for special education students. J. Educ. Technol. Soc. **21**(3), 213–227 (2018)
22. Wei, X.D., Zhang, K.: A study on strategies of game design for second language education. E-Educ. Res. **43**(05), 70–75+108 (2022)
23. Chou, Y.S., Hou, H.T., Chang, K.E., Su, C.L.: Designing cognitive-based game mechanisms for mobile educational games to promote cognitive thinking: an analysis of flow state and game-based learning behavioral patterns. Interact. Learn. Environ. **31**(5), 3285–3302 (2023)
24. Jiang, X.N., Li, Y., He, W., Chen, S.H.: The design and case analysis of popular science games based on knowledge classification theory. Mod. Educ. Technol. **31**(06), 49–55 (2021)
25. Gresalfi, M.S., Barnes, J.: Designing feedback in an immersive video game: supporting student mathematical engagement. Educ. Tech. Res. Dev. **64**, 65–86 (2016)

26. Wang, Y.H.: Can gamification assist learning? a study to design and explore the uses of educational music games for adults and young learners. J. Educ. Comput. Res. **60**(8), 2015–2035 (2023)

27. Hao, K.C., Lee, L.C.: The development and evaluation of an educational game integrating augmented reality, ARCS model, and types of games for English experiment learning: an analysis of learning. Interact. Learn. Environ. **29**(7), 1101–1114 (2021)

28. Chan, H.Y., Liu, S.W., Hou, H.T.: Interacting with real-person non-player characters to learn history: development and playing behavior pattern analysis of a remote scaffolding-based situated educational game. Interact. Learn. Environ. 1–21 (2023)

29. Agbo, F.J., Oyelere, S.S., Suhonen, J., Tukiainen, M.: Design, development, and evaluation of a virtual reality game-based application to support computational thinking. Educ. Tech. Res. Dev. **71**(2), 505–537 (2023)

30. Neto, L.V., Junior, P.H.F., Bordini, R.A., Otsuka, J.L., Beder, D.M.: Details on the design and evaluation process of an educational game considering issues for visually impaired people inclusion. J. Educ. Technol. Soc. **22**(3), 4–18 (2019)

31. Coburn, C.E., Penuel, W.R., Geil, K.E.: Practice partnerships: a strategy for leveraging research for educational improvement in school districts. William T. Grant Foundation (2013)

32. Li, W., Zhao, W., Ma, J.: Design and development of the secondary school physics education game based on Flash + XML. E-Educ. Res. **07**, 86–90 (2013)

33. Ramli, R.Z., et al.: Designing a mobile learning application model by integrating augmented reality and game elements to improve student learning experience. Educ. Inf. Technol. **29**(2), 1981–2008 (2024)

34. Wang, G.X., Wang, Y.: Using narrative games to enhance smart learning: game development and learning effectiveness verification. Distance Educ. China (10), 20–28+92–93 (2019)

35. Goli, A., Teymournia, F., Naemabadi, M., Garmaroodi, A.A.: Architectural design game: a serious game approach to promote teaching and learning using multimodal interfaces. Educ. Inf. Technol. **27**(8), 11467–11498 (2022)

36. Boel, C., Rotsaert, T., Valcke, M., Vanhulsel, A., Schellens, T.: Applying educational design research to develop a low-cost, mobile immersive virtual reality serious game teaching safety in secondary vocational education. Educ. Inf. Technol. 1–38 (2023)

37. Korozi, M., et al.: Designing an augmented tabletop game for children with cognitive disabilities: the home game case. Br. J. Edu. Technol. **49**(4), 701–716 (2018)

38. Benton, L., et al.: Designing for "challenge" in a large-scale adaptive literacy game for primary school children. Br. J. Educ. Technol. **52**(5), 1862–1880 (2021)

39. Beavis, C., O'Mara, J., Thompson, R.: Digital games in the museum: perspectives and priorities in videogame design. Learn. Media Technol. **46**(3), 294–305 (2021)

40. Zeng, J.L., Zhang, P., Shang, J.J.: Design-based research and applications in educational game design. E-Educ. Res. **08**, 32–40 (2022)

41. Filippas, A., Xinogalos, S.: Elementium: design and pilot evaluation of a serious game for familiarizing players with basic chemistry. Educ. Inf. Technol. **28**(11), 14721–14746 (2023)

42. Merilampi, S., Koivisto, A., Sirkka, A.: Designing serious games for special user groups—design for somebody approach. Br. J. Edu. Technol. **49**(4), 646–658 (2018)

43. Karoui, A., Marfisi-Schottman, I., George, S.: JEM Inventor: a mobile learning game authoring tool based on a nested design approach. Interact. Learn. Environ. **30**(10), 1851–1878 (2022)

44. Kara, E., Cagiltay, K.: Using E-textiles to design and develop educational games for preschool-aged children. Educ. Technol. Soc. **26**(2), 19–35 (2023)
45. Wu, L., Kim, M., Markauskaite, L.: Developing young children's empathic perception through digitally mediated interpersonal experience: Principles for a hybrid design of empathy games. Br. J. Edu. Technol. **51**(4), 1168–1187 (2020)
46. Donmez, M., Cagiltay, K.: Development of eye movement games for students with low vision: single-subject design research. Educ. Inf. Technol. **24**, 295–305 (2019)

Sense of Presence and the Illusion of Self-scaling in Virtual Learning Environments

Linfeng Wu⬤, Karen B. Chen⁽⊠⁾⬤, Matthew Peterson⬤, and Cesar Delgado⬤

North Carolina State University, Raleigh, USA
{lwu23,kbchen2,mopeters,cdelgad}@ncsu.edu

Abstract. Virtual reality (VR) enables users to have a sense of presence and potentially facilitates effective learning. The research team developed Scale Worlds
(SW), a virtual learning environment designed to help learners conceptualize size
and scale through virtual shrinking and growing by tenfold increments and experiencing scientific entities at extreme scales. The present work investigated two
crucial aspects of experiences in SW: the sense of presence and a novel self-
scaling illusion. Participants experienced SW via two devices: a head-mounted
display (HMD) with the absence of a virtual body and a Cave Automatic Virtual Environment (CAVE) where participants could see their own physical body.
Results showed that participants reported higher levels of presence and more
readily felt themselves shrinking and growing in SW-HMD than in SW-CAVE.
Findings include factors that contributed to the sense of presence and self-scaling
illusion in SW, and implications for designing those illusory experiences in VR
across various applications and platforms.

Keywords: Virtual Reality · Presence · Scale Cognition · Education Application

1 Introduction

Virtual reality (VR) has demonstrated effectiveness in education as it enables immersive
and interactive learning experiences [1, 2]. In VR, users have reported varying illusory
experiences where they felt as if they had entered altered situations and identities, and
responded accordingly [3]. The creation of these experiences in VR, such as the sense
of presence, can be important to enhance learning outcomes in virtual learning environments by facilitating deeper engagement and active participation among learners, such
as hands-on learning experiences and enhanced cognitive processes [4, 5].

Presence in VR is the sensation of being immersed in a computer-generated environment, feeling as if one is truly present in it [6–8]. Presence can be construed as
a fundamental manifestation of illusion, specifically the illusion of physical presence
despite the conscious awareness of its virtual nature [9, 10], and it thus contributes to
the powerful and captivating appeal of VR. With a greater sense of presence, users may
perceive VR to be a more enveloping and interactive reality than the surrounding physical world [5, 11]. This psychological experience profoundly affects user engagement,
cognition, and emotions during VR interactions [12–14]. Specifically in the context of

© The Author(s), under exclusive license to Springer Nature Switzerland AG 2025
P. Zaphiris et al. (Eds.): HCII 2024, LNCS 15378, pp. 195–210, 2025.
https://doi.org/10.1007/978-3-031-76815-6_14

learning, developing a sense of presence in VR can play an important role in enhancing learning outcomes through purposeful design of the learning environment mitigating cognitive load [15, 16]. Studies about formal learning in VR revealed that the association between the sense of presence and learning is positive and has increased as technology has evolved [5].

Learning size and scale has been an important topic in education due to its fundamental relevance across numerous scientific disciplines [17, 18]. Virtual reality has brought new inspiration to learning size and scale since it has the ability to visualize metaphors of intangible abstract science, technology, engineering, and mathematics (STEM) concepts [19, 20] such as creating visual illusions related to size and scale [21]. Studies have shown that individuals' perception of size and scale could be manipulated through the "body scaling effect," which refers to using their own body or limbs to base the size of the environment and nearby objects [22, 23]. Body change illusions (embodying participants in different sizes of virtual bodies) have been used to manipulate the perception of size and scale in the virtual environment [24–27]. In addition, in situations with the absence of a visible body, the perception of size and scale can be manipulated through the visual cues of nearby environmental features [28–30]. Drawing from these insights, the current study addresses the self-scaling illusion in a virtual learning environment called Scale Worlds (SW), which was designed to enhance learning size and scale.

Scale Worlds allows users to shrink or grow by powers of ten and experience entities from molecular to astronomical levels, to address challenges in the conceptualization of size and scale through VR. The present work stemmed from a larger user experience study that evaluated the usability of SW. In this paper, we focus on examining participants' sense of presence and self-scaling illusion in SW-HMD and SW-CAVE. By examining both quantitative and qualitative measures, the present work discusses the influence of these factors on users' perception and its implications for designing effective and impactful immersive virtual learning environments.

2 Related Works

2.1 Presence, Immersion, and Learning

In the context of VR, presence refers to the subjective feeling of "being there" in the virtual environment, to the extent that the individual perceives and interacts with a virtual space as if it were real [12, 13]. The sense of presence is a fundamental factor influencing a user's engagement, cognitive processes, and emotional responses during VR experiences [31, 32]. In relation to learning in VR, the sense of presence is connected to selective attention, which reduces the processing of distractions and thus enhances memory encoding [33]. A systematic review on the relationship between the sense of presence and learning in VR has shown that presence can enhance learning and has the potential to give a virtual experience the same value as a corresponding real one [5]. In contrast to the subjective nature of presence, immersion refers to the quantifiable characteristics of VR technology, which may support users in developing a sense of presence in VR [14, 34]. The assumption is that greater levels of immersive quality can lead to increasing sense of presence [35], and a meta-review has further identified specific characteristics of VR technology that have a relatively greater impact on the sense of presence, including user-tracking, utilization of stereoscopic visuals, and wider visual display fields [36].

Different VR hardware devices and systems may have different immersive qualities, which may lead to users' varying sense of presence [37]. Head-mounted displays provide individual users with a more personal and enclosed VR experience, and augment users' sense of presence through advanced tracking mechanisms and stereoscopic displays that precisely synchronize visual and auditory stimuli with users' head movements [38, 39]. On the other hand, cave automatic virtual environments (CAVEs), which employ multiple projectors in a room-sized enclosure, utilize active shutter glasses and precise tracking of user movements to enable a shared experience among multiple users within a physical space with a broader field of view and greater interactivity [40, 41]. While a study by Juan and Pérez [42] compared CAVEs to HMDs and found that CAVEs elicited greater presence and anxiety for acrophobia-related scenarios, another study indicated the difference in terms of features like immersion, presence, or other perceptual illusions between head-mounted displays (HMDs) and CAVEs were inconclusive [37]. The current study aimed to investigate participants' sense of presence across the two different versions of SW and to discern any potential factors contributing to the sense of presence in SW.

2.2 Visual Illusions Related to Size and Scale in VR

Understanding size and scale perception of objects in VR has become an active research topic and previous research has shown that visual cues of size in VR can affect the perception of sizes and distances [30]. It is known that people tend to use familiar objects, such as their own bodies or limbs, as references to compare with less-known features of the environment. This phenomenon is often referred to as the "body scaling effect," through which people base the size of the environment and nearby objects [22, 23]. Users can embody virtual bodies of different sizes and possibly develop body change illusions, which may produce changes in perception of size and scale in VR. Studies have shown that body change illusions impact size perception in VR environments, where objects may appear larger or smaller than their actual physical counterparts [24, 27]. A study about embodying an adult within a child-like virtual body has shown that people's mental representations of their own bodies and size perception are malleable through sensory cues in VR [24]. Study by Normand et al. [27] about body change illusion showed that multisensory stimulation can induce an illusion of larger belly size in VR and suggested applications including treatment for body size distortion illnesses.

In addition to having a visible virtual body, another way to influence the perception of size and scale is by manipulating the visual cues within VR. Individuals' object size estimations are affected by manipulating the size of nearby objects or the environment [30]. Furthermore, the effects of stereopsis on vection in VR indicate that a self-motion illusion could be created by rotating the visual cues of surroundings [43, 44]. Similarly, the team aimed to create a self-scaling illusion for participants in SW by manipulating the features of the environment, such as scaling animations of the environment from the backend transitions.

2.3 Scale Worlds for Learning Size Through Scaling

The exploration of size and scale is a pivotal subject of study due to its fundamental relevance across numerous scientific disciplines and its impact on our understanding of the physical world [17, 18]. Scale Worlds encompasses a wide range of scientific entities of different sizes that are distributed among distinct environments or "scale worlds" [45, 46], each of which corresponds to an exponent in scientific notation. In SW, the environment was designed to be a single, internally consistent world to provide an allocentric point of view, and the user is the only entity that is inconsistent (shrinking and growing). Similar to the vection illusion, it was intended for the users to evoke the illusion of self-scaling (i.e., feel they have shrunk or grown) when going to different scale worlds, as opposed to users noticing the environment (e.g., entities, posts, grids, floor) changing. This approach was adopted to ensure that participants could authentically experience scientific entities at extreme scales, as opposed to merely observing 3D entity models scaled to certain sizes. Thus, SW was purposefully designed to elicit self-scaling illusion, with environmental elements and design attributes strategically employed to support it.

Previous investigations primarily utilized HMDs and involved the concept of body scaling effect to induce the body change illusions in VR [24, 27]. Though research has shown that the body scaling effect exists even when the body is not visible [28, 29], there is limited research in this area when there is no virtual body present, and there is a paucity of studies conducted within CAVE systems where users could see their physical bodies. The current exploratory study preliminarily examined whether the illusion of self-scaling can be induced within SW-HMD, which lacks a virtual body presence, or in the SW-CAVE setting, where participants have visual access to their physical bodies. It explores the relationship between the sense of presence and the illusion of self-scaling in SW-HMD and SW-CAVE, and whether and how this relationship differs across platforms, along with the perceived advantages and disadvantages of the two versions regarding learning size and scale. The investigation holds significance as it could offer valuable insights aimed at enhancing learning outcomes within virtual learning environments through different VR technologies.

3 Methods

3.1 Participants

Fifteen first-year college students participated in this study (age 18.8 $\pm$ 0.56, six female, nine male). The rationale behind selecting first-year college students as participants stems from their status as a representative cohort for exploring size and scale concepts within the college context, as they could enroll in courses such as astrophysics (larger entities) and biochemistry (smaller entities). Exclusion criteria encompassed individuals with a history of epileptic seizure or blackout, propensity for motion sickness, or heightened sensitivity to flashing lights. The user experience sessions were completed in under two hours. All participants provided informed consent, which was approved by the Institutional Review Board of North Carolina State University.

3.2   Equipment

SW-HMD was delivered via Oculus Quest 2 and SW-CAVE was delivered via a C4 CAVE. Both versions of SW were developed in and rendered using Unity (version 2021.3.17f1). Oculus Quest 2 (Meta, Quest 2) provides a resolution of 3664 × 1920 (1832 × 1920 per eye) and is equipped with integrated inertial measurement units that monitor the user's head orientation, facilitating the provision of suitable visual perspectives. In SW-HMD, the participants interacted with virtual entities and the user interface (UI) using the Quest 2 native hand-held controller. The CAVE (Viscube, Visbox, St. Joseph, IL) in the current study comprises three walls and a floor, employing four stereoscopic projectors with a resolution of 1920 × 1800 (Barco F50, Barco) to generate images on corresponding surfaces. Real-time tracking of the user's active shutter 3D glasses is managed using a motion tracking system (DTrack 2, ART GmbH) (Fig. 1). Interaction is enabled through a wand, enabling manipulation and engagement with the UI.

Fig. 1. A screenshot in Unity of SW-CAVE (left) and a user holding the wand in the CAVE and being in the Human World (right).

3.3   Procedures

Upon obtaining participants' consent, the researcher introduced SW and provided an overview of the study: to understand students' experiences when using SW. Participants first experienced SW-HMD, followed by SW-CAVE. This sequence was dictated by the inclusion of a tutorial session within SW-HMD, because we anticipated SW-HMD to function as a standalone product to be distributed to learners, requiring minimal guidance from the developers. In contrast, the usage of SW-CAVE was envisioned to be guided by a facilitator during lab tours, leading to the omission of a tutorial session. Teleportation was implemented in SW-HMD to facilitate movement, while in SW-CAVE participants physically walked for movement. Participants spent approximately 25 min experiencing SW-HMD, including the tutorial. They were then directed to complete the Slater-Usoh-Steed (SUS) presence questionnaire [47] on paper to self-report their sense of presence. Subsequently, participants progressed to experience SW-CAVE for approximately 20 min and then completed the SUS in relation to their experience in SW-CAVE. Finally, the session ended with a semi-structured interview with a series of inquiries regarding their experience in SW. The semi-structured interview was audio recorded for later data processing and analysis.

3.4 Experiencing Scaling in SW

The current version of SW consists of 21 scale worlds ranging from molecular to astronomical levels. Participants were instructed to use either the controller (in SW-HMD) or the wand (in SW-CAVE) to interact with the UI to shrink or grow themselves by a power of ten, which will trigger an animation that proportionally alters the entire environment (including entities, posts, grids, and floor). Positions of the visible entities are ordered logarithmically and approach a zero point, from which all scaling motions are calculated (Fig. 2). In Unity, the position of the zero point is set as (0,0,0) which represents the coordinate origin and the center of the three-dimensional space. The scaling animations of zooming in or out start from this point, growing or shrinking the participant's surroundings, creating an illusion similar to vection [43], which we refer to as the self-scaling illusion. Participants were advised to stand at this point to experience scaling, ensuring that the sensation feels natural. The apportion of scientific entities and the scale armatures (e.g., posts) are designed to reinforce the sense of self-scaling, and to provide means by which users can estimate the size of the entities (and of themselves).

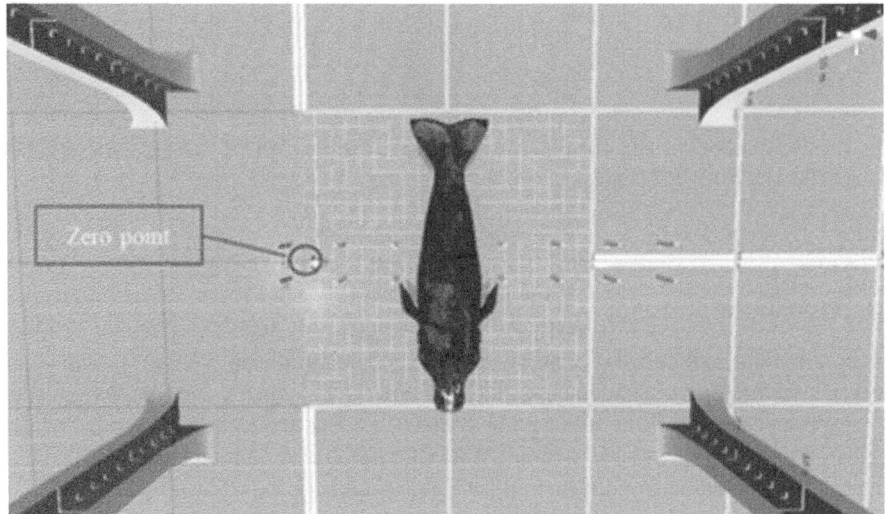

Fig. 2. Scale Worlds features to support the self-scaling illusion including entities, posts, grids, and floor.

3.5 Variables and Analysis

Subjective Sense of Presence

The Slater-Usoh-Steed (SUS) is a presence questionnaire [47] (Table 1) comprising six questions, stemming from three central themes: the perception of being immersed within the virtual environment, the level to which the virtual environment supersedes the real world, and the extent to which the virtual environment is recollected as a distinct "place." Each question was rated on a scale of 1 to 7, with higher scores indicating a higher level of presence.

The SUS presence score was calculated in two ways [47, 48]: mean score and count score. The SUS mean score is the average across the six questions. The SUS count is the number of scores of the six questions, where the responses had a score of 6 or 7 on a 1–7 scale. Both sets of scores are pivotal in assessing the degree of presence experienced by participants within the virtual environment, thereby offering insights into the perceived immersive quality of the VR experience.

Table 1. The six questions in SUS.

1. Please rate your sense of being in the VE, on the following scale from 1 to 7, where 7 represents your normal experience of being in a place	
(1) Not at all	(7) very much
2. To what extent were there times during the experience when the VE was the reality for you?	
(1) At no time	(7) Almost all the time
3. When you think back about your experience, do you think of the VE more as images that you saw, or more as somewhere that you visited?	
(1) Images that I saw	(7) Somewhere that I visited
4. During the time of the experience, which was strongest on the whole, your sense of being in the VE, or of being elsewhere?	
(1) Being elsewhere	(7) Being in the virtual space
5. Consider your memory of being in the VE. How similar in terms of the structure of the memory is this to the structure of the memory of other places you have been today? By "structure of the memory," consider things like the extent to which you have a visual memory of the VE, whether that memory is in color, the extent to which the memory seems vivid or realistic, its size, location in your imagination, the extent to which it is panoramic in your imagination, and other such structural elements	
(1) Not at all	(7) Very much so
6. During the time of the experience, did you often think to yourself that you were actually in the VE?	
(1) Not very often	(7) Very much so

Semi-structured Interview. The semi-structured interview (Table 2) centered on students' experience in SW and solicited their insights on the sense of presence, the perception of self-scaling, and the advantages and disadvantages of SW-HMD and SW-CAVE to support learning size and scale. This approach allowed for a comprehensive exploration of participants' perspectives, thereby complementing the quantitative data acquired from the questionnaire with a richer layer of qualitative insights.

Table 2. The specific phrasing and language of the three questions asked during the semi-structured interview.

Q1. Please explain your ratings regarding "the sense of being there" in the two versions of SW. What things helped to give you a sense of really being in the VE, and what things acted to "pull you out" of it?
Q2. Did you feel like you were growing or shrinking, or did you feel like you remained the same and the objects in SW were growing or shrinking? Why? Is there a difference between the two versions regarding this question?
Q3. What advantages or disadvantages of the two versions of SW did you notice for learning size and scale?

Question 1 (Q1) concerned participants' sense of presence for both versions of SW and participants were requested to provide explanations for the corresponding ratings [47]. Question 2 (Q2) concerned participants' perception of self-scaling illusions. Participants were asked whether they felt themselves were changing in size, which yielded a binary response (yes/no). Furthermore, participants were asked to elaborate on what supported them in perceiving such illusions during the scaling process in SW. Question 3 (Q3) concerns participants' perspectives on the advantages and disadvantages of the two versions of SW in terms of learning size and scale.

Qualitative data from the interview underwent thematic analysis. First, all the responses were transcribed into text [49] and then coded and grouped into themes [50, 51]. Themes characterized participants' experience in SW including the sense of presence, self-scaling illusion, and the advantages and disadvantages of the two versions regarding learning size and scale. In addition, participants' sentiment (e.g., liked/disliked, advantages/disadvantages) were teased out.

4   Results

4.1   Presence Score from SUS

The SUS mean scores were 4.80 ± 0.97 and 4.45 ± 1.08 for SW-HMD and SW-CAVE, respectively. The SUS count scores were 3.47 ± 1.45 and 2.50 ± 1.69 for SW-HMD and SW-CAVE, respectively.

4.2   Illusion of Self-Scaling

Twelve out of the 15 participants (12/15) reported that they perceived themselves shrinking or growing in SW-HMD while six of the 15 participants (6/15) reported the same in SW-CAVE.

4.3 Themes from Semi-Structured Interview

For Question 1 regarding the presence scores, five participants attributed the higher presence in SW-HMD to greater immersion. In SW-CAVE, participants reported mixed feelings about the visibility of their physical bodies regarding the sense of presence. Four thought the visibility helped enhance the sense of being in the virtual environment while the other two stated the opposite. Additionally, six participants emphasized that visual limitations, particularly the absence of a ceiling and side walls of the CAVE utilized in this study, contributed to decreased presence.

Regarding Q2, participants attributed the heightened immersion of SW-HMD as a contributing factor to the self-scaling illusion. In addition, six participants emphasized the absence of a visible body in HMD enhancing the sense of presence and the presence of a visible physical body in CAVE decreasing it.

In response to Q3, participants favored SW-HMD for learning size and scale, due to its higher level of immersion and freedom of movement, despite reporting greater eye fatigue. On the other hand, participants appreciated SW-CAVE for its ease on the eyes due to the glasses, as well as the ability to physically walk within it. However, they noted that the CAVE system's cost and space requirements made it less accessible compared to HMD. Further details regarding keywords and their corresponding counts are provided in Table 3.

Table 3. Recurring themes extracted from the semi-structured interview. For each question, the recurring themes and their corresponding frequencies noted as counts were listed.

			SW-HMD	SW-CAVE
Q1	Themes (count)		immersion (5) movement (2)	visibility of physical body (6) visual limitations (6)
Q2	Themes (count)		immersion (3) no virtual body (6)	visibility of physical body (6)
Q3	Themes (count)	pros	immersion (11) movement (2)	easier on eyes (5) physically walk (3)
		cons	fatigue on eyes (3)	less accessible (2)

5 Discussion

This study investigated the sense of presence and self-scaling illusion in SW-HMD and SW-CAVE, as well as the advantages and disadvantages of the two versions of SW regarding learning size and scale. Through a comprehensive approach that combined quantitative and qualitative data analysis, results showed that participants reported higher levels of sense of presence and more readily felt themselves shrinking and growing in SW-HMD than in SW-CAVE. Noteworthy recurring themes arose from the semi-structured interview regarding the advantages and disadvantages of the two versions for learning size and scale, providing insights for designing the illusory experiences and learning size and scale in the virtual environment across various applications and platforms.

When exploring the immersive virtual learning environment, participants reported a greater sense of presence in SW-HMD than in SW-CAVE. It was natural to speculate the difference in sense of presence between SW-HMD and SW-CAVE was attributed to the different quantifiable immersive characteristics, such as field of view and tracking latency [37, 42]. However, themes from the semi-structured interview revealed additional details that further explained the differences in sense of presence. Participants stated that teleportation in SW-HMD felt "not realistic" thus decreased the sense of presence, which was in line with the studies that have shown teleportation as a type of movement might lessen the sense of presence in VR [52, 53]. While this was not in the originally planned study objective, the semi-structured interview revealed different usage of VR terminologies by the participants. Immersion has emerged as the frequently cited rationale behind participants' sense of presence, yet it was referenced in various contexts. While the present study has used one of the many definitions of immersion (i.e., the objective characteristics of VR technology that allows users to feel as if they are present in a simulated environment [14, 34]), the literature includes different definitions and explanations of immersion [54]. Among those who indicated that SW-HMD provided "better immersion" and that thus they had a higher sense of presence, it seemed that they might have subjectively assumed a positive relationship between immersion and presence. For instance, one participant said, "you're a little more immersed, a little more present because you can't see anything else".

Participants' lack of experience with VR technology and terminologies might have affected the responses regarding the sense of presence. This phenomenon aligns with the argument that it is challenging to measure the sense of presence in VR using post-experience questionnaires since the application of questionnaires typically relies on previous experiences, which does not apply to presence that many people are not familiar with [55]. During the process of understanding the reasons behind participants' sense of presence in SW-HMD and SW-CAVE, it became necessary to examine the context of their verbalization during the semi-structured interview. For instance, participants reported mixed feelings about the visibility of a physical body (i.e., participant's real body) in SW-CAVE regarding sense of presence. Four of them believed that such visibility contributed to a heightened sense of presence, with one participant noting, "being able to see myself in the world." Conversely, the other two participants held opposing views, with one stating, "I'm there in my own physical body, and I don't feel like I'm in a virtual reality system." Certainly, there was a degree of unfamiliarity with VR terminology and concepts among the participants given that out of these 15 participants, 13 had rarely or never used an HMD and none of them had prior experience using a CAVE. In sum, participants' exposure to VR terminologies affected the verbalized responses, which highlighted the need for improved methods of measuring VR presence. And the context in thematic analysis of semi-structured interview data helped clarify the participants' intended meaning.

Scale Worlds intends to enable users to shrink or grow themselves as they travel to different scale worlds that contain scientific entities of size differences in tenfold increments [21]. Through this study, SW successfully evoked the self-scaling illusion with 80% of participants reporting this in SW-HMD and 40% in SW-CAVE. While humans cannot physically change their body sizes by powers of ten, SW enabled the participants to generate perceptual illusions that could potentially deceive their visual senses, prompting them to develop the self-scaling illusion instead of recognizing the environmental changes. The literature has demonstrated that individuals' perception of size and scale could be manipulated through the "body scaling effect" [22, 23], which was mainly accomplished through participants embodying different-sized virtual bodies [24, 27]. The present study did not embody participants in a virtual body in SW-HMD, it even showed users their physical bodies in SW-CAVE, which countered the approach in the literature. Scale Worlds instituted self-motion illusions (vection) to facilitate perspective switches and ultimately to relax the physical motion in VR [43]. The findings from the current study suggest that the self-scaling illusion can occur both without a virtual body (SW-HMD) and in the presence of a visible physical body (SW-CAVE). In addition, participants were more likely to perceive the self-scaling illusion in SW-HMD than SW-CAVE. The responses from the semi-structured interview further supported that a virtual body was not required to induce the self-scaling illusion, and the visibility of the real body as seen in the CAVE could potentially undermine the induced self-scaling illusion.

While it may be intuitive to assume that a heightened sense of presence is a prerequisite for inducing the self-scaling illusion, since participants would seemingly need to feel being in the VE to have the sense of self-scaling, the results challenged this assumption. No significant relationship between the sense of presence and self-scaling illusion was found after accounting for the main effects across HMD and CAVE. The data suggested that the extent of presence, assessed using the SUS, was not a requirement for the manifestation of the self-scaling illusion. This observation aligned with the findings from Q2 in the semi-structured interviews, where the theme of presence did not frequently emerge in explanations concerning the perceived self-scaling illusion. Gonzalez-Franco and Lanier's work on illusions in VR highlights the pivotal role of visual inputs in creating illusory experiences and described the minimum instrumentation requirements to support such illusions [3]. Both SW-HMD and SW-CAVE appeared to satisfy these minimum requirements, providing continuously updated displays with head tracking and congruent sensorimotor feedback. However, in the case of the C4 CAVE configuration, visual inputs were not limited to the VR display but also encompass the physical world, which potentially broke the illusion. During the SW-CAVE experience, participants occasionally experienced breaks in the illusion when they directed their gaze towards the physical world surrounding them. As one participant aptly put it, "In CAVE I could see my body so I can, like, remind myself I'm not changing size." Conversely, the HMD effectively mitigated this issue by isolating users from the physical world, thereby preserving the consistency of the illusion.

There have been studies showing that there is a positive association between the sense of presence and learning in virtual environments [56], where the association between the sense of presence and learning is more frequent using quantitative approaches of learning assessment [5]. While the investigation of the learning outcomes was within the scope of the overarching project, it is not implemented in the current study and should be for future studies. This study opted to garner participant insights through semi-structured interviews. Participants were asked about the comparative advantages and disadvantages concerning the two versions of SW in learning size and scale. While a clear-cut preference did not emerge, participants reported the merits and limitations of each. The recurring sentiment was that SW-HMD offered a more immersive experience compared to SW-CAVE. SW-HMD enabled more unrestricted movement via teleportation, facilitating diverse perspectives from different positions, while SW-CAVE only permitted limited physical movements within a confined space. Participants noted that the comfort of the active shutter glasses used in SW-CAVE contrasted with instances of eye fatigue encountered in SW-HMD. Participants highlighted SW-HMD's greater accessibility as a learning tool for students, which aligns with observations that a CAVE system will cost more and takes up more space [37, 42]. Additionally, participants liked the fact that they could physically walk in the CAVE with one participant saying, "I like it in the CAVE that I can physically walk around the objects to compare and look". In sum, both SW-HMD and SW-CAVE have their respective advantages and disadvantages in terms of a scale learning experience. Future research endeavors should incorporate comprehensive investigations into the learning outcomes of these versions.

6   Limitation

Some limitations in this study need to be acknowledged. The configuration of a CAVE can include six walls that surround the user to contribute to the sense of being "inside" a simulated world, creating a more immersive experience [57–60]. However, the absence of two surfaces (one ceiling and one side wall) of the CAVE employed in the current study (Fig. 1), could potentially affect the immersion level of the system and participants' sense of presence in the VR environment.

One other limitation was that this study did not employ randomization for the order the participants would try SW. This was intentional for participants to explore SW-HMD upon following the instructions in the tutorial. It is imperative to acknowledge that this study does not constitute a structured experiment; rather, it yields notable observations and dialogues pertaining to the sense of presence and the illusion of self-scaling in SW. Future research should address these aspects with a comprehensive experimental control, such as randomized controlled trials and larger sample size.

7   Conclusion and Future Work

The results indicated that participants generally perceived a higher sense of presence in SW-HMD than in SW-CAVE, as measured by SUS. Additionally, participants reported that they were more likely to perceive the illusion of self-scaling in SW-HMD where a virtual body was absent than in SW-CAVE where the physical body was visible. Employing a comprehensive approach that integrated both quantitative and qualitative data analysis, this study has unveiled attributes of the illusory experiences including the sense of presence and self-scaling in SW through two VR technologies. Although no significant relationship between the sense of presence and the self-scaling illusion was identified in the current study, it is recommended that future research with a larger sample size and a comprehensive experimental design be conducted. While SW serves as a virtual learning environment aimed at facilitating students' understanding of size and scale, this study did not investigate the relationship between the sense of presence, the self-scaling illusion, and learning outcomes, which should be a focus of future research.

Acknowledgments. This study was funded by the National Science Foundation (DRL-2055680). The research team, including the authors, along with Tyler Harper-Gampp, Brian Sekelsky, Rebecca Planchart, Meghan Jack, Amanda Williams and Robert Kulasingam have contributed to the development of Scale Worlds. Thanks to Catherine Reckard and Ren Watt for assisting with the data collection.

Disclosure of Interests. The authors have no competing interests to declare that are relevant to the content of this article.

References

1. Martirosov, S., Kopecek,P.: Virtual reality and its influence on training and education - Literature review. Ann. DAAAM Proc. Int. DAAAM Symp. 708–717 (2017), https://doi.org/10. 2507/28th.daaam.proceedings.100

2. Petersen, G.B., Petkakis, G., Makransky, G.: A study of how immersion and interactivity drive VR learning. Comput. Educ. **179** (2022). https://doi.org/10.1016/j.compedu.2021.104429

3. Gonzalez-Franco, M., Lanier,J.: Model of illusions and virtual reality. Front. Psychol. **8** (2017). https://doi.org/10.3389/fpsyg.2017.01125

4. Roussou, M.: Learning by doing and learning through play: an exploration of interactivity in virtual environments for children. Comput. Entertain. **2**(1), 10 (2004). https://doi.org/10. 1145/973801.973818

5. Krassmann, A.L., Melo, M., Pinto, D., Peixoto, B., Bessa, M., Bercht, M.: What is the relationship between the sense of presence and learning in virtual reality? a 24-year systematic literature review. Presence Teleoperators Virt. Environ. **28**, 247–265 (2022). https://doi.org/ 10.1162/PRES_a_00350

6. Insko, B.E.: Measuring presence: Subjective, behavioral and physiological methods. Being There Concepts, Eff. Meas. user presence Synth. Environ., 2003. http://www.scs.ryerson.ca/ ~aferworn/courses/CPS841/CLASSES/CPS841CL09/MeasuringPresence.pdf

7. Ee, L.A.G ., Rnst, N.A. E., Bdelqader, B.I.A., Rath, M.E.M.C.G.: Understanding Virtual Reality : Presence, Embodiment. 61, no. 2, pp. 178–195 (2018)

8. Slater, M.: Presence and the sixth sense. Presence Teleoperators Virtual Environ. **11**(4), 435– 439 (2002). https://doi.org/10.1162/105474602760204327

9. Wilkinson, M., Brantley, S., Feng, J.: A Mini review of presence and immersion in virtual reality. Proc. Hum. Factors Ergon. Soc. Annu. Meet. **65**(1), 1099–1103 (2021). https://doi. org/10.1177/1071181321651148

10. Skarbez, R., Brooks, F.P., Whitton, M. C.: A survey of presence and related concepts. ACM Comput. Surv. **50**(6) (2017). https://doi.org/10.1145/3134301

11. Slater, M., Wilbur, S.: A framework for immersive virtual environments (FIVE) Speculations on the role of presence in virtual environments. PRESENCE Teleoperators Virtual Environ. **6**(6) (1997)

12. Witmer, B., Singer, M.J.: Measuring presence in virtual environments: a presence questionnaire. ACM Comput. Surv. **54**(8), 225–240 (1998). https://doi.org/10.1145/3466817

13. Slater, M., Steed, A., McCarthy, J., Maringelli, F.: The influence of body movement on subjective presence in virtual environments. Hum. Factors **40**(3), 469–477 (1998). https:// doi.org/10.1518/001872098779591368

14. Servotte, J.C., et al.: Virtual reality experience: immersion, sense of presence, and cybersickness. Clin. Simul. Nurs. **38**, 35–43 (2020). https://doi.org/10.1016/j.ecns.2019.09.006

15. Huang, C.L., Luo, Y.F., Yang, S.C., Lu, C.M., Chen, A.S.: Influence of students' learning style, sense of presence, and cognitive load on learning outcomes in an immersive virtual reality learning environment. J. Educ. Comput. Res. **58**(3), 596–615 (2020). https://doi.org/10.1177/0735633119867422

16. Lombard, M., Ditton, T.B., Weinstein, L.: Measuring presence: the temple presence inventory. In: Proceedings of the 12th Annual International Workshop on Presence, pp. 1–15 (2009)

17. Jones, G.M.: Conceptualizing size and scale, pp. 147–154 (2013)

18. National Research Council, A framework for K-12 science education: Practices, crosscutting concepts, and core ideas (2012)

19. Chen, J.C., et al.: Developing a hands-on activity using virtual reality to help students learn by doing. J. Comput. Assist. Learn. **36**(1), 46–60 (2020). https://doi.org/10.1111/jcal.12389

20. Altmeyer, K., Kapp, S., Thees, M., Malone, S., Kuhn, J., Brünken, R.: The use of augmented reality to foster conceptual knowledge acquisition in STEM laboratory courses—theoretical background and empirical results. Br. J. Educ. Technol. **51**(3), 611–628 (2020). https://doi.org/10.1111/bjet.12900

21. Wu, L., Sekelsky, B., Peterson, M., Gampp, T., Delgado, C., Chen, K.B.: Immersive virtual environment for scale cognition and learning: expert-based evaluation for balancing usability versus cognitive theories. Proc. Hum. Factors Ergon. Soc. Annu. Meet. **66**(1), 1972–1976 (2022). https://doi.org/10.1177/1071181322661094

22. Langbehn, E., Bruder, G., Steinicke, F.: Scale matters! Analysis of dominant scale estimation in the presence of conflicting cues in multi-scale collaborative virtual environments. In: 2016 IEEE Symp. 3D User Interfaces, 3DUI 2016 – Proc., pp. 211–220, 2016, https://doi.org/10.1109/3DUI.2016.7460054

23. Ogawa, N., Narumi, T., Hirose, M.: Distortion in perceived size and body-based scaling in virtual environments. ACM Int. Conf. Proc. Ser. (2017). https://doi.org/10.1145/3041164.3041204

24. Tajadura-Jiménez, A., Banakou, D., Bianchi-Berthouze, N., Slater, M.: Embodiment in a child-like talking virtual body influences object size perception, self-identification, and subsequent real speaking. Sci. Rep. **7**(1), 1–13 (2017). https://doi.org/10.1038/s41598-017-09497-3

25. Banakou, D., Groten, R., Slater, M.: Illusory ownership of a virtual child body causes overestimation of object sizes and implicit attitude changes. Proc. Natl. Acad. Sci. U.S.A. **110**(31), 12846–12851 (2013). https://doi.org/10.1073/pnas.1306779110

26. Kilteni, K., Normand, J.-M., Sanchez-Vives, M.V., Slater, M.: Extending body space in immersive virtual reality: a very long arm illusion. PLoS ONE **7**(7), e40867 (2012). https://doi.org/10.1371/journal.pone.0040867

27. Normand, J.M., Giannopoulos, E., Spanlang, B., Slater, M.: Multisensory stimulation can induce an illusion of larger belly size in immersive virtual reality. PLoS One **6**(1) (2011). https://doi.org/10.1371/journal.pone.0016128

28. Van Der Hoort, B., Ehrsson, H.H.: Illusions of having small or large invisible bodies influence visual perception of object size. Sci. Rep. **6**(April), 1–9 (2016). https://doi.org/10.1038/srep34530

29. van der Hoort, B., Ehrsson, H.H.: Body ownership affects visual perception of object size by rescaling the visual representation of external space. Attention, Percep. Psychophys. **76**(5), 1414–1428 (2014). https://doi.org/10.3758/s13414-014-0664-9

30. Pouke, M., Center, E.G., Chambers, A.P., Pouke, S., Ojala, T., Lavalle, S.M.: The body scaling effect and its impact on physics plausibility. Front. Virtual Real. **3**(May), 1–12 (2022). https://doi.org/10.3389/frvir.2022.869603

31. Schultze, U.: Embodiment and presence in virtual worlds: a review. J. Inf. Technol. **25**(4), 434–449 (2010). https://doi.org/10.1057/jit.2010.25

32. Sanchez-Vives, M.V., Slater, M.: From presence to consciousness through virtual reality. Nat. Rev. Neurosci. **6**(4), 332–339 (2005). https://doi.org/10.1038/nrn1651
33. Makowski, D., Sperduti, M., Nicolas, S., Piolino, P.: 'Being there' and remembering it: presence improves memory encoding. Conscious. Cogn. **53**, 194–202 (2017). https://doi.org/10.1016/j.concog.2017.06.015
34. Slater, M.: Immersion and the illusion of presence in virtual reality. Br. J. Psychol. **109**(3), 431–433 (2018). https://doi.org/10.1111/bjop.12305
35. Slater, M., Lotto, B., Arnold, M.M., Sanchez-Vives, M.V.: How we experience immersive virtual environments: the concept of presence and its measurement. Anu. Psicol. **40**(2), 193–210 (2009)
36. Cummings, J.J., Bailenson, J.N.: How Immersive is enough? a meta-analysis of the effect of immersive technology on user presence. Media Psychol. **19**(2), 272–309 (2016). https://doi.org/10.1080/15213269.2015.1015740
37. Elor, A., Powell, M., Mahmoodi, E., Hawthorne, N., Teodorescu, M., Kurniawan, S.: On shooting stars: Comparing CAVE and HMD immersive virtual reality exergaming for adults with mixed ability. ACM Trans. Comput. Healthc. **1**(4), 1–22 (2020). https://doi.org/10.1145/3396249
38. Schafer, P., Koller, M., DIemer, J., Meixner, G.: Development and evaluation of a virtual reality-system with integrated tracking of extremities under the aspect of Acrophobia. In: IntelliSys 2015 - Proc. 2015 SAI Intell. Syst. Conf., pp. 408–417 (2015). https://doi.org/10.1109/IntelliSys.2015.7361173
39. Lubetzky, A.V., Wang, Z., Krasovsky, T.: Head mounted displays for capturing head kinematics in postural tasks. J. Biomech. **86**, 175–182 (2019). https://doi.org/10.1016/j.jbiomech.2019.02.004
40. Genova, C., et al.: A simulator for both manual and powered wheelchairs in immersive virtual reality CAVE. Virtual Real. **26**(1), 187–203 (2022). https://doi.org/10.1007/s10055-021-00547-w
41. Billen, M.I., et al.: A geoscience perspective on immersive 3D gridded data visualization. Comput. Geosci. **34**(9), 1056–1072 (2008). https://doi.org/10.1016/j.cageo.2007.11.009
42. Carmen Juan, M., Pérez, D.: Comparison of the levels of presence and anxiety in an acrophobic environment viewed via HMD or CAVE. Presence Teleoperators Virtual Environ. **18**(3), 232–248 (2009). https://doi.org/10.1162/pres.18.3.232
43. Riecke, B.E., Feuereissen, D., Rieser, J.J., McNamara, T.P.: Self-motion illusions (vection) in VR - Are they good for anything?, Proc. - IEEE Virtual Real., pp. 35–38 (2012). https://doi.org/10.1109/VR.2012.6180875
44. Luu, W., Zangerl, B., Kalloniatis, M., Kim, J.: Effects of stereopsis on vection, presence and cybersickness in head-mounted display (HMD) virtual reality. Sci. Rep. **11**(1), 1 (2021). https://doi.org/10.1038/s41598-021-89751-x
45. Tretter, T.R., Jones, M.G., Minogue, J.: Accuracy of scale conceptions in science: Mental maneu- verings across many orders of spatial magnitude. Res. Sci. Teach. **43**(10), 1061–1085 (2006). https://doi.org/10.1002/tea.20155
46. Tretter, T.R., Jones, M.G., Andre, T., Negishi, A., Minogue, J.: Conceptual boundaries and distances: Students' and experts' concepts of the scale of scientific phenomena. Res. Sci. Teach. **43**(3), 282–319 (2006). https://doi.org/10.1002/tea.20123
47. Usoh, M., Catena, E., Arman, S., Slater, M.: Using presence questionnaires in reality. Presence Teleoperators Virt. Environ. **9**(5), 497–503 (2000). https://doi.org/10.1162/105474600566989
48. Schwind, V., Knierim, P., Haas, N., Henze, N.: Using presence questionnaires in virtual reality. Conf. Hum. Factors Comput. Syst. - Proc., pp. 1–12 (2019). https://doi.org/10.1145/3290605.3300590

49. Creswell, J.W.: Research design : qualitative, quantitative, and mixed methods approaches (3rd ed.). Sage (2009)
50. Corbin, J., Strauss, A.: Basics of qualitative research: techniques and procedures for developing grounded theory. In: SAGE Publ. Inc., 2008. https://doi.org/10.4135/9781452230153
51. Creswell, J.W., Plano Clark, V.L.: Designing and conducting mixed methods research (Third Edit)," SAGE. (2018)
52. Martirosov, S., Bureš, M., Zítka, T.: Cyber sickness in low-immersive, semi-immersive, and fully immersive virtual reality. Virtual Real. **26**(1), 15–32 (2022). https://doi.org/10.1007/s10055-021-00507-4
53. Prithul, A., Adhanom, I.B., Folmer, E.: Teleportation in virtual reality; a mini-review. Front. Virtual Real. **2**(October), 1–7 (2021). https://doi.org/10.3389/frvir.2021.730792
54. Nilsson, N.C., Nordahl, R., Serafin, S.: Immersion revisited: a review of existing definitions of immersion and their relation to different theories of presence. Hum. Technol. **12**(2), 108–134 (2016). https://doi.org/10.17011/ht/urn.201611174652
55. Slater, M.: How colorful was your day? Why questionnaires cannot assess presence in virtual environments. Presence Teleoperators Virtual Environ. **13**(4), 484–493 (2004). https://doi.org/10.1162/1054746041944849
56. Krassmann, A.L., Melo, M., Pinto, D., Peixoto, B., Bessa, M., Bercht, M.: How are the sense of presence and learning outcomes being investigated when using virtual reality? A 24 years systematic literature review. Interact. Learn. Environ. (2023). https://doi.org/10.1080/10494820.2023.2184388
57. Johnson, A., Roussos, M., Leigh, J., Barnes, C., Vasilakis, C., Moher, T.: The NICE project: learning together in a virtual world. In: Proceedings of the VRAIS '98, pp. 176–183, (1998). http://www.evl.uic.edu/moher/papers/vrais98.pdf
58. Cruz-Neira, C., Sandin, D., Defanti, T.: The CAVE: Audio visual experience automatic virtual environment. Comm. ACM, **35**, 6, 64–72 (1992)
59. Cruz-Neira, C., Sandin, D.J., DeFanti, T.A.: Surround-screen projection-based virtual reality: the design and implementation of the CAVE. In: Proceedings of the ACM SIGGRAPH 93 Conference Comput Graph, pp. 135–142 (1993)
60. Muhanna, M.: Virtual reality and the CAVE : Taxonomy , interaction challenges and research directions (2015)

Early Childhood Apps Design with Augmented Reality for Learning

Xiao Zhen[1] and Jiandong Liu[2(✉)]

[1] Zhejiang Normal University, Jinhua, China
[2] The Hubei University of Economics, Wuhan, China
jiandong.liu.ai@gmail.com

Abstract. This paper explores the impact of Augmented Reality (AR) interaction on the learning experiences of young children in nature-based education. The research focuses on understanding how AR can improve learning by comparing two different representations: traditional 2D image demonstrations and 3D interactive AR demonstrations. The study was conducted with 43 participants, all aged between 4 and 6 years, who engaged with educational content centered around the topic of dinosaurs. To provide a comprehensive assessment, the children's learning experiences were evaluated on two aspects: their ability to acquire new knowledge and their development of critical thinking skills. The study's results suggest that AR interaction positively impacts learning outcomes to some extent. Specifically, children who engaged in 3D interactive AR presentations did not show significant improvements in knowledge acquisition compared to children who learned through traditional 2D images. The interactive attributes of AR lead to a deeper engagement with the learning content, which significantly contributed to the development of critical thinking skills. This suggests that the experience provided by AR can stimulate cognitive processes more effectively than traditional methods. This research contributes to understanding how AR can be integrated into educational content to develop a more interactive learning experience.

Keywords: Augmented Reality · Pre-school · Children Learning

1 Introduction

The education field is witnessing a transformation of integrating Augmented Reality (AR) into interaction-based learning methodologies [1]. This advance illustrates a promising future to improve the learning experience, especially for the current generation of children who, having been exposed to digital devices from anearly age, often find interactive learning approaches more engaging than traditional approaches. Such approaches leverage AR to make learning more interesting and attractive.

The AR approach is especially relevant to early childhood education, where children frequently face challenges in acquiring knowledge about nature. These challenges often exist in correlating concepts presented in textbooks with real- world observations in their surroundings [2]. AR enhances traditional teaching approaches by overlaying digital information, such as images and interactive elements, onto the real-world environment, creating a more engaging learning experience. Additionally, AR-based educational activities reinforce knowledge through interaction, improving understanding of complex concepts [3]. By integrating AR technology, teachers can create engaging and effective learning approaches that address the challenges pre-school students face in learning about nature.

Although AR technologies in education have been studied for years [4], the underlying theoretical mechanisms remain a subject of ongoing research. Consequently, it is crucial to examine the factors influencing student motivation, as these elements play a pivotal role in the learning process. Empirical studies have consistently demonstrated a significant increase in motivation levels when learners engage with AR, compared to traditional learning modes that do not incorporate AR. The use of AR technology in the learning process not only leads to more active participation but also enhances the overall effectiveness of educational media, making it a valuable tool for enriching the learning experience [5–8]. This promotes a more enjoyable learning experience for children.

Therefore, given the significance of the topic, this paper is dedicated to investigating the impact of augmented reality (AR) interactions on children in nature-based education. Nature education is centered on allowing learners to ac- quire knowledge and contribute to learning outcomes through interactions with the natural world. Nature education has a high demand for interactive learning and is one of the most suitable areas to explore as an AR-assisted learning outcome.

2   Related Work

2.1   Nature Education

The importance of nature education was first clearly emphasized in the Stock- holm Declaration of the 1972 United Nations Conference on the Human Environment [9]. The Declaration not only emphasized the urgency of environmental issues but also pointed out the key role of education in establishing the concept of harmonious coexistence between human beings and nature. With the increased attention to environmental issues, nature education has become a hotspot for academic research, with the core objective of promoting the dissemination of the concept of sustainable development through education and enhancing the ability of individuals to solve environmental problems.

Existing literature suggests that nature education is essential for environmental protection. Cheng [10] indicated that direct contact with nature is particularly important for children's development, stimulating emotional attachment to nature and environmental awareness. However, as urbanization accelerates, many children have less and less contact with the natural environment, a phenomenon known as "nature deficit disorder" [11]. This lack of exposure may decrease the development of environmental awareness, which in turn may affect future environmental behavior [15].

Research also suggests that nature education is particularly important for preschoolers [15], emphasizing that childhood experiences with nature can im- plant emotional attachments to natural objects in the minds of individuals. By incorporating nature-related education into the curriculum, children can grow up with a deep connection to, and concern for, natural things, which can help them in their future knowledge and understanding of natural things.

In recent years, dinosaurs have received increasing attention as part of nature education [16]. Dinosaurs are not only a point of interest for many children, but also an important entry point for science education. Using dinosaur-related content for nature education can stimulate children's interest in earth's history, biodiversity, and evolution [16]. By exploring dinosaurs and their causes of ex- tinction, children can gain a deeper understanding of the importance of environ- mental change and ecological balance. This type of education not only cultivates children's interest in nature but also helps them develop a sense of responsibility and action towards environmental protection.

2.2 Augmented Reality (AR)

Augmented Reality (AR) is a technology that displays virtual information in the real world as seen by the user through a display device [17]. This fusion of virtual and real elements allows the user to experience an enhanced version of the environment. According to Milgram [18], the concept of AR lies somewhere between the real and the virtual and is part of a continuum from fully real to fully virtual environments.

Azuma [19] further defines AR as an environment that integrates virtual and real-world elements, allowing real-time interaction and three-dimensional experiences. This widely accepted definition distinguishes AR from Virtual Reality (VR), which fully immerses the user in a computer-generated environment, isolated from the real world around them. Practical applications of AR include providing guided tours in museums, outdoor tourist attractions, and campuses, allowing users to instantly access pertinent information about the place.

To achieve the fusion of real and virtual objects, AR relies on image recognition technology to ensure a seamless overlay of augmented content with real- world objects. This technology enables users to experience vivid simulations on the device display, making AR applications more engaging and interactive.

2.3 AR in Nature Education

Augmented Reality (AR) represents the fusion of the digital and physical worlds, and its application in assisted learning is significantly different from traditional learning methods [20]. AR technology allows students to interact with the learning content, which in turn enhances their concentration and learning. AR utilizes the user's visual and spatial abilities to enhance the learning experience by adding extra information to the real world, rather than having students merely face a static textbook or PowerPoint [20].

In addition to AR, Virtual Reality (VR) is an ever-explored virtualization tool that has been widely used in education [21]. However, there is a significant difference between Virtual Reality (VR) and Augmented Reality (AR) in terms of the approach to enhancing the learning experience. VR brings students fully into a computer-generated digital environment through a display, enabling them to explore and interact with virtual objects. VR technology is commonly used for immersive simulations and can provide a better level engagement experience that allows students to gain a deep understanding of complex concepts [21].

In contrast, Augmented Reality (AR) technology allows students to perceive digital components of a physical environment through a screen or mobile device by connecting digital elements with the real world [22]. Students can interact with physical objects with digital annotations or access 3D models that pop up in the actual environment. AR serves as an information layer that enhances the tangible experience and is particularly well-suited for guided tours, interactive visualizations, and real-time data integration. Augmented reality maintains a connection to the real world and facilitates the integration of physical and digital interactions [23].

3 Experiment

3.1 Experiment Design

Natural Education Lesson Materials. To present the nature of education content, we employed video as the primary instructional tool. Videos were chosen for their ability to deliver comprehensive educational material in a format that is accessible and appealing to children. The teaching theme focused on dinosaurs; a subject that is inherently fascinating to preschoolers yet remains outside their everyday experiences. By selecting dinosaurs as the topic, we minimized the potential for participants' pre-existing knowledge to influence the experimental results, ensuring a more controlled and unbiased assessment of the intervention.

During the instructional process, we presented a video lesson centered around various aspects of dinosaurs, including their physical characteristics, habitats, and behaviors. These video lessons were crafted to be both informative and captivating, utilizing high-quality animations and narrations designed to hold the attention of pre-school children. To reinforce the educational content and assess the effectiveness of the instruction, each video lesson was accompanied by a series of corresponding questions. These questions were strategically integrated into the lessons.

By using a diverse array of question formats, we aimed to obtain a comprehensive picture of the learning outcomes. This approach enabled us to determine not only the participants' immediate retention of the material but also their ability to apply and generalize the knowledge to new contexts.

Representation Modes. The 2D picture as representation mode was chosen for comparison with the AR mode because the picture mode is most commonly used for educational purposes [24].

The use of 2D images for knowledge description during the course learning process is for more effective learning of knowledge concepts, e.g., Fig. 1 and Fig. 2 are screenshots of the instructional video and 2D images about Tyrannosaurus rex and Triceratops. As a mode as opposed to 2D images, the AR mode makes learning target more intuitive. For example, Fig. 3 shows the use of AR technology to demonstrate the Tyrannosaurus rex and Triceratops. In addition to being able to observe the behavior of the object from multiple perspectives as shown in Fig. 3, the AR mode allowed participants to interact with the object by tapping on the screen. Since the AR content in this study is pre-designed, users do not need to use special equipment and only need to be on a tool that

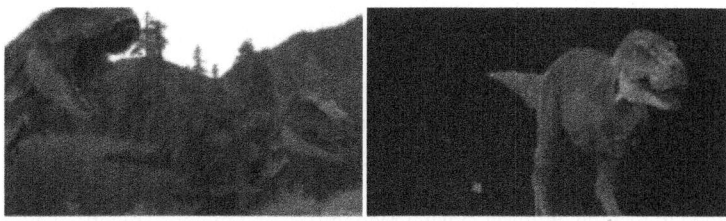

Fig. 1. Dynamic movements (Left) and static poses (Right) of Tyrannosaurus Rex

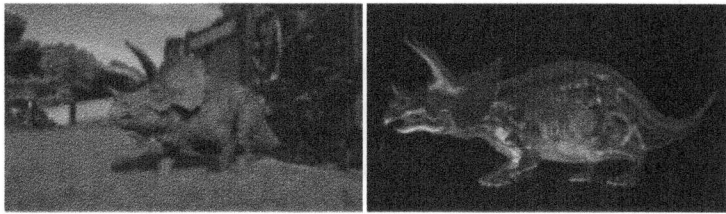

Fig. 2. Dynamic movements (Left) and static poses (Right) of Triceratops

can support video playback and on-screen interaction in order to use the AR- based instructional content. During the teaching step, the learning content will be presented as a video. When the AR content is played, the AR application is launched to enable interaction.

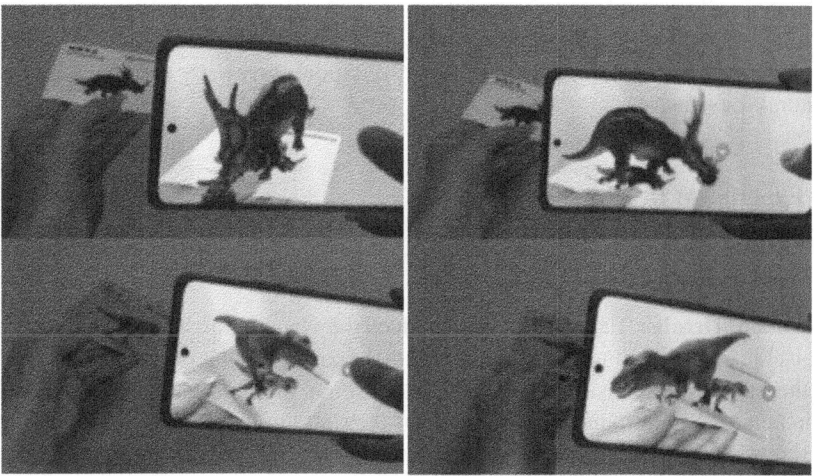

Fig. 3. AR representations with the interaction button.

Evaluation Method. The evaluation of the children's learning effectiveness was meticulously structured through a two-part question series, immediatelyfollowing the viewing of the video presentations. This assessment was crucial in determining the efficacy of both the augmented reality (AR) and traditional 2D image representations in nature-based education.

First Question Type (Q1): In the first part of the assessment, the children were presented with multiple images, each depicting different dinosaurs. Among these, one dinosaur had been featured in the video they had just watched. The task required the children to identify this specific dinosaur from the group of images. This question type was designed to test the children'svisual recognition and memory recall—key cognitive skills that underpin early educational development. The ability to correctly identify the dinosaur was indicative of how well the children could remember and recognize visual information that was presented to them.

Second Question Type (Q2): The second part of questions was more challenging and aimed at assessing higher-order cognitive skills. The children were asked to describe the appearance and distinctive features of a specific dinosaur, previously introduced in the video. This task tested their ability to synthesize the information presented and articulate it in a detailed and accurate manner. It required the children not only to recall the visual details but also to communicate these details effectively, illustrating their comprehension and verbal expression skills. For instance, they might have been asked to describe the size or any dis- tinctive features like the plates of a Stegosaurus or the horns of a Triceratops, as demonstrated in the AR or 2D video.

The results from these questions were meticulously recorded, including both the accuracy of the children's responses and the time they took to respond. These metrics were essential for evaluating the impact of the technological medium on the children's learning performance. By analyzing the children's ability to recognize and describe the dinosaurs accurately and quickly, the researchers could infer the effectiveness of augmented reality in enhancing visual memory and cognitive articulation compared to traditional methods. This detailed analysis was fundamental in understanding how different educational technologies can be optimized to improve early childhood education in natural sciences.

3.2 Experiment Description

Participants. A total of 43 participants were selected from a kindergarten. Participants were aged 4 to 6 years old.

Experiment Details. Each lesson was conducted by two researchers. One of them was responsible for conducting the experiment with the participants as presented in Fig. 4, and the other one was responsible for collecting data. First, the children sat in a chair and the researchers briefly introduced the purpose of the study to them. Then, each participant was shown a teaching video using two presentation modes. Apart from the presentation mode, the content used in the two teaching videos was exactly the same. When the teaching video proceeded to explain specific knowledge, the different presentation modes would be awakened. For example, after the video explained the morphological characteristics of dinosaurs, the participants saw a detailed presentation of a dinosaur. Participants in the 2D presentation mode would learn by browsing different pictures, while participants in the AR presentation mode would learn through AR interaction. After learning the content of the video, participants were asked questions related to it.

For example, in question 1, the researchers showed the children a set of images, each depicting a different dinosaur. Among them, one dinosaur appeared in the video they had just watched. This task required the children to identify this specific dinosaur from the set of pictures. As the main criterion for evaluating the children's problem-solving ability, another researcher recorded their answers and reaction times. After the study, each child was asked to talk about their learning experience in the two presentation modes.

Measurement. Response efficiency and effectiveness in solving the learning tasks were measured. For efficiency, we measured the response time, which is defined as the time between the moment when the researcher proposed a question and the time at which answers were provided by the participants. As for effectiveness, we simply employ the accuracy rate of question answering.

Data Collection. The response time data was collected by a researcher with a timer. The accuracy rate was also recorded by a researcher.

4   Result

This study first examines the effectiveness and outcomes of preschoolers learning about dinosaurs and compares the AR model with the graphical model. The effectiveness of the two models was balanced by the time and accuracy of students 'answers. Under the AR model, the average time for answering the naturaleducation question Q1 for children was 1.19 and 1.27 seconds for two different types of dinosaurs, which are 1% improved and 4% deteriorated. In 2D image mode, they spent an average of 1.21 and 1.22 seconds for two different types of dinosaurs. As for question Q2, participants with 2D image representation took 2.51 and 2.98 seconds to answer questions, and participants with AR representation took 2.39 and 2.87 seconds to answer questions.

At the end of the experiment, all children were interviewed to understand their learning experience in AR and image modes. Most children liked having both virtual

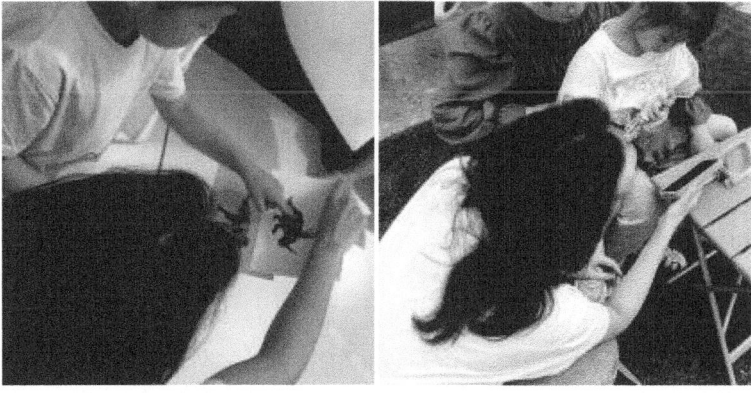

Fig. 4. Pre-schoolchildren participating in experiments.

and real-world scenes in AR mode. They showed better mastery of dinosaur-related knowledge. The interview results showed that when asked "Which representation mode do you like?", 30 children chose AR representation. Two explanations dominated. The first reason is that the AR mode is more attractive to interact with, which allows children's learning behavior to getsustained attention. The second reason is that the AR mode can provide a more detailed learning process.

In contrast, the AR mode has a more obvious improvement in learning effects in more difficult knowledge learning.

5 Discussion

The experiment results show that increased participation in nature-based education with AR mode is associated with knowledge acquisition and critical thinking skills. It is important to note that the design of our study does not establish a causal relationship between AR mode and critical thinking, as the findings are based on theoretical assumptions supported by experimental evidence. Nonetheless, the significance of cultivating both knowledge acquisition and critical thinking, as complementary drivers of children's learning capacity, through nature-based education should be further investigated as a highly promising approach to nurturing self-driven individuals.

6 Future Directions

We suggest considering several future directions for improving the design of AR- based applications in early childhood learning.

First, there is still a lot of room for exploration on how to design AR models to better stimulate children's learning. At present, we have proved through ex- perimental comparison that the AR model's promotion effect on learning mainly exists in increasing the duration of attention for a single learning session and in- creasing the learning efficiency per unit time. However, for different learning contents, the direction that the AR model needs to focus on is also different. For learning content with high logical ability requirements, such as mathematics and physics, a clearer explanation process will have a better improvement in learning effects. However, for general education content, extending the duration of attention for a single learning session can more effectively complete the learn- ing content. Therefore, for different learning contents, using different AR mode designs will more effectively improve students' learning effects.

In addition, taking eye trackers and brain activity signals as learning effect measurement indicators into consideration can more accurately analyze the core factors for improving learning effects under AR mode. In most studies on the learning effects of AR modeon preschool children, only the question-and-answer results of participants are used as analysis data.

7 Conclusion

There has been an increasing level of interest in applying AR to create attractive and effective education experiences. However, the application of AR technology in education for children remains to be fully explored, especially when it is being used with knowledge learning. This paper has investigated the effects of AR as a representation mode on pre-school children's learning of the concept of knowledge.

This study examined AR technology as a mode of representation in assisting children's learning of natural concepts when compared with a conventional 2d image mode. AR interaction may develop the independent learning ability of pre- school children by encouraging them to obtain more information from learning objects.

One limitation of the study is the conventional design of AR applications and question scenarios, which has been illustrated above. The designs of AR mode and questions are selected from conventional pre-school learning class materials and the interaction function is also designed by an experienced expert. The whole experiments are designed to explore the impact of AR technology on the learning process. There is increasing research indicating that collaborative design approaches should be more utilized in AR-enhanced applications so that more diversified AR interaction functions can be proposed. Another limitation of the study is that only pre-defined learning contents can support AR mode. Thus, the alignment of 2D image content and 3D AR content is also important. The best approach is to construct 3D AR content based on 2D images. However, the 3D AR content employed in this study is pre-designed by human experts which would involve personalbias to a certain extent. Thus, generation approaches like NeRF which can generate 3D content based on image input should be employed in future studies.

References

1. Ramli, R.Z.: Designing a mobile learning application model by integrating augmented reality and game elements to improve student learning experience. Personal Ubiquitous Comput. **29**, 1981– 2008 (2024)
2. Van Steenbrugge, H., Valcke, M., Desoete, A.: Mathematics learning difficulties in primary education: Teachers' professional knowledge and the use of commercially available learning packages. Educ. Stud. **36**(1), 59–71 (2010)
3. Chen, Y.C., Wang, S., Chiang, Y.: Exploring the Effect of Presence in an AR-based Learning Environment. In: 13th Global Chinese Conference on Computers in Education, Taipei (2016)
4. Ardiny, H., Khanmirza, E.: The role of AR and VR technologies in education developments: opportunities and challenges. In: 2018 6th RSI International Conference on Robotics and Mechatronics (icrom), pp. 482–487. IEEE (2021)
5. Atwood-Blaine, D., Huffman, D.: Mobile gaming and student interactions in a science center: the future of gaming in science education. Int. J. Sci. Math. Educ. **15**, 45–65 (2017)
6. Furió, D., Juan, M,-C., Seguí, I., Vivó, R.: Mobile learning vs. traditional classroom lessons: a comparative study. J. Comput. Assist. Learn. **3**(31), 189–201 (2015)
7. Radu, I.: Augmented reality in education: a meta-review and cross-media analysis. Pers. Ubiquit. Comput. **18**, 1533–1543 (2014)
8. Radu, I., MacIntyre, B., Lourenco, S.: Comparing children's crosshair and finger interactions in handheld augmented reality: relationships between usability and child development. In Proceedings of the The 15th International Conference on Interaction Design and Children (IDC '16). Association for Computing Machinery, New York, NY, USA, 288–298 (2016). https://doi.org/10.1145/2930674.2930726
9. Handl, G.: Declaration of the united nations conference on the human environment (stockholm declaration), 1972 and the rio declaration on environment and development, 1992. United Nations Audiovisual Library of International Law **11**(6), 1–11 (2012)

10. Cheng, J.C.H., Monroe, M.C.: Connection to nature: children's affective attitude toward nature. Environ. Behav. **44**(1), 31–49 (2012)
11. Dwyre, Vanessa J: Nature Deficit Disorder and the Need for Environmental Edu- cation. (2015)
12. Wu, H.K., Lee, S.W.Y., Chang, H.Y., Liang, J.C.: Current status, opportunities and challenges of augmented reality in education Comput. Educ. 62(5) 41–49 (2013)
13. Radu, I.: Exploring the usability of augmented reality interaction techniques during children's early elementary-school years. Georgia Institute of Technology, Location (2016)
14. Malinverni, L., Valero, C., Schaper, M.M. and Pares, N.: A conceptual framework to compare two paradigms of augmented and mixed reality experiences. In Proceedings of the 17th ACM Conference on Interaction De- sign and Children (IDC '18). Association for Computing Machinery, New York, NY, USA, 7–18 (2018). https://doi.org/10.1145/3202185.3202750
15. Asah, S.T., Bengston, D.N., Westphal, L.M, Gowan, C.H: Mechanisms of children's exposure to nature: predicting adulthood environmental citizenship and commitment to nature-based activities. Environment Behav. **50**(7), 807–836 (2018)
16. Ardoin, N.M., Bowers, A.W.: Early childhood environmental education: a systematic review of the research literature. Educ. Res. Rev. **31** 100353 (2020)
17. Salmi, H., Thuneberg, H., Vainikainen, M.-P.: Learning with dinosaurs: a study on motivation, cognitive reasoning, and making observations. Int. J. Sci. Educ., Part B 7(3), 203–218 (2017)
18. Al-Ansi, A.M., Jaboob, M., Garad, A., Al-Ansi, A.: Analyzing augmented reality (AR) and virtual reality (VR) recent development in education. Social Sci. Human. Open 8(1), 100532 (2023)
19. Milgram, P., Takemura, H., Utsumi, A., Kishino, F.: Augmented reality: a class of displays on the reality-virtuality continuum. Telemanipulator Telepresence Technologies, **2351** 282–292 (1995)
20. Azuma, R.T.: A survey of augmented reality. Telemanipulator Telepresence Technol. **6**(4) 355–385 (1997)
21. Lin, H.-C., Chen, M.-C., Chang, C.-K.: Assessing the effectiveness of learning solid geometry by using an augmented reality-assisted learn- ing system. Interact. Learn. Environ. **23**(6), 799–810 (2015)
22. Chen, J., Zhou, Y., Zhai, J.: Incorporating AR/VR- assisted learning into informal science institutions: a systematic review. Virt. Real. **27**(3), 1985–2001 (2023)
23. Jamali, S., Shiratuddin, M.F., Wong, K.: An overview of mobile-augmented reality in higher education. Int. J. Recent Trends Eng. Technol. **11**(1), 229–238 (2014)
24. Lin, S., Cheng, H.F., Li, W., Huang, Z., Hui, P., Peylo, C.: Ubii: Physical world interaction through augmented reality. IEEE Trans. Mob. Comput. **16**(3), 872–885 (2016)
25. Passig, D., Eden, S.: Cognitive intervention through virtual environments among deaf and hard-of-hearing children. Eur. J. Spec. Needs Educ. **18**, 173–182 (2003)

New Cultural and Tourism Experiences

Evaluating the Effectiveness of an Augmented Reality Platform in Promoting Sustainable Tourism in the Peruvian Amazon Jungle

Johan Baldeón[(✉)][iD], Darwin Auccapuri[iD], Emilio Díaz[iD], Andrés Masuda[iD], and Rodolfo Gálvez[iD]

Pontificia Universidad Católica del Perú, Lima, Peru
{johan.baldeon,dauccapuri,ediazm,masuda.a,rjgalvezm}@pucp.edu.pe
https://www.pucp.edu.pe/

Abstract. This work explores the potential of Augmented Reality (AR) to boost the sustainability of tourist experiences in the Peruvian Amazon, leveraging a comprehensive UX evaluation of the "Pacaya Samiria" AR platform. Motivated by the increasing role of technology in tourism, we delve into the multifaceted impact of AR on visitor behavior and environmental stewardship. The meticulously designed "Pacaya Samiria" AR platform immerses visitors in the Amazon's biodiversity and cultural heritage while promoting eco-awareness. Employing advanced methodologies and UX expertise, we conducted a rigorous evaluation using focus groups and the User Experience Questionnaire (UEQ). This allowed us to assess the platform's strengths (immersion, education), weaknesses (technical challenges, cultural relevance), and overall impact on visitor perceptions and behaviors. Key findings highlight the crucial role of context-sensitive design and content curation for effective AR implementation in remote ecotourism settings. While "Pacaya Samiria" demonstrates promise, opportunities for optimization exist, particularly in addressing technical limitations and enhancing cultural integration. This research contributes to Sustainable HCI by offering actionable insights into how AR can support environmental conservation and enrich visitor experiences in ecotourism destinations. By unveiling the intricate dynamics of UX in the Amazon, we inform future initiatives harnessing technology for global sustainable tourism development.

Keywords: User experience · UX evaluation · augmented reality · sustainable tourism · cultural sensitivity · focus group method · Amazon jungle

1 Introduction

Tourism stands as a cornerstone of economic growth for many nations, continuously adapting to meet the evolving needs and expectations of travelers [32,43].

P. Zaphiris et al. (Eds.): HCII 2024, LNCS 15378, pp. 223–241, 2025.
https://doi.org/10.1007/978-3-031-76815-6_16

With the integration of cutting-edge technologies, the tourism sector has the potential to undergo significant transformation, enhancing visitor experiences while championing sustainability [36]. Nowhere is this potential more promising than in the depths of the Peruvian Amazon jungle, a region renowned for its unparalleled biodiversity and rich cultural heritage.

As digital technologies increasingly shape travel experiences, the evaluation of User Experience (UX) in tourism platforms has garnered significant attention [1,13,15,34]. Augmented Reality (AR) applications, in particular, have emerged as powerful tools for enriching visitor experiences at sites of natural and cultural significance [30,38]. In the domain of Human-Computer Interaction (HCI), conducting thorough UX evaluations is essential for the success of any tourism platform utilizing AR, given its direct impact on visitor satisfaction and loyalty [16]. However, the effective implementation of such technologies must contend with the unique challenges posed by remote and demanding environments [2,6,22,27,31].

It's essential to recognize the role of context in UX evaluation [10,25,28,34], where cultural and environmental factors significantly influence users' interactions and perceptions. Yet, there remains a gap in comprehensive studies exploring the intersection of immersive technology, sustainability, and cultural context in remote ecotourism settings, such as the Amazon jungle in Peru. This paper aims to address this gap by examining the UX of an AR platform within the Pacaya Samiria Amazon Lodge Private Reserve in Peru's Amazon jungle. The primary objectives are to identify areas for improvement and provide actionable recommendations to enhance the UX.

The significance of this work lies in its endeavor to evaluate emerging technologies in unique environmental contexts, such as remote ecotourism settings. Traditional UX evaluation methods may fall short in capturing the nuanced and dynamic experiences users encounter when interacting with AR applications in such environments. Focused on advancing ecotourism, scientific inquiry, and sustainable ecosystem utilization, this study transcends conventional usability assessments, delving into the intricate dynamics of culture, technology, and ecological preservation.

Methodologically, this work employs a focus group [45] approach alongside the User Experience Questionnaire (UEQ) [23,24,41]. The focus groups gather qualitative data on visitors' perceptions and behaviors, while the UEQ quantitatively measures the UX of the platform. Data analysis encompasses both qualitative and quantitative techniques [3].

Findings from this study reveal several strengths of the "Pacaya Samiria" platform [33], including its immersive and interactive nature, educational value, and contributions to environmental conservation. However, weaknesses such as technical issues and the need for more culturally sensitive content are also identified. Moreover, the platform demonstrates a positive impact on visitors' perceptions and behaviors, fostering increased interest in environmental conservation and sustainable tourism practices.

This work underscores the necessity for continuous evaluation and improvement of the platform to ensure its efficacy and sustainability. It highlights the potential of emerging technologies like AR to provide immersive experiences while promoting sustainable tourism in remote ecotourism settings. Additionally, it emphasizes the importance of considering unique cultural and environmental factors in shaping users' interactions and perceptions. Through its insights into the UX of the "Pacaya Samiria" platform, this study contributes to Sustainable HCI and Cultural HCI, advocating for technology's role in supporting environmental conservation and cultural sensitivity in HCI research.

2   Related Work

Sustainable tourism stands at the intersection of environmental conservation, cultural preservation, and economic development, emphasizing the responsible management of resources and experiences to meet the needs of present and future generations [9]. Augmented Reality (AR) technology has emerged as a promising tool in the tourism industry, offering immersive and interactive experiences that have the potential to enhance visitor engagement and promote sustainable practices.

Sustainable Tourism Practices and Challenges: The concept of sustainable tourism, rooted in the Brundtland Report's [50] definition of sustainable development, emphasizes the triple bottom line of economic, environmental, and socio-cultural sustainability.

The growing demand for sustainable tourism has led to a surge in research exploring frameworks and practices that minimize environmental impact, benefit local communities, and ensure economic viability [14,49]. Studies have identified challenges such as balancing visitor needs with conservation efforts, managing waste and resource consumption, and fostering responsible behavior among tourists [11,18,35,44].

AR in Tourism for Sustainability: AR technology overlays digital information onto the physical world, offering novel ways to engage and educate tourists. Studies by Kim [19] and Buhalis and Foerste [4] have explored the potential of AR to enhance visitor experiences by providing contextually relevant information, fostering emotional connections, and promoting environmental awareness. Additionally, AR has been shown to facilitate cultural immersion and interpretation, as demonstrated in research by Lee et al. [5] on AR-enhanced heritage tourism.

The application of AR in ecotourism has gained traction, with studies demonstrating its potential to enrich visitor experiences, enhance environmental awareness, and promote sustainable practices [30,38]. These studies showcase the ability of AR to overlay digital information onto physical environments, fostering deeper engagement and understanding of natural and cultural heritage.

Implementing AR effectively in remote and demanding environments like the Amazon jungle presents unique challenges. Studies have identified issues related to technical limitations, infrastructure constraints, and ensuring cultural appropriateness [2,6,22,27,31]. Addressing these challenges is crucial for successful AR adoption in such settings.

AR applications are increasingly explored in tourism for enhancing visitor experiences and promoting sustainability [21,29,52]. Studies highlight potential benefits like raising awareness of environmental issues [37], promoting responsible behavior [39], and fostering cultural understanding [7,46]. However, challenges such as technical limitations, accessibility concerns, and potential negative impacts on cultural heritage require consideration [51].

UX Evaluation of AR in Remote Settings: User Experience (UX) evaluation plays a vital role in assessing the effectiveness of AR applications in tourism. Traditional usability testing methods, such as heuristic evaluation and user testing, may need adaptation to account for the unique characteristics of AR interfaces. Recent studies, such as those by Law et al. [26] and Hassenzahl [17], advocate for holistic approaches to UX evaluation that consider emotional, hedonic, and pragmatic aspects of user interaction. Moreover, the User Experience Questionnaire (UEQ) developed by Laugwitz et al. [23] offers a standardized tool for quantitatively measuring UX dimensions such as attractiveness, perspicuity, and efficiency.

A substantial body of research underscores the crucial role of UX in tourism platforms, emphasizing its impact on visitor satisfaction, loyalty, and overall experience [1,12,13,15,20,34,47,48]. These studies highlight the need for user-centered design approaches that consider the specific needs and expectations of tourists in various contexts.

Research has increasingly highlighted the importance of considering cultural and environmental factors in UX evaluations, acknowledging their critical role in shaping how users interact with and perceive technology. Modern UX evaluations emphasize the need to go beyond traditional [10,25,28,34]. This is particularly relevant for tourism platforms operating in unique settings like the Amazon jungle, where cultural sensitivity and environmental considerations are paramount.

Limited research exists on UX evaluation of AR applications in remote and environmentally sensitive settings (e.g., mountain areas, rainforests). Existing studies primarily focus on usability testing in controlled environments [2]. While user satisfaction and engagement are explored [27], few studies address the specific contextual factors influencing UX in remote settings, such as connectivity limitations, cultural sensitivity, and environmental impact considerations.

Gap and Significance. While existing research explores AR's potential for sustainable tourism and UX evaluation in remote settings, a gap exists in studies examining the intersection of immersive technology, sustainability, and cultural context in remote ecotourism settings. This study addresses this gap by evaluating the UX of the "Pacaya Samiria" AR platform within the unique context of the Peruvian Amazon jungle, considering both its contribution to sustainable tourism practices and its impact on visitors' perceptions and behaviors in this culturally and environmentally sensitive setting.

This study's novelty lies in its multifaceted approach:

– **Contextualized UX evaluation**: Examining AR's UX within the specific cultural and environmental context of the Amazon jungle.
– **Focus on sustainable tourism**: Assessing the platform's contribution to promoting responsible behavior and environmental awareness.
– **Actionable recommendations**: Providing insights and recommendations for improving the platform's UX and sustainability impact.

By addressing this gap, this study contributes to the growing body of knowledge in Sustainable HCI and Cultural HCI, highlighting the potential of AR for promoting sustainable tourism practices while considering the unique challenges and opportunities presented by remote ecotourism settings.

3   Description of the "Pacaya Samiria" AR Platform

The "Pacaya Samiria" AR platform lets visitors experience the "experience economy" by offering innovative and interactive ways to explore the region's biodiversity. See Fig. 1 for examples of the app's user interface.

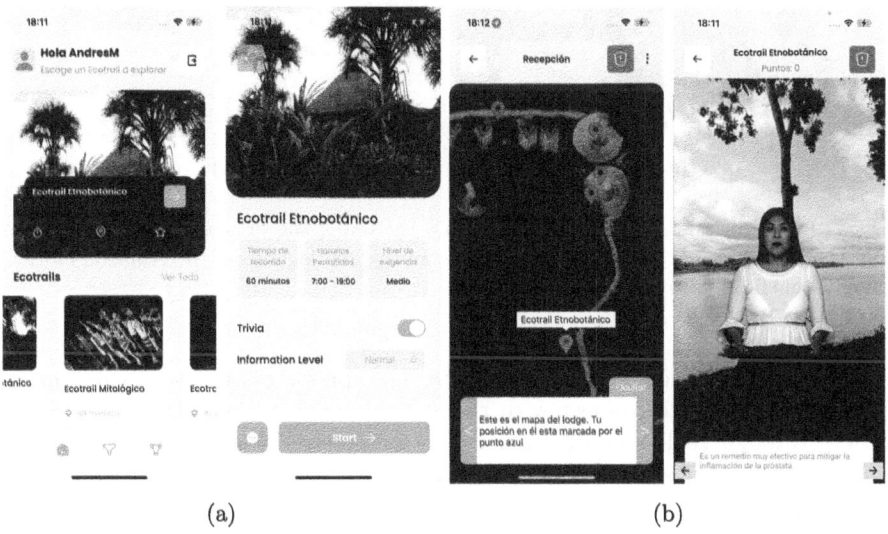

(a)   (b)

Fig. 1. User interfaces of the "Pacaya Samiria" AR platform. (a) The Ecotrails catalogue and the intro of an Ecotrail. (b) The map of an Ecotrail with geolocalization and the AR of a character.

The User-Centered Design (UCD) approach has been applied to emphasize understanding user needs, goals, and context, and to design a system that is usable, useful, and desirable.

The "Pacaya Samiria" AR platform offers five unique "Ecotrails" themed around ethnobotany, mythology, fauna, local worldview, and even an interactive game. These Ecotrails aren't just virtual paths; they're gateways to understanding the region's rich biodiversity and culture. Visitors can delve into expert-curated information, making their exploration truly immersive. Figure 2a and Fig. 2b show the use of the "Pacaya Samiria" App and how users can experience cultural heritage.

(a)   (b)

Fig. 2. (a) Using the App "Pacaya Samiria". (b) Using the "Pacaya Samiria" App to tour the Mythological Ecotrail that presents myths and legends of the Amazon culture using augmented reality.

But the engagement doesn't stop there. The app fosters a sense of community by allowing guests to connect with their social networks and share their experiences through real-time streaming. This immersive journey isn't just about learning, it's about sharing and connecting.

The app offers gamified activities for those seeking a playful twist where users can interact with charming AR characters and earn rewards, adding another layer of fun and satisfaction to their lodge visit.

The platform uses the Internet of Things (IoT) and cloud computing to provide real-time information about the ecolodge and automatic positioning assistance. The solution architecture allows the AR app to receive short-range radio signals (Bluetooth) from beacons or Bluetooth low-energy devices distributed in each Ecotrail in the Pacaya Samiria Amazon Lodge Private Reserve to trigger events related to thematic routes with AR and customize the activities. The app can access services on the cloud to get information about the login information, points, and comments.

A reliable and sustainable telecommunications infrastructure ensures connectivity in the remote jungle. This system includes solar panels, batteries, a tall tower, and communication equipment. The energy system uses solar panels and batteries for sustainable operation.

The platform seeks to foster a greater appreciation of Amazonian cultural identity through the creation of authentic and respectful tourist experiences and promote the active participation of local communities, their traditions, crafts, and ancestral knowledge, which can generate a greater sense of belonging and pride in their cultural heritage.

4   Methodology

4.1   Research Design

This study employs a mixed-methods approach to evaluate the effectiveness of the "Pacaya Samiria" Augmented Reality (AR) platform in promoting sustainable tourism in the Peruvian Amazon Jungle. The research design integrates qualitative and quantitative data collection methods to provide a comprehensive understanding of visitor experiences and perceptions.

The "Pacaya Samiria" AR platform was selected based on its reputation for providing immersive and educational experiences that highlight the biodiversity and cultural heritage of the Peruvian Amazon Jungle. The study site, the Pacaya Samiria Amazon Lodge Private Reserve, was chosen for its ecological significance and popularity among ecotourists seeking authentic and sustainable experiences in the Amazon rainforest.

4.2   Data Collection Methods

Focus Groups. Focus groups [45] are conducted with visitors who have experienced the "Pacaya Samiria" AR platform during their visit to the reserve. Semi-structured interviews facilitate in-depth discussions about visitors' perceptions, emotions, and behaviors related to the AR experience. Focus groups allow for the exploration of nuanced perspectives and the identification of common themes among participants. The survey designed in Table 1 explored the effects of the "Pacaya Samiria" AR platform on visitors' perspectives, including identity, inclusivity, and sustainable tourism practices. The researchers surveyed visitors to collect demographic and travel data. Additionally, interviews were conducted with local communities, tourism professionals, and government officials to gauge the project's impact on these same themes. By analyzing the interviews, patterns and trends related to identity, inclusivity, and sustainable tourism were identified. Throughout the study, strict ethical protocols were followed to protect participant privacy and anonymity.

Table 1. The designed survey for measuring the impact of the "Pacaya Samiria" AR platform on perceptions about identity formation, inclusivity, and sustainable tourism practices.

Objective 1: To investigate the role of the "Pacaya Samiria" AR platform in fostering identity formation among visitors and collaborators of the ecolodge.

1. Demographic information:

– Age, gender, nationality, educational background, occupation.

2. "Pacaya Samiria" AR platform experience:

– Have you visited the Pacaya Samiria ecolodge in the Amazon Jungle of Peru?

• Yes / No

– If yes, how many times have you visited?

– How would you describe your overall experience using the "Pacaya Samiria" AR platform in terms of fostering a sense of personal identity?

• Not at all fostering / Slightly fostering / Moderately fostering / Very much fostering / Extremely fostering

– Please provide specific examples or instances where you felt a stronger connection to your own identity during your visit.

3. Collaborative activities:

– Have you participated in any collaborative activities in the Pacaya Samiria ecolodge?

• Yes / No

– If yes, how would you describe the impact of these collaborative activities on your sense of identity formation?

• No impact / Little impact / Moderate impact / Significant impact / Profound impact

– Please provide specific examples or instances where your participation in collaborative activities enhanced your sense of identity.

Objective 2: To analyze how the "Pacaya Samiria" AR platform promotes inclusivity in the tourism industry and local communities.

4. Inclusivity in the tourism industry:

– How inclusive do you perceive the "Pacaya Samiria" AR platform to be in terms of engaging visitors from diverse backgrounds?

• Not at all inclusive / Slightly inclusive / Moderately inclusive / Very inclusive / Extremely inclusive

– In what ways do you think the "Pacaya Samiria" AR platform promotes inclusivity? Please provide specific examples.

5. Community engagement:

– To what extent do you think the "Pacaya Samiria" AR platform has engaged and benefited the local communities?

• No engagement/benefit / Little engagement/benefit / Moderate engagement/benefit / Significant engagement/benefit / Profound engagement/benefit

– Please provide specific examples of how the "Pacaya Samiria" AR platform has positively impacted the local communities.

(continued)

Table 1. (*continued*)

Objective 3: To assess the impact of the "Pacaya Samiria" AR platform in reducing inequality by promoting sustainable tourism practices and supporting the local economy.

6. Sustainable tourism practices:

    – How important do you consider sustainable tourism practices in the context of the "Pacaya Samiria" AR platform?

        • Not important at all / Slightly important / Moderately important / Very important / Extremely important

    – In what ways do you think the "Pacaya Samiria" AR platform promotes sustainable tourism practices? Please provide specific examples.

7. Economic impact:

    – To what extent do you think the "Pacaya Samiria" AR platform has contributed to the local economy and reduced inequality in the region?

        • No contribution/reduction / Little contribution/reduction / Moderate contribution/reduction / Significant contribution/reduction / Profound contribution/reduction

    – Please provide specific examples of how the "Pacaya Samiria" AR platform has supported the local economy and reduced inequality.

8. Overall assessment:

    – Based on your experiences and observations, how would you rate the overall impact of the "Pacaya Samiria" AR platform in fostering identity formation, promoting inclusivity, and reducing inequality?

        • Very low impact / Low impact / Moderate impact / High impact / Very high impact

9. Additional comments:

    – Is there any additional feedback or comments you would like to share regarding the role of the "Pacaya Samiria" AR platform in fostering identity formation, promoting inclusivity, and reducing inequality?

10. Consent:

    – By completing this survey, you are giving consent for your responses to be used in the research study. Your participation is voluntary, and your identity will remain confidential.

User Experience Questionnaire (UEQ). The UEQ [23,24,41] is administered to visitors immediately after their AR experience. This standardized questionnaire assesses various dimensions of user experience, including attractiveness, perspicuity, efficiency, dependability, stimulation, and novelty [42]. Participants rate each dimension on a Likert scale, providing quantitative data on their overall satisfaction and perceived usability of the AR platform. The study employed the UEQ version 10, detailed further in [40, Fig. 1]. This questionnaire uses a 7-point scale where respondents rate their agreement with pairs of opposing statements (e.g., "attractive" vs. "unattractive"). Each item is rated from -3 (strongly agreeing with the negative term) to +3 (strongly agreeing with the positive term). The order of positive and negative starting points is randomized for each item.

To explore the platform's cultural sensitivity, the study adapted several UEQ questions: (1) Participants identified their cultural background. (2) They then rated the importance of technology reflecting their cultural background. (3) They also assessed how well the platform catered to their cultural preferences and interests. (4) Additionally, they reflected on how their cultural background influenced their interaction with the content. (5) Finally, they evaluated the alignment of the content with their cultural preferences and values, and if it inspired an appreciation for the Amazon's cultural diversity.

The Technology Acceptance Model (TAM) [8] framework was used to predict and explain user behavior towards new technologies. TAM focuses on two key factors: (1) Perceived Usefulness (PU): This refers to how helpful users believe the technology will be in their tasks. For this study, questions related to the platform's ability to enhance experiences and promote ecological awareness align with PU. (2) Perceived Ease of Use (PEOU): This refers to how easy users believe the technology is to learn and use. Questions regarding navigation, content access, and overall user-friendliness assess PEOU for the platform's AR application.

The UEQ questionnaire used in this study incorporates these TAM aspects:

- **Usefulness and Ease of Use**: The questionnaire assesses both PU and PEOU through questions about the platform's features, information provision, and overall user experience.
- **Attitudes and Behavioral Intentions**: The questionnaire gauges participants' overall satisfaction, likelihood of future use, and recommendations for others.
- **Social Influence and Facilitating Conditions**: The questionnaire explores the influence of others and any technological or environmental challenges faced while using the platform.
- **Perceptions of Technology**: The questionnaire investigates participants' general comfort level with technology and their perspectives on using digital tools in eco-tourism settings.

4.3 Participant Recruitment, Sample Size and Ethical Considerations

Participants are recruited from visitors to the Pacaya Samiria Amazon Lodge Private Reserve who voluntarily opt to experience the "Pacaya Samiria" AR platform during their visit. A purposive sampling approach is employed to ensure diversity in participant demographics, including age, gender, nationality, and previous travel experience. The sample size is determined based on the principle of data saturation, with approximately 10–15 participants per focus group session and a total sample size of 50–100 participants across multiple sessions. This study adhered to rigorous ethical guidelines, placing utmost importance on protecting participants' privacy and confidentiality. All participants freely provided informed consent before participating, and their identities remain completely anonymous in any presented findings. This ensures their privacy and fosters trust in the research process.

4.4   Data Analysis Procedures

Qualitative data from focus groups are transcribed and thematically analyzed using a rigorous coding process. Themes and patterns related to visitor experiences, perceptions, and suggestions for improvement are identified through constant comparison and iterative analysis. Quantitative data from the UEQ are analyzed using descriptive statistics to calculate mean scores for each dimension of user experience.

Table 2 and Fig. 3 showcase the user experience evaluation for the "Pacaya Samiria" AR platform. The UEQ scale, with its range of -0.8 to 0.8, indicates neutral user experience between those values. Scores below -0.8 reflect a negative evaluation, while values above 0.8 indicate a positive one.

These results reveal positive user feedback for the platform, particularly in the areas of Attractiveness, Pragmatic Quality (user-friendliness), and Hedonic Quality (enjoyment). This suggests that users found the platform appealing, easy to use, and enjoyable overall. Table 3 and Fig. 4 present benchmark scores for the six UEQ scales. These "benchmarks" are created by averaging the scores gathered from user questionnaires. In simpler terms, they represent the typical or average UX for each aspect measured by the questionnaire. The results consistently fall into the "Excellent" rating category, indicating a highly positive user experience across all measured domains. This positive experience can be attributed, in part, to the sustainable telecommunications infrastructure, which ensures reliable and eco-friendly connectivity within the ecolodge. The integration of qualitative and quantitative findings enables a comprehensive evaluation of the "Pacaya Samiria" AR platform's effectiveness in promoting sustainable tourism and enhancing visitor satisfaction in the Peruvian Amazon Jungle.

Table 2. User Experience Questionnaire Scale Measurement

UEQ Quality	UEQ Scale	Variable	UEQ Scale: Mean	UEQ Scale: Variance
Attractiveness	2.345	Attractiveness	2.345	0.10
Pragmatic Quality	2.393	Perspicuity	2.464	0.28
		Efficiency	2.321	0.16
		Dependability	2.393	0.11
Hedonic Quality	2.304	Stimulation	2.286	0.37
		Novelty	2.321	0.25

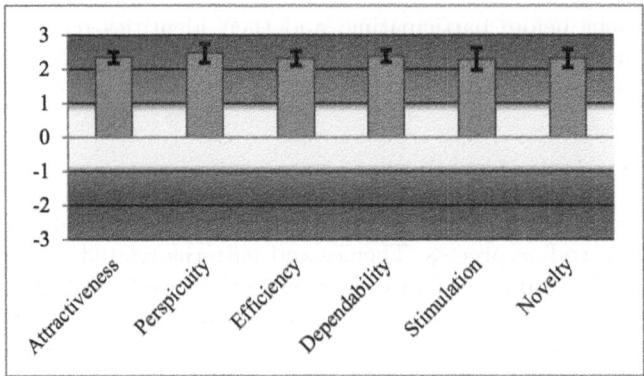

Fig. 3. UEQ Scale from 6 scale chart.

Table 3. Benchmark Measurement Result

Scale	Mean	Comparisson to benchmark	Interpretation
Attractiveness	2.345	Excellent	In the range of the 10% best results
Perspicuity	2.46	Excellent	In the range of the 10% best results
Efficiency	2.32	Excellent	In the range of the 10% best results
Dependability	2.39	Excellent	In the range of the 10% best results
Stimulation	2.29	Excellent	In the range of the 10% best results
Novelty	2.32	Excellent	In the range of the 10% best results

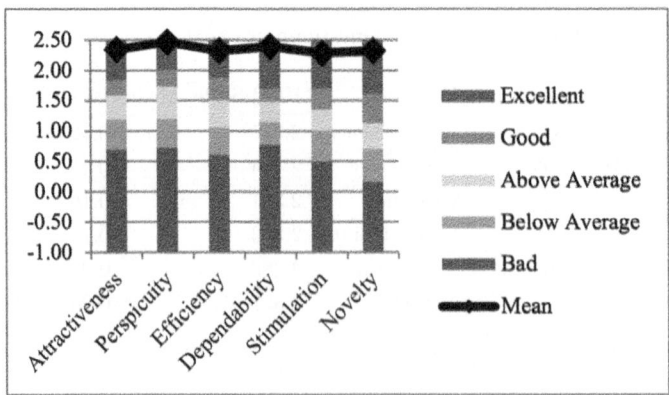

Fig. 4. Benchmark results.

5   Results

5.1   Evaluation of the "Pacaya Samiria" AR Platform

The evaluation of the "Pacaya Samiria" AR platform yielded valuable insights into its effectiveness in promoting sustainable tourism and enhancing visitor experiences in the Peruvian Amazon Jungle. The findings are presented below, highlighting both strengths and weaknesses identified through qualitative and quantitative analysis.

Strengths. Immersive and Educational Experience: Participants overwhelmingly praised the platform for its ability to provide an immersive and educational experience. They appreciated the interactive nature of the AR content, which allowed them to engage with the biodiversity and cultural heritage of the Amazon jungle in a captivating manner.

- **Environmental Awareness**: The AR platform effectively raised awareness about environmental conservation among visitors. Participants expressed a heightened sense of appreciation for the fragile ecosystem of the Amazon jungle and a greater understanding of the importance of sustainable tourism practices.
- **Engagement and Interactivity**: The interactive features of the AR platform, such as virtual guided tours and interactive quizzes, enhanced visitor engagement and participation. Participants reported feeling actively involved in the learning process, which contributed to a more memorable and enjoyable experience.

Weaknesses:

- **Technical Issues**: Some participants encountered technical issues, such as connectivity problems and glitches in the AR application. These technical challenges detracted from the overall experience and led to frustration among certain visitors.
- **Content Diversity**: While the AR content provided valuable insights into the flora, fauna, and indigenous cultures of the Amazon jungle, some participants expressed a desire for greater diversity in content. They suggested incorporating additional themes and narratives to cater to a wider range of interests and preferences.

5.2   Qualitative Analysis

Qualitative analysis of focus group discussions revealed several key themes related to visitor experiences with the "Pacaya Samiria" AR platform. Participants expressed a sense of wonder and awe at the immersive nature of the AR content, describing it as a transformative and enriching experience. They also highlighted the platform's potential to foster connections between visitors and the natural environment, emphasizing the importance of emotional engagement in promoting sustainable tourism practices.

5.3   Quantitative Analysis

Quantitative analysis of data from the User Experience Questionnaire (UEQ) provided further insights into visitor perceptions of the AR platform. Overall, participants reported high levels of satisfaction with the platform, with mean scores indicating positive ratings across all dimensions of user experience. Specifically, participants rated the platform highly in terms of attractiveness, perspicuity, efficiency, dependability, stimulation, and novelty, reflecting its effectiveness in engaging and captivating visitors.

The results of the evaluation demonstrate the potential of the "Pacaya Samiria" AR platform to promote sustainable tourism and enhance visitor experiences in the Peruvian Amazon Jungle. While the platform exhibits notable strengths in providing an immersive and educational experience, addressing technical issues and diversifying content are key areas for improvement. By leveraging the insights gained from this evaluation, stakeholders can optimize the AR platform to better meet the needs and expectations of visitors while contributing to the conservation of the Amazon rainforest.

6   Discussion

The evaluation of the "Pacaya Samiria" AR platform in promoting sustainable tourism in the Peruvian Amazon Jungle has provided valuable insights into the intersection of technology, visitor experiences, and environmental conservation. This discussion section interprets the findings in relation to the research questions and objectives, explores their implications for sustainable tourism development and AR experience design, and discusses theoretical and practical contributions to the fields of User Experience (UX) evaluation and Sustainable Human-Computer Interaction (HCI).

The findings indicate that the "Pacaya Samiria" AR platform exhibits strengths in providing an immersive and educational experience for visitors, while also raising awareness about environmental conservation. Despite encountering technical issues and a desire for more diverse content, participants reported high levels of satisfaction with the platform overall. These results align with the research objectives of assessing the effectiveness of the AR platform in promoting sustainable tourism and enhancing visitor perceptions and behaviors.

The positive reception of the AR platform highlights its potential to contribute to sustainable tourism development in ecotourism settings. By fostering connections between visitors and the natural environment, the platform can encourage responsible behavior and promote conservation efforts. Moreover, the platform's ability to engage visitors in educational experiences can enhance their appreciation for the cultural and ecological significance of the Amazon rainforest, ultimately supporting the long-term viability of tourism in the region.

Addressing technical issues and diversifying content are crucial considerations for optimizing the effectiveness of AR experiences in ecotourism settings. Improving connectivity and minimizing glitches will enhance the reliability and usability of the platform, thereby maximizing visitor satisfaction. Additionally, incorporating a broader range of themes and narratives can cater to diverse visitor interests and preferences, ensuring that the AR experience remains engaging and relevant for all participants.

This study makes several theoretical and practical contributions to the fields of UX evaluation and Sustainable HCI. The mixed-methods approach employed in the evaluation demonstrates the importance of integrating qualitative and quantitative methods to provide a comprehensive understanding of visitor experiences. Furthermore, the findings highlight the potential of AR technology to support sustainable tourism initiatives and promote environmental awareness in ecotourism destinations. By elucidating the complex dynamics of technology, culture, and sustainability, this research contributes to a deeper understanding of how emerging technologies can be leveraged to enhance visitor experiences while advancing conservation efforts.

7   Conclusion

The evaluation of the "Pacaya Samiria" Augmented Reality (AR) platform in promoting sustainable tourism in the Peruvian Amazon Jungle has yielded significant insights into the potential of technology to enhance visitor experiences and support conservation efforts in ecotourism settings. This section summarizes the main findings, acknowledges the study's limitations, suggests avenues for future research, and offers recommendations for stakeholders involved in the design and implementation of AR platforms for sustainable tourism.

The evaluation revealed that the "Pacaya Samiria" AR platform offers an immersive and educational experience for visitors, fostering environmental awareness and promoting sustainable tourism practices. Despite encountering technical challenges and limitations in content diversity, participants reported high levels of satisfaction with the platform overall. These findings underscore the transformative potential of AR technology in enhancing visitor experiences while advancing conservation goals in ecotourism destinations.

It is important to acknowledge several limitations of the study. First, the sample size may not fully represent the diverse range of visitors to the Peruvian Amazon Jungle, potentially limiting the generalizability of the findings. Second, the study's focus on a single AR platform may overlook alternative technologies or approaches that could also contribute to sustainable tourism development. Additionally, the evaluation was conducted at a specific point in time and may not capture the long-term impacts of the AR platform on visitor behavior and environmental conservation efforts.

Future research could explore the long-term effects of AR platforms on visitor perceptions, behaviors, and environmental outcomes in ecotourism settings. Longitudinal studies tracking visitor engagement and conservation behaviors over time would provide valuable insights into the sustained effectiveness of AR interventions. Additionally, comparative studies evaluating different AR technologies and approaches could shed light on best practices for designing immersive and sustainable tourism experiences.

Stakeholders involved in the design and implementation of AR platforms for sustainable tourism should prioritize addressing technical issues, enhancing content diversity, and ensuring cultural sensitivity in their initiatives. Collaborative partnerships between technology developers, environmental organizations, and local communities are essential for co-designing AR experiences that resonate with visitors and contribute to the preservation of natural and cultural heritage. Furthermore, ongoing monitoring and evaluation efforts are needed to continuously refine AR platforms and adapt to changing visitor preferences and environmental conditions.

In conclusion, the evaluation of the "Pacaya Samiria" AR platform underscores the importance of technology in promoting sustainable tourism and fostering environmental stewardship in the Peruvian Amazon Jungle. By addressing the study's limitations and pursuing future research directions, stakeholders can harness the transformative potential of AR technology to create immersive and impactful experiences that inspire visitors to engage in responsible tourism practices and contribute to the conservation of precious ecosystems.

References

1. Abbasi, V.: Introduction of a gamified platform to enhance museum visiting experience. Proc. Inst. Civ. Eng. Urban Des. Plann. **175**, 169–178 (2022). https://doi.org/10.1680/jurdp.22.00007
2. bin Ahmad Radzi, M.Q.A.N., Shah, D.S.M., Othman, M.F.S., Nor, M.N.R.M., bin Masaat, M.F.F.: Review on application of augmented reality (AR) in the ecotourism sector. Int. J. Acad. Res. Bus. Soc. Sci. **11** (2021). https://doi.org/10.6007/IJARBSS/v11-i11/11377
3. Bryman, A.: Social Research Methods. Oxford university press, 5th edn. (2016)
4. Buhalis, D., Foerste, M.: SoCoMo marketing for travel and tourism: empowering co-creation of value. J. Destination Mark. Manag. **4**(3), 151–161 (2015). https://doi.org/10.1016/j.jdmm.2015.04.001, smart Destinations
5. Chung, N., Lee, H., Kim, J.Y., Koo, C.: The role of augmented reality for experience-influenced environments: the case of cultural heritage tourism in Korea. J. Travel Res. **57**(5), 627–643 (2018). https://doi.org/10.1177/0047287517708255
6. da Costa, C.L., Prata, W.: Animal trail: an augmented reality experience in the amazon rainforest. In: Stephanidis, C. (ed.) HCI International 2019 - Posters, pp. 366–373. Springer International Publishing, Cham (2019). https://doi.org/10.1007/978-3-030-23528-4_50
7. Cranmer, E.E., tom Dieck, M., Jung, T.: The role of augmented reality for sustainable development: evidence from cultural heritage tourism. Tourism Manag. Perspect. **49**, 101196 (2023). https://doi.org/10.1016/j.tmp.2023.101196
8. Davis, F.D.: A technology acceptance model for empirically testing new end-user information systems: Theory and results. Ph.D. thesis, Massachusetts Institute of Technology (1985)
9. Edgell, Sr, D.L.: Managing Sustainable Tourism. Routledge, London, England, 3 edn. (2019). https://www.routledge.com/Managing-Sustainable-Tourism-A-Legacy-for-the-Future/Edgell-Sr/p/book/9780367331382
10. Fan, X., Li, X., Song, L., Zhang, Y., Liu, M., Miao, Q.: Usability evaluation of AR human-machine interface based on user experience. In: 2022 International Conference on Virtual Reality, Human-Computer Interaction and Artificial Intelligence (VRHCIAI), pp. 23–29 (2022). https://doi.org/10.1109/VRHCIAI57205.2022.00011

11. Fennell, D.A.: Routledge Handbook of Ecotourism. Routledge (2021). https://doi. org/10.4324/9781003001768
12. Firmansyah, B., Jonathan, M., Andreas, J., Philip, S., Hidayaturrahman: Application of UI/UX in tourism information service problems: A review. In: Proceedings of the 8th International Conference on Sustainable Information Engineering and Technology, p. 462–472. SIET 2023, Association for Computing Machinery, New York, NY, USA (2023). https://doi.org/10.1145/3626641.3627603
13. Fitriani, W.R., Azzahro, F., Hidayanto, A.N., Putra, S.P., Soesman, G.G., Hapsari, I.C.: Determining smart tourism application features based on pain points of tourism stakeholders. Int. J. Innov. Learn. **32**, 1 (2022). https://doi.org/10.1504/ijil.2022.123803
14. Gössling, S., Hall, C.M., Weaver, D.: Sustainable Tourism Futures: Perspectives on Systems. Restructuring and Innovations. Routledge (2009). https://doi.org/10.4324/9780203884256
15. Hamid, R.A., et al.: How smart is e-tourism? A systematic review of smart tourism recommendation system applying data management. Comput. Sci.e Rev. **39**, 100337 (2021). https://doi.org/10.1016/j.cosrev.2020.100337
16. Han, D.I., tom Dieck, M.C., Jung, T.: User experience model for augmented reality applications in urban heritage tourism. J. Heritage Tourism **13**, 46–61 (2018). https://doi.org/10.1080/1743873X.2016.1251931
17. Hassenzahl, M.: The thing and i: understanding the relationship between user and product, pp. 301–313. Springer International Publishing, Cham (2018). https://doi.org/10.1007/978-3-319-68213-6_19
18. Hughes, M., Weaver, D., Pforr, C.: The Practice of Sustainable Tourism: Resolving the Paradox. Routledge (2015). https://doi.org/10.4324/9781315796154
19. Kim, J.H.: The impact of memorable tourism experiences on loyalty behaviors: the mediating effects of destination image and satisfaction. J. Travel Res. **57**(7), 856–870 (2018). https://doi.org/10.1177/0047287517721369
20. Kontogianni, A., Alepis, E.: Smart tourism: state of the art and literature review for the last six years. Array **6**, 100020 (2020). https://doi.org/10.1016/j.array.2020.100020
21. Kounavis, C.D., Kasimati, A.E., Zamani, E.D.: Enhancing the tourism experience through mobile augmented reality: challenges and prospects. Int. J. Eng. Bus. Manag. **4**, 10 (2012). https://doi.org/10.5772/51644
22. Kurnaz, H.A., Ön, F., Yüksel, F.: Sustainability, big data, and corporate social responsibility, chap. A New Age in Tourist Guiding: Digital Tourism and Sustainability. CRC Press (2022). https://doi.org/10.1201/9781003138051
23. Laugwitz, B., Held, T., Schrepp, M.: Construction and evaluation of a user experience questionnaire. In: Holzinger, A. (ed.) HCI and Usability for Education and Work. pp. 63–76. Springer Berlin Heidelberg, Berlin, Heidelberg (2008). https://doi.org/10.1007/978-3-540-89350-9_6
24. Laugwitz, B., Schrepp, M., Held, T.: Konstruktion eines fragebogens zur messung der user experience von softwareprodukten. In: Mensch & Computer. pp. 125–134 (2006). https://doi.org/10.1524/9783486841749
25. Law, E.L.C., Heintz, M.: Augmented reality applications for k-12 education: a systematic review from the usability and user experience perspective. Int. J. Child Comput. Interact. **30**, 100321 (2021). https://doi.org/10.1016/j.ijcci.2021.100321
26. Law, E.L.C., van Schaik, P., Roto, V.: Attitudes towards user experience (UX) measurement. Int. J. Hum. Comput. Stud. **72**(6), 526–541 (2014). https://doi.org/10.1016/j.ijhcs.2013.09.006, interplay between User Experience Evaluation and System Development

27. Liang, L.J., Elliot, S.: A systematic review of augmented reality tourism research: what is now and what is next? Tourism Hospitality Res. **21**, 15–30 (2021). https://doi.org/10.1177/1467358420941913

28. Maulana, F.I., Wijaya, I.B.A., Pramono, A., Harjo, A.A., Suwondo, L., Livianty, V.: User experience evaluation of kindteractive application to improve user experience of kindergarten interior introduction. In: 2022 8th International HCI and UX Conference in Indonesia (CHIuXiD), vol. 1, pp. 65–70 (2022). https://doi.org/10.1109/CHIuXiD57244.2022.10009773

29. Mohanty, P., Hassan, A., Ekis, E.: Augmented reality for relaunching tourism post-Covid-19: socially distant, virtually connected. Worldwide Hospitality Tourism Themes **12**(6), 753–760 (2020). https://doi.org/10.1108/whatt-07-2020-0073

30. Navarro, I., Sánchez, A., Gimenez, L., Pérez, M.Á., Vidal Peig, T., Besné, A., Redondo, E.: Heritage augmented reality applications for enhanced user experience. In: Zaphiris, P., Ioannou, A. (eds.) Learning and Collaboration Technologies: Games and Virtual Environments for Learning. pp. 302–312. Springer International Publishing, Cham (2021). https://doi.org/10.1007/978-3-030-77943-6_20

31. Nobre, I., Nobre, C.: Amazon 4.0: a third way for the amazon. Futuribles: the digital, a social and political issue **434**(1), 95–108 (2020). https://doi.org/10.3917/futur.434.0095

32. Oh, C.O.: The contribution of tourism development to economic growth in the Korean economy. Tour. Manage. **26**, 39–44 (2005). https://doi.org/10.1016/j.tourman.2003.09.014

33. Pacaya Samiria: Pacaya Samiria - Apps on Google Play — play.google.com. https://play.google.com/store/apps/details?id=pe.com.pacayasamiriamockup. Accessed 24 Aug 2023

34. Palos-Sanchez, P., Saura, J.R., Correia, M.B.: Do tourism applications' quality and user experience influence its acceptance by tourists? Rev. Manag. Sci. **15**, 1205–1241 (2020). https://doi.org/10.1007/s11846-020-00396-y

35. Pan, S.Y., Gao, M., Kim, H., Shah, K.J., Pei, S.L., Chiang, P.C.: Advances and challenges in sustainable tourism toward a green economy. Sci. Total Environ. **635**, 452–469 (2018). https://doi.org/10.1016/j.scitotenv.2018.04.134

36. Pencarelli, T.: The digital revolution in the travel and tourism industry. Inf. Technol. Tourism **22**, 455–476 (2020). https://doi.org/10.1007/s40558-019-00160-3

37. Rane, N., Choudhary, S., Rane, J.: Sustainable tourism development using leading-edge artificial intelligence (AI), blockchain, internet of things (IoT), augmented reality (AR) and virtual reality (VR) technologies. SSRN Electron. J. (2023). https://doi.org/10.2139/ssrn.4642605

38. Refae, S., Ragab, T., Samir, H.: Augmented Reality (AR) for urban cultural heritage interpretation: a user experience evaluation. In: Visvizi, A., Troisi, O., Grimaldi, M. (eds.) Research and Innovation Forum 2022, pp. 283–298. Springer International Publishing, Cham (2023). https://doi.org/10.1007/978-3-031-19560-0_23

39. Samaddar, K., Mondal, S.: AR and VR-based travel: a responsible practice towards sustainable tourism. Int. J. Tourism Cities (2023). https://doi.org/10.1108/ijtc-05-2022-0135

40. Schrepp, M.: User Experience Questionnaire Handbook. ueq-online.org. https://www.ueq-online.org/Material/Handbook.pdf. Accessed 3 May 2023

41. Schrepp, M.: User Experience Questionnaires: How to Use Questionnaires to Measure the user Experience of Your Products? (2021)

42. Schrepp, M., Hinderks, A., Thomaschewski, J.: Applying the user experience questionnaire (ueq) in different evaluation scenarios. In: Marcus, A. (ed.) Design, User Experience, and Usability. Theories, Methods, and Tools for Designing the User Experience, pp. 383–392. Springer International Publishing, Cham (2014). https://doi.org/10.1007/978-3-319-07668-3_37

43. Sofronov, B., et al.: The development of the travel and tourism industry in the world. Annals of Spiru Haret University. Econ. Ser. **18**, 123–137 (2018). https://doi.org/10.26458/1847

44. Spenceley, A.: Handbook for sustainable tourism practitioners: the essential toolbox. Edward Elgar Publishing (2021). https://www.e-elgar.com/shop/gbp/handbook-for-sustainable-tourism-practitioners-9781839100888.html

45. Stewart, D.W., Shamdasani, P.N.: Focus groups: Theory and Practice, 3rd edn. Applied Social Research Methods, Sage Publications, Christchurch, New Zealand (2014)

46. Tscheu, F., Buhalis, D.: Augmented reality at cultural heritage sites. In: Inversini, A., Schegg, R. (eds.) Information and Communication Technologies in Tourism 2016, pp. 607–619. Springer International Publishing, Cham (2016)

47. Videva, J., Marchiori, E., Cantoni, L.: Assessing usability and user experience of immersive web VR platforms for tourism destinations. e-Review of Tourism Res. **17**(2) (2019). https://ertr-ojs-tamu.tdl.org/ertr/article/view/509

48. Vila, T.D., González, E.A., Vila, N.A., Brea, J.A.F.: Indicators of website features in the user experience of e-tourism search and metasearch engines. J. Theor. Appl. Electron. Commer. Res. **16**(1), 18–36 (2021). https://doi.org/10.4067/S0718-18762021000100103

49. Weaver, D.: Sustainable Tourism. Routledge (2005). https://doi.org/10.4324/9780080474526

50. World Commission on Environment and Development: Our Common Future. Oxford paperbacks, Oxford University Press (1987). https://books.google.es/books?id=iu6b4FzPoSAC

51. Yung, R., Khoo-Lattimore, C.: New realities: a systematic literature review on virtual reality and augmented reality in tourism research. Curr. Issue Tour. **22**(17), 2056–2081 (2017). https://doi.org/10.1080/13683500.2017.1417359

52. Özkul, E., Kumlu, S.T.: Augmented reality applications in tourism. Uluslararası Güncel Turizm Araştırmaları Dergisi **3**(2), 107–122 (2019). https://doi.org/10.30625/ijctr.625192

Exploring the Current State and Future Development of Online Exhibitions of Art in the Post-COVID Era – A Case Study of ART TAIPEI

Pan Chu[✉] and Cheng-Min Tsai

Department of Visual Communication Design, National Taiwan University of Arts, Taipei City, Taiwan
pampam0516@gmail.com

Abstract. The pandemic compelled significant art museums, galleries, and art fairs to innovate exhibition formats that presented them virtually to audiences in 2019. To enhance the usability and user experience of online platforms, interview guidelines were formulated based on a literature review and case analysis. Four experts, including planners from ART TAIPEI and executives involved in online exhibitions, were invited for interviews. The purpose was to understand the platform development process for online exhibitions in the post-pandemic era and to establish guidelines for future online art fairs. These results indicate that online exhibitions are no longer limited to physical exhibitions to visitors during the post-pandemic era. Rather, their goal is to enhance physical exhibitions by incorporating interactive elements. These include adding features such as 'following' and 'collection' options and introducing filters that allow viewers to quickly refine their preferences. These elements enhance the online exhibition experience and platform usability, enabling viewers to swiftly find their targets during physical exhibitions. For format, online exhibitions should be based on a two-dimensional map to provide visitors with a sense of spatial orientation and maintain a clear direction during browsing. In addition, 3D model exhibitions can serve as promotional highlights to attract a broader audience. In summary, future online platforms for art fairs should transition into hybrid forms of virtual and physical exhibitions, and incorporating interactive functionalities to engage in physical exhibitions is crucial.

Keywords: Online Exhibitions of Art · Post-COVID · user interface · user experience

1 Introduction

1.1 Background and Motivation

Since the 2019 pandemic, the government has enforced isolation policies, resulting in temporary closures, exhibition postponements, and cancellations of art museums, galleries, and fairs. To ensure public access to the artwork that cannot be displayed

P. Zaphiris et al. (Eds.): HCII 2024, LNCS 15378, pp. 242–255, 2025.
https://doi.org/10.1007/978-3-031-76815-6_17

owing to the closure of physical exhibition spaces, galleries, and museums have progressively embraced digital exhibition methods. Over the past few years, various online art exhibitions have emerged in response to persistent challenges posed by the pandemic.

Since 1990, art fairs have proliferated in a mushroom-like manner. These annual events are crucial to the contemporary art market where galleries and artists showcase their works worldwide. Art fairs provide a platform for mutual exchange and facilitate the establishment of collaborative relationships between artists and galleries (Yogev & Grund 2012). If online exhibitions help art fairs overcome time and space constraints, they would increase the efficiency of galleries and artists.

For many galleries worldwide, Art Basel, founded in 1970, is the most prestigious in selling works of art and is the most significant international art fair for contemporary art. In 2020, for the first time during self-isolation, an online event was held for the public (Rusakov & Vorozheikin 2022). This "online viewing room (OVR)" platform has features for selection and filtering, enabling visitors to quickly choose galleries based on gallery names, types of artworks, and artist names. The viewing rooms appeared simple with only a white wall and a chair. Detailed information about the artwork and sales inquiries is provided on the right-hand side (Fig. 1).

Fig. 1. Art Basel online viewing room (2020). https://is.gd/WKaFFc

Other international art fairs such as Frieze and ART FAIR ASIA FUKUOKA have begun to create online viewing rooms. However, there is currently a relatively low utilization of online viewing rooms at art fairs in Taiwan. In an industry that emphasizes interpersonal interaction and tangible experiences, online platforms' inter-activity and experiential aspects are crucial. Therefore, this study conducts a case analysis of an online exhibition held by Taiwan's most representative art fair, ART TAIPEI, in 2020. It aims to summarize the functionalities required for online art fair exhibitions and provide recommendations for the future implementation of online viewing rooms by ART

TAIPEI. The insights gained can benefit other entities when planning online viewing rooms.

1.2 Purpose

A thriving digital industry has emerged in response to the COVID-19 pandemic. The ascent of virtual networks has effectively transcended time and space constraints. This study aimed to enhance the ART TAIPEI online viewing room and its essential components to boost user engagement. Building on the background and motivation outlined above, the Purpose of this study were as follows:

1. To understand contemporary online art exhibition platforms' development process and current status.
2. To summarize the challenges of ART TAIPEI online viewing room status.
3. Analyzing and proposing user needs and essential elements of the user interface for establishing an online viewing room for ART TAIPEI and providing suggestions for improvement.

2 Literature Review

2.1 Art Fairs

Art fairs typically last from a few days to a week, allowing galleries and artists to showcase and sell their artworks. The first art fair, in the form we recognize today, took place in 1967 with the inauguration of Art Market Cologne (Kunstmarkt Köln). Art Market Cologne, later renamed Art Cologne, had a profound impact on the international art market (Zmpogko 2018).

Annual art fairs play a crucial role in contemporary art markets. These fairs serve as significant platforms for interaction among galleries, artists, collectors, and other art lovers. They are also a substantial commercial platform in the art market (Yogev & Grund 2012). The concentration of many art galleries in one space allows the sharing of information and testing of the water on what sells (Vermeylen 2015). According to "THE ART MARKET 2023," jointly published by Art Basel and UBS in Nov. 2023, art fairs account for 35% of the total annual turnover of art dealers. Among dealers with annual turnovers exceeding USD$10 million, 40% of their sales are reported to occur primarily at international fairs (Art Basel and UBS 2023).

2.2 Online Exhibition

During the lockdown, art fairs innovated new exhibition formats by presenting their shows virtually to maintain connections with visitors. A unique aspect of online exhibitions is that users can enter a virtual environment by simply clicking on web links. This feature allows users to view comprehensive information about the displayed artwork without leaving their homes. In addition, participants can communicate with organizers and exhibitors online in real-time, providing a sense of presence at the exhibition venue (Wu & Yang 2020).

Online exhibitions offer tremendous convenience, allowing galleries to overcome limitations of time and space by expanding the number of visitors and reaching potential buyers through online platforms. They allow visitors to participate more easily and establish direct connections with the galleries. Thus, even when it became possible to organize real-life events, most art fairs were held in hybrid virtual and physical forms. Additionally, online art fairs can provide supplementary access to information that is unavailable during live events (Zagrebelnaia 2021).

While the current pandemic is gradually fading, "THE ART MARKET 2023: A report by Art Basel & UBS" revealed that online sales in 2022 were maintained at 16%, exceeding the 13% recorded in 2019 (Art Basel and UBS 2023). Many galleries have adopted a hybrid approach in which dealers maintain digital marketing and sales strategies alongside live events and exhibitions. Therefore, enhancing the usability of online exhibitions to enable participants to immerse themselves in the art world through virtual displays has become a future developmental trend in the exhibition industry and galleries.

2.2.1   Types of Online Exhibitions

With the advancement of technology and the impetus of the pandemic, the development of digital showcasing has surged rapidly. Exhibition organizers have increasingly emphasized technology exhibitions and online exhibition systems have evolved into various forms. Different modes of online exhibitions can affect their effectiveness.

Online platforms typically utilize predesigned templates that can be personalized for different content. Some platforms provide 360° panorama pictures only; some allow one to move between hotspots and explore a 3D-modeled space, and others provide maximum freedom in terms of movements (Resta, Dicuonzo, Karacan, & Pastore 2021).

This study gathers information on current online exhibitions from art fairs that classify them into "360 Virtual Tours," "3D Model-Ing Exhibitions," and "Web Exhibitions". The following section presents case studies of these online exhibition types, highlighting their functionalities and features.

1. 360 Virtual Tours

360 Virtual Tours involve capturing 360° panorama pictures to faithfully recreate the details of the physical exhibition space. It is the online exhibition method most commonly used by cultural and art institutions in the country (Lin 2022). This online exhibition surpasses others in terms of authenticity as it requires physical space for photography. Users can experience a sense of presence at a venue without physically attending.

With advancements in 360° panoramic pictures and image-stitching technology, tools for capturing such images have become readily available. Even smartphones can capture 360° panoramic images through simple operations. This user-friendly approach empowers stakeholders in the exhibition industry to present their exhibitions effortlessly to audiences who cannot attend in person or recreate past exhibitions (Fig. 2).

2. 3D Modeling Exhibitions

The key difference between 3D Modeling Exhibitions and 360 Virtual Tours is that 3D Modeling Exhibitions do not require physical exhibition spaces. Rather, they utilized

Fig. 2. ART FAIR ASIA FUKUOKA 2023 (2023). https://artfair.asia/en/

3D modeling techniques to create a virtual space, allowing exhibition organizers to define the layout of the exhibition area. This flexibility extends to all elements within the exhibition, such as the color of the display panels, flooring, and the overall spatial arrangement.

In addition to offering more flexibility, the models developed for 3D Modeling Exhibitions allow the creation of diverse thematic exhibitions by adjusting internal display items or textual content (Hu 2023). The UBS Art Virtual Exhibition is a typical 3D modeling exhibition (Fig. 3).

3. Web Exhibitions

Web Exhibitions use presentation formats that include images and text in a flat graphical manner. In modern contexts, exhibition organizers may enhance their experiences by integrating multimedia elements such as videos and music and even incorporating game design (Wang 2022).

This online exhibition platform was built without specific settings or specialized tools. This is relatively easier and quicker than other methods. Additionally, it seamlessly aligns with the audience's familiar web browsing habits. Consequently, it has recently gained widespread popularity and has become a prevalent choice for art fairs and galleries (Fig. 4).

Different online exhibition methods provide audiences with diverse feelings and experiences. This study analyzes the characteristics of three types of online exhibitions, focusing on the fidelity of reproducing physical exhibitions, interface aesthetics, and minimalism; the capability to quickly filter artworks; the potential for content updates to

Fig. 3. UBS Art virtual exhibition. https://reurl.cc/09py3b

Fig. 4. Artsy Online Art Gallery Shows. https://www.artsy.net/shows/online

make exhibitions reusable; intuitive usability; interactive experiences; personalization; and Responsive Web Design. These are summarized in Table 1.

2.3 Usability and User Experience

Usability is a user-centered design concept that is typically associated with a product's functionality. Usability is a quality attribute that assesses the ease of use. The word "usability" also encompasses methods for improving ease of use during the design process (Nielsen 1994, 2012). For websites and applications, usability matters because

Table 1. Characteristics of Three Types of Online Exhibitions

	360 Virtual Tours	3D Modeling Exhibitions	Web Exhibitions
Reality	✓	✗	✗
Minimalist	✗	✓	✓
Filters	✗	✗	✓
Reusable	✗	✓	✓
Intuitive	✗	✗	✓
Interactive	✓	✓	✗
Personalization	✗	✓	✗
RWD	✓	✓	✓

if users cannot achieve their goals efficiently, effectively, and satisfactorily, they are likely to seek alternative solutions to reach their goals (Komninos 2020).

The most widely used evaluation method usability of user interface design is Nielsen's ten heuristics, which was established in 1990 (Benaida 2023). In 2020, Nielsen refined his original article, providing more explanation and clarity while adding new examples. The ten usability heuristics for User Interface design include visibility of system status, the match between the system and the real world, user control and freedom, consistency, and standards, Error Prevention, Recognition rather than recall, flexibility and efficiency of use, aesthetic and minimalist design, helping users recognize, diagnose, and recover from errors, help, and documentation (Nielsen 1994, 2020).

Punchoojit and Hongwarittorrn (2017) pointed out that a usable product seeks to achieve three primary outcomes: (1) the product is easy for users to become familiar with and competent in using during the first contact, (2) the product is easy for users to achieve their objective by using it, and (3) the product is easy for users to recall the user interface and how to use it in later visits.

With the rapid development of online exhibitions, people increasingly regard online user experience as a vital criterion for evaluating the capabilities of event-planning units. Measures need to be taken to ensure that online exhibition platforms fulfill user expectations and improve usability. This study integrates the results of interface usability expectations and Nielsen's ten established heuristics as criteria for the subsequent design and evaluation of online exhibition platform interfaces.

3   Research Method

This study conducted a case analysis of the most iconic art fair in Taiwan, ART TAIPEI, which organized an online exhibition in 2020. The study was divided into three stages. In the first stage, a literature review gathers information on currently available online exhibitions domestically and internationally. This process aims to clarify the conceptual definitions of online exhibitions, their processes, and the current state of practice. The second stage involved interviewing. An interview outline was developed based on information compiled from previous research. Invite planners of the ART TAIPEI online exhibition and operators to conduct in-depth interviews. To understand the operational performance, business conditions, and potential development of the platform user interface. In the final stage, this study aims to discover the key elements influencing the ART TAIPEI online exhibition platform and provide suggestions for improvement.

3.1   Introduction to the Case of ART TAIPEI

ART TAIPEI is a significant annual international art event held in Taiwan. According to the book "The 30 Years of Taiwan Art Gallery Association" published by the Taiwan Art Gallery Association (TAGA) in 2022, it was established in June 1992. In November of the same year, it held the first "ART GALLERIES FAIR R.O.C 1992 TAIPEI". To move towards the international market and adapt to changing market trends, it officially changed its name to "ART TAIPEI" in 2005 and has retained it since.

Since its inception, ART TAIPEI has faced various challenges, including the Asian financial crisis and factors such as the COVID-19 pandemic. While art fairs in other countries were suspended, the ART TAIPEI continued to be held, making it one of Asia's longest-standing and most representative art expos (Chu 2018). Therefore, this study selected an online exhibition hosted by ART TAIPEI 2020 as a case study and combined the aforementioned literature to investigate the current status and future trends of online exhibitions.

3.2   In-Depth Interview

From Nov. 2023 to Feb. 2024, four experts were invited to participate in in-depth interviews for this study, which aimed to put forth enhancement recommendations for the online viewing room of ART TAIPEI and offer insights for future art fair organizers involved in creating an online viewing room. Interviews were conducted with four individuals to ensure that the vital components of online exhibitions met industry standards and fostered development opportunities. Four individuals were members of the ART TAIPEI executive and online platform production teams. As outlined in Table 2.

Interviews were conducted on four dimensions. An outline of the interviews is presented in the following table (Table 3).

4   Results

4.1   Results of Case Study

In response to the global impact of the pandemic, ART TAIPEI moved its exhibition online in 2020 and named it the ART TAIPEI Online Viewing Room. Website design primarily focuses on user browsing through computer interfaces. The ART TAIPEI online viewing room presents exhibitions in 360 Virtual Tours accessible by clicking on

Table 2. Interview Participants

Number	Company	Department	Position Title
1	TAGA	ART FAIR	Secretary General
2	ART TAIPEI	International Exhibition Affairs and Exhibition	Art Director
3	ART TAIPEI	creative marketing	Creative Marketing Director
4	iStaging	Business Dept	Business Development, Assistant Director

Table 3. Interview Outline

No.	Dimension	Questions
1	Management	1. What challenges did you face while planning ART TAIPEI 2020? 2. What feedback did you receive from the audience during ART TAIPEI 2020? 3. What suggestions do you have for the future development of ART TAIPEI online viewing room?
2	Platform Execution	1. What are the advantages and features of the ART TAIPEI online viewing room? 2. What challenges did you face during the ARTSY? 3. In what areas does the ART TAIPEI online viewing room need improvement? 4. What suggestions do you have for the future development of the ART TAIPEI online viewing room?
3	Media Marketing	1. What are the advantages and features of the ART TAIPEI online viewing room? 2. What is the key to increasing brand marketing or media promotion? 3. In what areas does the ART TAIPEI online viewing room need improvement? 4. What suggestions do you have for the future development of the ART TAIPEI online viewing room?
4	Platform Development	1. What challenges did you face during the production of the ART TAIPEI online viewing room? 2. What are current online exhibitions' common types and pros/cons? 3. What possibilities do you see for developing the ART TAIPEI online viewing room? 4. What suggestions do you have for the future development of the ART TAIPEI online viewing room?

the designated URL on the official ART TAIPEI website. The user's navigation begins at the entrance of the exhibition venue, allowing them to freely explore preferred exhibition areas by clicking or dragging the mouse and providing an immersive experience similar to that of a physical exhibition.

For functionality, labels were incorporated into the artwork to meet viewers' intuitive needs. Users can click on these labels to instantly access detailed information about the artwork, including pricing, the artist's background, and gallery details. Additionally, the platform integrates voice-guided elements featuring audio explanations from gallery owners or artists, thereby enhancing user interaction and experiential engagement (Fig. 5).

Fig. 5. ART TAIPEI 2020 (2020).

4.2 Results of In-Depth Interview

The interviews were centered on the four dimensions of art fairs. This study consolidates the feedback and suggestions from interviewees into three primary perspectives.

(1) Areas for Improvement in ART TAIPEI 2020, (2) Essential Elements for the online viewing room of ART TAIPEI, and (3) Future Development Directions for the online viewing room of ART TAIPEI. The results are presented in the following table (Table 4).

Table 4. Summary of interview results

Perspectives	Feedback and Suggestions
Areas for Improvement in ART TAIPEI 2020	1. Elderly users have mentioned that the 360° interface, lacking walls and allowing rotation, can lead to disorientation during use 2. The exhibition has cluttered items, such as display lights, tables, chairs, and panels, causing visual distractions 3. Due to time constraints in opening the exhibition, the setup is usually rushed, leaving no time to capture 360° panorama pictures 4. The ART TAIPEI team solely uploads the content, which faces workforce shortages. Furthermore, artworks sell rapidly, posing a challenge for timely replacements
Essential Elements for the online viewing room of ART TAIPEI	**Layout:** 1. Keep the layout design simple, focusing on artwork and textual information 2. The website layout begins with a 2D map, providing a clear view of the relative positions of exhibition areas 3. Ensure a webpage-list-style layout, facilitating quick access to artworks 4. It is recommended that exhibition spaces for 3D modeling with curated content and storytelling be established to enhance the presentation of artwork and promotional highlights **Function:** 1. The online exhibition offers 5–6 modular exhibition hall styles, allowing galleries to choose according to their preferences 2. Enable galleries or artists to update images or textual information themselves 3. Adding a "follow" or "favorite" feature that allows users to add their preferred galleries to a list. Galleries can then periodically send messages to enhance interaction 4. Introduce filters to help users find desired artwork types and galleries quickly 5. Access backend browsing data for industry analysis, achieving tangible results to improve the platform's effectiveness

(continued)

Table 4. (*continued*)

Perspectives	Feedback and Suggestions
Future Development Directions for the online viewing room of ART TAIPEI	1. The online viewing room should progress in a direction that complements online and offline experiences 2. Most users browse on mobile devices three times more than on other platforms. Therefore, future layouts should prioritize mobile-friendly designs 3. Given the transient nature of art fairs, it is recommended that future online viewing rooms focus on curatorial branding for increased sustainability

5   Conclusion

Based on literature reviews and interviews, this study synthesizes crucial research findings and proposes recommendations for future research.

5.1 Discussion

The research findings show that contemporary online exhibition platforms are evolving toward holding hybrid virtual and physical forms. The advantages of online exhibitions include the pre-event promotion of artwork and galleries to a broader audience, expansion to the international stage, and attraction of visitors to physical venues. Additionally, online exhibitions provide visitors with detailed information about artworks and galleries, making it easier to collect or explore their favorite galleries and artworks. Exhibition organizers can also use platform analytics to conduct industry analyses, leading to tangible results.

Analysis and interviews suggested that the 360 Virtual Tour of the ART TAIPEI 2020 online viewing room accurately replicated the physical venue. However, onsite clutter often causes images to appear messy. Moreover, owing to the lack of a clear navigation path, users can easily lose their sense of direction. Operationally, time constraints during an event and the fast-paced exhibition setup make it challenging to capture panoramic images. Moreover, issues such as insufficient workforce and rapid artwork sales delay updating the artwork with current photos. Therefore, high-fidelity 360 Virtual Tours may not be the most suitable format for current online art fairs.

In summary, based on the analysis and feedback from the interviews, this study identified key elements and suggestions for future online art fairs.

4. Format of online exhibitions

Interviewees from the ART TAIPEI executive team emphasized the importance of maintaining a list-style presentation on an online exhibition webpage with which users are more familiar, allowing for the most direct display of artwork and gallery information. Pre-event online promotions of exhibitions are crucial. Utilizing 3D Modeling

Exhibitions as promotional highlights can attract a broader audience and expand their reach on the international stage.

5. The layout for online exhibitions

The layout should be based on a 2D map, offering visitors a sense of spatial orientation and maintaining clear direction during browsing. The design of individual booth interfaces should avoid using cluttered elements such as exhibition lights, tables, chairs, and display boards. This ensures that viewers can better appreciate the detailed artwork and gallery information.

6. Enhance Interactive Features

Respondents highlighted the need for increased platform interactivity, including features like 'follow' or 'bookmark,' allowing visitors to add their favorite galleries to a list. In addition, there is a desire to introduce filters that enable visitors to search quickly for specific artwork types, prices, years, artists' names, colors, and galleries. These elements enhance platform usability.

5.2 Future Work

In the post-pandemic era, online exhibitions have evolved beyond serving as alternatives for audiences unable to attend them. They were transformed into a hybrid form, combining the virtual and physical for maximum benefit. Therefore, this study proposes the following recommendations for constructing future online exhibition platforms.

1. This study primarily focuses on the ART TAIPEI 2020 online viewing room, with its platform designed for computer users. However, as the pandemic gradually subsided, more people began to use mobile devices. The number of mobile users exceeded that of computer users by threefold. Consequently, it is suggested that future platform layout designs prioritize mobile user experience.
2. Online exhibitions provide additional channels for audience participation. They also serve as complementary tools for physical exhibitions. Thus, future research should emphasize the enhancement of interactive features with physical exhibitions, making online exhibition platforms more comprehensive support systems.
3. Art fairs are characterized by their short-term nature. Future online exhibition platforms should be built around curatorial company brands to provide galleries and artists with long-term display opportunities. This platform offers sustained exposure and contributes to the long-term development of fair-art brands.

Acknowledgments. The authors would like to thank the reviewers for providing insightful comments. We also appreciate the support of ART TAIPEI for providing this research case. Finally, I would like to acknowledge and give my warmest thanks to all interviewees who offered guidance and suggestions. The suggestions provided by the interviewees were invaluable for the subsequent analysis.

References

Benaida, M.: Developing and extending usability heuristics evaluation for user interface design via AHP. Soft Comput. **27**, 9693–9707 (2023). https://doi.org/10.1007/s00500-022-07803-4

Chang, C.Y.: The 30 years of Taiwan art gallery association. Artist Mag. (2022)

Chu, Y.T.: The Cultural politics and mechanism of art fairs: a case analysis of art Taipei. J. Natl. Taitung Univ. Coll. Humanit. **8**(1), 77–115 (2018). https://www.airitilibrary.com/Article/Detail?DocID=P20130128005-201806-202108230011-202108230011-77-115

Clare, M.: The Art Market 2023. Art Basel and UBS (2023). https://is.gd/rZnbOo

Hu, W.C.: A study on the influence of user behavior and experience on online exhibitions. Natl. Taichung Univ. Sci. Technol. (2023). https://www.airitilibrary.com/Article/Detail?DocID=U0061-2808202310120600

Komninos, A.: An Introduction to Usability. Interaction Design Foundation – IxDF (2020). https://www.interaction-design.org/literature/article/an-introduction-to-usability

Lin, W.Y.: Potential Users' Behavioral Intention of Virtual Exhibition Platform. National Taiwan University of Arts (2022). https://hdl.handle.net/11296/3uc289

Nielsen, J.: 10 Usability Heuristics for User Interface Design. Nielsen Norman Group Logo Nielsen Norman Group (1994). https://www.nngroup.com/articles/ten-usability-heuristics/

Nielsen, J.: Usability 101: Introduction to Usability Nielsen Norman Group Logo Nielsen Norman Group (2012). https://www.nngroup.com/articles/usability-101-introduction-to-usability/

Nielsen, J.: 10 Usability Heuristics for User Interface Design. Nielsen Norman Group Logo Nielsen Norman Group (2020). https://www.nngroup.com/articles/ten-usability-heuristics/

Punchoojit, L., Hongwarittorrn, N.: Usability studies on mobile user interface design patterns: a systematic literature review. Adv. Hum. Comput. Interact. (2017). https://doi.org/10.1155/2017/6787504

Resta, G., Dicuonzo, G., Karacan, E., Pastore, D.: The impact of virtual tours on museum exhibitions after the onset of COVID-19 restrictions: visitor engagement and long-term perspectives. SCIRES-IT **11**(1), 151–166 (2021). https://www.researchgate.net/publication/35290657

Rusakov, S.S., Vorozheikin, Y.P.: Art fairs in the context of virtualization. Challenges and prospects of the interaction between culture, science and arts in the modern context: scientific monograph (2022). https://doi.org/10.30525/978-9934-26-206-7-10

Vermeylen, F.: The India art fair and the market for visual arts in the Global South. In: Cosmopolitan Canvases: The Globalization of Markets for Contemporary Art Oxford, pp. 34–51 (2015). https://doi.org/10.1093/acprof:oso/9780198717744.003.0002

Wang, C.Y.: A Preliminary Study on the Applicability of the "Evaluation Survey of the Ideal Online Exhibition Model" and A Discussion of Post-COVID Museum Online Exhibition Development. Fu Jen Catholic University (2022). https://hdl.handle.net/11296/38etat

Wu, Y.L., Yang, G.L.: Development status and feasibility analysis of domestic and foreign virtual exhibition. MICE Prospects **1**(1), 38–55 (2020). https://tpl.ncl.edu.tw/NclService/JournalContentDetail?SysId=A20008917

Yogev, T., Grund, T.: Network dynamics and market structure: the case of art fairs. Sociol. Focus **45**(1), 23–40 (2012). https://doi.org/10.1080/00380237.2012.630846

Zagrebelnaia, A.: State of the art fair post-Covid: audience development strategies in a post-digital context. Eur. J. Cult. Manag. Policy **11**(2), 34–51 (2021). https://nbn-resolving.org/urn:nbn:de:0168-ssoar-76435-7

Zmpogko, E.: What Do Art Fairs Do? The Case of Art Dubai. Research Centre for Communication and Culture (CECC) (2018). http://hdl.handle.net/10400.14/27103

Enhancing Painting Exhibition Experiences with the Application of Augmented Reality-Based AI Video Generation Technology

Yuexi Dong[✉] [ID]

Beijing Jiaotong University, Beijing, China
9888@bjtu.edu.cn

Abstract. Traditional painting exhibitions often rely on flat presentation methods, such as walls and stands, limiting their impact. Augmented Reality (AR) technology presents an opportunity to transform these experiences by turning static, flat artwork into dynamic, multi-dimensional presentations. However, creating and integrating video or dynamic content can be time-consuming and challenging, requiring meticulous planning, design, and production. In the context of urban renewal and community revitalization, particularly in China's first-tier cities where real estate development has saturated the market, there is a growing trend to repurpose traditional commercial and office spaces with cultural and artistic exhibitions. These exhibitions not only enhance the spatial quality but also elevate the user experience, making the spaces more competitive. However, these non-traditional exhibition venues often lack the amenities of professional galleries, relying on walls, windows, and corners for displays, and requiring quick setup times. For visitors, who are often office workers or shoppers with limited time, the use of personal mobile devices for interaction is common. WeChat, China's most widely used mobile application, provides a platform for convenient digital interactive experiences through mini-programs, which can support lightweight AR applications. AI video generation technologies, such as Conditional Generative Adversarial Networks (ControlNet) and Latent Consistency Models (LCM), have seen significant advancements. These technologies now allow for the creation of 3D models and video content from text and images. Tools like Meshy and Pika provide the ability to generate various video styles and offer precise control over video content. New AI video applications like Stable Video further expand the possibilities by rapidly converting static images into dynamic videos, facilitating easy adjustments and edits. This paper explores the application of AR-based AI video generation technology in enhancing the experience of painting exhibitions. By integrating these technologies, traditional paintings can be transformed into interactive, engaging displays that enrich the viewer's experience. The study demonstrates the potential of these innovations to make art exhibitions more appealing and competitive in various public spaces, thereby improving both artistic expression and audience engagement.

Keywords: Augmented Reality · AI-Generated Art · Digital Exhibition Design · Art and Technology

1   Introduction

Traditional painting exhibitions are often constrained by their flat presentation methods, primarily utilizing walls and stands. Augmented Reality (AR) technology offers a way to enhance these experiences by expanding static, flat artwork into dynamic, multi-dimensional presentations [1]. However, creating and integrating video or dynamic content requires significant effort and time, involving prior planning, design, and production.

In the context of urban renewal and community revitalization, particularly in China's first-tier cities where real estate development has reached saturation, there is a growing trend to transform traditional commercial and office spaces with cultural and artistic exhibitions. These exhibitions enhance the spatial quality and user experience, making the spaces more competitive. However, these non-traditional exhibition venues often lack the facilities of professional galleries, relying on walls, windows, and corners for displays, and requiring quick setup times. For visitors, typically office workers or shoppers with limited time, the use of personal mobile devices for interaction is common. WeChat, the most widely used mobile application in China, provides a platform for convenient digital interactive experiences through mini-programs, which can support lightweight AR applications [2].

AI video generation technologies, such as Conditional Generative Adversarial Networks (ControlNet) and Latent Consistency Models (LCM), have advanced rapidly. These technologies now enable the creation of 3D models and video content from text and images [3]. Tools like Meshy and Pika allow for the generation of various video styles and precise control over video content. New AI video applications like Sora and Stable Video further expand the possibilities by converting static images into dynamic videos quickly, facilitating easy adjustments and edits.

This paper explores the application of AR-based AI video generation technology in enhancing the experience of painting exhibitions. By integrating these technologies, traditional paintings can be transformed into interactive, engaging displays that enrich the viewer's experience. The study demonstrates the potential of these innovations to make art exhibitions more appealing and competitive in various public spaces, thereby improving both artistic expression and audience engagement.

2   Related Work

The application of AR and AI in enhancing art exhibitions has been the subject of previous studies. Researchers have explored how AR can transform static art displays into immersive, interactive experiences. For example, van Krevelen and Poelman provided an extensive review of AR applications, highlighting its potential to overlay digital content onto physical artworks, thereby enriching viewer engagement [4]. Chang et al. examined the use of AR in museum settings, emphasizing its ability to enhance educational value and user interaction through interactive displays [5].

AI-driven content creation has also seen significant advancements. The introduction of GANs by Goodfellow et al. has become a cornerstone in AI-generated imagery, allowing for the creation of realistic images and videos from textual descriptions or existing images [6]. Recent developments in GANs and other AI technologies have enabled platforms like Runway ML to facilitate the creation and modification of artworks with minimal effort, making AI tools more accessible to artists and curators.

In the context of art exhibitions, the combination of AR and AI technologies has shown promising results. For instance, Höllerer et al. demonstrated how AR could be used to create dynamic, interactive exhibitions that go beyond traditional static displays, thereby enhancing the visitor experience [7]. Similarly, recent work by Isola et al. on image-to-image translation using conditional GANs has further expanded the possibilities for transforming static artworks into dynamic visual experiences [3].

These preliminary studies have laid the groundwork for integrating AR and AI in art exhibitions. However, this research specifically focuses on the application of AR-based AI video generation technology to enhance the experience of painting exhibitions. By leveraging AI to quickly generate dynamic video content from static paintings and integrating it with AR for interactive displays, this study aims to make art exhibitions more engaging and competitive. The significance of this research lies in its potential to revolutionize the presentation of traditional artworks, thereby improving both artistic expression and audience engagement.

3   Case Study: "Multiverse" Exhibition

The "Multiverse" exhibition, held at Beijing's Intime Commercial Center, serves as an exemplary case study of the application of AR-based AI video generation technology in enhancing traditional painting exhibitions. This exhibition featured a collection of static paintings created two years prior, focusing on themes of astronauts and outer space. See Fig. 1.

Fig. 1. "Multiverse" Exhibition.

To transform these static paintings into dynamic, interactive displays, the exhibition leveraged AI video generation tools such as Stable Video. By inputting textual descriptions and static images into the AI tools, dynamic videos were generated, bringing the paintings to life with motion and depth. The generated videos included detailed adjustments such as camera panning, zooming, and object rotation, which enriched the visual experience and expanded the narrative potential of the artworks.

The exhibition also utilized AR technology to integrate these AI-generated videos into the physical space. Platforms like Kivicube were employed to upload the AI-generated video content and create AR models that could be accessed via QR codes. Visitors used their mobile devices to scan these QR codes, instantly viewing the augmented video content overlaid onto the original paintings. This seamless integration of AR and AI allowed for a more immersive and engaging viewer experience, attracting and retaining the attention of the audience. See Fig. 2.

Fig. 2. Visitor scanning an AR exhibition piece to view AI-generated video content.

In the "Multiverse" exhibition, two sets of experimental scenarios were constructed to compare traditional video editing with AI-generated video content. The first set contrasted colorful abstract landscapes and figurative paintings, while the second set compared monochromatic animal models of varying complexity. The results indicated that AI-generated videos could produce creative and unexpected dynamic expressions quickly, particularly in scenes with prominent subject matter.

The use of AR and AI significantly enhanced the overall exhibition experience. Visitors responded positively to the interactive elements, spending more time exploring the dynamic content. This case study demonstrates the potential of AR-based AI video generation technology to transform traditional art exhibitions, making them more competitive and appealing in various public spaces. By bridging the gap between static and dynamic art presentations, the "Multiverse" exhibition highlighted the advantages of integrating these advanced technologies into the art world.

4 Comparative Experiment: AI vs. Traditional Video Generation

To evaluate the effectiveness of AI-generated video content compared to traditional video editing methods, a comparative experiment was conducted using a series of static paintings as the base material. A series of static paintings served as the base material for the experiment, with the goal of assessing the quality, efficiency, and creative potential of AI-generated videos in enhancing the viewer experience of art exhibitions. Two researchers selected, produced, and compared the videos.

4.1 Methodology

- **Selection of Paintings:** A diverse set of paintings, including colorful abstract landscapes, figurative artworks, and monochromatic animal models, was chosen for the experiment. These paintings varied in complexity and subject matter to provide a comprehensive assessment.
- **Traditional Video Editing:** A professional video designer manually created dynamic videos based on the selected paintings. This process involved editing, adding effects, and integrating motion to bring the static images to life. The time and effort required for each video were recorded.
- **AI-Generated Videos:** AI video generation tool Stable Video, was used to automatically generate dynamic videos from the same set of paintings. The AI tools were trained to recognize key elements in the paintings and create motion effects accordingly. The time taken for AI-generated videos was also recorded.
- **Evaluation:** The generated videos were evaluated based on criteria such as visual quality, creativity, narrative enhancement, and overall impact on viewer engagement. A panel of art experts and exhibition curators provided qualitative feedback on each video.

4.2 Results

- **Visual Quality:** Both AI-generated and traditionally edited videos demonstrated high visual quality. AI-generated videos showed a comparable level of detail and realism to traditional methods.
- **Efficiency:** AI-generated videos were significantly faster to produce compared to traditional editing methods. The AI tools were able to generate videos in a fraction of the time it took for manual editing, making them more efficient for rapid content creation.
- **Creativity:** AI-generated videos exhibited a higher degree of creativity in terms of unexpected motion effects and dynamic transitions. Traditional videos, while well-executed, often followed conventional editing styles.
- **Narrative Enhancement:** AI-generated videos effectively enhanced the narrative of the paintings by adding dynamic elements that complemented the artwork's theme. Traditional videos were limited by the designer's interpretation and editing skills.

4.3 Insights

The experiment provides insights into the potential of AI-generated videos to revolutionize the creation of dynamic content for art exhibitions. This study reflects a subjective exploration by the researchers, showcasing their personal choice and approach to comparing AI and traditional methods. AI offers a faster, more efficient, and creatively diverse approach compared to traditional editing methods. By integrating AI video generation technology, art exhibitions can be made more engaging and competitive, enhancing the overall viewer experience.

5 Conclusion and Future Work

The integration of AI video generation tools can significantly enhance the dynamic video production process for art exhibitions, providing designers with efficient and creative solutions for transforming traditional static paintings into dynamic, engaging videos. These tools offer distinct advantages in scenarios with short time requirements, complex video models, scenery-dominated scenes, small movement demands, short video durations, and lower video quality requirements, complementing traditional manual video production methods.

Moreover, as art exhibitions expand beyond traditional gallery settings to encompass public spaces such as commercial, office, and outdoor areas, the importance of enhancing exhibition experiences with digital interactive elements becomes increasingly evident. Fragmented viewing times and the prevalent use of mobile devices among viewers underscore the need for convenient, user-friendly interactive solutions. In China, the widespread use of WeChat, particularly its support for lightweight AR applications through mini-programs, presents an ideal platform for enhancing short-term, "passing-by" viewing experiences at art exhibitions.

The combination of AI video generation and AR technologies has shown promising results in enhancing the viewing experience and interactivity of art exhibitions. While the current study has primarily relied on subjective comparisons, future work should involve more systematic experiments to rigorously evaluate the effectiveness of this approach. This innovative method holds potential for broadly converting traditional paintings into dynamic displays, thereby enriching interactive experiences in various traditional institutions and spaces.

Acknowledgments. The author would like to thank all the staff involved in the exhibition and the visitors for their participation and support.

Disclosure of Interests. The authors have no competing interests to declare that are relevant to the content of this article.

References

1. Azuma, R.T.: A survey of augmented reality. Presence Teleoperators Virtual Environ. **6**(4), 355–385 (1997)
2. Billinghurst, M., Clark, A., Lee, G.: A survey of augmented reality. Found. Trends® Hum. Comput. Interact. **8**(2–3), 73–272 (2015)
3. Isola, P., Zhu, J.Y., Zhou, T., Efros, A.A.: Image-to-image translation with conditional adversarial networks. In: Proceedings of the IEEE Conference on Computer Vision and Pattern Recognition, pp. 1125–1134 (2017)
4. van Krevelen, D.W.F., Poelman, R.: A survey of augmented reality technologies, applications, and limitations. Int. J. Virtual Real. **9**(2), 1–20 (2010)
5. Chang, K.-E., Chang, C.-T., Hou, H.-T., Sung, Y.-T., Chao, H.-L., Lee, C.-M.: Development and behavioral pattern analysis of a mobile guide system with augmented reality for painting appreciation instruction in an art museum. Comput. Educ. **71**, 185–197 (2014)
6. Goodfellow, I., et al.: Generative adversarial nets. In: Advances in Neural Information Processing Systems, pp. 2672–2680 (2014)
7. Höllerer, T., Pavlik, J.V., Feiner, S., Goebel, M.: Situated documentaries: embedding multimedia presentations in the real world. In: Proceedings of the 12th ACM International Conference on Multimedia, pp. 1040–1041 (2013)

STAR: A See-Through Augmented Reality Exhibit Showcase for Transparent Displays

Aikaterini Gerakianaki[1], Emmanouil Zidianakis[1(✉)], Vassiliki Neroutsou[1],
Anastasia Ntagianta[1], Konstantina Manoli[1], Stavroula Ntoa[1], Ilia Adami[1],
Margherita Antona[1], and Constantine Stephanidis[1,2]

[1] Foundation for Research and Technology – Hellas (FORTH), Institute of Computer Science,
N. Plastira 100, Vassilika Vouton, 700 13 Heraklion, Crete, Greece
{kgerak,zidian,vaner,dagianta,cmanoli,stant,iadami,antona,
cs}@ics.forth.gr
[2] Computer Science Department, University of Crete, Heraklion, Crete, Greece

Abstract. Motivated by the potential of Augmented Reality (AR) applications for transparent displays, this work presents a See-Through Augmented Reality (STAR) Exhibit Showcase, an interactive system that provides information and multimedia content for physical exhibits through a seamless User Experience (UX). The research described addresses underlying key inquiries about the effect of ambient light conditions, multi-user interaction, and methods for achieving accessibility. To validate the system, a case study was implemented for the city of Kalamata, demonstrating the potential of AR in promoting and enhancing user engagement with local products. Two heuristic evaluation sessions were conducted to identify usability problems and improve the UX.

Keywords: See-through · Augmented Reality · Exhibit Showcase · Transparent Display

1 Introduction

Augmented Reality (AR) is the technology that merges the virtual world with the real world and was invented in the late 1950s [1]. This combination is achieved by overlaying virtual models in the real world, where users can dynamically interact with these virtual objects [2]. AR moved from theoretical research to the stage of mass and industry application in 2015.

Typically, AR is utilized through devices such as mobile phones, tablets, and smart goggles, enabling users to access and engage with augmented environments seamlessly. In addition, see-through transparent screens can connect the virtual and physical worlds without noticeable disruption. This type of display allows digital information to be overlaid on the transparent screen without hindering the view of the surrounding environment and without sacrificing aesthetics, adding a modern and elegant finish.

AR use in combination with a see-through display, can further transform the latter into interactive showcase windows, panels, or cabinets overlaying information regarding

P. Zaphiris et al. (Eds.): HCII 2024, LNCS 15378, pp. 263–279, 2025.
https://doi.org/10.1007/978-3-031-76815-6_19

an exhibited item placed behind it. By filling the gap between the physical and digital worlds, transparent screens provide immersive and enriched experiences. Transparent displays have been present for a while now, however, the utilization of AR applications remains at a relatively early stage in research and production.

This work presents the STAR Showcase, an interactive system that augments physical exhibits using a transparent display. The system aims to enhance User Experience (UX), as users are able to get information about the displayed exhibits (e.g. museum items, traditional products, etc.) in an intuitive, efficient, and enjoyable manner. To support and validate the proposed system, an AR product showcase was developed for the city of Kalamata in Greece. The presented work addresses fundamental questions regarding the user experience with AR applications for transparent displays, including the impact of external environmental factors on such applications, the implications of multi-user interaction, and accessibility considerations, and highlights key design and interaction considerations.

The paper is structured as follows. Section 2 presents the related work and the background information to set the premises for this research work. Section 3 dives into the design process and describes the implementation of the STAR Showcase. Section 4 describes the heuristic evaluation process and its results, while Sect. 5 presents the installation of the STAR Showcase in a real-world setting/in actual operational conditions. Finally, Sect. 6 concludes the document and discusses future work.

2 Background and Related Work

AR technology allows users to view virtual objects superimposed into the real world [3]. For example, AR can be used to integrate digital information with physical environments and real-world surroundings which is exemplified in applications such as geolocated historical content [4], exploration of archival documents [5], historical experiences like mobile tour guides [6], etc. The screens used to augment information in the real world often include a light engine and an optical combiner [7]. These components are essential for developing interactive games, designing advertisements, and enhancing UX.

Transparent displays have gained attention and application in various sectors. These sectors include museums, public spaces, and semi-public places (i.e. places that are privately owned but can be accessed by members of the public). AR technology on transparent displays is truly significant in the area of exhibitions and product presentations. The adoption of transparent displays is limited due to challenges such as cost and technological limitations [8]. As noted in the study of Syed et al. [9], AR technology will dramatically impact our lives in the future.

Existing research mainly focuses on the functionality of transparent displays in enhancing UX. This technology also provides the "wow" effect while various AR applications have been described to be "fun".

WaveWindow [10] is an interactive see-through display that allows users to interact with digital content that overlays physical items behind the semi-transparent screen. This study explored factors that affect interaction with see-through displays in public environments, such as user demographics and interaction types. Performance anxiety and social inhibition were observed as a barrier to interaction. Additionally, it was noted that through the visibility of interaction, these barriers were overcome. Furthermore, it was reported that collaborative interactions often enhanced engagement with the group members encouraging each other and taking turns (particularly in families with children). TransWall [11] is a transparent display, that allows people on either side to interact with direct touch, the development of this display illustrates a significant advancement in the realm of interactive see-through displays. MUSTARD [12] allows users to inspect objects behind a glass panel while delivering view-independent information through the glass.

Colley et al. [8] provide a perspective on deploying see-through AR signage in real-world scenarios. This research study emphasizes the significance of clear communication of purpose in AR displays. The study showed the effectiveness of interactive display systems in engaging passersby in various scenarios. Users approaching the installation from the front or behind exhibited prolonged observation periods. People who approached from the front interacted with the AR content. Moreover, the study by Li et al. [13], proposed three monocular and four biovular configurations. Notably, this study considers monocular vision restricted to an extremely near-distance level. At the same time, the absence of stereovision makes the screen correspond to the retinal imaging plane of the viewing eye.

The Transparent Touch [14] system features a touch screen that is superimposed in front of the objects being interacted with. These objects are represented on-screen representations rendered on a second screen behind the transparent screen. The display system can thus be classified as a combination of AR and spatial display. In their 2014 study, Li, Greenberg, Sharlin, and Jorge [13] mention that transparent displays are not always transparent. They all require a critical trade-off between the graphics displayed on the screen and the clarity of what people can see through the screen. This work mentions that factors affecting transparency are graphics density and brightness, screen materials, projector brightness, environmental lighting, and personal lighting.

According to the reviewed literature, AR applications for transparent displays mainly focus on hardware development [12, 13]. Additionally, they facilitate the display of objects from a predefined specific angle, failing to provide a holistic view of the objects [12, 14]. Moreover, the prospect for multiple users to engage with real objects at the same time remains a largely unexplored area. Regarding accessibility, while there has been a growing focus on accessibility standards and solutions, the accessibility of AR applications for transparent displays is still in its infancy. This work aims to advance transparent AR displays along the aforementioned areas, offering a 360° product view, supporting multi-user interaction, and also taking into account system accessibility for users with disabilities. In addition, this work contributes to the AR literature by offering insights into the UX of intuitive and efficient applications that augment physical exhibits with transparent displays, as these were recorded through the iterative design and evaluation of the STAR display.

3 System Description

3.1 STAR Showcase Overview

The STAR system is an interactive showcase panel suitable for various exhibition environments, such as museums, libraries, galleries, retail shops, etc. It incorporates a transparent touch screen positioned in front of a stand with four rotating posts for displaying objects. Users can interact with the objects by initiating their rotation for a 360-degree viewing and accessing detailed information through User Interface (UI) elements which are displayed on the touch screen, augmenting the physical products with digital information (Fig. 1). Users can also send detailed information about exhibits via e-mail.

Fig. 1. STAR Showcase: System Overview Design

Users who cannot interact with the touchscreen directly due to visual or physical impairments may navigate through the system using a handheld remote-control device (fully presented in Sect. 3.3) that supports two navigation options, namely scanning and screen reading. Additionally, the system also provides dyslexia-friendly options to adjust the font size, word spacing, and line spacing.

The STAR system addresses a broad audience, including public visitors such as families, tourists, and casual learners who can explore exhibits through its interactive features. Some example contexts of use include retail stores which can employ STAR to enhance the customer shopping experience by providing additional information for specific products (i.e. price, characteristics, materials, etc.); corporate users who can leverage its capabilities for exhibit presentations during demonstration events; educational institutions that can integrate it into classrooms and labs to present educational material in an engaging way while fostering student interaction; and of course museums, galleries, and other exhibition settings which can use it to display any background information regarding their exhibits (i.e. historical information, origins, creator information, etc.).

No matter the context of use, for the successful implementation of the system in a public setting, in addition to providing a UI that ensures smooth operation and readability, the system should be robust, handling incorrect inputs without malfunctions and remaining operational even in the event of hardware component failures. To ensure this result, we followed an iterative design process, implementing multiple prototype iterations and formative evaluations the results of which are discussed in Sect. 4.

3.2 Iterative Prototyping

The iterative prototyping process involved a thorough, step-by-step review and analysis of design mockups, ensuring that the STAR Showcase design evolved gradually and efficiently.

The initial idea aimed to provide information about the exhibits through a square dialog box placed in the center of the transparent display (Fig. 2). This approach was abandoned early during the first design review since the depicted information prevented the displayed exhibits from being visible enough through the transparent display.

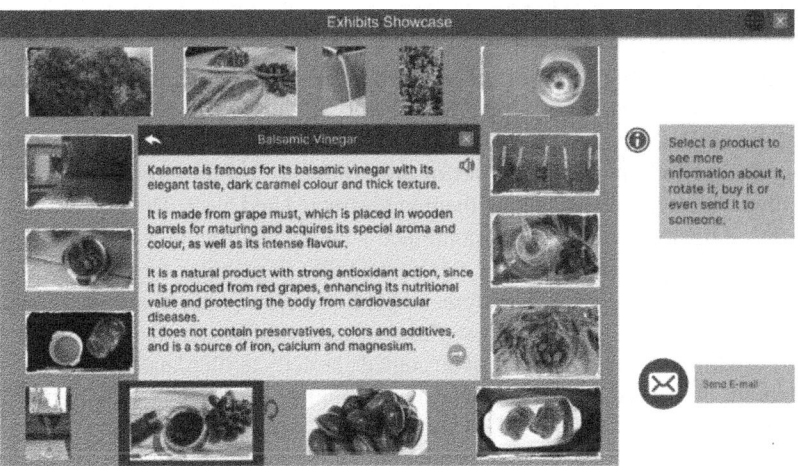

Fig. 2. Initial prototype idea

In the second design iteration, the idea of incorporating a stand with four rotating posts on which objects can be placed was explored. By mechanically rotating the posts, users would obtain a 360-degree view of the exhibits. This rotating-posts solution could be applied to different contexts of use, such as in museums, retail stores, and gallery spaces for their exhibits. The first version of the high-fidelity mockups of the rotating posts is illustrated in Fig. 3 (left). A working prototype of the system with the rotating posts was implemented based on the high-fidelity designs (Fig. 3-right).

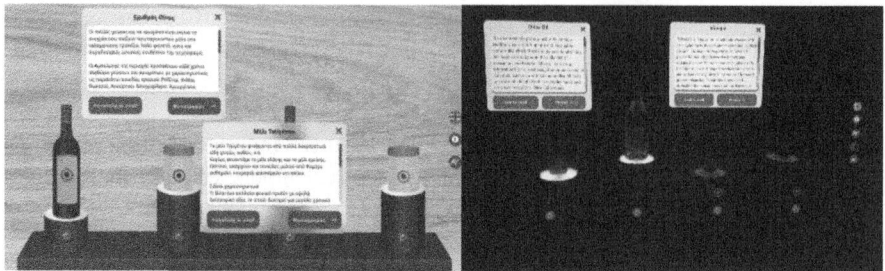

Fig. 3. First version of high-fidelity mockups for STAR Showcase (left)/First version of high-fidelity mockups presented using the actual setup (right).

Afterward, an expert-based heuristic evaluation (fully presented in Sect. 4.1) was conducted by deploying the designed mockups on the actual transparent display, which revealed several usability issues such as low contrast, unclear icons, unclear interaction, etc., and produced various suggestions to improve the design prototypes. In addition, the first heuristic evaluation revealed that there was insufficient visibility of the exhibit due to poor lighting. As a result, the addition of a swivel spotlight was considered in each rotating post. The initial idea was to put the light on the lower part of the stand support, however, this was quickly rejected, as a simple test proved that the combination of the light with the external light of the environment caused reflections that did not help alleviate the problem. As a result, it was decided to place the spotlights in the upper part of the display case (Fig. 4). As shown in (Fig. 4 B) the absence of spotlights made it difficult to view the details of the exhibit; when spotlights were positioned in the lower part of the exhibit, the light reflection further hindered visibility (Fig. 4 C). However, placing the spotlight in the upper part of the exhibit so that the exhibit was bathed in light, illuminated the labels making them unobstructed and clear. The placement of the spotlights at the top of the window combined with the addition of a black background minimized reflections and improved exhibit visibility (Fig. 4 D).

Another challenge that such systems in public or semi-public spaces must address, aside from insufficient lighting, is the glare caused by reflections from glass windows (Fig. 5). Additionally, spotlights must be angled correctly to illuminate the exhibit without creating blurring or shadows. Also, the brightness of the light must be carefully controlled. To address this, the STAR Showcase allows installation experts to adjust the brightness to low, medium, or high depending on the external light conditions via the Content Management System (CMS) fully presented in Sect. 3.4.

To further address the visibility and reflection issues identified in the first heuristic evaluation, the transparency and the gradient of the UI elements that display the exhibit information were also updated, as illustrated in (Fig. 6). These adjustments, in combination with the corrected spotlight angles and brightness levels, significantly improved the visibility of both the exhibit details and the information displayed on the screen. Consequently, the system became less dependent on the ambient lighting from the surrounding area.

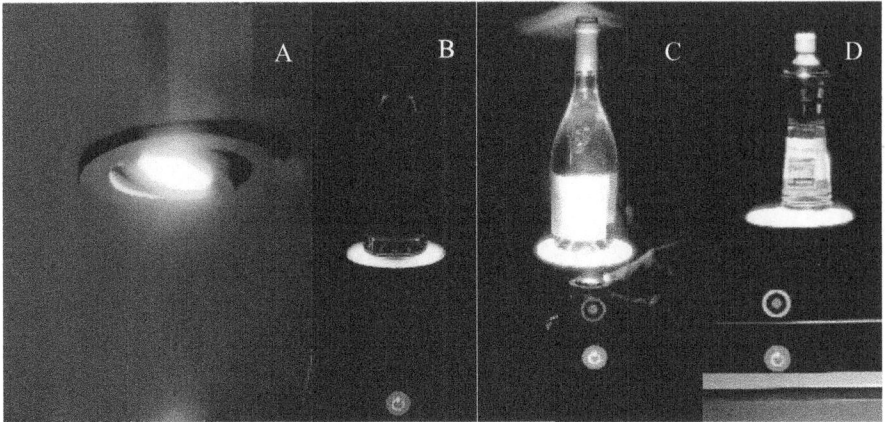

Fig. 4. Swivel spotlight (A)/Exhibit without spotlight (B)/Exhibit with a spotlight at the bottom (C)/Exhibit with a spotlight at the top (D)

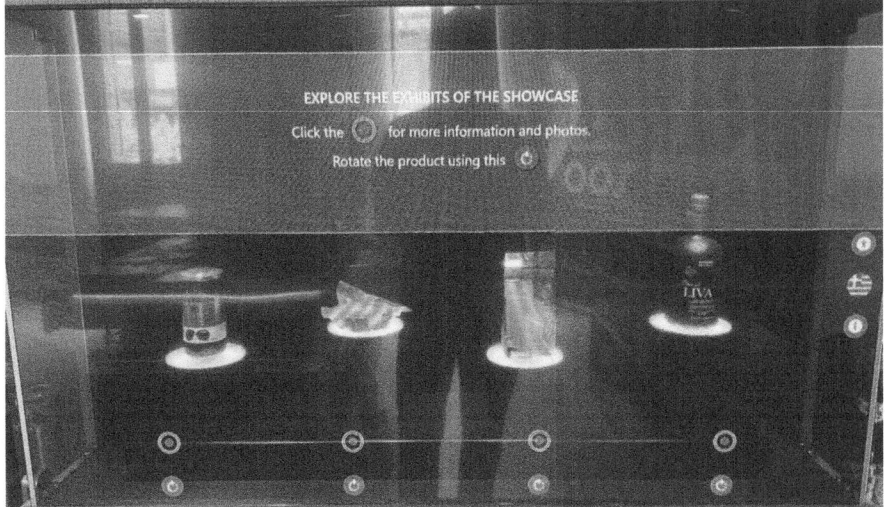

Fig. 5. Reflections from ambient light

3.3 Accessibility Features

As mentioned earlier, the STAR Showcase system was designed to include accessibility features for users with impairments (i.e., vision, physical, cognitive, etc.). The design of these features was based on the guidelines set by the World Wide Web Consortium (W3C) [15] and the Web Content Accessibility Guidelines (WCAG) [16], as well as guidelines reported in the literature for designing accessible interactions for users with disabilities [17–19].

To this end, the STAR Showcase system provides users with a dedicated assistive wireless device (Fig. 7) that acts as an alternative interaction modality that allows users

Fig. 6. Final high-fidelity for STAR Showcase (left)/Final high-fidelity design for STAR Showcase in the Transparent Display (right)

to navigate and explore the exhibit collection information, without relying on traditional touch input. The system navigation via the handheld device has two modes, scanning and reading. Scanning addresses people with mobility disabilities while reading is for people with visual disabilities. The scanning mode allows the user to navigate through each interactive element on the screen sequentially by using the back and forward arrow buttons on the device. The user can select an item by pressing the provided OK button. The reading mode works similarly to the scanning mode in the navigation, but in addition, it announces every element displayed on the screen and reads the displayed exhibit information. It should be noted that when the accessibility mode is enabled, the system disables touch instructions so that no other user can disrupt the experience of the user with the assistive wireless device.

Fig. 7. STAR Showcase Accessibility Wireless Handheld Device

Furthermore, the system also provides a suite of accessibility options that allow users to customize the presentation of the information based on their needs and/or preferences. These options are available through a dedicated "Accessibility menu" and include settings for dyslexia-friendly viewing, text size, line spacing, font family, and color contrast. These features are designed to benefit not only users with disabilities but can also improve the UX for all individuals.

3.4   Content Management System

The STAR system incorporates a comprehensive CMS for the administrative management (addition, removal, editing) of all the data (descriptions and multimedia content) regarding the displayed exhibit collections (Fig. 8).

Fig. 8. CMS for STAR Showcase

The implementation of the STAR Showcase including CMS was conducted using the web application technologies Angular [20], ElectronJs [21], Node.js [22], and Docker [23]. As illustrated in Fig. 9, the user application displays the content retrieved from the CMS server such as the collections of exhibits, exhibit information, multimedia content, and more.

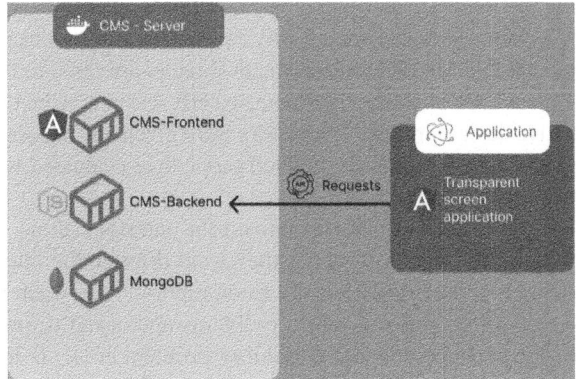

Fig. 9. System's Software Overview

Through CMS, administrators can browse existing exhibit collections, add new ones, copy existing ones, edit, and delete them. Furthermore, they can adjust the exhibit's time rotation as well as light intensity to accommodate the ambient light in the environment around the showcase (Fig. 10).

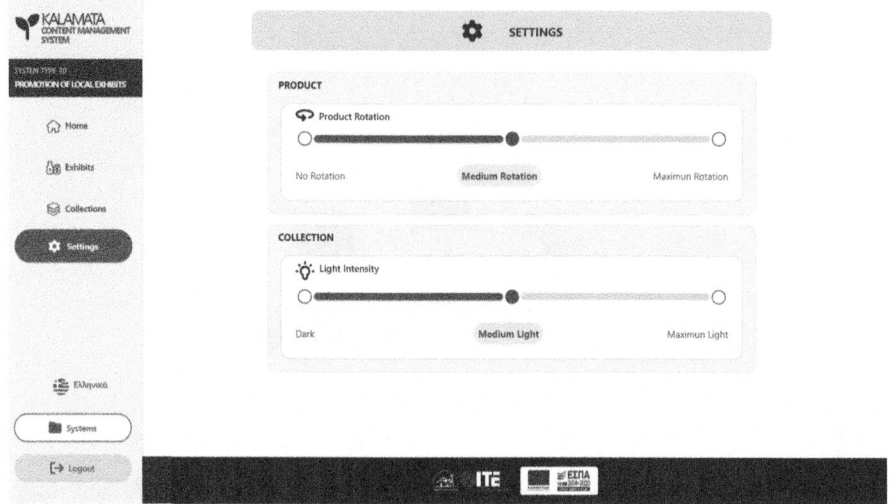

Fig. 10. Adjustment of STAR Showcase Settings

4 Heuristic Evaluations

Heuristic Evaluation (HE) is a usability inspection method for identifying usability problems in a UI design so they can be attended to as a part of an interactive design process. During HE a small set of Human-Computer Interaction experts or domain expert evaluators examine the interface and judge its compliance against established usability principles, known as heuristics, and specifically Jacob Nielsen's ten usability heuristics [24]. It is recommended that in this process the evaluators are three to five [25].

In the case of the STAR Showcase system, two HE sessions were conducted in the context of the iterative design process. Evaluators were given any necessary background information about the system, while the defined scope they evaluated was the interface without the accessibility navigation.

In each HE session, each evaluator examined the interface alone. Each evaluator verbalized their comments to an observer as they went through the interface of STAR, to reduce the workload on the evaluators of written reports. After each HE session, the evaluators were given a list of the usability problems and asked to rate their severity on a 0–4 scale (0- the problem was not a usability problem at all, 1- the problem was cosmetic, 2- the problem was a major problem, 3- it was a major problem, 4- the problem was a usability catastrophe) [26].

4.1 First Heuristic Evaluation Session

The first HE involved a group of four Human-Computer Interaction experts and researchers with backgrounds in User Interaction/User Experience (UI/UX) design. The first session of HE took place after the second design iteration.

The HE was performed both individually and in a group format. During this process evaluators verbalized their thoughts and used the think-out-loud protocol [24, 27] which encourages evaluators to express their thoughts, actions, feelings, and experiences when they interact with the system interface. This approach allowed a comprehensive heuristic evaluation of the STAR Showcase, recording spontaneous thoughts during the interaction process, both in cases where the potential user used the system alone or collaboratively. The HE identified key usability issues early in the design phase. Key areas for improvement included visual clarity, navigation, feedback mechanisms, and technical functionalities. The method proved crucial in uncovering critical usability issues and guiding necessary redesign efforts to enhance the UX and its satisfaction.

More specifically, the first HE inspection indicated a total of 44 issues regarding the *Visibility of the System, Match between the system and the real world, Consistency and Standards, User control and freedom, Error Prevention, Flexibility and efficiency of use,* and *Aesthetic and minimalist design.* Those issues included problems like poor contrast and visibility particularly when objects were obscured by the information dialogs, and lack of feedback for email actions which led to evaluators' frustration. Also, some abrupt and uneven movements of the underlined servo motors that mechanically hold and rotate the posts were observed resulting in an uneven rotation of the exhibited object. Additionally, the system behavior such as dialog boxes' rapid movements and unresponsive elements were identified as sources of increased user frustration. Accessibility settings were noted as nonintuitive. In detail, the settings were difficult to navigate and lacked clear structure making it challenging for users to find and adjust the options.

The results of this first heuristic evaluation led to further design and system adjustments, which were ultimately integrated into the second version of the system working prototype. The updated version went through a second heuristic evaluation the results of which are discussed next.

4.2 Second Heuristic Evaluation Session

The second HE was conducted at the end of the design iterations and involved a group of three Human-Computer Interaction experts and researchers with backgrounds in UI/UX design. These experts were not the same as the ones who participated in the first HE.

The second HE indicated 33 issues most of which had to do with the *Visibility of the System Consistency and Standards, User control and freedom, Error Prevention,* and *Flexibility and efficiency of use.* In detail, the second HE revealed critical issues such as unclear indicators for disabled arrows on photos and not understandable accessibility settings, both graded as 4 in Nielsen's grading (the highest grade).

During the heuristic evaluation, it was noted that some design choices may not be suitable for a multi-user environment. For example, sequential pop-up windows tend to be attention-grabbing, and distracting from the physical objects in view. The challenges for many users included potential conflicts if users wanted different languages. After this HE session, the evaluators discussed along with the designer and developer possible solutions to the identified problems. It was decided to redesign the photo layout and to develop new features for the users who will be using the system simultaneously, allowing them to adjust their individual preferences such as accessibility needs or language preferences. The experts also mentioned that interactions of more than two concurrent users may also degrade the UX due to the specific screen size. In case of three or more users, the personal interactive space becomes limited, making it difficult for users to view information and interact with the display conveniently (Fig. 11). As a result, considering the limitations due to the screen size (55″) of the specific transparent display, the ideal maximum number for multiple concurrent users was set to two (Fig. 12).

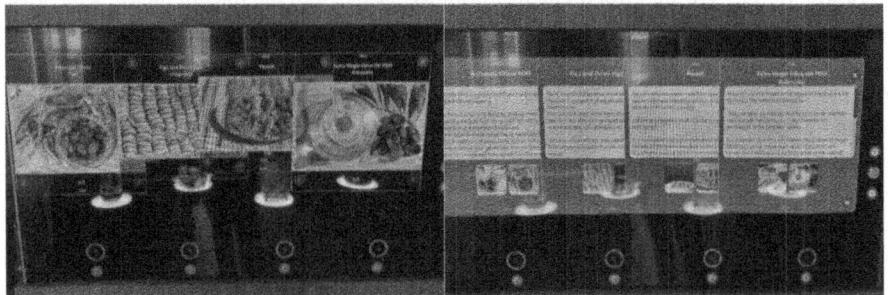

Fig. 11. Multiple Open Modals of STAR Showcase Application

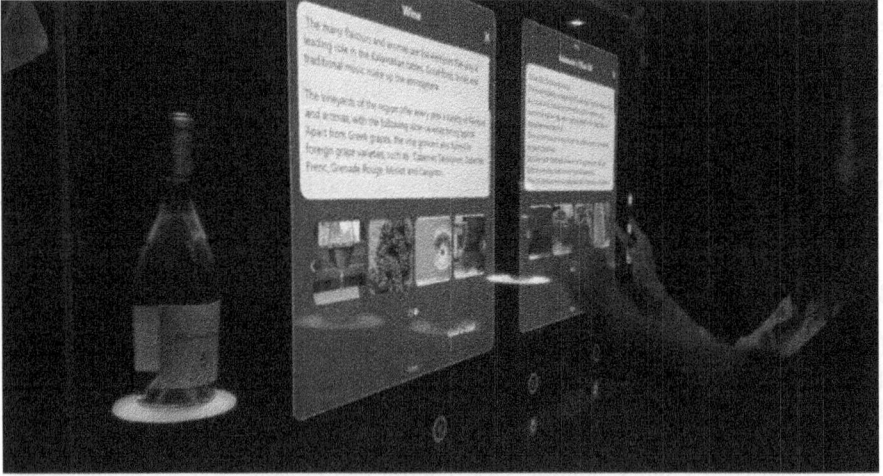

Fig. 12. Multiple users in STAR Showcase

4.3 Usability Assessment

At the end of each round of the heuristic evaluation, the evaluators were asked to assess the STAR showcase user-perceived usability by filling in the System Usability Scale

(SUS) [28] and the Usability Metric for User Experience (UMUX) [29] questionnaires, aiming to quantify usability and UX to some extent.

The results of the questionnaires are illustrated in Fig. 12. SUS and UMUX scores significantly improved between the first and second evaluation sessions. The SUS score increased by 12.7% indicating a substantial improvement, while the UMUX score rose by 22.22%.

In conclusion, the evaluation results show that the changes made to the overall system improved the usability and UX.

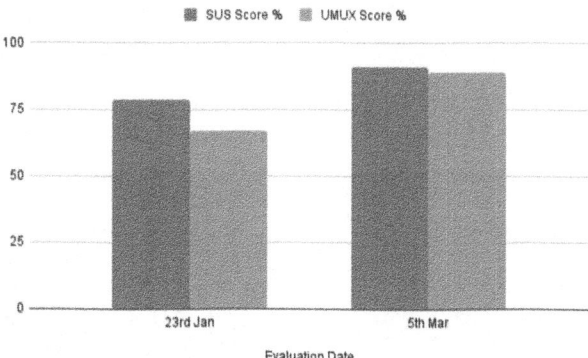

Fig. 13. Evaluation results

5 Case Study: Kalamata Traditional Products

A STAR showcase was developed for the city of Kalamata as a case study demonstrating the practical application of the proposed system (Fig. 14). The showcase presents various local products of Kalamata which is a city in southern Peloponnese in Greece that has a rich agricultural heritage and high-quality traditional products. The collection of the products comprises four products: 1) Kalamatas Olives PDO, 2) Figs and Dried Figs (Tsapeles), 3) Pasteli, and 4) Extra Virgin Olive Oil PDO Kalamata.

This case study (Fig. 15) offers a compelling example of how technology can enrich a physical exhibit with digital information regarding the historical and cultural context of the displayed item. In this case, each of the displayed local products is enriched with information ranging from their cultivation and production processes to their nutritional value and use in cooking recipes.

6 Conclusion and Future Work

This study presented the STAR Showcase, a See-Through Augmented Reality exhibit showcase built for transparent display that augments virtual information on real exhibits. The system aims to augment physical exhibits with digital information in a seamless manner. To support and validate the proposed system, the implementation of a use case was conducted in Kalamata, demonstrating the practical application of the system in a real environment.

Fig. 14. STAR Showcase developed for the city of Kalamata

Fig. 15. Kalamata's Local Products Case Study

The development of the STAR underscored the importance of iterative prototyping and expert feedback in refining usability and functionality. During the design process, experts' feedback proved invaluable in improving the system interface and overall functionality. Iterative prototyping was also instrumental in emphasizing the need to test all the design adjustments on the fly and in the environment setting. Finally, this work highlights the importance of considering multi-user interaction, allowing us to address challenges for a more seamless UX.

The iterative prototyping process was guided by the active feedback and the provision of expert insights, ultimately leading to several improvements regarding UI and supported functionality provided by the system. Each design iteration, steered by the outcomes of heuristic evaluation revealed issues leading to continuous improvements. The design process focused also on meeting the diverse needs, preferences, and limitations of the end users. In addition, practical tests led to key adjustments, such as optimal spotlight placement to enhance the visibility of the exhibits. Addressing multi-user interaction challenges and considerations of social dimensions were crucial for the design's effectiveness.

Two heuristic evaluations were conducted by experts in the field of HCI revealing various findings such as usability problems and considerable questions about its complete design and usability in multi-user collaborative environments.

Regarding future work, the STAR system needs to be tested with real users and the accessibility device has to be tested with users with disabilities. In addition, the system should extend its capabilities to support more types of multimedia content relevant to the exhibits like videos, 360 photos, 3D models, etc. Last but not least, expanding accessibility features is a priority for future development efforts. This may include the integration of features such as voice commands, eye tracking, gestures, and more.

Acknowledgments. We sincerely thank the Archaeological Museum of Messara for granting access to their site and providing the transparent screen to test the STAR Showcase. The authors would like to also thank Spyros Paparoulis, Michalis Roulios, and Nikolaos Stivaktakis for their contribution to the realization of the STAR Showcase. Their support contributed significantly to this research.

Funding. This work was conducted under the project "SUPPLY AND INSTALLATION OF INFORMATION TECHNOLOGY EQUIPMENT AND ELECTRONIC CITIZEN INFORMATION AND COMMUNICATION SYSTEM VISITORS TO THE CITY OF KALAMATA" of the Act: "Creation of modern means of promotion of the cultural and tourist resources of Kalamata" PRIORITY AXIS: 'Environmental protection - transition to an environmentally friendly economy', which has been included in the Operational Programme "Peloponnese 2014–2020" and co-financed by the ERDF, Integration Decision no. 3135 of 24-09-2019, MIS code 5041844.

References

1. Arena, F., Collotta, M., Pau, G., Termine, F.: An overview of augmented reality. Computers **11**(2), 28 (2022)
2. Fan, X., Chai, Z., Deng, N., Dong, X.: Adoption of augmented reality in online retailing and consumers' product attitude: a cognitive perspective. J. Retail. Consum. Serv. **53**, 101986 (2020)
3. Sun, D., Xu, L., Zhang, L., Cui, N.: How augmented reality affects people's perceptions: adoption of AR in product display improves consumers' product attitude. J. Phys. Conf. Ser., 012037 (2019)
4. Methimakis, M., et al.: Geolocalized AR exploration of shepherd settlements in the Psiloritis mountain. In: Proceedings of the 17th International Conference on PErvasive Technologies Related to Assistive Environments, pp. 112–117 (2024)
5. Hourdakis, A., et al.: Augmented reality application to highlight health policies about refugee students in the interwar period. An example of empathetic study of an archival collection (2023)
6. Foukarakis, M., et al.: A mobile tour guide with localization features and AR support. In: Stephanidis, C., Antona, M., Ntoa, S., Salvendy, G. (eds.) HCII 2023. CCIS, vol. 1957, pp. 489–496. Springer, Cham (2024). https://doi.org/10.1007/978-3-031-49212-9_60

 7. Xiong, J., Hsiang, E.-L., He, Z., Zhan, T., Wu, S.-T.: Augmented reality and virtual reality displays: emerging technologies and future perspectives. Light Sci. Appl. **10**(1), 216 (2021)
 8. Colley, A., Ventä-Olkkonen, L., Alt, F., Häkkilä, J.: Insights from deploying see-through augmented reality signage in the wild. In: Proceedings of the 4th International Symposium on Pervasive Displays, pp. 179–185 (2015)
 9. Syed, T.A., et al.: In-depth review of augmented reality: tracking technologies, development tools, AR displays, collaborative AR, and security concerns. Sensors **23**(1), 146 (2022)
10. Perry, M., Beckett, S., O'Hara, K., Subramanian, S.: WaveWindow: public, performative gestural interaction. In: ACM International Conference on Interactive Tabletops and Surfaces, pp. 109–112 (2010)
11. Heo, H., Kim, S., Park, H., Chung, J., Lee, G., Lee, W.: TransWall. In: ACM SIGGRAPH 2013 Emerging Technologies, SIGGRAPH 2013. Association for Computing Machinery, New York (2013). https://doi.org/10.1145/2503368.2503382.
12. Karnik, A., Mayol-Cuevas, W., Subramanian, S.: MUSTARD: a multi user see through AR display. In: Proceedings of the SIGCHI Conference on Human Factors in Computing Systems, pp. 2541–2550 (2012)
13. Li, J., Greenberg, S., Sharlin, E., Jorge, J.: Interactive two-sided transparent displays: designing for collaboration. In: Proceedings of the 2014 Conference on Designing Interactive Systems, DIS 2014, pp. 395–404. Association for Computing Machinery, New York (2014). https://doi.org/10.1145/2598510.2598518
14. Kratky, A.: Transparent touch – interacting with a multi-layered touch-sensitive display system. In: Antona, M., Stephanidis, C. (eds.) UAHCI 2015. LNCS, Part II, vol. 9176, pp. 114–126. Springer, Cham (2015). https://doi.org/10.1007/978-3-319-20681-3_11
15. Brooks, T.: World wide web consortium (W3C). In: Encyclopedia of Library and Information Sciences, pp. 5695–5699 (2010)
16. Caldwell, B., et al.: Web content accessibility guidelines (WCAG) 2.0. In: WWW Consort. W3C, vol. 290, no. 1–34, pp. 5–12 (2008)
17. Nurgalieva, L., Jara Laconich, J.J., Baez, M., Casati, F., Marchese, M.: A systematic literature review of research-derived touchscreen design guidelines for older adults. IEEE Access **7**, 22035–22058 (2019). https://doi.org/10.1109/ACCESS.2019.2898467
18. Ntoa, S., Margetis, G., Adami, I., Balafa, K., Antona, M., Stephanidis, C.: Digital accessibility for users with disabilities. In: Designing for Usability, Inclusion and Sustainability in Human-Computer Interaction. CRC Press (2024)
19. Guerreiro, T., Nicolau, H., Jorge, J., Gonçalves, D.: Towards accessible touch interfaces. In: Proceedings of the 12th International ACM SIGACCESS Conference on Computers and Accessibility, ASSETS 2010, pp. 19–26. Association for Computing Machinery, New York, October 2010. https://doi.org/10.1145/1878803.1878809
20. Google LLC: Angular Documentation (2024). https://angular.io/docs
21. OpenJS Foundation: Electron Documentation (2024). https://www.electronjs.org/docs
22. OpenJS Foundation: Node.js Documentation (2024). https://nodejs.org/en/docs/
23. Docker, Inc.: Docker Documentation (2024). https://docs.docker.com/
24. Nielsen, J.: Finding usability problems through heuristic evaluation. In: Proceedings of the SIGCHI Conference on Human Factors in Computing Systems, pp. 373–380 (1992)
25. Nielsen, J.: Severity ratings for usability problems. Pap. Essays **54**, 1–2 (1995)
26. Nielsen, J.: Reliability of severity estimates for usability problems found by heuristic evaluation. In: Posters and Short Talks of the 1992 SIGCHI Conference on Human Factors in Computing Systems, pp. 129–130 (1992)

27. Alhadreti, O., Mayhew, P.: Rethinking thinking aloud: a comparison of three think-aloud protocols. In: Proceedings of the 2018 CHI Conference on Human Factors in Computing Systems, pp. 1–12 (2018)
28. Brooke, J., et al.: SUS-a quick and dirty usability scale. Usability Eval. Ind. **189**(194), 4–7 (1996)
29. Bosley, J.J.: Creating a short usability metric for user experience (UMUX) scale. Interact. Comput. **25**(4), 317–319 (2013)

Research on Emotional Design and Multidimensional Expression of Cultural and Creative Products in a Multicultural Background

Wenrui Ji and Jing Li[✉]

Beijing Institute of Technology, Beijing, People's Republic of China
774909461@qq.com

Abstract. In a multicultural context, Emotional cultural and creative products are more likely to elicit consumer recognition and resonance, This article is based on practical cases-The research focuses on the creative product design of Lingnan lion dance culture in China, Explore the emotional design and multidimensional expression forms of its cultural and creative products, By constructing emotional and multi-dimensional design strategies for cultural and creative products, Seeking more dimensional forms of expression, Construct emotional connections and situational interactions between people and products. Through sensory and experiential interaction, the cultural connotation and interactive fun of cultural and creative products can be enhanced, in order to achieve the goal of enriching the diversity and immersive experience of cultural and creative products.

Keywords: Cultural and creative products · Emotional design · Multidimensional expression

1 Introduction

Cultural and creative products, as a special type of cultural consumer goods, have been highly favored by the market and recognized by consumers in recent years. Its core lies in using products as carriers to understand and study their cultural characteristics, empower them with specific ideas and wisdom, creatively transform cultural connotations, and enrich the spiritual needs of consumers [1], Transforming cultural resources into high value-added products that are in line with social consumption needs. At the same time as its development, The homogenization of its product design has also become a bottleneck for the development of this market, In this situation, exploring the local cultural characteristics and humanistic emotions of the development subject can be a design approach.

In the context of multiculturalism, product design must integrate local cultural characteristics and spiritual emotions in order to achieve sustainable development, The intervention of emotional experience can not only guide product design, but also enhance the value of product design to a certain extent. "Emotional design" is proposed by American cognitive psychologist Donald Arthur Norman and belongs to the category of design psychology [2]. In the theoretical research of cultural and creative product design, the intervention of emotional design can help oneself make better and more reasonable value judgments. Professor Donald Arthur Norman proposed three levels of emotional design: the instinctive level, the behavioral level, and the reflective level. It is not difficult to see from the three-level theory that the design of cultural and creative products needs to seek design possibilities through cultural, emotional, and situational exploration and understanding. The form of cultural and creative products needs to gradually evolve from a process that emphasizes formal functions to a process that follows emotions and experiences. In a multicultural context, cultural and creative products from different regions should adhere to and uphold their own cultural characteristics and spiritual emotions. Based on this research, the idea is: Firstly, construct a cultural system for the design framework of cultural and creative products, and analyze the living context and emotional needs of consumers in the cultural system of product development; Furthermore, through the emotional experience needs of users, the emotional context of regional culture is constructed; Exploring the multidimensional expression forms of emotional design in cultural and creative products by combining the ideas of emotional design in cultural and creative products.

2 Theoretical Background

2.1 Analysis of Multicultural Background

"Multiculturalism" originates from cultures with different starting points, and due to the diverse lifestyles of different regions and races, it presents diverse cultural attitudes, promoting the formation of multiculturalism. Multiculturalism is a composite complex of ideological cohesion, encompassing the common characteristics of cultural diversity, and is also a trend in the development of global culture today [3]. Commonality is a bridge for communication and exchange between different cultural backgrounds, and the commonality of human culture is manifested as the wisdom created by humans in long-term practical activities, regardless of the type of culture, It has a common development direction and law, and has both unified and diverse characteristics. The unity of culture is based on diversity, and the diversity of culture is based on unity, thus forming a dialectical relationship between cultural unity and diversity [4]. So although different ethnic cultures, due to their different starting conditions of development, exhibit diversity in their subsequent development process, and even have significant differences with each other, there are still common characteristics in diversity. Among them, human cultural emotions and needs in a multicultural context have certain common characteristics. On the basis of human cultural emotional commonalities, the locality and uniqueness presented by different cultural backgrounds reflect the dialectical relationship between cultural diversity and unity.

2.2 Analysis of Emotional Product Design

The so-called emotional design starts from an emotional perspective, establishes to a certain extent the emotions between people and products, making products have an affinity and a kind of spiritual care. In cultural and creative product design, the focus of this design concept is on the audience's experience rather than the product's functionality, it is a design form that can achieve emotional dialogue and communication [5].

Emotional design starts from the perspective of exploring the relationship between human emotions and design, deeply analyzing the role of human emotional factors in product design, and striving to better integrate emotional factors into design, so that products fully reflect the "people-oriented" design concept. Professor Donald Arthur Norman's "Emotional Design" theory divides emotional design into three levels: instinctive level design, behavioral level design, and reflective level design. The design at the instinctive level focuses on the sensory stimulation that the product's appearance brings to people. The design of behavioral hierarchy refers to the participation of consumers in the process of using products, as well as the sense of achievement and pleasure they obtain. The design of the reflective level is the highest level, referring to the deeper emotional, conscious, understanding, personal experience, and cultural background intertwined in the minds of consumers due to the effects of the first two levels. By incorporating emotional design into the above three levels of design, it stimulates people's associations and resonates with them during the process of using the product, thereby achieving spiritual pleasure and emotional satisfaction [6]. Emotional design embodies a people-oriented approach, Culture is the core of emotional products, and emotional analysis of products needs to be analyzed from a cultural perspective, So some Taiwanese scholars have also pointed out the different ways in which culture is stratified based on different perspectives. Divide culture into the outer layer, the middle layer, and the inner layer from a spatial perspective. The outer layer refers to the sum of visible, palpable, and explicit material cultures; The middle layer is the sum of audible, visible, and untouchable behavioral cultures; The inner layer refers to the sum of implicit, intangible, and imperceptible consciousness, conceptual culture, and concepts [7]. This further indicates that product emotionalization can be divided into three levels: material level, behavioral level, and reflective level. It is the sum of explicit cultural factors and implicit cultural factors. The three levels of emotion exist independently as different dimensions of the emotional system, but they interact with each other to form our overall emotional experience of the world [8].

Compared to designs that overly emphasize product functionality while ignoring human emotional needs, the emergence of emotional design is a significant breakthrough. It has reversed the situation where product functionality technology surpasses human emotions, bringing the object centered design pattern back to human centered design. Donald Arthur Norman wrote in "Emotional Design 3": "The emotional elements of a product's success or failure may be more crucial than the practical elements. Good products focus on functionality, while excellent products focus on emotions".

2.3 Multidimensional Design Expression Analysis

Multidimensional design expression refers to the need to consider multiple dimensions and factors in the design process, emphasizing emotional communication and interaction between people and products. The interaction between products and people is brought about by the design and usage characteristics of the products. The interactive properties can prolong the time spent between people and products, allowing consumers to have a deeper understanding of the products and maximizing their functionality [9]. With the development of digital media, relying solely on visual and auditory transmission of information is not enough. People need an efficient way of natural language interaction. With the rapid changes in machine interfaces, simulation technology, and graphics processing software, trends such as naturalization (limbs, NLP language) and virtualization (AR, VR, MR) are flourishing [10]. The multidimensional scalability of these technologies enriches the expression of emotional design in products.

Multidimensional expression can be broadly divided into aesthetic dimension, practical dimension, and cultural dimension. Among them, the aesthetic dimension refers to the use of diverse forms of expression to render the cultural value of the product from multiple dimensions, achieving emotional resonance with users; Under the practical dimension of people-oriented philosophy, apply user needs and interaction methods to product design; The cultural dimension reflects humanistic care and the value of culture. In the context of multiculturalism, incorporating multidimensional expressions into cultural and creative design can solve the problems of current cultural and creative product convergence and single market experience. Xue Xiaoxia once evaluated cultural and creative products from two dimensions: "endogenous" and "exogenous", and proposed a multidimensional expression of cultural and creative products. Li, J. et al. proposed a multi-level and multi-dimensional theoretical approach in their research on multi-dimensional museum cultural and creative design, dividing it into two aspects: appearance design and product significance value from the perspectives of material and spiritual needs. The dimensions of appearance design are divided into two-dimensional pattern dimensions and three-dimensional modeling dimensions; From the perspective of product meaning and value, the dimensions include cultural connotation, practical function, and interaction [9].

Analysis overview: It is not difficult to see from the above literature that multiculturalism has the characteristics of cultural diversity and unity, The unique culture of each region is a sample that constitutes multiculturalism, and the needs and expressions of human emotional culture share common characteristics. The design of cultural and creative products under different cultural backgrounds is gradually evolving towards emotional and experiential directions with common characteristics. Starting from the uniqueness of multiculturalism and the emotional design of products, the emotional design of cultural and creative products is constructed. Combining with the current era of integration and interactive development of cultural and creative and technology, the dimensions and space of interactive cultural and creative product design can be expanded.

3   Design Thinking Framework

Based on the theoretical background of previous research, the author has constructed a multi-dimensional emotional design approach for cultural and creative products (see Fig. 1). Divide cultural product design into two parts: external system and internal system, External systems focus on environmental and human design requirements; The internal system of the product focuses on cultural characteristics and product requirements. The internal and external systems are mutually coordinated and balanced [11]. In the trend of evolving from emphasizing formal functions to following emotions and experiences, the focus of design will shift to people, emotions, and experiences, thus constructing an emotional context that originates from culture, reviews tradition, and identifies with belonging. Products that reflect cultural identity can bring more sustainable emotional projection. So in the design process, by fully considering the cultural spirit in the design, emphasizing the output of emotional value, users can form recognition of the product's emotional culture [12]. Next, around the emotional context of the product, the various elements of emotional encoding for cultural products are deconstructed one by one. The author will focus on the code extraction centered on symbolization; On the extraction of coding centered on narrative and context. in the context of multi-dimensional expression of needs, cultural and creative product design can be placed in a contextualized interactive experience. Through different dimensions, time space, perceptual space, emotional space, environmental space, information space, etc. can be extended and overlaid.

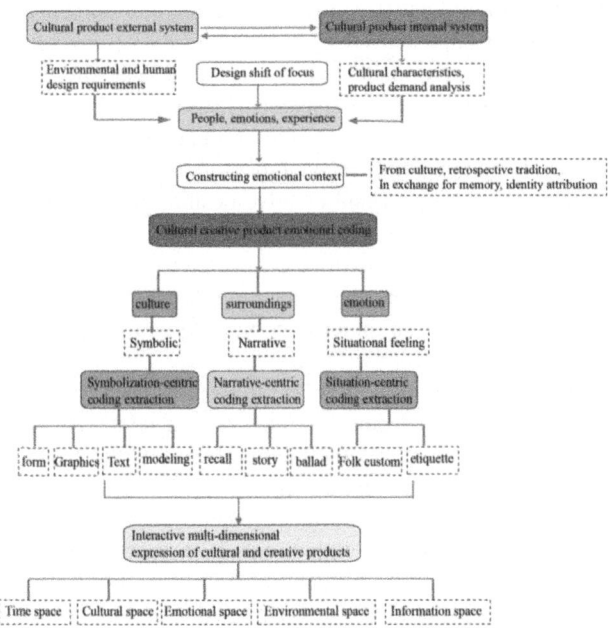

Fig. 1. Emotional multi-dimensional design thinking diagram

4 Practice

This article combines practical cases - creative product design of Lingnan's lion dance culture, Interpret from two aspects: cultural and creative emotional design and multi-dimensional expression design.

4.1 Emotional Design Strategies for Lingnan's Lion Dance Cultural

Lingnan culture is an important component of the splendid culture of the Chinese nation, lion dance culture as a symbol of Lingnan culture, has a history of thousands of years,

The lion dance of lingnan posture and appearance are exquisite, Rich in inner spirit, passed down from generation to generation, enduring for a long time, it has rich and profound cultural influence both domestically and internationally [13].

When conducting emotional design and development of cultural and creative products, Firstly, incorporate user demand characteristics into the design thinking framework. According to Donald Arthur Norman's hierarchy theory of emotional design (see Fig. 2), Construct an emotional design framework based, behavioral layer, and reflective layer. Firstly, the analysis of the instinctive level, namely the visual perception level, of lion dance culture includes the physiological, safety, and aesthetic needs of users; The behavior layer centered on experience includes cognitive needs, belongingness needs, and respect needs; Finally, it boils down to the reflective level, reflected in spiritual needs, self-actualization needs, and transcendent needs. The visual elements such as the form, type, pattern, and craftsmanship of lion dance at the instinctive level correspond to the sensory dimension; The performance programs, action rituals, and other behavioral layers in the lion dance culture under the experiential dimension reflect the satisfaction of respect and cognitive needs, Creating a sense of belonging and participation in specific activities and festivals, which are categorized as explicit factors induced by the atmosphere; Finally, in the reflection layer, by satisfying the user's spiritual and material needs through experience, emotional connection and emotional memory are achieved, and these emotional rituals belong to implicit factors. The explicit and implicit factors ultimately come down to the cultural aspect of emotional product design, namely cultural cognition, cultural identity, and cultural inheritance.

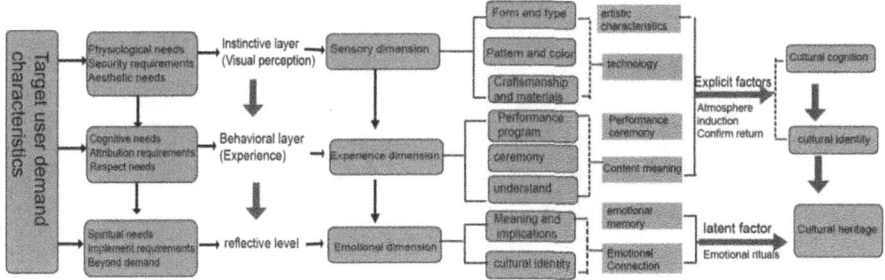

Fig. 2. Lingnan's lion dance culture and creative emotional design thinking chart

4.2 Extraction and Expression of Product Design Elements

Based on the sorting and analysis of the dominant gene morphology materials mentioned above, extract typical features of each dominant substance form, using representative images as samples, according to the extraction of core representative features, simplify and summarize the main morphological elements, and extract some dominant genes of lion culture for illustration (see Fig. 4).

In the design process, specific cultural connotations are visually transformed to create a brand culture with its own characteristics. Based on the cultural characteristics of "Lingnan's lion dance", a series of cultural and creative product application designs are carried out (see Fig. 5) (Fig. 3).

Fig. 3. Lingnan's lion dance Design element extraction

Fig. 4. Lingnan's lion dancel and Creative Expression

4.3 Sensory Interaction in Multidimensional Expression Design of Products

Based on the emotional design of Lingnan's lion dance cultural and creative products in the early stage, the following practical interpretations will be conducted from two aspects: sensory interaction and experiential interaction expressed in multiple dimensions (see Fig. 6). In emotional design mind maps, emotional design at the behavioral level requires establishing connections between people and objects, and "sense of participation" and "sense of experience" are important connections that form emotional resonance [14]. Integrating traditional culture and art with new media technology, through multisensory interaction, can generate more three-dimensional and effective emotional interaction with users, enhancing the excitement of product interest, The forms of interaction can be divided into sensory interaction and experiential interaction, The sensory interaction adopts the technical feature of combining AR virtual and real, which increases the fun of virtual experience and multimedia integration. The characteristic of AR technology is to "overlay" virtual information on the real environment, and present the scene of virtual information and the real environment after overlapping and merging to the user as a new technology [15].

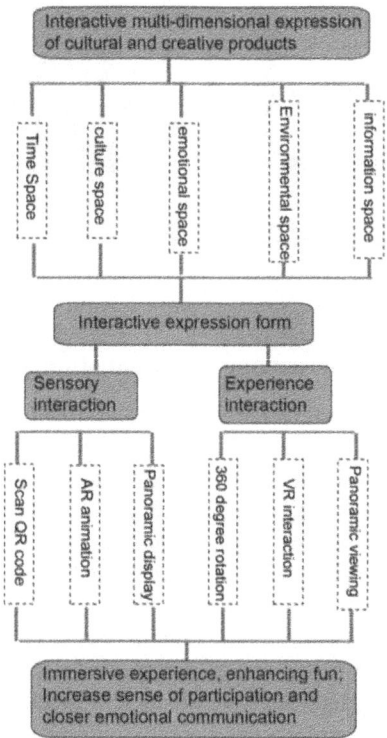

Fig. 5. Interactive Multidimensional Expression Mind Map

For example, AR technology has been added to lion dance culture and creative products, If the user scans the cover of the Lion laptop in their official account, There will be vivid lion dance movements, The fun interaction of lion dance can be achieved through AR special effects camera technology in the APP, Scan the lion head in the picture, It will automatically recognize the user's facial features, You can place the lion's head element in the appropriate position to interact with the face. Using mobile applications, Align the lion head pattern printed on the lion dance cultural and creative product, Complete the finishing touch of the lion dance (see Fig. 7).

Fig. 6. The application of AR technology in cultural and creative products

4.4 Multidimensional Expression and Experiential Interaction

With the support of many digital technologies, integrating culture into mobile interaction can make traditional culture more interesting and engaging. Enhanced emotional experience, the environment where virtual and real intersect provides users with a more easily perceivable and empathetic "presence" experience, not only can it enhance user willingness, but it also expands the display dimension of traditional cultural products [16]. For example, the Han Xizai Night Banquet Image APP developed by the Beijing Palace Museum utilizes modern technology to showcase traditional art scrolls, or utilizes AR, VR interactive devices, etc. to combine single visual information with five senses, which can enhance the communication experience with characters in all aspects. For example, the Han Xizai Night Banquet Image APP developed by the Beijing Palace Museum utilizes modern technology to showcase traditional art scrolls, or utilizes AR, VR interactive devices, etc. to combine single visual information with five senses, which can enhance the communication experience with characters in all aspects. With the development of digital technology and the diversification of digital media and communication forms, it adapts to the needs derived from multiple dimensions.

In terms of multi-dimensional expression of lion culture products, while continuing traditional lion culture, Zhao Weibin, the inheritor of lion dance, and technology companies are also actively exploring the path of presenting intangible cultural heritage lion dance under the "art+" and "technology+" models, combining traditional culture with new media such as VR animation to make it more contemporary and technological (see Fig. 8). Due to the beauty of both static imagery and the majesty of dynamic performances in Lingnan lion dance, the presentation form is limited to a certain range of small venues, and the dissemination power is limited, by utilizing VR animation design techniques, people can immerse themselves in VR virtual characters and VR virtual scenes, increasing their immersive experience. Users can perform lion awakening role-playing through VR controllers and eye masks, and integrate with lion dance under interactive commands. When participants jump or perform lion dance movements, the appearance of the lion also corresponds to jumping, squatting, kicking and other related movements.

This interaction allows people to immerse themselves in VR lion dance scenarios. Expanding the dimensional expression of lion dance culture through sensory and experiential interaction. This interaction allows people to immerse themselves in VR Lingnan lion dance scenarios. Expanding the dimensional expression of Lingnan lion dance culture through sensory and experiential interaction [17].

Fig. 7. Intangible cultural heritage experience hall in guangdong intangible cultural heritage block (Network source)

5   Conclusion

In the context of multiculturalism, emotional design of cultural and creative products contains cultural belonging, respect for needs, cultural identity, and cultural inheritance. Therefore, emotional cultural and creative products are more likely to attract consumer recognition and resonance. Under the premise of emphasizing emotional design of cultural and creative products, seek more dimensional expressions to enrich the diversity of cultural and creative products. Based on the psychological needs of users, this article constructs a multi-dimensional emotional design strategy for cultural and creative products. Taking Lingnan lion dance Design as an example, based on the emotional design thinking of Lingnan lion cultural and creative products, By summarizing and extracting visual symbols of explicit and implicit elements in the instinctive layer (visual layer), interactive emotional symbol design is constructed, and a series of emotional cultural and creative product designs are developed. On this basis, based on the demand for interactive multi-dimensional expression of cultural and creative products, the fun of cultural and creative products is enhanced through sensory and experiential interaction, increasing the sense of user participation, making them have an immersive experience and closer emotional communication.

References

1. Li, H., Wang, X., Li, W.: Research on the design of cultural and creative products at the palace museum based on cultural elements. Packag. Eng. **43**(2), 325–332 (2022)
2. Liu, W., Li, Z., Guo, Q.: Research on the design of cultural and creative products based on the emotional needs of generation Z: taking Zhao Wangcheng ruins park as an example. Packag. Eng. **44**(22), 368–380 (2023)
3. Chen, R., Jiang, W., Feng, H., Yang, Z.: A study on the aesthetic value and realistic social function of creation epics from a multicultural perspective: taking the "Cham" of the Yi ethnic group in Chuxiong as an example. Comp. Study Cult. Innov. **7**(33), 101–105 (2023)
4. Dai, D.: Research on the nationalization characteristics of product design in a multicultural background. Art Des., 175–177 (2010)
5. Zhou, X., Cao, X., Wu, J.: Research on emotional oriented cultural and creative product design. Packag. Eng. **44**(04), 339–342 (2023)
6. Donald Arthur Norman: Emotional Design. China CITIC Press, Beijing (2015)
7. Xu, Q., Lin, R.: Cultural product design program. J. Des. **16**(4), 1–18 (2011)
8. Yao, Z., Zhu, X.: Research on emotional design based on design and requirement levels. Sci. Technol. Inf. **19**(10), 23–25 (2021)
9. Li, Ji., Lv, Ji.: Research on multidimensional museum cultural and creative design- taking Nanjing museum as an example. Art Educ. Res. (11), 114–117+120 (2021)
10. Tian, J.: Research on interactive dynamic design centered on emotional user experience. Pop. Stand. **13**, 58–60 (2021)
11. Qi, F., Xiao, D., Li, H., et al.: Research on design and evaluation of Huxiang cultural and creative products based on situational systems. Packag. Eng. **39**(06), 119–126 (2018)
12. Hu, H., Liu, B., Huang, Y.: Research on railway cultural and creative product design based on analytic hierarchy process. Design **36**(21), 14–17 (2023)
13. Xie, Z., Li, N.: The History, Culture, and Skills of Lions Awakening in the South China Sea. Guangming Daily Press, Beijing (2019)
14. Yu, J., Liang, X.: Digital emotional interaction design of festival culture: a case study of new year cultural creation in the palace museum calendar. Design **36**(15), 50–53 (2023)
15. Yu, R., Tang, C., Hu, S.: Research on innovative design and development of cultural tourism products based on AR technology. Hundred Sch. Arts **29**(04), 181–185 (2013)
16. M, X., S, M., et al.: How the immersive technology affect the perception of affective value in digital culture: an empirical study based on the moderating effect of self-categorization. J. Xi'an Jiaotong Univ. (Soc. Sci.) **41**(5), 144–154 (2021)
17. Li, L.: Research and application of animation digital art in Lingnan lion awakening virtual simulation. Art Outlook (9), 196 (2019)

Research on Embodied Interaction Design of Traditional Crafts Based on Experiential Learning – A Case Study of Lime Sculpture Craft

Yining Li, Wen Luo, and Chen Wang[(✉)]

South China University of Technology, Guangzhou 510006, People's Republic of China
wangchen@scut.edu.cn

Abstract. Digital technology, through virtual construction and digital display, has enriched the public's experience of traditional craftsmanship, making it more engaging and immersive. However, current digital applications tend to focus on creating "experiences" while neglecting the deepening of "learning," lacking exploration of the intrinsic knowledge of traditional craftsmanship. This study aims to start from the essence of embodiment in traditional craftsmanship, based on experiential learning theory, to explore the application of embodied interaction media for presenting traditional craft content, thereby enhancing the audience's learning and understanding of traditional craft knowledge. The paper first analyzes the current state of research on digital display and embodied interaction of traditional crafts. Then, it introduces experiential learning theory to analyze the embodied cognition and experience model of traditional crafts, dividing it into three levels: situational perception, behavioral interaction, and meaning-making, and proposes corresponding design strategies. Finally, taking the traditional lime sculpture of Guangzhou as an example, the study conducts design practice and prototype experiments. The experimental results are positive both in terms of user experience and learning outcomes. Embodied interaction design for traditional crafts based on experiential learning can effectively promote learners' understanding and comprehensive cognition of traditional crafts.

Keywords: Traditional Craft · Experiential Learning · Embodied Interaction · lime Sculpture Craft

1 Introduction

Traditional crafts, as the crystallization of cultural heritage and human wisdom, embody rich knowledge content. Effectively conveying the embodied knowledge of traditional crafts is a prerequisite and key for their dissemination and inheritance. Traditional crafts, formed by artisans through long-term embodied experiences, are essentially a type of tacit knowledge that is difficult to codify, emphasizing practice and experience, reflecting the production, life, and cultural spirit of specific periods and places [1]. The interpretation and dissemination of traditional crafts require people to personally participate in

P. Zaphiris et al. (Eds.): HCII 2024, LNCS 15378, pp. 291–308, 2025.
https://doi.org/10.1007/978-3-031-76815-6_21

the practice of traditional crafts to understand embodied knowledge, and through craft inheritors or interpretive media to reveal their meanings and relationships. However, the current display of traditional crafts mainly relies on static methods such as textual descriptions and physical displays, supplemented by dynamic forms such as videos, explanations, and live performances. This traditional format of "crafts + text + video + explanation" detaches from the context of traditional crafts, lacking in engagement, making it difficult for the audience to experience the craftsmanship and cultural spirit embedded in traditional crafts.

In recent years, digital technology and smart technology have opened up new possibilities for displaying and experiencing the intangible and invisible content of traditional crafts. This breakthrough transcends the limitations of conventional static displays in terms of time and space, and overcomes the one-way nature of traditional dissemination, enabling exhibition experiences to be more immersive, interactive, and intelligent. H. Zhang and F. Tian [2], through the application of new media technology, have achieved digital recording and interactive design and development of the underglaze five-color craft. This has allowed the traditional craft display to break away from the conventional "physical object + text" format. E. Selmanovic, et al. [3] utilized virtual reality technology to develop interactive storytelling for intangible cultural heritage, aiming to improve the accessibility of such content. S. Rizvic, et al. [4] designed interactive storytelling using virtual reality and augmented reality to narrate the historical stories of Bosnian intangible cultural heritage. N. C. Yazli, et al. [5] developed a digital craftsman to narrate traditional handicraft content, applying it in interactive programs to represent and showcase both the tangible and intangible aspects of the craft. Y. J. Gao and Z. W. Xu [6] employed digital virtual technology to break down the key steps of the carving technique. They used a hierarchical method to organize and output these steps, thereby enabling the digital capture of technique essentials and creating an interactive experience of the carving context. L. Fan, et al. [7] conducted intelligent interactive development for traditional arts and crafts, using Jinshan Farmer's Paintings as a case study. They utilized human-computer interaction to inspire a sense of engagement.

In addition to enhancing the audience's experience in terms of immersion and engagement during exhibitions, the challenge of presenting the embodied knowledge of traditional crafts has drawn the attention of scholars to the design concept of embodied interaction. The concept of embodied interaction stems from scholars' exploration of applying perceptual phenomenology and embodied cognition theory to human-computer interaction (HCI). In 2001, Paul Dourish coined the term "embodied interaction" to describe a new paradigm of interaction design. This paradigm emphasizes the physical, bodily, and social aspects of people's interaction with digital technology [8]. It aligns with the focus of traditional crafts on bodily sensory experiences and practical knowledge in specific contexts. Embodied interaction can use digital technology to create immersive scenarios for traditional crafts, allowing learners to immerse themselves in these settings and simulate the embodied practices of traditional crafts from a first-person perspective. This approach fosters empathy and understanding of traditional crafts, as depicted in Fig. 1. The current concrete forms of embodied interaction in the digital application of traditional crafts can be categorized into gesture-based interaction, virtual reality interaction, augmented reality interaction, and immersive spatial interaction.

For example, P. Koutsabasis and S. Vosinakis [9] designed, developed, and evaluated a kinesthetic application for Cycladic sculpture, where users become ancient artisans in a virtual environment, interacting with hand gestures to complete simple carving tasks. This approach enables users to understand the major stages of statue-making and the tools and materials used, through embodied interaction. J. Yi, et al. [10] proposed an embodied interactive learning model for traditional handicraft education based on WebAR technology, improving the learning environment in traditional handicraft education. S. Y. Zhong, et al. [11] proposed an immersive virtual reality design model for Guangdong porcelain based on embodied interaction, conveying knowledge about Guangdong porcelain at three levels: physical embodiment, phenomenological embodiment, and knowledge construction. These studies focus on embodied interactive design for specific traditional craft cases from various technological application perspectives. However, there is limited research on cognitive development in the context of embodied interaction for traditional crafts, and the exploration and application of the embodied knowledge inherent in traditional crafts are still in the preliminary research stage.

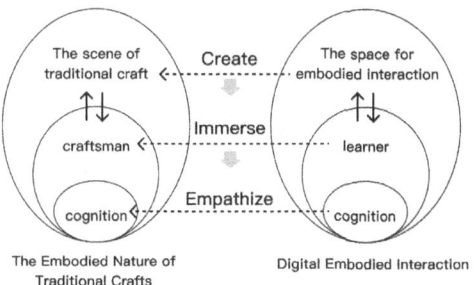

Fig. 1. The Alignment between Embodied Interaction and Traditional Crafts

How can media and technology related to embodied interaction best leverage their strengths for experiential learning of embodied knowledge in traditional crafts? Experiential learning theory offers a relatively systematic and comprehensive framework—the Kolb's Experiential Learning Model—that systematically summarizes the relationship between experience and learning. It reveals how contextualized knowledge can be acquired through concrete experiences and reflective observations in specific contexts, and how it can be internalized and extended through practical behavior. This model can provide theoretical guidance for the application and design planning of media in embodied interaction for experiential learning in traditional crafts, thereby establishing the experiential learning significance of traditional craft-based embodied interaction applications. Therefore, this study aims to build on previous research by incorporating experiential learning theory, focusing on users' cognitive development process regarding traditional craft knowledge during embodied interaction. The goal is to explore common embodied interaction design practices and strategies for traditional crafts to promote the learning and understanding of embodied knowledge in traditional crafts through digital experiences.

2   Methodology

Experiential Learning Theory originates from educator John Dewey's notion of "learning by doing," emphasizing the process by which learners immerse themselves in a knowledge context and acquire knowledge through firsthand practice and reflective abstraction. Educational psychologist Kolb [12], building on earlier research, proposed a classic experiential learning cycle, indicating that experiential learning is a continuous cyclical process comprising four stages: concrete experience, reflective observation, abstract conceptualization, and active experimentation. During experiential learning, learners progress through these four stages, with their bodies and minds continually interacting with the environment. This interaction leads to the internal accumulation of experience in the brain to adapt to changing environments, ultimately resulting in knowledge acquisition—evidenced by changes in behavior and behavioral potential.

2.1   Layer Goals of Embodied Cognition and Experiential

This study, based on Kolb's classic experiential learning model, designed an embodied interactive learning process for traditional crafts. In a created traditional craft context, learners undergo specific situational perception and contextual tasks, followed by appropriate interactive behaviors. They then reflect on and associate the scientific principles and artistic characteristics involved in their behavioral experience based on the feedback received, forming abstract concepts of traditional crafts in their minds—evidenced by the potential for future behavior changes. They then apply this knowledge through behavioral practice, developing it into personal experience. This process can be divided into three levels: "Situational Perception Layer," "Behavioral Interaction Layer," and "Meaning Formation Layer," serving as cognitive experiential goals for learners at different stages of the experiential process to guide design (Fig. 2 left).

Situational Perception Layer. Learners need to understand the relationship between their bodies and the traditional craft context, achieving both sensory and psychological immersion. Based on what they see, hear, and need in the context (new environmental stimuli), they determine "what can I do, what do I need to do, and what outcomes could occur." This leads to a basic understanding of the physical properties of materials and the fundamental uses of tools, connecting them to prior abstract concepts, thereby forming an initial intuitive image of traditional crafts.

Behavioral Interaction Layer. At this level, learners respond to the context through physical movements and receive immediate feedback. In this process, they gain an experiential understanding of the traditional craft process through bodily behaviors and movements. They reflect and make associations based on the "knowledge metaphors of interactive actions" and the "feedback from interactions," leading to a deeper practical understanding of how the physical properties of materials and the use of tools impact the formation of traditional craft forms.

Meaning Formation Layer. This layer represents the ultimate goal of the embodied interactive experience, relying on the systematic accumulation of perception and behavior from the previous layers. Learners combine their personal experiences with what they have seen, done, and felt, engaging in self-reflection and internalization, leading to a comprehensive understanding of the abstract concepts of "traditional craft form and its technical content, scientific principles, aesthetics, and other related aspects."

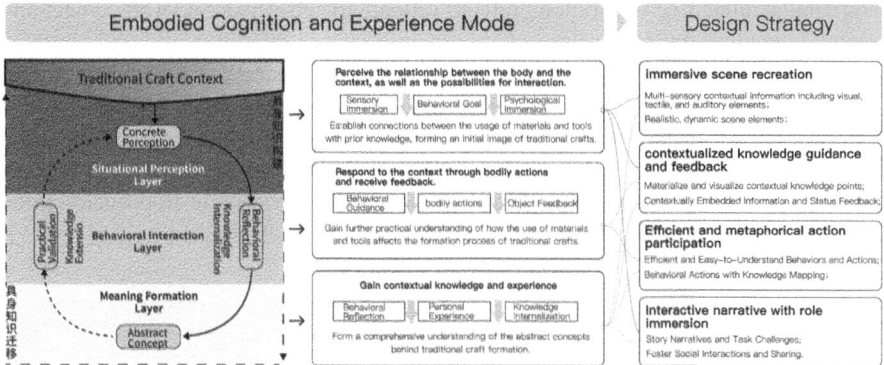

Fig. 2. Mode and Strategy

2.2 Embodied Interaction Design Strategies

Combining the characteristics of relevant digital technologies, this study breaks down the cognitive and experiential goals for the three levels and proposes an embodied interactive design strategy for traditional crafts under the framework of experiential learning (Fig. 2 right).

At the situational perception level, dynamic multi-sensory scene design and narrative design are employed to induce both sensory and psychological immersion in learners, while enhanced information is used to facilitate their perception of the context.

At the behavioral interaction level, learners reflect on knowledge through metaphorical gestures and object feedback, necessitating the metaphorical design of related action instructions and the presetting of guidance and state feedback associated with knowledge to promote reflection. The natural efficiency of actions during the interactive process determines the effectiveness of traditional craft learning through metaphorical interaction.

The achievement of the meaning formation level is predicated on the design quality of the previous two levels. It is promoted through systematic and narrative task flows, task challenges, and social interactions based on contextualized knowledge and "action-knowledge" metaphors, enhancing learners' deeper understanding of traditional craft knowledge. Moreover, achieving the meaning formation level solely through digital embodied interactive learning is insufficient; it requires learners to practice or discuss the knowledge gained during the experience in real life to achieve ultimate knowledge internalization and transfer. The proposed embodied interaction design strategy for traditional crafts comprises four key points: Immersive scene recreation, Contextualized knowledge guidance and feedback, Efficient and metaphorical action participation, and Interactive narrative with role immersion.

3   Prototype Design and Implementation

This study, based on the proposed model and design strategy, designed and developed an embodied interactive application prototype for Guangzhou lime sculpture craft (a traditional architectural decoration craft) to validate the effectiveness of the model and strategy in guiding design.

In the early stages of design, the study chose the Oculus Quest 2 virtual reality device, which can provide embodied perception and natural motion interaction, as the interactive platform, in line with the requirements of embodied interaction characteristics. The study then extracted experiential elements from the Guangzhou lime sculpture craft process based on the three levels of embodied cognition and experience in traditional crafts, including scene elements, action elements, and knowledge elements.

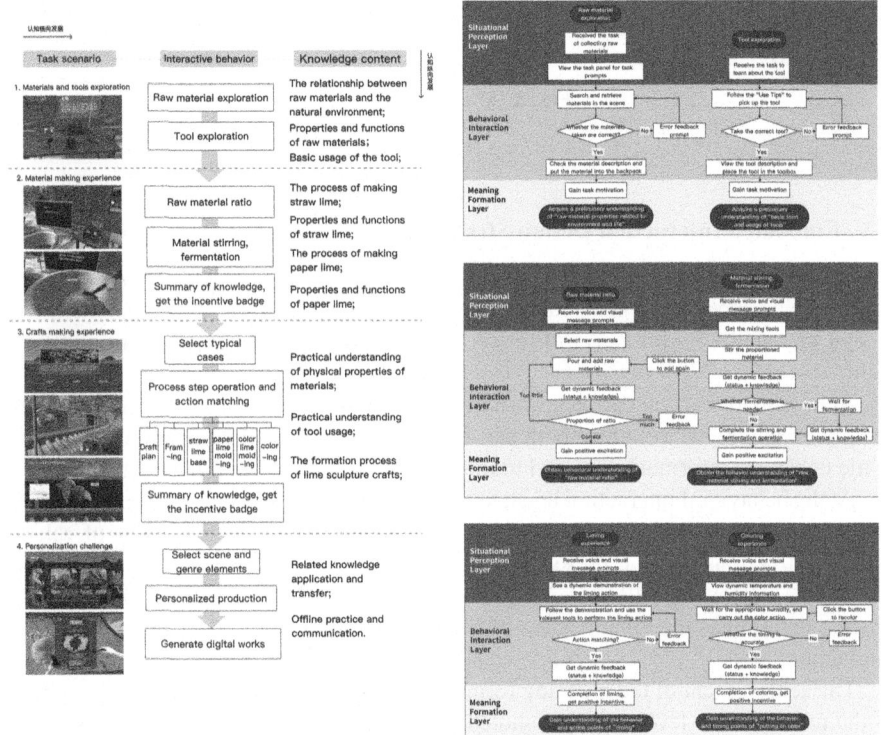

Fig. 3. Experiential Flow

During the design process, the study developed the experiential flow corresponding to the lime sculpture craft process and divided it into four main scenes based on the embodied interactive learning process for traditional crafts. This design approach aims to facilitate learners' cognitive development through systematic experience and accumulation, resulting in a comprehensive understanding of the knowledge behind lime sculpture craft. In each experiential scene, the design adhered to the lateral cognitive development process, moving from situational perception to behavioral interaction to meaning formation (Fig. 3). And then, the design was guided by the embodied interactive design strategy for traditional crafts to design and develop scene interaction prototypes, achieving the cognitive and experiential goals of lime sculpture craft embodied interaction.

3.1 Immersive Scene Recreation

The embodied interaction design of traditional lime sculpture craft first requires the recreation design of craft production and application scenarios, enabling learners to perceptually immerse themselves in the practical environment of traditional lime sculpture craft. This includes experiencing the dynamic realism of the surrounding environment and perceiving the body's mobility. The design and implementation primarily involve scene spatial construction, object perception implementation, and body perception implementation.

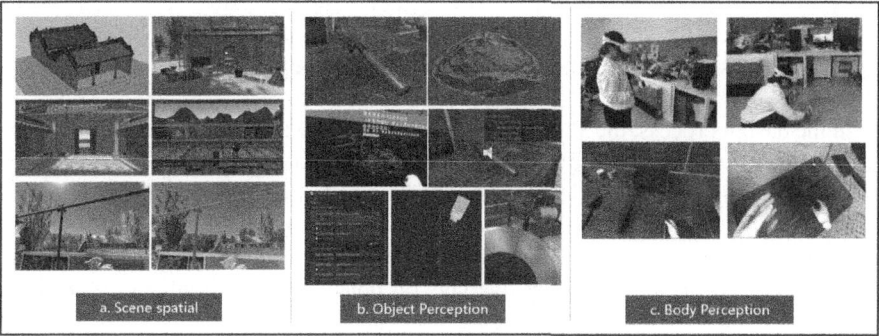

Fig. 4. Immersive scene recreation

Scene Spatial Construction. The production space of Lingnan lime sculpture corresponds to its craft process, including the material preparation space and the sculpture production space, with main spatial carriers such as Cantonese ancestral halls, arcade houses, and Lingnan dwellings. This design selects the more typical Cantonese ancestral hall architecture and its environment as the spatial carrier, and then constructs a realistic scene space through the design of experiential flow and placement of objects. (Fig. 4a). Additionally, lime sculpture craft has strict requirements for environmental temperature, humidity, and time. Therefore, when simulating the lime sculpture process, it is necessary to replicate the dynamic changes of temperature and humidity over time in the environment, allowing learners to experience how the weather characteristics of the Lingnan region affect the lime sculpture craft during the simulated experience of the production process.

Object Perception Implementation. To provide a more immersive and realistic sensory experience for users during object interaction, this design utilizes Unity's physics engine to set physical constraints for interactive objects, allowing for realistic collision effects between objects. Additionally, by adding appropriate event-triggered sound effects and vibration feedback, it enhances learners' multisensory perception of visual, auditory, and tactile sensations during interactive events. (Fig. 4b).

Body Perception Implementation. The perception of bodily movement in virtual reality is primarily achieved through head tracking and hand tracking. Subsequently, full-body tracking is realized through the correlation of the head, hands, and body skeleton joints. Since various handheld tools are predominantly used in the process of grey sculpture crafting, this design opts for controllers to track hand movements and execute corresponding interactions. These controllers serve as real-world counterparts to the handheld tools in the virtual lime sculpture experience.

3.2 Contextualized Knowledge Guidance and Feedback

Unlike the previous section on object interaction feedback, this section focuses on the visual and tangible design and implementation of contextual interaction guidance and feedback related to the knowledge points of the lime sculpture craft. The aim is to enable learners to perceive the knowledge points of the lime sculpture craft and their association with user actions during embodied interactive learning, thereby promoting learning and reflection.

In the design process, the various knowledge points of the lime sculpture craft were deconstructed to form contextualized text and audio materials. Through appropriate visual and multi-sensory design, these knowledge points were integrated into the learners' experiential context, providing guidance before actions, immediate feedback and explanations during actions, and feedback after actions. In terms of action guidance, visual image processing and audio overlays on objects and environments were used to visualize contextual knowledge, helping users understand the behavior requirements related to the contextual knowledge. During actions, besides overlaying information for behavior knowledge explanation, different behaviors can be associated with object and context state feedback. For instance, presetting feedback such as "if too much brown sugar is added, the material becomes too sticky and unusable, prompting the user to go back a step and re-add" has been used. After actions are completed, motivational feedback reinforces the learners' perception of acquiring knowledge points.

The relevant designs primarily include UI guidance and feedback, voice guidance and feedback, as well as animation guidance and dynamic object generation during the experiential process (Fig. 5).

3.3 Efficient and Metaphorical Action Participation

In traditional craft embodied interaction, learners' behavioral actions can be classified into basic actions and key actions based on the degree of mapping to craft knowledge. The corresponding design and implementation of action participation aim to construct a natural and efficient interaction conceptual model in the context of lime sculpture embodiment, enabling learners to perform related interactive behaviors with natural basic actions. Simultaneously, metaphorical design is applied to key actions to establish connections between behavioral actions and the informative feedback, facilitating

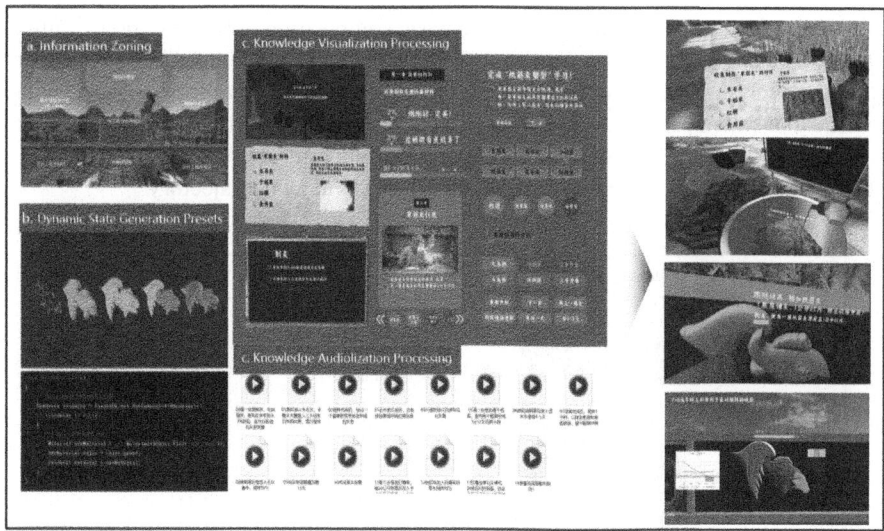

Fig. 5. Contextualization of Craft Knowledge

learners to grasp the essential behavioral and action points of the clay sculpture making process through bodily perception.

Basic Action Design. The main basic actions in this design are positional transfer and object grabbing and placing. This design sets up an interactive method of jumping positions through ray casting. Users in the virtual embodied space can move over a large range through rays without the need for frequent body movements and rotations to switch positions and perspectives. At the same time, this interaction method reduces to some extent the dizziness caused by the asynchronous visual image and body during movement, enabling users to complete key interaction operations more efficiently. Small-scale body movements and actions still retain the six degrees of freedom interaction mode to ensure the immersion of the experience. The object grabbing interaction is designed based on the hand tracking function of the controller and the headset camera (Meta XR SDK). The grip button on the side of the controller is designed with a gripping action metaphor. In this design, only by adding interaction components (Interactor) for hand models and grabbing interaction components (Interactable) for objects, and setting Attach Transform according to the gripping position of the object, can the object grabbing interaction be achieved.

Key Action Design. In the lime sculpture craft embodied interaction, key actions primarily include "pouring, stirring, cutting" in the material preparation experience, and "painting, applying lime, plastering lime, trimming" in the sculpture creation experience. Examples of key action design and implementation are shown in Fig. 6. Through embodied simulation and knowledge mapping in key action design, learners are encouraged to engage in behaviors and actions during the experience, further deepening their understanding of the hierarchical levels of actions in lime sculpture craft. For instance, the action of sketching is designed for learners to use a brush to outline key positions in the composition, enabling them to perceive the basic composition of lime sculpture. Different hand movements are preset for various lime processing actions: the hand movement preset for applying lime involves pressing the target position from front to back, while the hand movement preset for plastering involves more extensive back-and-forth motion according to the model's form; and the hand movement preset for trimming involves small, up-and-down hooking movements based on the model's trajectory.

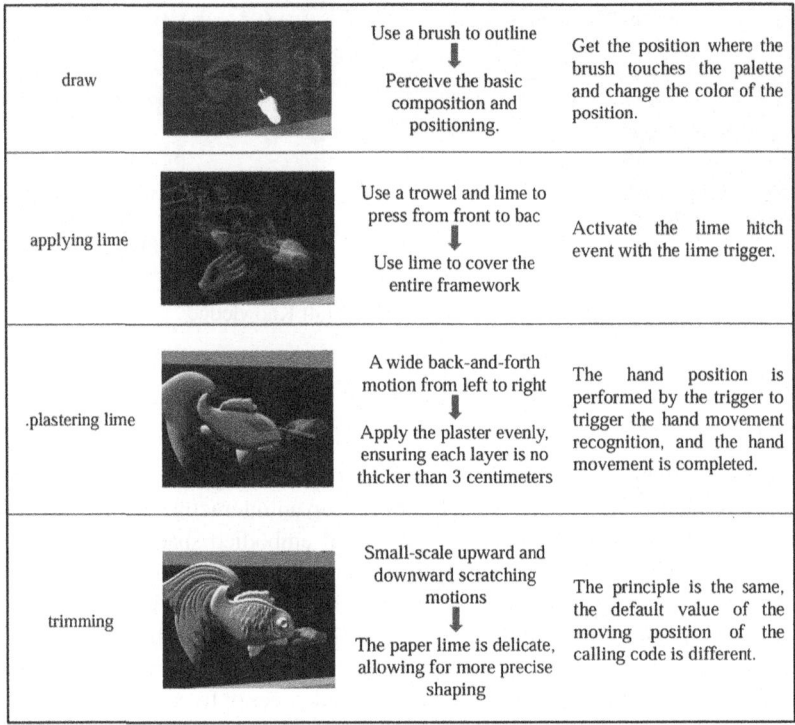

Fig. 6. Metaphorical Design of Key Actions

3.4 Interactive Narrative with Role Immersion

The sensory embodiment of the scene and the natural interactive behaviors provide learners with the sensory and behavioral foundation to experience the narrative process from a "first-person perspective." Additionally, designers can construct the learners' behavioral goals and meanings within the embodied interactive context through the design of narrative plots and characters.

This design incorporates corresponding storylines based on the apprenticeship model of the lime sculpture craft. In the embodied interaction learning process, learners assume the role of an apprentice in the lime sculpture craft, enhancing the sense of immersion through guided interactions and feedback that foster a continuous dialogue and emotional connection with the "master." Upon entering the experience, learners are informed of the era and background through a combination of voiceover narration and scene design, setting the stage for their mission to "travel through time to undertake the responsibility of promoting and revitalizing the traditional culture of the lime sculpture craft." This introduction helps learners understand the historical and cultural context of the lime sculpture craft, thereby enhancing their sense of immersion and mission. Subsequently, learners complete identity registration and beginner guidance through dialogue with the "master" (Fig. 7). The progression of tasks in the subsequent experience is advanced through interactive exchanges.

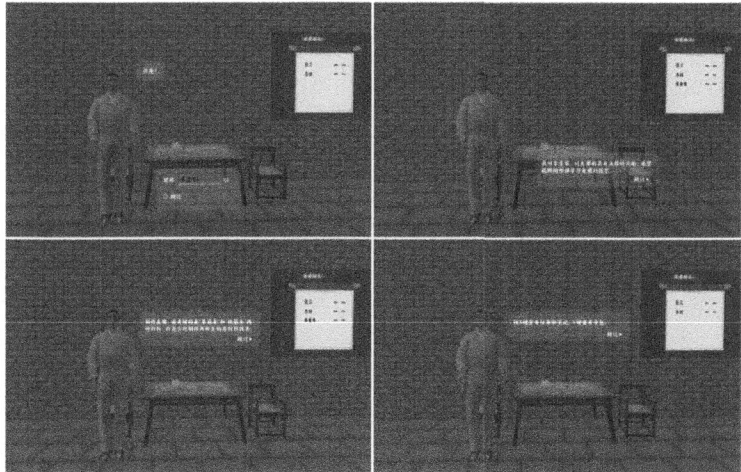

Fig. 7. Identity registration and beginner guidance

4   Prototype Experiment Evaluation

After completing the prototype development, the author recruited 26 participants (college students with no prior knowledge of lime sculpture craft) to undergo prototype experience and testing. The experiment evaluated the prototype's user experience and learning effect regarding traditional craft knowledge through post-experience questionnaire scales, interviews, and knowledge quizzes.

4.1   Level of User Experience

Testing at the user experience level was conducted primarily through questionnaires and interviews. The questionnaire utilized a 5-point Likert scale and was created based on the three-level model of embodied cognition and experience discussed earlier. It was divided into four sections: situational perception, behavioral interaction, meaning formation, and user satisfaction, comprising a total of 22 items. After completing the test tasks, participants were asked to fill out the questionnaire. The descriptive statistics for the questionnaire results (N = 26) are presented in Table 1. Each section's Cronbach's alpha coefficient exceeded 0.7, indicating good internal consistency among the evaluation items, and there were no outliers in the data. The average scores for each section were all above 4, suggesting that the overall user evaluation was relatively positive and that participants could establish a fairly complete experiential learning process during the experience. However, upon further analysis of the minimum values, a few participants indicated that the prototype still had deficiencies in areas such as "immersion," "route guidance," "knowledge presentation," and "value guidance."

Table 1. Descriptive Statistics for the Embodied Cognition and Experience Scale Results

Evaluation Dimension	Items	Min	Max	Mean	SD	Med
Situational Perception (Cronbach. α: 0.745)	A1.	2	5	4.23	0.765	4
	A2.	4	5	4.42	0.504	4
	A3.	2	5	4.19	0.634	4
	A4.	4	5	4.42	0.504	4
	A5.	4	5	4.50	0.51	4.5
Behavioral Interaction (Cronbach. α: 0.802)	B1.	4	5	4.31	0.471	4
	B2.	3	5	4.08	0.628	4
	B3.	4	5	4.35	0.485	4
	B4.	2	5	4.39	0.697	4
	B5.	4	5	4.50	0.51	4.5
	B6.	3	5	4.50	0.583	5
Meaning Formation (Cronbach. α: 0.865)	C1.	4	5	4.42	0.504	4
	C2.	2	5	4.00	0.849	4
	C3.	3	5	4.42	0.578	4
	C4.	2	5	4.50	0.762	5
	C5.	2	5	4.35	0.846	5
Satisfaction (Cronbach. α: 0.881)	D1.	4	5	4.58	0.504	5
	D2.	3	5	4.58	0.578	5
	D3.	4	5	4.58	0.504	5
	D4.	4	5	4.62	0.496	5
	D5.	4	5	4.50	0.51	4.5
	D6.	4	5	4.58	0.504	5

4.2 Level of Learning Effect

Testing at the learning effect level was conducted using a controlled experiment. The author recruited an additional 26 university students for a control group test; these 26 students were also completely unfamiliar with lime sculpture craft. The experimental group underwent learning using the prototype designed in this study. The control group learned about lime sculpture by watching educational videos and reading text-based materials with equivalent knowledge content; their learning duration was the same as that of the experimental group. Both groups took tests to measure their knowledge of lime sculpture and their emotional levels (PANAS) before and after the learning session, and post-learning task load (NASA-TLX) was measured for both groups. After the experiment was completed, the test results from both groups were analyzed. The normality test indicated that the sample data from both groups showed a normal distribution, allowing for an independent samples t-test. The analysis results for the pre-test and post-test data for the control and experimental groups are presented in Tables 2 and 3.

Pre-test Analysis. From the analysis results in the Table 2:

Table 2. Results of Independent Samples t-Test Analysis for Pre-test

Measurement Index	Group (Mean ± SD)		t	p
	Experimental (n = 26)	Control (n = 26)		
Positive Emotions	33.19 ± 6.42	25.85 ± 7.00	3.945	0.000**
Negative Emotions	18.85 ± 7.72	18.88 ± 7.55	-0.018	0.986
Scores for Knowledge	38.92 ± 7.39	38.69 ± 8.32	0.106	0.916

$*p < 0.05$ $**p < 0.01$.

Subjective Emotions. There was a significant difference at the 0.01 level for "positive emotions" ($t = 3.945$, $p = 0.000$), with the experimental group having a significantly higher mean (33.19) compared to the control group (25.85). This indicates that participants in the experimental group had a more positive attitude towards learning the lime sculpture craft through this prototype before the experiment.

Knowledge Level. There was no significant difference between the two groups in the "knowledge level - pretest" ($p = 0.916 > 0.05$), indicating that both groups had an equivalent level of knowledge about the lime sculpture craft before the experiment.

Post-test Analysis. From the analysis results in the Table 3.

Subjective Emotions. The independent samples t-test results were consistent with the pretest. Further comparing the changes in emotions between the pretest and posttest (Fig. 8), both the control group and the experimental group showed an increase in the average level of positive emotions and a decrease in the average level of negative emotions after completing the learning experiment. Using a Paired Samples t-test to compare the pretest and posttest data, it was found that only the experimental group's

Table 3. Results of Independent Samples t-Test Analysis for Post-test

Measurement Index	Group (Mean ± SD)		t	p
	Experimental (n = 26)	Control (n = 26)		
Positive Emotions	36.00 ± 6.87	28.00 ± 9.23	3.546	0.001**
Negative Emotions	14.12 ± 5.43	16.54 ± 7.16	-1.375	0.175
Scores for Knowledge	84.62 ± 9.29	63.69 ± 8.52	8.464	0.000**
Task Load	3.84 ± 1.53	4.12 ± 1.50	-0.621	0.538

$*p < 0.05 **p < 0.01$.

negative emotions showed a significant difference at the 0.01 level between the pretest and posttest (the difference value conforms to normal distribution) (difference = 4.73, t = 4.756, p = 0.000 < 0.01). This indicates that learning the lime sculpture craft through this prototype can alleviate negative emotions.

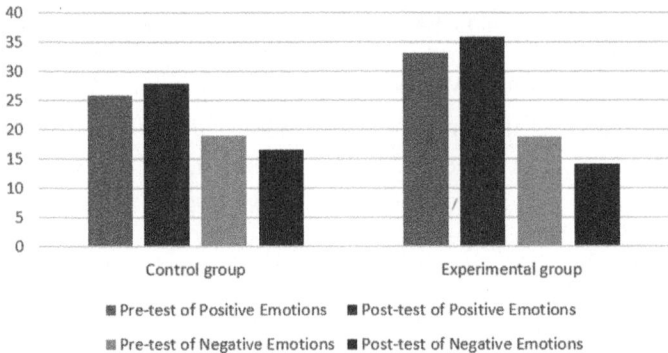

Fig. 8. Changes in Average Scores for Pre-test and Post-test of Subjective Emotions

Knowledge Level. The results of the control group and the experimental group showed a significant difference at the 0.01 level (p = 0.000 < 0.01). Specifically, the average post-test score of the experimental group (84.62) was significantly higher than that of the control group (63.69). This indicates that learning the lime sculpture craft through this prototype is more effective and has a clear advantage over the "video + text" self-learning method.

Task Load. The task load scores of the control group and the experimental group did not show a significant difference (p = 0.538 > 0.05). Further comparison of the scores and weights of the task load indicators for the two groups (Fig. 9), reveals that the "Physical Demand" in the experimental group was significantly lower than that in the control group. Conversely, the "Own Performance" and "Frustration" in the experimental group were significantly better than those in the control group. This indicates that, compared to the traditional "video + text" learning method, learning the lime sculpture craft through this prototype emphasizes bodily participation and effectively enhances learners' satisfaction and confidence.

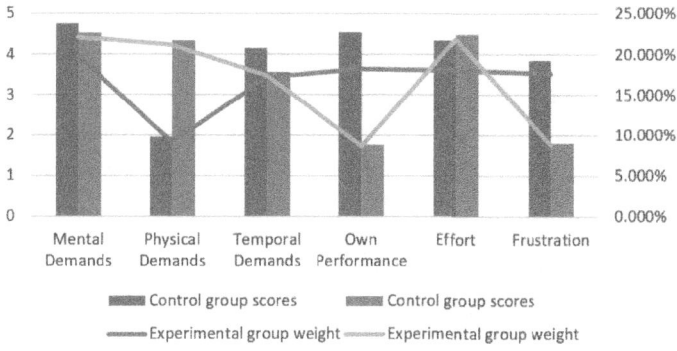

Fig. 9. Task Load Index Scores and Weights

4.3 Interview Analysis

To address potential problems, further interviews were conducted with participants who performed poorly during the experience. The following issues were identified:

Device Performance: The lagging and frame drops in the virtual reality visuals detracted from the realism of the experience and caused dizziness.

Interaction Guidance: Since participants were completely unfamiliar with the lime sculpture craft, the guidance for using certain tools was not sufficiently clear and intuitive. And the error feedback and correction prompts need further optimization.

Redundant Interaction Actions: Some knowledge feedback occurred during the selection of complex tools or other interactions, which did not correlate well with the knowledge feedback. This may cause participants to overlook the learning content and increase their cognitive load.

Lack of Real Experience: While the virtual embodied experience of the lime sculpture craft processes was provided, some participants lacked confidence in their ability to perform the actual craftwork. They suggested that combining the virtual experience with offline practice could further enrich the learning experience.

5   Results and Discussion

5.1 Positive Results

The experimental results show that the model and strategy constructed in this study can effectively guide the design of embodied interactive applications for traditional crafts. The designed embodied interactive application demonstrates good usability and can effectively facilitate learners in establishing a complete experiential learning process for traditional crafts during embodied interaction. Moreover, it promotes a positive learning experience and learning outcomes in traditional crafts:

1. Learners are more inclined towards the embodied interaction learning approach in traditional crafts, harboring a more positive attitude towards it. Moreover, it effectively reduces learners' negative emotions after experiencing it, achieving an entertaining learning experience.
2. Embodied interaction learning emphasizes bodily participation, which can effectively enhance learners' immersion and satisfaction.
3. Through embodied interaction learning, better learning outcomes can be achieved, aiding learners in quickly forming a systematic framework of traditional craft knowledge, thereby promoting their contemplation of the practical value and artisan wisdom of the craft.

5.2 Issues and Insights

In the experiment and evaluation, the problems existing in the current design and the key difficulties that should be paid attention to were also reflected: ① The usability issues mainly focus on "newcomer guidance, item guidance, timely error feedback, and correction in some contexts"; ② The complex and redundant body interactions and multimodal feedback in the current design increase the cognitive load of the experiencers during the learning process. It is necessary to establish effective connections with traditional craft knowledge through reasonable interaction behavior and guidance design and continuously optimize the interaction efficiency and knowledge presentation efficiency through continuous testing.

To address the above issues and key difficulties, this study, combined with reflections from design practice, summarized the following optimization points for design strategies:

In terms of Action Design, Key Actions Need to Be Clearly Distinguished from Basic Actions. Key actions should avoid redundant actions beyond knowledge metaphors. For the behavior interaction of basic actions, it should be simplified as much as possible, following the basic design principles of interaction systems—close to user cognitive experience; improve the controllability, consistency, and efficiency of operations; provide timely error feedback and correction guidance to increase interaction efficiency and avoid increasing cognitive load with complex or excessive basic action guidance. For example: setting reasonable task routes and guidance for users to efficiently experience craft tasks; selecting object items by directly holding them and switching items by simple arm shaking.

Regarding Multimodal Information Guidance and Feedback, Two Points Need to Be Noted: ① Avoid Presenting Too Much Information Simultaneously in Visual or Operational Focus. The "space proximity principle" or "time proximity principle" can be used to present text or audio explanations adjacent to the appearance of relevant knowledge, or highlighting clues using "highlights," "arrows," "bold," etc. Additionally, using concise design to distinguish different types of knowledge can effectively reduce the cognitive load of embodied interactive learning. ② Pay attention to users' multimodal attention allocation and avoid simultaneously opening multiple perceptual channels. For example, during key actions, users mainly operate through visual and kinesthetic senses. At this time, auxiliary knowledge points should be presented through auditory channels other than visual channels, or presented with more intuitive animated demonstrations, rather than using textual forms that require more attention and cognitive load. For key knowledge points that require more text-based explanations, users' attention should be focused on learning the knowledge points by stopping other behaviors and using auditory channels supplemented by speech.

6 Summary and Prospects

The essence of "embodiment" in traditional craftsmanship implies that effective communication of the knowledge within traditional crafts in displays and dissemination requires creating contexts that allow learners to deeply understand traditional craftsmanship through firsthand experiences. The approach proposed in this study emphasizes learners' intuitive perception and interaction with contexts related to traditional craftsmanship, enabling learners to effectively learn and reflect on the embodied knowledge of traditional craftsmanship through experiential learning and reflection in embodied perception and behavioral interaction. Subsequent prototype experiments in design practice have demonstrated that designing traditional craftsmanship embodied interactions based on this method promotes user experience and learning effectiveness. This method can be applied to the design of digital experiential applications for popularizing traditional craftsmanship education: on one hand, it can be applied to digital designs in public educational contexts such as museums and cultural centers to deeply convey the value of traditional crafts related themes to audiences, realizing the public educational application of traditional craftsmanship culture; on the other hand, it can also be applied in the digital teaching design of craft-related courses in relevant colleges and universities, forming typical teaching applications that combine traditional craftsmanship with modern information technology.

Furthermore, due to the current limitations of technology in realizing the ideal state of embodied interaction, this design pattern and practice still have immature aspects, such as the realization of realistic tactile perception during the experiential process and the correlation between behavior and knowledge. In subsequent research, further optimization and improvement will be conducted based on this foundation, and interactive solutions to problems arising from technological limitations will be sought.

Acknowledgments. This study was funded by the Research on the Lineage of Decorative Arts in Lingnan Traditional Architecture (23BG104), the Research on the Revitalization and Modern Transformation of Lingnan Lime Sculpture (GD23LN07), the Teaching Research on Interactive Display Design in the Digital Context (2023GXJK216), the Research on the Conservation and Inheritance of Lime Sculpture Craftsmanship of Cantonese Traditional Architectural (2022ZD08).

Disclosure of Interests. The authors have no competing interests to declare that are relevant to the content of this article.

Institutional Review Board Statement. Not applicable.

Informed Consent Statement. Informed consent was obtained from all subjects involved in the user experience studies.

Data Availability Statement.   Not applicable.

References

1. Sun, F.C.: The "body" value and "living" space in the conservation of traditional craftsman-ship. National Arts Bimonthly, pp. 55–63 (2020)
2. Zhang, H., Tian, F.: Digital exhibition of traditional craft based on new media technology: a case study of Liling underglaze five-colored porcelain, Zhuangshi, pp. 106–109 (2019)
3. Selmanović, E., et al.: Improving accessibility to intangible cultural heritage preservation using virtual reality. J. Comput. Cult. Herit. **13**, 1–19 (2020)
4. Rizvić, S., Bošković, D., Okanović, V., Kihić, I.I., Prazina, I., Mijatović, B.: Time travel to the past of Bosnia and Herzegovina through virtual and augmented reality. Appl. Sci. **11**, 3711 (2021)
5. Cadi Yazli, N., et al.: Modeling craftspeople for cultural heritage: a case study. Comput. Animat. Virtual Worlds **33**, n/a (2022)
6. Gao, Y.J., Xu, Z.W.: Digital virtual technology empowering the preservation of the 'endan-gered secret technique' in Guangzhou ivory carving: protection of intangible cultural heritage, Zhuangshi, pp. 142–144 (2022)
7. Fan, L., Li, D., Zhuo, J.G., Yan, S.D., Gong, S.Y.: Research on AI empowering the inheritance of traditional arts and crafts: a case study of Jinshan farmer paintings, Zhangshi, pp. 94–98 (2022)
8. Svanæs, D.: Interaction design for and with the lived body. ACM Trans. Comput. Hum. Interact. **20**, 1–30 (2013)
9. Koutsabasis, P., Vosinakis, S.: Kinesthetic interactions in museums: conveying cultural her-itage by making use of ancient tools and (re-) constructing artworks. Virtual Real. **22**, 103–118 (2018)
10. Ji, Y., Tan, P., Hills, D.: Chinese traditional handicraft education using AR content. Leonardo **53**, 199–200 (2020)
11. Zhong, S., Ji, Y., Dai, X., Clark, S.: Research on immersive virtual reality display design mode of cantonese porcelain based on embodied interaction. In: Kurosu, M. (eds.) HCII 2021. LNCS, vol. 12764, pp. 198–213. Springer, Cham (2021). https://doi.org/10.1007/978-3-030-78468-3_14
12. Kolb, D.A.: Experiential Learning: Experience as the source of Learning and Development Second Edition, 2nd edn. Pearson Education, London (2015)

Co-creation Cultural Tourism Game Design Based on Scene Theory

Ziyun Lin, Zhongqing Yao, Zhiquan Zeng, and Yun He[✉]

School of Design, South China University of Technology, Guangzhou 510006, China
hebin@scut.edu.cn

Abstract. This research aimed to explore co-creation game design based on scene theory to enhance tourists' cultural tourism experiences in the Xiguan area of Guangzhou. Through methods such as literature analysis, autoethnography, and co-creation workshops, the study delved into the scene characteristics of the Xiguan area and tourists' experience needs. A game design framework based on the virtual newspaper 'Xiguan Daily' was developed, integrating a virtual co-creation platform with real scenes. This framework encouraged players to explore the Xiguan area through AR technology and create virtual newspaper articles with AI assistance. The game design emphasized three mechanisms: exploration, kiosk interaction, and newspaper creation, and its feasibility was assessed through paper prototype testing. Game design effectively enhanced users' sense of cultural participation and depth of experience, providing a new perspective and practical reference for cultural tourism game design.

Keywords: Gamification · Game Design · Co-creation · Cultural Tourism · Scene Theory

1 Introduction

1.1 Cultural Tourism

The relationship between culture and tourism is crucial, as cultural attractions are a significant driver of the tourism industry. In recent decades, this connection has been defined as cultural tourism, in which the visitor's essential motivation is to learn, discover, experience and consume the tangible and intangible cultural attractions/products in a tourism destination [1]. Tourists increasingly say that they want to experience local culture, to live like locals and to find out about the real identity of the places they visit. However, traditional Cultural Tourism often offers visitors conventional, one-sided, and superficial cultural experiences, making it necessary to explore a new approach to Cultural Tourism.

1.2 Gamification

Gamification is widely accepted that refers gamification as contextualizing game design outside its original domain and it focuses on changing players' behaviour, engagement

© The Author(s), under exclusive license to Springer Nature Switzerland AG 2025
P. Zaphiris et al. (Eds.): HCII 2024, LNCS 15378, pp. 309–322, 2025.
https://doi.org/10.1007/978-3-031-76815-6_22

with their environment and co-players who may also be fellow customers or service providers towards achieving meaningful interaction and engagement and potentially achieve rewards. Games of travel provide a means of dynamic interaction through suggested tasks, and link with surrounding physical locations, challenge the player virtually, providing instant feedback for the player's achievements, responding to the players emotions in a fun and rewarding way before, during and after trip [2]. Gamification in Cultural Tourism can enhance tourists' engagement in cultural tourism activities, allowing them to explore the cultural essence of the destination actively and with interest. This approach helps create a deeper, unique, and memorable experience for tourists.

1.3 Content and Significance of the Research

Guangzhou Xiguan, located in Guangzhou, Guangdong Province, China, is an area rich in historical significance and one of the birthplaces of Lingnan culture. As an old urban area, Xiguan boasts an extensive historical and cultural district with abundant cultural and scenic resources.

This research used the Guangzhou Xiguan region as a case study to introduce Scene Theory and Co-creation in exploring a novel and profound cultural tourism model, and designing a cultural tourism game. The research aims to expand the media of cultural tourism scenes and provide tourists with a more enriched cultural tourism experience.

2 The Current Applications of SceneTheory and Co-creation

2.1 Scene Theory

Scene Theory is widely applied across various academic disciplines, including psychology, communication studies, and urban studies. In psychology, Scene Theory primarily focuses on the impact of the environment on individual behaviors and emotions. It emphasizes the influence of physical elements, contexts, and interactions within environmental scenes on individuals' perceptions, emotions, and behaviors. Scene Theory in communication studies (The media situation theory), on the other hand, examines the influence of media, social, and cultural environments on the processes and outcomes of information dissemination [3]. Scene Theory in urban studies (A theory of scenes), focusing on the dynamics of urban cultural development and the consumption of urban cultural values, investigates the construction of physical spaces and the influence of scene culture on users' behavior [4]. Although these three theories have different research orientations, they all play significant roles in the study of cultural and tourism experiences discussed in this paper.

Since the proposition of Scene Theory, numerous studies have applied this theory to the Cultural Tourism. In terms of constructing multimedia scenes, Shao employed diversified narratives and interactive experiences to shape the scene encounters. They also investigated the potential of utilizing technologies such as VR, AR, and tactile interactions to enrich interpersonal dynamics within scenes [5]. Concerning enhancing the experiences in Scenes, Chen applied the Scene Theory to elevate users' multilayered cultural tourism experiences. They delved into four dimensions: sensory, functional, interactive, and identity layers, analyzing the connections between scenes, experiences, and products [6]. Regarding scene analysis and deconstruction, Luo utilized tools from the Scene Theory to comprehend the constitution of community scenes and proposed corresponding scene creation strategies based on the requirements of scene elements for target characteristic scene types [7].

2.2 Co-Creation

Co-creation refers to the process where two or more parties collaborate to create new things together.

In cultural tourism, there are numerous cases where the co-creation model is applied. For example, Atembe discussed the potential of using mobile devices and mobile technology to facilitate co-creation of on-site tourism experiences, especially as these devices were increasingly carried into tourism settings. This exploration was conducted through methods such as workshops and focus groups [8]. Matthys employed 3D modeling and 3D scanning technologies to involve city residents in the reconstruction of urban history, enabling the recreation of city history in VR/MR/XR environments. By organizing workshops, they invited residents to participate in the co-creation of cultural heritage [9]. This demonstrated the bidirectional impact of co-creation: it enriches tourists' travel experiences and simultaneously adds value to urban spaces through the contributions of the tourists.

2.3 Conclusion

Based on the analysis, we discovered the application space for Scene Theory and Co-creation in Cultural Tourism. Leveraging Scene Theory allowed for the analysis and deconstruction of the composition types of scenes in the Xiguan area. By regarding Co-creation Space as another scene medium, it can provide tourists with a richer cultural tourism experience and accomplish a value transmission. The conclusions of this analysis were also applied in the process of constructing and researching the game design framework.

3 Co-creation Cultural Tourism Game Design Process Based on Scene Theory

3.1 Framework for Feasibility

Based on Scene Theory, we introduced a virtual environment, named Co-creative Virtual Space, to interact with the real environment and jointly affect users, thereby achieving a co-creative cultural tourism experience through user participation in this Co-creative Virtual Space. This co-creative virtual space was constructed based on an open and realistic environment and jointly acted on users in the real cultural tourism environment, enabling users to generate diverse emotions and behaviors and encouraging users to participate and act on the co-creative virtual space, thus initiating a cyclic progression. In this cyclic, through such a pattern, the Co-creative Virtual Space and the cultural tourism experience were continuously enriched, allowing users to have a better cultural tourism experience and cultural dissemination (Fig. 1).

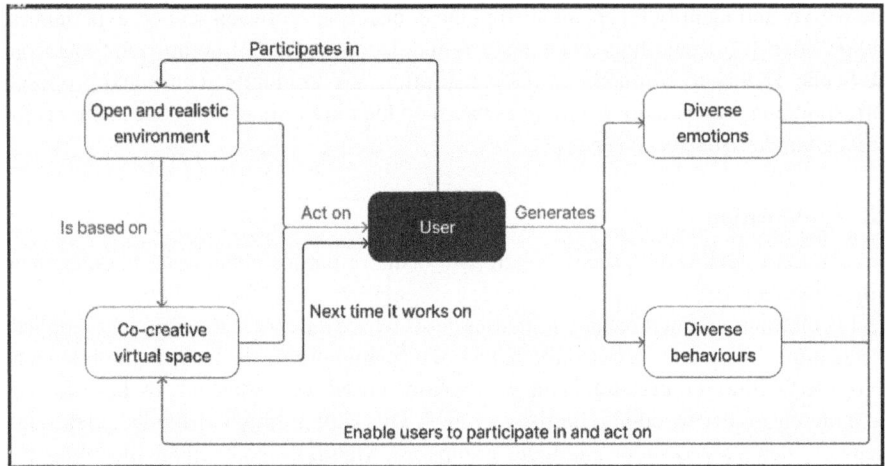

Fig. 1. Framework for Feasibility

3.2 Scene Type Characterization

To gain deeper insights into the Xiguan area, we employed an auto-ethnography app-roach, a qualitative research method leveraging personal experiences to enhance under-standing of social phenomena [10]. This allowed us to gather information about the conditions of cultural tourism resources in Xiguan, alongside documenting our subjec-tive experiences in the setting. Through field research in Xiguan, we recorded the data and personal impressions using notes, recordings, videos, and photos. These collected materials were then utilized for qualitative analysis of different scenes within the Xiguan area.

The elements of scenes in Scene Theory (A theory of scenes), including Neighbor-hoods, Physical Structures, Diverse Populations, Activity Combinations, and Cultural Values, were translated into five characteristic factors: Scene Characteristics, Partici-pants, Daily Activities, Featured Events, and Cultural Values, according to the require-ments and characteristics in the scenes. Combined with field research data, the Xiguan area can be divided into seven different types of scenes (Fig. 2).

3.3 Visitor Experience Analysis in the Scene

Through the questionnaire (Fig. 3), we found that people have different preferences in travel. From the Scene Theory, people with different values prefer different scenes and generate varied behaviors and feelings within those scenes. Therefore, this study employed co-creation workshops to investigate the behaviors and feelings of people with different travel habits, aiming to uncover their pain points and needs [11]. Design tools from the field of human-computer interaction were applied in the workshop design, including Non-participatory Observation and Cultural Probe. Particularly, in the final stage of the workshop, we utilized a Focus Group that collected data through group interaction on our topic [12].

Scene Type	Scene Characteristics	Participants	Daily Activities	Featured Events	Cultural Values
Scenario 1: Restored residential areas	Alleyways, Old Buildings, Dilapidated Streets	Local Residents, Out-of-Town Tenants	Lifestyle: Daily Work and Life Interaction; Chatting Leisure: Watching, Leisurely Walking, Daily Pet Walking, Photography	Festivals and Events, Folk Worship	Authenticity
Scenario 2: Unrestored residential areas	Alley, Dilapidated Roads/ Streets, Neighbourhood Clusters Interspersed with Blocks	Local Residents, Out-of-Town Tenants	Lifestyle: Residential living, Daily Shopping, Leisure: Sitting and Playing Chess and Cards	None	Authenticity
Scenario 3: Large Public Places	Large Green Areas, Large Area of Public Space, Large Distribution of Art Area	Local Residents, Foreign Tourists, Sanitation Workers, Photo Enthusiasts	Interaction: Chatting, Parent-Child Activities, Recreation and Fitness Leisure: Walking, Chatting, Taking Photos, Stopping to Watch, Feting Local Specialities	Spontaneous Singing and Dancing Performances, Various Special Resident Activities	Authenticity
Scenario 4: Emerging Business District	Modern Design Stores, Trendy Brands, Chain Stores, Clustered in a Certain Area	Visitors, Shopkeepers, Photo Enthusiasts	Life type: Daily work, Social Chatting and Talking Leisure: Daily Consumption, High-End Resting pace, Leisure Food and Drink, Photo shooting	Night Market Stalls, Characteristic Consumption, Creative Bazaar	Theatricality
Scene 5: Museums	Indoor scenes, Irregular distribution, Adaptation to original space remodeling	Visitors, Volunteers	Interaction: Talking and Chatting, Parent-Child Activities Recreational: Staying and Watching, Leisurely Walk	Featured Exhibitions, Theme Lectures	Theatricality
Scene 6: Living Commercial Street	a Mix of Indoor and Outdoor Scenes, Distributed Along a Line Around a Neighbourhood	Local Residents, Shop Operators, Visitors	Lifestyle: Daily Consumption, Grocery Shopping, Snacks, Social Talking and Chatting	Folklore Activities	Theatricality
Scene 7: Cultural and Creative Storefronts	Indoor Scenes, Distributed in a Protected Neighbourhood, Spatial Distribution of Points	Traditional Culture Enthusiasts, Visitors	Lifestyle: Daily Work, Education and Training Interaction: Chatting, Tea party, Cultural Content Output Leisure: Experiencing Related Culture, Staying and Watching Consumption: Purchase Related Items, Pay to Learn	Organisation of Lectures, Organising tea Parties, Experiential Consumption	Authenticity

Fig. 2. Scene Characterization of Xiguan Area

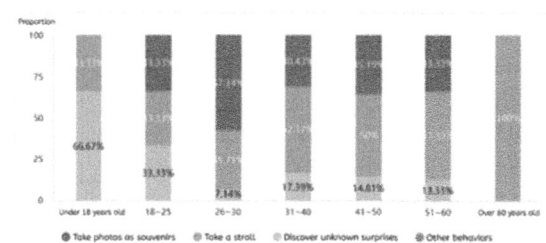

Fig. 3. Analysis of Questionnaires on Traveling Habits of Different Groups

We invited five participants (divided into three groups based on different travel habits) to join our co-creation workshop (Fig. 4). During the workshop, participants arranged their travels according to their usual habits but were instructed to explore interesting aspects of their journeys with an observational perspective and record using tools such as smartphones. Throughout the workshop, researchers conducted non-participatory observations and documented participants' behaviors. After completing the experiential journey, participants gathered with researchers to share discovered issues and discuss their underlying causes. Subsequently, researchers posed questions for participants to discuss, aiming to gather their insights.

Through analyzing the participants' behaviors during the exploration, we identified commonalities and differences among them. Firstly, although the participants had varied activity spaces within the scenic area, they all exhibited curiosity when listening to others' experiences in different locations. This helps to argue the possibility of using co-creation

Fig. 4. Photos from the Co-creation Workshop

to facilitate the sharing of individual experiences during exploration, enabling a deeper collective immersion into local culture. Furthermore, we observed that some participants actively shared their observations and discoveries during the exploration, while others needed prompting to express themselves. Therefore, in the co-creation process, it is essential to provide guidance and incentive mechanisms to stimulate the desire to share and encourage active participation in activities where individuals share their experiences during exploration.

3.4   Design Strategies with MDA Gamification Methodology

Design Strategy at the Mechanistic: Active Exploration, Easy Sharing. In the gamification design of cultural tourism, games should encourage tourists to actively explore tourist destinations, observe events in the tourism scene, and deeply experience the local cultural connotations. Simultaneously, emphasis should be placed on encouraging tourists to actively share their observations, experiences, and feelings, providing them with certain support for sharing and creation.

Design Strategy at the Dynamic: Fusion of Real and Virtual, Proactive. In the gamification design of cultural tourism, sensitivity and curiosity towards the surrounding environment should be enhanced. Fusion of virtual and real can be achieved through various technologies, diminishing the blocking effect of smartphones on user perception. Additionally, attention should be given to game feedback, providing prompts and encouragement to maintain user engagement.

Design   Strategy   at   the   Aesthetic: Unique   Style,   Featuring Xiguan Characteristics. In the gamification design of cultural tourism, tourists should experience the fusion of traditional Xiguan aesthetics and modern minimalism. In UI design, visual consistency in color schemes and configurations, as well as uniformity in model and pattern styles, should be maintained.

4 Game Design

4.1 Game Design Framework

Based on the results and game design strategies, we conducted a game design practice in the Xiguan area of Guangzhou. Xiguan has a historic "Newspaper Street". Therefore, we used "newspapers" as the co-creative medium and created the "Xiguan Daily" virtual co-creative game platform, with co-creation being through newspaper production. We integrated the design concept of Xiguan Daily and supplemented the framework as shown in Fig. 5.

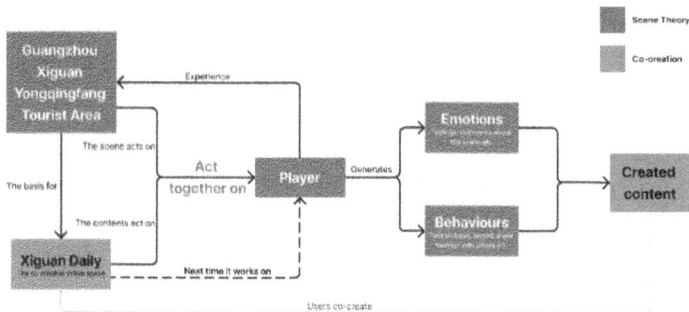

Fig. 5. Game Design Framework

The blue part in the diagram represents the operation of scene theory within the entire system, while the yellow part indicates the path of co-creation.

When players experience a scene in Xiguan, they simultaneously receive information from both the physical scene and the virtual newspaper. These pieces of information prompt players to generate various emotions and behaviors during gameplay. For instance, players might become curious about a landmark, actively explore its story, and share it in the newspaper. Alternatively, they might be intrigued by interesting things left by other players in the newspaper and decide to explore further. These emotions and behaviors are reflected in the co-creation platform through the newspaper creation process, facilitating value exchange among players. This cyclic process continually enriches the co-creation content of the Xiguan Daily and enhances it as a virtual scene medium.

4.2 Game Introduction

Xiguan Daily aims to allow everyone to personally experience and share their own stories of Xiguan, enriching the virtual co-creation platform through newspaper articles. It facilitates bidirectional communication between local culture and tourists, providing them with novel and profound cultural tourism experiences. The primary target user of this game is young people aged 20–30 interested in humanities. Here is a brief overview of the gameplay:

Players explore the streets of Xiguan while using AR to locate "newsstands" within the scene. At these "newsstands," players can engage in dialogue with an AI NPC to tell their stories and craft newspaper articles based on the cultural encounters they experience. These articles are then published alongside those created by other players in the Xiguan Daily, a virtual newspaper. Players can also obtain newspapers from different scenes at the newsstands, sparking their interest in the cultural stories of other scenes and prompting them to explore further, thus completing the cyclic.

4.3   Main Mecchanics of the Game

Explore. One of the main goals for players is to explore and discover various cultural stories in Xiguan, and find newsstands scattered throughout different scenes to read or create newspapers, making exploration one of the main mechanisms of the game.

In order to enrich players' immersive exploration experience and social needs, we designed a system that allows players to customize their character avatars, using AR to connect players with the virtual environment. In Fig. 6, the player's movements also reflect their avatars walking in AR, adding enjoyment of the process. The arrow beneath the avatar serves as an indicator of the approximate direction to the newsstands, which players can check on their phones while walking. The approximate direction randomized the players' route, avoiding a fixed journey route as with navigation. If players want to see the exact location of the newsstand, they can open the homepage and select "Search for newsstand" to use the map.

As players approach the location of newsstand, the system will alert them through sound and vibration, prompting the walking player to scan into the virtual newsstand using AR, and select to read newspapers or create newspapers.

Virtual Newsstand.   Newsstand are interactive elements within virtual game environments, it's the main place to co-creative newspaper content for players. Players interact with these newsstands through AR. While the newsstands are virtual elements, their locations are based on the real-world. In our delineated scenes, each type of scene hosts a newsstand (Fig. 6). This newsstand distributes newspapers relevant to their respective scenes. Players, while at a newsstand within a particular scene, can choose to read newspapers from other scenes, generating interest in exploring the next scene after reading.

Virtual Newspaper.   The virtual newspaper in the co-creation and reading platform is the main mechanism of Xiguan Daily.

Xiguan Daily is a virtual newspaper (Fig. 7), and different "publishing units" and "issues" (all fictional) are divided according to the scene types, with content of each newspaper differentiated based on the scene. The layout of the newspaper consists of covers created by different players, including images uploaded by players, titles, bylines (the players' usernames), and like button. The specific process of creating newspaper covers will be described later. Additionally, each newspaper will have a fixed area to introduce historical stories that have actually occurred in the scene, helping players better understand the local history and culture.

When creating newspapers, utilizing AI in the creative process is one of the key components. As revealed by the user research, most players lack the ability to create newspaper articles and find writing lengthy texts to be cumbersome. Moreover, rather

Fig. 6. Explore

Fig. 7. Reading the newspaper

than writing, players prefer to share their experiences through conversation while on their journey.

At the onset of newspaper creation, players engage in dialogue with AI NPC, telling their stories in the journey. The AI NPC listens to the player's stories attentively and guides them to articulate their experiences fully through inquiries. Once the dialogue is complete, the entire conversation content is recorded by the newspaper creation AI Agent, which then create it into newspaper articles. During training, the newspaper creation Agent combines the scene type feature analysis figure (Fig. 2), matching the features of the scene where the player is located, along with historical and cultural elements, to create newspaper articles. After generating the articles, the newspaper creation Agent autonomously designs the layout for the newspaper cover, which players can modify based on provided materials. To facilitate program layout, the newspaper cover comes in three fixed size formats (Fig. 8), allowing players to choose the layout according to their preferences.

Fig. 8. Creating the newspaper

4.4 Game Play Process

Before traveling, players can preview the map of the Xiguan area in Guangzhou on the app and customize their virtual character's appearance.

Upon arriving in Xiguan, new players will enter tutorial when opening the game. A virtual newsstand will appear in front of them for interaction. The app will guide players to read a newspaper and write a short passage based on their current view using the app's creation feature. This tutorial helps players understand the gameplay and boosts their enthusiasm for exploring Xiguan.

During the tour, players can interact with their virtual character by taking photos and controlling its actions. While exploring Xiguan, players can follow directional cues under their virtual character to find the nearest virtual newsstand. Additionally, players can click the "Find Newsstand" button to open a map showing all virtual newsstands.

When a player approaches a newsstand, its model will appear on their phone via AR technology. By clicking the interaction button, the app will switch to the newsstand's UI through an AR animation.

In the virtual newsstand UI, players can click the "Buy Newspaper" to select from a list of newspapers created by others. By clicking the "Create Newspaper" button, the app will enter the newspaper creation UI, where players can create contents through AI dialogue and use creative tools to edit the layout and images. Completing a newspaper rewards the player.

After creating a newspaper at one virtual newsstand, players can seek out the next newsstand.

Post-tour, players can review their created newspapers and those collected from others in the "My" section of the app.

The service blueprint is shown in Fig. 9.

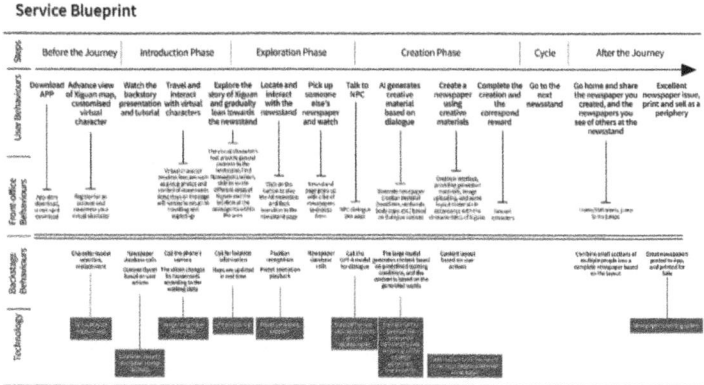

Fig. 9. The Service Blueprint

4.5 Game Visual Design

The visual design of the Xiguan Daily drew inspiration from the fusion of old and new features found in Xiguan. Classic Cantonese color schemes were employed, stylized for effect.

In Fig. 10, the newsstand character design was inspired by the image of paperboy from the Republic of China era. For player-customized virtual avatars, a library of assets was provided for mixing and matching, as illustrated in the example below. The virtual newsstand was modeled after the stand styles found in Xiguan, incorporating architectural design symbols from the area to evoke vivid memories for players (Fig. 11).

4.6 Prototype Test

We conducted tests on two users who participated in the co-creation workshop and three users who did not participate, using paper prototypes and prototypes created with Figma (Fig. 12). The testing focused on four sections: instructional guidance, newsstand interaction, reading newspapers, and newspaper creation. For instructional guidance, newsstand interaction, and reading, we utilized Figma prototypes, while paper prototypes were used for newspaper creation.

Fig. 10. LOGO, Characters and newsstand

Fig. 11. UI design

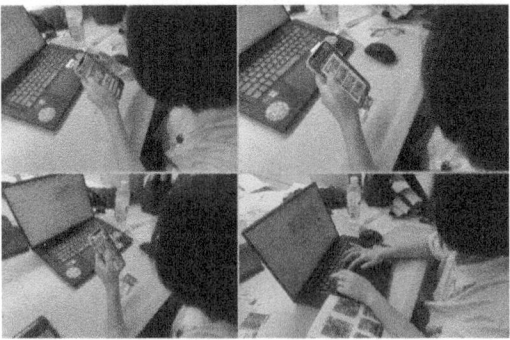

Fig. 12. Testing Process

The prototype testing process was designed to simulate real-world exploration. The specific steps are as follows:

1. Participants familiarize themselves with the current scene by viewing images of the scene to form an initial impression.
2. Participants receive instruction based on the game's tutorial, experiencing the processes of reading and creating newspapers.
3. Participants simulatedly experience AR and interact with the newsstand.
4. Participants are interviewed about their experiences during the test.
5. Participants complete the SUS scale (Fig. 13).

After testing, the SUS results (Fig. 14) were compiled as shown in Figure x, with an average final score of 88. According to the SUS score interpretation, the system's usability is rated as EXCELLENT.

Fig. 13. SUS scale

User	Q1	Q2	Q3	Q4	Q5	Q6	Q7	Q8	Q9	Q10	Final score
User A	4	2	5	1	5	1	5	1	4	1	92.5
User B	5	2	4	1	4	1	3	2	4	1	82.5
User C	5	2	5	2	5	1	3	2	4	1	85
User D	4	2	5	1	5	1	4	1	3	1	87.5
User E	5	2	5	1	5	1	4	1	4	1	92.5

Fig. 14. SUS Test Result

5 Conclusion and Future Work

The design of Xiguan Daily provides a new medium for the Xiguan region. This game guides tourists to explore local cultural life in depth, fostering a bidirectional communication with local culture, and enhancing the richness and depth of the cultural tourism experience. Additionally, the game exemplifies the potential of co-creation models in cultural tourism. Thus, this co-creation-based tourism game model can be extended beyond Xiguan to other tourist attractions, improving tourism experiences and cultural dissemination.

This research conducted a usability test on the game using paper prototypes and high-fidelity prototypes, yielding positive preliminary feedback. However, the AI-assisted creation and AR features of the game are difficult to fully test with paper prototypes. Therefore, future work involves developing a functional version of the game and testing each feature iteratively through interviews and focus group. Additionally, a workshop will be held in Xiguan to gather data on player co-creation, informing adjustments to the game's features and AI model training details.

References

1. Richards, G.: Cultural tourism: a review of recent research and trends. J. Hosp. Tour. Manag. **36**, 12–21 (2018)
2. Xu, F., Weber, J., Buhalis, D.: Gamification in tourism. In: Xiang, Z., Tussyadiah, I. (eds.) Information and Communication Technologies in Tourism 2014, pp. 525–537. Springer, Cham (2013). https://doi.org/10.1007/978-3-319-03973-2_38
3. McLuhan, M.: Understanding Media: The Extensions of Man. MIT Press, Cambridge (1994)
4. Silver, D., Clark, T.N., Rothfield, L.: A theory of scenes (2007). http://tnc.research.google pages.com/atheoryofscenes
5. Ming-hua, S., Tian-tian, Y.: Scene-empowered red culture tourism development: theoretical logic and multidimensional paths. J. Lanzhou Univ. (Soc. Sci.) **50**(06), 95–104 (2022)
6. Weize, C.: Research on experience design of digital cultural and creative products of the grand canal poetry road culture based on context theory. Zhejiang Gongshang University (2023)
7. Xuelei, L., et al.: Research on community-oriented renovation of industrial relics from perspective of the theory of scenes. Archit. Cult. **04**, 153–155 (2023)
8. Atembe, R., Akbar, B.: Tourism, tourists co-creation experiences onsite-enabled by mobile devices, p. 20–28 (2014)
9. Matthys, M., et al.: An "animated spatial time machine" in co-creation: reconstructing history using gamification integrated into 3D city modelling, 4D web and transmedia storytelling, **10**(7), 460 (2021)
10. Wall, S.: An autoethnography on learning about autoethnography. Int. J. qual. Methods **5**(2), 146–160 2006
11. Holmlid, S., et al.: Co-creative practices in service innovation p. 545–574 (2015)
12. Morgan, D.L.: Focus groups. Ann. Rev. Sociol. **22**(1), 129–152 (1996)

The Visual Guidance of Scenic Windows in Spatial Sequences: A Case of New Garden of Qinghui Garden

Chen Liu[1], Mingjie Liang[1(✉)], and Junxi Feng[2]

[1] South China University of Technology, Guangzhou 510006, China
mjliang@scut.edu.cn
[2] Hainan University, Hainan 570228, China

Abstract. This research employs eye-tracking technologies to study the role of scenic windows in spatial sequences in the New Garden of Qinghui Garden, especially in terms of guiding visitors' gazes. The results indicate that elements such as leaking windows, empty windows, Manchurian-style windows, and doorways in the New Garden of Qinghui Garden can effectively attract visitors' visual attention and guide their gazes. These elements not only enhance the sense of penetration and depth of space but also cleverly guide visitors to experience and appreciate the predetermined landscape sequence along the main tourist routes. Therefore, this experiment validates the significant impact of windows on visual guidance in the New Garden of Qinghui Garden, providing useful references for landscape design and the creation of spatial sequences.

Keywords: Scenic Windows · New Garden · Qinghui Garden · Spatial Sequences · Visual Guidance · Eye-tracking Technologies

1 Research Background

As one of the four famous gardens in Lingnan during the Qing Dynasty, Qinghui Garden in Shunde District has retained its relatively intact appearance to this day. After two major expansion projects, particularly the second in the 1990s, it underwent protective renovation and expansion on the original site, increasing the garden area by three-quarters. Three new gardens were established: Guangda Garden, Chuxiang Garden, Xiaopenglai Garden. This expansion integrated the stylistic features and spatial layout of three other famous gardens, namely, Ke Garden in Dongguan, Liang Garden in Foshan, and Yuyin Garden in Panyu District, forming a distinctive 'compilation-style' garden. The term 'compilation-style' garden refers to a layout strategy that combines one or two main scenic areas with several independent small gardens, forming the feature of large-scale gardens with small-scale ones inside [1].

The spatial layout of the 'large-scale gardens with small-scale ones inside' in the New Garden of Qinghui Garden not only enriches the space, providing a multi-faceted experience for visitors [2], but also cleverly combines sightlines and pathways to guide visitors to appreciate the subtleties of each landscape. The variation in sightlines and the twists and turns of pathways in the garden constantly bring surprises to visitors, reflecting the richness of the 'compilation-style' garden in terms of landscape themes, spatial layout, and viewing experience.

In classical garden design, to create profound viewing effects, designers meticulously combine landscape elements and employ the techniques of 'concealment' and 'reveal.' Through partial concealment and appropriate unveiling, they not only avoid a complete view of the landscape but also enhance its allure. This design technique of 'concealing before revealing' not only creates subtle and profound viewing effects [3], but is also crucial for effectively organizing complex spatial structures and guiding visitors' visual perception [4].

This study aims to explore the guiding role of scenic windows in the spatial sequence of Qinghui Garden's New Garden on the visitors' gaze. To validate this, eye-tracking experiments were conducted, selecting focal points along the main pathways of the New Garden of Qinghui Garden, capturing photographs of the garden space, and analyzing research data from both subjective and objective perspectives. Eye-tracking technology was initially applied in various fields such as medicine, education, transportation, and human-computer interaction [5, 6], gradually expanding into areas like geography, tourism, and landscape research [7–9]. This technology can collect and analyze behavioral data of individuals in landscape environments [10], revealing the inherent connection between visual attention points and spatial characteristics, providing a scientific and quantitative basis for landscape design and gaze guidance.

In the field of landscape architecture, eye-tracking technology is primarily used in studies such as landscape evaluation and perception, yielding rich results [11–13]. The precise tracking and recording capabilities of eye trackers make them an ideal tool for studying visual attention and eye movement behavior, which are closely related to human cognitive processes. Therefore, data captured through eye-tracking can reveal how visitors experience and perceive garden spaces under the guidance of different window views. Additionally, the results of this study aim to provide practical guidance for the inheritance of modern landscape design and traditional garden art, as well as insights for landscape designers on enhancing visitor experiences through gaze guidance.

2 Methods

2.1 Research Methods

This study primarily employs eye-tracking technologies: utilizing an eye tracker to capture and record the physiological activities of subjects' eyes while viewing photographs of the New Garden.

2.2 Experimental Preparation

1. Image Selection: Due to limitations in human and material resources, it was not feasible to conduct on-site field experiments. Therefore, images were chosen as a medium for conducting on-site research. The research material consisted of live scene

photos taken by the author at selected points along the three main pathways of the New Garden in Qinghui Garden(Guangda Garden, Chuxiang Garden, Xiaopenglai Garden). The images had a uniform pixel size of 4608X3072 and a resolution of 350. The experimental photo materials comprised three sets of photos, with each garden having one set, totaling six photos per set (see Fig. 1).

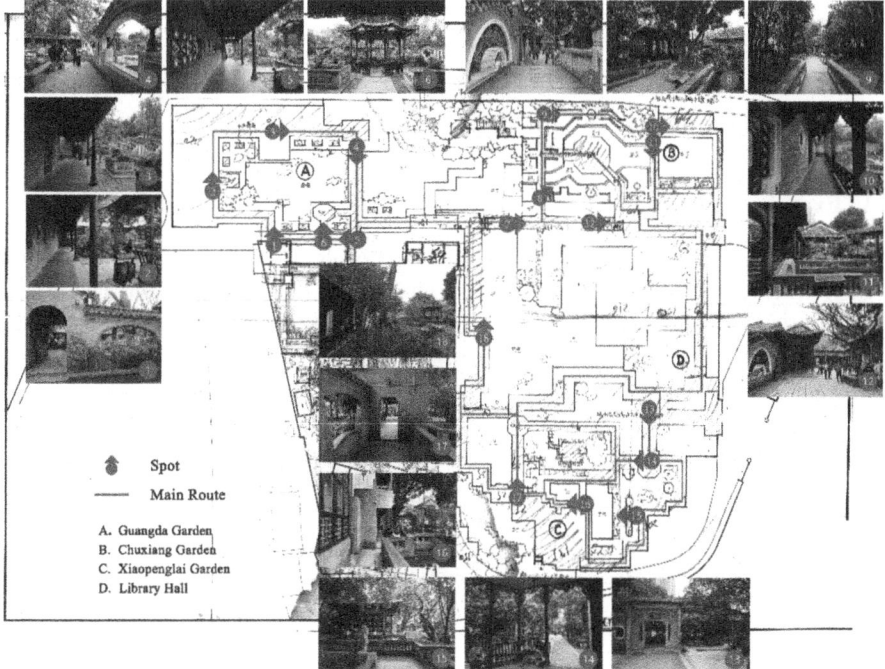

Fig. 1. Three sets of photos taken at designated points in the New Garden of Qinghui Garden.

2. Participant Selection: Forty university students with diverse academic backgrounds from different colleges were recruited for the experiment, including 11 males and 25 females. After excluding participants with low eye tracking sampling rates (<50%), the effective sample size was 36. Participants had normal uncorrected and corrected vision ranging from 0.8 to 1.5.

3. Instrumentation: Eye-tracking data from 40 participants were recorded using the aSee Glasses eye tracker (see Fig. 2). The eye tracker serves as a crucial auxiliary tool and effective quantitative indicator in visual research. By recording the attention and focus of different participants during information processing, the eye tracker can objectively and accurately reveal the cognitive characteristics of participants during observation. Additionally, a 14-inch HP laptop was used as the hardware and software device to support the eye tracker and for subsequent data analysis. An external 27-inch Dell monitor was connected for participants to view images during the eye-tracking experiment. The data obtained from the experiment were analyzed using eye-tracking

analysis methods, with further processing conducted using aSee Studio software. During the experiment, the eye-tracking sampling rate was set to 120Hz.

Fig. 2. Eye-tracking Device.

2.3 Experimental Procedures

The experiment mainly involves recording the fixation points of participants' eyes while they view images and conducting statistical analysis on the collected data. The experimental process includes point selection, photo shooting and processing, eye tracker calibration and validation, eye-tracking experiments, experimental recording, and data analysis (see Fig. 3).

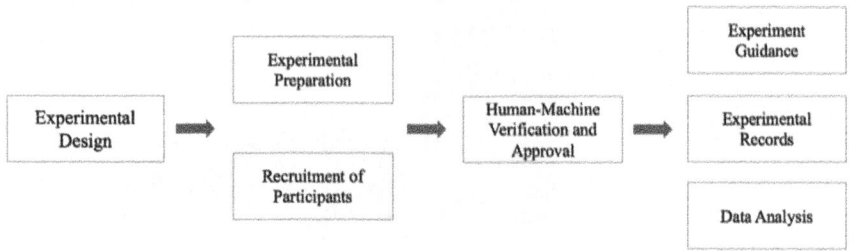

Fig. 3. Experimental Steps.

The first step is eye tracker calibration. After the participants are seated, the author will assist them in correctly wearing the eye-tracking device, guide them to sit approximately 65 cm away from the image display screen, and help the participants complete the calibration of the eye tracker.

The second step is experimental recording. Before the experiment begins, the author will provide detailed explanations of the experimental procedure and specific requirements to the participants. Each participant will then view 18 images (see Fig. 4), in a fixed order, during which the eye tracker records their eye movement data.

The third step is data statistical analysis. After the experiment, data processing is conducted using aSee Studio software. Eye movement data from all participants are extracted for heat maps and gaze plots analysis. Invalid data are removed, and the final number of participants with valid eye movement data is determined to be 36 individuals.

Fig. 4. Eye-tracking Experiment.

2.4 Indicator Selection

In order to objectively verify the effectiveness of the visual guidance provided by the scenic window in this article, eye-tracking experiments will be conducted and analyzed using heat maps and gaze plots. The eye-tracking experiments will be conducted indoors, and the testing time for subjects will be distributed across different time periods. To enhance the accuracy of the eye-tracking data, the author will utilize relative time as an analysis indicator (Table 1).

Table 1. Eye-tracking Indicators and Their Meanings.

Eye-tracking Indicators	Meanings
Heat Map	By visualizing the fixation points' positions and average fixation duration, it intuitively reflects the attractiveness of the stimulus materials and the subjects' level of interest, thereby evaluating the strength of visual stimulation in the photo content
Gaze plot	Displaying the movement path of the eye and changes in fixation points when subjects observe visual stimulus materials
Relative Time (ms)	An indicator that records the temporal sequence and duration of eye movements relative to the start time of the experiment, used for analyzing the dynamic changes in visual attention

3 Results and Discussions

3.1 Participant Demographic Data

The research officially commenced its experiments in early March 2024, collecting a total of 36 valid eye-tracking datasets (Table 2). Among these, there were 11 male and 25 female participants, mostly undergraduates. In terms of academic backgrounds, 20 participants were from humanities disciplines, among them 16 majoring in art and design. The majority of participants were from Outside Guangdong province areas, with

32 viewing the New Garden photos for the first time, and only 4 having visited the New Garden previously. Regarding the experimental data, the sampling rate exceeded 90% for the vast majority of participants, indicating high efficiency and data reliability, suitable for further analysis. By individually matching and superimposing the 36 eye-tracking datasets with the 18 experimental images, ensuring accurate correspondence between the appearance time of each image and its corresponding eye-tracking data, three sets of 18 heat maps and gaze plots were generated.

Table 2. Basic Information of Participants.

Basic Information		Number of Participants	Percentage (%)
Gender	Male	11	30.6
	Female	25	69.4
Educational Background	Undergraduate	26	72.2
	Graduate	10	27.8
Major Background	Humanities	20	55.6
	STEM	16	44.4
Whether Revisited	No	32	88.9
	Yes	4	11.1

3.2 Discussions

1. Heat map and gaze trajectory analysis of a photo in the Guangda Garden reveals distinct 'clusters' and convergence areas of fixation points formed by the interests of 36 subjects. These areas mainly concentrate on the distant Manchurian-style windows within the left-side doorway sightline and the route and windows at the farthest point within the sightline through the right-side empty window. Combined with the plan view mentioned earlier, it can be observed that the clusters in the heat map and the dense gaze trajectory areas are located along the paths in the Guangda Garden (see Fig. 5).

a. Original Image   b. Heat Map Analysis   c. Focus Map Analysis

Fig. 5. Eye-tracking Experiment Analysis of the Guangda Garden.

2. By analyzing the heat map and gaze trajectory of a photo within the Chuxiang Garden, it can be observed that the areas of interest for subjects mainly concentrate on the left-side leaking window, the Manchurian-style window at the end of the corridor, and the Manchurian-style window of the Zhuangyuan Hall on the right side. Contrasting with the plan view mentioned earlier, it can be seen that the clusters in the heat map and the dense gaze trajectory areas are also located along the paths in the Chuxiang Garden (see Fig. 6).

a. Original Image   b. Heat Map Analysis   c. Focus Map Analysis

Fig. 6. Eye-tracking Experiment Analysis of Chuxiang Garden.

3. Analysis of the heat map and gaze trajectory of a photo within the Xiaopenglai Garden reveals that the subjects' areas of interest mainly concentrate in four areas: first, the leaking window of the left cloud wall; second, the farthest leaking window in the corridor visible through the doorway; third, the leaking window of the right corridor; and the fourth area is the Manchurian-style window of the Liuxiang Pavilion. The gaze trajectory similarly shows that subjects' gazes are mainly focused on different areas of the corridor. This corresponds with the plan view mentioned earlier, indicating that the clusters in the heat map and the dense gaze trajectory areas are located along the paths in the Xiaopenglai Garden (see Fig. 7).

a. Original Image   b. Heat Map Analysis   c. Focus Map Analysis

Fig. 7. Eye-tracking Experiment Analysis of Xiaopenglai Garden.

The analysis of the heat maps and gaze trajectories above reveals the strong interest of the subjects in the scenic windows, manifested in distinct clusters and concentrated areas of trajectory networks. These areas closely align with the positions of the scenic windows, highlighting the effectiveness of the windows in attracting visitors' visual attention. The

Fig. 8. Eye-tracking Experiment Analysis. (a) Guangda Garden. (b) Chuxiang Garden. (c) Xiaopenglai Garden.

(b)

(c)

Fig. 8. (*continued*)

distribution of gaze trajectory maps further indicates that the scenic windows are at the visual network's center throughout the landscape, demonstrating their strong visual connection within the garden space. This confirms the importance of scenic windows in guiding visitors' gazes and experiences.

Visual processing of the relative time and fixation point positions of the 36 subjects was conducted to generate heat maps and gaze plots of photos captured at main points along the paths of the Guangda Garden, Chuxiang Garden, and Xiaopenglai Garden (see Fig. 8).

4 Conclusion

Based on the analysis of the heat maps and gaze plots, the following conclusions can be drawn:

1. Subjects' visual attention is mainly focused on linear perspective-guided spaces, especially on landscape elements with multi-level spatial penetrability. This indicates that elements such as leaking windows, empty windows, Manchurian-style windows, and doorways in the New Garden, due to their ability to provide visual penetration and spatial extension, can become key attractors of visual focus.
2. Within narrower sightlines, subjects tend to observe distant scenery through visual channels such as empty windows, indicating the important role of windows in guiding sightlines and expanding visual space.
3. In open areas of the field of view, subjects' gaze points are more concentrated on distant objects, such as Manchurian-style windows, indicating that windows in the New Garden not only serve as visual focal points but also guide sightlines to more distant important landscape nodes.
4. The concentrated gaze points are mostly located on the main pathways of the New Garden, indicating that the design of the New Garden cleverly utilizes elements such as windows to guide visitors to experience and appreciate the predetermined landscape sequence along the main tour routes.

In summary, the experimental results validate the significant impact of windows in the New Garden on guiding sightlines. Designers have enhanced the sense of spatial penetration and depth by the positioning, form, and layout of windows, effectively guiding visitors' sightlines and tour paths, thus creating an engaging effect.

References

1. Zhou, W.Q.: History of Chinese Classical Gardens. 1st edn. Tsinghua University Press, Beijing (1990)
2. Chu, X.Z., Song, J.H., Wang, S.R., Ding, J.F.: Research on the touring experience of the master-of-nets garden based on Isovist analysis. Urban Archit. **20**(18), 197–199+212 (2023)
3. Peng, Y.G.: Analysis of Chinese classical gardens. China Building Industry Press, Beijing (1986)
4. Underwood, G.: Cognitive Processes in Eye Guidance. Oxford University Press, New York (2005)

5. Li, S.P., Zhang, X.L., Kim, F.J., et al.: Attention-aware robotic laparoscope based on fuzzy interpretation of eye-gaze patterns. J. Med. Devices **9**(4), 041007 (2015)
6. Tinker, M.A.: Experimental studies on the legibility of print: an annotated bibliography. Reading Res. Q. **1**(4), 67–118 (1966)
7. Xu, F.: The impacts of wind energy development on landscape planning in the context of carbon neutrality. Landscape Archit. **29**(5), 52–58 (2022)
8. Zhang, R.S., Yan, X.Y., Wang, C., et al.: Research on emotional interaction between people and built environment driven by multi-modal data: take Wudaokou Jingzhang railway park as an example. Urban Dev. Stud. **29**(7), 55–66 (2022)
9. Zhao, Y., Lin, J.H., Liu, Y.: Research on visual evaluation of tourism scenery based on eye movement experiment: a case of Tangjia ancient town in Zhuhai. Hum. Geogr. **35**(5), 130–140 (2020)
10. Cheng, S., Zhang, X.H., Cheng, Y.N.: Prospect of the application of digital landscape technology in the field of landscape architecture in China. Landscape Archit. **28**(1), 46–52 (2021)
11. Li, X., Li, Y., Ren, Y.P., et al.: Research on the Urban spatial visual quality based on subjective evaluation method and eye tracking analysis. Archit. J. **S2**, 190–196 (2020)
12. Wei, F., Chen, L., Zan, P., et al.: Between industrial remains and the green: research on public perception of rewilded postindustrial landscape. Chin. Landscape Archit. **38**(8), 36–41 (2022)
13. Wu, Y.L., Dong, W.H., Zhang, W.J.: Research on influencing factors of built environment perception in neighborhoods: evidence from behavioral experiment. City Plann. Rev. **46**(12), 99–109 (2022)

Design of Customer Intelligent Guidance APP in Exhibition Venues

Xiao Liu[1,2(✉)], Chen Wan'er Zhang[1], Huiru Wang[1], Xia Wang[3], and Xiaohua Yang[1]

[1] School of Cultural Industries and Tourism, Xiamen University of Technology, Xiamen, Fujian, China
xiaoanneliu@163.com
[2] Research Centre for Cultural Industries, Xiamen University of Technology, Social Science Research Base of Fujian Province, Xiamen, China
[3] School of Foreign Languages, Ningbo University of Technology, Ningbo, Zhejiang, China

Abstract. Exhibition venues are the prerequisites and physical carriers in terms of infrastructure and technologies in MICE industry. As public places with high density of visitors flow, there always lurk such risks as traffic congestion in popular booths and crowd gathering in entrances and exits. The services for accurate positioning and navigation guidance are gradually in demand for exhibition venues. This paper firstly analyses the core technological bases of customer intelligent guidance APP, namely, face recognition, crowd density detection, as well as indoor positioning and navigation. Then, technical structures are dealt with, which include overall architecture and databases of visitors, exhibitors, organizers and electronic maps. 7 first-level modules are hence designed. The venue map is displayed on the website port. The system backstage is built on Spring Boot, and the local data are saved in the form of map with the implementation of Serializable. This App is thereby programmed with algorithms and tested with great results.

Keywords: Smart Guidance · Exhibition venues · design · technical structures

1 Introduction

There is enough natural soil for the integration of exhibition industry and digital technologies. The wide application of new generation digital technologies, such as Artificial Intelligence (hereinafter referred to as AI), Big Data, Virtual Reality (hereinafter referred to as VR), etc., has stimulated the driving force for the development of the exhibition industry, giving birth to one-stop virtuality-reality combination MICE technical platform and meta-universe technology scene. Rapid changes in the field of technologies have pushed the upstream and downstream enterprises to reshape their organizational structure, work methods and business processes, which brought profound transformation in the exhibition industry. Moreover, due to the outbreak of COVID-19 and the limitation of on-site exhibition scene, the development process of digital exhibition has accelerated from technological concept to practical application [1]. Service in the exhibition industry shows the characteristics of personalization, autonomization, digitalization, networking, virtualization and experientialization [2]. In the context of "Internet + MICE",

© The Author(s), under exclusive license to Springer Nature Switzerland AG 2025
P. Zaphiris et al. (Eds.): HCII 2024, LNCS 15378, pp. 334–344, 2025.
https://doi.org/10.1007/978-3-031-76815-6_24

the Smart MICE industry emphasizes information sharing, resource integration, and integrated innovation. One of this industry modes is related industries collaboration, which is the business cooperation among the MICE, transportation and public security. With their all-round cooperation, issues on passenger flow and security can be solved and predicted [3]. Exhibition venues are the prerequisites and physical carriers in terms of infrastructure and technologies in MICE industry. Exhibition venue construction is an important topic in MICE management research, which has gradually attracts the attention of academia and industry.

According to the research results, factors of exhibition service satisfaction include reception services, professional services, supporting services and backstage services [4]. These services in exhibition venues provide automatic positioning, friend location search, nearby information search etc. [5] As public places with high density of visitors flow, there always lurk such risks as traffic congestion in popular booths and crowd gathering in entrances and exits. The demands for accurate positioning and navigation service are becoming more prominent with the development of the MICE industry. Therefore, this paper aims to design an intelligent guidance APP for exhibition venues, providing data of target booth navigation path and visitor flow density. The findings will enhance user experience and provide suggestions for the construction of smart exhibition venues.

2 Core Technological Bases

2.1 Face Recognition Technology

Face recognition is developing rapidly in the field of biometric recognition, and has become an important branch of Artificial intelligence in the domain of image recognition domain. In the research area of low-resolution, a methodology of Multidimensional Scaling (MDS) is proposed for face recognition with simple and easy algorithm [6]. However, it is restricted by the factors of posture, expression and illumination. A coupled discriminative dictionary and transformation learning approach for face recognition is tested with better effect [7]. An approach to robust low-resolution face recognition is put forward via low-rank representation and locality-constrained regression [8].

At the present time, face recognition technology is gradually integrated with the security inspection system of various venues, such as museums, art galleries, libraries, and exhibition venues, and is widely used in these entrances and exits for visitors' identification and authentication. With this technology, users could access and identify automatically by scanning their face or the QR code to replace the traditional manual scanning. In this way, crowd gathering can be effectively alleviated with higher efficiency and more security. Taking the Cross-Strait Book Trade Fair held at the Xiamen International Convention and Exhibition Center as an example, the "Face Recognition System" has been fully implemented in 2019. Compared with manual security checks, the average time for passenger security checks is reduced from 30 s to 2 s. The accuracy and efficiency of security checks and verification are significantly improved.

2.2 Crowd Density Detection

Crowd density is highly related to crowd safety [9]. Crowd density is used to measure the concentration of the crowd in a certain space. The higher the data of crowd density is, the more crowd the space is, which may lead to the stampede or other accidents. With the increasing demand of public space safety and comfort level, the technology of crowd density detection gradually becomes a research focus in the academia. Crowd density methods can be divided into two types, namely the shallow learning-based methods and the deep learning-based methods [10]. The former include pixel-based method [11], texture-based method [12] and corner point-based method [13]. Based on neural network model [14], the deep learning-based methods usually contain back-propagation neural network [15], rank-based spatial pyramid pooling neural network [16], feature map fusion convolutional neural network [17] and convolutional neural Networks [18]. In general, it is easy to operate by the shallow learning-based methods, while the deep learning-based methods could solve the issues of crowd overlap with strong robustness, timely data acquisition and high accuracy.

2.3 Indoor Positioning and Navigation

With the development of the mobile Internet, the research of digital electronic indoor map is gradually conducted with the functions of display, positioning and navigation [19]. As early as the 1990s, some of the institutions and scholars began to make the researches on indoor positioning technology systems, which were only used in specific environment with short propagation distance. In 2009, Micello, Inc. (acquired by HERE Technologies) made indoor maps for the exhibitions with Application Programming Interface. In 2013, iBeacon, released by Apple, Inc. is characterized by energy-saving, positioning-accuracy, wider signal cover and applications. In China, the appearance of Baidu Map marked the beginning of precise positioning industry in 2005. Generally speaking, indoor positioning and navigation technologies started relatively late with higher speed. In MICE industry, the technology of iBeacon has realized the functions of route navigation, positioning, guide for booth and shopping. Based on the routes of visitors, the information of consumption preference and booth duration could be analyzed in order to provide suggestions for resource allocation, marketing decisions, and customer value [20]. In China, "i-showcom" exhibitor-visitor smart interaction platform (designed by EastFair Corporation) and one-stop digital MICE SaaS cloud platform (designed by 31 Conference Corporation) are related to electronic map navigation and positioning, which ignore the needs of crowd guidance. In all, how to relieve the congestion for visitors in the exhibition venues is still an urgent issue to be solved for MICE industry.

2.4 Research Review

Firstly, the application of crowd density detection algorithm still faces some challenges. The results of Davies et al. (1995) [11] were not accurate by the means of pixel-based estimation in high-density crowds. The estimation methods were interfered by the background texture in the extraction of image features [12]. In the process of acquiring image features, it is easy to cause image distortion based on convolutional neural networks in real-time crowd density estimation [18].

Secondly, the application scope and area of crowd density detection also need to be explored, especially in the exhibition centers, venues, stadiums and other crowed places. The placement and accumulation of exhibits as well as the construction of booths are likely to be affected by the light, posture change, and facial expression variation, so crowd image is sheltered for the reasons above. The mobility of the crowd increases the difficulty of video image acquisition which leads to low recognition and high error.

Thirdly, besides the limitation of the crowd density detection technology itself, the application achievements of this technology are relatively few. In the implementation process, there is no complete standard for face recognition technology in the current situation [21]. Two-way intelligent evacuation instruction system was proposed [22], but they did not consider the impact of individual behavior difference on route selection. An OGRE (Object-Oriendted Graphics Rendering Engine) passenger flow guidance effect display module was designed [23]. Based on image acquisition technology, a subway platform passenger flow guidance system was designed [24], which made the automation of passenger flow guidance realizable with low precision of the passenger flow information. Only Fu (2011) [25] noticed the application of performance-based design in the evacuation of large-space exhibition venues, which is mostly related with our research. The current patents focus on cell phone positioning devices, video monitoring technologies, and safety evacuation signs, achieving limited research findings on customer guidance in exhibition venues.

3 Technical Structure

This study will develop an intelligent guidance APP in exhibition venues which is based on Android platform. This APP will adopt iBeacon guidance system design, in order to provide the functions of real-time positioning and navigation, short-time and safe route recommendation, real-time monitoring of passenger flow density, help, etc. Furthermore, it will be combined with the smoothed multi-objective D* Lite smoothing algorithm [26] to collect customers' route preferences, provide "APP + Web" interaction, route for target booth navigation and data for passenger flow density. The purpose of this APP is to enhance customers' experience for the exhibitions and provide references for the construction of intelligent venues.

3.1 Overall Architecture

This customer intelligent guidance APP includes User Interface, Web-based Online Map Editing and Back-end Database. In the part of User Interface, there are seven core functional interfaces, including Exhibitions, Hot Topics, Guidance, Mine, Help, Communication and Scan QR Code. Web-based Online Map Editing is to design the online map of booth distribution in exhibition venues. User information is stored in Back-end Database to achieve data collection and transmission of Web-based Online Map Editing. The overall architecture of this system is shown as Fig. 1.

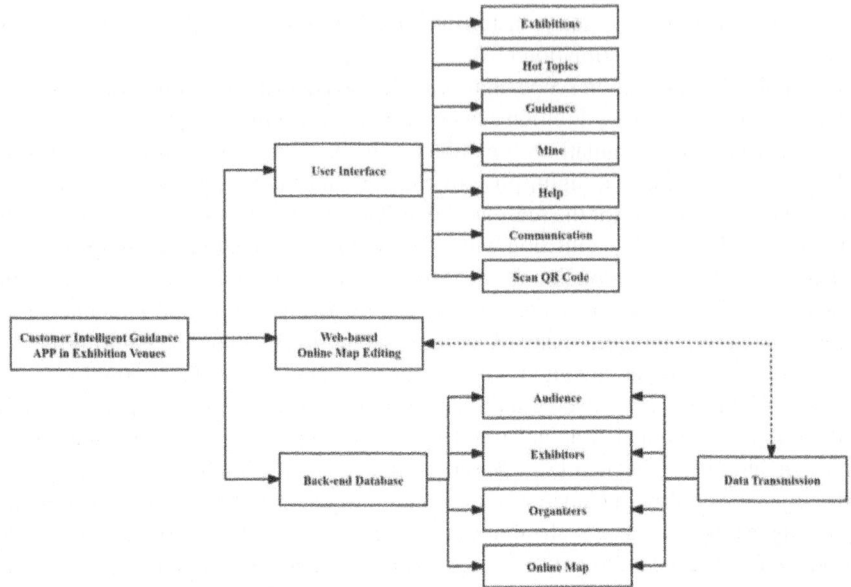

Fig. 1. Overall Architecture of Customer Intelligent Guidance APP in Exhibition Venues

Taking the research design of Li et al. (2011) [27] and Zhao et al., (2014) [28] as references, the approaches of this APP are as follows. Firstly, on the Web-based Online Map Editing, the layout of booth location is converted into electronic map by map vectorization, without any transformation by the protocol. Secondly, APK executable files generated by compiling the test system are installed in the Android intelligent terminal device. This APP will analyze the users' preference, distribution and other data by the function of heat map. The user's real-time path information could be obtained by Inertial Measurement Unit (IMU) data and Pedestrian Dead Reckoning (PDR) algorithm. Thirdly, the user's location can be transmitted to the API interface by the APP server via the blue-tooth function. The data format is processed, encapsulated and stored in the back-end database after receiving the location data signals in the server. Furthermore, based on iBeacon positioning technology, the user's location is transformed into the point in the matrix, with this point as the starting point and the destination as the end point. The path from the origin to the destination is obtained through D*Lite algorithm and returned to the APP for interface display. Both of the shortest-time path and the shortest-distance path are recommended for the users.

3.2 Database Design

According to the source of data, this APP database will store the data from the following four parts.

(A) Audience
This APP database will collect the data information of audience in the aspects of name, gender, age, education background, telephone, interests and preference, reservation, etc.

(B) Exhibitors
This APP database will collect the data information of exhibitors in the aspects of company name, personal name, gender, age, education background, telephone, booth, exhibit, etc.

(C) Organizers
This APP database will collect the data information of organizers in the aspects of exhibition scale, exhibition type, exhibition time, exhibition location and the basic information of the organizers.

(D) Online Map Database
This APP database will collect the data information of online maps in the aspects of latitude and longitude, style, color, name, tilt angle, etc.

After collecting the information above by the APP database, APP operators could edit the exhibition map data, exhibition news information, booth information, and upload them to the APP terminal by online map editor. Based on the accurate delivery of exhibition information, APP users could upload real-time information by the function of feedback, in order to put forward improvement suggestions.

3.3 Module Functions

The first-level modules of the APP include: Exhibitions, Hot Topics, Guidance, Mine, Help, Communication, Scan QR Code. Each first-level model includes several second-level and third-level modules. It is shown Table 1.

Table 1. Module functions of Customer Intelligent Guidance APP in Exhibition Venues

First-level modules	Descriptions	Second-level modules	Third-level modules
Exhibitions	Exhibition information and passenger flow	Previous exhibitions	
		Insights	
		Real-time data	Real-time passenger flow density

(*continued*)

Table 1. (*continued*)

First-level modules	Descriptions	Second-level modules	Third-level modules
			Passenger flow analysis
			Duration
		Overview	
		Search	
Hot Topics	Audios, videos and convenient service	Focus	
		Videos	
		Recommendations	
		Cultural activities	
		More	Tickets
			Hotels
			Food
			Online store
Guidance	Map guidance and heat map display	Restroom	
		Stairs	
		Elevators	
		Emergency exits	
		Service counter	
		Heat map[1]	
Mine	Personal records and feedback	Identification	
		Favorites	
		Tracks	
		Errors	
		Feedback	
		Settings	Usage mode
			Location

(*continued*)

---

[1] The function of "Heat map" is to collect and display the visitor distribution and passenger flow. When click any of the second-level modules in the "Guidance", there are two paths shown on the APP interface in the colors of red and green. The red path means the shortest-distance one, while the green path describes the safest one to avoid the traffic jam.

Table 1. (*continued*)

First-level modules	Descriptions	Second-level modules	Third-level modules
			Privacy
			Clear the cache
			About us
Help	Get help by call		
Communication	Communicate with exhibitors or organizers		
Scan QR Code	Get information about exhibitions		

4 Algorithm and Application Test

The venue map is shown on the website port. This APP system backstage is built on Spring Boot. The local data are saved in the form of map with the implementation of Serializable. Here are some codes of the main functions.

(A) Path Collection
The App utilizes the Arraylist to insert, access and output objects with these following codes.

```
ArrayList<Node> arrayList = new ArrayList<Node>();
while (parent != null) {
System.out.println(parent.x + ",  " + parent.y);
arrayList.add(new Node(parent.x,  parent.y));
parent = parent.parent;}
for (int i=0;i<arrayList.size();i++){
    System.out.println(arrayList.get(i).x+"=="+arrayList.get(i).y);}
long end=System.currentTimeMillis();
System.out.println("\n");
System.out.print((start-end)/1000);
```

(B) Path Display
The first step in this function is to determine whether it contains a path. If not, there is no path to show in the APP. Function codes are as follows.

```java
public static Node find(List<Node> nodes, Node point) {
    for (Node n : nodes)
        if ((n.x == point.x) && (n.y == point.y)) { return n;}
    return null;}
public static boolean exists(List<Node> nodes, Node node) {
    for (Node n : nodes) {
        if ((n.x == node.x) && (n.y == node.y)) { return true;}}
    return false;}
public static boolean exists(List<Node> nodes, int x, int y) {
    for (Node n : nodes) {
        if ((n.x == x) && (n.y == y)) { return true;}}
    return false;}
public static class Node {
    public Node(int x, int y) { this.x = x; this.y = y;}
    public int x; public int y; public int F;
    public int G;
    public int H;
    public void calcF() { this.F = this.G + this.H;}
    public Node parent;}}
```

(C) Application Test

When this Customer Intelligent Guidance APP is developed, it is tested on Android system platform of several brands, such as Xiaomi, Huawei and VIVO. This test is based on 2019 China International Fair for Investment & Trade (CIFIT). After the layout data of 2019 CIFIT is input into the back-end database, the interface is shown immediately. Click "Heat map", and the APP can display crowd density and recommend paths for visitors. Click any booth in the map interface, and it can move to the sub-interface with more detailed information of this booth. Users can add it to "Favorites" or share it. If the users click "Real-time data" in "Exhibitions", the real-time data of passenger flow density, passenger flow and duration can be shown. And if the users click any safety identification module in "Guidance", two paths will be presented. The red one means the shortest-time path, while the green one provides the shortest-distance and the safest path. Click "Help", and the phone number will be shown.

In all, this APP is simple and clear with convenient operation. Seven main functions can run smoothly with steady operation. There is no stuck or delay in the process of uploading the data. The expected requirements of system design and development have been achieved.

Fundings. This work was supported by Fujian Provincial Social Science Fund under No. FJ2023MGCA024 (Key Program) entitled "Dynamic mechanism and path of transformation and upgrading for Fujian convention and exhibition industry in the trend of immersive experience", Humanities and Social Science Fund of Ministry of Education of China under No. 2021RUS0001 entitled "Mechanism of CIIE and the construction of Hainan Free Trade Port" and Enterprise authorized project under No.SKHX23014 entitled "Smart MICE service collaborative innovation system development and platform construction".

References

1. 2023 Annual report of China's exhibition industry. https://exhibition.ccpit.org/cms/article/file/showFile?path=Article/2024/01/17/10-25-1528609.pdf
2. Lv, Z.-Y., Zhang, X.-W., Li, C.-H., Qin, X.-Z., Zhang, X.-Y.: Research on the connotation and general character technology system of fusion of information resources management and cloud service. Intell. Theory Pract. **35**(9), 26–32 (2012). (In Chinese)
3. Liu, X.: Research on the innovation of wisdom exhibition industry development mode in Fujian province in the era of "Internet+." J. KaiFeng Coll. Educ. **37**(7), 250–252 (2017). (In Chinese)
4. Zhang, T.: A study on satisfaction measurement for MICE service-the case of Macao international trade and investment fair. Tourism Forum. **4**(1), 24–27 (2011). (In Chinese)
5. Tian, H.: The development trend of China's exhibition industry under the perspective of intelligent exhibition. Small Medium-sized Enterprises Manag. Technol. **30**, 58–59 (2020). (In Chinese)
6. Biswas, S., Bowyer K.W., Flynn, P.J.: Multidimensional scaling for matching low-resolution face images. IEEE Trans. Pattern Anal. Mach. Intell. **34**(10), 2019–2030 (2012)
7. Mudunuri, S.P., Biswas, S.: A coupled discriminative dictionary and transformation learning approach with applications to cross domain matching. Pattern Recogn. Lett. **71**(1), 38–44 (2016)
8. Gao, G.-G., et al.: Robust low-resolution face recognition via low-rank representation and locality-constrained regression. Comput. Electr. Eng. **70**, 968–977 (2018). (In Chinese)
9. Fruin, J.J.: Pedestrian planning and design. Metropolitan Assoc. Urban Designers Environ. Planners, 26–40(1971). New York
10. Zhang, J.-J., Shi, G.-Z., Li, J.-C.: Current researches and future perspectives of crowd counting and crowd density estimation technology. Comput. Eng. Sci. **40**(2), 283–288 (2018). (In Chinese)
11. Davies, A.C., Jia, H.Y., Velastin, S.A.: Crowd monitoring using image processing. Electron. Commun. Eng. J. **79**(1), 37–47 (1995)
12. Marana, A.N., Velastin, S.A., Costa, L.F., Lotufo, R.A.: Automatic estimation of crowd density using texture. Saf. Sci. **28**(3), 165–175 (1998)
13. Albiol, A., Silla, M.J., Mossi, J.M.: Video analysis using corner motion statistics. In: the Proceedings of IEEE International Workshop on Performance Evaluation of Tracking and Surveillance, pp. 31–38(2009)
14. Chow, T.W.S., Yam, Y.F., Cho, S.Y.: Fast training algorithm for feed forward neural networks: application to crowd estimation at underground stations. Artif. Intell. Eng. **13**(3), 301–307 (1999)
15. Wen, X.-B., Man, J.-F., Li, Q.-Q.: Human segmentation and tracking for crowded people in video surveillance. Small Microcomput. Syst. **33**(4), 892–895 (2012). (In Chinese)
16. Shi, Z.-L., Ye, Y.-D., Wu, Y.-P., Lou, Z.-Z.: Crowd counting using rank-based spatial pyramid pooling network. J. Autom. **42**(6), 867–874 (2016). (in Chinese)
17. Tang, S.-Q., Tao, W., Zhang, L.-L.: A deep crowd counting algorithm based on multi-column feature map fusion. J. Zhengzhou Univ. **50**(2), 70–74 (2018). (In Chinese)
18. Li, B.-P., Han, X.-Y., Wu, D.-M.: Real-Time crowd density estimation based on convolutional neural networks. J. Graph. **39**(4), 729–734 (2018). (In Chinese)
19. Xu, H-Y., Li, Z-H., Wang, J-Y.: Present status and prospect of indoor map application. Surv. Mapp. Bull. **9**, 119–121 (2014). (In Chinese)
20. Tian, Y., Qin, R.-T.: Application of precise positioning real-time navigation system in convention and exhibition. South. Entrepreneur **1**, 233–234 (2018). (In Chinese)

21. Qin, H., Li, T.-F., Guo, H.-Y., Xu, Y.: A study on the application of face recognition technology in libraries. J. Univ. Lib. **36**(6), 49–54 (2018). (In Chinese)
22. Liu, B., Liu, Y.-B., Wu, X.-C.: On software design principles of intelligent evacuation indication system. Fire Sci. Technol. **31**(3), 303–305 (2012). (In Chinese)
23. Liu, F.-Y.: Design and implementation of a module showing the effect of subway station passenger evacuation. J. Lanzhou Univ. (Nat. Sci. Ed.) **50**(4), 570–576 (2014). (In Chinese)
24. Pang, M-Y. Du, Y-J., Li., C-J.: A study on passenger flow guidance system for metro platforms based on image acquisition technology. Metro Express Traffic **30**(2), 37–41(2017). (In Chinese)
25. Fu, R.-S.: The application of performance-based design on large space exhibition's evacuation. Fire Sci. Technol. **30**(2), 112–115 (2011). (In Chinese)
26. Yu, C.-B., Sun, M.-N., Yang, R.-M.: Design and implementation of indoor navigation system using iBeacon technology. J. Chongqing Univ. Technol. (Nat. Sci. Ed.) **32**(5), 162–168 (2018). (In Chinese)
27. Li, Z., Jiang, Z.-H., Qin, J.: Research and implementation of online electronic map service system. Comput. Eng. Des. **32**(7), 2344–2347 (2011). (In Chinese)
28. Zhao, R., Zhong, B., Zhu, Z.-L., Ma, L., Yao, J.-F.: Overview of indoor localization techniques and applications. Sci. Electron. **27**(3), 154–157 (2014). (In Chinese)

Computer Vision and AI Tools for Enhancing User Experience in the Cultural Heritage Domain

Pavan K. Rachabathuni, Paolo Mazzanti⬤, Filippo Principi,
Andrea Ferracani, and Marco Bertini[✉]⬤

Università degli Studi di Firenze - DINFO - MICC, Florence, Italy
{PavanK.Rachabathuni,Paolo.Mazzanti,Filippo.Principi,
Andrea.Ferracani,Marco.Bertini}@unifi.it
http://www.micc.unifi.it

Abstract. To enhance the museum experience for visitors, it's crucial to adopt a people-centered approach. This means engaging with visitors dynamically, providing transformative learning experiences from pre-arrival to post-departure. Using interactive and immersive experiences can evoke emotions, inspire creativity, and facilitate participatory learning. Incorporating advanced technologies like artificial intelligence (A.I.) and computer vision (C.V.) can deepen the connection between artworks and visitors, resulting in a "phygital museum." This helps to reimagine museums with diverse spaces, tools, and interactions for various audiences. AI/CV tools help visitors interact with collections, inspiring insights and enriching data [15].

According to the "contextual mode" of learning proposed by Falk and Dierking [7], the more interactive and participatory the museum experience is, the more it will have a lasting impact on the visitor and thus improve his or her learning on the subject. Visitors are driven by their motivations, emotions, interests, and prior knowledge, and this background has a huge influence on the experience the visitor gets from the stay, including the memory they will have of it and recommendations to other users and friends. Emotions play a motivating role at every stage of the museum experience, from the decision to visit the museum to post-visit enjoyment, and visitors' emotional engagement is a prerequisite for effective and authentic learning. Digital tools can enhance the museum experience by triggering a multisensory experience, enabling physical connections, personalizing the visit to the user's needs, enhancing playful and social interaction, and sharing personal experiences.

In this paper we report on the design and functionalities of a set of CV and AI tools designed to enhance the user experience in cultural heritage institutions like museums. The tools are open source.

Keywords: Computer Vision · User Experience · Gamification · Phygital Museum

---

P. K. Rachabathuni, P. Mazzanti and F. Principi—Equal contribution.

P. Zaphiris et al. (Eds.): HCII 2024, LNCS 15378, pp. 345–354, 2025.
https://doi.org/10.1007/978-3-031-76815-6_25

1   Introduction

Contemporary literature highlights the importance of engaging audiences in dynamic experiences that enable visitors to enjoy, learn, discover, and interact [7,15]. To achieve this, it is necessary to create new forms of engagement that cater to diverse audiences, with particular attention to younger and local communities. Utilizing a range of digital tools, cultural heritage sites can motivate audiences with an interactive and human-centered approach. Visitors are increasingly familiar with using digital tools and new languages to interact with museum collections, creating and sharing new stories before, during, and after their visit. New technologies, particularly AI/CV tools, hold great potential for motivating and creating a stronger relationship between artworks and visitors. When applied in a playful approach based on gamification and learning-by-doing techniques, these tools can foster interaction and emotional relationships between visitors and artworks, making the content more memorable [4].

Within the ReInHerit project[1], a toolkit has been developed using A.I. and C.V. technologies. The main goal is to allow visitors to interact with collections and exhibitions playfully, using different approaches like gamification, or asking visitors to interact with chat-based systems, or to inspect artworks using virtual magnifying lenses. This encourages visitors to explore artwork content more deeply during and after their visit, creating new narratives and, in some cases, also producing user-generated content for social media sharing, as a memento of the visit. Smaller museums often lack resources for innovative digital services, and only larger institutions can develop applications using A.I. and computer vision tools. Making the toolkit open source aims to bridge this technological gap.

The ReInHerit toolkit has been designed for young visitors who are more likely to use digital tools in a museum setting. The emphasis is on creating mobile-first and web-first applications, prioritizing mobile devices. This approach makes it easier to implement a Bring-Your-Own-Device (BYOD) approach for seamless integration. For this reason, the interfaces and interactions have been designed to be usable both on small and larger screens, to account also for the case in which the organizations prefer to provide the experience through installations, instead of mobile apps.

The strategy used to design the toolkit is based on the following pillar topics:

- Interactivity: to enhance visitor engagement, motivate learning, create a stronger relationship between artworks and visitors;
- BYOD: mobile device applications have been specifically developed as primary targets, simplifying adherence to the Bring-Your-Own-Device (BYOD) approach;
- Artificial Intelligence and Computer Vision: to develop new types of human-computer interactions;

---

[1] https://www.reinherit.eu.

– Open-Source: to align with a sustainable management perspective, streamlining maintenance and facilitating the reuse of applications by different organizations.

In particular, in this paper we report on the following applications:

– Strike-a-Pose and Face-fit: these two applications are designed to employ gamification and interaction with an artwork to increase the engagement of the visitors of a museum: visitors are asked to replicate an artwork using the pose of their body pose and their facial expression and pose; CV is used to automatically evaluate the similarity to the pose of the artwork. User-generated materials are provided for social media sharing and as mementos of the museum visit, where the user is depicted replicating the poses or painted with his own expression within an artwork.
– Smart Lens: this app transforms a mobile phone in a virtual magnifying lens to observe the details of an artwork and getting the related information; the user is asked to observe more proactively an artwork and think about its parts. Computer vision is used to recognize the relevant artwork details selected by the exhibition curators to provide the associated multimedia information.
– Multimedia Chatbot: this system merges CV and natural language processing capabilities of Multimedia Language Models (MLM) to implement a chatbot usable in web/mobile interfaces; the system also provides speech-to-text functionalities to allow for a more natural interaction during a visit. The goal is to provide descriptions and information on artworks using natural language and interacting in a chat, thus again eliciting a proactive interaction from the user, answering his real interests, and using a type of interaction that has become common especially for younger users.

2 The Toolkit

In the following sections we are going to present the applications developed and published in the Toolkit. Source code and documentation of all the applications is available on the ReInHerit Digital Hub[2]. In Sect. 2.1 we describe two applications implemented following the paradigm of serious gaming (Strike a Pose and Face-Fit). In Sect. 2.2 we face the problem of providing information about details of artworks through object detection on mobile devices. In Sect. 2.3 we present a system (i.e. Viola Chatbot) which engages users on artworks through an AI-powered conversational chat-bot.

2.1 Strike-a-Pose and Face-Fit

Gamification is the process of exploiting strategies and game dynamics into scenarios that are not a game. It has already been proved to be useful to enhance

---

[2] https://reinherit-hub.eu/.

skills and competences in a variety of domains such as marketing, industry training and entertainment. Certainly also cultural heritage can benefit from a gamification approach which represents an opportunity to engage visitors to museums content through the design of more entertaining, social and challenging digital learning scenarios [3,9,13], to help museums to move from the traditional "look and do not touch" toward a "play and interact" approach. In fact, it has been observed that the availability of tools like gamified e-guides to visitors contributes to the sustainability of museums [2]. The two applications presented in this section use gamification as a strategy to elicit an emotional response from users and to trigger a learning process. More detials regarding the design is provided in [5].

Strike-a-Pose (Fig. 1) is a web-based application that enables users to compare and evaluate their own poses to those present in famous paintings or statues. The system can be accessed via visitors' smartphones using the "Bring Your Own Device" (BYOD) approach or through a dedicated environment that uses a fixed station equipped with a large screen and a camera. The application uses a gamification paradigm that makes the process of learning about works of art fun and engaging for users. After registering, users are challenged to replicate the poses of selected artworks from the museum's collections. The application provides users with skeleton displays of both the artwork and their own bodies to facilitate matching various points and segments. The application presents users with sets of challenges that require replicating poses using different body parts, such as using only the torso to allow wheelchair users to participate. Once all the poses have been matched, the application allows users to generate a video of the interactive experience, which can be saved for social sharing.

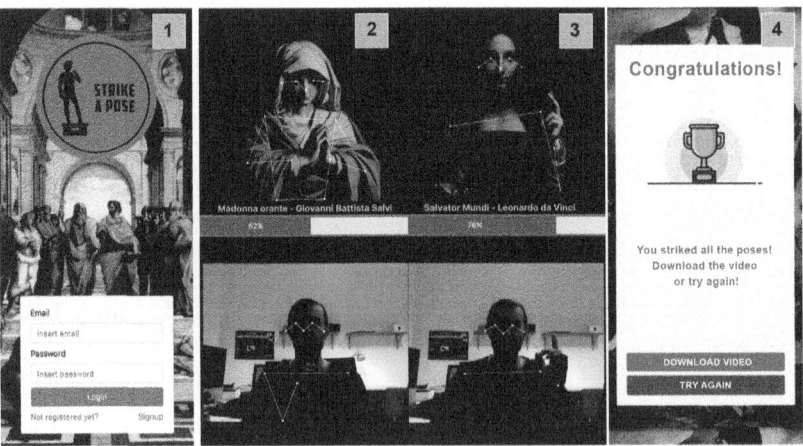

Fig. 1. Strike a Pose App for smartphone. 1) Login. 2–3) The user trying to strike the pose in the painting (playing in "easy" mode, with visible skeletons). 4) Challenge completed: download the video.

The application was developed using JavaScript on the client-side and Python on the server-side. Pose detection on human bodies is achieved using TensorflowJS detection API[3], which exploits the pose detection model, MoveNet. MoveNet is a fast and accurate model that detects 17 key points of a body. The model is used in the variant "Lightning" for latency-critical applications, running faster than real-time on most modern desktops, laptops, and phones. The model runs completely client-side in the browser. Server-side, an SQLLite database is used to store artwork collections, challenges, and artwork metadata and descriptions. Communication between the knowledge-base and the interface is ensured through RESTful APIs developed in Flask[4]. The video is created server-side. The interface designed for smartphones uses a vertical layout, while the one for installations has a horizontal layout, to accommodate different screen aspect ratios.

To ensure that the coordinates of the keypoints were not related to the entire image but only to the pose, both for the user's pose and the pose of the character in the painting, they have been normalized. The algorithm used to test the similarity of the user's pose to the pose of the character in the painting is based on the Euclidean distance between the set of points. The match is verified if the distance is below a predefined threshold for a certain time interval.

Face-Fit (see Fig. 2) is a software application developed in JavaScript and Python that allows users to personalize and gamify famous paintings, particularly portraits. The app is designed for both smartphones and desktop installations in museums. It lets users replicate the head pose and expression of portraits by famous painters and transfer their own face onto the artwork to create a new image. The development of the app was informed by a usability study that followed an iterative design approach with three groups of five people [12].

To use the app, the user stands in front of a camera-equipped smartphone or installation and chooses a painting from a vertical carousel of portraits. The app presents a ghost image of the user's face over the painting, which the user must try to superimpose perfectly. The ghost image was introduced to solve issues related to keeping the user focused on the task while still making the game fun. Initially, visual suggestions were provided to help users find the right pose, but these were found to distract users from the painting and the game.

The app uses the Mediapipe library[5], which employs Tensorflow Lite technology, to detect facial landmarks in real-time, even on mobile devices [8]. The landmarks are used to compute the rotation angles of the user's head with respect to the camera, which are then compared to the pose of the face in the painting. The match is verified when the Euclidean distance of the 3D rotation angles is below a predefined threshold. A second check is then performed to compare the shapes of the three most significant features of the human face - eyes, eyebrows, and mouth - detected in both images. These features convey the seven universal facial expressions as identified by Ekman *et al.* [6]. Image matching and face-

---

[3] https://www.tensorflow.org/js.

[4] https://flask.palletsprojects.com/.

[5] https://google.github.io/mediapipe/.

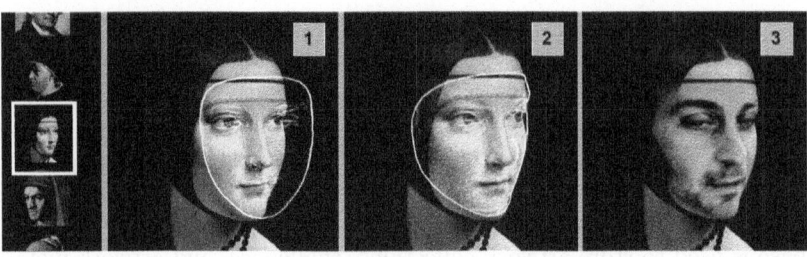

Fig. 2. Face-Fit App for museum installation. 1) trying to match the pose and expression of Leonardo's *Lady with an Ermine*. 2) Face matched. 3) Challenge completed: image generated.

swapping between the user's face and the painting is achieved through affine transformation to corresponding mesh triangles.

To adapt the style of the user's image to that of the painting, the app uses color correction based on statistical analysis by Reinhard *et al.* [14]. Once the user completes a challenge, they can obtain the generated images for sharing on social media and unlock descriptions of the matched artworks.

2.2   Smart Lens

Smart Lens (see Fig. 3) is a mobile application with the purpose to automatically recognize details of artworks. The user can employ his mobile phone (or tablet) as if it was a lens to inspect and analyze details of interest, that are recognized using a variety of computer vision techniques such as Content-based Image Retrieval (CBIR), classification, or object detection. As details are recognized, the app provides multimedia information about them. The app can be used as a smart guide to a collection or for a set of artworks that are of particular relevance and require thorough analysis. An additional benefit is that it is possible to collect anonymized information on the details and artworks of interest, providing curators with statistics and information on how the exhibitions are experienced by visitors.

The application allows the recognition of artwork details using three alternative methods: Content-based Image Retrieval (CBIR), classification, and object detection.

Content-based Image Retrieval (CBIR): the CBIR mechanism allows the recognition of the works and their details through the comparison between the visual features extracted from a dataset of images (the collection of details stored in a database, i.e., in the guide) and those obtained from the frame produced by the user's camera. To allow the recognition of the details of the works, the features have been extracted not only from the entire work but also from some of its parts obtained through a rigid subdivision.

Classification: this approach allows the recognition of the framed detail/work through a classification network on which a fine-tuning operation

Fig. 3. Smart-Lens App for smartphone. 1) Home. 2) The user frame the artwork with the device camera. Bounding boxes of the details and image details previews are shown. 3) After the selection of a detail the user can hace insights about it and listen to the audioguide.

has been performed on the paintings and their details present in the dataset. This requires retraining of the neural network, typically achievable even using CPUs. In this version, the classification of the entire frame is performed, and it is identified with the most probable class only if the degree of confidence is greater than a specific threshold for each image.

Object Detection: in this version, the recognition is entrusted to a network for object detection on which fine-tuning has been performed on the details of the work. This retraining is more expensive than the previous one and requires a GPU. In this case, only the details within the work are identified by taking the most probable bounding-box (i.e., a rectangle that most probably contains the object of interest) for each class provided that its degree of confidence exceeds a specific threshold for each detail.

The interface is entirely made in HTML5 and CSS and has a fluid behavior adapting to the size of any screen (tablet or smartphone). It is dynamically modified through JavaScript scripts that allow you to show the results of the matches with the images framed by the camera in real-time. In the camera view, the work or detail is framed, and the recognition operation is carried out in real-time. Tensorflow[6] networks were used for Retrieval and classification, and SSD/MobileNetV3 for Detection. For each work or detail, a textual description, the relative image, and any audio and video content are provided. If an audio

---

[6] https://www.tensorflow.org/.

file is not available, the application will allow the text-to-speech of the textual information shown on the screen, allowing, in any case, the use of the application as an audio guide.

The application can be used to perform artwork recognition, without considering the details. To use the application, a server is needed to host the backend and the web app itself. A QR code can be used to avoid typing the URL of the web app; this approach has been used during a set of exhibitions organized by the Museum of Cycladic Art in Athens, The Graz Museum and the Museum of the Bank of Cyprus Cultural Foundation, that used Smart lens to let visitors of the exhibitions to learn more in depth about details of selected artworks.

2.3   Multimedia Chatbot: Viola

Viola is a new mobile and web application that has been developed to provide a unique form of interaction through a chatbot on cultural heritage subjects. The web app allows users to ask questions about the content and context of artworks using natural language, either by typing or using voice-to-text input. This type of interaction has gained popularity recently with the emergence of chat systems like ChatGPT. This task can be considered as a form of Visual-Question Answering (VQA).

The chatbot has been designed to use two different types of backends: a version is based on GPT -based LLMs, while a second newer version employs Multimodal Language-and-Image Models (MLLMs). In particular we have developed a MLLM that extends a LLaVa model [11] with GLIP [10], and uses Retrieval Augmented Generation (RAG) to reduce hallucinations in the answer, so to produce scientifically accurate answers using curated artwork information, providing broader historical and cultural context.

To train the MLLM we have developed a new dataset, based on the VIS-COUNTH [1] dataset, that provides approximately 500K images of Italian cultural assets, including paintings, statues, finds, prints, and churches, along with 6.5M question-answer pairs. The issue with this dataset is that these questions are based on predefined templates applicable to different cultural assets, thus limiting the types of questions, and the answers often tend to repeat the same words used in the questions. Therefore training a MLLM on this dataset limits the model's ability to learn the context of the cultural assets. To address these limitations, we have thus created a new dataset developed from VISCOUNTH. In this novel dataset we have created about 55,000 question-answer pairs related to 2,890 images of cultural assets images. The question-answer pairs have been created using the capabilities of GPT-4.

An example of the app is shown in the figure below (Fig. 4). The app is web-based and consists of a backend system where the visual question answering system is executed to enable chat-based functionalities, and an HTML5-based frontend interface for end users.

The system can be easily reused by modifying the database information, including images of the gallery and textual information related to the visual and contextual aspects of the artworks. A backend functionality allows museum

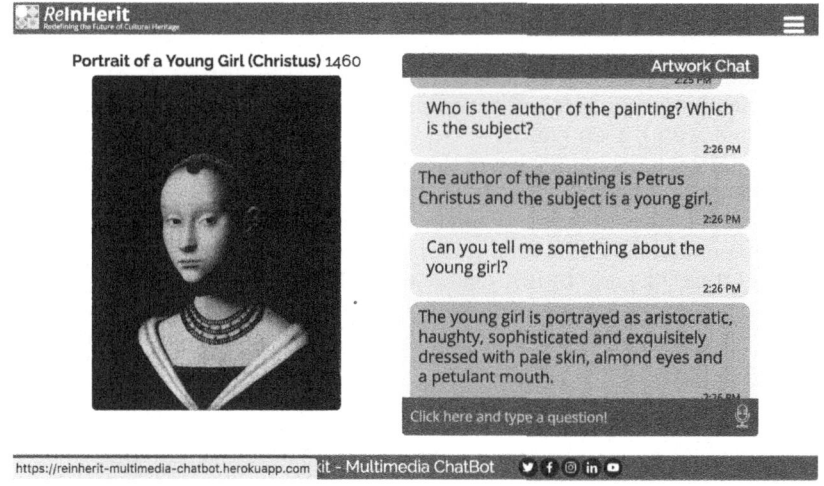

Fig. 4. Multimedia Chatbot Viola answering some questions about a portrait

curators to manage collections aand to add the descriptions used in the RAG functionality of the chatbot to ensure the accuracy o the answers provided by it. Furthermore, VIOLA can serve as a foundation for more complex systems, such as chat-based retrieval systems, serious games, or other interactions based on natural language processing.

3   Conclusions

In conclusion, the ReinHerit project and its Toolkit model confirm and reinforce the concept of an innovative interactive museum that focuses on visitors and the use of digital tools throughout the entire visitor journey. The museum is considered as a generator of unique and informal educational experiences that attract diverse audiences and stimulate their learning. Museum studies emphasized the potential of Digital Learning to offer museums new educational approaches, employing various digital technologies for content mediation, storytelling, and engagement with different visitor types and styles.

The ReinHerit Toolkit model focuses on visitor-centered interactive experiences facilitated by innovative digital tools, such as AI and computer vision. It emphasizes the promotion of emotional and playful digital learning and encourages visitors to use their own smartphones (BYOD) through web applications to enhance their interaction throughout the visitor experience.

Acknowledgments.. This work was partially supported by the European Commission under European Horizon 2020 Programme, grant number 101004545 - ReInHerit.

Disclosure of Interests. The authors have no competing interests.

References

1. Becattini, F., et al.: VISCOUNTH: a large-scale multilingual visual question answering dataset for cultural heritage. ACM Trans. Multimedia Comput. Commun. Appl. **19**(6), 1–20 (2023)
2. Bieszk-Stolorz, B., et al.: Impact of the availability of gamified e-guides on museum visit intention. Procedia Comput. Sci. **192**, 4358–4366 (2021)
3. Bonacini, E., Giaccone, S.C.: Gamification and cultural institutions in cultural heritage promotion: a successful example from Italy. Cultural Trends **31**(1), 3–22 (2022). https://doi.org/10.1080/09548963.2021.1910490
4. Del Bimbo, A.: Emotions in digital. In: of European Museum Organisations, N. (ed.) Emotions and Learning in Museums, pp. 24–30. Network of European Museum Organisations, online (2021)
5. Donadio, M.G., Principi, F., Ferracani, A., Bertini, M., Del Bimbo, A.: Engaging museum visitors with gamification of body and facial expressions. In: Proceedings of the 30th ACM International Conference on Multimedia, pp. 7000–7002. MM '22, Association for Computing Machinery, New York, NY, USA (2022). https://doi.org/10.1145/3503161.3547744
6. Ekman, P., et al.: Universals and cultural differences in the judgments of facial expressions of emotion. J. Pers. Soc. Psychol. **53**(4), 712 (1987)
7. Falk, J.H., Dierking, L.D.: The Museum Experience Revisited. Left Coast Press Inc. (2012)
8. Kartynnik, Y., Ablavatski, A., Grishchenko, I., Grundmann, M.: Real-time facial surface geometry from monocular video on mobile GPUS. In: CVPR Workshop on Computer Vision for Augmented and Virtual Reality 2019. Long Beach, CA (2019). https://arxiv.org/abs/1907.06724
9. Khan, I., Melro, A., Amaro, A.C., Oliveira, L.: Systematic review on gamification and cultural heritage dissemination. J. Digit. Media Interact. **3**(8), 19–41 (2020)
10. Li*, L.H., et al.: Grounded language-image pre-training. In: CVPR (2022)
11. Liu, H., Li, C., Li, Y., Lee, Y.J.: Improved baselines with visual instruction tuning (2023)
12. Nielsen, J.: Iterative user-interface design. Computer **26**(11), 32–41 (1993)
13. Paliokas, I., et al.: A gamified augmented reality application for digital heritage and tourism. Appl. Sci. **10**(21) (2020). https://doi.org/10.3390/app10217868, https://www.mdpi.com/2076-3417/10/21/7868
14. Reinhard, E., Adhikhmin, M., Gooch, B., Shirley, P.: Color transfer between images. IEEE Comput. Graphics Appl. **21**(5), 34–41 (2001)
15. Villaespesa, E., Murphy, O.: This is not an apple! Benefits and challenges of applying computer vision to museum collections. Museum Manag. Curatorship **36**(4), 362–383 (2021). https://doi.org/10.1080/09647775.2021.1873827

RoboInsight: Towards Deploying an Affordable Museum Guide Robot with Natural Language Processing, Image Processing and Interactive Engagement

Nusrat Jahan Shawon, Nizar Ahmed, Yasin Arafat, Mumtahina Arbi, Farzana Rahman, and Mohammad Shidujaman(✉) 📵

Department of Computer Science and Engineering, School of Engineering, Technology and Sciences, Independent University, Bangladesh (IUB), Dhaka, Bangladesh
shidujaman@iub.edu.bd

Abstract. In the contemporary era, museums serve as crucial repositories of cultural heritage, offering visitors a gateway to the past. As technology evolves, there is a growing need for innovative solutions that enhance the museum experience. This paper explores the history and significance of integrating robotics, image processing, and natural language processing in a museum guide bot. Our project "RoboInsight" presents a pioneering solution, combining line following capabilities for precise navigation, image processing for exhibit recognition, and multilingual chatbot functionality. Visitors can interact with the guide bot in Bangla or English, gaining insightful information about museum exhibits through seamless conversations. This innovation not only enriches the visitor experience but also provides an accessible and engaging platform for cultural exchange. Despite challenges, including navigation complexities and language nuances, the potential benefits are vast. The project not only addresses current museum-related needs but also sets the stage for future advancements in interactive cultural museum robot exploration.

Keywords: Museum Guide Robot · Natural language processing (NLP) · Image recognition · Human-museum robot interaction · Cultural preservation

1 Introduction

In the realm of cultural heritage, museums stand as bastions of our collective past, housing artifacts, artworks, and historical treasures that encapsulate the essence of human civilization. By leveraging cutting-edge techniques such as natural language processing and image processing to provide real-time information and interactive experiences, we aim to create a transformative museum experience that transcends traditional boundaries [1]. These repositories of culture serve as vital conduits for preserving and transmitting our shared heritage across generations, fostering a deeper understanding and appreciation of our roots. However, in today's fast-paced and technologically driven world, the

P. Zaphiris et al. (Eds.): HCII 2024, LNCS 15378, pp. 355–374, 2025.
https://doi.org/10.1007/978-3-031-76815-6_26

traditional museum experience faces challenges in engaging modern audiences effectively [4]. Static exhibits and audio guides, while informative, often fail to captivate visitors in a dynamic and interactive manner, especially those accustomed to digital experiences.

Against this backdrop, the integration of cutting-edge technologies [15] has emerged as a promising solution to revolutionize the museum-going experience. By leveraging robotics, artificial intelligence, and natural language processing, museums can offer visitors immersive and personalized journeys through their collections, transcending the constraints of physical space and time [16]. Our project, the Museum Guide Robot, epitomizes this vision of a technologically enhanced museum experience that seamlessly blends analog artifacts with digital technology to bridge the past with the present (Fig. 1).

Fig. 1. Visitors are being guided by guide robots (picture generated by AI)

In today's fast-paced digital age, where information is readily accessible at our fingertips, the Museum Guide Robot represents a beacon of innovation in the field of cultural preservation. With the Museum Guide Robot, we are not only creating a tool for navigating museum exhibits but also paving the way for a deeper understanding and appreciation of our shared history, art, and culture. Our project's motive is deeply rooted in the belief that technology has the power to revolutionize the way we interact with and understand our cultural heritage. By leveraging cutting-edge techniques such as natural language processing and image processing, we aim to create a transformative museum experience that transcends traditional boundaries [10]. Through the seamless integration of robotics and artificial intelligence, our project seeks to empower visitors to engage with museum collections in a more immersive, interactive, and personalized manner. The genesis of our project lies in recognizing the evolving needs and expectations of museum visitors in an increasingly interconnected world. Museums, traditionally guardians of cultural heritage, must adapt to remain relevant in the digital age. The Museum Guide Robot signifies a paradigm shift, merging robotics with artificial intelligence and natural language processing to offer a novel approach to exploring exhibits and interacting with artifacts. Moreover, it democratizes access to cultural heritage by catering to diverse needs and preferences, ensuring inclusivity for visitors with disabilities and enhancing engagement for all. This innovation inspires curiosity, sparks imagination, and fosters a lifelong appreciation for the arts and humanities [32, 33].

As we embark on this technological journey, we envision a future where the Museum Guide Robot becomes an indispensable companion for museum visitors worldwide [34]. Its seamless integration into museum environments, coupled with its ability to adapt and evolve over time, ensures its relevance and longevity in an ever-changing landscape [8]. By harnessing the power of technology to preserve, promote, and reinterpret our cultural heritage, we believe that the Museum Guide Robot has the potential to redefine the museum experience and shape the way we engage with our past, present, and future.

2 Literature Review

2.1 Receptionist Robots

In the realm of modern workplaces, the integration of artificial intelligence (AI) and robotics has led to the emergence of office robot receptionists, aiming to streamline visitor interactions, enhance workplace efficiency, and improve overall productivity. One notable endeavor in this field introduced ROBOR, a robotic receptionist designed by B G Ramya et al., which offers practical services while exhibiting engaging personality traits [1].

ROBOR's functionalities extend beyond traditional reception duties, encompassing visitor detection, interaction, message conveyance, and guest information management. These capabilities are made possible through the integration of advanced AI algorithms and sensor systems, highlighting the significance of natural behaviors and motions in fostering effective communication between humans and robots [1]. In a parallel development, a demonstration by Patrick Holthaus and Sven Wachsmuth showcased iCub's proficiency as a receptionist. Through interaction strategies such as spatial attention mechanisms, iCub effectively navigates visitor inquiries with speech and gestures, indicating the potential for humanoid robots to serve as receptionists in diverse workplace settings [2]. While both initiatives emphasize social competence and natural behaviors in human-robot interactions, they differ in implementation and underlying robotic platforms. The Roboceptionist Project focuses on practical solutions for robotic receptionists, while the iCub demonstration explores the capabilities of humanoid robots in receptionist roles [1, 2].

In addition to these advancements, recent efforts have introduced novel approaches for enhancing the functionality and adaptability of office robot receptionists. For instance, a study by researchers introduced innovative features in guide robots for shopping malls, emphasizing natural interaction with customers and effective provision of shopping-related information [13]. This expansion of functionalities underscores the evolving landscape of office robot receptionists, where versatility and adaptability are key drivers of success (Table 1).

2.2 Natural Language Processing (NLP) in Robotics and Humanoid Robots

In recent years, the integration of Natural Language Processing (NLP) with robotics has transformed human-robot interaction, paving the way for enhanced functionality and adaptability in various applications. Researchers have explored this intersection, aiming to bolster the capabilities of robots and refine their interactions with humans.

Table 1. Receptionist Robots

Papers	Objective	Findings	Structure
[1, 2]	Introduction of office robot receptionists aiming to streamline visitor interactions and enhance workplace efficiency	ROBOR and iCub demonstrate capabilities in visitor detection, interaction, and information management. Focus on practical solutions for robotic receptionists and exploration of humanoid robots in receptionist roles	
[30]	To determine if a humanoid robot enhances user experience as an automated receptionist compared to a smart display	No significant difference in user experience was found between the robot and the smart display, suggesting physical embodiment is not crucial for reception effectiveness	
[31]	To develop ASKA, a humanoid robot for university reception, enhancing user interaction with advanced speech recognition and natural gestures	ASKA achieved 90.9% word recognition for reception tasks, 78.9% for out-of-domain tasks, and a 61.7% correct response rate, effectively engaging users	

Recent advancements in language processing methodologies, spanning classical, machine learning, and deep learning approaches, have enabled significant progress in tasks like sentiment analysis and machine translation [3]. Simultaneously, innovative humanoid robots have emerged, showcasing proficiency in understanding, and communicating in multiple languages [4]. These robots leverage sophisticated voice and image recognition technologies, emphasizing the integration of natural language processing (NLP) into artificial intelligence (AI) robotics [5]. Personal assistant robot prototypes equipped with advanced speech recognition and NLP capabilities aim to enhance productivity in collaborative work settings [6]. Additionally, NLP-driven Computer-Based Test (CBT) guides, tailored for visually impaired students, provide real-time assistance during exams [7]. Proposed frameworks enhance Human-Robot Interaction (HRI) through proficient NLP modules capable of parsing multiple languages [8].

Recent research addresses energy and policy considerations for deep learning in NLP, emphasizing the environmental and financial costs associated with training state-of-the-art NLP models [13]. This study quantifies carbon emissions and cloud computer costs, advocating for efficient practices and equitable access to computational resources. An easy-to-use framework for state-of-the-art NLP, FLAIR, has been introduced, streamlining the training and distribution of sequence labeling, text classification, and language models [14]. FLAIR offers a unified interface for diverse word and document embeddings, facilitating experiment setup and model training (Table 2).

2.3 Human-Robot Interaction (HRI) and Social Bots

In recent years, Natural Language Processing (NLP) has emerged as a crucial technology for improving Human-Robot Interaction (HRI), enabling more seamless communication and task execution. One notable study introduces a comprehensive framework for enhancing HRI through an NLP module proficient in parsing both English and Turkish [9]. Leveraging statistical and rule-based strategies, including Combinatorial Categorial Grammar (CCG) parsing and Boxer for semantic interpretation, the NLP system extracts ontologies from natural language using Formal Concept Analysis (FCA) and Wordnet. The integration of visual feedback and the NLP module in a semantic-driven system architecture showcases a clear pathway for task execution in robotics, highlighting the importance of object tracking for robotic applications [25].

Another noteworthy application of NLP is demonstrated in the development of chatbot systems. One study presents an implementation of a chatbot system using AI and NLP, designed to assist users with various queries and tasks [10]. Leveraging NLP, the chatbot can understand and analyze user queries, directing them to relevant information effectively. The system utilizes Artificial Intelligence Markup Language (AIML) for natural conversation with users, enhancing user experience and engagement. Similarly, another study focuses on building a chatbot for healthcare using NLP, providing patients with 24/7 assistance for scheduling appointments, getting medical advice, and more [11]. By leveraging NLP techniques, the chatbot can make natural communication with users via text or voice interactions, offering personalized support based on a patient's medical history and treatment recommendations [27, 28].

In the context of college inquiries, an intelligent college enquiry bot using NLP and deep learning techniques is introduced [12]. This web application utilizes NLP and Long Short-Term Memory (LSTM) networks & Recurrent Neural Network (RNN) to interact with users, aiding with admissions, fee structures, department details, and more. The incorporation of deep learning techniques enhances the chatbot's ability to understand and respond to user queries accurately (Table 3).

2.4 Museum Guide Robots and Cultural Heritage Preservation

In recent years, advancements in robotics and natural language processing (NLP) have significantly impacted cultural heritage preservation and museum guide services. These innovations aim to enhance visitor experiences, provide accessibility, and promote engagement with cultural artifacts.

Table 2. NLP in Robotics and Humanoid Robots

Papers	Objective	Findings	Structure
[8]	NLP integrated with robotics improves how robots understand and respond to human language, using methods from sentiment analysis, machine translation, and other NLP tasks	Proficient humanoid robots communicate in multiple languages Advanced personal assistant robots with speech recognition and NLP capabilities developed Innovative NLP-driven Computer-Based Test (CBT) guides for visually impaired students introduced Comprehensive frameworks proposed for enhancing Human-Robot Interaction (HRI) through NLP Energy and policy considerations addressed for deep learning in NLP Introduction of FLAIR framework for state-of-the-art NLP	
[23]	The paper aims to survey recent literature on chatbot development, focusing on AI advancements and deep learning models, with a specific interest in healthcare assistance	The paper proposes a functional architecture for intelligent chatbots in healthcare, emphasizing training mechanisms to overcome current limitations and improve patient care, symptom analysis, and medical education	
[7]	Introduces an NLP-based Computer-Based Test guide to improve exam accessibility for visually impaired students through real-time assistance	The system effectively facilitates accessible testing, achieving high precision and recall scores. It enhances the testing experience for visually impaired students, minimizing malpractices	

The MAGICAL project, which integrates GPT-4 into museum guide services, aims to create personalized museum experiences by categorizing instructions and leveraging

Table 3. Human-Robot Interaction (HRI) and Social Bots

Papers	Objective	Findings	Structure
[9]	Utilization of NLP for improving human-robot interaction and developing chatbot systems in various contexts	Introduction of comprehensive frameworks for enhancing HRI through NLP modules proficient in parsing multiple languages. Implementation of chatbot systems using AI and NLP for healthcare and college inquiries	
[17]	Test neural networks' capability to guide robots in urban settings with GPS and compass sensors amid moving obstacles	Specific neural connections enable robots to swiftly avoid collisions and reach targets in real-world environments	
[12]	This paper presents an intelligent chatbot for college inquiries, employing NLP and LSTM networks to efficiently handle various user queries related to admissions and college affairs	The chatbot achieves nearly 99% accuracy, reducing staff workload and response time, while offering potential for future student engagement enhancements with AI/ML/DL technologies	

multilingual capabilities [16]. Additionally, the development of mobile robots tailored for visually impaired individuals represents a significant step forward in enhancing accessibility within museum settings, employing innovative navigation methods and obstacle avoidance techniques [17]. Furthermore, research on emotion detection for social robots based on NLP transformers and emotion ontology holds promise for deepening human-robot interactions in museums, enabling robots to detect and respond to visitors' emotional cues [18, 19].

The integration of NLP techniques and robotics in museum guide services and cultural heritage preservation signifies a transformative shift towards enhanced accessibility, engagement, and inclusivity. These advancements hold promise for creating immersive and enriching experiences for visitors, while also contributing to the preservation and dissemination of cultural heritage for future generations [20–22] (Table 4).

Table 4. Museum Guide Robots and Cultural Heritage Preservation

Papers	Objective	Findings	Structure
[21]	Advancements in robotics and NLP impacting cultural heritage preservation and museum guide services	Introduction of large language models (GPT-4) as personalized museum guides. Development of guide mobile robots tailored for visually impaired individuals. Research on emotion detection for social robots based on NLP transformers and emotion ontology	
[24]	Develop an automated WhatsApp responder using Python, ChatterBot, and NLTK to improve communication efficiency	The Chatbot provides realistic responses using NLP and machine learning, with potential for improved accuracy and scalability	
[26]	Develop an automated, gamified platform using semantic web technologies to enhance museum visitor engagement with minimal maintenance	The platform effectively automates question generation, increasing visitor interaction and showing potential for broader application in cultural institutions	

2.5 Exploring Existing Museum Guide Robots

In the realm of robotics, various models serve distinct purposes, employing advanced technologies and sensor systems for efficient operation. Pepper, designed as a receptionist robot and personalized service assistant, integrates ROS (Robot Operating System) and Human Interaction Architecture for seamless human-robot interaction, facilitated by ultrasound transmitters and receivers, laser sensors, and obstacle detectors. ASIMO (Advanced Step in Innovative Mobility), renowned for its independent walking and stair climbing capabilities, as well as gesture recognition and voice interaction, relies on advanced motion control algorithms and an array of sensors including floor surface sensors, ultrasonic sensors, joint-angle sensors, and force sensors. EMIEW3 (Excellent Mobility and Interactive Existence as Workmate 3) specializes in actual service tasks and autonomous travel, boasting voice and image recognition alongside remote brain configuration, supported by similar sensor technology to ASIMO. Promobot, tailored for customer service and marketing, employs navigation and face recognition algorithms along with machine learning techniques, utilizing lidar sensors, depth cameras, and touch sensors for operation. Lindsey, facilitating campus tours and visitor assistance, utilizes navigation algorithms, speech recognition, and object recognition, complemented by depth cameras, touch sensors, and infrared sensors [29].

On the other hand, Temi V3 serves as a personal assistant and telepresence device, integrating navigation algorithms and natural language processing for seamless communication, supported by depth cameras, touch sensors, and infrared sensors. Persephone, a tour guide robot, employs similar technology to Temi V3, focusing on navigation and speech recognition for guiding purposes. Lastly, Robohon offers personal assistance, entertainment, and educational services, incorporating speech and gesture recognition, as well as emotion recognition algorithms, utilizing nine-axis sensors and illuminance sensors for enhanced interaction (Table 5).

Table 5. Exploring Existing Museum Guide Robots

Name	Application	Algorithm	Sensor	Structure
ASIMO (Advanced Step in Innovative Mobility)	Independent Walking and Stair Climbing, Gesture Recognition and Voice Interaction, IC Communication Technology	advanced motion control algorithms	Floor Surface Sensors, Ultrasonic Sensors, Joint-Angle Sensors, and Force Sensor	
Pepper	Receptionist Robot, Personalized Service	ROS Integration, Human Interaction Architecture	Ultrasound Transmitters and Receivers, Laser Sensors, Obstacle Detectors	
EMIEW3 (Excellent Mobility and Interactive Existence as Workmate 3)	Actual Service Intent, Autonomous Travel Technology, Voice and Image Recognition, Remote Brain Configuration		Floor Surface Sensors, Ultrasonic Sensors, Joint-Angle Sensors, and Force Sensor	

(*continued*)

Table 5. (*continued*)

Name	Application	Algorithm	Sensor	Structure
Promobot	Customer Service, Information and Guidance, Entertainment and Marketing	Navigation Algorithm, Face Recognition Algorithm, Speech Recognition and NLP, Machine Learning Algorithms	Lidar Sensors, Depth Cameras, Touch Sensors	
Lindsey	Campus Tours, Visitor Assistance	Navigation Algorithm, Speech Recognition and NLP, Object Recognition	Depth Cameras, Touch Sensors, Infrared Sensors	
Temi V3	Personal Assistant, Telepresence	Navigation Algorithm, Speech Recognition and Natural Language Processing (NLP), Speech Recognition and Natural Language Processing (NLP)	Depth Cameras, Touch Sensors, Infrared Sensors	
Persephone	Tour Guide	Navigation Algorithm, Speech Recognition and Natural Language Processing (NLP),	Depth Cameras, Touch Sensors, Infrared Sensor	

Embarking on a journey through AI, NLP, and robotics reveals remarkable advancements in chatbots, human-robot interaction, and museum guide robots. The fusion of AI and NLP has empowered intelligent agents to navigate complex inquiries in various fields. Moreover, humanoid robots now possess unprecedented abilities to comprehend and engage in human dialogue, ushering in a new era of seamless interaction. However, continued research and innovation are crucial to overcome challenges and shape a future where intelligent technologies enrich human experiences.

3   Methodology (Explanations with Block Diagrams)

Embarking on a journey to revolutionize museum experiences, the development of our museum guide bot follows a meticulously planned trajectory, navigating through the realms of design, implementation, testing, and validation. Picture this, a cutting-edge creation poised to seamlessly navigate the labyrinthine corridors of art and history, armed with the prowess of line following robotics, the discerning eye of image processing, the linguistic finesse of natural language processing (NLP), and the charm of multilingual communication capabilities.

Our project's designed system is translated into a functional prototype. Equipped with sensors and actuators for navigation and interaction with museum visitors, the museum guide bot incorporates line following algorithms to enable autonomous navigation along predefined paths to users requesting assistance. Additionally, it integrates image processing capabilities to recognize and analyze museum artifacts or exhibits based on user queries. NLP modules are integrated into the museum guide bot to facilitate natural and intuitive communication with museum visitors. Supporting both Bangla and English languages, the bot enables users to interact in their preferred language, understanding queries, providing relevant information about exhibits, and engaging in general conversations (Fig. 2).

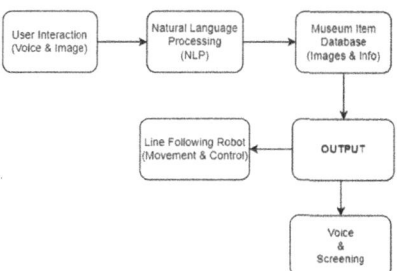

Fig. 2. Block Diagram of the System

In Fig. 3, we can see it's composed of interconnected components essential for the functionality of the museum guide bot. Visitors interact with the bot through voice commands or image uploads, initiating a process where the bot utilizes natural language understanding (NLP) techniques for voice queries and image descriptions. The heart of our guide bot lies in a line-following robot, autonomously navigating predefined museum tracks with sensors and actuators, facilitated by sophisticated control algorithms. The NLP module enables the bot to comprehend both Bangla and English languages, extracting relevant keywords to retrieve specific information from a comprehensive museum artifact database. Upon processing user queries, the bot generates informative responses containing historical facts and intriguing anecdotes, conveyed audibly and visually through voice and screen output.

Once the implementation phase concludes, rigorous testing and validation procedures take center stage to ascertain the museum guide bot's functionality, reliability, and user-friendliness. This entails subjecting the bot to a battery of tests, ranging from simulated scenarios to real-world trials within the dynamic environs of museum settings, thereby evaluating its performance across diverse situations and user interactions. Throughout the testing phase, an invaluable stream of feedback flows in from museum visitors, offering invaluable insights into the bot's performance. This feedback becomes the bedrock for iterative refinements, where the bot's responses are fine-tuned, bolstering its ability to accurately recognize exhibits, enhancing its language understanding capabilities, and optimizing its navigation efficiency to ensure seamless traversal through the museum's labyrinthine halls.

With each iteration, the museum guide bot evolves, imbibing the wisdom gleaned from real-world encounters to better serve its patrons. Upon successful testing and validation, the bot earns its rightful place within the museum's hallowed halls, where it stands as a beacon of technological prowess, ready to enrich the visitor experience with its wealth of knowledge and unparalleled guidance. As it takes its place amidst the treasures of human history and art, meticulous maintenance procedures are put in place to uphold its operational integrity, ensuring uninterrupted service to museumgoers. Moreover, a roadmap for future updates and enhancements is charted, poised to seamlessly integrate new features, and adapt to the ever-changing landscape of museum exhibits and visitor needs.

4   System Design (Hardware and Software Architecture)

Embark on a journey into the heart of our innovation as we unveil the intricate design and development of our Museum Guide Robot, "RoboInsight." Representing a significant advancement in interactive museum experiences, RoboInsight seamlessly integrates cutting-edge hardware components with sophisticated software functionalities. Leveraging advanced image processing algorithms, natural language processing (NLP) techniques, and intuitive user interaction modules, RoboInsight offers visitors a seamless and enriching journey through the museum's exhibits. This fusion of art and engineering redefines the museum experience, fostering a deeper appreciation for the collections with informative commentary and historical context. Our quest for innovation extends to the user-friendly structure of our prototype, meticulously designed to engage visitors while enhancing their understanding and appreciation of the exhibits. Through the fusion of state-of-the-art hardware and intelligent software, RoboInsight transforms visitor engagement within the hallowed halls of cultural heritage, exemplifying the harmonious synergy between art and engineering.

After careful consideration, we divided the design into three parts: the head, body, and lower part. In Fig. 4, we can see the head component stands out as the primary interface, housing the display and camera to provide users with a seamless visual experience. Meanwhile, the body segment contains the central processing unit, comprising the Raspberry Pi, along with speakers, a microphone, and various hardware components crucial

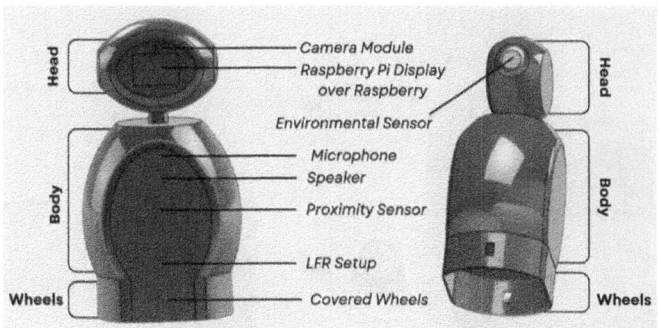

Fig. 3. 3D Design of RoboInsight

for intelligent processing and communication. Finally, the lower part integrates motor drivers, motors, and wiring, facilitating the robot's mobility as it navigates the museum's diverse terrain, ensuring visitors can engage with exhibits effortlessly. This thoughtful integration of hardware and software components underscores our commitment to enhancing visitor experiences within cultural institutions.

4.1 Hardware Architecture

Our Museum Guide robot represents the pinnacle of technology in cultural engagement, boasting a meticulously crafted hardware architecture tailored for museum environments. Powered by the versatile Raspberry Pi 4B, it orchestrates navigation, interaction, and data processing efficiently. Integrated seamlessly, a high-resolution camera module enables precise object detection and recognition within exhibits. Bolstered by advanced line-following mechanisms and a four-wheel drive system, the robot maneuvers gracefully around obstacles, guided by integrated IR and proximity sensors. These sensors facilitate real-time detection of exhibit boundaries and visitor engagement, ensuring a safe and dynamic museum experience.

Central to our hardware architecture is the inclusion of a comprehensive audiovisual interface, comprising built-in speakers and a microphone system. This setup empowers the robot to deliver immersive audio narratives, enriching the visitor experience with informative commentary, historical anecdotes, and interactive prompts tailored to each exhibit. Leveraging an LM386 audio amplifier module, the robot ensures crystal-clear communication even amidst bustling museum environments, guaranteeing every visitor a seamless and enriching interaction (Table 6).

This table provides a concise overview of each component of "RoboInsight", including its specific role and how it integrates into the robot's system.

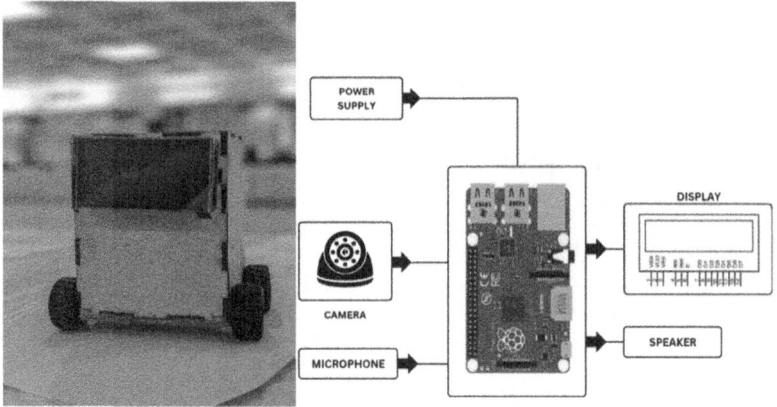

Fig. 4. First Prototype and Internal Hardware Structure of ROBOINSIGHT

Table 6. Component List.

Component	Specification	Function	Price (Taka)	Price (USD)
Raspberry Pi 4B	-	Central processing unit	11994	$143.40
Camera (Raspberry Pi camera module v2 - 8 Megapixel, 1080p)	Raspberry Pi camera module v2 - 8 Megapixel, 1080p	Visual data acquisition	4690	$56.07
Display LED (3.5-inch Raspberry Pi display)	3.5-inch Raspberry Pi display	Visual interface	3800	$45.24
Proximity sensor (Sharp GP2YOA21YKOF Analog distance sensor)	Sharp GP2YOA21YKOF Analog distance sensor	Visitor detection/navigation	682	$8.13
Environmental sensor (DHT22 Temperature and Humidity sensor)	DHT22 Temperature and Humidity sensor	Environmental monitoring	590	$7.03
IR sensor (QTR-8RC Reflectance sensor array)	QTR-8RC Reflectance sensor array	Obstacle detection	1490	$17.77

(continued)

Table 6. (*continued*)

Component	Specification	Function	Price (Taka)	Price (USD)
Microphone (Adafruit electret microphone amplifier)	Adafruit electret microphone amplifier	Audio input	1016	$12.10
Amplifier (LM386 Audio amplifier module)	LM386 Audio amplifier module	Audio output enhancement	100	$1.19
Speaker	-	Audio output	300	$3.57
Motor Driver	-	Motor control	1000	$11.90
Wheels	-	Mobility	1500	$17.86
Motor	-	Mobility	3600	$42.86
Wires	-	Connectivity	500	$5.95
Total	-		31262	$372.50

4.2 Software Architecture

Our museum guide bot's software architecture is a meticulously designed suite of modules crafted to facilitate information processing, decision-making, and seamless interaction with visitors. These components synergize with our hardware infrastructure, ensuring a cohesive and immersive user experience. Key modules include the Natural Language Processing (NLP) module, which interprets queries in Bangla and English, the Image Processing module, employing OpenCV and deep learning for artifact analysis, the Database Management module, facilitating efficient retrieval of historical facts, and the Output Generation module, providing auditory and visual feedback through text-to-speech synthesis and visual display. Our bot stands as a testament to innovation, seamlessly blending cutting-edge technology with cultural heritage to deliver personalized assistance and captivating narratives, heralding a transformative era in museum exploration where curiosity meets technology and knowledge intertwines with discovery.

Speech to Text & Speech (English & Bangla). Experience the convenience of speech-to-text technology, seamlessly integrated into our museum guide bot. This innovative feature simplifies your museum visit by instantly transcribing your spoken questions into text responses. Engage with exhibits effortlessly as you receive real-time information in both textual and voice formats, making your cultural experience more interactive and informative. Whether you prefer reading or listening, our system ensures that you can access information with ease, enhancing your overall museum exploration (Fig. 5).

Image Detection and Information Delivery into Text & Speech: to Text & Speech (English & Bangla). Step into a new era of museum exploration with our innovative guide bot, poised to transform the visitor experience. By harnessing cutting-edge image processing technology, our system enables effortless access to detailed exhibit information with just a snapshot. When you take a picture of an artifact, our system detects and

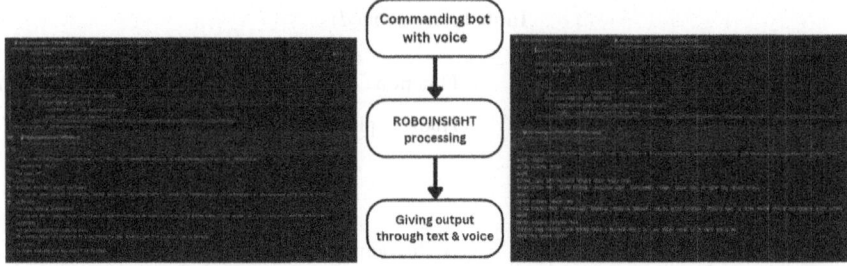

Fig. 5. Speech to Text Output from Serial Monitor and Speech output in Real-Time (In English & Bangla)

analyzes the image, providing instant spoken descriptions of what you're seeing. This breakthrough not only breaks down language barriers but also enhances engagement by offering personalized and immersive experiences (Fig. 6).

Fig. 6. Image to Text & Speech

This advancement marks a significant leap forward in museum accessibility and interaction. By converting visual information into spoken narratives, our system ensures that every visitor, regardless of language fluency or visual impairment, can fully appreciate and engage with the exhibits. It's a seamless and enriching experience for all, bringing cultural heritage to life in a whole new way.

Chatbot System with API. Experience the convenience of conversational interaction with our museum guide bot, which adeptly handles queries in both Bangla and English. This system embodies innovation, offering a seamless blend of API integration and custom data processing to deliver accurate and engaging responses tailored to visitor inquiries (Fig. 7).

By organizing the content into two distinct sections, we provide clarity on the functionalities and features of each system within the museum guide bot. This approach ensures that visitors can fully appreciate the capabilities of both the image detection and information delivery system, as well as the chatbot system, fostering a memorable and enriching museum experience.

Fig. 7. Chatbot System with API

5 Discussion and Future Works

5.1 Discussion

The ROBOINSIGHT project represents a significant leap forward in the integration of robotics and artificial intelligence within the museum context. By leveraging line-following capabilities for navigation, advanced image processing for exhibit recognition, and multilingual chatbot functionality, ROBOINSIGHT has shown how technology can enhance the cultural and educational experience of museum visitors.

One of the core strengths of ROBOINSIGHT is its ability to cater to a diverse audience by providing information in both Bangla and English. This multilingual support not only makes the exhibits accessible to a broader demographic but also promotes cultural exchange and understanding. The interactive nature of the bot, facilitated through natural language processing, ensures that visitors engage with the exhibits in a more meaningful and personalized manner.

However, the project is not without its challenges. Navigational complexities within the dynamic and often crowded environment of a museum pose significant hurdles. The accuracy of line-following technology must be continuously refined to ensure the bot can traverse the museum effectively without disruption. Furthermore, the nuances of language processing, especially in a multilingual setting, require sophisticated algorithms to interpret and respond to user queries accurately. Addressing these challenges is crucial for the seamless operation of ROBOINSIGHT.

The current hardware used in ROBOINSIGHT, while functional, presents another area for potential improvement. As technology advances, more robust and efficient hardware solutions could be adopted to enhance the bot's performance, reliability, and overall user experience. The integration of cutting-edge technologies will be instrumental in overcoming existing limitations and paving the way for more sophisticated applications.

5.2 Future Work

The future of ROBOINSIGHT is promising, with several key areas identified for further development and enhancement:

Integration of ChatGPT API. One of the immediate future plans is to incorporate the ChatGPT API to minimize response times. By utilizing this advanced natural language processing tool, ROBOINSIGHT can offer quicker and more accurate responses to visitor inquiries, thereby enhancing the overall interaction experience. The ChatGPT API's ability to handle complex queries and provide nuanced answers will significantly improve the bot's conversational capabilities.

Upgrading Hardware Systems. To address the current limitations related to hardware, future iterations of ROBOINSIGHT will explore the use of more advanced and efficient hardware components. This includes better processors, enhanced sensors, and more reliable power sources. Upgrading the hardware will not only improve the bot's operational efficiency but also enable the incorporation of additional features that require higher computational power.

Cost-Effectiveness. Another critical aspect of future development is making ROBOINSIGHT more cost-effective. Reducing production and maintenance costs without compromising on quality and functionality will be essential for widespread adoption. Exploring alternative materials, optimizing the design, and leveraging economies of scale are potential strategies to achieve this goal.

Expanding Language Capabilities. While ROBOINSIGHT currently supports Bangla and English, expanding its language capabilities to include other regional and international languages will further broaden its accessibility. This will involve training the natural language processing system on a wider array of linguistic datasets and refining its ability to understand and respond to different dialects and accents.

Interactive and Personalized Experiences. Future enhancements could also focus on creating more personalized visitor experiences. By incorporating machine learning algorithms, ROBOINSIGHT could analyze visitor interactions to provide tailored recommendations and insights, making each visit unique and engaging.

While ROBOINSIGHT has already made significant strides in enhancing the museum experience, there is substantial potential for further innovation and improvement. By addressing current challenges and focusing on the outlined future work, ROBOINSIGHT can continue to evolve, offering even more robust, efficient, and engaging solutions for cultural and educational exploration.

6 Conclusion

The development of the museum guide robot, RoboInsight, represents a significant step forward in redefining the visitor experience within cultural institutions. Through a combination of advanced hardware components and sophisticated software functionalities, RoboInsight has demonstrated its ability to enhance engagement, foster learning, and provide personalized assistance to museum visitors. The project's results and analysis have shown the robot's proficiency in navigation accuracy, interactive engagement, and operational efficiency, as well as its potential for further improvements in exhibit recognition accuracy and language support. Looking ahead, future work in enhancing the robot's artificial intelligence capabilities, integrating augmented reality and virtual reality experiences, expanding multilingual support, and fostering collaboration with cultural institutions and researchers holds promise for further elevating the impact of museum guide robots in shaping the future of interactive museum experiences. By continuing to innovate and evolve, RoboInsight and similar projects pave the way for a more immersive, accessible, and educational journey through cultural heritage for visitors worldwide.

References

1. Ramya, B.G., Chaitra, N., Rai, P., Murali, A.: An office robot receptionist using artificial intelligence (2019)
2. Holthaus, P., Wachsmuth, S.: The receptionist robot. In: Proceedings of the 2014 ACM/IEEE international conference on Human-robot interaction , p. 329 (2014)
3. Sen, O., et al.: Bangla natural language processing: a comprehensive analysis of classical, machine learning, and deep learning-based methods. IEEE Access **10**, 38999–39044 (2022)
4. Akib, A.A.S., Ferdous, M.F., Biswas, M., Khondokar, H.M.: Artificial intelligence humanoid bongo robot in Bangladesh. In: 2019 1st International Conference on Advances in Science, Engineering and Robotics Technology (ICASERT), pp. 1–6. IEEE (2019, May)
5. Saini, V., Joseph, N.: Artificial intelligence in robotics using NLP (2022)
6. Valerie, M., Salamah, I.: Innovative personal assistance: speech recognition and NLP-driven robot prototype. Jurnal Nasional Teknik Elektro (2023)
7. Tubo, F.N., Onyenwe, I.E., Asogwa, D.C.: Development of an NLP-driven computer-based test guide for visually impaired students
8. Kilicaslan, Y., Tuna, G.: An NLP-based approach for improving human-robot interaction. J. Artif. Intell. Soft Comput. Res. **3**(3), 189–200 (2013)
9. Macaluso, I., et al.: Experiences with CiceRobot, a museum guide cognitive robot. In: AI* IA 2005: Advances in Artificial Intelligence: 9th Congress of the Italian Association for Artificial Intelligence, Milan, Italy, 21-32 September 2005. Proceedings 9, pp. 474–482. Springer, Heidelberg (2005)
10. Lalwani, T., Bhalotia, S., Pal, A., Rathod, V., Bisen, S.: Implementation of a Chatbot System using AI and NLP. Int. J. Innov. Res. Comput. Sci. Technol. (IJIRCST) **6**(3) (2018)
11. Kevin, B., VIkin, B., Nair, M.: Building a Chatbot for healthcare using NLP. Authorea Preprints (2023)
12. Nikhath, A.K., Rab, M.A., Bharadwaja, N.V., Reddy, L.G., Saicharan, K., Reddy, C.V.M.: An intelligent college enquiry bot using NLP and deep learning-based techniques. In: 2022 International Conference for Advancement in Technology (ICONAT), pp. 1–6. IEEE (2022)
13. Kanda, T., Shiomi, M., Miyashita, Z., Ishiguro, H., Hagita, N.: An affective guide robot in a shopping mall. In: Proceedings of the 4th ACM/IEEE international conference on Human robot interaction (pp. 173–180) (2009)
14. Strubell, E., Ganesh, A., McCallum, A.: Energy and policy considerations for deep learning in NLP. arXiv preprint arXiv:1906.02243 (2019)
15. Wang, K.J., Zheng, C.Y., Shidujaman, M., Wairagkar, M., von Mohr, M.: Jean Joseph v2. 0 (REmotion): make remote emotion touchable, seeable and thinkable by direct brain-to-brain telepathy neurohaptic interface empowered by generative adversarial network. In: 2020 IEEE International Conference on Systems, Man, and Cybernetics (SMC), pp. 3488–3493. IEEE (2020)
16. Shidujaman, M., Samani, H., Raayatpanah, M.A., Mi, H., Premachandra, C.: Towards deploying the wireless charging robots in smart environments. In: 2018 International Conference on System Science and Engineering (ICSSE), pp. 1–6. IEEE (2018)
17. Capi, G., Kaneko, S., Hua, B.: Neural network-based guide robot navigation: an evolutionary approach. Procedia Comput. Sci. **76**, 74–79 (2015)

18. Zhang, B., Okutsu, M., Ochiai, R., Tayama, M., Lim, H.O.: Research on design and motion control of a considerate guide mobile robot for visually impaired people. IEEE Access **11**, 62820–62828 (2023)

19. Trichopoulos, G., Konstantakis, M., Alexandridis, G., Caridakis, G.: Large language models as recommendation systems in museums. Electronics **12**(18), 3829 (2023)

20. Mehzabin, K.M., Islam, M.Z., Nur, M.A., Shidujaman, M., Samani, H., Mi, H.: Roopkotha: A companion robot for enhancing interactive storytelling with natural interaction. In: 2024 International Conference on Image Processing and Robotics (ICIPRoB), pp. 1–6. IEEE (2024)

21. Hellou, M., Lim, J., Gasteiger, N., Jang, M., Ahn, H.S.: Technical methods for social robots in museum settings: an overview of the literature. Int. J. Soc. Robot. **14**(8), 1767–1786 (2022)

22. jobaida, n., et al.: design and Development of a Low-Cost Voice Interactive Children Educational Robot 'TINY' with natural language processing. In: 2024 International Conference on Image Processing and Robotics (ICIPRoB), pp. 1–6. IEEE (2024)

23. Ayanouz, S., Abdelhakim, B.A., Benhmed, M.: A smart Chatbot architecture-based NLP and machine learning for health care assistance. In: Proceedings of the 3rd international conference on networking, information systems & security, pp. 1–6 (2020)

24. Nagender, Y., Patil, K.H.: Whatsapp auto responder using natural language processing and AI. Int. J. Comput. Eng. Technol. **8**(5), 15–22 (2017)

25. Rousi, R., Kolari, S., Shidujaman, M.: Beauty in interaction: a framework for social robot aesthetics (Pandemic Edition). In: Robotics for Pandemics, pp. 19–62. Chapman and Hall/CRC (2021)

26. López-Martínez, A., Carrera, Á., Iglesias, C.A.: Empowering museum experiences applying gamification techniques based on linked data and smart objects. Appl. Sci. **10**(16), 5419 (2020)

27. Zidianakis, E., et al.: The invisible museum: a user-centric platform for creating virtual 3D exhibitions with VR support. Electronics **10**(3), 363 (2021)

28. Iio, T., Satake, S., Kanda, T., Hayashi, K., Ferreri, F., Hagita, N.: Human-like guide robot that proactively explains exhibits. Int. J. Soc. Robot. **12**, 549–566 (2020)

29. Duguleană, M., Briciu, V.A., Duduman, I.A., Machidon, O.M.: A virtual assistant for natural interactions in museums. Sustainability **12**(17), 6958 (2020)

30. Wolter, R., Hindriks, K.V., Samur, D., Jonker, C.M.: A study on automated receptionists in a real-world scenario. In: Advances in Practical Applications of Agents, Multi-Agent Systems, and Trustworthiness. The PAAMS Collection: 18th International Conference, PAAMS 2020, L'Aquila, Italy, October 7–9, 2020, Proceedings 18, pp. 340–352. Springer International Publishing (2020)

31. Lee, M.K., Kiesler, S., Forlizzi, J.: Receptionist or information kiosk: how do people talk with a robot? In: Proceedings of the 2010 ACM conference on Computer supported cooperative work, pp. 31–40 (2010)

32. Li, M., et al.: Generative AI for sustainable design: a case study in design education practices. In: International Conference on Human-Computer Interaction, pp. 59–78. Springer Nature, Cham (2024)

33. Velentza, A.M., Ioannidis, S., Georgakopoulou, N., Shidujaman, M., Fachantidis, N.: Educational robot European cross-cultural design. In Human-Computer Interaction. Interaction Techniques and Novel Applications: Thematic Area, HCI 2021, Held as Part of the 23rd HCI International Conference, HCII 2021, Virtual Event, July 24–29, 2021, Proceedings, Part II 23, pp. 341–353. Springer International Publishing (2021).

34. Liu, J., Sun, G., Shidujaman, M.: Integrating virtual and real: a holistic framework for mixed reality interactive design in museum exhibitions. In: International Conference on Human-Computer Interaction, pp. 367–387. Springer Nature, Cham (2024)

Sentiment Classification Model for Landscapes

Nelson Silva⑩, Pedro J. S. Cardoso⑩, and João M. F. Rodrigues$^{(\boxtimes)}$⑩

NOVA LINCS & ISE, Universidade do Algarve, 8005-139 Faro, Portugal
{a60678,pcardoso,jrodrig}@ualg.pt

Abstract. Automatic sentimental evaluations for the outdoors, whether they are man-made or natural environments, can provide valuable insight for applications like tourism, marketing, and urban planning, because they help to learn how people perceive, appreciate, and engage with the surroundings. Often, these places are portrayed in social media posts accompanied by a written description that may or may not convey the same emotion as the image. In this work, we study the automatic sentimental evaluations of pairs of photos and texts, where the depicted images are from natural environments – landscapes. During the analysis, the sentiments derived from the image and text are evaluated independently. These individual sentiments are then merged to form the overall sentiment associated with the pair. The analysis provides the sentiment (positive, negative, or neutral) associated with the image, the text, the combination of the image and the text, and the disparity between the sentiments represented in the two. Overall, an ensemble of deep-learning models was used for images, and an ensemble of machine-learning models for text and for the combination of images and text, the latter applied if the disparity justifies that ensemble. According to preliminary findings, for the landscape photo-text combination, in our private dataset, we achieved an accuracy of 78.75%.

Keywords: Sentiment Analyses · Affective Computing · Human-Centred AI · Outdoor Images sentiments · Image-text sentiments

1 Introduction

The goal of Human-Centered Artificial Intelligence (HCAI) [1] is to create technologies that assist people in carrying out various daily tasks, while also advancing human values, such as rights, fairness, and dignity [1]. By promoting humans' autonomy, well-being, and control over future technologies, HCAI also seeks to strike a balance between human control and (full) automation, as an interdisciplinary field combining computer science, psychology, and neuroscience. In a related field, Affective Computing (AC) integrates the disciplines of emotion recognition and sentiment analysis, being supported by various types of physical information, such as text, audio (speech), visual data (e.g., facial expression, body posture, or environment), or physiological signals (e.g., EEGs – electroencephalography or ECGs – electrocardiograms). Within this framework, AC can be built on either unimodal or multimodal data [2].

P. Zaphiris et al. (Eds.): HCII 2024, LNCS 15378, pp. 375–393, 2025.
https://doi.org/10.1007/978-3-031-76815-6_27

The applications of HCAI and AC are numerous. For instance, a machine, in *lato sensu*, should be developed to collaborate or learn to work with humans, like an inter-personal connection. However, feelings and sentiments are essential to interpersonal connections, and those must be integrated into any machine that interacts with humans.

On the other hand, social media platforms have a growing importance today, influencing people to visit places, search and buy products, change lifestyles, change their way of thinking about a subject etc. Within the volume of daily posts on many of those platforms, the necessity and opportunity to analyse and understand the emotion and sentiment that those messages carry have emerged. Video, photos, and short texts are the fastest and simplest type of publication to attract *users to click*, buy, and read about a particular subject or product, which is why social networks, such as Instagram or X (previously Twitter), become quite popular in recent years.

In this context, significant developments have been made in sentiment detection through text and image (photo) analysis. Even though sometimes the image transmits a different sentiment from the text, image and text can be used to complement each other in the analysis of sentiment in a post, being this information important for marketers, and in the development of machines (e.g., robots and interfaces) that follows the HCAI principles.

In this paper, we focus on classifying sentiments in natural environments, i.e., landscape posts supported by photo-text data, a multimodal approach. For example, this classification problem is completely different from the detection of emotions and sentiments from facial expressions, speech, or body posture [3]. Sentiment analysis becomes more intricate when we segment these settings into *indoor* and *outdoor* spaces, which probably should be dealt with separately to attain more accurate methods. Further, in making this differentiation, there is the aspect that indoor spaces are typically man-made and *outdoor* environments are splitable into *urban* (man-made) and *natural* (land-scapes) environments. For the types of problems previously presented, but even with more emphasis in the latter case (namely, landscapes sentiment analysis), colour, texture, edges, line type, and orientation play a key role in the attraction and sentiment that the photo carries. In fact, when trying to extract sentiments from natural environments, colour data may be one of the most important features at play [4].

In summary, this work presents a model for a landscape sentiment classifier based on image (photo) and associated text, frequently observed in posts on social media platforms, the *Landscape Sentiment Classification* model (LSCm). The LSCm aggregates image and text information, returning the sentiment classification and discrepancy between the image and text-predicted sentiments.

The main contribution of this work is three-fold: (i) classify sentiments in natural scene images (landscapes), (ii) classify the sentiments linked with the text associated with a landscape, and (iii) combine image and text classification, returning the information about its discrepancy.

The present section introduces the goal of the work as well as the list of main contributions, Sect. 2 presents the contextualization and state of the art, Sect. 3 introduces the datasets used, Sect. 4 details the model, and Sect. 5 outlines the tests, results and respective discussion. Finally, Sect. 6 presents the conclusions and future work.

2   Contextualization and State-of-the-Art

The term *interpersonal relationship* refers to the association, warmth, friendliness, and dominance between two or more people, expressed when relationships are formed, reciprocated, or deepened [5]. Simultaneously, impersonal human-machine interactions hinder broader communication, making difficult the reciprocal or close ties between humans and machines (devices and/or interfaces). In this context, automatic emotion and sentiment analysis methods are the automated processes of analyzing information to estimate the emotion [6] (e.g., categorized as happiness, sadness, fear, surprise, disgust, anger, and neutral) or sentiment [7, 8] (typically limited to positive, negative, and neutral). Sentiment classification has been a popular research topic in recent years, and significant progress has been made. Here we should notice that sentiments and emotions are interdependent, nevertheless are different concepts [8, 9]. The sentiment is a mental attitude related to positive, negative, or neutral evaluation/thought of something, and can be influenced by factors such as emotion, past experiences, cultural background, personal beliefs, age, or even gender [9]. The categorization of user emotions and sentiments goes beyond the traditional approach of identifying facial expressions, which focuses on alterations in the facial features and actions of a subject.

However, the examination of what feeling or attitude is evoked by a landscape, which is an umbrella term for the geographic features that mark or are typical of a certain location, and is sometimes referred to as a picture of natural scenery, is far more complex. It is therefore important to think about the category and context of such images while analysing them. An image of a beach or the ocean will often have blue as the predominant colour, which is typically connected to serenity, while an image of a forest will emphasize green tones, which are typically connected to harmony. Colour should not be the single feature to analyse, as the meaning of colour might vary depending on where it is used; for instance, red can in some cases signify rage, love, or frustration [4, 10–12]. In addition, just like for music, different people may emotionally interpret colour dissimilarly.

There are several types of emotion classification and different authors divide them into several levels/sublevels [9]. As mentioned before, the six basic emotions (usually complemented with the neutral emotion) was a classification done by the famous psychologist Paul Ekman [6], based on universal facial expressions, but is not the focus of this work. Other authors also proposed alternative classifications, like Robert Plutchik [13] that defined eight basic/primary emotions, based on adaptative biological processes, namely: joy, trust, fear, surprise, sadness, disgust, anger, and anticipation. Plutchik developed a colour wheel, called Plutchik's wheel, to represent these emotions, with each emotion being associated with a specific colour. In this case, emotions can be classified into different intensities and combinations, i.e., the primary emotions are then combined in different ways to create secondary and tertiary emotions, which are represented by different shades and hues of colours, totalling 24 emotions.

The emotions shown in Plutchik's wheel are divided into two main sentiments: *positive* and *negative*. The positive sentiment emotions are joy, trust, anticipation, and surprise, while the sadness, disgust, fear, and anger emotions are considered negative. However, the classification of emotions into positive and negative sentiments can be somewhat subjective and may depend on individual and cultural factors, as already mentioned [12]. The sentiment is often longer and more stable than emotion, which can change rapidly in response to changing stimuli and contexts [14].

Several authors worked in sentiment classification. Ortis *et al.* [9], in 2019, presented an overview of image sentiment analysis. The authors discussed the major issues and outlined opportunities and challenges in the area. Gaspar and Alexandre [15] presented a multimodal sentiment analysis (image and text) model for the classification of the content of composite comments in social media. The method is divided into three main parts: a text analysis, an image classifier, and a method that analyses the class content of an image, checking the probability that it belongs to one of the possible classes. They worked with the T4SA dataset [16], which has three million tweets (images and text) classified into three sentiments: *positive, negative,* and *neutral.* Oliveira *et al.* [16] presented the OutdoorSent, a framework to classify the sentiment of generic outdoor images shared by users on social networks. The authors also evaluate how the merging of deep features and semantic information derived from the scene attributes can improve classification and cross-dataset generalization performance. The same authors also propose a dataset of geolocalized urban outdoor images extracted from Flickr and labelled (by at least five volunteers) the samples as positive, negative, or neutral.

A colour cross-correlation net for image sentiment analysis was presented in [4]. The architecture not only leverages contents and colors simultaneously, but also considers their correlations. The authors used a pre-trained convolutional neural network to extract content features and colour moments to collect colour features from multiple colour spaces. Then, they propose a cross-correlation method to model the relationships between content and colour features, with an attention mechanism and sequence convolution, in which sentiment expressing of content and colour can be enhanced by each other, integrating these two types of information for better results in the end.

Chatzistavros *et al.* [17] presented a deep-learning architecture for sentiment analysis on 2D images of urban and indoor spaces. In [18] is analyzed the sentiment from disaster images in social media. In [19], based on a gated attention mechanism, a multimodal (text and image) sentiment classification model is presented, where the image feature is used to emphasize the text segment by the attention mechanism, allowing the model to focus on the text that affects the sentiment polarity. Moreover, the gating mechanism enables the model to retain useful image information, while ignoring the noise introduced during the fusion of image and text.

It is important to stress, that there are a huge number of models available to do text analysis [8], which usually follow the following steps: (i) *Text processing:* The text is cleaned to increase the sentiment prediction accuracy using techniques such as tokenization, stop word removal, stemming, lemmatization, emote and emoji conversion, and removing useless information; (ii) *Feature Extraction:* Relevant features, in this case, words, are extracted from the pre-processed text. The most common way to do this is using techniques such as bag-of-words and *n*-grams; (iii) *Model Development:* Train a machine learning model (e.g., Random Forest or Decision Tree) or a deep learning model to learn from data and later classify new unseen text sentiment correctly; And, in the case when sentiment is analysed, (iv) *Sentiment Classification Evaluation:* Use other models and adjust models to get the best performance possible.

Even though landscape images are included in "all" datasets and even though almost all authors used outdoor images in their work, those images showed a wide range of scenarios, many of which included man-made structures, people, or plants/animals close-ups. In the present work, we focused only on landscapes – natural outdoor scenes. We also propose ensemble/stacking modelling, which typically allows to increase in the accuracy of predictive analytics and data mining applications. In this context, ensemble modelling or fusion is the act of executing two or more related but separate analytical models and then combining the results into a single score or spread. In the present case, we can relate different results from different/complementary models to achieve the best accuracy or to complement information. Examples of these techniques can be found in [14] or in [19].

The next section will briefly describe the sub-datasets created to test the model and the pre-processing steps applied to the data before analysing it.

3 Dataset

In the present study, we use three sub-datasets from two well-known datasets. The first sub-dataset (a) is going to be used to develop *Image Sentiment Classifier* models (see Sect. 4.1), being constructed as a restriction to the Flickr dataset [20]. The second sub-dataset (b) was used to develop *Text Sentiment Classifier* models (see Sect. 4.2), being constructed from the T4SA dataset [16]. Finally, the third sub-dataset (c) was used to build the integrated model, the *Multimodal Sentiment Classifier* model (see Sect. 4.3), being also formed using the T4SA dataset.

The decision to use these two well-known datasets (Flickr and T4SA) is based on the lack of a single dataset that offers the simultaneous ground truth for text and image sentiment. Further, it were used sub-datasets of those, as the full datasets have outdoor and indoor images, man-made scenarios, scenarios with persons etc., while we are only focused on landscapes. In more detail, the development of the *Image Sentiment Classifier* models involved the use of the Columbia Multilingual Visual Sentiment Ontology (MVSO) dataset, created from the Flickr dataset. This database covers a visual sentiment ontology consisting of 3.244 adjective-noun pairs and SentiBank, which is a set of 1.200 trained visual concept detectors, providing a mid-level representation of sentiment, associated training images acquired from Flickr, and a benchmark containing 603 photo tweets covering a diverse set of 21 topics [20], being available at https://www.ee.columbia.edu/ln/dvmm/vso/download/flickr_dataset.html.

A subset was derived from Flickr dataset, specifically choosing landscape photos. This sub-dataset is designated as (a) *FlickrCollmg*. Since in the original dataset, the sentiment polarity of the images changes between -2 and 2, we considered for our models that a negative sentiment is between -2 and -0.5, a neutral sentiment is between -0.5 and 0.5, and a positive sentiment is between 0.5 and 2. With 153k landscape images, the *FlickrCollmg* sub-dataset is not balanced, so, ~ 80k balanced images were randomly selected from those 153k images (see Table 1).

The second and third dataset is based on the T4SA dataset [16], available at http://www.t4sa.it/#dataset. The dataset's collection process took place in 2016 and 2017, being the total number of tweets in the dataset of ~ 3.4 M, corresponding to ~ 4 M images, as each tweet may have more than one image. Each tweet (text and associated images) has been labelled according to the sentiment polarity of the text, namely negative (-1), neutral (0), or positive (1). The dataset's authors removed corrupted and near-duplicate images and selected a balanced subset of images, named B-T4SA. Figure 1 illustrates the architecture of the T4SA data collection process.

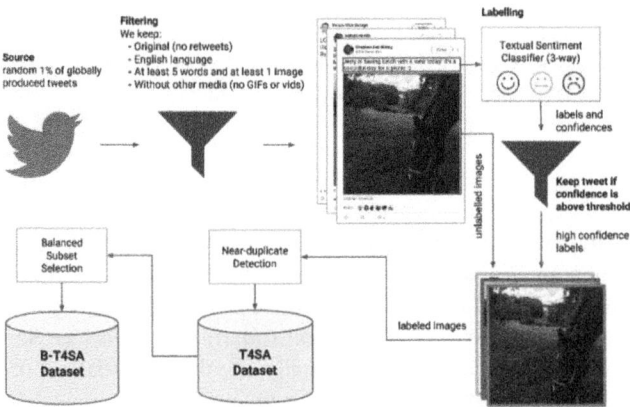

Fig. 1. T4SA dataset collection process [16]. Image retrieved from http://www.t4sa.it/#dataset.

It is important to stress again that this dataset has outdoor and indoor images, where the outdoor images include landscapes, man-made images, images with persons etc. In our study, a sub-dataset of text posts was selected from the B-T4SA. These were used to train the *Text Sentiment Classifier* models, and it was designated as (b) **B-T4SAtext**, consisting of 379k unbalanced samples, from which 50k balanced samples were randomly selected (see Table 1. Summary of the used data.). To this sub-dataset was applied the following pre-processing steps for text analysis: (i) the replacement of emojis/emoticons for words (e.g., 😍 was replaced by "smiling face with hearts"); (ii) convert all text to lowercase; (iii) remove stop words (e.g., 'i', 'me', 'after', 'moreover'), proves useful as they do not contribute to sentiment analysis and their exclusion avoids unnecessary computations; (iv) removed HTML tags, images, mentions, links, punctuation etc., because they do not carry sentiments; (v) apply a lemmatizer, which removes inflectional endings from a token to turn it into the base word lemma (e.g., the word 'dancing' would be lemmatized to 'dance'); and (vi) apply stemming, which is the process of removing suffices from words to obtain their root form (e.g., the word 'dancing' would be stemmed to 'danc'). Both stemming and lemmatizations serve the purpose of reducing word forms to their base or root forms to generalize the words, resulting in more accurate predictions in sentiment detection.

The final sub-dataset was designated (c) **B-T4SAland**, consisting of only 850 samples (see Table 1. Summary of the used data.), being once again based on B-T4SA. For this dataset, the 850 posts (including image-text) were randomly selected, ensuring that the photos/images were of landscapes. Once the T4SA did not provide sentiment labelling (ground truth) for the images, those photos were presented and classified by a group of 6 persons (3 male, 3 female), with ages between 21 and 55 years, all with Portuguese nationality. The dataset was filtered to include only those cases where a minimum of five out of the six individuals unanimously agreed on the sentiment classification (positive, negative, or neutral). For each of those selected landscape images, the corresponding text was selected and the respective sentiment label was retrieved from the B-T4SA dataset. This approach resulted in an unbalanced (sub-)dataset and other relevant occurrences, such as, the diversity of images/text sentiments pairing, where positive/neutral/negative classified images were paired with positive/negative/neutral texts classification. This is the reason why Table 1. Summary of the used data. Shows, e.g., 639 images vs. 252 texts with positive sentiment or 96 images vs. 571 texts with neutral sentiment.

Table 1. Summary of the used data.

Sentiment	Image - *FlickrCollImg*		Text - *B-T4SAtext*		*B-T4SALand*	
	Original	**Balanced**	Original	**Balanced**	**Image**	**Text**
Positive (+)	89.746	**27.278**	127.086	**16.667**	639	252
Negative (-)	36.480	**27.278**	21.643	**16.667**	115	27
Neutral (=)	27.278	**27.278**	230.471	**16.667**	96	571
Total	153.504	**81.834**	**379.200**	**50.001**	**850**	**850**

Fig. 2. Examples of landscape images used for training and testing where the upper row images are from Flickr and the bottom rows from B-T4SAland. From left to right are images classified as positive, neutral, and negative.

To summarize, the number of images and text data divided per sentiment for each sub-dataset is represented in Table 1. Examples of photos are shown in Fig. 2, upper row images from Flickr and bottom rows *B-T4SAland*, from left to right columns show positive, neutral, and negative sentiments. Examples of text are presented in Table 2, negative, positive, and neutral for the original post and the pre-processed text. The next section introduces the developed models.

Table 2. Examples of texts used for the models' development

Tweet/Sentiment	Text	PreProcessed Text
Negative	"RT @Reuters: Special Report: Iraq militia massacre worse than U.S. acknowledged. https://t.co/Khzqwl oPam https://t.co/8HtpZYQZQh"	special report iraq militia massacr wors u acknowledge
Positive	"Have a look at the most spectacular #NationalParks in #California. #traveler https://t.co/wiIfw7nnH7 https://t.co/sxnJnQH0cC"	look spectacular nationalpark california travel
Neutral	"Live Next Door To Parents https://t.co/FfJrf5n8D1 https://t.co/2bZRdn kPQY"	live next door parent

4   Landscape Sentiment Classification Model

The *Landscape Sentiment Classification model* (LSCm) is used to extract sentiments from photos-images and texts, following the principles presented in [15]. However, our model exhibits distinctions when ensembles are employed. Namely, image and text sentiment classification results from the combining of various methods, i.e., components are combined into an ensemble to yield the ultimate result. In this context, the possible outputs are (see Fig. 3. Proposed model for LSCm.): (i) sentiment resulting from the image (*isc*), generated by the *Image Sentiment Classification* (ISC) block; (ii) sentiment resulting from the text (*tsc*), generated by the *Text Sentiment Classification* (TSC) block; (iii) sentiment resulting from the combination of image and text (*msc*), generated by the *Multimodal Sentiment Classifier* (MSC) block; and (iv) sentiment discrepancy between image and text (*dis*). So, for each paired (image - text) the model returns the following vector [*isc*, *tsc*, *msc*, *dis.*].

Figure 3 shows a simplified diagram block of the model. At the top is presented the generic LSCm, where " +" represents a positive sentiment, "-" a negative sentiment, " =" the neutral sentiment, and *dis.* is the discrepancy between the sentiment returned from the image and the text, for each pair of image-text presented in the input. In the middle of the figure are the image and text sentiment classifier blocks, ISC and TSC, respectively. The bottom part of the figure represents the schematized combination of all the inputs to return the final output in the multimodal sentiment classifier block (MSC). Details of these blocks will be presented in the following sections.

4.1   Image Sentiment Classifier Block

The landscape *Image Sentiment Classification* block is based on the work of Oliveira *et al.* [16], which creates a deep learning (DL) sentiment classifier model based on a traditional DL architecture backbone (such as VGG, ResNet, Inception etc.) followed by a "handcrafted" network head, based on fully connected layers.

In this scenario, three primary models are introduced (predefined), distinguished by the applied backbone architecture. Specifically, one utilizes the DenseNet121 (121 layers) architecture as the backbone [20], another uses the Xception architecture (71 layers) [21], and the third one uses the ResNet-50 architecture (50 Layers) [22]. It is worth noting that all the backbones were trained using the ImageNet dataset. Different strategies of fine-tuning were used for these models, including different numbers of fully connected layers at the network's head.

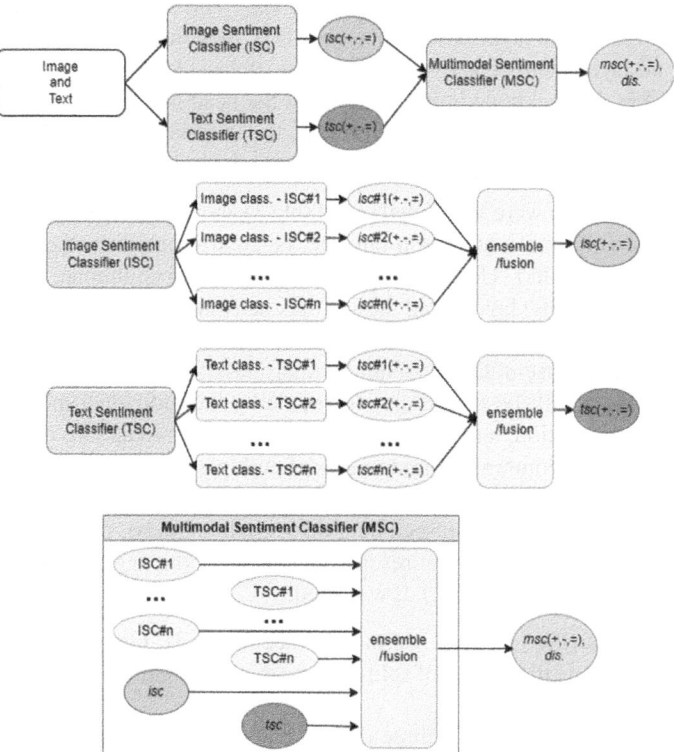

Fig. 3. Proposed model for LSCm.

The models are depicted in the 2nd row of Fig. 3 and Table 3 shows the optimized hyperparameter values, each pre-defined architectures sub-model summarized as follows:

(a) **ISC_DL#1:** the backbone is a DenseNet121. Furthermore, let $L_{i,j}$ represent a dense layer, where i is the layer number and j is the number of units. Then, in ISC_DL#1, the head has 5 layers. In the initial layer, L_{in}, the number of units equals the number of outputs of the backbone. The second dense layer has n units with X_2 activation function ($L_{2,n}$) and dropout D_{d2}, a dense layer $L_{3,m}$ with D_{d3}, and a dense layer with 24 units ($L_{4,24}$), all with X_i activation functions. The last layer has 3 units with a soft-max activation function (Ls). The layer of 24 units is based on our hypothesis derived from Plutchik's wheel of emotions. We hypothesize that due to the importance of colour in sentiment analysis and the relation between emotion and sentiment, and once there are 24 emotions in Plutchik's wheel, it is expected that a layer of 24 units can help the network to learn those emotions and relate them with the 3 sentiments, which appears in the last layer. I.e., it will allow to classify the sentiment of the image into positive, negative, or neutral according to the responses of these "emotions".

(b) **ISC_DL#2:** the backbone is Xception and the head has 6 layers. The first dense layer has L_{in}, the number of units equals the number of outputs of the backbone. Then, a dense layer with n units ($L_{2,n}$) and D_{d2}. The third layer has also m units and D_{d3}. The fourth layer has o units, with D_{d4}, then the dense layer with 24 units ($L_{5,24}$), all layers with X_i activation functions, the last layer is the Ls.

(c) **ISC_DL#3:** the backbone is ResNet-50 and the head has 5 layers. The first dense layer is L_{in}, the second layer $L_{2,n}$ with D_{d2}, the third layer $L_{3,n}$ with D_{d3}, a fourth layer $L_{4,24}$, all with X_i activation functions, and the last layer is the Ls.

These architectures were fine-tuned (see Table 3) and several hyperparameters were tested, such as number of units, drop-out rate, batch size, number of epochs etc. (see section Tests and Results). The only fixed values were the penultimate (with 24 units) and the last (with 3 units) layers, and the softmax activation function.

Them, the results from the three classifiers (ISC_DL#1, ISC_DL#2, and ISC_DL#3) are to be combined/ensembled to obtain a final classification. So, the inputs of the ensemble sub-block will be the predictions made by the individual models, resulting from the softmax function, and the output will be the final prediction, *isc*. Ensembling leverages the idea that combining the strengths of multiple models can result in improved overall performance and accuracy, compared to using a single model, as well as a better generalization (reacts better to unseen data than single models), reduces "overfitting", and increases the robustness of the results obtained. For the aggregation of sentiment classification (ensemble sub-block), it was used:

1. **Random Forest (ISC_RFa):** k estimators (see Table 3), Gini impurity as criteria function to measure the quality of split, and the minimum number of samples required to split an internal node was 2.
2. **Neural Network (ISC_NNa):** three dense layers, where the first layer has 9 units (L_{in}), then a dense layer with n units ($L_{2,n}$) with X_i activation functions, and the third layer the Ls.

A search tuner function was used to find the best (hyper-)parameters for the proposed models (see Table 3).

4.2 Text Sentiment Classifier Block

In the landscape *Text Sentiment Classification* block, the first step consists of converting the text (see Sect. 3) into structured data, in a way that can be used by machine learning (ML) methods. To achieve this, a Bag of Words (BOW) was applied to extract 5.000 features, with one to two n-grams, from the processed texts. Figure 4. Features extraction from text for sentiment detection. Image retrieved from http://www.datasciencelovers. com/tag/tf-idf/.illustrates the feature extraction from text for sentiment classification.

Using a fine-tuning procedure, the BOW was used to train two ML models (see Table 3):

(a) **Random Forest (TSC_RFc)**: created with k estimators and Gini impurity as criteria function to measure the quality of the splits.
(b) **Neural Network (TSC_NNc)**: 4 dense layers where the first has 5.000 units (L_{in}), then two layers with n units ($L_{2,n}$) units and m units ($L_{3,m}$) are added, with X_i activation functions. The last layer uses 3 units with a softmax activation function (Ls), used to predict the probability of a text carrying a positive, negative, or neutral sentiment.

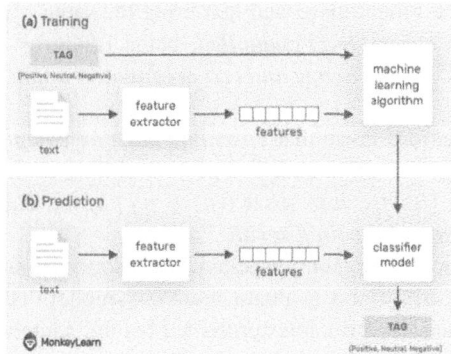

Fig. 4. Features extraction from text for sentiment detection. Image retrieved from http://www. datasciencelovers.com/tag/tf-idf/.

Furthermore, the (c) Natural Language Toolkit (TSC_NLTK) method, available in the literature at https://www.nltk.org/, was used as a third model.

The block diagram of the proposed TSC block is presented in the 3rd row of Fig. 3. For the aggregation of text sentiment classification (the ensemble sub-block) was used:

(i) (**Random Forest (TSC_RFt)**: k estimators and "Gini criteria" function;
(ii) (**Neural Network (TSC_NNt)**: 4 dense layers, the first layer has 9 units (L_{in}), then a dense layer with 3 units ($L_{2,n}$), a third layer with m units ($L_{3,m}$) all with X_i activation function, and the fourth layer the Ls.

As before, a search tuner function was used to find the best (hyper-)parameters for the proposed models (see Table 3).

4.3 Multimodal Sentiment Classifier Block

The *Multimodal Sentiment Classifier* block, as largely mentioned in the text, is based on classifications resulting from text and image. Going back to the block diagram in Fig. 3, bottom row, the ensemble block has 3 inputs from ISC and 3 inputs from TSC. Also, *isc* and *tsc* are used to compute the *discrepancy*:

(a) **If the input sample (image and text) has similar sentiments**, i.e., $isc = tsc$, then $msc = isc = tsc$, and LSCm = [$isc, isc, isc, dis. = 0\%$] is the resulting output.

(b) **If the input sample (image and text) has different sentiments** ($isc \neq tsc$), considering μ_I the average results (between 0–100) from all ISC models that returned the same sentiment, μ_T the average of all TSC models that returned the same sentiment, and the threshold $\mu_t = 85$ (empirically calculated):

(b.1) If $\mu_I \geq \mu_t$ and $\mu_T \geq \mu_t$ then both ISC and TSC are certain of the sentiment and, in this case, most probably the person who posted the image-text intended different sentiments. The ensemble block is not computed, resulting LSCm = [$isc, tsc, \times, dis. = 100\%$]. This case means that **the image and text have different sentiments.**

(b.2) If $\mu_I < \mu_t$ and $\mu_T < \mu_t$ and $\mu_I \sim \mu_T$ (~ means approximately, with a difference of ± 2 percentual points) then image and text bring the same contribution, i.e., $dis. = 50\%$. In this case, the **ensemble is computed,** being LSCm = [$isc, tsc, msc, dis. = 50\%$]. This case means that **the image and text are indeterminate if they have the same sentiments.**

(b.3) All other situations mean that **ensemble must be computed**, once there is no certainty about what the person intended to post. Resulting in this case the $dis. = (\mu_I + \mu_T)/2$, and LSCm = [$isc, tsc, msc, dis. = ((\mu_I + \mu_T)/2) \%$]. This case means that **the image and text complement the final result.**

As there is no balance in the sentiment classes, the Stratified K-Fold cross-validation technique was used to train and evaluate the MSC model. The ensemble block is computed following the same principles presented before, namely:

1. **Random Forest (MSC_RFe):** k estimators and Gini as criteria function;
2. **Neural Network (MSC_NNe):** 4 dense layers, where the first layer has 18 units (L_{in}), a dense layer with n units ($L_{2,n}$), a third layer with m units ($L_{3,m}$), with X_i activation function, and the fourth layer the Ls with softmax as activation function.

A search tuner function was used to find the best structure and parameters, see Table 3. In the following section test and results will be presented.

5 Tests and Results

The procedure implemented to evaluate the model is divided into three steps: (a) evaluate image sentiment classification, (b) evaluate the text sentiment classification, and (c) evaluate the ensemble of both text and image models, i.e., evaluate the LSCm model. The models were trained and tested using a combination of the Google Colab (with 12.7GB de RAM and 107.7GB disc space) and Kaggle platform (with 14.8 GB RAM e GPU T4 x2). For the Random Forest models, the Gini impurity was the criteria function to measure the quality of split and the minimum number of samples required to split an internal node was 2. The model was trained in two ways: (a) by using the sentiment values of -1 (negative), 0 (neutral), and 1 (positive), predicted by the individual models, and (b) by using the sentiment-predicted probabilities from the individual models. As the results were very similar, so the option (b) was chosen.

Table 3 shows the ISC, TSC and MSC parameters, hyperparameters, and accuracies of the models. In more detail, the first column shows the used models, the second column summarizes the number of units used in the layers (resulting from the optimizations), as well as the estimators, and the third column shows how many layers the backbone has, as well as some hyperparameters used to train the new data, dropout, and activation functions. The accuracy is presented in the last column.

Lines 3 to 6 present the information related to the ISC models, lines 8 to 11 the information related to TSC models, line 13 the results of the MSC model, and line 14 the LSCm's results. The last line shows the results from the analysed image-text, in percentage, the different types of combinations of sentiment classification, where: $dis. = 0\%$ corresponds to ISC and TSC reporting the same sentiment; $dis. = 100\%$ corresponds to ISC and TSC reporting different sentiments; and other $dis.$ Values when the sentiment is undetermined, i.e., the image and text point to opposite sentiments, but this is not completely clear.

Table 3. ISC, TSC, and MSC parameters, hyperparameters, and accuracy of the models.

Model	Number units / estimators	Backbone layers trained // hyperparameters + dropout + activation function			Accuracy
Image Sentiment Classification					
ISC#1 (DL)	$n = 2048$ $m = 1024$	8 Opt: SGD (1e-2) Epochs: 20 Batch size: 32	$d_1 = 50\%$ $d_2 = 50\%$	$X_i = \text{ReLU}$ $i = \{1,...,4\}$	54.55%
ISC#2 (DL)	$n = 4096$ $m = 4096$ $o = 2048$	8 Opt: SGD (1e-2) Epochs: 20 Batch size: 32	$d_1 = 70\%$ $d_2 = 50\%$ $d_3 = 30\%$	$X_i = \text{ReLU}$ $i = \{1,...,5\}$	54.79%
ISC#3 (DL)	$n = 1024$ $m = 512$	All Opt: SGD (1e-4) Epochs: 20 Batch size: 32	$d_1 = 50\%$ $d_2 = 50\%$	$X_i = \text{ReLU}$ $i = \{1,...,4\}$	54.73%
ISC – RFa **ISC – NNa**	$k = 100$ (est.) $n = 57$	Opt: Adam (7e-4) Epochs: 20 Batch size: 32	—	$X_i = \text{ReLU}$ $i = \{1,..., 3\}$	55.46% **55.89%**
Text Sentiment Classification					
TSC#1 (RF)	$k = 100$ (est.)	—	—	—	90.10%
TSC#2 (NN)	$n = 300$ $m = 100$	Opt: SGD (1e-2) Epochs: 10 Batch size: 8	—	$X_i = \text{ReLU}$ $i = \{1,..., 3\}$	88.55%
SC#3 (NLTK)	—	—	—	—	84.34%

(continued)

Table 3. *(continued)*

Model	Number units / estimators	Backbone layers trained // hyperparameters + dropout + activation function			Accuracy
TSC – RFt **TSC – NNt**	$k = 100$ (est.) $n = 100$ $m = 20$	Opt: SGD (1e-2) Epochs: 10 Batch size: 2	—	$X_i = $ ReLU $i = \{1,..., 3\}$	91, 95% **92,10%**
Multimodal Sentiment Classification					
MSC - RFe **MSC – NNe**	$k = 100$ (est.) $n = 100$ $m = 24$	Opt: Adam (1e-2) Epochs: 10 Batch size: 32	—	$X_i = $ ReLU $i = \{1,..., 3\}$	**100.00%** 98.46%
LSCm	—	—	—	—	**78.75%**
Sentiment Disparity Between Image and Text					
	Ground-Truth		Prediction		
dis. $= 0\%$ *dis.* $= 100\%$ *dis.* $= \#\%$	32,11% 4,47% 64,41%		38,00% 4,24% 57,76%		

Going back to the evaluation procedure of the model, in more detail: (a) the image models were trained with *FlickrCollmg*, composed of 81.834 images (see Table 1), where 80% of those images were used for training and 20% for testing. As the dataset had images with different scales, (a.1) image pixel values were normalized between 0 and 1 and (a.2) resized to 224 × 224 pixels. The (b) text models were trained with *B-T4SAtext*, composed of 50.001 text tweets, where 80% of the samples were used for training and 20% for testing. The (c) MSC was trained using *B-T4SALand* and a stratified K-fold cross-validation technique, but only using the samples where the image and the text have the same sentiment, resulting in 273 samples. For the final results, LSCm's results (see Table 3, 14th line), the inference is done over the already trained models, mentioned above, using *B-T4SALand* dataset, with 850 samples.

In Table 3, the high accuracy of the MSC models is justified by the fact that they are solely employed to determine and enhance sentiment accuracy based on the results of the six individual models (3 TSC and 3 ISC). So, for nearly 100% of the cases, the previously predicted sentiment will remain the same. At this point, it is also important to stress again how the accuracy of LSCm is computed, as it aggregates results from the MSC model (a), (b.2), and (b.3), and checks these predictions against the ground truth, once (b.1) image and text reflect or could reflect different sentiments.

One of the main focuses of the paper is to understand if the image and text in a post represent the same sentiment, and present the alignment between real sentiments (ground truth) and predicted sentiments, for both text and image data. In the figure, " − 1" are negative sentiments, "0" are neutral sentiments, and "1" are positive sentiments. At the top of Fig. 5, the confusion matrices compare the real vs. predicted sentiments of the text (left) and image (right) samples, while at the bottom the confusion matrices show the difference in real and predicted sentiment between the text and image.

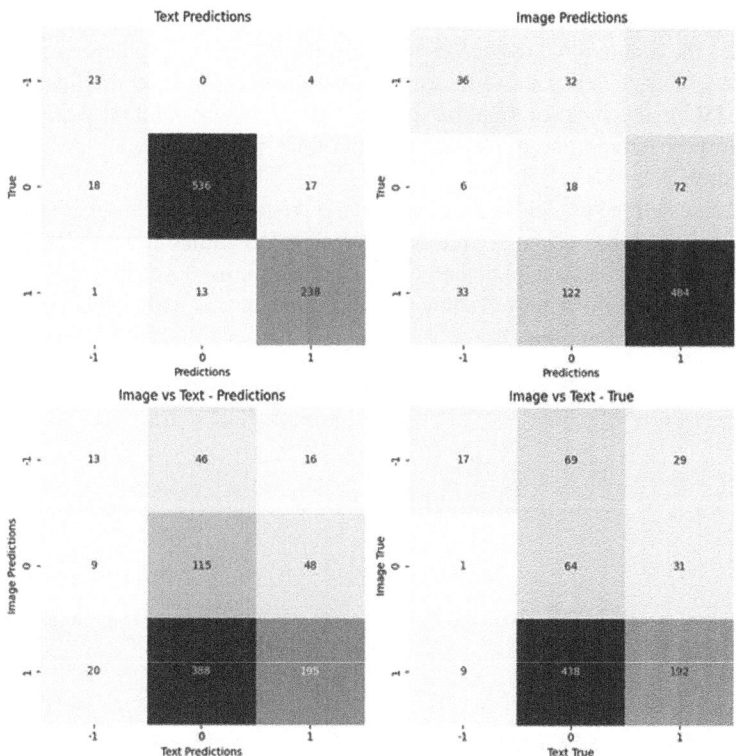

Fig. 5. Confusion matrices of images, text, and text-image classifications (3 sentiments).

By analysing text and images isolated (Fig. 5, top), it is evident that the main error of the model is to assign positive images to neutral images. Furthermore, by observing the bottom row, where we can compare our predictions and the real results for the text-image combination, we can see that the results are quite similar. One example is "Image vs. Text - True" matrix, which reflects that 192 pairs show the same positive sentiments, 438 show indeterminacy (i.e., both image and text can report the same sentiment or opposite sentiments), and 9 show different sentiments. Now looking at the same line but in the confusion matrix for "Image vs. Text - Predictions", we have respectively 195, 388 and 20, being only 3 more pairs are assigned to positive sentiment.

If we analyse the disparity for the ground truth data and our previsions, Table 3 bottom line, we see the same trend. So, results that point to an indeterminacy of the image and text sentiment should be used to complement the global sentiment of the post. The left side of Fig. 6 shows the discrepancy bar chart (3 sentiments) and on the right the prediction confidence percentage level bar chart (3 sentiments).

Table 4 exemplifies the *confidence* in how the MSC predicts a sentiment. The MSC model uses the 6 individual estimators to determine a certainty probability for the final sentiment so that, if all of those return the same predictions then the final sentiment and the MSC is the same (normal behaviour), which results in a high accuracy of the model. In the example, the model predicts the final sentiment with 90% certainty of being positive.

We also tested the model for 2 sentiments, i.e., from the sub-datasets *FlickrCollImg*, *B-T4SAtext*, and *B-T4SALand* we removed the neutral samples and retrained the models again, using the same parameters, except for the output layer that was adapted in accordance. The results achieved show the same tendency as with 3 sentiments, as can be observed in Fig. 7 and Fig. 8.

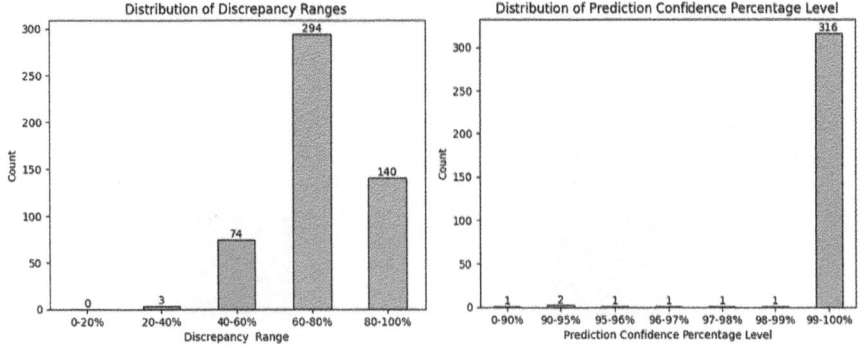

Fig. 6. On the left, discrepancy bar chart (3 sentiments) and, on the right, the prediction confidence percentage level bar chart (3 sentiments).

Table 4. Example of prediction confidence percentage level sample.

	NEGATIVE	NEUTRAL	POSITIVE
ISC#1	0%	25%	75%
ISC#2	10%	10%	80%
ISC#3	10%	40%	50%
ISC (ensemble)	0%	18%	82%
TSC#1	10%	20%	70%
TSC#2	25%	25%	50%
TSC#3	0%	70%	30%
TSC (ensemble)	0%	26%	74%
TSC - ISC	POSITIVE – POSITIVE		
MSC	0%	10%	90%
LSCm	POSITIVE		

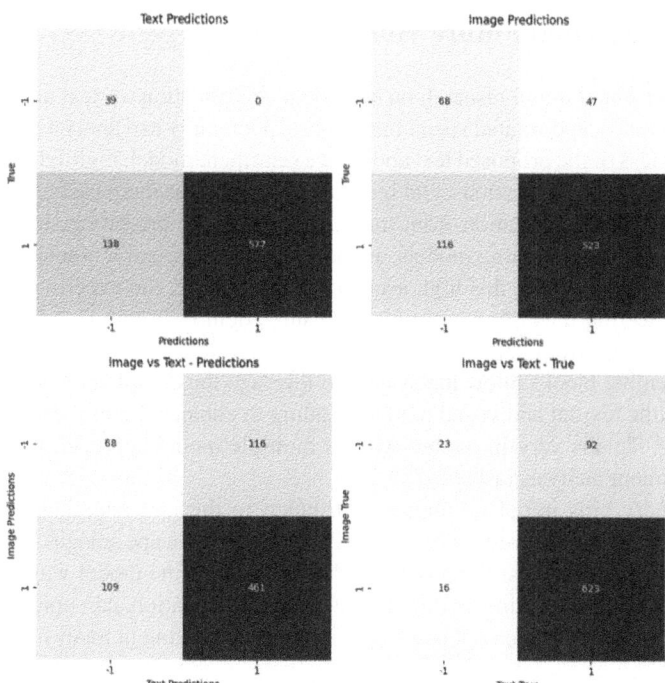

Fig. 7. Confusion matrices of images, text, and text-image classifications (2 sentiments).

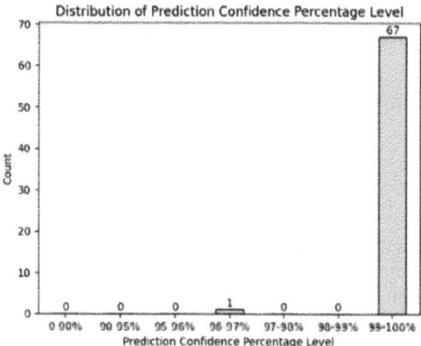

Fig. 8. On the left, is the discrepancy bar chart (2 sentiments) and, on the right, the prediction confidence percentage level bar chart (2 sentiments).

6   Conclusions and Future Work

This work presented initial research on sentiment classification for text and image data, especially in landscape-related social media posts. Our study and analysis demonstrated the effectiveness of the proposed text and image sentiment model, highlighting its potential applications and implications. Our results indicate that the model achieves high accuracy in sentiment classification from image-text data. The pre-processing techniques, incorporation of deep learning models, and advanced feature extraction techniques used have led the system to get this high accuracy. Furthermore, the experiments on image sentiment detection have shown promising results, demonstrating that the system can classify sentiments from landscape images.

The ensemble blocks allow the system to leverage the complementary information provided by the textual and visual models, leading to enhanced sentiment classification performance. This is very important when a multiple model approach is used, in this case in sentiment analysis tasks.

In summary, this initial prototype contributed to the understanding of sentiment detection from pair image-text data, with a focus on landscape images. Although the accuracy of the system is still not optimal the potential of the model was shown. Continuing to improve and refine landmark sentiment classification, can open up new possibilities for enabling more sophisticated and nuanced sentiment analysis in interfaces and/or robots.

Looking ahead, there are several directions for future research. The focus should be on improving the sentiment detection model in images and getting more and, also extremely relevant, better datasets of image-text related to landscapes. We also intend to test the same models in pairs text-image of indoor, and outdoor man-made scenes as well as scenes with persons and finally combine all the information.

Acknowledgements. This work is supported by NOVA LINCS (UIDB/04516/2020) with the financial support of FCT.IP.

References

1. Shneiderman, B.: Human-Centered AI. Oxford University Press (2022)
2. Wang, Y., et al.: A systematic review on affective computing: emotion modelsd databases, and recent advances. Inf. Fusion **83–84**, 19–52 (2022). https://doi.org/10.1016/j.inffus.2022. 03.009
3. Li, S., Deng, W.: Deep facial expression recognition: a survey. IEEE Trans. Affect Comput. **3045**, 1–20 (2020). https://doi.org/10.1109/TAFFC.2020.2981446
4. Ruan, S., Zhang, K., Wu, L., Xu, T., Liu, Q., Chen, E.: Color enhanced cross correlation net for image sentiment analysis. IEEE Trans. Multimedia **1**, 1–14 (2021). https://doi.org/10. 1109/TMM.2021.3118208
5. Zhang, Z., Luo, P., Loy, C.C., Tang, X.: From facial expression recognition to interpersonal relation prediction. Int. J. Comput. Vis. **126**(5), 550–569 (2018). https://doi.org/10.1007/s11 263-017-1055-1
6. Ekman, P.: Are there basic emotions? Psychol. Rev. **99**(3), 550–553 (1992). https://doi.org/ 10.1037/0033-295X.99.3.550

7. Noroozi, F., Corneanu, C.A., Kaminska, D., Sapinski, T., Escalera, S., Anbarjafari, G.: Survey on emotional body gesture recognition. IEEE Trans. Affect. Comput. **12**(2), 505–523 (2021). https://doi.org/10.1109/TAFFC.2018.2874986
8. Nandwani, P., Verma, R.: A review on sentiment analysis and emotion detection from text. Soc. Netw. Anal. Min. **11**(1) (2021). https://doi.org/10.1007/s13278-021-00776-6
9. Ortis, A., Farinella, G.M., Battiato, S.: An overview on image sentiment analysis: methods, datasets and current challenges. In: Proceedings of the 16th International Joint Conference on e-Business and Telecommunications, SciTePress, 2019, pp. 296–306 (2019). https://doi.org/10.5220/0007909602900300
10. Fugate, J.M.B., Franco, C.L.: What color is your anger? Assessing color-emotion pairings in english speakers. Front. Psychol. **10** (2019). https://doi.org/10.3389/fpsyg.2019.00206
11. Amencherla, M., Varshney, L.R.: Color-based visual sentiment for socialcommunication. In: Proceedings of the 15th Canadian Workshop on Information Theory (CWIT) (2017). https://doi.org/10.1109/CWIT.2017.7994829
12. Peng, Y.F., Chou, T.R.: Automatic color palette design using color image and sentiment analysis. In: Proceedings of the IEEE 4th International Conference on Cloud Computing and Big Data Analysis (ICCCBDA) (2019). https://doi.org/10.1109/ICCCBDA.2019.8725717
13. Plutchik, R.: "Chapter 1 - A General Psychoevolutionary Theory Of Emotion," In: Plutchik, R., Kellerman, H. (eds.) Theories of Emotion, Academic Press, pp. 3–33 (1980). https://doi.org/10.1016/B978-0-12-558701-3.50007-7
14. Munezero, M., Montero, C.S., Sutinen, E., Pajunen, J.: Are they different? Affect, feeling, emotion, sentiment, and opinion detection in text. IEEE Trans. Affect Comput. **5**(2), 101–111 (2014). https://doi.org/10.1109/TAFFC.2014.2317187
15. Gaspar, A., Alexandre, L.A.: A multimodal approach to image sentiment analysis. In: Proceedings of the Intelligent Data Engineering and Automated Learning–IDEAL 2019: 20th International Conference, Manchester, UK, 14–16 November 2019, Proceedings, Part I 20, pp. 302–309 (2019)
16. Vadicamo, L., et al.: Cross-media learning for image sentiment analysis in the wild (2017). http://www.t4sa.it
17. Chatzistavros, K., Pistola, T., Diplaris, S., Ioannidis, K., Vrochidis, S., Kompatsiaris, I.: Sentiment analysis on 2D images of urban and indoor spaces using deep learning architectures (2022). https://www.mturk.com/
18. Hassan, S.Z., et al.: Visual sentiment analysis from disaster images in social media. Sensors **22**(10), 3628 (2022)
19. Du, Y., Liu, Y., Peng, Z., Jin, X.: Gated attention fusion network for multimodal sentiment classification. Knowl. Based Syst. **240** (2022). https://doi.org/10.1016/j.knosys.2021.108107
20. Huang, G., et al.: "Densely connected convolutional networks". In: Proceedings of the IEEE Conference On Computer Vision And Pattern Recognition, pp. 4700 4708 (2017). https://doi.org/10.1109/CVPR.2017.243
21. Chollet, F.: "Xception: deep learning with depthwise separable convolutions". In: Proceedings of the IEEE Conference On Computer Vision And Pattern Recognition, pp. 1251–1258 (2017). https://doi.org/10.1109/CVPR.2017.243
22. He, K., et al. "Deep residual learning for image recognition". In: Proceedings of the IEEE Conference On Computer Vision And Pattern Recognition (2016)

GoraNiNora: Context-Dependent Information for Safe Mountain Visits

Domen Vilar[1(✉)], Veljko Pejović[1,2], and Bojan Blažica[2]

[1] Fakulteta za računalništvo in informatiko, Univerza v Ljubljani, Večna pot 113, 1000 Ljubljana, Slovenia
dv6526@student.uni-lj.si, veljko.pejovic@fri.uni-lj.si
[2] Jožef Stefan Institute, Ljubljana, Slovenia
bojan.blazica@ijs.si

Abstract. The rise in mountaineering accidents, notably from snow avalanches, highlights the need for enhanced safety measures in mountain tourism. This study leverages mobile computing to address the gap in mountaineers' practical knowledge through GoraNiNora[3], a mobile app providing context-sensitive educational content. Developed on the basis of survey results involving 950 mountaineers and in collaboration with eight professional mountaineering experts, GoraNiNora utilizes real-time location and weather data to offer tailored advice improving a user's safety and knowledge. A usability evaluation confirms the app's effectiveness and user-friendliness, suggesting that GoraNiNora could contribute to safer mountain tourism by enriching mountaineers' knowledge and experience.

Keywords: mountain safety · context-aware notification system · mobile application · Android · mobile sensing

1 Introduction

The allure of mountaineering has significantly grown, driven by the search for adventure and escape from the rapid pace of daily life. This increase in mountain tourism has, however, led to a rise in mountaineering accidents, particularly problematic in the context of winter mountaineering without proper experience. Accident statistics of the Mountain Rescue Association of Slovenia (GRZS) show that the number of interventions in the mountains has doubled in the last ten years. If in 2010 there were only around 300 GRZS interventions, in 2020 there were already more than 600 [11,15]. The integration of Information and Communication Technology (ICT) in outdoor activities presents a promising avenue to address mountaineeringsafety, as ICTs, thanks to ubiquitous connectivity and sensors embedded in mobile devices can provide timely and context-relevant information. Nevertheless, the existing mountaineering-oriented mobile

---

GoraNiNora literaly translates to "The Mountain is Not Crazy".

© The Author(s), under exclusive license to Springer Nature Switzerland AG 2025
P. Zaphiris et al. (Eds.): HCII 2024, LNCS 15378, pp. 394–404, 2025.
https://doi.org/10.1007/978-3-031-76815-6_28

apps often lack context-awareness, failing to deliver real-time, location-specific, and quality educational content and safety information.

In this paper we present the design and development of *GoraNiNora*, a mobile app that bridges the above gap and provides dynamic, real-time mountaineering advice based on the user's current location and weather conditions, while conserving battery life. GoraNiNora was designed after a comprehensive study that includes in-depth interviews and surveys with mountaineers to understand their needs and the practical knowledge gaps that exist. Based on these insights, a context-aware app was designed and developed. Our evaluation of the app focuses on its usability and effectiveness in delivering educational content. By addressing the limitations of existing solutions and incorporating advanced mobile computing technologies, GoraNiNora represents a promising research direction within the field of human-computer interaction, particularly in the context of outdoor safety and education. The implications of our findings extend beyond mountaineering, offering insights into the design and development of context-aware mobile applications for a variety of outdoor activities.

2   Background and Related Work

The increasing popularity of outdoor activities, particularly mountaineering, has been accompanied by a corresponding rise in the development of mobile applications aimed at enhancing the safety and experience of participants. In 2012, three apps appeared: iSis, Sng, and SnoWhere [9], which the developers touted as life-saving apps. The applications detected whether the user was involved in an avalanche and notified the contacts and competent services in that area. These apps did not warn the users of the dangers in the mountains and did not educate them, but only took action when the a user was already in danger. The Canadian Avalanche Center was well aware of this, and very quickly issued a warning and advised against the use of such applications instead of avalanche beacons [10]. The following year, 2013, the applications were withdrawn from the market due to the realization that people's lives depended on their correct functioning. In summary, the solutions mentioned above are either *reactive* focus on rescue or are a source of very general educational content that prevents their practical use. With GoraNiNora, we develop a versatile practical *proactive* tool that improves the safety of participants in the mountains.

The fields of context-aware computing and resource-efficient mobile computing have made significant strides in past decades due to advancements in mobile sensor technology and algorithms enabling applications to adapt their behavior based on the user's context [14,17]. These technologies offer the potential for creating more personalized and relevant user experiences, for instance, by adapting to a user's physical activity [18]. However, their application in the domain of outdoor safety and education remains challenging. Critically, it is important to fully understand the domain in which the app will be used, so that the key dimensions of the context and the key affordances of mobile computing and sensing can be identified.

3 Methodology

The development of "GoraNiNora" was informed by a comprehensive research methodology that included surveys, in-depth interviews, and usability testing. This approach enabled the collection of valuable insights into the needs and preferences of mountain tourists, as well as the practical challenges they face.

3.1 Survey

The success of the development solution is also influenced by the interaction between the users and the developers of the solution [16]. To obtain a detailed overview of the habits of users regarding the use of avalanche devices, their education in the field of mountaineering safety, and the equipment used while in the mountains, we conducted an online survey. We used the online tool 1KA for the survey and published it on the Slovenian mountaineering association website and in two Facebook groups (*Turno smuanje – Sneak* and *Ideje kam v hribe*) geared towards local mountaineers and touring skiers. We have collected answers from 950 respondents (72% male, 28% female, avg. age 36.9 years).

The most common activities that the respondents engage in are mountaineering and ski touring. We are interested in how well-equipped the mountaineers and touring skiers are. *The avalanche trio*, which consists of an avalanche beacon, shovel, and a probe, is used by as many as 85 % of the touring skiers and only 65 % of the mountaineers. *The avalanche backpack* is also more common among touring skiers. From this data, we can conclude that people think that avalanches are dangerous only for ski touring, which is far from the truth, since avalanches threaten all visitors to the mountains in winter. The mountain climbers are very well equipped with crampons (95%) and ice axes (88%), while 80% of touring skiers use the above equipment. Finally, our survey shows that a first aid kit is also commonly present. We can estimate that Slovenian mountain visitors often go to the mountains relatively well equipped. Only the avalanche backpack is a relatively less used piece, probably due to its price, as it is the most expensive of all the listed equipment.

Regarding to use of tracking technology, somewhat surprising is that as many as 64% of respondents use GPS to track their route. This means that a mobile application that we develop would not consume additional energy to obtain the location, since it would not be the only one that would request the location from the Android system via the *Location API* (Application Programming Interface) [6]. On the other hand, such a prevalence of mobile phone use is problematic, as nearby electronic devices may disturb the avalanche beacon. This is not generally known, and, of those surveyed, 46% believe that electronic devices do not disturb the avalanche beacon, while among those who believe that electronic devices disturb the beacon, only 35% knew that the disturbance is the highest when the beacon is in the reception mode. We can conclude that users of avalanche beacons are not well acquainted with its operation, thus that there is an opportunity for improving the general training and education when it comes to the use of mountaineering equipment.

When it comes to obtaining relevant information, 99% of respondents get information about snow conditions online; 55% of respondents inquire about the situation from friends; 34% of respondents use mobile applications; and 12% of respondents use the radio. As many as 88% of respondents follow the report on the risk of avalanches before each tour, which means that information about the current situation is important to them. 93% of respondents go to the hills in pairs or groups, so the application could take into account that a user often does not venture into the mountains alone. Finally, only 55% of our respondents review the avalanche safety information every year. Those who do, usually attend avalanche safety lectures and full-day workshops in the field.

We believe that the respondents' lack knowledge about avalanche safety, confirmed by their answers indicating that the operation of the avalanche beacon necessary for a successful rescue is not widely understood, that the avalanche safety information is generally not revisited every year, and the fact that, on the average, users rate their experience level as 3.1 out of 5, point to the need of providing concise in-context information through our mobile app solution.

3.2   Interviews

We conducted interviews with eight experts in the field of mountain safety. We looked for people who are professionally engaged in work related to mountains or who have many years of experience in mountaineering. The purpose of the interviews was to learn as much as possible in the field of safety, technologies and in general the use of mobile devices in the mountains, so to identify critical information that should be supplied to our users. The interviews were up to one hour long. We spoke with experts from the Environmental Agency of the Republic of Slovenia (ARSO), the Mountaineering Association of Slovenia (PZS), the Administration of the Republic of Slovenia for Protection and Rescue (URSZR), the head of the Zelenica-Tri Avalanche Protection Service, two volunteer mountain rescuers, guide and head of the Crossrisk project [8].

The approach to reducing accidents in the mountains with a mobile app that is supposed to replace the beacon and notify contacts in the event of an accident is flawed, was unanimously voiced by the experts. The experts are of the opinion that such an application gives the user the impression of safety, as the user is sure that the application will notify the emergency services in the event of an avalanche. Not only can such application fail to react in case of an avalanche, it can also give the user a false impression of safety and reduce the motivation for keeping oneself informed and prepared.

Our intention is develop an application for use in the mountains, thus, it is very important to know what the limitations of using mobile devices in the mountains in winter. Our interviewees noted that due to low temperatures and poor signal coverage in the mountains, the battery drains faster. Furthermore, the mobile device is usually kept as close to the body as possible due to heat and is therefore inaccessible. We also wear gloves in winter which makes it difficult to operate a mobile device. Therefore, *the interaction time with the device should be as short and infrequent as possible.*

Regarding the content, our interviewees agreed that the most important thing is to educate people, as in this way mountaineering-related accidents can be avoided naturally. There are swaths of educational materials about safety in the mountains, yet they are scattered around the Web and people have to locate the info themselves. Since a user may not even know which information is relevant for a particular situation, it may be difficult to extract the important knowledge before the trip. Thus, *there is an opportunity for a mobile app to provide relevant content to a particular use at a particular place and time.*

3.3   System Requirements

Based on interviews and survey analysis, we formulated functional requirements focusing on the user's point of view and the desired affordances of the app:

- **Display contextually-relevant and general alerts.** The main purpose of the application should be to deliver context-dependent information to users when visiting the mountains, as well as information of more general importance, on the basis of which the user can decide to visit the mountains. Thus, we positioned alerts at the core of GoraNiNora. We decided to split the alerts into general and contextually-relevant alerts. *General alerts* are pertaining to a wider geographical area a user plans to visit. With these alerts, we want to warn the user in advance about various dangerous situations one can expect based on the general properties of the area. *Contextually-relevant alerts*, on the other hand, are to be displayed only when the application detects that the user is in the mountains.
- **Automatic context detection.**   To issue relevant alerts, the app must accurately detect the context of a user. We identified a user's physical activity and her location as the key aspects of the context that need to be detected. Furthermore, there is a need for the app to automatically detect that a user is indeed venturing into mountains, as well as the need to obtain latent context, such as the information about the slope that a user is on, weather, and other factors.
- **View alert history.** To support the educational side of the engagement, the app should allow the user to revisit the earlier alerts and inspect them in more detail.
- **Usability in the outdoor environment.** GoraNiNora is to be used predominantly in outdoor winter environments, where there is a need for larger font size and a stronger contrast among elements. Due to this, additional restrictions are placed on the amount of content that can be shown in a single interaction instance.

4   System Design and Implementation

This section describes the system architecture, including its components and functionalities, and highlights the application's innovative approach to context-aware computing and battery efficiency.

4.1   Perception of Relevant Context

Mobile devices have a multitude of built-in sensors, such as accelerometer, gyroscope and GPS, which, combined with machine learning, allow the device to accurately determine the context of the user. In our application, the relevant context is determined by the location, current weather and avalanche conditions in the area where the user is located. The 1 table describes more precisely

Table 1. Data available for context recognition.

Data	Description	Source	Sampling frequency	Availability
Altitude	Height above sea level	GPS	60 s, when in mountains.	GPS signal coverage
Location	Geographical coordinates	GPS	60 s, when in mountains	GPS signal coverage
User physical activity	Walk or still.	Activity Recognition Transition API [1]	Handled by the underlying API, no control over it	Always
Slope	Angle of the slope in degrees °	ArcGIS API [2]	60 s, when in mountains.	GPS signal coverage, Internet connection
Exposure	Exposure in degrees from (0° to 360°)	ArcGIS API [2]	60 s, when in mountains	GPS singal coverage, Internet connection
Temperature	Altitude-dependent temp	ARSO weather [4]	Low (at least once per day)	Internet connection
Wind	Altitude-dependent wind speed	ARSO weather [4]	Low (at least once per day)	Internet connection
Weather	Cloudiness, weather events, and precipitation intensity	ARSO weather [4]	Low (at least once per day)	Internet connection
Problem	Avalanche problem in the snowpack	ARSO avalanches [3]	Low (once per day at most)	Internet connection
Pattern	Typical avalanche patterns	ARSO avalanches [3]	Low (once per day at most)	Internet connection
Danger	Avalanche danger level from 1 to 5	ARSO avalanches [3]	Low (once per day at most)	Internet connection

the data that the application captures to define the context, where the data is acquired through a mix of on-device sensing and remote API querying.

An important part of the context detection is the automatic recognition of hill walking. GoraNiNora monitors the GPS signal and a user's physical activity, and in case the user has walked at least 50 m in elevation in the last 30 min indicates hill walking. This is signaled to a user through a notification. Furhter, the application enables manual toggling of the hill walking mode.

4.2   Defining and Triggering Warning Alerts

In the previous section we identified the need for showing relevant alerts to the user. In GoraNiNora we achieve this through the notification mechanism. If, and which, alerts will be shown is defined through a set of rules that describe the conditions that must be satisfied for the application to display a certain alert or warning to the user. We obtained these rules from discussions with experts and professional literature in the field of mountain safety. As detailed above, the warnings are divided into *contextually-relevant* and *general* alerts. Contextually-relevant alerts take into account the current location, slope, slope orientation, and altitude. The context is further expanded with the weather forecast, current avalanche problems, patterns, and known hazards. More specifically, using the user's current location GoraNiNora queries remote APIs of the avalanche bulletin and the weather forecast. The application then matches the acquired information with the predefined rules for displaying warnings, and displays any contextually-relevant warnings to the user.

General warnings are the ones that the user can look at every time she opens the application, even if she is not in the mountains. Depending on the geographical area that a user selects using a drop-down menu, the app displays general alerts for the region. With general warnings, we want to warn the user in advance about various situations in the mountains. For example, in case of rain or newly fallen snow, we want to inform the user in advance so that he can adjust the upcoming winter tours.

The rules for displaying general and current warnings are shipped with the app in a JSON file and are written to an on-device database when the application is first started. In the current prototype, the application will not retrieve new rules from an external source, yet, at a later stage, this rules could be handled by a public authority in charge of mountain safety.

4.3   User Interface

In accordance with the best practices of Android application development, the user interface is based on Fragments created in the context of various activities. The basic Fragments of the application are shown in Fig. 1, and a detailed description of the warnings is shown in Fig. 2.

Fragment for displaying warnings (Fig. 1b) takes care of displaying contextually-relevant and general warnings fired during the current day. The Fragment also displays information on whether uphill walking has been detected

  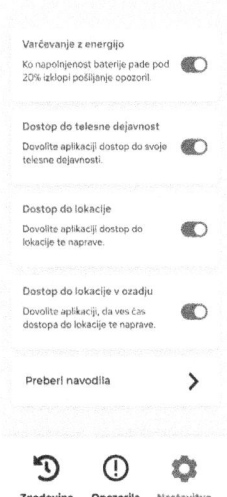

(a) History tab to display historical alerts.

(b) Alert tab to display contextually-relevant and general alerts.

(c) Settings tab to edit app permissions, display instructions, and turn on power saving.

Fig. 1. Three main tabs of GoraNiNora.

and enables manual switching to the walking mode, if needed. *Fragment for displaying history* (Fig. 1a) is responsible for displaying contextually-relevant and general alerts that the application has detected in the previous days. *Fragment to display settings* (Image 1c) ensures that the user can view the application's permissions, read the instructions again, and enable energy saving.

Activity to show current alerts by clicking notification notifies the user of currently detected alerts via a user-clickable Android notification. Clicking on the notification, the current contextually-relevant warnings are displayed (Image 2). *Activity to display alert details* takes care of the detailed description of the alert when it is clicked.

4.4 Use of Sound and Vibration to Deliver Alerts

From the analysis of user needs, we learned that the mobile device can be inaccessible while walking in winter, as we want it to be as close to the body as possible in a warm place. Even handling the device is very difficult due to the use of gloves. Therefore, we opted for an audio signal and vibration to be triggered when warnings are detected to signal potential danger. In this way, the user is informed about the received current alert can read it, or the application itself reads it with the help of the automatic text-to-speech translator. In the current version of the application issues the default notification sound and vibration,

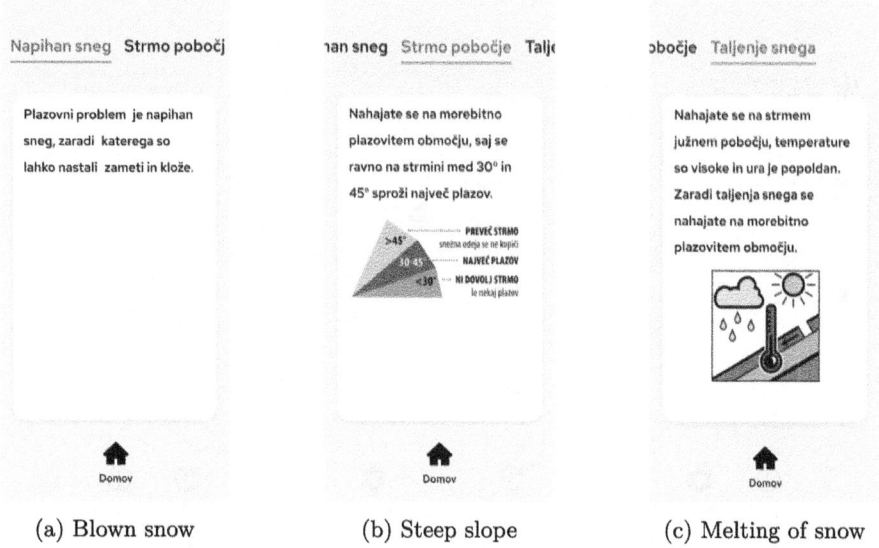

(a) Blown snow   (b) Steep slope   (c) Melting of snow

Fig. 2. Examples of context-relevant alerts in GoraNiNora.

thus does not allow the user to distinguish between GoraNiNora-related and other notifications. In future, we plan to analyze the most appropriate warning methods in the context of a winter visit to the mountains.

4.5 Battery Efficiency

Recognizing the importance of battery conservation in outdoor settings, GoraNi-Nora is designed to be able to take advantage of context-aware and approximate computing techniques to optimize energy consumption [17]. The application intelligently adjusts its data collection and processing activities based on the current battery level and the availability of critical information, thereby extending the device's battery life without compromising the delivery of essential safety information.

5 Usability Evaluation

The testing took place with ten volunteers (7 male and 3 female) aged between 15 and 65 years. The purpose of testing was to determine if GoraNiNora is sufficiently simple and understandable to use. User experience and interface testing was done using interactive mockups in Figma [5].

Participants were asked to use GoraNiNora during a mountaineering activity designed to simulate typical usage scenarios. The System Usability Scale (SUS) [12,13] was employed to quantitatively measure the application's usability. Post-activity interviews were conducted to gather qualitative feedback on the user experience, the perceived relevance of the educational content, and suggestions for improvements.

The SUS scores (average 89.75, standard deviation 5.83) indicated a high level of usability [7]. The usability evaluation also revealed areas for improvement. Testers tried to interact with the legend differentiating contextually-relevant from general alerts, mistaking it for a filter function, indicating a desire for alert filtering capabilities. Users expressed interest in seeing only contextually-relevant alerts during hiking and general alerts otherwise. However, to simplify interaction, especially with gloves, and prioritize the display of contextually-relevant alerts, a decision was made against implementing a filtering feature. Additionally, the notification indicating the app had detected hiking activity was not sufficiently noticeable in its original blue color, leading to oversights by some testers. This feedback led to the adoption of a more visible green color for this alert. Finally, one tester suggested that trust in the alerts could be enhanced by clarifying who is responsible for setting and managing the content of these alerts, proposing that this information be included in the app's instructions or settings.

6   Discussion

In this study we analysed the potential for mobile technologies to enhance mountain safety. We discovered that while mobile devices may not currently serve as the best tool for accident detection, they hold significant promise for educational purposes. With the advancement of sensor technology in wearable devices, such as smartwatches, and the increasing prevalence of these devices, we anticipate a future where applications could accurately detect imminent dangers in real-time. The integration of augmented reality and on-device machine learning could enable users to identify hazardous slopes directly, thereby avoiding potential dangers.

Our application GoraNiNora represents a stride towards this future by offering context-dependent notifications to users based on data sensed on a smartphone and matched against predefined rules. This approach not only addresses the immediate need for educational content tailored to the mountaineer's current situation, but also opens up possibilities for predictive models that could identify new hazards based on the collected field data. However, it's crucial to acknowledge that the current set of rules within our system is not exhaustive. The expertise of professionals in the field will be invaluable in expanding these rules to cover a broader range of scenarios.

7   Conclusion

In this paper we designed and implemented GoraNiNora to demonstrate the significant potential of mobile apps to enhance the safety and knowledge of outdoor enthusiasts. By leveraging sensor data to deliver context-sensitive information, such as location and physical activities, and querying a number of external

APIs, GoraNiNora acquires both general and contextually-relevant information and issues alerts to a mobile user. As we move towards a future where mobile and wearable technologies become increasingly sophisticated, the possibility of creating an ecosystem of applications that can accurately predict, warn, and, most importantly, educate users of potential hazards in real-time becomes more tangible.

Acknowledgement. The authors thank the survey respondents, the interviewees, and the usability testers. This work was supported by the Slovenian Research Agency (grant P2-0098 and project J2-3047).

References

1. Activity recognition API. https://developers.google.com/location-context/activity-recognition
2. ARCGIS summarize elevation. https://developers.arcgis.com/rest/elevation/api-reference/summarize-elevation.htm
3. ARSO plazovi. https://vreme.arso.gov.si/plazovi
4. ARSO weather forecast. https://meteo.arso.gov.si/met/sl/service/
5. Figma. https://figma.com
6. Location services. https://developers.google.com/android/reference/com/google/android/gms/location/LocationServices
7. Measuring usability with the system usability scale (sus). https://measuringu.com/sus/
8. Project crossrisk. https://crossrisk.zrc-sazu.si/
9. Snowsafe blog. https://www.snowsafe.co.uk/avalanche-transceiver-app/
10. There's not an app for that: CAC issues warning about avalanche apps (2013). https://newatlas.com/cac-warning-avalanche-search-apps/29575/
11. Accident statistics GRZS (2022). https://www.grzs.si/resevanje/statistika-nesrec/
12. Blažica, B., Lewis, J.R.: A Slovene translation of the system usability scale: the SUS-SI. Int. J. Hum. Comput. Interact. **31**(2), 112–117 (2015)
13. Brooke, J., et al.: SUS-A quick and dirty usability scale. Usability Eval. Ind. **189**(194), 4–7 (1996)
14. Chen, G., Kotz, D.: A survey of context-aware mobile computing research (2000)
15. Eidenbenz, D., et al.: Survival probability in avalanche victims with long burial (60 min): a retrospective study. Resuscitation **166**, 93–100 (2021)
16. Inukollu, V.N., Keshamoni, D.D., Kang, T., Inukollu, M.: Factors influencing quality of mobile apps: role of mobile app development life cycle. Int. J. Softw. Eng. Appl. (IJSEA), vol.5, no.5, September 2014 (2014)
17. Pejović, V.: Towards approximate mobile computing. GetMobile: Mob. Comput. Commun. **22**(4), 9–12 (2019)
18. Yamabe, T., Takahashi, K.: Experiments in mobile user interface adaptation for walking users. In: The 2007 International Conference on Intelligent Pervasive Computing (IPC 2007), pp. 280–284. IEEE (2007)

Comparative Research on Digital Design for Spring Festival and Christmas

Junwen Xiao[1,2](✉)

[1] Wuhan University of Technology, 122 Luoshi Road, Wuhan, Hubei,
People's Republic of China
xjw1999720@gmail.com
[2] University of Wales Trinity Saint David, Alexandra Road, Swansea, UK

Abstract. As the core carrier of culture, festivals concisely and profoundly display the essence of regional culture through diverse forms such as clothing, food, rituals, music and dance. These elements not only have the value of academic research, but also are important symbols of cultural identity and cultural inheritance. The Spring Festival and Christmas are the most important traditional festivals in China and the Europe and America, and their festive elements are also regarded as important traditional cultural symbols in China and Europe and America. The differences between the festive elements of the Spring Festival and Christmas stem from four aspects: world outlook and way of thinking, religious attitude, interpersonal relationships, and cultural inheritance methods. However, currently, comparative studies on the festive digitization of Spring Festival and Christmas are rare. Therefore, the purpose of this study is to explore the different advantages and uniqueness of the two cultures in digital design by analyzing how Chinese, European and American designers deal with design challenges with unique cultural backgrounds. Promote the digital design of traditional festivals between the two cultures through comparative research, and use traditional festivals as an opportunity to promote cross-cultural exchanges between the two cultures.

Keywords: Cultural differences · Comparative Research · Digital Design · Festival

1 Introduction

In the context of globalization, economic exchanges and social culture are increasingly integrated. As an important part of the culture of each country, the frequency of festival culture exchanges has also increased significantly. The Spring Festival, as the most solemn and distinctive traditional festival of the Chinese nation, carries a profound cultural heritage and national sentiment; and Christmas, as the most popular religious and cultural festival in the Western world, has also had a far-reaching impact on the world. The cultural exchange and integration of these two major festivals not only reflects the mutual respect and reference between different cultures, but also promotes the diversified development of global culture.

© The Author(s), under exclusive license to Springer Nature Switzerland AG 2025
P. Zaphiris et al. (Eds.): HCII 2024, LNCS 15378, pp. 405–416, 2025.
https://doi.org/10.1007/978-3-031-76815-6_29

At the same time, with the rapid development of information technology and digital technology, traditional festival forms are undergoing profound changes. As an emerging technical means, digital technology is gradually penetrating into various fields of festival culture, bringing new possibilities for the presentation and dissemination of festival activities. As the most representative festivals in the East and the West, the Spring Festival and Christmas use digital technology in festival design, which not only reflects the integration of festival culture and modern technology, but also provides us with a unique perspective to examine and compare festivals under different cultural backgrounds.

Therefore, this paper aims to explore the similarities and differences between the two in terms of design concepts, technical means, and forms of expression through a comparative study of the digital design of the Spring Festival and Christmas, and to analyze the role of digital design in the inheritance and innovation of festival culture, in order to provide theoretical support and practical guidance for the digital development of festival culture. At the same time, this paper also hopes to promote the exchange and integration of festival culture under different cultural backgrounds and promote the diversified development of global culture through this study.

2 Digitalization of Festival Culture

2.1 Digitization

Digitalization is a technical means of converting information, materials or processes in the real world into digital form, and using digital devices such as computers for processing, storage, transmission and display. The process of digitalization includes steps such as sampling, quantization and encoding, through which continuously changing analog signals can be converted into discrete digital signals. The application scope of digitalization technology is very wide, including various fields such as audio, video, images, and text. The advantage of digitalization is that it can improve the accuracy, reliability and processability of information, while reducing the cost of information transmission and storage. In the field of traditional cultural protection, digital research and practice have achieved remarkable results.

2.2 Digital Technology and Festival Culture

Traditional festival culture is often preserved through oral inheritance, paper records, etc., while digital technology provides a new solution for the preservation and inheritance of festival culture. Digital technology can digitally collect, store and process various elements of festival culture, such as music, dance, drama, folk activities, etc., so that they can be permanently preserved in digital form. At the same time, digital technology provides more colorful forms and channels for the display and dissemination of festival culture. The popularity of the Internet and mobile devices provides a more convenient and extensive way for the dissemination of festival culture. In addition, through the processing and processing of digital technology, traditional festival culture is combined with modern elements, creating more festival cultural products with the characteristics of the times, which are digital products that better meet the aesthetics and needs of modern people. The innovations brought by these digital technologies have injected new vitality and impetus into the inheritance and development of festival culture.

The digitization of festival culture is the process of innovatively protecting, inheriting and promoting traditional festival culture using digital technology and information platforms. This process not only involves converting traditional cultural elements into digital formats, but also includes enhancing the interactivity and accessibility of festival culture through new media means, thereby attracting a wider audience. With the development of information technology, especially the widespread application of new media technology, the digitization of festival culture has become an important way of cultural inheritance and innovation. Digital technology makes the collection, classification, storage and display of festival cultural resources more efficient and systematic.

3   Cross-Cultural Communication and Festival Research

In the context of cross-cultural communication, the communication and celebration of the Spring Festival and Christmas have influenced each other and promoted understanding and respect between different cultures. The international communication of the Spring Festival helps to promote Chinese culture, while the global celebration of Christmas demonstrates the openness and inclusiveness of Western culture [1]. In addition, as China's status on the international stage rises, the influence of the Spring Festival, as an important part of Chinese culture, is also expanding [2]. By comparing the digitization of the Spring Festival and Christmas, we can better understand the differences and commonalities between Chinese and Western cultures and promote communication and integration between different cultures. Therefore, this paper will conduct a comparative study on the digital design of the Spring Festival and Christmas from the following aspects.

3.1   Differences Between the Spring Festival and Christmas Celebrations

Explore the fundamental differences between the Spring Festival, the most distinctive traditional festival of the Chinese nation, and Christmas, a religious and cultural festival popular in the Western world, in terms of cultural heritage, values, and social significance. Analyze how the collectivism and community participation of the Spring Festival and the personal religious experience of Christmas affect the digital expression of the two.

3.2   Comparison of Festive Elements Between the Spring Festival and Christmas

Compare traditional elements of the Spring Festival such as red envelopes, temple fairs, dragon and lion dances with Christmas elements such as Christmas gifts, Christmas markets, Christmas carols, etc., and analyze their symbolic meanings and social functions in their respective cultures, and how they are innovatively transformed and utilized in the digital age.

3.3   Comparison of the Digitization of Festive Elements Between the Spring Festival and Christmas

Compare the different strategies and applications of the Spring Festival and Christmas in digital practice. For example, the digitization of Spring Festival red envelopes through mobile payment platforms, and how to use AR technology to enhance interactivity; and how Christmas greeting cards are digitally disseminated through email and social media platforms, and how digitalization affects people's emotional expression and social habits.

3.4   The Role of Digital Design in the Inheritance and Innovation of Festival Culture

Study how digital design can help the traditional festival culture of the Spring Festival and Christmas to be more effectively inherited and innovated. Analyze how digital technology can make the collection, classification, storage and display of festival cultural resources more efficient and systematic, and how to enhance the interactivity and accessibility of festival culture through new media.

4   Cultural Differences Between Chinese New Year and Christmas

4.1   Origin and Cultural Background of the Festival

The Spring Festival, the Chinese Lunar New Year, originated in ancient agricultural society and is closely related to seasonal festivals and sacrificial activities. It reflects the respect for family and ancestors in Chinese culture, as well as the wish for future prosperity and harmony. Christmas, a Christian festival, commemorates the birth of Jesus Christ and reflects the deep respect for religious beliefs in Western society [3]. The difference in the origins of these two festivals shows the different orientations of Chinese and Western cultures in religious beliefs and values.

4.2   Festival Customs and Cultural Values

Although the Spring Festival and Christmas originate from different cultural backgrounds, they both emphasize the themes of family reunion and gratitude. During the Spring Festival, Chinese families celebrate the New Year through activities such as New Year's Eve dinner, distributing red envelopes, and posting Spring Festival couplets, which reflects the pursuit of harmony and auspiciousness in Chinese culture. Christmas expresses family affection and friendship through the decoration of Christmas trees, exchanging gifts and family gatherings. These customs show the social and cultural commonality of festivals as cultural inheritance and social cohesion. At the same time, the celebrations of the Spring Festival focus more on collectivism and community participation, while Christmas focuses more on family and personal religious experiences [4].

4.3 Religious Beliefs and Festivals

The religion and beliefs of the Spring Festival reflect the diversity and inclusiveness of Chinese culture, including tolerance of Buddhism and Taoism and respect for ancestors. In contrast, Christmas celebrations are deeply influenced by Christian doctrines, reflecting the central position of religious beliefs in Western culture. In terms of festival activities, Spring Festival celebrations such as dragon and lion dances and firecrackers show the vitality and enthusiasm of Chinese culture. Christmas is dominated by religious and cultural activities such as church activities and Christmas concerts, reflecting the importance of religious beliefs in Western culture.

5 Chinese New Year and Christmas Festive Elements

The Spring Festival is one of the most important traditional festivals in China. It symbolizes family reunion, bidding farewell to the old and welcoming the new, and the beginning of hope. During the Spring Festival, it is a traditional custom for elders to distribute red envelopes (also known as lucky money) to younger generations. This custom has rich cultural significance and implications. It is traditionally believed that the coins in the red envelopes can drive away evil spirits and protect the younger generations from misfortune and disaster. The red envelopes also symbolize the elders' blessings to the younger generations, hoping that they will be safe, healthy, happy, and bring good luck in the new year. Christmas, as the most important festival in Europe and the United States, originally originated from religious traditions, but now has extraordinary influence worldwide. Giving gifts is an important part of Christmas.

5.1 Similarities and Differences Between Chinese New Year and Christmas Elements

In the academic field of cross-cultural comparative studies, in-depth analysis of the festive elements of the Spring Festival and Christmas not only helps to reveal the uniqueness of the two cultures, but also promotes the understanding of cultural integration and inheritance in the context of globalization. The following is a comparative study of the festive elements of the Spring Festival and Christmas, aiming to explore the similarities and differences between the two in terms of cultural traditions, social significance and symbolic connotations.

Red Envelopes and Christmas Gifts. The red envelopes (Hongbao) during the Spring Festival are a gift from elders to younger generations, reflecting the Confucian culture of respecting the old and loving the young and wealth inheritance. The exchange of red envelopes is not only the transfer of material wealth, but also a blessing and expectation for the younger generation.

Christmas cards usually contain holiday greetings and family information, and are a medium for emotional communication in European and American societies. The sending of Christmas cards reflects the importance of personal expression and emotional communication in Western culture.

Spring Festival Performances and Christmas Activities. The Spring Festival performances are rich and colorful, covering a variety of art forms such as opera, dance, and music. They are not only a display of visual art, but also an important form of community unity and cultural inheritance.

Christmas activities include various forms of performing arts such as Christmas carols, Christmas plays, concerts, light shows, etc. They originated from Christian religious rituals, and later gradually evolved into secular celebrations, becoming a symbol of community cohesion and social harmony.

Temple Fairs and Christmas Markets. Temple fairs are traditional market activities during the Spring Festival, integrating religious, cultural and entertainment elements. Temple fairs are not only places for commodity trading, but also platforms for cultural exchange and community interaction.

Christmas markets are mainly about commodity trading and social activities, reflecting the market economy and consumer culture of Western society. The holding of Christmas markets reflects the importance Western society attaches to holiday consumption and social activities.

5.2 Comparison

Through the above comparison, we can see that although the Spring Festival and Christmas differ in cultural background, celebration methods and symbolic meaning, both emphasize the importance of family reunion, cultural exchange and social harmony. The comparative study of these festival elements not only enriches our understanding of the two cultural traditions, but also provides an academic perspective for further exploring the mutual influence and integration between different cultures. Future research can continue to explore the evolution of the Spring Festival and Christmas in different cultural backgrounds, as well as their mutual reference and integration in the era of globalization.

6   The Digitization of Festival Elements and Their Digital Design

The process of digital transformation, the traditional festival elements of the Spring Festival and Christmas have undergone innovative transformation and formed a unique digital form. This transformation not only marks the adaptation and development of the two festival cultures in modern society, but also reflects the important role of digital design in inheriting and innovating traditional festivals.

6.1   Red Envelope and Christmas Card

Driven by the wave of digitalization, the culture of red envelopes during the Spring Festival has achieved an innovative transformation. Through mobile payment platforms, especially the "Collect Five Blessings" activity launched by Alipay, red envelopes have been transformed from traditional physical forms to electronic forms. Users can obtain red envelopes by collecting five blessing cards online and using AR scanning technology. This process not only retains the traditional meaning of red envelopes, but also adds interactivity and fun, making the "Collect Five Blessings" activity a Spring Festival event that everyone can participate in, enhancing the festive atmosphere of the festival [5].

The launch of the WeChat red envelope function has further promoted the digital development of the Spring Festival red envelope culture. Since its launch in 2014, WeChat red envelopes have given new life to the traditional custom of sending red envelopes in the digital age with its simple interactive mode. It not only makes the delivery of red envelopes more convenient, but also promotes the popularity of remote video calls to wish a happy new year, allowing relatives and friends in different places to share the joy of the festival.

In terms of design, although Alipay's "Collect Five Blessings" activity follows the traditional Chinese style of the Five Blessings, it has made innovations in the interactive mode. The activity encourages users to complete the collection tasks through four core driving forces - progress and achievement, ownership and sense of possession, scarcity and desire, and unknown and curiosity - and gives red envelope rewards to users who complete the tasks. This design cleverly combines traditional culture with modern technology, improving user participation and satisfaction.

At the same time, WeChat red envelopes remain simple and intuitive in their interactive mode, but their innovation in red envelope styles is also worth noting. The WeChat platform allows artists or institutions to publish artistically designed red envelope covers for users to download. This personalized design not only enhances the cultural connotation of red envelopes, but also brings users a richer visual experience.

James Carey, an American communication scholar, once proposed the "ritual view" of communication. He believed that communication is not only the transmission of information, but also the construction of a meaningful cultural world through communication [6]. In this sense, Alipay's "Collect Five Blessings" and WeChat red envelopes have become a new ritual of the Spring Festival. They not only inherit traditional culture, but also create new festival elements in a digital form, making the celebration of the Spring Festival more diverse and modern [7].

Christmas cards are an important element of Christmas celebrations. Because they are gifts like red envelopes, the digitization of Christmas cards is compared with the digitization of Spring Festival red envelopes. As a tool to express holiday greetings, Christmas cards have an important purpose. They provide an opportunity for people to connect with their social circles. Digital Christmas cards are sent via email or social media platforms. Some brands even provide interactive cards that display video or audio messages by scanning QR codes, adding interactivity and personalized experience to the holiday.

Judging from the styles and decorations of Christmas cards, electronic Christmas cards obviously provide users with more choices than physical greeting card stores. Many websites offer hundreds of different electronic Christmas card templates for users to choose from. What's more interesting is that websites such as Canva and Smilebox also provide online electronic card customization functions, where users can choose their favorite decorations, music and upload meaningful photos as part of the card. Although many applications and websites have launched the production of electronic Christmas cards, a survey conducted by Daniel Gooch and Ryan Kelly in 2016 found that people use paper Christmas cards more than electronic Christmas cards [8]. Some people think that "paper cards seem to express my care and efforts better than electronic cards." In fact, people think that electronic cards are not as effective and sometimes even completely inappropriate: "They don't belong to proper Christmas cards" "They are not humane and there is no effort." Supporters of paper cards also believe that paper cards can make the house more festive. In contrast, electronic cards are mainly seen as a computer-based media, rather than something that can be viewed and shared.

The culture of the red envelopes during the Spring Festival and the tradition of greeting cards during Christmas present different characteristics in the digital transformation. China's Spring Festival red envelopes have been digitized through mobile payment platforms such as Alipay's "Collect Five Blessings" and WeChat red envelopes. These platforms use AR technology, the interactivity of social networks, and personalized design to strengthen the sense of participation and fun of the festival. They are closely related to the popularity of mobile payments in China and the deep integration of social media, which has led to a wave of participation by all people. In contrast, although Christmas e-cards offer a rich selection of styles and personalized customization, many people still prefer the unique touch and human touch of traditional paper greeting cards. Paper greeting cards are considered to be more able to express personal emotions and efforts, and add to the festive atmosphere of the family. This difference may be due to differences in cultural values, technology acceptance, social habits, and market environment. The improvement of China's mobile payment infrastructure provides technical support for the digitization of Spring Festival red envelopes, while the Western Christmas greeting card tradition is influenced by people's emotional attachment to traditional celebrations and the recognition of the value of physical objects.

6.2 Spring Festival Performances and Christmas Programs

Spring Festival performances and Christmas activities have not only been inherited and protected with the advent of the digital age, but have also been revitalized and charmed with the help of modern technology, and have acquired innovative forms of expression.

Lion and dragon dances and fireworks shows are the most well-known Chinese New Year performances. In addition, due to China's vast land area, different regions have different performance customs. Shehuo performances (a general term for a variety of recreational and acrobatic activities), a traditional cultural activity that brings together elements of recreational and acrobatic activities, are deeply rooted in the folk beliefs of Northwest China. Historically, the display of this type of folk art is often limited to specific regions, especially communities at the township level, and is less known to the outside world. However, with the vigorous development of short video platforms in recent years, Shehuo performances have ushered in a new display window and a wider audience group [9].

Digitalization has not only broken geographical boundaries, but also provided a new display platform for community fire performances. Through the modern medium of short videos, the colorful charm of community fire art has been able to transcend regions and reach audiences across the country and even the world. These short and concise video works, with their intuitive and vivid characteristics, capture and show the essence and climax of community fire performances, allowing the audience to feel the original passion and enthusiasm even outside the screen. The community fire performance videos on short video platforms not only record the moments of the performance, but also often include an introduction to the culture and history behind the performance, providing viewers with an opportunity to gain an in-depth understanding of the rich folk customs in Northwest China. In addition, these videos can also stimulate the interest of the audience, prompting them to further explore and participate in related cultural activities [10]. Through interviews, we investigated people's views on the dissemination of Spring Festival folk performances such as community fire on digital short video platforms. Most people expressed their approval of such dissemination: "I didn't know there were such performances in the Northwest before. To a certain extent, these performances and the culture behind them can represent the spirit of the Chinese nation."

The performances during the Spring Festival are an important part of the culture of the Spring Festival, and the Christmas programs are in stark contrast. Digital transformation has greatly enriched the performing arts of Christmas programs, bringing innovative forms of expression and wider audience participation to traditional celebrations. During the COVID-19 pandemic, many theater companies and artists have made large-scale reshaping of live theater performances and explored various media to connect with the audience, including experiments with virtual reality and video games. In the virtual performance space, artists use VR, AR and 3D simulation technology to create an immersive viewing experience, allowing the audience to enjoy the performance as if they were on the scene even at home [11]. Online live events have become a new bridge connecting artists and audiences, allowing Christmas concerts, stage plays and dance performances to reach global audiences through the Internet.

Digitalization not only enhances the interactivity of performing arts, but also allows audiences to directly participate in performances through online voting, social media interaction and other tools, which enhances the sense of participation and interactivity of performances. At the same time, the communication power of social media platforms has also become an important channel for promoting Christmas performing arts, helping artists and performance groups attract fans and build brand image.

Take Actors Theatre of Louisville ('ATL'), for example, who adapted Charles Dickens' A Christmas Carol and used XR technology to help audiences get closer to Scrooge's experience. In early discussions with partner studio Agile Lens, which created the ghost animation, the team realized that the same 3D assets could be used to create a VR stage for the game. This led to two parallel productions of the show, one on stage and the other entirely in VR, with the two stages forming a digital twin of A Christmas Carol [12].

The digital transformation of the Spring Festival and Christmas has its own characteristics in design. The digital design of the Spring Festival tends to use short video platforms, emphasizing the instant sharing of art and social interaction, so that traditional performances such as lion and dragon dances and community performances can be quickly spread, breaking through geographical restrictions and reaching a wider audience. This design pays more attention to popularization and socialization, emphasizing the sharing and dissemination of culture.

The digital design of Christmas focuses more on creating personalized and immersive experiences, providing novel viewing methods through technologies such as AR and VR, such as transforming A Christmas Carol into an XR experience. It emphasizes innovation and exploration in art, enhances audience participation through online live broadcasts and social media interactions, and helps artists build brand images.

The design of the Spring Festival highlights the popularization and education of traditional culture, while the design of Christmas highlights the innovation and personalization of artistic experience. The digital designs of the two festivals reflect the integration of respect for traditional culture and innovative spirit, and show the innovation paths and development directions under different cultural backgrounds.

6.3   Digital Temple Fairs and Christmas Markets

Spring Festival temple fairs and Christmas markets are also important elements of the Spring Festival and Christmas. Their digitization, as a model of the combination of traditional festivals and modern technology, has brought consumers a new shopping experience and cultural participation method. Through the construction of e-commerce platforms, digital temple fairs enable traditional handicrafts, festival foods, etc. to be displayed and sold online, breaking through geographical and time limitations, allowing consumers around the world to easily participate in the fun of shopping during the Spring Festival. This model not only enhances the diversity of goods and the convenience of shopping, but also enhances the interactivity between buyers and sellers through instant messaging functions. At the same time, it also provides a platform for the display and dissemination of traditional culture.

Thanks to the rapid development of China's Internet and e-commerce industries over the past 25 years, digital Spring Festival temple fairs have become part of people's daily lives. In Chinese culture, the Spring Festival symbolizes the end of the old year and the beginning of the new year, so many consumers tend to buy new and more expensive daily necessities during this period. Whether it is Alibaba or JD.com, large e-commerce platforms will launch grand online shopping festivals around the Spring Festival and name these activities in the form of temple fairs. These digital temple fairs attract consumers by offering rich discounts and vouchers. From the perspective of interactive design, these shopping platforms not only incorporate traditional Spring Festival decorations and patterns into their website designs to create a strong festive atmosphere, but also cleverly digitize traditional Spring Festival games such as guessing lantern riddles. Consumers who participate in these games can not only experience the fun of traditional culture, but also have the opportunity to get additional discounts and vouchers, further enhancing the interactivity and fun of the shopping experience [13].

In the process of digitalization of Christmas markets, early research has laid the foundation for the development of this field. For example, Simon Marquis conducted in-depth research on Christmas e-commerce in 2000 [14]. In 2020, Dave further pointed out that the booming e-commerce has fundamentally changed the pattern of Christmas shopping and has had an impact on traditional gift-giving behavior [15]. At present, many online shopping platforms have launched online Christmas market activities to cater to consumers' shopping needs. However, through interviews, we found that consumers are more inclined to buy holiday items online before Christmas when discussing Christmas shopping. Especially during the Black Friday shopping festival, consumers can enjoy greater discounts, which has become an important consideration in their shopping plans. Therefore, for online shopping companies, combining Black Friday with digital

Christmas markets can not only attract consumers' attention, but also create new shopping experiences and market opportunities. This strategy can not only meet consumers' expectations for holiday shopping, but also further stimulate their shopping enthusiasm by providing more attractive discounts and offers.

With the development of cutting-edge technologies such as augmented reality (AR), virtual reality (VR), 5G, and artificial intelligence, the prospects of digital temple fairs and Christmas markets are becoming more and more exciting. The application of these technologies will enable consumers to enjoy a more realistic and interactive shopping experience, and at the same time, personalized services will more accurately meet the unique needs of each consumer. However, most of the virtual reality digital Spring Festival temple fairs and Christmas markets currently constructed using technologies such as VR, AR, and artificial intelligence are still in the experimental stage. Take Zhang Yu and Xu Zhepeng's study on the digitization of Wushan Temple Fair culture in February 2024 as an example. The study introduced interactive technologies such as VR, AR, and MR, aiming to achieve the comprehensive benefits of "reducing the cost of visiting the exhibition, breaking the geographical constraints, enhancing the fun experience, and strengthening the cognitive level." Although the study has made significant contributions to the digitization of traditional temple fair culture using innovative technologies, the project has not yet stepped out of the experimental stage [16]. Despite this, we have reason to be optimistic about the future. With the continuous maturity of technology and the gradual promotion of applications, emerging technologies will surely bring more innovative and interesting experiences to the digital transformation of Spring Festival temple fairs and Christmas markets. We expect these technologies to perfectly combine the charm of traditional festivals with the convenience of modern technology, bringing more colorful holiday celebrations to consumers around the world.

7   Conclusion

Through an in-depth comparative study, this paper reveals the similarities and differences between the digital design of the Spring Festival and Christmas, and how these designs have influenced and promoted the inheritance and innovation of festival culture. The digital transformation of the Spring Festival is reflected in the red envelope culture of mobile payment platforms, the dissemination of social performances on short video platforms, and the digital temple fairs on e-commerce platforms; while the digitalization of Christmas is reflected in e-cards spread through email and social media, online Christmas markets, and Christmas programs that use VR/AR technology to enhance the viewing experience. The digital design of both festivals demonstrates the integration of respect for traditional culture and innovative spirit, while also adapting to the technological development trend of modern society.

The analysis in this paper shows that digital technology not only provides a new platform and channel for the dissemination of traditional culture, but also makes festival culture more vivid and closer to modern people's lives by enhancing interactivity and accessibility. Digital design plays an important role in the inheritance and innovation of festival culture. It enables traditional cultural elements to survive and develop in new forms, and also provides new opportunities for the diversified development and exchange of global culture.

With the continuous advancement of technology, we expect digital design to bring more innovative forms of expression to traditional festivals such as the Spring Festival and Christmas, and further promote the exchange and integration of different cultures. Future research can continue to explore how digitalization affects festival activities in different cultural backgrounds, and how to more effectively use digital means to protect and inherit festival culture.

Here, we are optimistic that digitalization is not only a technical means, but also a cultural force. It is reshaping our understanding and celebration of traditional festivals on a global scale. Let us look forward to the arrival of a more diverse, interactive and shared festival culture era, and let us contribute to the development and prosperity of global culture.

References

1. Yan, Y.: A comparative study of Chinese and Western traditional festivals in the context of cross-cultural communication—taking Spring Festival and Christmas as examples, Sci. Technol. Inform. (2020)
2. Liu, D.: Comparative study of Spring Festival and Christmas, MS thesis, Henan University (2014)
3. Ouyang, Q.: Comparative analysis of Spring Festival and Christmas holiday elements. J. South-Central Univ. Nationalities (Humanit. Soc. Sci.) 5, 71–74 (2010)
4. Zhang, H.: See the differences between Chinese and Western cultures through the spring festival and Christmas, Group Lit. World 3, 280–282 (2012)
5. Shen, X., Zhao, Q.: A brief analysis of App product experience design from the perspective of gamification—take "Alipay Collection of Five Blessings" as an example. Popular Lit. Art 01, 74–75 (2020)
6. Carey, J.W.: A Cultural Approach to Communication, Communication as Culture, pp. 11–28. Routledge, New York (2009)
7. Tang, J.: Looking at Alipay's "collecting five blessings" activity from the perspective of media ritual theory, Today's media 8, (2019)
8. Gooch, D., Ryan, K.: Season's greetings: an analysis of Christmas card use. In: Proceedings of the 2016 CHI Conference Extended Abstracts on Human Factors in Computing Systems (2016)
9. Deming. A.,: Recognition and negotiation: shehuo performance during the spring festival in Jiezi township, J. Wenzhou Univ.·Soc. Sci. 25(6), 3–8 (2012)
10. Qi, X.: Application research on digital protection of intangible cultural heritage in central and western Guanxi. J. Baoji Univ. Arts Sci. (Soc. Sci.) (2015)
11. Gochfeld, D., et al.: A tale of two productions: a Christmas carol on stage and in VR. Proc. ACM Comput. Graph. Interact. Tech. 5(4), 1–9 (2022)
12. Amy, W.: Robert Barry Fleming on the 2020–2021 Season. (October 30, 2020). Retrieved Jan 18, 2020 (2020). https://www.actorstheatre.org/archive/robert-barry-fleming-2020-season/
13. Han, R., Yuanhuifen, Wang, X.: Analysis on the design path of intangible cultural heritage products based on experience - taking Wuwei ink gauze lantern as an example, J. Chaohu Univ. 23(2), 1–7 (2021)
14. Marquis, S.: The first digital Christmas will be the last for some dotcoms, Marketing, 18 (2000)
15. Eslit, E.R.: The future of festivity: Christmas, technology, and the post-pandemic realm (2023)
16. Zhang, Y., Xu, Z.: Design and research of Wushan temple fair cultural app from the perspective of intangible cultural heritage inheritance and innovation, Zhuang Shi 02 (2024)

Author Index

P. Zaphiris et al. (Eds.): HCII 2024, LNCS 15378, pp. 417–418, 2025.
https://doi.org/10.1007/978-3-031-76815-6

SPRINGER NATURE

GPSR Compliance

The European Union's (EU) General Product Safety Regulation (GPSR) is a set of rules that requires consumer products to be safe and our obligations to ensure this.

If you have any concerns about our products, you can contact us on ProductSafety@springernature.com

In case Publisher is established outside the EU, the EU authorized representative is:

Springer Nature Customer Service Center GmbH
Europaplatz 3
69115 Heidelberg, Germany

The manufacturer's authorised representative in the EU is Springer
Nature Customer Service Centre GmbH, Europaplatz 3, 69115 Heidelberg,
Germany. If you have any concerns regarding our products, please
contact ProductSafety@springernature.com

Printed and bound by CPI Group (UK) Ltd, Croydon, CR0 4YY

24/04/2026

02096375-0008